DANTE

DANTE

The Story of His Life

MARCO SANTAGATA

Translated by Richard Dixon

THE BELKNAP PRESS OF

HARVARD UNIVERSITY PRESS

Cambridge, Massachusetts

London, England

2016

First printing

Library of Congress Cataloging-in-Publication Data

Names: Santagata, Marco, author.
Title: Dante : the story of his life / Marco Santagata ; translated
   by Richard Dixon.
Other titles: Dante. English
Description: Cambridge, Massachusetts : The Belknap Press of
   Harvard University Press, 2016. | First published as Dante :
   il romanzo della sua vita. Milano : Arnoldo Mondadore
   Editore, 2012. | Includes bibliographical references and
   index.
Identifiers: LCCN 2015039151 | ISBN 9780674504868 (alk. paper)
Subjects: LCSH: Dante Alighieri, 1265–1321. | Poets, Italian—To
   1500—Biography.
Classification: LCC PQ4339 .S2613 2016 | DDC 851/.1—dc23 LC
record available at http://lccn.loc.gov/2015039151

Contents

Translator's Note

The translations throughout this book are my own, though I have consulted numerous other translations. Most helpful of these have been the parallel translation of *The Divine Comedy of Dante Alighieri*, edited and translated by Robert M. Durling, with introduction and notes by Ronald L. Martinez and Robert M. Durling (New York: Oxford University Press), *Inferno*, 1996; *Purgatorio*, 2003; *Paradiso* 2011; and *The Divine Comedy* translated by Mark Musa (New York: Penguin Books) I: *Inferno*, 1971; II: *Purgatorio*, 1981; III: *Paradiso*, 1984. For other works by Dante, I have also found most useful the online resource of the Società Dantesca Italiana at www.danteonline.it.

My special thanks to Giuliana Paganucci for helping me with the meaning of particular words, and to Peter Greene for his comments and suggestions for improvements to the translation.

Abbreviations of Dante's Works

Inf.	*Inferno*
Purg.	*Purgatorio*
Para.	*Paradiso*
VN	*Vita Nova*
Ep.	*Epistles*
Conv.	*Convivio*
VE	*De vulgari eloquentia*
Mn.	*Monarchia*
Ec.	*Eclogues*

Part One

FLORENCE

I

Childhood

1265–1283

I was born and raised
in the great city on the lovely River Arno

I' fui nato e cresciuto
sovra 'l bel fiume d'Arno a la gran villa

—*Inf.* XXIII 94–95

The "glorious stars"

DANTE ALIGHIERI was born in Florence in May 1265 under the sign of
Gemini.[1] At the baptismal font he was given the name Durante.[2] It was
a name he would never use: in his writings he called himself and always
signed himself just Dante; the poets with whom he corresponded called
him Dante; Dante is the only name to appear in private and public documents written during his lifetime; and Dante is the form on which all
"interpretations" of his name have been built. In the Middle Ages there
was a widely held belief that the name of a person, if properly interpreted
(*interpretatio nominis*), would reveal the destiny of its bearer, or rather,
that the actions carried out by the person bearing it would reveal the
inner meaning of the name itself. This interpretation was not at all influenced by the actual etymology of the name. In the same way that the
name Beatrice tells us this woman is "blessed" and "a source of beatitude" for others, so the name Dante indicates that its holder, through

his works, generously "gives" (*dà*) to others his great intellectual gifts received from God.[3]

Dante tells us himself in *Paradiso* that he was born under Gemini. During his ascent to the Empyrean, finding himself in that very constellation, he asks the Twins to help him on the final difficult stretch of his journey and recalls how the sun had reached them at the moment when he had "first breathed the Tuscan air" (*Para.* XXII 117; "quand' io senti' di prima l'aere tosco"). At the very moment of his first breath, when the influence of the stars operates with greater force, those "glorious stars" had infused in him all the talent, "whatever it might be," with which he felt endowed. But though he considers astrological problems on many occasions, and though he insists on the "virtue" of the stars that had presided over his birth, Dante never specifies what particular influence they had on him. The astrologers of the time claimed that if Mercury and Saturn were present in the "house" of Gemini (a conjunction that had actually taken place in 1265), those born under the sign were endowed with excellent intellectual qualities and special abilities in writing. Dante may also have thought this. Certainly, apart from (infrequent) assertions of modesty, he was convinced that the twins of Gemini had provided him with a remarkable talent.[4]

We can be sure, however, that if he had been born under another sign, he would have claimed to have been greatly blessed all the same. The most remarkable aspect of Dante's personality is, in fact, his feeling of being different and predestined. In whatever he saw, did or said—the first feeling of love, the death of the woman he had loved, political defeat or exile—he glimpsed some sign of destiny, the shadow of an unavoidable fate, the mark of a higher will. It was an idea he first cultivated in his youth, and one that would grow stronger until it became a conviction that he had been invested by God with the prophetic mission of saving humanity. How can we avoid asking, then, what kind of self-image such an egocentric man, so sure of his exceptional nature, must have possessed in daily life? Above all, how did his self-opinion influence how others saw him?

The popular portrait of Dante as scornful, proud, haughty, a man of rock-solid convictions who, for love of truth, challenges those in power and pays for it personally, obviously originates from the *Commedia*: both from what he says there about himself—"be like a solid tower, that never crumbles from the battering of winds" (*Purg.* V 14–15; "sta come torre ferma, che non crolla / già mai la cima per soffiar di venti") and "four-square against the blows of destiny" (*Para.* XVII 24; "ben tetragono ai colpi di ventura")—and from the poet's asserted role as judge of humanity. Indeed, you need an uncommon degree of self-confidence to hand out scathing judgments, to hurl ferocious jibes and utter slanderous accusations against people of rank, many of whom, moreover, were still alive or had direct descendants who were still living. Such a portrait, however, does not altogether correspond with the human and psychological reality of a man obliged to steer his way between conflicting political factions, to temper the wills of patrons who were often themselves divided and hostile, nor with the reality of an exile without material resources, endlessly and fruitlessly searching for a replacement for his lost home.

His contemporaries offer little help to anyone wishing to reconstruct the true Dante. Almost none of those who knew him wrote about him; only a few of the next generation had anything reliable to say about him.

Giovanni Villani, about ten years younger, was an acquaintance, if not a friend of Dante. In his history of Florence (1321), he dedicates a whole paragraph to him in which he draws a brief, caustic profile of his character. Villani acknowledges that Dante had honored the city with his works but insinuates that in the *Commedia,* perhaps exasperated by his exile, he "took delight" in "grumbling and complaining" more than he ought. He then says Dante's learning had made him "presumptuous, contemptuous, and disdainful," and ends by noting that, like an "ungracious" scholar, he was unable to talk easily to uneducated people. In short, he portrays Dante as impatient and ill-tempered. Giovanni Boccaccio, who didn't know Dante but spoke to many who did, was an unreserved admirer, so that the portrait he paints is one entirely of praise, if not out-and-out glorification. Certain features, however, are similar to those drawn by Villani, except that Boccaccio puts a positive light on the less endearing qualities. Dante's peculiarities, such as talking little and only when asked, his love of solitude, losing himself in thought and fancy to the point of being unconscious of what was happening around him, being "proud and very disdainful," are the very aspects of the sage and the philosopher, of someone who is aware of his own greatness. So far as his pride, even though Dante accuses himself of this sin, Boccaccio, like a scrupulous historian, requires the supporting evidence of "contemporaries," namely of those who knew him in life. And he also cites oral testimony providing evidence of a negative side of Dante's personality, that of "animosity," which he is indeed ashamed to have to reveal. Boccaccio concludes that, if moved on points of politics, Dante would get angry until he lost his self-control, just like a "furious" madman—and sometimes for futile reasons. It seems that in the Romagna region (where Dante spent the final years of his life and where Boccaccio had also lived) it was commonly said that Dante worked himself into such a state of anger if he heard a young woman or even a small boy speak ill of the Ghibellines that he'd throw stones at them if they didn't stop. This hardly seems likely. What is believable, however, is that in Romagna a picture was passed down of Dante being irascible and fiercely partisan. These outbursts, according to Boccaccio, were triggered by hatred of the Guelfs, who had thrown him out of Florence, a hatred which in response had turned him into a "proud Ghibelline." Dante never was a Ghibelline, but it is clear from all he did that tolerance was never one of his strengths.[5]

Boccaccio also sketches a physical portrait: long face, aquiline nose, large eyes, and jaws that protruded in a pronounced, jutting lower jaw. These would become classic features in later portraits, especially during the fifteenth century. But where did Boccaccio get this information? It is striking that certain of these features are to be found in the frescoed figure (apparently earlier than 1337) in the chapel of the Palazzo del Podestà (the Bargello) in Florence: there is no documentary evidence to confirm that the portrait, once attributed to Giotto, is of Dante, but its partial resemblance to a later, confirmed one (1375–1406) that has recently come to light in the old audience hall in the Palazzo dell'Arte dei Giudici e Notai (the Palace of the Guild of Judges and Notaries), also in Florence, suggests that the earlier portrait really does depict Dante.[6] Boccaccio would have been able to view that fresco, but also perhaps others now lost. He adds further details, such as his low stature, dark complexion, and the fact that in later years he was "rather hunched," which he couldn't have deduced (particularly the last of these) from any paintings, but about which he must have been told by people who had known Dante. And in fact he names Andrea Poggi, "an illiterate man, but of natural good sense," with whom he spoke several times "about

Dante's habits and ways." Andrea, who came of age in 1304, not only knew Dante but was a nephew (the son of a sister of Dante whose name we don't know) and, moreover, a nephew who bore an extraordinary similarity to him in mien, "in personal stature," and even in bearing, given that he too "was somewhat hunched, as Dante was said to have been." This suggests that something of the original figure of Dante must have remained in Boccaccio's description, in the same way that something of his facial features must, in the light of certain similarities, have remained in the picture at the Palazzo del Podestà. Which means, therefore, that despite the inevitable tendency to produce a uniform image (the fourteenth-century graffito picture on a ground floor wall of the Florentine convent of SS. Annunziata, formerly Santa Maria di Cafaggio, if it was of him, was almost a caricature), we have at least a rough idea of how Dante looked.[7]

The "ancient circle" and the "new folk"

Dante was born in the family home on the piazza behind the church of San Martino al Vescovo, in the *sestiere* of San Pier Maggiore, almost opposite the Torre della Castagna, which still stands, a few steps away from the abbey and church still known as the Badia Fiorentina, and the Palazzo del Podestà. The Alighieri house was therefore about halfway between the Duomo and the present-day Piazza della Signoria, to the east of what is now Via dei Calzaiuoli. When Dante was sentenced to exile and to the confiscation and destruction of his property in 1302, his house was not razed to the ground: its destruction was prevented by the fact that he jointly owned the property with his half-brother Francesco.[8] It was still there in the early decades of the fifteenth century.

Leonardo Bruni tells of a great-grandson of Dante called Leonardo, a descendant of his eldest child Pietro, who, having come to Florence "with other young men" from Verona, where the family had then been living for two generations, had visited Bruni to find out about his illustrious great-grandfather: on that occasion, Bruni had shown him "the properties belonging to Dante and his forebears" and had given him information "about many things unknown to him." The house—"very respectable," according to Bruni—would have been of modest size. Yet in the *Vita Nova,* the autobiographical account of his love for Beatrice,

Dante refers several times to a "room" of his own where he could go alone to think, to weep, and also to sleep. His insistence on a space exclusively for his use is quite striking—not only were there no separate areas for single members of a family in medieval houses, but those living in the small Alighieri house at the time when the *Vita Nova* is set included (apart from Dante) his wife, his stepmother, and his half-brother. It is hard to believe, therefore, that he had a room of his own. Only very rich people could afford spaces set aside for study, or as a bed chamber, which others couldn't enter. If the availability of his own domestic space denoted the status of a gentleman, it is more than likely that, by emphasizing the room, Dante wanted to suggest his own aristocratic tenor of life: this too would be one of the many signs of distinction by which he was seeking to hide his lowly origins and give himself a higher social rank.[9]

Though the house was modest, San Pier Maggiore was what, today, we would call a good neighborhood. Living there were magnate families—some aristocrats, others awarded the dignity of knights—as well as ordinary folk with no noble coats of arms, indeed most of humble origin but well-to-do. Magnates or not, they were influential families. Some, like the Portinari, Beatrice's family, were to have an important part in Dante's life; others, like the Cerchi and Donati, would indeed play a decisive role: the disastrous conflict between the factions led by these two families would lead to his banishment. San Pier Maggiore, like all *sestieri,* was divided by economic interests, especially those of banking and commerce, as well as political interests: at an early stage it was pro-papal Guelfs against pro-imperial Ghibellines; later Black (Donati) Guelfs against White (Cerchi) Guelfs. And yet the rival families lived shoulder-to-shoulder in fortified houses with towers, each abutting the other, and were for this very reason always anxious to keep control over their own residential area and ready to exploit every opportunity to expand it. Ideally, marriages were contracted between those living in nearby houses so as to gradually extend ownership of land. The greater the portion under direct control, the stronger the influence over the whole district. The greatest risk was that other families would move into someone's territory. One of the causes of the struggle between the Donati and Cerchi mentioned above—which only ended at the close of the century, and with disastrous results—was this very problem of invasion of territory. The Cerchi, extremely rich but of humble origin, had managed to take over a large part of the area. In 1280 they had also bought up properties owned by the Guidi (Palatine counts, appointed by the Holy Roman emperor, who were among the most distinguished feudal dynasties in the territories between Tuscany and Romagna). They had rebuilt the area and were living a life of luxury. The Donati, ancient aristocrats with less wealth, regarded themselves as the leading figures in the *sestiere* and, seeing their supremacy under threat, began to hate and disdain their upstart neighbors who were brazenly flaunting their economic power.[10]

Florence, the city where Dante would live until he was thirty-six, was nothing like the city that later became famous worldwide for its architectural monuments.[11] Obviously, there was no bell tower by Giotto, no Brunelleschi dome, no Medici palaces, nor even the churches of Santa Maria Novella or Santa Maria del Fiore. Dante's Florence was a medieval city: a tangle of narrow streets, of buildings in stone and wood, one against the other, a jumble of houses, factories, workshops, and storehouses interspersed here and there with vegetable plots, vineyards, and gardens. The churches were many but small; the towers numerous, and sometimes remarkably tall. The great family clans built them partly as a sign of their power, but above all to defend the houses and the workshops beneath them, and as high lookout posts from which they could control a vast area around them. Defense and intimidation were both necessary operations in a city where quarrels between individual citizens and factions degenerated almost daily into violence and unrest.[12] In short, the city was shaped by its towers and campaniles, not by civic or religious monuments. Only by the end of the century would work begin on some of the great building projects that still shape modern-day Florence. In May 1279, the Dominicans in the monastery of Santa Maria Novella solemnly laid the first stone of a church they intended to become one of the greatest in Italy; in 1284 the old Badia was modernized (perhaps by the great architect Arnolfo di Cambio); in October 1295 the Franciscans began to build Santa Croce; a year later, the transformation began of the small cathedral of Santa Reparata into the magnificent Santa Maria del Fiore, designed by Arnolfo; in February 1299 work commenced on the Palazzo dei Priori (later known as Palazzo della Signoria and, finally, as Palazzo Vecchio), designed once again by Arnolfo. These were projects that would take years of work, sometimes even centuries.

During his later years in Florence, Dante saw the building sites and walked beneath the scaffolding. But those majestic buildings hadn't yet had time to capture his imagination as new symbols of the city—not even the Duomo of Santa Maria del Fiore which, although far from complete, was already being used (and celebrated as the new glory of the city) while he was still living in Florence. Dante never mentions it. His central image of the city, carried with him into exile, was the Baptistery of San Giovanni. Up to the beginning of the 1300s his "fine San Giovanni" (*Inf.* XIX 17; "bel San Giovanni") was not only the largest and most lavishly decorated building in Florence, but also the quintessential city shrine, where the most important religious ceremonies took place, where the Commune kept its *carroccio* (a four-wheeled war altar) and its war trophies. No other building could compete with this religious and civic symbol.

In short, the Florence in which Dante was born and had spent the early part of his life was not a city conspicuous for the grandeur of its monuments or the opulence of its noble residences. Pisa, its historic rival, offered quite a different spectacle for the number, size, and richness of its buildings—first and foremost its marble Duomo and baptistery complex. But Florence was not small as a city—by 1280 it had around forty to fifty thousand inhabitants, making it one of the largest in Europe—and, above all, it was expanding fast, while Pisa was in decline.[13]

By the mid-1200s the wall around the city, which had replaced the ancient Roman-Byzantine wall at the end of the previous century, was already inadequate, and monasteries, churches, and hamlets of considerable size had sprung up outside the boundary. So work began in 1285 to build a third fortified circle, which was not completed until 1333. This, in the end, had a circumference of eight and a half kilometers; by that time, the population was almost double that of 1280.

So Florence was a dynamic city, driven by extraordinary economic growth. The heart of the Florentine economy was finance. The number of its banks and trading companies (the two almost always went together) was impressive: they were based in the city, but operated throughout Europe and the Mediterranean by way of a system of branch offices and alliances that could cover the most important markets, from Flanders, England, and France, down to the kingdom of Sicily and northern Africa. At the heart of Florentine finance was the florin. This twenty-four carat gold coin with the city's symbol (the fleur-de-lis) on one side and the image of John the Baptist, its protector, on the other was first minted in November 1252 and soon became a sort of dollar of the time, the main coinage in international trade and currency even among the Saracens. Remigio dei Girolami, the famous Dominican theologian and preacher, went as far as proclaiming that the florin was one of the seven gifts that Providence had bestowed on Florence.[14] Florence's economic development and growing role as a regional power led to a conspicuous phenomenon of urban growth, fueled not only by the influx of manual workers from rural areas, but also by the arrival in the city of land owners and feudal lords, along with craftsmen, judges, advocates, and notaries from other urban centers.

Dante liked none of this. Florins, for him, were an "accursed flower" (*Para.* IX 130; "maladetto fiore") blossoming from corruption. It was the tangible symbol of society's perversion. The new men of power, who had become powerful through business, had put profit in place of the civic and military virtues of the old magnate families. The enormity, the chaos, the bustle of a city in which nobles and ordinary people were all involved in some financial business made him long for the smaller Florence of a hundred years earlier, for the city that had lived soberly but peacefully, with dignity and modesty, "within the ancient circle" (*Para.* XV 97; "dentro da la cerchia antica") of the walls, and when the working day was measured out by the chime of the bells of the Badia. The Florentines felt themselves then to be part of a close-knit community who respected immutable social hierarchies, "loyal citizens" (*Para.* XV 97–99, 130–132; "fida cittadinanza") unacquainted with the upheavals produced by the arrival of outsiders from rural areas ("the new folk") and by the "quick gains" (*Inf.* XVI 73; "i sùbiti guadagni") of families with no past. No one at that time could have imagined that the Guidi family, nobility par excellence, would have had to demean themselves by taking up residence in the city, in the very neighborhood of the Alighieri family; but worse still, that those houses would then be bought up by the Cerchi, a family of lowly origins that had moved in from the Val di Sieve.[15] And the good residents of the ancient district of San Pier Maggiore would have found it even more difficult to imagine that it would be infected by the "stench of the peasant from Aguglione" (*Para.* XVI 56; "puzzo / del villan d'Aguglion"), the jurist Baldo who had come from the Castle of Aguglione in Val di Pesa. Dante, during his exile, would have scathing words for the Cerchi, and especially for Baldo of Aguglione. His views came from disappointment, since Dante had been one of the Cerchi's men in Florence, and from personal hatred, since he had once had some kind of short-lived political understanding with Baldo. And yet Dante, though appearing in character and training to be a man of the city when compared to such brilliantly international and impartial humanists as Petrarch, was in reality never in tune with Florentine society, even when he enjoyed the rights of citizenship. He was against modernity itself: in other words, against economic progress and social mobility.

Among the many contradictions in his character is the inconsistent way in which he views innovation according to its effect on art and culture, or on politics and society. Dante felt—and it was a highly original idea—that the passage of time played a crucial role in transforming cultural phenomena. Natural languages were inconstant and ever-changing, the arts and literature were themselves also moving: Franco Bolognese went further than Oderisi da Gubbio's art of illumination, Giotto supplanted Cimabue, Cavalcanti took the glory of language from Guinizelli, the "new sweet style" ("dolce stil novo") surpassed all the lyrical production of Giacomo da Lentini, Guittone d'Arezzo, and Bonagiunta da Lucca. And yet, the intellectual who demonstrated such an acute perception of the historicism of cultural phenomena, when he turned his gaze to the social, economic, and political dynamics of his own period, wanted to stop the course of history and turn the clock back. He rejected out of hand a production system based on manufacture, commerce, and finance that had caused upheaval in the social fabric of the communes: the "population, now mixed" (*Para.* XVI 49; "cittadinanza, ch'è or mista"). He rejected the new forms of ruling government (which he calls "tyrannies"), the decline of feudal jurisdictions, and the central position of finance in relations between states and signorias. He regarded social dynamism as bringing a degeneration of customs and a perversion of values. The loss of the role and power of the old ruling classes for him represented the collapse of the mainstays of society. He saw the bitter competition between cities and the establishment of signorias as disastrous for the peaceful coexistence of Christianity. He was convinced that salvation could only come from a return to former times: to the domestic serenity of pre-mercantile Florence, to the time when Christianity rested on the balance between the two "suns" (papacy and empire), to a hierarchic and stable social structure based on the feudal aristocracy. He longed to turn back or stop time, to rebuild an unchanging world, guaranteed by an immutable institutional design, resembling in this respect the eternal celestial court of Paradise.[16]

Destruction and reconstruction

During the last twenty years of his time in Florence, Dante witnessed a period of great upheaval. The city was scattered with construction sites, crisscrossed with scaffolding, populated by workmen, and teeming with carts piled with building materials. But in the years before then, he would have seen quite a different picture of the city. He had seen Florence with its roads torn up, strewn with debris, houses unroofed, towers ruined or lopped off. He had even risked not seeing any of it. Bitter conflict, an out-and-out civil war between Guelfs and Ghibellines, had wrought continual havoc and the city had stood on the brink of total destruction.

The rule of one party or other during the thirteenth century didn't bring with it a normal alternation of power. In Florence, as in other cities, the spoils system meant that losers had their property and possessions confiscated and sometimes even lost their lives. If they managed to save their skins, they were banished from the city or went into exile; their homes were plundered, their houses and workplaces taken away from them or destroyed. This followed judicial proceedings of dubious fairness. But there were countless private vendettas and settling of scores carried out regardless of the law. And this was why even those not banished often chose to leave the city of their own free will. Vexatious litigation and private persecutions led to a gulf of enmity between the parties, which became wider and wider as successive victories and defeats led to repeated episodes of forfeiture and banishment. Spiraling hatred ended up dividing the larger family clans and even causing rifts in smaller ones. Coexistence in the city was precarious, marred by sudden outbursts of collective violence and individual *coups de main,* even during periods of relative calm when factions were attempting to work together.

The division into Guelfs and Ghibellines wasn't just a domestic phenomenon. Both parties had allies in other cities, and had close relationships with the leading international champions of Empire and

Church. Internecine conflicts were therefore bound up with questions of external policy, and the consequences were of no small importance. An example of this was the proposition to destroy Florence made by envoys of Manfred, king of Sicily—leader of the Ghibelline party around the middle of the century—at a congress held at Empoli by the victors at the Battle of Montaperti in September 1260, during which the Florentine Ghibelline exiles, the Sienese and Manfred's imperial forces had inflicted a disastrous defeat on the Florentines governed by the Guelfs. The proposal was not accepted due to the opposition of the Ghibellines of Florence, headed by their charismatic leader Manente degli Uberti, nicknamed Farinata (immortalized by Dante in Canto X of *Inferno*). Florence was not razed to the ground, but it was partially destroyed. The Ghibellines, once back inside the city, vented their fury on the losers with orders of banishment, removal from office, confiscation and the destruction of property. Only two years earlier it had been the Guelfs who had destroyed the houses of the Ghibellines so that, by the end of 1260, much of Florence must have been reduced to rubble. But that wasn't the end of it. Seven years later, after Manfred's defeat at Benevento in 1266, the roles were reversed. The Ghibellines were removed from office and exiled, their possessions confiscated and many of their properties demolished.[17] The debris from these and earlier destructions would remain visible for many years. Young Dante, walking the city streets, would have seen a half-derelict Florence, strewn with debris. Scars in the urban fabric that would remain unhealed for many years, in certain cases forever. The sites of some of the buildings pulled down at that time would never be built upon again. The houses and towers of the Uberti family—the most powerful and illustrious Ghibelline family—close to the present Palazzo Vecchio, in the San Pier Scheraggio district, were razed to the ground and the rubble remained there for decades. The space they occupied was never built upon, so that the area ended up as part of what is now Piazza della Signoria, by the Palazzo dei Priori.[18]

In 1280, the warring parties reached a hard-won reconciliation: it would mark the beginning of reconstruction. The Ghibellines would rebuild the houses that had been demolished; they would begin major civic and religious building projects, and the rubble that had cluttered the streets for twenty years would be used to consolidate the ramparts of the new city wall.

Dante was living in a city that had two faces to it, but one common feature: instability. We might ask whether the sight of a city caught up in a cycle of destruction and reconstruction, in a state of constant upheaval, hadn't increased Dante's desire for stability, helping to form his great backward-looking vision of a return to antiquity, to a Florence static in its urban and social structure.

Guelfs and Ghibellines: The roots of hatred

Dante was a second-level politician. Contemporary accounts say nothing about his public activities or they mention them only in passing. And yet politics conditioned his life more than anything else. Having lived in a city that was firmly Guelf, he was expelled as a result of divisions that had torn apart the party ruling in the final years of the 1200s; as an exile, wandering between cities and castles of northern central Italy, he was also caught up in hostilities between Guelfs and Ghibellines which he had not experienced personally in his home city.

The words "Guelf" and "Ghibelline" are the Italian transposition of names used in twelfth-century Germany to describe respectively those who upheld the claims to the imperial crown of the Bavarian and Sassonian house of the Welfen, and those who supported the Hohenstaufen, the lords of the castle of Wibeling. In northern central Italy the two words began to be used during the conflict between the popes and Emperor Frederick II, where they ended up denoting the factions that supported the pope (Guelfs) and the emperor (Ghibellines). Even though the division of cities and feudal guilds into two parties was linked to questions that went beyond local considerations, the composition of the factions was determined by social and cultural interests peculiar to each city. In short, in most cases, to declare oneself a Guelf or a Ghibelline gave an ideological cover to the conflicts endemic in city society, between great families, each of whom headed their own system of alliances and economic relationships.

In Florence, a city that obtained considerable international protection through its financial activities, there was a particularly close link between domestic events and foreign policy. Rivalries between parties were intimately bound up with financial and commercial relations at an international level, and this meant that, from the Battle of Montaperti onward, what had been a fight limited to the governing class was transformed into a conflict involving the citizenry as a whole. The fate of the whole city was at stake—not just that of a particular ruling group. The oligarchy was made up of magnate families, the so-called "Grandi." The magnates, defined not only by their noble blood, but also by their wealth and style of living, were to be found in both parties, even though, generally speaking, the aristocracy of feudal extraction were closer to the empire, whereas the moneyed aristocracy, more open to the so-called *popolo*—merchants, rich craftsmen, and property owners who constituted the backbone of Florentine society—tended toward the pope's party.[19]

With Frederick II of Swabia, of the House of Hohenstaufen (1194–1250), the fight for supremacy between the Germanic emperors and the papacy—begun during the time of his grandfather Frederick I, nicknamed Barbarossa, and continued by his father Henry VI—became primarily an Italian question. Frederick II, in fact, had unified in one person the titles of king of Sicily (1198) and emperor of the Romans (1220), and this was what the popes had feared more than anything else. The kingdom of Sicily—which, apart from the island, included the whole of southern Italy—had formally been the feudal property of the pope, but in reality it enjoyed full autonomy; the empire could also claim rights over northern central Italy, but the commune cities and the signories behaved like entirely independent city-states. The papacy feared that an emperor who had control of both Germany and southern Italy would be tempted to join together the two dominions, re-establishing his power over the rest of the peninsula. If this were to happen, the territories of central Italy and Romagna over which the pope exercised his own direct authority (the so-called "possessions of Saint Peter") would be surrounded. The pontiff's influence over Italian affairs would be much reduced. The fear was justified, since this was exactly what Frederick II sought to do. It was this political design that earned him the labels of heretic and devil's messenger during his lifetime, and his reputation as an enemy of the Church and of Christianity would follow him for years.

Florence was a supporter of the pope by tradition (and out of interest); its main rivals in Tuscany, Pisa and Siena, supported the emperor. Though Frederick II had managed to impose a substantial Ghibelline hegemony over the region, Florence had long resisted. Nevertheless, a military contingent sent by the emperor under the command of Frederick of Antioch had succeeded in overthrowing its government in January 1249 and had forced the ruling Guelfs to leave the city. But the Ghibelline victory was to be short-lived. Frederick II died suddenly in December 1250; the Ghibellines, already in serious difficulty due to a popular revolt even before the emperor's death, were ousted from power. A government was established (later known as the "Primo Popolo" to distinguish it from the "Secondo Popolo" of the 1280s) led by the business classes (in other words, the *popolo*) and centered on the artisan guilds. It was they who appointed the new magistrate, the *capitano del popolo,* who now stood alongside the traditional *podestà*.[20] Though not overtly partisan, it was nevertheless a government with a strongly Guelf influence, so much so that a group of Ghibellines had already been expelled from the city by July 1251. This influence became more marked over subsequent years, and would complicate coexistence with the Ghibelline party. Nevertheless, Florence was to enjoy relative stability for almost ten years and, since disorder was the norm in this city, it is understandable that the Florentine chroniclers over the next decades (all committed Guelfs) have mythologized this period as a kind of golden age in the life of the commune (it was during this time that the florin was minted and the Palazzo del Capitano del Popolo was built).

Stability in Italy (and consequently in Florence) was shattered in 1258 when Manfred, natural son of Frederick II, violating all the rights of the legitimate heir Conradin, obtained the crown of the king of Sicily and Puglia and resumed his father's policy, with the support of Ghibelline forces from the rest of Italy. The Ghibellines of Florence, led by Farinata degli Uberti, immediately broke the truce, but their attempt to overthrow the city government was thwarted: banished from the city, they took refuge in Siena. War between the two factions was inevitable. It would end on September 4, 1260, with the Battle of Montaperti, mentioned earlier. In that battle the Guelfs of Florence and their allies (headed by those from Lucca) were routed by the joint forces of Siena, the

German cavalry sent by Manfred and the Ghibelline fugitives from
Florence. It marked the course of Florentine history and would remain
etched upon the city's memory for decades. The Florentines, especially
the Guelfs, wouldn't forget the massacre of their fellow citizens (Dante
would recall the Arbia, the river that ran through the battlefield, "stained
red" [*Inf.* X 86; "colorata in rosso"] by the blood of the fallen), nor the terrible fate of most of the thousands of prisoners incarcerated in the jails of
Siena. As many as eight thousand would die in prison, and the survivors
would not be released until ten years later, in August 1270. Immediately
after the defeat, the Guelfs left the city en masse, and most took refuge
in allied Lucca. The Ghibelline oligarchy took complete control of the
government: it abolished the magistracy of the *capitano del popolo* and
proceeded with orders of confiscation, destruction, and banishment
against the vanquished. After Montaperti, Manfred's imperial forces
seemed to have total control of Tuscany. In 1264, Lucca also expelled the
Guelfs so that the Florentine fugitives were forced to emigrate once
again, many of them to Bologna.

At this point the papacy took the initiative. Faced with the reemergence of the threat averted at the time of Frederick II, Clement IV made
two countermoves: on the one hand he put pressure on the Florentine
bankers, who were very anxious to preserve their substantial interests
in the administration of the papal court; on the other he sought the
intervention of a non-Italian power. In 1265 he offered the crown of
the southern kingdom to Charles of Anjou, Count of Provence and
the brother of King Louis IX of France. This gesture would not only
change the course of the war against the Swabians but would affect the
course of Italian history for centuries. Arriving in Italy in January 1266,
Charles was crowned as king of Sicily in Rome and began hostilities
against Manfred. The war ended quickly when Manfred was defeated
and killed at Benevento in February the same year. In Florence, after an
attempt at joint government by the two factions, the French cavalry arrived in the city in April 1267. The Ghibellines fled and the city was
handed over to Charles of Anjou who, in May, assumed the office of *podestà* for seven years (a role he would exercise through deputies). A last
attempt to rally the Italian Ghibellines, made by Conradin of Swabia,
nephew of Frederick II, who landed in Pisa in April 1268 to declare war

against Charles of Anjou, was crushed in August at Tagliacozzo. Conradin was taken prisoner and beheaded in Naples a few months later.

The fall of the Swabians did not mark the end of the conflict between the papal and imperial parties, which would rumble on for over half a century, though mixed with periods of relative calm and never reaching the tragic climaxes of the Swabian period. But it marked the end of the Ghibelline presence in Florence. The Guelf government would identify itself more and more with city institutions, to the point where party organizations became the effective organs of city government. Florence would become closely bound to the Anjou court of Naples and the papal court. Bankers and financiers would obtain substantial economic benefits, but the city would be kept under control. Dependence on the Angevins of Naples would be relaxed only in the early 1290s, when Florence gave itself a new institutional structure at whose core was a college of magistrates formed by people—priors—elected for a limited time.

The Alighieri family: History and legend

The Alighieri family were Guelfs, and so the fact that Dante was born in Florence in May 1265, many months before the Guelf victory at Benevento, may mean either that, after Montaperti, his mother didn't follow his father into exile, or that his father didn't leave, or wasn't even banished. The second possibility, given Dante's father's low public standing, seems the more plausible. Although several Alighieri were banished during the years of Ghibelline triumph (including Geri del Bello or di Bello, a cousin of Dante's father who, in 1269, obtained modest compensation for damage to his house), we can say that Dante did not belong to a family of hard-line Guelfs.[21]

The first recorded information about an Alighieri ancestor in Florence relates to a Cacciaguida who lived in the twelfth century. Dante, who makes Cacciaguida into one of the most important characters in the *Commedia,* would also start off the family history, as he knew it, from this great-great-grandfather who, according to him, had married a woman from the Po Valley from where the name Alighieri was supposed to originate. We can say little for certain about Cacciaguida, nor can we entirely accept all of what Dante tells us about him. His claims that his great-great-grandfather had been knighted by no less than an emperor, described no better than "emperor Conrad" (*Para.* XV 139; "imperador Currado") and that he died fighting under the crusader banner in the Holy Land arouse certain doubts. It might be traced back to Dante's desire, particularly apparent at the time of the *Commedia,* to give dignity to a family which, in reality, could boast no noble roots nor any knights among it, least of all of imperial investiture. Cacciaguida's reference to his brothers Moronto and Eliseo (of whom, however, some documentary evidence exists) could also be part of the same strategy, since it suggests a relationship between the Alighieri and the Elisei family, one of the oldest noble families of Florence. Cacciaguida also talks of a son called Alighiero, Dante's great-grandfather, whom he describes in the *Commedia* as having been purging himself of the sin of pride for over a hundred years. And the mention of pride, a typically noble sin, seems to be just another feature intended to complete the picture of a once high-ranking family that Dante is tracing back.[22]

Of this Alighiero (whom we shall call Alighiero I to distinguish him from Dante's father, referred to below as Alighiero II) we know almost nothing, "except that he had houses in San Martino del Vescovo and from him were born Bello and Bellincione who, in due time, divided those houses between them."[23] Bello was a man of sufficient prestige to be given the title of knight; Bellincione, who practiced the profession of "changer"—in other words, a small-time moneylender—was also a respectable figure, though he didn't share his brother's prominence. With the sons of Alighiero I, the family split into two branches. The eldest son of Bellincione was Alighiero II. Dante was born from his first marriage to a woman called Bella (Gabriella). Since Bellincione must have had a certain social prestige, it would be no surprise for him to arrange his son's marriage to a woman of standing. The wife of Alighiero II could therefore have been Bella di Durante degli Abati, from a wealthy and powerful family who lived in the same district. This would explain the close links that Durante had with Dante and his brothers, both in guaranteeing loans granted to them as well as in obtaining their surety on debts contracted by him. And it would also explain the origin of the name Durante, a homage by Alighiero II to his worthy father-in-law. It is true that the Abati were proud Ghibellines; but it is also true, as already indicated, that marriages frequently took place between families politically divided—indeed it was used as a means of settling disputes. In general, looking at the Alighieri family tree, it can be seen that the oldest generations of both branches had, as was common among families of moderately high standing, a store of family names to draw upon, especially among the males: Alighiero, Bellincione, Bello, Cione, Bellino, and Belluzzo. But from Dante's siblings onward, this practice of reuse was lost: an indication that the clan identity was fading.

For unknown reasons, the prestige enjoyed by Bellincione diminished during the life of his son Alighiero II. Evidence for this comes from the fact that, after the death of his first wife and, most probably, also his father, Alighiero II contracted a second marriage with a woman called Lapa, daughter of a merchant, Chiarissimo Cialuffi, whose family were wealthy but of no importance in Florence. Alighiero II had three children from Bella: Tana (Gaetana), born around 1260, who married Lapo Riccomanni, perhaps around 1275 but before 1281, and was still alive in 1320; a second unnamed daughter, who we know married a certain Leone Poggi, whose son Andrea Poggi gave information about his famous uncle to Boccaccio; and finally, the third child, Dante. From Lapa, he had just one son, Francesco.

We have very little recorded information about Alighiero II: he was perhaps born around 1220 and most likely died shortly after 1275.[24] Dante would therefore have been born when he was already getting on in years. Various legal documents show him to have been a businessman, money lender and land dealer, especially in the Prato area—first in partnership with his father and brothers, then by himself. The financial dealings and land transactions of Alighiero II must have been profitable enough, but it is perhaps too much to suggest, as is often claimed, that on his death he left his children comfortably off. The property assets of the brothers Dante and Francesco, which had still not been divided when Dante was banished from the city in 1302, comprised: the family home in San Martino (a small house, it would seem); a farm with its main building, sheds and various pieces of surrounding land at San Miniato di Pagnolle, not far from Florence; another farm in the parish of San Marco in Camerata, in the Mugnone valley; and, lastly, a cottage with vegetable plot and small piece of land situated in the "popolo" (parish) of Sant'Ambrogio, behind the third circle of city walls, toward the Affrico torrent. They certainly weren't large properties. Alighiero II therefore didn't have an accumulated investment in real estate. Leonardo Bruni's assessment would therefore seem quite reasonable when he concludes that Dante, before being exiled, "although he was not greatly rich, he was not poor either, but had moderate and sufficient wealth to live honorably."[25] The problem, however, is to establish what for Dante was an honorable life and whether his wealth was sufficient to enable him to lead it.

A bad reputation

Alighiero II has a bad reputation: certain shameful suspicions hang over him, above all that of usury. They come, however, not from any public records, nor from contemporary gossip, but from his own son Dante, though indirectly. I am referring to an exchange of sonnets (a *tenzone*) that took place in the early 1290s between Dante and his slightly older friend Forese Donati, nicknamed Bicci. Forese, who died in 1296, belonged to one of the city's most important families: he was the brother of Corso and Piccarda, and therefore a distant relation of Gemma, Dante's wife.

The exchange between the two took place as a tenzone. Medieval lyric poetry was generally in the form of a dialogue and tended to be directed to an interlocutor, historical or imaginary, named or implied. It is no surprise, then, that the tenzone was one of the most popular genres. A poet would send a poem (in Italy almost always a sonnet) to a fellow poet or group of poets, in which he posed a question and sought an answer. The recipient (or recipients) would reply with another poem, which generally continued the same rhyme pattern as the original poem; the person who began the tenzone could then answer, thus often prompting a further response from the correspondent (or correspondents). Dante made frequent use of the genre of the tenzone, but his exchange with Forese differed from the others since it was a tenzone of insults. It consists of six sonnets (three by Dante and three by Forese) in which the two exchange insults and innuendos about their private life and their close family. Tenzoni of this kind were frequent in the world of court jesters and Provencal troubadours: they were, in effect, fanciful, light-hearted exchanges, peppered with jibes designed to bring laughter to the audience before whom the contestants performed their verses. But in Italy this was almost entirely absent. The contest between Dante and

Forese must be regarded as a literary joke, a game, but a joke that, at a certain point, seems to have got out of hand. I say "seems" because the allusions to matters of private life, and to certain Florentine customs and expressions about which we know nothing today, prevent us from giving a clear interpretation to much of the literal meaning of the sonnets.[26]

Dante begins (*Anyone who heard his poor wife cough / Chi udisse tossir la malfatata*) by first making a sarcastic comment about Forese's lack of virility and then insisting on his poverty (a shameful situation in the Middle Ages). Forese replies (*The other night I had a great coughing fit / L'altra notte mi venn'una gran tosse*), admitting that he is poor, but that Alighiero, Dante's father, was poorer than him, so poor that he had to be buried in a mass grave in unconsecrated ground, a fate, as we know, not only for heretics and moneylenders but also for those who couldn't afford the cost of a tomb. The information, however, should not be taken literally but as a piece of hyperbole in the game of abuse being played out between them. Dante then moves target (*You'll get well tied in Solomon's knot / Ben ti faranno il nodo Salamone*): he accuses Forese of being so greedy and gluttonous (a serious accusation at that time) as to be at risk of imprisonment (we remember how in *Purgatorio* Forese will be placed among the gluttons); Forese replies (*Go and pay back San Gal before you tell / Va rivesti San Gal prima che dichi*) that Dante eats at the cost of others, that he has gone as far as stealing from charitable institutions, and that he risks ending up not in prison, but in a poor house. At this point Dante insinuates (*Young Bicci, son of I know not whom / Bicci novel, figliuol di non so cui*) that Forese is the son of no one and that to satisfy his greed, as everyone knows, he steals; the reply is deadly (*I know of course you're Alighieri's son / Ben so che fosti figliuol d'Allaghieri*): it's better to be son of no one than son of "Allaghieri," a father from whom Dante has inherited cowardice, so as to leave unavenged an insult he had received, indeed, to have hurried to make immediate peace.

The accusations exchanged between the two are all, without exception, part of the repertory of abuse and insults used in this kind of tenzone: they are elements in a literary game built around recurring themes and therefore not to be interpreted in a directly biographical manner. We cannot assume that the insinuations about Alighieri II's abject poverty and lack of noble spirit are true; they are, in fact, to be placed on the same level as the obviously exaggerated insinuations about Dante himself. Such an exchange is interesting not for the validity of the insults, but for the fact that, despite an air of tavern jest or party humor, Forese's malicious comments about Dante, his father, and the Alighieri family in general stand in stark contrast to the family portrayed in Dante's works. This contrast is further accentuated by the fact that, while Dante talks about past generations in his writings, the tenzone refers to members of the Alighieri family who are still alive or recently dead. On the one hand we have Cacciaguida, related to the aristocratic Elisei family, a crusader and knight of imperial investiture, and Alighiero I, who atones in Purgatory for the sin of pride which, as already mentioned, is a characteristic sin of aristocrats; on the other, we have an impoverished and morally bankrupt Alighiero II and a Dante on the road to the poor house, who has no hesitation in stealing from other paupers and shrinks from avenging the insult inflicted on his father. The contrast couldn't be greater. A past distinguished by noble spirit and blood is set against a shabby and plebeian present. It is clear that both images are distorted: the first, by a visionary reactionary tendency, fueled by an equally visionary desire for advancement and self-ennoblement; the second, by the crescendo of tit-for-tat insults. And yet the two images are a measure, though exaggerated, of that distance between ideal and real that Dante's somewhat fanciful reconstructions obstinately seek to cancel out.

The "path of knowledge"

Dante makes no mention of his childhood. We would be surprised if he did. Childhood is conspicuously absent, in fact, in medieval literature. This doesn't mean that people at that time were not interested in childhood and in the adult-child relationship. Nevertheless, with rare exceptions, literature did not permit descriptions of childhood experiences, especially personal recollections.

Dante showed an interest in childhood. He records the attempts of young children to articulate their first words: *pappo* (food), *dindi* (money), and observes that this way of speaking brings delight to fathers and mothers; he studies their behavior and their psychology: their need to feel protected and consoled by the mother, the shame they feel for

wrongs committed, their tears when punished.[27] And yet he doesn't in-
dulge in recollections and memories of his earliest years, partly, he
says, because it would be "fanciful talk" and more importantly because
the teachers of rhetoric did not allow writers to talk about themselves,
except when to do so is "useful" to others—and neither an account of
the experiences of a child or young boy nor that of the private business
of a person can be of benefit to anyone, unless they have some particular moral and exemplary value. Fortunately for us, in his later years,
possessed of an irrepressible autobiographical urge, Dante had to talk
directly or indirectly about himself.[28]

But so far as his childhood, he makes only a few vague references
about himself and his family. We cannot therefore even speculate about
the effects of his mother's death on him when he was still extremely
young, nor about his relations with his father's second wife and what it
had meant for Dante to lose his father at little over the age of ten.

Around the age of five or six, like many children of the better-off
classes, he would have begun his education. This statement is hypothetical since there is a complete lack of information on this important aspect of his life. Nor can we make up for this absence by looking at the
schooling practices of his contemporaries. While Florence's archives are
bursting with documents of every kind that make it possible to follow
the public life of the city and of a vast number of its citizens almost day
by day, the documents and records relating to schooling in the last decades of the 1200s have been almost entirely lost. This absence can perhaps be put down to the chances of history, but the suspicion remains
that education and culture were not uppermost in the minds of the rich
and industrious Florentines.

The Alighieri family were not wealthy enough to afford a private
tutor. Dante therefore presumably started attending a public school
in the early 1270s. Though their existence is only documented toward
the end of the century, we can reasonably assume that at least some
schools were already operating in earlier decades. They were private fee-
paying schools, run by lay "teachers of children" (*doctores puerorum*) with
whom, over five or six years, the pupils learned reading, writing, and the
basic rudiments of Latin. The fact that in 1277 a *doctor* from Rome ran a
school in the San Martino district, very close to Dante's house, doesn't
allow us to conclude that this was the school he attended. The teaching

was conducted in the vernacular and perhaps only in the recent past had it included some Latin (the Psalms, Aesop, and little else). In the *Convivio,* Dante explains that the vernacular tongue introduced him "onto the path of knowledge" and thanks to this he "entered Latin," a language that then opened the way "to progress further" (*Conv.* I XIII 5; "questo mio volgare fu introduttore di me nella via di scienza, che è ultima perfezione, in quanto con esso io entrai nello latino e con esso mi fu mostrato: lo quale latino poi mi fu via a più inanzi andare"): but that doesn't mean he is referring to his first period of education and nor to his grammar education, which is equivalent to our secondary school.[29]

Teaching was mainly by rote, with the assistance of very few written texts; the rod (*ferula*) played a central role in teaching at that time (and also long after). Around the mid-1300s, Petrarch wrote to his friend Zanobi da Strada, head of a grammar school in Florence, to persuade him to give up teaching and cultivate higher pursuits, namely to devote himself to study and poetry. According to Petrarch, schoolmasters must enjoy "the dust and the cries and tears of those who groan under the rod [*sub ferula*]": let this profession therefore be for those who take pleasure in "commanding inferiors and always having someone to frighten, torment, afflict, rule over, someone who hates them so that they might be feared."[30] Petrarch is certainly overdoing it, but the association of the rod with schooling returns so many times among writings in the early centuries, even among preachers, that we cannot but think that our ancestors recalled their schooldays as a time of suffering. Petrarch's words also show that the teaching profession enjoyed very little prestige. Moreover, it was poorly paid.[31]

Once the first cycle of schooling had ended, around the age of ten, there were two options for children in Florence and the other commune cities: one led them toward the professions and the other toward the "liberal arts." The first, much more frequently exercised option was based on so-called "abacus" or "algorism" schools. Future merchants, bank clerks, and artisans would be taught subjects, in Italian, which today we would call accounting, economics, and international finance. They would also learn those rules of Latin necessary to draft letters. The second option, however, made mastery of Latin the goal, which was essential for entering a university. The grammar school courses lasted around five years and, after a period devoted almost entirely to Latin (based on the grammar of the fourth-century teacher Aelius Donatus), it also extended indirectly into ancient literature, thanks to the vast number of references quoted in the more complex grammar of Priscian (fifth–sixth century AD). We have no information about lay grammar schools in the second half of the 1270s (the earliest evidence dates from 1299), but we know of their existence in monastic institutions: there is documentary evidence of the presence of two grammar masters for novice monks in the Servite convent of Santa Maria di Cafaggio between 1286 and 1290.[32] Dante refers, once again in his *Convivio,* to the "art of grammar" (*Conv.* II XII 3–4; "l'arte di gramatica") that had enabled him to understand Boethius and Cicero, where "grammar" indicates both the Latin language and the practice of studying it. It is therefore possible that he attended a school, but this presumed course of studies also remains a mystery. We therefore don't know what Latin classics he may have read at this time. In Florence, where interest in the great Latin writers was very late to develop, books by classic authors were in short supply. In any event, as I have already said, the general impression is that no particular concern was given to education even in the last decades of the 1200s. And not just in the sphere of liberal studies. There are no documents, for example, about the activities of the schools of notaries and the schools of law, which we would have expected in a commercial city where the number of notaries, judges, and advocates was so high that they established their own guild. Cities like Arezzo, Siena, and Pistoia showed more interest in lay culture.

If there were no grammar schools—or at least none of any importance—there could obviously be no schools of rhetoric, schools where, once knowledge of the language had been acquired, pupils learned to compose texts, particularly in prose, that followed established rhetorical traditions, the so-called *artes dictaminis.* More than oratory, the main scope of this advanced learning was epistolography, the art of composing official letters on behalf of institutions, or private letters that had a certain literary pretension. Dante turned out to be an excellent Latin prose writer and a great epistolographer. Assuming he completed a formal grammar education around the age of fifteen, where and under whom did he attain his linguistic and rhetorical skill? His education progressed not through a course of studies, but also not by simple self-instruction. The only person in Florence who had the culture, experience, and authority to be able to transmit these skills was Brunetto Latini.

Fulguration and fainting

The young child who learned to read and write under the guidance of a *magister puerorum* probably had certain health problems. We can deduce this from Dante's writings in later years. No other medieval writer talks about the illnesses he suffered as frequently as Dante does. Sometimes he refers to them directly while at other times, and more often, he mentions bouts of sickness when he speaks of his relationship with Beatrice and alludes to them through a metaphorical game that lessens the more overtly autobiographical aspects and suggests a symbolical interpretation of events.[33]

An example of the first kind is the account of an eye ailment he says he suffered as a result of too much study. By force of reading, he had weakened "the visual powers" to the point that the stars "seemed all veiled in white haze," and only "by long rest in dark cool places, and refreshing the eye with clear water" did he recover his "former good state of vision" (*Conv.* III IX 15; "in tanto debilitai li spiriti visivi che le stelle mi pareano tutte d'alcuno albore ombrate. E per lunga riposanza in luoghi oscuri e freddi, e con affreddare lo corpo dell'occhio coll'acqua chiara, riunì sì la vertù disgregata che tornai nel primo buono stato della vista"). Dante suggests he had suffered this affliction during the period when he devoted himself to philosophical study, more exactly between 1293 and 1295.[34] We know he venerated Saint Lucy. Since the particular devotion to a saint almost always depends on the kind of protection traditionally attributed to him or her, that of Dante for Saint Lucy will have depended on the fact that the saint is invoked as protector of sight, due to the connection between her name and light (*luce*). The eye ailment (which oculists would describe as accommodative asthenopia) may help to explain why in the *Commedia*, Saint Lucy is given the important role of intermediary between Dante and Beatrice.[35]

More often than not, the reference to ailments is found when there is talk of love.

In the *Vita Nova* Dante describes having been struck down by a "painful illness," an attack of fever that had left him delirious: "and then,

I was overcome with such confusion, that I shut my eyes and began to struggle like a person raving." (*VN* 14, 1, 4; "una dolorosa infermitade; E però, mi giunse uno sì forte smarrimento, che chiusi gli occhi e cominciai a travagliare come farnetica persona"). The episode, which we can regard as real, has no connection with the passion of love, nor would it have anything to do with the story narrated in the book if Dante hadn't used it, under the form of a premonitory nightmare, to introduce the description of the death of Beatrice. To nurse him in his illness is a "young and gracious lady" who is "very closely related by birth" (*VN* 14, 1–12; "donna giovane e gentile . . . di propinquissima sanguinità congiunta"): a very close female relative who could be a sister. The love story told in the *Vita Nova* begins in 1283: his sister Tana was already married by that time, as was presumably his other unidentified sister who had married Leone Poggi, so that the ailment must relate back to his childhood. Dante reuses it, placing it in a later period for narrative purposes. In other words he provides a credible context (introduced by the account of that illness) for the canzone *Donna pietosa e di novella etate* (*A kindly lady and of tender years*), which, according to him, refers in the opening lines to that same sister.[36]

His physical crisis, almost a fainting, provoked by the appearance of Beatrice, fits fully into the symptoms of love. On the occasion of a wedding, Dante went with a friend to a house where many women were assembled and there, even before he had seen her, he physically perceives the presence of his beloved ("I seemed to feel a strange throbbing that began in the left side of my breast and spread to all parts of my body"). As soon as he sees Beatrice, from a shudder he falls into a faint: "then my spirits were so destroyed by the strength that Love acquired on seeing itself so close to that most gracious lady . . . And my friend, misunderstanding though acting in good faith, took me by the hand, and leading me away from the sight of these women he asked what was wrong. Then I, feeling somewhat rested, and my dead spirits coming back to life, while those driven out having come back to their rightful place, I said to my friend: 'I have set foot in that part of life beyond which no one can go, still hoping to return'" (*VN* 7, 4–8; "mi parve sentire uno mirabile tremore incominciare nel mio petto dalla sinistra parte e distendersi di subito per tutte le parti del mio corpo . . . Allora fuoro sì distrutti li miei spiriti per la forza che Amore prese veggendosi in tanta propinquitade alla gentilissima donna . . . onde lo ingannato amico di buona fede mi prese per la mano, e traendomi fuori della veduta di queste donne mi domandò che io avesse. Allora io riposato alquanto, e resurressiti li morti spiriti miei e li discacciati rivenuti alle loro possessioni, dissi a questo mio amico queste parole: 'Io tenni li piedi in quella parte della vita di là dalla quale non si puote ire più per intendimento di ritornare'").

In his poetry, the appearance of women often produces similar traumatic effects: the epiphany of the beloved, actual or only sensed, provokes in the subject (unique among thirteenth-century versifiers) an instant bewilderment in which loss of sight can be associated with a loss of consciousness. It is odd, though, that a very similar crisis, according to what Dante tells us, had affected him in childhood. It is he himself, in fact, who traced his first psychophysical crisis back to his first months of life, which he described in a canzone perhaps written in the first half of the 1290s, *E' m'incresce di me sì duramente* (*I feel such deep pity for myself*): on the day that Beatrice was born, he, still only a few months old, had lost consciousness "so suddenly that I fell to the ground," as if struck by lightning. The symptoms are the same as the crisis in which the victim is the man in love who speaks in the so-called "montanina" canzone, *Amor, da che convien pur ch'io mi doglia* (*O Love, since I must suffer more and more*), which dates to a period far away from that of *E' m'incresce di me* (perhaps late in 1307, during one of Dante's stays in the Casentino area) and therefore not referring to Beatrice. Here the poet writes that, obsessed by the thought of his lady, he goes to where he can see her with the same heart as a condemned man approaching the gallows, and that when he is before her, at the very moment when he is looking for someone who might give him comfort, from her eyes there is a sudden splendor that takes away his senses and leaves him "lifeless." Unlike the first, this canzone describes at length the resolution of the crisis, presented as a "coming back to life": after the blow that had "struck [him] down" like "thunder," the subject slowly regains consciousness, but it is followed by a shudder of fear and for some time his face remains pale and upset by the shock he has experienced.[37]

The psychophysical crises described here, and the way they were resolved—crises that have nothing to do with the conception of love as a pathology, so-called love sickness (*amor heroes*) and well known to medical science of the time—are unique to Dante and show all the signs of an apoplectic or epileptic fit.[38] Dante describes a similar crisis in medical terms in Canto XXIV of *Inferno,* in a context devoid of the slightest connection to themes of love. Vanni Fucci, a thief, after a serpent bite has instantly reduced him to ashes, is restored just as instantly to human form. His fall had been sudden and his return to his own human form had been just as sudden; but the reemergence of consciousness and the restoration of mental balance are slower, so that Dante, in describing the process, resorts to this simile:

> And as a man in a fit will fall, not knowing why
> by force of a demon that pulls him down to earth,
> or some oppilation that can bind the man,
> > then, struggling to his feet, will look around,
> confused and overwhelmed by the great anguish
> he has suffered, moaning as he stares about—
> > so did this sinner when he finally rose.

> E qual è quel che cade, e non sa como,
> per forza di demon ch'a terra il tira,
> o d'altra oppilazion che lega l'omo,
> > quando si leva, che 'ntorno si mira
> tutto smarrito de la grande angoscia
> ch'elli ha sofferta, e guardando sospira:
> > tal era 'l peccator levato poscia.

—*Inf.* XXIV 112–118

Toward the end of the nineteenth century, Cesare Lombroso's school of psychiatry diagnosed Dante as having been affected by epilepsy. With very few exceptions, this diagnosis has never been accepted by Dante scholars. And yet, the precision and emotional involvement with which Dante describes these attacks suggests that beneath the literary text lies a strong dose of experience. The illness seems to have afflicted him from early childhood. In the canzone *E' m'incresce di me* he writes that he has taken the recollection of the fulguration that struck him the day Beatrice was born from the book of memory ("as we find / in the ever-fading book of the mind"): in the "mind" of a child just a few months old there can be no fixed memories of any kind, and therefore we must think that, unless it's a pure invention (possible, but unlikely), Dante is referring to accounts heard from relatives or people who nursed him immediately after his birth.[39]

Predestination

In the Middle Ages, epilepsy had the same nature of a sacred affliction that it had had among the ancients, for whom it was caused by a divine intervention which was almost always punitive. But its sacrality had been transformed into something diabolic: the epileptic was possessed by the devil. Not only was it a shameful illness, often confused with madness, but it was also socially dangerous because it could be transmitted not only through heredity but also by contagion. The diabolical nature of evil suggested a series of therapeutic prescriptions for which, alongside fanciful and sometimes cruel remedies, there was much space for amulets, prayers to saints, magic rituals, and exorcisms. The epileptic therefore had to cope with great prejudice that often turned into wrath and persecution.[40] It is against this background that Dante's references to the sickness must be considered. There was a very widely held view— expressed, for example, by Hildegard of Bingen, the twelfth-century Benedictine nun—that the devil, thanks to his power, doesn't provoke the epileptic attack directly but exercises his influence when the body is unbalanced due to the humors that clog the brain and therefore that he acts on a susceptible body through the "breath of his power of suggestion" ("flatu suggestionis suae"). But in the lines "by force of a demon that pulls him down to earth, / or some other oppilation that can bind a man," Dante seems to be making a distinction: the loss of senses and the consequent fall to the ground can be caused by possession by the devil or by an occlusion or obstruction ("oppilation"). His use of the rare technical term suggests that, alongside the more popular conception, he had a more strictly medical conception of the complaint. Oppilation, in fact, was one of the scientific explanations produced by medieval medicine: it was said to be an excess of humors, of varying nature, that led to the total or partial obstruction of the ventricles of the brain.[41]

But Dante didn't stop at mitigating the diabolical aura of the disorder; in *E' m'incresce di me,* in the stanza in which he recounts his experience of fulguration as a child, he presents the crisis suffered in the first months of life as the sign of having been destined from birth to an exclusive love, a tangible sign, impressed upon his body, of a predestination decreed by a supreme power. In short, the nexus between love and illness is a powerful mark of distinction: he alone, among all the versifiers of his century, had received this gift (or this affliction). If that psychophysical crisis is to be understood in a medical sense as an epileptic crisis, then we find ourselves in front of a Dante who transforms an illness which marks the patient in a strongly negative manner into a phenomenon that distinguishes him in a positive sense.

So even illness—or at least this specific illness—is one of the factors that strengthens his personal conviction that he is exceptional. The visionary gift that he displays in many of his works, and in particular in the *Commedia*—a gift that medieval culture regarded as integral to mysticism—could be deeply rooted in the pathological experiences marked by such states of hallucination as those of epilepsy: an hypothesis to explore with caution, but nevertheless preferable to the idea suggested by one scholar that he used stimulants or narcotics.[42]

Dante detected the seal of fate in many other occurrences in his life, not just in illness, and his task as an intellectual was to reveal their hidden significance. His tendency to recognize the "signs" and to interpret them would accompany him throughout his life. Signs, however, are always engraved upon objects, upon his person or his actions.

One day—no date is given but it must have fallen in a period fairly close to his journey of 1300 into the afterworld—an incident occurred during a baptism ceremony in San Giovanni. A (newborn?) child fell into one of the terracotta amphorae containing the holy water and was in danger of drowning. Dante promptly smashed the container and saved the child. That gesture caused an outcry—perhaps it was regarded as sacrilege. Years later, when he wrote the *Commedia,* Dante remembered it and recounted it in *Inferno,* in the canto about the simoniacs. Here he compares the holes that perforate the walls and the bottom of the bolgia to those excavated in the baptismal font to contain the amphorae:

> They seemed no wider nor deeper to me
> than those inside my fine San Giovanni,
> made as a place for the baptizers;

and then, unexpectedly, he adds:

> and one of which, not many years ago,
> I smashed for one who was drowning inside:
> and may this be a seal to undeceive all men.

> Non mi parean men ampi né maggiori
> che que' che son nel mio bel San Giovanni,
> fatti per loco d'i battezzatori;
>   l'un de li quali, ancor non è molt' anni,
> rupp' io per un che dentro v'annegava:
> e questo sia suggel ch'ogn' omo sganni.

—*Inf.* XIX 16–21

He recounts it to reestablish the truth of the facts ("and may this be a seal to undeceive all men"), but above all because in the meantime he had realized that his past gesture repeated a similar one performed by the prophet Jeremiah. The inhabitants of Jerusalem had given themselves to prophetic cults, and then God had commanded Jeremiah to break an amphora in the valley in front of the Gate of the Potsherds to proclaim to them that their city would be destroyed. Dante was therefore persuaded that his own gesture had also been prophetic, and communicated it to readers through a "figural" procedure: the breaking of the amphora of holy water replicates the gesture and, at the same time, the message of the biblical prophet.[43] In the same way that Jeremiah had railed against the idolatry of the Jews, he, in the *Commedia,* railed against the modern idolatry (simony) of the church. In that sacred place, God had given him the task of denouncing ecclesiastical corruption: he had given him a prophetic mission.

The epileptic crisis as a sign of predestination is not explored beyond the bounds of amorous discourse. Yet medieval theologians, following ancient philosophers and physicians, also detected a condition during states of trance, including those of epilepsy, that was favorable to the manifestation of prophetic or divinatory powers. But for them it remained to be decided, case by case, whether the prophetical inspiration came from God or Satan. We may think it was the very ambiguity of the aura surrounding the figure of an epileptic-prophet that convinced

Dante to limit the compass of that *signum* only to the sphere of love.[44] The role of the prophet with a mission to save Christianity required much clearer and unambiguous credentials.

May Day

In the documentary desert of the 1270s, two dates stand out: 1274 and 1277. Both relate to women who counted much in Dante's life, but whose destinies were completely different, if not opposite: the first was Beatrice, the second Gemma Donati, his wife. Beatrice would have central place in Dante's poetic imagination; Gemma would remain just a fleeting figure in the background.

At the beginning of the *Vita Nova,* Dante declares he had met Beatrice for the first time, and had fallen immediately in love with her, when he was almost at the end and she just at the beginning of their ninth year (1274). Later on, he says he saw her again for the second time when they were both eighteen (1283).[45] The *Vita Nova,* completed around the mid-1290s, tells the story of the author's poetry and, at the same time, of his love for Beatrice, claiming that this woman had always inspired his poetry, even secretly at times, and that from his childhood Dante had always remained faithful to this love, despite certain appearances to the contrary. His claim that this was his only love is also one of the formative elements in his portrayal, or rather self-portrayal, of Dante as someone exceptional. In reality, things weren't quite like that: if we look at the love poems written by Dante before the *Vita Nova,* we quickly realize that Beatrice didn't enjoy a particularly prominent position among his many poetical inspirations, and that her myth is effectively generated with the *Vita Nova.* Her relationship with Dante, whatever its nature, began in fact at the end of the 1280s and was interrupted by her death in June 1290. But the *Vita Nova* is an autobiography, so its story could not openly contradict what Florentine readers knew about its author's poetical and love life, yet it had to appear credible. To give credibility to a story that had been largely invented, Dante sprinkled it with references to real life, interpreting events experienced by him in the light of the fictitious plot. In short, he constructs a "false" account, assembling much "true" material.[46]

Was it true, then, that he'd met Beatrice at the age of nine? No one, obviously, could question a detail that was so personal and which, moreover, dated back to a time readers of the story could have no knowledge about. Besides, Dante doesn't specify where and in what circumstances the meeting took place. It was Giovanni Boccaccio who gave it an exact context. In his *Trattatello in laude di Dante* he would put together the story about how, on May Day 1274, Beatrice's father, Folco Portinari, had gathered many people, including Alighiero and his young son Dante, at his house to celebrate, and that on that occasion the boy had fallen in love forever with the young Bice. It is an invention by Boccaccio who, among other things, without realizing it, dates a festive custom to a time, in the 1270s, when it hadn't yet come into fashion.[47] But it was probable, and therefore credible to readers, that there may have been celebrations and party gatherings between families who lived in the same district and who were also linked by political connections—the Portinari and Alighieri families both sided with the Cerchi party.

Dante was interested in the date, and was interested in expressing it through the number nine. That number would be repeated over and over again in the story: it would become one of the key symbols, up to the point where Beatrice herself would become identified with the number nine. And yet it was the very recurrence of this symbolic number—which to our minds is a sure indication of invention—that made the veracity of the date plausible, if not certain. For us, it is natural to think that an author first gives a particular symbolic value to a particular number and then constructs the narrative sequences of the book around that symbolism. And yet it was more probable that a medieval author first discovered certain numerical coincidences in reality and only afterwards clothed them with symbolic meaning and transformed them into significant and even structural aspects of his work. We should remember what Petrarch did with the number six, which would have a very similar role in his *Canzoniere* as that given by Dante to the number nine in the *Vita Nova*. Petrarch would develop the symbolic significance of six starting from a "realistic" element, namely the coincidence between the date of his first meeting with Laura (April 6, 1327) and that of her death (April 6, 1348). It is reasonable to think that Dante may also have been encouraged by biographical coincidences, that he might even have remembered real events, as is typical of his approach, and may afterwards have recognized a symbolic value in them.[48]

We are surprised by the very young age of the two. And in fact, though Dante, at nine, was indeed very young by the standards of the time, this is not so for Beatrice. The marrying age was around fourteen or fifteen (the legal minimum being twelve, though the limit was sometimes reduced). A contemporary of Dante, Francesco da Barberino, in his *Reggimento e costumi di donna*—a treatise on female comportment written in verse and interspersed with passages in prose, written between 1318 and 1320—tells the story of Corrado di Savoia who falls in love with a knight's daughter called Gioietta, "who was nine years old," and marries her. In other words, Beatrice's nine years are not to be interpreted, by our standards, as indicating that she was still a child, but as an indication that she was, as Barberino says, "a girl who begins to feel a certain shame," in other words "begins to have good and bad feelings."[49]

We can therefore accept that Dante met Beatrice in 1274, but we really can't believe him when he claims that the love of his life—the only love of his life—began on that occasion. And yet he would always remain faithful to this invention of his, to the point of it becoming one of the classic features of his intellectual and literary biography. Dante seems incapable of imagining a book in which his person, or at least a person bearing his name, doesn't play a significant role, but that character can equally be a literary construction, and therefore a true fictional character, or it can be the direct transposition of his biographical self—and it can often be both at the same time. In short, he talks about himself without distinguishing between fiction and reality. When in *Purgatorio* he writes that Beatrice had "transfixed" him before he was "out of boyhood" (*Purg.* XXX 41–42; "m'avea trafitto / prima ch'io fuor di puerizia fosse"), he is referring to the literary fiction of the *Vita Nova,* but when, in a sonnet replying to Cino da Pistoia (datable to between 1303 and 1306) he describes himself as an expert in love through having lived at its service from his ninth year (*Rime* 47b 1–2; "Io sono stato con Amore insieme / dalla circulazion del sol mia nona"), he assumes this invention as a real biographical fact.[50]

The brief life of Bice Portinari

The *Vita Nova* indicates by implication when Beatrice was born (1266) and is clear, though convoluted (in doing so, he refers to three different calendars) about the date of her death, specifying its hour, day, month, and year: an hour after sunset on June 8, 1290.[51] The book also mentions her father and a brother, but to reconstruct what little we know about her life we have to go to other sources.[52]

We know she was the daughter of Folco Portinari, a leading member of a prominent family involved in trade and finance, living in the same *sestiere* as the Alighieri family. The Portinari, like the Alighieri, were politically close to the faction headed by the Cerchi family (of whose bank Folco was a member), a faction which had been the backbone of the party of the Whites in the last years of the century, in opposition to that of the Blacks, led by the Donati family. Folco had held important public offices (several times a prior) and, above all, his name was linked to the founding of the city's main charitable institution, the hospital of Santa Maria Nuova in 1286, though it would not be opened until two years later. He died on December 31, 1289. The *Vita Nova* dedicates a whole paragraph to his death, in which the reference to the deceased's great kindness is to be interpreted as a direct reference to the hospital he founded. Dante was closely attached to the Portinari family: he considered Beatrice's brother, Manetto, to be his next best friend after Guido Cavalcanti.[53]

Beatrice, therefore, belonged to the city's high society, and on her marriage to Simone dei Bardi she became part of an even more illustrious family. The Bardi, known today for having commissioned Giotto to paint the frescoes that decorate their chapel in Santa Croce (1325–1330), were the heads of one of the main Florentine banking companies. Already powerful in the 1280s, their company would further grow until it became one of the largest in Europe. Its sudden collapse in 1343 would have serious repercussions for the whole Florentine financial system.

Simone, son of Geri di Ricco, belonged to one of the two main branches of the family: unlike the other, descended from his uncle, Iacopo de Ricco, who was involved in major finance and held key positions in the city's political life, Geri's family branch seemed concerned in external affairs, in what we might describe as the family's foreign policy. While many in Iacopo's branch were priors, no one of Geri's branch ever seems to have held that appointment. In the records, the name Simone di Geri is accompanied by the word *dominus,* indicating that he had been given the title of knight. In the city's stratified society, a knight enjoyed great prestige. This is confirmed by literary texts: for example, the so-called "canzone del pregio" (*Amor mi sforza e mi sprona valere*) by Dino Compagni draws a scale of hierarchy: kings down to barons, judges, and knights, then jurists, notaries and doctors, next financiers (*mercatanti*), and finally artisans.[54] In short, by marrying the knight Simone dei Bardi, Beatrice had become part of Florence's most aristocratic elite. Great was the distance between her social position and that of Dante, scion of a family of such mediocre status that it had produced only one prior between 1282 (the date when the office of prior was instituted) and 1300, and that was Dante himself. Simone held prestigious public appointments in various cities, including that of *capitano del popolo* (Orvieto, 1310) and *podestà* (Volterra, 1288). In 1290, the year when Beatrice died, he was *capitano del popolo* of Prato.

We don't know when Beatrice and Simone married: perhaps even before 1280.[55] It would naturally have been an arranged political marriage. In a city torn apart by unending strife, the marriage alliance between rival families was one way of trying to keep the peace, and of limiting damage in the event of conflict; so it is no surprise that the prudent Folco Portinari had sought a bond with the Bardi, who were ardent supporters of the Donati. We don't know whether the couple had any children. The only certainty is that, when they married, Beatrice moved to her husband's house.

The houses of the Bardi family stood in the Oltrarno area, along the road (which today bears their name) that runs east, parallel with the river, as far as Porta San Niccolò, below San Miniato hill. That gateway was known as the gate to Rome, since the Via Cassia, the ancient consular road for Siena and Rome, began there. It was therefore what we would now call a major communication route and, in fact, various hospitals stood there (one for men was opened in 1283, near the homes of the Bardi family, and another for women was opened the following year). Toward the end of the *Vita Nova*, Dante describes a group of pilgrims who cross Florence during Holy Week along a street "that goes more or less through the middle of the city" who, by their manner, show that they know nothing of the great loss it has suffered, namely the death of Beatrice. Here Dante makes an exception to his rule of not using familiar names of people or places (not even Florence is ever named): he tells his readers that the pilgrims are on their way to Rome to see Saint Veronica's

veil. They are therefore traveling the road that crossed Florence from
west to east, on which stood the house where Beatrice had lived during
her marriage and where she had almost certainly died. Villani, the
chronicler, tells us that the houses of the Bardi family stood close to the
Church of Santa Lucia dei Magnoli (also known as Santa Lucia dei
Bardi).[56] We don't know in which church Beatrice was buried: the most
probable were either this or the nearby Santa Maria Sopr'Arno (demolished in 1869); in any event, its physical proximity made it more likely
that she attended the church of Santa Lucia. Here, then, may be a further
reason for the choice of Saint Lucy as intermediary in the *Commedia*: the
saint is linked, on the one hand, to Dante for the particular devotion he
professed toward her (in which his problems with eyesight probably
played a part), and on the other to Beatrice, who must have prayed
many times in the church dedicated to the saint.

Simone dei Bardi, like all his relatives, was a loyal follower of the
Donati faction. His brother Cecchino, whom the chronicler Dino Compagni presents as one of Corso's men, must have been a particularly ardent supporter. Between Corso Donati and Guido Cavalcanti there
was, according to Compagni, a fierce hatred, to the point where Corso
had tried to kill Guido while he was on a pilgrimage to Santiago di Com-
postela. That, at least, was what Cavalcanti believed, who was waiting
for his moment of revenge. One day, while he was riding his horse
through the city with several members of the Cerchi family, Guido came
across Corso, who was also in the company of his followers, including
Cecchino dei Bardi. Guido spurred his horse and shot an arrow at his
enemy, but missed the target. Guido thought he was being backed by
his companions in the attack but found himself alone and had to escape
from Corso and his gang.[57]

When the Donati faction took the name Blacks, the Bardi also became
Blacks: they always sided not just with that faction, but indeed with the
more hard-line part of it, headed by the Della Tosa family. Dante therefore had every reason to regard them as personal enemies. And yet it is
surprising that in the *Commedia,* where he is never short of sarcasms,
jibes, and insults against his political enemies, and even against his one-
time friends, he never once mentions the Bardi family. Is this a sign of
respect or complete *damnatio memoriae*?

A prestigious marriage

Dante was still a child when his father—or perhaps his closest relatives after his father's death—decided he should marry. The choice eventually fell on Gemma, a young girl the same age or perhaps a few years younger than Dante, from the powerful Donati family, who also lived in San Pier Maggiore. Once again, since the Alighieri and Cerchi families were related, there would have been no shortage of political reasons for the marriage, as well as financial ones (the girl's family held lands in Pagnolle adjoining those of the Alighieri). Gemma was related, though only distantly (she was a third cousin), to Corso, Forese, and Piccarda, in other words, to the branch of the Donati family that would lead the victorious Guelf faction over the next decades. Her parents could also boast an illustrious ancestry. Her father, Manetto, was son of Ubertino Donati, and his mother a daughter of Bellincione Berti.[58] Dante had such great respect for the nobility of Ubertino that in *Paradiso*, in order to emphasize it, he would say that Ubertino had disapproved of the fact that his father-in-law Bellincione had married off another daughter of his to a member of the Adimari family, who were haughty but insignificant ("di picciola gente").[59] Even assuming that Dante was exaggerating, as usual, the aristocratic nature of his wife's family, this was nevertheless a prestigious marriage for the Alighieri family, and it became all the more so when Manetto, who in 1280 had been one of the guarantors of the so-called Peace of Cardinal Latino, was knighted, after Dante's engagement with Gemma.

The prenuptial negotiations resulted in one document, signed before a notary on February 9, 1277 (Dante was just short of twelve), in which Gemma was promised to Dante and the amount of the dowry was settled. That document has unfortunately not survived, and we therefore can't establish who acted on Dante's behalf, whether it was his father Alighiero or a guardian. Alighiero II could, in fact, have already died, and the negotiation would therefore have been carried out by the orphans' guardian. An alliance with the Donati was socially prestigious, but brought little advantage from an economic point of view. Gemma's dowry, in fact, was only 200 small florins.[60] Dowries were calculated in proportion to the wealth of the future husband, and this was because his wealth guaranteed its return in the event of the husband dying. Gemma's extremely modest dowry confirms that Alighiero II (or his estate) had no substantial assets by the second half of the 1270s. In practical terms, Gemma brought only a prestigious name as her dowry. It seems unlikely that a small-time moneylender like Alighieri II, needful of liquid assets for his profession, would have contemplated such a marriage: his interests and his way of thinking would have indicated instead a contract with a woman less noble but of greater economic means. Someone like Durante degli Abati, on the other hand, might have been more interested in the name rather than in florins, and he might perhaps have found it convenient to make an alliance, however distant, with the Donati.[61]

The wedding, as we shall see, took place later—perhaps between 1283 and 1285.

There has been much discussion among Dante scholars about whether the marriage was happy. The discussion was sparked by Boccaccio, who painted an unflattering portrait of Gemma in his *Trattatello*. According to him, Dante's relatives persuaded him to get married to console him after the death of Beatrice—which is obviously fanciful—and they made a great mistake. The relationship brought him only trouble and pain, says Boccaccio, because this is the fate of all men of genius (*filosofanti*) who reconcile themselves to marriage: those who have tried it know "what sorrows rooms conceal, which from outside, to those eyes not keen enough to penetrate their walls, are supposed to be joys." The only support he gives for his allegations is the conjecture (though still unproved and actually to be regarded as groundless) that, after Dante's exile, the two never met again. In the absence of any firm evidence we can only refrain from making any judgment about Dante's marriage. But it ought to be said that any disagreements between them couldn't have been particularly serious. This is indicated by the fact that Dante and Gemma's father and brothers were always on good terms. For example, Manetto Donati was several times guarantor of loans given to Dante in the 1290s, and even for substantial amounts: in December 1297, as will be mentioned below, he guaranteed a debt contracted by Dante and his brother Francesco for the sizeable sum of 480 gold florins. And even after his exile, there is no sign of conflict between husband and wife. Besides, Dante, despite his political quarrel with Corso, treated the Donati family with respect, even with favor.

2

A Strange Florentine

1283–1295

If you follow your star,
you cannot fail to reach a glorious port

Se tu segui tua stella
non puoi fallire a glorïoso porto

—*Inf.* xv 55–56

A difficult coexistence

MANY FLORENTINE Ghibellines had left after the political upheaval of 1267, most of them interned or exiled, though many had gone voluntarily.[1] Over the next few years, those who remained in the city were barred from public office and subjected to fundamental forms of discrimination; attempts at reconciliation, though encouraged (such as that of 1273 promoted by Pope Gregory X), had no lasting effect. The political climate began to change around 1280 when Pope Nicholas III sent his nephew Cardinal Latino Malabranca as papal legate. After long negotiations in February, an agreement was formalized (the Peace of Cardinal Latino), after which the Ghibellines who had emigrated or been exiled could return to the city and a system of political guarantees was established. It is worth noting that the influential citizens named by the parties to assure respect for the terms of the pact included Brunetto Latini and Guido Cavalcanti, who would both play a major part in

Dante's life. The agreement involved changes in the city statutes and the appointment of new magistrates. The aim was to form a compromise government that would ensure a tolerable coexistence, though not exactly an equilibrium, since the Guelfs were in the majority. But very soon the objective proved illusory: the widespread hostility that divided the two parties led to continual tension and sporadic outbreaks of violence between the leading families. Above all, the fact that the Ghibellines still remained in a minority favored the perpetuation of private vendettas and public persecution.

An example was the trial in 1283 against Farinata degli Uberti (who had died in 1264) and his surviving heirs. This was yet another chapter in the long campaign of persecution against the family which had led the Ghibelline party and was accused of bearing prime responsibility for the massacre at Montaperti. The Florentine inquisitor, the Franciscan friar Salomone da Lucca (of the Mordecastelli family), accused Farinata and his wife Adaletta (both deceased) of being members of a Cathar sect, and convicted them of heresy. While the corpse of Farinata was dug up and his bones burned at the stake, his sons Lapo, Federico, and Maghinardo, and the children of Azzolino degli Uberti, Lapo and Itta, received the sentence imposed upon other members of the family, namely the confiscation of their inheritance. Two years later, Salomone convicted Bruno (another dead Uberti) as a heretic and ordered the confiscation of the property inherited by his grandchildren Bruno and Guiduccio. The Franciscan also convicted other dead people of Cathar heresy during the three years in which he held the office of inquisitor.[2] It ought to come as no surprise that trials were held against the dead. During the Middle Ages, and for many centuries in the modern period, the law allowed not only the conviction of a dead defendant but also the infliction of punishments upon their bodies. The corpses of heretics, if buried in consecrated ground, were exhumed and delivered to the secular authority for the prescribed penalties. One spectacular case (told also by Dante in Canto III of *Purgatorio*) was the digging up of the corpse of Manfred on the order of Pope Clement IV, which took place at night and with lights dimmed, in accordance with the procedure laid down for the excommunicated dead.

The Cathars, who in Italy were called *patari* or *patarini*, were the last major heretical movement of the Middle Ages. Their popularity spread after 1000, particularly in southern France, and they disappeared around the mid-thirteenth century. They claimed that the world was the scene of perpetual conflict between spirit, created by God, and matter, created by Satan, and they led a vigorously ascetic lifestyle: if the world is a work of evil, the faithful must withdraw from it by abstaining, for example, from sexual relations and thus by refusing to procreate. Church propaganda, on the other hand, portrayed them as depraved and as indulging in the vilest debauchery. From the mid-1200s it was common practice for inquisitors and papal legates to accuse Ghibelline enemies of heresy, often without even specifying what kind, so that it was widely believed that heterodoxy and Ghibellinism were one and the same thing. The Uberti were probably therefore convicted for mainly political reasons.

But Salomone da Lucca didn't only proceed against people and families loyal to the Ghibellines: for example, he convicted and confiscated the property of two members (both deceased) of the Bagnesi family, known as being a family faithful to the Guelf cause. Salomone made no distinction between those who were dead or alive, nor between men and women: both Rovinosa, one of the women of the Bagnesi family, and the wife of Farinata were convicted, though already dead. Alongside political vengeance or perhaps (though doubtful) the good faith of a sincere friar who was anxious to wipe out all trace of heresy, we then have to put other, far less noble interests into the equation. The confiscated properties were, indeed, variously subdivided, and parts of them ended up at auction. We know the names of the Florentine families who became wealthy through the purchase of assets confiscated from convicted people. Behind many trials, blatant financial intrigue can be glimpsed. In most cases, it would seem, the supposed *patarini* were nothing of the kind and the trials were means of appropriating the property of families who were politically weak. And the personal interests of those associated with the inquisitors, if not the inquisitors themselves, have also to be borne in mind.[3]

Magnates and the people

During the 1280s, unlike what had happened in the past, injustices and full-blown persecutions against the losers didn't take the form of open

and bloody conflict. This was because a new force began to establish itself, bringing with it a different approach to civic life in Florence.

The new protagonist was what, today, we would call the trading
middle class. At that time it was organized into so-called *arti,* or guilds.
These corporations, which were created toward the end of the twelfth
century as craft associations and developed over time to include almost
the whole of the city's economic and professional activities, were subdivided in the early 1280s into seven large guilds—the Arte di Calimala
(merchants), the Arte del Cambio (bankers and money-changers), the
Arte della Lana (wool), the Arte di Por Santa Maria (silk), the Arte dei
Medici e Speziali (physicians and apothecaries), the Arte dei Vaiai e Pel-
licciai (tanners), and the Arte dei Giudici e Notai (judges and notaries)—
as well as five medium-sized guilds and twelve small ones. The seven
large guilds, of which the Arte di Calimala—a sort of employers' feder-
ation—was the most important, organized the main economic activities (industry, international commerce, finance), while the others brought
together auxiliary activities (today we'd call them services), crafts and
small businesses. All were regulated by their own charter and managed
by governing bodies who had the power to resolve internal questions.
The guilds took part in city assemblies with their own representatives,
and in the period under consideration here, they also had their own
militias. The political weight of the larger guilds, who represented the
interests of the most powerful capitalist class, far exceeded that of the
others.

By 1282, the major guilds, whose prime concern was that of domestic
peace to ensure economic development, had already managed to impose, alongside the new magistracy created out of the Peace of Cardinal
Latino, a government body made up of three priors, directly appointed
by them. The following year the number of members in the Collegio
dei priori—who held office, then as always, for only two months—was
increased to six, all taken from the seven major guilds, but appointed
in such a way that each of the city's *sestieri* was represented. The change
was hardly noticed but, for a city that until then had been changing its
statutes and forms of government with impressive speed, this new
system—which, with few modifications, would remain unchanged for
decades—was a real revolution. The government of the priors sanctioned,
also formally, Florence's full identification with the Guelf cause. From

this moment on, the political conflict in Florence would no longer be between the two historic parties of Guelfs and Ghibellines but would be acted out—no less bitterly and ruthlessly than earlier—between the two factions into which the Guelfs would be split.[4]

The guilds had also appointed an official, called the *capitano e difensore delle arti,* with equal powers to assist the *podestà* and the *capitano del comune* (a magisterial office created with the peace settlements of 1280). Conflicts between the two *capitani* were inevitable, but were resolved by dismissing the *capitano del comune* one month prior to the end of his mandate and merging the duties of the two posts in one single figure of *capitano delle arti e degli artefici e conservatore della pace del comune.* This episode would be of no particular interest to us if it were not for the fact that the *capitano* who was given early dismissal in February 1283 was Paolo Malatesta (nicknamed Paolo il Bello), the same person who would be killed a couple of years later by his brother Giovanni (nicknamed Gianciotto, since he was lame), who had discovered his affair with his wife Francesca da Polenta of Rimini (this is the tragic love story told by Dante, and only by him, in Canto V of *Inferno*).[5]

The new system of government was what the financial oligarchy wanted. It had represented their interests in the early days but, within just a few years, the smaller guilds had begun to assume increasing importance, and even in the main guilds began to develop a policy of limiting the power of the *grandi* or magnates—in other words, of those who were aristocrats by birth or through wealth. It was a long and intermittent process, but one that moved toward the expansion of the social power base and the recognition of middle class and even lower-middle class needs. Over the years, a succession of rules were introduced against the magnates (particularly severe were those imposed in 1286 which required every individual recognized as a magnate, upon reaching the age of fifteen, to pay a heavy security, known as a *sodamento*). Then, exactly ten years after the creation of the office of prior, a radical reform excluded them even from appointment as political representatives. The struggle between families and guilds, which had marked political life up until then, was transformed now into open class conflict.

This led to the promulgation of the so-called *Ordinamenti di giustizia* in 1293, thanks to the action of the wealthy merchant Giano Tedaldi della Bella (who had properties near the church of San Martino, in other words, not far from where Dante lived). They were a series of regulations, introduced over two years from 1293 to 1295, that excluded magnates from political office, in particular from the most important office of prior (though not from administrative roles such as ambassador, for example, or from military appointments). The problem then was to establish who should be considered a magnate. Families of the ancient feudal nobility certainly belonged to the magnate category. They had distinguished themselves in over forty years of conflict between Guelfs and Ghibellines, but by the 1290s they no longer formed the backbone of the city's aristocracy. The *grandi* at this time—against whom the *popolo minuto* (ordinary people, such as craft workers, small and medium businessmen, and money changers) directed their resentment—had themselves originally been ordinary people, but had amassed enormous wealth and had adopted the manner and style of the nobility, characterized by arrogance, disdain, disregard for the law, and an overbearing manner exhibited daily in the city streets. The ruling groups of the guilds, including those of the Arte di Calimala, felt compelled to break the hold this small group of influential clans still had over city government, even though political representation had become much broader.

The greatest aspiration of the oligarchs was to achieve noble status, to rise to the same social rank as families of feudal birth. That is why everyone wanted a knighthood: only that title could provide a way of moving up in rank. Our picture of the knight is typically that of a member of a feudal society, in the same way that our picture of the merchant is typically one associated with civic life. Indeed, until at least the early 1200s, the *milites,* in numerical terms, were a very significant portion of city society, where they ranked at the very top. Knights, namely those who could afford a costly battle outfit, including horse, were the heart of the city's military power: they were therefore essential both for its defense as well as for its territorial expansion. This role brought them great economic benefits, gained from the profits of war and, above all, from the fact that, being a compact and united group, they were able to siphon off a large portion of public finances to their advantage. Though not necessarily of noble blood, knights could therefore maintain a close bond with the nobility in their manner and ideals, enabling them to play a key role in public affairs and enjoy real class privileges.

By the final decades of the 1200s, things were different. The cavalry, the central core of the army, still consisted of wealthy men (a large number belonging to the magnate classes), but the majority had no knighthood. It still, however, bore considerable attraction. It didn't bring great financial rewards, but it provided a series of privileges, almost all honorary, for its members: to wear spurs, have pommels on their swords, and ride a horse with a gold bit; to decorate themselves (and their wives) with precious stones in exemption from the restrictions of sumptuary laws; to have a greater number of guests at weddings and of clerics at funerals than were normally allowed, and so on. We can well understand, then, why their title would no longer be *miles,* but *dominus* (in Italian *messere*), a title also held by judges. Among the rich, especially among those with no noble ancestry, there was great competition to be dubbed a knight. The number of knights was considerable (in 1283, three hundred *cavalieri di corredo* in the city and the surrounding area, to which were added the mass of *donzelli,* candidates for the cavalry; ten years later the number stood at around two hundred and fifty), but incomparably lower than the number of *milites,* or actual knights, in the previous century, which could reach a third of the city's population. According to the chroniclers, it would seem that the position of cavalier was regarded as a sort of public license to behave in a manner that was evidently regarded as aristocratic, in which luxury and privilege were flaunted: knights kept sumptuous court night and day, gave lavish gifts on feast days, surrounded themselves with jesters and courtiers, entertained any illustrious person who might be visiting Florence and escorted them on horseback around the city and beyond. Being a knight was therefore a status symbol, a step up from merchant, manufacturer, or banker to that of "lord."[6]

This is why the *Ordinamenti di giustizia* stipulated, in the criteria for defining a magnate, a blood relationship, even distant, to a knight (later increased to two knights), either living, or dead for less than twenty years. In accordance with the regulations, the magnate families deprived of political rights were listed by name: seventy-two in all. The name of the Alighieri family, of course, was not among them.[7]

A Ghibelline uprising

Guelf supremacy had been established over most of Tuscany (with the obvious exception of Pisa). But the Ghibellines of neighboring Romagna, headed by Guido da Montefeltro, who had installed himself in Forlì, had strongly resisted all papal attempts throughout the 1270s to control the region after the defeat of the Swabians. An army of Angevin and French forces had had to intervene in the early 1280s and had succeeded in occupying Forlì in 1283, but only after disastrous setbacks: the massacre of French knights in the city, carried out by Montefeltro on May 1, 1282, caused horror—"a bloody heap of French" (*Inf.* XXVII 44; "di Franceschi sanguinoso mucchio"), Dante would write. That same year, a revolt against the Angevins, the so-called Sicilian Vespers, had erupted in Palermo, with the cry "Death to the French"—"bad government," Dante would write, had "moved Palermo to shout: 'Die, die!'" (*Para.* VIII 73–75; "se mala segnoria, che sempre accora / li popoli suggetti, non avesse / mosso Palermo a gridar: 'Mora, mora!'"). The effects of the revolt would involve Charles of Anjou and his successors in a war lasting twenty years, at the end of which they would finally lose Sicily, which passed under the rule of an Aragon dynasty. These events had weakened the Guelf faction and the power of the king of Naples. Added to this, Rudolf of Habsburg, king of the Romans, while awaiting his imperial coronation after a long period of absence, had developed a new interest in Tuscan affairs and, in early 1281, had sent his chancellor Rudolf of Hoheneck there on a mission as vicar general. While Guelf power was being consolidated in Florence, in many other parts of Tuscany there was a restirring of Ghibelline support.

The epicenter of Ghibelline agitation for almost a decade had been Arezzo. Here, around the mid-1280s, after repeated domestic upheavals, power had been assumed by the Ubertini, a family of feudal descent who had vast landholdings in the Casentino valley. Under the rule of bishop Guglielmino degli Ubertini, Arezzo became the rallying point for Ghibelline fugitives from Siena and Florence. Conflict between Florence and Arezzo was therefore inevitable. The first significant act of war, from October 1285 until the following April, was Florence's long siege of the castle of Poggio Santa Cecilia, owned by Siena but occupied by the Ghibellines with the support of Arezzo. Once the Florentines and Sienese had recaptured the castle, the situation turned into a state of localized war until 1287, when, after a brief interlude of Guelf rule, the Ubertini regained full control of the city. A league of the Guelf cities of Tuscany was then formed against Arezzo, which could rely on the support of the Ghibelline fugitives and of the new imperial vicar general, Percivalle di

Lavagna. This brought a reestablishment of the factions that would divide the region for over half a century. After an initial victory by Arezzo (commanded by Buonconte da Montefeltro, Guido's young son) at Pieve al Toppo in June 1288, the decisive battle was fought on the plain of Campaldino, near the castle of Poppi, on June 11 of the following year. The Guelfs won a crushing victory, thanks to the valor of Corso Donati who, at the head of a rearguard cavalry division, disobeying orders, had burst onto the field, surprising the Arezzo forces who, in the first encounter, had put the Florentine light cavalry into disarray. Bishop Guglielmino was killed in the fray (his weapons were hung up as trophies in the Baptistery of San Giovanni in Florence, while his body was buried by the battlefield, in the small nearby church of Certomondo which, by a stroke of irony, the Guidi family had built in 1262 to celebrate the Ghibelline victory at Montaperti); so too was Buonconte da Montefeltro (whose death Dante would recount in Canto V of *Purgatorio*).[8] What would seem a battle between cities was, in reality, a battle between parties. The Florentines regarded it as a victory not so much over Arezzo as over the Ghibellines: they recorded it with an inscription in the "Palagio" (the Bargello) that read: "Sconfitti i Ghibellini a Certomondo" ("The Ghibellines defeated at Certomondo").[9]

Shortly afterward, the Florentine armies turned their attentions to Pisa. After the disastrous defeat at the hands of the Genoese in the naval battle of Meloria (August 6, 1284), Pisa, the strongest Ghibelline bastion in Tuscany, in the face of a hostile alliance between Genoa, Lucca, and Florence, had made Ugolino della Gherardesca, count of Donoratico, the effective ruler of the city. He had then given joint power to his nephew Nino Visconti, ruler of the Giudicato of Gallura, in Sardinia. Both had Guelf sympathies (especially Visconti) but their politics seemed especially linked to the Guelfs because their preference for the ranks of the aristocracy produced an aversion to the "popolo" of Pisa, who were traditionally Ghibelline. It is true, however, that Gherardesca had behaved in a conciliatory manner toward Lucca and Florence, and it was exactly this receptiveness that gave the Ghibelline archbishop Ruggieri degli Ubaldini (nephew of Cardinal Ottaviano, whom Dante placed in Hell, along with Farinata and Federico II) the pretext for accusing Ugolino of treason.

The fate of Ugolino and members of his family is well known, since it is retold in Canto XXXIII of *Inferno*. The count was imprisoned with his sons Gherardo and Uguccione, and grandsons Nino il Brigata and Anselmuccio, in the Torre dei Gualandi on July 1, 1288, in a room where falcons were kept when they were molting ("muta"—which is why the tower is also called "la Muda"), and forced to pay large sums of money in ransom. It was the custom, not just in Pisa, to allow three days for payment, after which prisoners were given no more food. After eight months, once the Gherardesca money had finished, the prisoners were left to die of hunger and without the last rites. Legend has it that the falcon room was next to the chamber where the Elders met, so that the councilors could hear the groans of the dying men. Their corpses were not removed from the tower until March 18, 1289. By that time, Pisa had appointed Guido da Montefeltro as *capitano* of the city: after the surrender of Romagna in 1283, he had temporarily yielded to papal authority before returning to the Ghibelline cause. Montefeltro's skill as a condottiere enabled the Pisans to quickly recover many castles and strongholds that had been surrendered to Lucca and Florence.

Florence, having won at Campaldino, and spurred on by Nino Visconti, who had managed to escape from Archbishop Ruggieri's plot, organized an expedition against Pisa. It succeeded in taking several castles, including that of Caprona (August 6, 1289), and pushed on almost as far as the walls of the enemy city, but then stopped without any real gains. The war against Pisa would last until 1293.[10]

Father and children

In 1283, Dante signed over to Tedaldo di Orlando Rustichelli the benefit of a modest loan of 21 lire that his father had made to Donato di Gherardo del Papa and to the brothers Bernardo and Neri di Torrigiano.[11] This means that Dante was acting at that time as head of the family. The Alighieri brothers, until that year, were not of legal age, and had been assisted by a guardian. It could have been the guardian who had paid the dowry of their sister Tana when she married Lapo di Riccomanno, just before or after 1275.[12] In that case, the prenuptial negotiations were probably commenced several years earlier by Alighieri II, who would have settled the amount of the dowry and, as was customary, would have deposited the sum in a bank. Lapo's father, a Ghibelline who had been interned in 1268, was a member of a leading mercantile company registered with the Arte di Calimala. Tana's dowry could hardly fail to match her husband's wealth, and in fact it totaled 366 gold florins. It was not a princely dowry, but it certainly weighed considerably on the Alighieri finances. In comparison, the 200 small florins that Gemma brought as a dowry to Dante at about the same time seem paltry (one gold florin was worth 29 small florins, so that Gemma's dowry amounted to little more than 12 gold florins).

It is thought that the marriage between Dante and Gemma, who had been "promised" to each other since 1277, was celebrated not long after 1283. Dante was eighteen and Gemma (who would live long, until around 1343) was perhaps about fourteen.

Three or four children were born from this union. Four, if we accept that the son Giovanni "Dantis alagherii de Florentia" recorded in a legal document in Lucca dated October 21, 1308 is actually the eldest son of Dante and not that of another "Dantino di Alighiero da Firenze" who lived in Padua well into the thirteenth century; three, if we reject the connection: and thus, in probable order of birth, Pietro, Iacopo, and Antonia. It has to be said that the presence of a son in Lucca in 1308 would be consistent with Dante's life story; but it is strange that there is no other trace of him.[13] Pietro and Iacopo, according to the legal proceedings they would become involved in because of their father, must have been born not much before 1300. They left Florence between 1311 and 1315, in compliance with the Florentine law requiring the sons of those who had been banished to leave the city when they turned fourteen, and probably joined their father in exile. They were with him in Ravenna toward the end of 1318, but the date of their reunion may have been a few years earlier. Antonia would also have been in Ravenna but, as the banishment did not apply to daughters, we don't know whether she had followed her father straight away or had remained in Florence with her mother. Nor do we know whether Gemma left the city when her husband was expelled. Opinions vary, but it seems almost certain that she was obliged at some point to leave. The problem as to whether and where she joined her husband remains open. If Antonia was with Dante during the last years of his life, then it is most likely that Gemma had also moved there.[14] This doesn't prevent us speculating about whether Dante and his wife had also lived together in other, earlier periods.

His children were with him in Ravenna at the time of his death. Pietro, after studying law at Bologna, where he could have known the student Petrarch, would later follow a distinguished career as a judge in

Verona (another city, apart from Bologna, where he might have been acquainted, if not friends, with Petrarch, who sent him a short letter in Latin verse). Iacopo, having returned to Florence in 1325 and taken minor orders, obtained a canonship, also in Verona, and various benefices in Valpolicella. Pietro died in 1364, and we know that Iacopo was still alive in November 1347. As for Antonia, it seems almost certain that she became a nun, taking the name Suor Beatrice, in the monastery of Santo Stefano in Ravenna, though we don't know whether this was before or after her father's death.[15]

Dante's sons felt an enormous admiration—one might say reverence—toward their father. Both studied and promoted his works: Iacopo wrote a vernacular commentary on *Inferno* sometime around his father's death; Pietro wrote a long Latin commentary on the whole poem between about 1338 and 1341. Their intellectual admiration may well have been fueled by a certain vanity and perhaps also by thoughts of personal advantage, yet beyond the understandable pleasure of being able to boast the name of such a father, nothing suggests they were moved by anything other than genuine feelings of love. And this wasn't only true of Dante's learned sons: wasn't Antonia's decision to take the name Beatrice also, in effect, an implied homage to her father? Lacking all information, as we do, about the life of the Alighieri family before and after exile, we certainly cannot presume to understand its emotional dynamics. One indication alone, for what it is worth, suggests some closeness between parents and children. How would we otherwise interpret the fact that Pietro and Iacopo, when they decided to name their own children, chose names from among their closest family, parents included? And so Pietro, father of seven children, baptized two with the names Gemma and Dante, another with that of his sister, Antonia, and a fourth adapting the family name—Alighiera. Iacopo was less varied, giving two of his three (illegitimate) children the name Alighiero and Alighiera. This is very little on which to build the picture of a united family that got on well together but, against the commonly held idea of Dante detached from everyday life, submerged in sublime thoughts and poetical fantasies, it is perhaps enough to provide an outline of a father who succeeded in being loved and who, despite countless misfortunes, enabled those he loved to maintain a sense of family. Besides, it would seem that his family (his own and his family of origin) were much more important to him than we might imagine. This is suggested by the fact that, contrary to the rule forbidding any mention of family in literary texts, which was obeyed by writers of the time—and thus belying the current image we have of his poetry—Dante sometimes alludes to members of his close family: to a sister who nurses him when he is ill in the *Vita Nova,* even to his wife, Gemma, in an important canzone. These are unconventional gestures even for a writer like him, intolerant of every preset rule and constantly aiming for the new.

Far from politics

In the fifteen years separating the Peace of Cardinal Latino (1280) from the reforms of Giano della Bella (1293–1295) Dante had reached adulthood, established his own family, become head of what remained of his family of origin, and had moved into the limelight, making his name as a poet and an intellectual. But he had kept well away from politics. For many years, the very person who, from the age of thirty onward, would become possessed by the demon of politics, showed a complete disinterest in it. He had obviously chosen to occupy himself with other matters—that of learning and writing. So for a long time he was just a spectator in Florentine public life. But, judging from the accounts left in the *Commedia* of events that took place during that period and the people he met or even just glimpsed, he was an attentive and interested spectator.

Florence continued to be one of the great crossroads of Italian history, as it had been in the 1270s. All the people who mattered either visited or passed through. Most were Angevins, and their presence was often the result of developments in the long war in Sicily.

Clemence of Austria, the thirteen-year-old daughter of Rudolph, king of the Romans, passed through in April 1281 on her way to Naples, where her fiancé Charles Martel (eldest son of Prince Charles of Anjou, future king of Sicily), who was barely ten years old, was waiting for her. The following year, with the outbreak of revolution in Sicily, it was Charles Martel himself who passed through Florence on his return journey to Naples from the court of Philip III of France, to whom he had turned for military reinforcements. War in Sicily had been dragging on for a couple of years when Charles I and Peter of Aragon, the two contenders for the crown, agreed to leave their fates to the judgment of God in the form of a duel between the two of them. A fairly odd solution, if it weren't for the fact that neither sovereign seriously thought of seeing it through: for both it was just a way of playing for time. Once the winter of 1284 was over, the king of Naples nevertheless made his way toward Bordeaux, a convenient place for the duel, entering Florence on March 14. He was seeing the city he had controlled for almost fifteen years for the last time: he would die in January 1285. The duel, of course, turned into a farce. Charles, heir to the throne, was captured in 1284 during a naval battle and taken to Catalonia, where he would remain in prison for five years, even after the death of his father. When news began to spread of his imminent release, Mary of Hungary, his wife, set off for Provence and, in November 1287, she too stayed in Florence. But Charles would not be released for another year: he arrived back in Italy in 1289, and in May would pass through Florence on his way to Rieti, where the pope would crown him king of Sicily and Jerusalem (even though the island was in Aragonese hands and Jerusalem in the hands of Muslims). From that moment the lame prince, despised by his father, would become Charles II of Naples, but for Dante he would be "the Cripple of Jerusalem" (*Para.* XIX 127; "Ciotto di Ierusalemme").

In Spring 1294, a sort of Angevin triumph was staged in Florence. The whole court, in fact, assembled there. Charles Martel arrived in March, accompanied by his wife, Clemence, and their three children: they waited twenty days for the arrival of their father, Charles II, who was on his way from Provence with his sons, who had been held hostage by the Aragonese. The event was memorable for the long, solemn and sumptuous celebrations held around it. If we can accept what Dante says in *Paradiso,* an affectionate relationship began between him and Charles Martel (who would die the following year), on which Dante had placed much hope. It is hard to believe that a bond of friendship could have been established between an Angevin prince (and a crowned king of Hungary to boot, though more in name than fact) and a simple citizen of Florence. But Dante would probably have had an opportunity to get close to him during the celebrations organized by the city, or perhaps even to recite some of his poems to him. By that time he was already well known as a poet, and could therefore have been invited to some banquet or celebration as one of the city's leading intellectuals.[16]

During those same years, Dante was also on friendly terms—according, once again, to the *Commedia*—with Nino Visconti, one of the leading figures in the events in Pisa involving Count Ugolino and, in particular, in the war between Florence and Pisa that followed it. He meets his soul in *Purgatorio* and addresses him using the friendly *tu* to express joy at finding him safe: "Noble judge Nino, how I rejoiced when I saw you were not among the damned!" (*Purg.* VIII 53–54; "giudice Nin gentil, quanto mi piacque / quando ti vidi non esser tra' rei!"). Their acquaintance, if it existed, could have begun after the political upheaval in Pisa, when Visconti visited Florence to back the Guelf league against that city. Another key figure in Pisan affairs, Guido da Montefeltro, passed through Florentine territory after the signing of the peace of 1293 and was received with great honor. He too would be a leading figure in the *Commedia,* but Dante must never have met him: when Dante comes across Guido's soul in the fictional world of the poem, he is not recognized by him.[17]

Lastly, brief mention should be made of a character whom Dante could not have forgotten. This was Guido il Vecchio da Polenta, the father of Francesca, who held the post of *podestà* in Florence from July to November 1290, only a few years after his daughter had been murdered, around 1285. Paolo Malatesta, the other victim, had been the city's *capitano* between 1282 and 1283: the decade seems to have been pervaded by memories of this bloody deed.

"The violent death" unavenged

During this time the Alighieri family also suffered a murder in the family. On April 15, 1287 the monks at the convent of Santa Maria di Cafaggio accompanied the body of Geri del Bello for burial, receiving alms of fourteen soldi for doing so. He had been killed that day or the day before by Brodario, a member of the Sacchetti family.[18] Geri, first cousin of Dante's father, and perhaps the only member of the family to have been exiled by the Ghibellines after Montaperti, was certainly, along with his brother Cione, one of the Alighieri most in the public eye. He must have been violent and quick to start a fight, since he and Cione had been tried and convicted in early November for acts of violence committed in Prato.[19] Dante sees him in *Inferno* among the sowers of discord, but doesn't talk to him.

Having reached almost the boundary of the ninth *bolgia* of Hell, and being rebuked by Virgil for having slowed his pace, Dante justifies himself by saying that he was trying to identify a relative who ought to be among those damned. To which Virgil replies that he has seen him: "for I saw him at the foot of the bridge / pointing at you and making fierce threats with his finger, / and I heard him called Geri del Bello." (*Inf.* XXIX 25–27; "ch'io vidi lui a piè del ponticello / mostrarti e minacciar forte col dito, / e udi' 'l nominar Geri del Bello"). Dante knows what has led Geri to hold such a scornful and even menacing attitude toward him:

> "Oh my guide, his violent death
> That is not yet avenged," I said,
> "by anyone who shares in his shame,
>
> > has made him scornful, so that he went
> without a word to me, as though I judge:
> and this has moved me more to pity."

> "O duca mio, la vïolenta morte
> che non li è vendicata ancor," diss'io,
> "per alcun che de l'onta sia consorte,
>
> > fece lui disdegnoso; ond' el sen gio
> sanza parlarmi, sì com' ïo estimo:
> e in ciò m'ha el fatto a sé più pio."

—*Inf.* XXIX 31–36

In 1300, Geri's death had still not been avenged by his relatives. Aware of the additional pain the soul of the dead man must feel for this, Dante feels pity for him. He seems almost to hope that someone would at last decide to wipe away the "shame" that weighs on the family. In reality, he is not so much interested in the lack of revenge as in emphasizing that the Alighieri family has a duty to carry it out.

We should not be surprised that Dante appears as a champion of vengeance. The private vendetta was one of the customs that a feudal society had passed on to city society. It would seem, though, that Tuscan cities, especially Florence, were particularly partial to such a practice: many Florentines complained about the spread of the phenomenon;

others, non-Florentines, suggested it was a peculiarity of that city.[20] As revenge for the medieval mind was an act of justice, city laws had not gone as far as stopping it but only curbing it with a series of provisions that required the act of vengeance to be proportionate to the offense committed. For the nobility, insults had to be avenged in order to preserve honor, and it was therefore, first and foremost, a duty rather than a right. But the city laws provided for the possibility of a reconciliation between the parties and the signing of a document of peace (*carta di pace*). It was essential, however, that the reconciliation should not be a surrender or, worse still, that it should seem like a way of evading the responsibility of defending the family honor. It is revealing that in the tenzone between Forese and Dante, Forese accuses Dante of hurrying to make peace when he should have avenged an offense against his father. It is not clear what offense had been committed against his father, but Forese's insult is clear: Dante, he claims, had shown himself to be of the same substance as his father, namely a coward.[21]

We don't know why Brodario killed Geri; the fact that Dante places him among the sowers of discord could have something to do with his violent death. The most reasonable explanation is that he was killed "not because he himself had killed one of that family, but for the discord he had sown in it, or between it and another family"; in effect, if Geri "had himself first killed one of his adversaries, the death would have been a cause for just revenge, and it would not have left the Alighieri family with the duty that Dante recognizes." The Sacchetti were an old noble Guelf family in the *sestiere* of San Pier Scheraggio. Dante names them in *Paradiso* as one of the twelfth-century families who were already great—"Already great was the column of Vair, / Sacchetti, Giuochi, Fifanti, and Barucci" (*Para.* XVI 103–104; "Grand' era già la colonna del Vaio, / Sacchetti, Giuochi, Fifanti e Barucci"). Though they had seen a certain political decline during the 1280s, they were declared magnates in 1293 following the *Ordinamenti di giustizia*.[22] It is very important that the Sacchetti were nobles when we consider the meaning of Dante's reference to the need for vengeance. Noble families could not avoid carrying out their right and duty of revenge. The Alighieri—merchants, moneychangers, small-scale traders—were not nobility, and yet Dante considers that, through their inaction, they had failed in their duty. With the unavenged Geri, he adds another element to the myth that he is constructing in the *Commedia,* and beyond, about the nobility of his origins.[23]

Geri would eventually be avenged. It would be carried out much later, around 1317, by Bambo and Lapo, the sons of his brother Cione, when they killed an unidentified Sacchetti at the door of his house.[24] It was commonly known that a vendetta could be postponed for years and years, so much so that it became proverbial—according to the *Ottimo commento,* there was a saying among Florentines: "a hundred-year vendetta keeps you as young as a child at your mother's breast." And there is no shortage of examples of killings avenged after a long period of time: Ghino Velluti, a Guelf, killed by Tommasino dei Mannelli in fall of 1267, would be avenged by a group of his relatives on Saint John's Day, 1295—twenty-eight years later—with the killing of a young member of the Mannelli family. A thirty-year wait was, however, fairly exceptional. But the oddest thing is that peace between the Alighieri and Sacchetti families was established so many years after the murder. It was not until October 10, 1342 that, "in ducali palatio" (in other words, in the residence of Gualtieri di Brienne, Duke of Athens, who a month earlier had been proclaimed ruler of the city for life), Pietro of the late Daddoccio dei Sacchetti and his son Uguccione, on the one part, and Francesco Alighieri, also on behalf of his absent nephews Pietro and Iacopo, on the other, solemnly declared and signed in writing, also on behalf of their present and future relations, that a real and sincere peace would remain between them forever.[25] There's a suspicion that it was Dante's brother and children who asked for the solemn peace. The assassination carried out by Geri's nephews should in theory have settled the score; the Sacchetti family were not therefore held by any duty of honor to strike back against any of the Alighieri—unless they felt that the killing of their relative couldn't be considered, so to speak, a legitimate revenge: in other words, that the murder committed by Bambo or by Lapo or by both, after such a long time, was substantially unmotivated . . . or worse still, for the Alighieri, that it had been caused by some sort of provocation or by something that they had interpreted as a provocation. In short, the Sacchetti might have seen it as a cause for vengeance. They could have complained publicly and even, perhaps, issued some threat. The *Com-*

media was famous by this time, and who knows what gossip was circling in Florence about the killing of poor Sacchetti. And perhaps it was even being suggested that the great poet was morally responsible for it. A contract for peace would therefore have enabled Dante's brother and children to sleep more soundly at night.

Mounted cavalier

Dante had kept out of politics, as we have seen, until the age of thirty, but he didn't shirk his duties as a citizen. Among these was the duty to serve in times of war. Some suggest that his military experience continued throughout the wars with Arezzo and Pisa, in other words from the siege of Poggio Santa Cecilia (1286) up to Campaldino and Caprona (1289). Dante indeed makes scattered references in his writings to places, events, and people that could relate to those war campaigns. In the *Commedia* he mockingly records a certain Lano of Siena, ambushed at Pieve al Toppo, whose feet "were not very nimble," in other words not able to save him "at the jousts of Toppo." (*Inf.* XIII 120–121; "non furo accorte / le gambe tue a le giostre dal Toppo!") And the cavalry maneuvers at the beginning of Canto XXII of *Inferno* refer to the Arezzo area, which he seems to have witnessed in person: "I have seen knights breaking camp, / and starting their attack and standing muster, / and sometimes running off to save themselves; / I have seen horsemen in your lands, / O Aretines, I have seen raiding-parties" (*Inf.* XXII 1–5; "Io vidi già cavalier muover campo, / e cominciare stormo e far lor mostra, / e talvolta partir per loro scampo; / corridor vidi per la terra vostra, / o Aretini, e vidi gir gualdane"). Nothing assures us, however, that Dante was there, armed, at Poggio Santa Cecilia or had carried out raids at Arezzo.[26]

But it is certain that he was at Campaldino on June 11, 1289. In *Purgatorio* he describes, perhaps referring to an idea going round at the time, how the corpse of the Ghibelline leader Buonconte di Guido da Montefeltro, who died in battle and was never found, had been dragged as far as the Arno by the waters of the Archiano torrent, which had swollen after a night storm. Appearing immediately before that, in the same canto, is Iacopo del Cassero—later killed at Oriago, on the road between Padua and Venice, by assassins from the Este family—who had also taken part in the battle, commanding a contingent from Fano that had sided with the Florentines.[27] Leonardo Bruni quotes, in translation, some lines of a lost letter in which Dante states he was one of the horsemen in arms at the battle of Campaldino, "where he had much fear and in the end very great joy for the various events of that battle." He "outlines the form" of the battle, the "various events": from the rout by the front ranks where he was mustered, up to the victory, won thanks to the precipitous retreat, which had had the effect of compacting the Florentine forces on foot and horseback, while separating the Aretine cavalry that was pursuing them from its own infantry. Dante therefore belonged to the detachment of *feditori,* who were responsible for the first attack. *Feditori,* armed light cavalry, were a prestige corps to which many nobles and magnates belonged. On that occasion, the task of selecting the *feditori* for the *sestiere* of San Pier Maggiore was given to Vieri dei Cerchi, head of the family to which the Alighieri were politically allied. In the lost letter, it would seem that Dante had emphasized his own bravery, yet his name doesn't appear among those who were compensated for having put themselves at particular risk during the action.

It is equally certain that on August 6, less than two months after Campaldino, Dante was below the walls of Caprona, not far from Pisa. With his own eyes, he saw frightened Pisan soldiers leaving the castle after having negotiated their surrender—"so once I saw frightened foot soldiers / who left Caprona by negotiation / seeing around them so many enemies" (*Inf.* XXI 94–96; "così vid' ïo già temer li fanti / ch'uscivan patteggiati di Caprona, / veggendo sé tra nemici cotanti"). The Florentine troops did no harm to these foot soldiers, but Guido da Montefeltro, the Pisan commander, accused them of treachery for surrendering after only three days of siege, without resistance.[28] A few days later, Dante would have followed the army as it pushed on to Cisanello, less than three kilometers from the walls of Pisa. But the Florentines, as we have seen, did not attack the city: they went back to Florence shortly after, having achieved no significant gain.

That experience of war gave Dante the opportunity to make his first real travels in Tuscany. It was then that he first visited places such as the Casentino and Arno valleys, which would become more familiar to him many years later when he would visit them as an exile.

The aristocratic ideal and indigence

Service in the cavalry brought much honor. Most mounted soldiers, who made up the most important part of a medieval army, came from the higher classes of society. In the previous century, when the *milites* (noble or otherwise), in terms of their number, wealth, and power, formed one of the most significant parts of the city's social structure and political life, knights regarded war as their raison d'être. Not only did they obtain direct economic advantage from military expeditions, but they enjoyed a sort of insurance against the harm they might suffer while carrying out their profession. Recruitment contracts with the city administration (in which, moreover, they often played a crucial role) provided indemnity for the loss of horses and weaponry, for any ransoms paid in the event of being taken prisoner, and so forth. In short, up until the early decades of the 1200s, for knights going to war, it was all gain. But matters had changed by Dante's time. Although there were still rewards and benefits for bravery in the event of victory, each individual in the heavy cavalry had to pay the considerable costs of buying and maintaining a destrier and at least a rouncy (a warhorse and a packhorse) and, in the light cavalry, the cost of at least one good horse, as well as buying weapons and protective gear (tunic, quilted jacket, hauberk, cuirass, shield, surcoat, helmet, etc.) and the pay for any servants.[29] Going to war, from the financial point of view, was pure loss. This is why wealthy people formed the backbone of the cavalry, many of whom were on the list of magnates. They were not looking for financial gain but for the social prestige still enjoyed by mounted cavalrymen, without forgetting the political advantages that came from it: it is no surprise that, in their struggle against the middle classes, they came out stronger each time they were called upon to fight a war.

Young Dante would have felt honored to be fighting next to Florence's most illustrious citizens. Being an *equitator,* a mounted soldier, was quite different to being an *eques,* a knight, but was nevertheless a mark of belonging to the city's aristocracy. This was all the more true since he had been co-opted into it, and therefore hadn't had to get there through political acts of self-advancement.

Dante must have wondered many times what place he held in Florentine society. He had married a Donati, the daughter and granddaughter of knights, but while his maternal grandfather (if he was Durante degli Abati, as seems likely) had belonged to a more distinguished family, he himself carried the name of a family of modest rank, now more than ever. He was in love—or rather, he claimed to be in love—with a woman married to a knight belonging to Florence's financial aristocracy. His circle of friends were also of high caliber. His best friend was none other than Guido Cavalcanti, a man who was not only learned and cultured but also heir to one of the city's largest fortunes. The Cavalcanti were magnates of great political influence—"the most powerful in people, possessions, and wealth in Florence"—and Guido was the son of one of the main leaders of the Guelf party. There was a vast social gap between them: Guido was in a position to challenge, armed, even Corso Donati himself. Manetto Portinari, Beatrice's brother, who was Dante's "next best friend" (VN 21, 1; "immediatamente dopo lo primo") was not from such a high-ranking family as Guido, but still belonged to the top mercantile and financial class. Another great friend, Cino, was one of the old Sigibuldi family of Pistoia whose wealth he would further increase once he had become one of the most eminent jurists of the time, as can be seen from the size of Cino's deposits in the Bardi family bank.[30]

Dante did not belong to the aristocracy either by birth or money. If he hadn't been Dante, the families he frequented as a friend would have seen him as a "client" on whom they would have bestowed a few favors and some money. If he treated Guido, Manetto, Cino and others as equals, it was only by virtue of his personality and his genius. His objective state of subservience would perhaps have given him a feeling of insecurity and certainly a strong desire to better himself, since he was ambitious. The most typical aspect of his personality, to regard and present himself as being different, unique, and exceptional, seems to be rooted in his modest social position as much as in his own self-esteem. His urge to do well and his sense of social inadequacy may also be underlying reasons behind his continual examination of the question of nobility—nobility in general, but also that of his own family.[31]

Dante immediately chose a way of life in keeping with the image of the different and out-of-the-ordinary person he wanted or felt himself to be. His distance from city politics is a characteristic trait, but what best represents the idea of the "aristocratic" life he so desired is his attitude to labor, to economic activities and the value to be placed on money.

We are struck, and his fellow citizens must have been struck even more, by the fact that Dante had no job. It is true that he didn't have enough capital to enter the financial or mercantile world. Nothing would have prevented him, however, from following the path of small business—buying and selling, financial speculation—as his father and all his family had done; nor even to enter a career in the professions, much in demand in Florence (Brunetto Latini, for example, was a notary, and so was his friend Lapo Gianni).[32] Dante was the first Alighieri to live on capital. It is clear that he did not live the idle life of a "young lord." He wanted to live as a nobleman, or at least a life in keeping with his idea of nobility, well away from "base" economic concerns and fully devoted to the liberal arts, in other words to study and poetry. But it is one thing to live on income from the large landholdings of true noblemen or from the "high rents," as Compagni wrote, from real estate on which the non-noble Cavalcanti could exist: it is quite another thing to rely solely on the rent from a couple of farms. Dante must, at the very least, have found himself forever short of money. Fairly soon he would discover that such a regimen was not sustainable. It would be the expenses he had to face from the mid-1280s onward—for the family he had established, for his military campaigns as a cavalryman, and for his stays in Bologna—that brought the Alighieri brothers into financial difficulty, well before the ruin brought about by his exile.[33]

"Sweet and charming" rhymes of love

In Spring 1283, exactly nine years after their first meeting, while Dante is strolling in a street in Florence, he meets Beatrice, accompanied by two older women, as was fitting for a married woman, and Beatrice greets him.[34] With this act she shows a reciprocation of the love Dante felt for her since he was a young boy. That Beatrice had greeted Dante on that occasion is not improbable; but it is unlikely that a sentimental relationship developed between them once they had reached eighteen. The *Vita Nova*, which makes this claim, suggests the contrary. We read there, in fact, that after that date, for "several years and months" (*VN* 2, 9; "alquanti anni e mesi") Dante had written love poems addressed to at least two other women. In the story he claims that these women were used by him as a "screen" to hide his true love and to divert the attention of curious Florentines; in reality, those love poems demonstrate that for many years after 1283 Beatrice had not yet appeared on his sentimental and poetical horizon. If he resorted to those and other expedients in the *Vita Nova*, it was because he wanted to place his entire production of love poetry under the sign of Beatrice, altering the reality, but in a way that appeared credible.

By using 1283 as the date when his adult love story began, he was able to keep very close to the biographical truth and, at the same time, tie together three separate beginnings: that of his love affair, that of his friendship with Guido Cavalcanti, and that of the public history of his poetry. In 1283 he was eighteen, and this enabled him to respect the rule expressed by Andrea Cappellano in *De amore* according to which a man cannot be a true lover before that age. *De amore,* a treatise written at the end of the twelfth century by a certain Andrea, a chaplain (*cappellano*) in the French court, was regarded as a sort of bible of courtship. For us it is almost impossible to understand how anyone can speak of requited love on the basis of just one exchange of greetings. But we must bear in mind that a woman's greeting in the society of that time was regarded in many respects as a tender act. Francesco da Barberino, in *Reggimento e costumi di donna,* questioned several times whether or not it was proper for women to respond to a greeting, and in what way to respond. He is strict in forbidding the "young lady who has already reached the marrying age" to greet someone she has met in a public place ("and if it should be that she is with her mother in a public place, she should offer no greeting"), but even with regard to a married woman he is full of cautions and fine distinctions.[35]

Having received the greeting, Dante returns home in a state of bliss and, after a dream, composes a sonnet (*A ciascun'alma presa e gentil core*—*To every loving heart and captive soul*) describing its mysterious content, and sends it to "many famous troubadours of that time" (*VN* 1, 20; "molti famosi trovatori in quel tempo"), asking them to explain the meaning of the dream. Among the many who sent him a sonnet in reply was Guido Cavalcanti: "and this was almost the start of the friendship between him and me, once he learned that I was the one who had sent it to him" (*VN* 2, 1; "e questo fu quasi lo principio dell'amistà tra lui e me, quando elli seppe che io era quelli che li avea ciò mandato"). Dante, therefore, following a recognized practice, had sent his sonnet anonymously and Guido had replied not knowing the identity of the author, which was only revealed later. Dante is once again mystifying the situation: he had certainly written and circulated that sonnet in 1283 and Cavalcanti had then replied, but their poetical collaboration must have dated from several years later and become much closer at the end of the 1280s (though Dante covers himself and writes that this was "almost the start of the friendship": he could hardly falsify this detail when he was in fact dedicating his story to Guido).[36] Immediately after writing that he had sent the sonnet to many famous poets, Dante adds an important piece of information. He says that before that sonnet he had already taught himself the art of versifying (*VN* 1, 20; "e con ciò fosse cosa che io avesse già veduto per me medesimo l'arte del dire parole per rima") but that he had revealed it publicly only on that occasion. In short, he claims to have become an effective member of Florentine literary society in 1283. Perhaps, once again, he shouldn't be taken too literally, but this general indication of time seems fairly reliable.

By cross-referencing the dates from the *Rime* with the information given in the *Vita Nova* we can chart Dante's career as a writer of vernacular verse from the early 1280s to the mid-1290s. At an early stage we find him in contact with writers of "courtly" verse who, so far as we can suppose, practiced poetry as amateurs, as a sort of intellectual game. The first sonnet in the *Vita Nova,* requesting an interpretation of his dream, is of this kind. This type of enigmatic composition, sent to a number of poets almost to provoke and stimulate their interpretative wit, was much in favor—Dante himself responded to a circular request to interpret a dream by Dante da Maiano, a writer of outmoded Sicilian-style verse, about whom we know very little and with whom Dante exchanged another two tenzoni. The list of verse writers, apart from Dante, who replied to that request gives us an idea of the poetic environment in which young Dante moved: alongside the few popular writers of lyric verse who are still known today, such as the two Florentines Chiaro Davanzati (with whom Dante seems to have exchanged poetical writings) and Guido Orlandi, are the names of two unknown writers, Salvino Doni and Ricco di Varlungo, and the Ghibelline notary Cione Baglioni. Those who had replied to Dante's sonnet certainly included poets of prestige, such as Davanzati and Cavalcanti, but there was also the little-known Terino da Castelfiorentino, who we know to have been in correspondence with Monte Andrea and Onesto degli Onesti of Bologna.[37] The other verse writers to whom Dante turned (Lippo, Meuccio, a certain *messer* Brunetto) have names that are too vague and common to enable us to identify precisely who they were; that same circle of pre-*Stilnovo* verse writers may have included Puccio Bellondi, with whom a Dante exchanged tenzoni in sonnet form, but this Dante may well have been Dante da Maiano.[38] In short, there is a feeling that Dante the verse writer first moved in tune with those of the old school, in a circle of relationships that had a very provincial flavor.

Matters changed in the mid-1280s, once Dante had formed a close and effective relationship, and discipleship, with Guido Cavalcanti after the time he spent around 1285 in Bologna, a great university city and therefore also a place where vernacular poetry was much cultivated. It was probably around this period that a small but close-knit group of innovative poets was formed, which included Dante, Cavalcanti, Cino, Lapo Gianni, and perhaps Gianni Alfani. It was Dante himself who, many years later, with them in mind, would coin the definition *dolce stil novo* ("new sweet style"), which has remained a part of history (*Purg.* XXIV 57).

The *Vita Nova* doesn't just give an outline of how Dante's conception of love developed over time (from the idea of love as a search for mutual exchange to that uncommon search for love as an end in itself, *caritas*) and of how, at the same time, the various "manners" of his love poetry came about (from his phase of old troubadour-courtly style to that of Cavalcantian painful love and finally the discovery of the ecstatic poetry of "praise"). It also maps out the changes in his public image as a poet, a gradual rise from the earliest anonymous verse to a position of fame in the early 1290s. Once he had revealed his identity in 1283, for an unspecified period of time, which was at least a few years, Dante appears to be a verse writer who, on the one hand, composed love poems addressed to different women—"certain small things in rhyme" (*VN* 2, 9; "certe cosette per rime") written for the women who provided the screen—and, on the other, made social use of poetry, meant as a cultivated and refined entertainment for an audience of friends and, above all, fellow poets or as a rhetorical exercise and a demonstration of bravura for rather exhibitionistic intellectuals. His sonnets—such as the one that opens the *Vita Nova*—belong to this second category. They invite the reader to solve intentionally obscure conundrums or try to solve puzzles posed by others. There were also compositions typical of a parlor game, written for a different audience of upper-class young men who were not necessarily poets, such as the "letter in the form of a sirventes" in which he says he has listed the names of the sixty most beautiful women in Florence.[39] It is striking that here is a poet who hasn't yet found his own clear voice. Cavalcanti must have been crucial in his development. Dante recognizes this, so much so that he would write that Guido was his John the Baptist, the one who had prepared the way.[40]

The *Vita Nova* is untruthful when it claims that Beatrice was his only love (and therefore his only true inspiration), but it is credible when it suggests that it was the new poetry linked to the name of that woman—his style of praise—that brought Dante to fame. This came in the early 1290s. It seems to have happened thanks to the canzone *Donne ch'avete intelletto d'amore* (*Ladies, who have intelligence of love*), the poem with which—according to the poet Bonagiunta da Lucca in *Purgatorio*—Dante had begun the "new rhymes" (*Purg.* XXIV 50; "nove rime"), thus marking the watershed between poets of the older generations—he himself, Giacomo da Lentini, Guittone d'Arezzo—and the new ones who use "rhymes of love . . . sweet and charming" (*Purg.* XXVI 99; "rime d'amor . . . dolci e leggiadre"). That canzone, says Dante with evident satisfaction, was "quite well-known among the people" (*VN* 11, 1; "alquanto divulgata tra le genti"). Although it presents Beatrice as still being alive, it was written just after her death, in June 1290. Yet by 1292 it was also known in Bologna, when Pietro Alegranze, a notary in that city (though originally from Florence) transcribed part of it, apparently between September 28 and October 2, into a register of public records (collections of civil law documents held by a particular municipal office, available for public consultation). It was after the publication of *Donne ch'avete* that friends and acquaintances began to ask Dante to compose verse for them. He writes in the *Vita Nova* that an unidentified friend who had read or heard the canzone, "having perhaps, on hearing it, an expectation of me that was more than fit," asked him to explain in rhyme "what is love" (*VN* 11, 1; "che io li dovesse dire che è Amore, avendo forse per l'udite parole speranza di me oltre che degna"). And once again, after he had circulated the canzone *Gli occhi dolenti per pietà del core* (*These eyes, grieving in pity for my heart*) on the death of Beatrice, Manetto Portinari asked him for "something for a lady who had died" (*VN* 21, 2; "alcuna cosa per una donna che s'era morta"). If the head of the Portinari family had commissioned a "lament" or *planctus* for a dead lady, this means, even taking account of the friendship between them, that Dante enjoyed considerable public renown by that time. This renown was further proved by two anonymous "gentlewomen" who asked him to send them his "words of rhyme" (*VN* 30, 1; "parole rimate"). From all this we can deduce that by the time Dante had completed the *Vita Nova* in 1295, he was well established as a lyric writer, both outside Florence as well as beyond the circle of those who wrote verse. And he was well aware of this, to the point of presenting himself as someone who had surpassed Guido Cavalcanti: if Cavalcanti was John the Baptist, then he was the Messiah.

Brunetto Latini: A "supreme master of rhetoric"

Whether or not he had attended a public grammar school, by about the age of fifteen he would have had the problem of deciding how to continue his studies.[41] Schools leading to one of the professions were not for him, nor were university studies in law or medicine. Another possibility would have been philosophy at Bologna, but it wasn't until the 1290s, when Gentile da Cingoli arrived from Paris, that philosophy became separated from theology, medicine, and law. At university, however, he could probably have found what he was looking for, namely courses in rhetoric, which at that time was considered essential for studying law, and was therefore taught as an introduction. So far as we know, there were no schools of rhetoric in Florence.[42] Anyone there with an interest in literature had no choice but to study privately. But there were major problems, even studying privately: books of Latin classics were hard to find in Florence and there were very few educated laymen versed in classical language and literature.

Living in the same *sestiere* of San Pier Maggiore was judge Bono Giamboni: he was at least thirty years older than Dante and died shortly after 1292. Giamboni is known in particular as the author of the moral and allegorical vernacular treatise *Il libro de' vizî e delle virtudi,* but he was also responsible for numerous "vernacularizations," or free adaptations, sometimes complete rewritings, of works by Latin writers of the Middle Ages and the late Latin period. He could also have written two of the four known vernacular translations, known as *Fiore di rettorica,* of a text attributed to Cicero, *Rhetorica ad Herennium,* which had been crucial for the study of rhetoric in the Middle Ages. We have no evidence of any contact between Dante and the elderly judge, but we know that Giamboni was on fairly close terms with Lamberto, a member of the Abati family, whose title of *messere* suggests someone of high rank. There was also an Abati called Durante, presumably Dante's grandfather, who was also a judge: so it would seem certain that he knew Giamboni, and probable that his relations with him were not just formal. It is quite possible, then, that Durante's grandson would have met Giamboni and been struck by his learning. It was a learning that didn't come from the classical Latin texts, but showed at least a knowledge of Boethius's *De consolatione Philosophiae,* a book which would be of vital importance to Dante.

We can safely say that young Dante's master was Brunetto Latini. He was the same age as Giamboni (he was born between 1220 and 1230 and died in late 1293) and was the intellectual who best typified the commune of Florence. An eminent notary, a diehard Guelf, he lived in exile in France during the period of Ghibelline rule between Montaperti and Benevento (1260–1266). Once back in Florence, he held key offices for the remainder of his life (including being the effective head of the commune's chancery). Above all, he was the undisputed reference point in the city's political and administrative life: as well as being a man of letters, he was also a wise man of government. Giovanni Villani wrote that he was "a supreme master in rhetoric" and "an initiator and master in refining the Florentines, making them discerning in good speech, and in knowing how to lead and govern our republic according to Politic." The crucial aspect of Latini's cultural action was in his nobly pedagogical conception of culture, regarded by him as an essential instrument for civil coexistence and therefore to be placed at the service of his fellow citizens. Brunetto was the author of many works, the most important being a large encyclopedia in French entitled *Il Tresor*—when his soul meets Dante in Hell, he would say "remember my *Tesoro*" (*Inf.* XV 119; "sieti raccomandato il mio Tesoro") as he bids him goodbye. Also noteworthy are his abridged version of the encyclopedia in Tuscan verse, called *Il Tesoretto,* and a short poem on friendship, *Il Favolello.*[43] From the point of view of Dante's education, the vernacular versions of *De inventione* and certain orations by Cicero and a vernacular tract devoted to *Rettorica* occupy a special place. Rhetoric, the twofold aspect of political and civil oratory (the art of city *rettori*) and the art of writing, above all epistolary texts, was one of the pillars of his civil education.

Dante would place Brunetto in Hell among the sodomites. Latini was "a man of the world" according to Villani, following what Brunetto said about himself: "I've kept myself / rather profligate."[44] Perhaps it was a sin about which he made no secret if one of his canzoni for the Florentine versifier Bondie Dietaiuti is interpreted as a love poem: this is not clear, however, and it would be the sole example in the whole of thirteenth-century poetry of a homoerotic composition.[45] In *Inferno* Dante is upset to see him running naked and burned on blazing sand. His pity upon meeting Brunetto is stirred by strong filial *pietas*: while Dante retains a "kind paternal image" (*Inf.* XV 83; "buona imagine paterna") of him, Brunetto twice addresses Dante as "son" (*Inf.* XV 31, 37; "figliuolo"). Dante never displays such an intimate relationship with any of the other dead Florentines he meets in the *Commedia*. The intimacy seems to go right back to Dante's early youth. Brunetto was a father and a "master" to him, a master who taught "how man makes himself eternal" (*Inf.* XV 84; "come l'uom s'etterna"), how he defeats death through writing.

Brunetto would have conducted his cultural and spiritual teaching by example, through his writings but also, we can assume, with actual lessons in language and style and with recommended reading. Among these texts were Italian authors, with Cicero in first place. Thanks to him, Dante may have known *De amicitia,* another book that was fundamental in his education. It was Brunetto's teaching of Latin prose rhetoric that would turn out, in time, to be most profitable. In his adult life, Dante would frequently offer his knowledge of Latin and the rules of rhetoric, which were vital to the art of letter writing, as a service to the lords who gave him hospitality and to his companions in exile. Carrying out chancery or secretarial tasks, writing letters and documents, would become a kind of job for him, and even a way of supporting himself during tight financial times in exile. Brunetto, as a notary, professionally practiced the *ars dictandi,* namely the practice of composing epistles in Latin, and was the greatest "dictator" active in Florence. It seems natural to imagine, more than anything else, that he would have transmitted the techniques of that professional art of writing to his young protégé.[46]

The shadow of the Garisenda

Dante learnt much from Brunetto's private lessons and the books he gave him to read. Yet it was a shame that his master's cultural horizon (and his library) lacked those very books that were most dear to him: it lacked classical poetry and perhaps we should even say literature in general. If he wanted to progress in a rhetorical study that wasn't directed just toward ethics and the public good, Dante had to leave Florence.

In the second half of 1287, the Bologna notary Enrichetto delle Querce transcribed one of Dante's sonnets, *Non mi poriano già mai fare ammenda* (*Never could I ever make amend*), into a register of public records, though written in a strongly Bolognese linguistic patina. The sonnet, which could have been written in Bolognese, but whose vernacular guise could be that of the notary who copied it, tells a story that isn't easy to interpret: the only certainty is that in it Dante describes himself looking with intense concentration at the Tower of Garisenda: "Never could I ever make amend / for the great failure of my eyes, unless they / weren't to go blind, on seeing the Garisenda / tower with its fine aspect" (*Rime* 7, 1–4; "Non mi poriano già mai fare ammenda / del lor gran fallo gli occhi miei, sed elli / non s'accecasser, poi la Garisenda / torre miraro co' risguardi belli"). Of all the monuments in Bologna, Dante mentions only this tower, here and in *Inferno*, where Antaeus the giant, when Dante sees him lean over, seems "like the Garisenda looks / from beneath the leaning side, when a cloud drifts / over it, so that it seems to fall" (*Inf.* XXXI 136–138; "Qual pare a riguardar la Carisenda / sotto 'l chinato, quando un nuvol vada / sovr' essa sì, ched ella incontro penda"). These, in both cases, are personal experiences—indeed, they are experiences typical of a Florentine in Bologna.[47] For Florentines, that tower (then much taller than it is now) was the most familiar building in Bologna, almost the symbol of the city. This was because the places where Florentines traditionally went to stay while they were in the city were owned by the Garisendi family and were close to the tower, at the crossroads of Porta Ravignana. It is likely that Dante lodged in one of the houses beneath the tower.[48]

The Garisenda sonnet establishes that Dante actually went to Bologna; the notary's transcription shows that he stayed there before the second half of 1287. When this exactly happened, and for how long, we don't know. He presumably stayed for just a few months, perhaps between 1286 and 1287.

Now, what else would have attracted a Florentine to Bologna, where he had no financial interests, unless it was to attend the university or frequent the university environment? Dante was over twenty and almost certainly had family responsibilities. People, at that time, went to university at the age of fifteen or even younger (Petrarch would begin studying law at Montpellier at the age of twelve, and would move to Bologna at sixteen). He wouldn't therefore have enrolled and attended regular courses. At most, he might have sat in on various lectures as an external student. Rather than law or medicine, he would have been interested in exercises in *artes dictaminis,* Latin prose writing (which was the first compulsory level for those wishing to study logic) and then natural philosophy. It would, in effect, be the course described by Boccaccio, where Dante "made his first start in his own city, and from there, since it is a place more fertile in nourishment, went to Bologna," adding that "he spent no small time there."[49] Whether or not he attended university classes, his period at Bologna must, in any event, have been profitable from many points of view. The writer of vernacular verse would have found a congenial atmosphere there (perhaps it was here that he befriended the university student Cino da Pistoia) as well as new stimulus, thanks to the local verse writers brought up under the aegis of Guido Guinizelli, a poet whom Dante would constantly describe as one of his masters. The student of Latin literature would finally have had the opportunity of reading the great classics, and thus, in addition to Cicero and Boethius, of getting to know the poetry of the four great classic authors: Ovid, Statius, Lucan, and Virgil.

1290: An unusual intellectual figure

Dante's intellectual experience by the end of 1280s was most uncommon for a Florentine. He was not a popularizer like Bono Giamboni or Brunetto Latini, nor a municipal verse writer who wavered between courtly tradition and moralizing, like Chiaro Davanzati; he was not a lyric poet involved in factional wars and in-fighting, like Monte Andrea, and certainly not an eclectic encyclopedist and allegorist like Francesco da Barberino.[50] Dante combined a strictly observed quality of amorous verse writing with a linguistic and literary competence in Latin that no one of the time could boast in mercantile Florence. All he had to do now was come out into the open and be recognized on both fronts.

Beatrice died on June 8, 1290. This was perhaps a sad event for Dante the man, but it was certainly a great opportunity for Dante the poet and man of letters. It was the death of Beatrice that prompted the idea of writing a completely new kind of book that would become the *Vita Nova*; and Dante's fame was established by several lyric compositions, such as the canzone *Donne ch'avete intelletto d'amore,* written shortly after the loss of his beloved. The tragic event also gave him the opportunity of appearing in public—officially, so to speak—as a Latin prose writer.

In the paragraph in the *Vita Nova* that announces the sudden death of Beatrice, Dante, by amplifying and thus manipulating an event we can regard as real, writes that the death of that woman had sent the whole city of Florence into grief and misery.[51]

> When she had gone from this world, the abovementioned city was left almost like a widow despoiled of all dignity. So I, still weeping in this desolate city, wrote to the princes of the land describing its state, taking the words from the beginning of Jeremiah *Quomodo sedet sola civitas* [How doth the city sit solitary].
>
> Poi che fue partita da questo secolo, rimase tutta la sopradetta cittade quasi vedova dispogliata da ogni dignitade. Onde io, ancora lacrimando in questa desolata cittade, scrissi alli principi della terra alquanto della sua condizione, pigliando quello cominciamento di Geremia profeta *Quomodo sedet sola civitas.*

—*VN* 19, 8

He goes on to say that, since this text is in Latin, he won't transcribe it into a book where he proposes, in full agreement with his friend Guido Cavalcanti, to use only the vernacular.

What text is Dante referring to? Sent to whom? The fact that it begins with the first verse of the Lamentations of Jeremiah indicates almost certainly that it was a message of condolence. A letter, or rather an epistle, sent immediately or almost immediately after the event ("still weeping") to the "princes of the land," meaning the leading figures of the city. The most important citizens of Florence, from an institutional point of view, were the priors, who were also called "signori." But why should the death of a fellow citizen, even from a respectable family, have been the subject of condolences to the priors of Florence? And especially on the part of someone with no official right to perform such an important act. It would be quite another matter if we supposed that Dante had in fact sent a letter of condolence not to the priors, but to one specific prior who was related to Beatrice. In this case he would have performed an act of courtesy, as was the custom then and now, and at the same time, in addressing someone of such high regard, he would have formulated his condolences as though they were to be made public. Indeed, among the six priors who began their two-month office on June 15, 1290 (less than a week after the death of Beatrice) was one "Cinus quondam domini Iacobi de Bardis (Ultrarni)." This Cino, one of the four children of Iacopo di Ricco, and therefore cousin of Simone, widower of Beatrice, was a person of great influence: in 1278 he was the head of the guild of merchants (Arte di Calimala). It seems most probable that Dante would have sent a letter of condolence to a close relative of the deceased, in the same way that it would be no surprise if he had wanted to offer a sample of his skill in the Latin language and the art of letter writing with a text that we must imagine to be high-sounding and refined—as suggested by the biblical incipit—and therefore intended for public circulation.[52] The fact that he recalls the episode in the *Vita Nova,* though disguising it, confirms that the letter must have aroused considerable interest among the upper echelons of Florentine society.

Around the middle of the 1290s, Florence woke to the fact that it had in its midst an intellectual figure who until then was almost unknown: a man of letters who was a master of the vernacular and Latin, who wasn't involved in public affairs but was interested rather in matters of poetry and rhetoric. A "sage" quite different from Brunetto Latini, whose pupil he professed to be. Florence realized this, and seems also to have honored him. In March 1294 the city organized a welcoming delegation led by Giano, son of Vieri dei Cerchi, to be sent to Siena to receive Prince Charles Martel and his consort and to escort them to Florence. It is suggested that Dante was one of these "ambassadors."[53] Unless the suggestion is completely unfounded, this honor could only have been granted to him for his intellectual merits. In short, his determination to be different and to pursue an unusual and solitary path was beginning to bear its first fruit.

"Drawing figures of angels"

Leonardo Bruni wrote that Dante "enjoyed music and sounds" and was the only early biographer to add: "and he drew excellently by hand."[54] It is no surprise that Dante was a competent musician. The writings of thirteenth-century Italian lyric poets circulated almost always by being read or recited and not, as the Provencal troubadours did, through sung performances with musical accompaniment, but there was still a practice of "clothing" poetry with notes. Dante makes several references to his lyric compositions having musical accompaniments, and there is a scene in *Purgatorio* where the musician Casella (about whom we know nothing, except that he was a friend) sings his canzone *Amor che ne la mente mi ragiona (Love that discourses in my mind)*.[55]

The art of drawing is quite another matter. Bruni doesn't say that Dante was a connoisseur or a cultivator of the fine arts but that he himself practiced it.[56] He could have taken the information that Dante painted, or rather drew, from the paragraph of the *Vita Nova* in which he describes the day of the first anniversary of Beatrice's death, June 8, 1291, when thinking of the lady's blessed soul, he sat in an unspecified place drawing "an angel on certain tablets." He was concentrating so much on this task that he didn't realize certain distinguished gentlemen had approached and were observing him. When he noticed their presence, he stood up and greeted them but then, once they had left, returned to "drawing figures of angels."[57] At first sight it might seem no more than an invention, but even if this were not the case, it certainly can't be assumed that these things happened at the time and in the way that Dante describes.

Yet the use of the technical words "tablets" *(tavolette)* is striking. Toward the end of the 1300s, the painter Cennino Cennini, a pupil of Agnolo Gaddi, wrote a practical treatise on the various techniques of drawing and painting in which, having established that "the basis of art . . . is drawing and coloring," he exhorts a prospective pupil to begin by drawing, and says that this practice begins with drawing *in tavoletta*. This consists of drawing using a "stylus" of "silver or brass" on wooden boards properly "plastered" with a layer of "well-ground bone."[58] Here it seems as though Dante is describing himself carrying out this preliminary exercise—an exercise which we should not imagine, in modern fashion, as being done in the open air. It would be more reasonable to think of him sitting in a closed, or semi-closed, surrounding which may have been a workshop (of a painter or apothecary). But since medieval workshops opened onto the street, the distinguished gentlemen could have easily observed him.[59] Besides, if even respectable city figures could see him at this work without finding it unusual, this means that Dante regarded it as more than a simple impromptu leisure activity: would he have portrayed himself as a "sketcher" if he wasn't known for such activity or practice?

Note Dante's insistence on his state of concentration. We have already seen him absorbed while looking at the Garisenda Tower, not noticing what was happening around him; one tercet in the *Commedia* can be read in this way: "this is why, when we hear or see a thing / that captivates the soul / time passes and we do not notice" (*Purg.* IV 7–9; "e però, quando s'ode cosa o vede / che tegna forte a sé l'anima volta, / vassene 'l tempo e l'uom non se n'avvede"). His capacity to withdraw from all around him seems to be a typical trait. In this respect, here is a story from Boccaccio: Dante was in Siena at the workshop of an apothecary when he was brought a famous "small book" that he had never read (apothecaries were also booksellers). Having taken the book, he sat down on a bench in front of the workshop and became absorbed in reading it, and was so absorbed that he failed to notice a festival raging around him from the ninth hour to vespers, with dancing, games, and even "great sport with weapons." Perhaps Boccaccio was making it up, but that reference to "sport with weapons," particularly between knights, would fit in well with the festivities organized in Siena to welcome Charles Martel.[60] The most interesting detail in Boccaccio's story is the reference to an apothecary's workshop. Apothecaries prepared not only medicines but also colors for artists—and colors, and their preparation, were certainly not matters of disinterest to Dante. Many passages in his writings show that his knowledge of colors and the ways of mixing them went beyond that of someone who had an ordinary interest in the fine arts; it was a knowledge that could grow only from practical experience.[61]

Even though several lines of the *Commedia* show him to be well-informed about the art of painting (he had a clear knowledge of the techniques of chiaroscuro and other specialist techniques, such as graffito filled with black glaze), Dante obviously never practiced it professionally but, let us say, he was an amateur who knew many of the practical aspects of these arts. He wouldn't therefore have gone to a painter's workshop, but he must have had someone like Cennino Cennini, someone who taught him at least the basic techniques. A knowledge (at least in theory) of how to grind or macerate natural materials to make pigments and how to mix them cannot be simply self-taught: it can only be learned though spending time in places, such as an apothecary's, that specialized in such matters.[62] Is it a mere coincidence that Boccaccio describes him in an apothecary's workshop and that the *Vita Nova* makes an implied reference to an open workshop, which could be that of an apothecary? And once it is accepted that he spent time in workshops of this kind, who could have introduced him there? One might suspect it was through his master Brunetto. The famous notary, in fact, used to go to such places: a document of 1270 shows him interested in a spice business in Bologna. Another document from the end of 1293, which also tells us that by that time Brunetto was dead, states that his son Cresta, also a notary, traded in spices. This must have been a business developed by Brunetto as, let us say, a secondary but permanent job, and passed on to at least one of his children, once again as a sideline business. But what did apothecaries trade in? Drugs, spices and medicinal remedies, coloring materials for painters and for the dying industry. Continuing our conjecture, might we not imagine that Dante had joined the Arte dei Medici e degli Speziali once he had entered the political arena? After all, from at least 1295 Florentine painters formed one of its sections (there is no documentation for the years before that). Through university links between physicians and philosophers, it had become the guild for those we would today call intellectuals, but it was also connected with the world of apothecaries and painters.[63]

"Most noble and beautiful Philosophy"

Dante began to study philosophy in the early 1290s. He would fully devote himself to it, to the point where, in *Convivio*, barely ten years later, he would have a command of philosophical language that only those deeply involved in the subject could have. At the end of the 1200s, studying philosophy was a much less obvious choice than it might seem to us today. It was still a recent area of study and, moreover, confined to the halls of universities and the more important monastic *Studia*. It had developed at the University of Paris with the rediscovery of Aristotle, thanks to translations, and had reached Bologna University in the early 1290s with the arrival of *magistri* from Paris, such as Gentile da Cingoli. The new discipline followed a human and rational path of research, quite separate in its methods and aims from that of theology. Philosophers in both Paris and Bologna therefore sought to create a space of their own inside an institution which had until then been dominated by theologians, doctors, and lawyers.[64]

This form of study was rather unconventional, and for someone living in Florence, almost unheard of. Here, anyone who devoted themselves to literary rhetoric was already an intellectual who stood out in the crowd; but anyone studying ethics and metaphysics instead of (or as well as) natural science, which was the core subject in the faculty of medicine, would have been considered unique. Dante, who then studied literary rhetoric as well as philosophy, was exceptional altogether.

Who in Florence would have encouraged him to make such a choice? Certainly not Brunetto, for whom the word philosophy held the traditional value of love of knowledge, and knowledge meant the encyclopedic accumulation of ideas. Guido Cavalcanti must have played a crucial role once again.

In the 1300s, Cavalcanti had the reputation of being an atheist and an "epicurean," intent on his "speculations," "on trying to determine if there was a way of proving that God did not exist"; but he was also famed as a "logician" and "philosopher."[65] Dante himself played a part in establishing Cavalcanti's bad reputation as an unbeliever: in the canto in *Inferno* devoted to the heretics, or rather, the epicureans "who make the soul die with the body" (*Inf.* X 15; "che l'anima col corpo morta fanno"), Guido is named by Cavalcante his father, so that, it has been said, "the impression of the naive reader is that Cavalcante's epicureanism taints his son." We know nothing about old Cavalcante's philosophical leanings, and Dante himself must have known very little about them. If he places him in those fiery arches together with Farinata the Ghibelline, and in the company of such great Ghibellines as Federico II and Cardinal Ottaviano degli Ubaldini, it is certainly not because he had rejected the survival of the individual soul as Averroes had done; his condemnation, just like that of Farinata, resulted from the political strategies that Dante was pursuing around 1307, the date when the canto was probably composed. But Dante knew Guido's philosophical tendencies and therefore names him intentionally, well aware that the reputation of unbelief would fall upon him.[66]

Cavalcanti's fame as a philosopher was widespread, but in truth it was based on a single text, the doctrinal canzone *Donna me prega, per ch'eo voglio dire* (*A lady bids me, so I will speak*). It must have been fueled above all by his relations with leading members of the new philosophy course at Bologna. In the 1290s, Iacopo da Pistoia dedicated his only surviving text, *Questio de felicitate,* to him, describing him as "pre aliis amico carissimo" (the dearest friend of all).

In short, no one else in Florence was better able to set Dante on the road of philosophical speculation than Guido. Yet Cavalcanti's interests in natural philosophy were strictly connected to problems of a medical kind, to the point where the famous "physic" (doctor) Dino del Garbo considered *Donna me prega* as worthy of lengthy commentary.[67] Dante, on the other hand, didn't seem much interested in a physical and pathological interpretation of the symptoms of amorous passion, and pursued other paths. We could say that, if Guido had played the role of John the Baptist in philosophy in the same way as he had already done in poetry, then Dante was the Messiah he heralded.

Convivio twice describes the steps Dante had taken in moving toward philosophy. The first description is allegorical. In the *Vita Nova* Dante had described how, after Beatrice's death, an unnamed woman showed such pity on him that, little by little, a real passionate love developed within, an irrational passion, a "wicked desire" that drove him to betray the memory of that blessed woman. But he then shamefully regretted that feeling and returned to his true and pure love for Beatrice. In the second book of *Convivio* he returns to the story in the *Vita Nova* and reveals that this *Donna pietosa* (a gentle and compassionate woman) was not a real woman, but was none other than the "most noble and beautiful Philosophy," "daughter of God" (*Conv.* II XII 9; "questa donna fu figlia di Dio, regina di tutto, nobilissima e bellissima Filosofia"). If he hadn't revealed her true identity in the *Vita Nova* it was because readers, convinced that he was in love with a real woman, would not have understood that this was an allegorical picture. He also says, by way of a complicated astrological aside, that that *Donna pietosa* (in *Convivio* always called *Donna gentile*) had appeared to him for the first time exactly 1168 days after the death of Beatrice. Since she had died on June 8, 1290, the *Donna gentile* ("Philosophy") had appeared to him on August 21, 1293. But he also adds that a little time was needed before his love for this new woman became complete, and therefore we can conclude that this happened between 1293 and 1294.[68]

In the second account, Dante takes for granted the allegorical identification of the *Donna gentile* with Philosophy and therefore points more decisively toward autobiographical aspects. He writes that after the death of Beatrice he had sought comfort in reading Boethius' *De consolatione Philosophiae* and Cicero's *De amicitia,* and that in those books he had found not only "remedy" for his tears but—as happens to someone who "goes in search of silver and quite unintentionally finds gold"—also "the words of authors, sciences, and books." From them he had understood how philosophy, "who was the lady of these authors . . . was a great thing." Then he had begun to dream about that woman, whom he imagined to be a *"donna gentile"* and compassionate. But to really see her, he had to "go where she was truly revealed, namely to the schools of the clerics and to the disputations of the philosophizers, so that in a short time, perhaps thirty months, I began to so feel her sweetness that my love for her drove away and destroyed every other thought." In short, in some two and a half years he had developed a happy and fulfilling relationship with philosophy.

Saying that he had at first only imagined the features of that woman was a way of getting around the arbitrary date—1168 days after Beatrice's death—that he had previously set for her appearance. A real woman can suddenly appear on a particular day, but philosophy—the subject being studied—is not something that can appear on a specific day. It can make its appearance only after prolonged study. So in the second account, the two and a half years ("perhaps . . . thirty months") that separate the beginning of his studies from his mastering the philosophical discipline do not have a precise starting point. But if we take as the end point the date suggested above (late 1293, early 1294) and we take away two and a half years, we can place Dante's first studies in philosophy more or less around the middle of 1291.[69]

The "schools of the clerics" and "disputations of the philosophizers"

When Dante states that he attended the "schools of the clerics" and the "disputations of the philosophizers," is he referring to two distinct institutions or to two educational activities carried out in the same place or in similar places, as monastic studies might be in Florence?

In Florence in the early 1290s, there were three religious *Studia:* one with the Augustinians at Santo Spirito (about which we have no records), another with the Franciscans at Santa Croce, and yet another with the Dominicans at Santa Maria Novella. They were obviously *Studia in theologia,* aimed at educating the higher ranks of the religious orders.

That of Santa Maria Novella, though it wouldn't rise to the status of *Studium generale* until the beginning of the 1300s, was already important during the time when Dante could have attended: at a provincial level its position was somewhere between the great *Studia generalia* and those of the convents, where the first selection of students took place. Being a theological institution, there were no courses in philosophy in the strict sense, but that doesn't mean there was no contact, at least indirectly, with the language and categories of Aristotle and the contents of some of his works (*Fisica* and *Metafisica*). But there must have been some contact, since the Dominican order did not allow lay students admitted to theology classes to attend those in philosophy, a subject evidently regarded as unsafe. The central figure there was Remigio dei Girolami, a former student of Thomas Aquinas in Paris, who for over forty years (he died in 1320), with a few interruptions, carried out the role of reader. Remigio, a "white" Guelf, had been one of the city's most influential figures, both at the cultural level and as an intermediary in political affairs: he has been described as "the authentic religious advocate of civic culture, in the same way as Brunetto in the previous generation had been its lay advocate."[70] There are no recorded dealings between him and Dante, but it is more than likely they must have happened: Dante could have followed some of his lectures and listened to some of his many sermons (for example, *De filio regis,* given in March 1294 in honor of Charles Martel).

The Franciscan institution of Santa Croce was a *Studium generale* and therefore, in order of importance, ranked second only to the three *Studia principalia* of Paris, Oxford, and Cambridge. Theology was also taught

here and, as in Santa Maria Novella, the teaching involved scriptural ex-
egesis and guided reading of Peter Lombard's *Sentences,* that body of
statements by the Fathers of the Church, collected and commented upon
around the middle of the twelfth century, which was one of the compulsory texts for any theology student. Two great intellectuals who were
readers at Santa Croce between 1287 and 1289—Pietro di Giovanni Olivi
from Provence, and the younger Ubertino da Casale—played a major
role in the history of the Franciscan movement and, more generally, in
the Church. Dante could not have attended their lectures since both had
left Florence before 1290, but it is always possible that he had heard some
of Ubertino's sermons. Dante never mentions Olivi, but in many respects
his vision of the history of the Church seems to coincide with that of
the Provencal theologian in its Franciscan and spiritual interpretation.
As for Ubertino, a leading champion of the Franciscan "spiritual" movement, namely of those who advocated a return to the rigor of Francis's
rule against the permissive interpretation of the so-called "conventuals"
led by the minister general, Matteo d'Acquasparta, Dante would have
Bonaventura da Bagnoregio say in *Paradiso* that they both betrayed the
rule: Matteo because he "is too loose" through permissiveness, Ubertino because he "is too narrow" through excessive rigor.[71]

When he states that he went to the "schools of the clerics" Dante must
be referring to attending one, or both, of these two *Studia*. He attended,
obviously, as an external lay student. The later mention of the "disputations of the philosophizers" probably also relates to this same
environment.

Disputationes were one of the classic forms of teaching in all faculties.
They dealt with questions relevant to their particular course, in a public
debate where the participants acted according to codified rules.[72] While
we have no evidence that philosophical disputations took place in Bologna, we do know that in the 1290s, in addition to those on medicine
and law, theological disputations were common among the mendicant
orders. Philosophical arguments might sometimes have arisen in theology courses as well as in public disputations (which were thus open
to laymen) but Dante could certainly never have followed systematic and
organized lessons on Aristotle in the Florentine *Studia*. For this, he
would have needed to go to Bologna.

There is no record of a second trip to Bologna. We know that on September 6, 1291, Dante is present as a witness at the office of a Florentine

notary appointed to draft a document of attorney; we presume that in March 1294 he is in Florence on the occasion of the visit of Charles Martel; from late 1295 there is a series of attendances at city assemblies and councils where he is a member. There is therefore a gap of about two or three years in the record of his life. From *Convivio* we can infer that his love of philosophy became "perfect" at some time between late 1293 and early 1294, in other words in the very middle of that documentary blank. And so it can be neither proved nor disproved that Dante had gained a full knowledge of the subject (the "perfect love") in Bologna, where he could have had contact with teachings specifically in philosophy and could have read books that would have been hard to find in the monastic libraries of Florence. Bellino di Lapo—a relative of his from the Bello branch of the family who died in 1299—lived at that time at San Giovanni in Persiceto, not far north of Bologna, practicing the trade of money changer, but he also had interests in Bologna. Dante, who was already sailing in rough financial waters, could therefore have looked to the support of these relatives.[73] But a second stay in Bologna is only hypothetical. Moreover, once back in Florence it is reasonable to imagine that he continued attending theology lectures at Santa Croce and Santa Maria Novella throughout the 1290s, up until his exile.[74]

The *Vita Nova* past and future

Dante completed the *Vita Nova* in 1295. He had worked on it for a long time if, as many indications lead us to believe, the project for the book took shape immediately after Beatrice's death.[75]

The work is new from many points of view. It is, for example, impossible to establish what literary genre it belongs to. It is impossible, in other words, to briefly describe a book that is at the same time a love story, a collection of poems, a literary autobiography, a poetical declaration, and a history of other people's poetry, in the same way that it is impossible to give a one-word description of the *Commedia*.[76] Entirely original, too, is the figure of the author that it delineates. The three directions along which Dante's studies had taken him for fifteen years—those of the vernacular poet, the student of the Latin tradition, and the learned philosopher—in fact converge and combine in this one figure.

The *Vita Nova* outlines the development of this author of vernacular verse, documenting it through an anthology of compositions, from the early "courtly" phase to the invention of the new subject of praise, and finally to a poetry that went beyond the ideological positions shared by his friends of the "dolce stile," a poetry that speaks to everyone and not just to the select audience of "gentle hearts," of connoisseurs with a certain education and particular sensibilities (an elite that ended up being his own group of companions).

His skill in rhetoric comes to the fore when he devotes a whole paragraph to a long digression on the history of modern vernacular lyric verse—something never before seen in the literature of that century. The reasons for this excursus would, at first sight, seem somewhat specious: Dante in fact declares that he wants to justify why in the sonnet *Io mi senti' svegliar dentro allo core* (*Within my heart I felt the stir*) he had personified Love by way of the rhetorical figure of a prosopopoeia, "as if it were a thing in itself," and thus had a body, whereas love is "an accident in a substance" (*VN* 16, 1; "come se fosse una cosa per sé . . . uno accidente in sustanzia"), in other words, a quality. But very soon it becomes clear that his aim is not to justify the use of a particular rhetorical figure but, much more ambitiously, to demonstrate that the vernacular versifiers could be equated with the "literati" poets, namely the Latin and Greek poets, the only ones who had been given the name of poet until the time of Dante. On the basis of the observation that vernacular verse writers used the same images as Latin poets—"if any rhetorical image or color is allowed to the poet, it should be allowed to writers of vernacular verse" (*VN* 16, 7; "se alcuna figura o colore rettorico è conceduto alli poete, conceduto è alli rimatori"), Dante coins the revolutionary definition of "vernacular poet" and states that "composing vernacular rhyme is just the same as composing Latin verse" (*VN* 16, 4; "dire per rima in volgare tanto è quanto dire per versi in latino"). For the first time in the West, vernacular poetry was given an equal dignity to that of Latin poetry.[77] In this same paragraph, Dante shows not only a complete mastery of rhetorical terminology, but quotes verses from Virgil's *Aeneid*, Lucan's *Pharsalia*, Horace's *Ars Poetica*, and Ovid's *Remedia Amoris*.

In this paragraph he also displays his skill as a philosophy scholar, using technical terms of that discipline (for example, "accident in a substance") as well as quotes from Aristotle. Quotes and a specialist lexicon also appear in other pages of this book, which is certainly not philosophical, as

Convivio would be, but in which the author, "almost as if dreaming, already saw" (*Conv.* II XII 4; "ingegno molte cose, quasi come sognando, già vedea") "many things" of philosophy.[78]

No other writer, and not just in Florence, could have boasted similar credentials. But for Dante this was not enough. Though the *Vita Nova* had had a long gestation period, some clues suggest that his final writing had been quick and hasty. We discover why Dante was in a hurry to finish the book only in the last lines, from which it is apparent that he was preparing another.[79]

After having transcribed a sonnet, *Oltre la spera che più larga gira* (*Beyond the widest-circling sphere*) in which he says he is thinking of Beatrice in Paradise but, due to the limitations of our intellectual capacity, he is unable to perceive any more than an indescribable intuition, Dante adds several lines which are worth reading (bearing in mind that these are the last lines of the book):

> After this sonnet, a marvelous vision appeared to me, in which I saw things that made me resolve not to say more about this blessed one until I can talk about her more worthily. And to achieve this I am trying as hard as I can, as she truly knows. So that, if it be the pleasure of Him through whom all things live, that my life continues for a few more years, I hope to write about her what has never been written of any other woman.

> Apresso questo sonetto apparve a me una mirabile visione, nella quale io vidi cose che mi fecero proporre di non dire più di questa benedetta infino a tanto che io potesse più degnamente trattare di lei. E di venire a cciò io studio quanto posso, sì com'ella sae, veracemente. Sì che, se piacere sarà di Colui a cui tutte le cose vivono, che la mia vita duri per alquanti anni, io spero di dire di lei quello che mai non fue detto d'alcuna.

—*VN* 31, 1–2

We will never know what he had in mind when, after the "marvelous vision," he determines with a certain solemnity not to write about Beatrice until he can "talk about her more worthily." But the difficulty is ours alone: Dante—like any other author—wouldn't have dared to end his first book with the promise of another to come unless he hadn't already decided the nature of this second work and drafted its basic outline. From those few lines we can infer that it would be centered on Beatrice, a work stylistically more elevated ("talk about her more worthily") than love poetry—therefore than the *Vita Nova*—as well as innovative and original: "what has never been written of any other woman." It is certainly not the *Commedia,* as many have claimed, and still claim. It cannot be that, since Dante states that now, at the moment in which he is writing, he is using all his efforts to achieve that result ("And to achieve this I am trying as hard as I can"), and it is impossible for him to have started planning what would be the *Commedia* in 1295.[80] We can surmise that this more worthy work could have been a poem, perhaps in Latin and perhaps, being based on the blessed soul of Beatrice, in the form of a paradisiacal vision. In short, a poem in which he would have publicly proven his qualities as a poet, rhetorician, theologian, and philosopher.

3

Municipal Man

1295–1301

. . . citizens of the divided city

. . . *li cittadin de la città partita*

—*Inf.* VI 61

A forgotten promise

THERE IS NO TRACE of the book promised at the end of the *Vita Nova*. Is this due to some accident of history, or did Dante never get as far as writing it? The question must remain unanswered, unless we give credit to those accounts that speak of a Latin poem begun by him and then left unfinished. These accounts, in truth, refer specifically to a first draft of the *Commedia* in Latin: it is clear that for readers of centuries ago it must have been almost automatic to associate the news of a presumed poem—passed down, moreover, through a doubtful oral tradition—with the poem actually written. If, however, we leave aside this simple misunderstanding, we could interpret them as evidence of the fact that Dante had actually spent time on the work promised at the end of the *Vita Nova*.

In the early 1340s the young Boccaccio transcribed in his commonplace book a part of a Latin epistle that a Benedictine monk named Ilaro from the Congregazione dei Pulsanesi had sent from the monastery of Santa Croce al Corvo, above the mouth of the River Magra in the

Lunigiana region, to Uguccione della Faggiola, lord of Pisa and Lucca, on a date unspecified, but sometime between the late summer of 1314 and the early spring of 1315. The letter is said to have been sent with the gift of a copy of *Inferno,* with marginal notes, dedicated to him. In the epistle, Ilaro states that an unnamed person (who from the description is clearly Dante) had passed through the diocese of Luni on his way "ad partes ultramontanas" (to the other side of the Apennines or the Alps?). After a private conversation, impressed by the devotion shown by the brother, he had pulled a small book from his pocket and had given it to him as a memento. And he then expressed the desire that the book (the first section of a three-part vernacular work, and thus identifiable as *Inferno*) should be sent, as soon as Ilaro himself had added a commentary to it, to Uguccione—which the brother was now doing. Finally, Ilaro informed Uguccione that, if one day he should wish "to seek out the other two parts of this work" ("Si vero de aliis duabus partibus huius operis aliquando Magnificentia vestra perquireret"), he could ask for that "which follows this" ("que ad istam sequitur") from Marchese Moroello Malaspina, and the third from Frederick of Aragon, King of Sicily. At this point Boccaccio (or the writer of the manuscript from which he is copying), who was clearly interested only in the section referring to Dante, ends the transcription.[1]

The problem is to establish whether the letter is genuine. This question is still open. The greatest doubts concern the very passages that would be of most interest to us. According to Ilaro, Dante confessed that he had begun writing the *Commedia* in Latin, but had soon moved to the vernacular because he had realized that "the poems of illustrious poets were scorned as if they were of no worth; and so men, for whom such things were written in better times, abandoned the liberal arts—alas!—to the common folk." Dante is therefore supposed to have interrupted the composition of the Latin poem because the level of culture almost demanded it, since "homines generosi," namely the nobles, the *potentes,* were unpracticed in Latin. Even more suspect are the two and a half hexameters that Dante is said to have recited to Ilaro, reputed to be the incipit of that abandoned poem: "Ultima regna canam, fluvido contermina mundo, / spiritibus que lata patent, que premia solvunt / pro meritis cuicunque suis." However these words are interpreted—"I will sing of the farthest realms, lying beyond the revolving universe, that open boundless to the spirits, and dispense rewards to each according to his merits" (Padoan); "I will sing of the last realms, lying beyond the corruptible world, that offer themselves vastly to the spirits, and repay each one as he deserves" (Bellomo)—these lines allude to the realm beyond this world: it isn't clear whether it is a generic hereafter or, more specifically, Paradise. Boccaccio was convinced of their authenticity, as he was about the rest of the epistle, but it is hard to believe these really belong to Dante. And the information about a *Commedia* first conceived in Latin is also hardly likely. That this comes from Dante himself is improbable, if not impossible. This is either an interpolation—meaning that the whole reference to the *Commedia*, and not just the hexameters, was added to the original letter—or it's a misunderstanding.[2] Dante could, in other words, have mentioned a poem in Latin begun and then abandoned, and Ilaro could have thought he was referring to the *Commedia*. A sensible conclusion could be that the parts relating to the supposed Latin poem were added, after Dante's death, to a genuine letter that accompanied the gift of a copy of *Inferno* to Uguccione. The epistle would therefore not be completely false, but corrected and altered at various points.

Although Brother Ilaro is such an unreliable witness that his very existence might be questioned, the authority of Filippo Villani is altogether different. In the preface to his commentary on the *Commedia* (written toward the end of the 1300s and interrupted after the first canto) Villani takes the content of Ilaro's epistle from Boccaccio (including the two and a half hexameters of the supposed incipit) but adds to it an entirely new detail. As confirmation of its truth he states that Dante— evidently before being banished from Florence—had told Villani's paternal uncle, the historian Giovanni Villani, that he had abandoned the Latin for the vernacular because, when he compared his lines to those of Virgil, Statius, Horace, Ovid, and Lucan, it seemed like placing a coarse rag beside purple cloth.[3] Like Boccaccio, Filippo also identifies the unfinished Latin poem as the *Commedia*, but his evidence is still very important since he states that the memory of Dante as a Latin poet was still alive in Florence. This certainly isn't very much, but it is perhaps enough to prevent us ruling out as entirely fanciful the possibility that this attempt at a Latin poem has something to do with the intention expressed at the end of the *Vita Nova*.

"I was less dear and less pleasing to him"

Whether or not he had started to write the work he had promised, it is a fact that, immediately after 1295, Dante's literary production radically changed. We would have expected him to follow the path of mystical and eschatological poetry, and yet here is a Dante more worldly than ever before and ignoring that myth of Beatrice he had spent so many years constructing. The love poet lets himself be inspired by several women, as though he had never (with the sole exception of the *Donna pietosa* or *gentile*) repeatedly proclaimed his loyalty to a single woman. But he even goes as far as writing poetry imbued with an eroticism and a sensuality that are the exact opposite of the rapturous atmosphere of his writings in praise of Beatrice: "if I had seized those lovely plaits / which had for me become a whip and lash / pulling them before the third hour [9 A.M.] / with them I'd pass afternoon and evening; / and I'd be neither piteous nor kind, / I'd behave in fact like a bear when he's having fun." (*Rime* 43, 66–71; "s'io avesse le belle trecce prese / che son fatte per me scudiscio e ferza, / pigliandole anzi terza / con esse passerei vespero e squille; / e non sarei pietoso né cortese, / anzi farei com'orso quando scherza").[4] Yet the project that Dante had announced at the end of the *Vita Nova,* however things had gone, seems to have remained alive in his mind, if only as something not yet done. We don't know whether he felt guilty about not fulfilling that promise, nor is it important; but we do know that in the *Commedia* he gives his own character a very heavy sense of guilt in relation to Beatrice. In Earthly Paradise he meets her at last, exactly ten years after her death. She is the same woman he loved in his youth and had celebrated in the *Vita Nova,* and yet here she seems profoundly changed. No longer a source of all sweetness, but "haughty" (*Purg.* XXX 70; "proterva"); she speaks, and her tongue is like a sword that strikes by its "point" as well as by its "edge" (*Purg.* XXXI 2–3; "per punta, / che pur per taglio"). She accuses a confused and bewildered Dante of having betrayed her: immediately after her death "he left me, and gave himself to someone else" (*Purg.* XXX 126; "si tolse a me, e diessi altrui"). This had led to a weakening of the feelings of love he had previously felt for her—"I was less dear and less pleasing to him" (*Purg.* XXX 129; "'fu' io a lui men cara e men gradita") and his unconsummated attraction to other women ("what mortal thing / must then have drawn you to desire it? . . . your wings should not have been weighted down, / to await another blow, from a pretty girl / or other passing new attraction" (*Purg.* XXXI 53–60; "qual cosa mortale / dovea poi trarre te nel suo disio? . . . non ti dovea gravar le penne in giuso, / ad aspettar più colpo, o pargoletta / o altra novità con sì breve uso"). There is therefore nothing vague about the accusation of unfaithfulness: Dante had forgotten the new poetical, literary, and human perspective that had opened out for him at the time of his beloved's death and had lapsed into a conception and a practice of poetry (pretty girls and other new attractions) that rejected the new amorous vision glimpsed in the book written during his youth. When Beatrice declares that Dante ought to have "risen up / after" her (*Purg.* XXXI 55–56; "levar suso / di retro") and had instead "weighted down" his wings, he is perhaps resorting to usual metaphors of a moral character, or perhaps he is alluding to something more concrete, to that failure to rise into the sky, in her footsteps, which a paradisiacal vision would have achieved literally.[5]

The shift doesn't just involve Dante's love poetry and Beatrice's prime role in it, but deeply affects the whole of his poetry. The same poet who, in the *Vita Nova,* had recently suggested—in agreement with his friend Cavalcanti and rejection of Guittone and his followers—that vernacular verse could only express ideas of love, is now composing poems on moral and secular themes.[6] What could have caused such a clear shift?

Brunetto Latini had died toward the end of 1293, and Bono Giamboni had died not long before. With the death of these two intellectuals, Brunetto especially, a great gap had opened in the cultural and civic life of Florence. For decades, Brunetto had personified the role of the sage who dispensed his wisdom to the city. He combined a notable bookish culture (unique in the city before Dante) and a remarkable practical ability when it came to government and private affairs. Florence's bankers and merchants could look to Brunetto as a model because he was one of them, but was equipped with what they lacked: a wide-ranging and refined culture. His death, though it left a void, also raised the question of succession. Dante was, objectively, the only lay intellectual who could take his place; in any event, he felt he was the true heir of his late master. Nevertheless, neither an elitist writer of lyric verse nor an even more remote Latin poet could aspire to the role of grand councilor or, as we might say today, political guru. That role required a committed intellectual who could deal with moral issues relating to city life. The individualist who cultivated his own garden of lyric verse or antique literature had to become a vernacular writer who dealt with problems felt by ordinary people. But this was just one part of what anyone aspiring to succeed Brunetto was required to do; the other and by no means secondary part concerned involvement in civic life. And this was exactly what Dante had so far been careful to avoid. To obtain that prestigious post, which he felt within his grasp, he had no choice but to become involved in city politics.

An "idler" in politics

During those same years, the unfolding of certain events in Florentine politics seemed have been tailor-made to help Dante take the leap.

The restrictions on public appointments, in force since 1293 against those belonging to the magnate class, had aroused understandably strong feelings among the ruling class. Following public disorder (January 23, 1294) started by the Donati—in particular Corso, who had been accused by the *popolo minuto* (the ordinary people) of having illegally escaped the proper sentence of death for two murders committed shortly before—the magnates were able to point the blame at Giano della Bella, who was at the heart of the anti-magnate government. In February 1295, the objective alliance between the *grandi* and the ordinary trading classes forced him to flee from Florence. But the attempt by the magnates to reverse the situation wasn't entirely successful. It is true that, as a consequence of Giano's downfall, the *Ordinamenti di giustizia* were reformed in a less restrictive sense (the so-called Relaxations, or *Temperamenti*), but the regulations remained substantially in force. The provisions of 1293 established that, as well as magnates (whose names were listed in a special register), those who had knighthoods and those who did not exercise a true profession were excluded from the office of prior. The provisions passed on July 6, 1295 kept the prohibition on knights but established that "to be considered as a craftsman and therefore to be admitted to the office of prior and to the enjoyment of all rights inherent in the position of craftsman, the real and personal exercise of the occupation itself is not necessary."[7] This regulation had a direct effect on Dante.

No law until 1293 would have prevented him from taking part in the city's magistracy; the impediment arose only in the years 1293–1295 insofar as he was not registered in a guild. (Dante never had the problem of ever being considered a magnate.) But from at least the 1280s, long before membership of a guild had become a requirement for access to public life, effective power was in the hands of the guilds, so that anyone who was not a member had great difficulty finding a way into public life. As Dante exercised no profession or business and so could not be registered with a guild, he was in effect excluded from active politics. His lack of involvement could have resulted from disinterest but must, more than anything else, have been the result of his preference for living on the rents from his property. From the summer of 1295 he now had the chance of joining a guild while continuing to live on income, and he immediately took advantage of it. He joined that category of people who would be regarded as "idlers"; in other words, jobless.

His enrollment in the guild of doctors and apothecaries is documented only in March 1297, but must have dated back to just after July 1295. It seems certain, in fact, that during the six months from November 1295 to April 1296 he had already represented his *sestiere* in the inner or special council of the *capitano del popolo* (consisting of thirty-six members and therefore also known as the Council of Thirty-Six). But it seems he made no spoken contribution and that he abandoned the meetings on several occasions: rather strange behavior for a "new recruit." It is certain, however, that he spoke on December 14, 1295, during a meeting of the Consiglio dei Capitudini. This council consisted of magistrates (consuls, or *capitudini*) from the twelve main guilds and had the task of preparing proposals and decisions to be submitted for the approval of the city councils. The session during which Dante spoke concerned the discussion of a proposal for a new system for electing priors. This or other bodies sometimes sought the advice of experts or "wise men" *(sapientes),* and it was in this very role as "wise man" that Dante was involved. It is equally certain that he took part, six months later, in the Consiglio dei Cento (Council of a Hundred). The council was elected every six months and, along with the College of Priors, was Florence's most important governing body (at whose sittings the priors and the *gonfaloniere di giustizia* took part): during the first six-month period it is recorded that Dante spoke on June 5, 1296.[8] But if Dante had been a member of the inner council of the *capitano del popolo,* whose mandate ended on April 30, he would have been prevented, by reason of incompatibility, from being elected to this second council, which came into operation on the first of that month. It is therefore reckoned that he had been co-opted by the *gonfaloniere* (Lapo Saltarelli who, as we shall see, was one of his political contacts) and the priors to stand in for a councilor who was for some reason unavailable.[9]

Whether as a "wise man" or as a stand-in, it seems that Dante had taken his first steps in politics without being elected. Someone, in some way or other, had chosen him, someone who would certainly not have looked at his financial means and professional prestige, but would have judged him fit to occupy public positions for his talent, now well known, as a philosopher and a poet. Nevertheless, it would be rather naive to imagine he could take part in Florentine public life—already turbulent in these years due to rifts in the ruling Guelf party—by representing his *sestiere* on his intellectual merits alone. The area in which he lived was the key starting point for a rise in politics, but what mattered was relations within it. San Pier Maggiore was split into two factions, whose rivalry was about to degenerate into open conflict between the Cerchi and Donati families. The latter were Dante's relatives through marriage, but his closest friends, such as Guido Cavalcanti and Manetto Portinari, were linked to the Cerchi. It was therefore the Cerchi—and in particular Vieri, the most powerful person in the *sestiere,* perhaps even in Florence—who decided that this man, no longer young in years, of modest family and humble means but of great intellectual talent, could be useful to their cause.

We know that Dante spoke once more during a council session in 1297 on an unspecified matter, after which there is no further trace of his involvement in city politics. We therefore don't know what path he trod, between alliances and rivalries, to become the first and only Alighieri to occupy the highest seat in the city hierarchy in that fateful year of 1300.

Instruction in "gentilezza"

In the first sessions in which he took part, Dante spoke as an "expert" on questions of a procedural nature; he spoke in favor of legislation against those, especially magnates, who committed acts of violence against the holders of public offices; he supported decisions in favor of neighboring Pistoia. He didn't have the opportunity of dealing with major problems of external and domestic politics. He took a modest role, therefore, that could give no idea of what real contribution a "philosopher" and "rhetorician" might make to city life. He could be recognized as Brunetto's successor only if his practical involvement were matched by an intellectual output capable of influencing the great issues that stirred debate and political conflict among city's various classes.

The problem of nobility—what it meant, which individuals and social classes could call themselves noble and, above all, what behavior was required of them—was central in the bitter political dispute of the 1290s, a period that began, not surprisingly, with the *Ordinamenti di giustizia* against the magnates. For an oligarchic group with no noble ancestry, the concept of nobility found its expression in the symbolic role of knighthood. The urge for this recognition indicated the eagerness of the great banking and commercial dynasties for social betterment. There again, it was precisely the arrogant and surly behavior which the new rich aristocrats borrowed from the ancient nobility that provoked the reaction of the *popolo*, namely the city's merchant class. The question of nobility therefore became mixed up with problems of public ethics. For Dante this also had a more personal relevance, if it is true that he was greatly influenced by the ideal of living as a nobleman.

At an early stage, when asked what was nobility, Dante had given the answer of an intellectual aristocrat. During the *Stilnovo* period he had shared with a close circle of friends the idea that only hearts that were *gentili* (in other words, noble) could feel love and, conversely, that love could not dwell in men who were "base" and "dull." In other words— as in the opening lines of a sonnet in the *Vita Nova*, relying on the authority of the Guinizelli of *Al cor gentil rempaira sempre amore* (*The noble heart will always be filled with love*)—the idea that "love and the noble heart are a single thing, / as the wise man writes in his verse" (*VN* 11; "amore e 'l cor gentil sono una cosa, / sì come il saggio in suo dittare pone").[10] This wasn't, in itself, an original idea, but from it came the new corollary introduced by Dante, Cavalcanti and, to some extent, Cino—that love poetry had to be for a limited, select readership, for those who were "noble" and "cultured" (*gentili* and *intendenti*). Thus the notion that nobility of spirit was a necessary and sufficient prerogative for experiencing love—a notion that in its history had been a sign of sensitivity, a way of breaking down ideological and social barriers—was transformed in the hands of these Florentine poets into an expression of detachment and closure. That small group dominated by the magnate Cavalcanti sought to establish itself as an intellectual elite, as a new aristocracy based on cultural merit and the conduct that followed from it.

Now, in the second half of the 1290s, Dante addressed the whole of the city's ruling class with two canzoni that were, so to speak, moral and instructive. In the first (*Le dolci rime d'amor ch'i' solia*—*The sweet rhymes of love I must forsake*) he defines nobility, the mirror of all "virtue"; in the second (*Poscia ch'Amor del tutto m'ha lasciato*—*Since love has wholly abandoned me*) he describes, under the label of "charm" (*leggiadria*), the behavior fitting for nobility. His intention was to show that "nobility" (*gentilezza*) could be acquired—and that courtesy, its translation into the sphere of social relations, can be practiced—in the context of the city as well, provided it is understood that this depends on neither breeding nor wealth. His proposal, therefore, was one of mediation, in the spirit of Brunetto.

In *Le dolci rime d'amor ch'i' solia,* rejecting a view that he attributes to Emperor Frederick II (though in fact it was Aristotle's), he insists that wealth is not the prime source of nobility and that you cannot be noble simply by birth:

> a certain ruler held nobility,
> as it appeared to him,
> to be possession of ancestral wealth
> and fine manners

> tale imperò che gentilezza volse,
> secondo 'l suo parere,
> che fosse antica possession d'avere
> con reggimenti belli

> —*Conv.* CANZ. III, 20–24

Wealth and ancestral nobility must be accompanied by individual virtue, consisting of the capacity to choose the appropriate position between two extremes. If seen against the background of Florentine social and ideological conflict, this view, which in itself was hardly original, might be regarded as being markedly "civic." In effect, it sanctions the right of what today would be called the middle class to claim noble rank, though of a new kind, and it recognized the worth of the ancient aristocracies, provided that they integrated into the community: a position, therefore, in which the whole of the city's composite ruling class could be recognized.

In the second canzone, the part describing the appropriate behavior for a true *leggiadro* (man of charm) is preceded by a bitter attack on false *leggiadri,* in other words those who behave in an unseemly and boorish manner in the conviction that theirs is the proper conduct of nobles, as they claim to be. Dante lists them by category. The spendthrifts, as they "squander their money," imagine "they are among honorable people," and thus spend money "on banquets and satisfying their sexual appetites," flaunting costly ornaments and clothing, "as though they were a commodity on display, waiting to be bought by dimwitted purchasers." Nor have they truly understood what noble behavior is when they laugh continually and inappropriately, thinking this to be the sign of a ready wit, or "express themselves in a complicated and elaborate way" and treat others haughtily, "satisfied that common folk will be struck by their words and by their arrogance." Enemies of nobility are also those who ignore the fidelity of love and the art of courtship, but abandon themselves to buffoonery in their discourse and, like a "furtive thief," steal bestial pleasures from women ("they never fall in love / with loving women; / in their talk they joke; they never move their feet / to court women in a manner of true elegance, / but like a thief at work, / so they go stealing furtive pleasure : . . like mindless animals." The *leggiadro,* on the other hand, "freely gives and takes, is pleasing in conversation, loves and is loved by wise people while being indifferent to the judgment of those who are not; he is not arrogant but knows how to show his worth when necessary."[11]

None of the arguments, for or against, can be regarded as new. But what is altogether new is a canzone in which a large amount of space is given over to philosophical arguments that could only be put forward by someone who was highly familiar with such texts as Aristotle's *Nicomachean Ethics.* And new, above all, is the fact that a philosophical argumentative layout is used for a discussion that has concrete aims that readers can easily identify. It is Dante himself who identifies the enemies of *leggiadria* in "false knights": "O false knights, evil and wicked, / its enemies" (*Rime* 27, 112–113; "Oh falsi cavalier, malvagi e rei, / nemici di costei"). But Florentines of that period needed no such assistance to understand: the enemies were the rich men with no past who had been given the title of knight, parvenus who aped the way of life of the highest class, who kept a sumptuous table, surrounded by buffoons and hangers-on (like Ciacco, the main character in Canto VI of *Inferno*), who flaunted their wealth, treated the *popolo* with arrogance and very often claimed (sometimes with force) a sort of legal immunity. They formed that magnate class against whom the people of Florence had risen in the 1290s, pushing it to the margins of political life. Dante's argument would have pleased Brunetto Latini for the very reason that it was not directed against the knights and nobility themselves, but against their degeneration. It certainly pleased a political intellectual like Lapo Saltarelli, mentioned earlier, who was involved in drafting Giano della Bella's *Ordinamenti di giustizia* against the magnates and was a leading member of the Cerchi faction (he was also related by marriage to Vieri dei Cerchi, being his father-in-law).[12] In short, with his *canzoni morali*, Dante was taking sides. And in doing so, he obviously couldn't please everyone.

The rift with Guido Cavalcanti

Guido Cavalcanti must not have been pleased. Having been accustomed since his youth to playing a leading part in public life (remember that in 1280 he was one of the guarantors of the Peace of Cardinal Latino), he had been marginalized by the *Ordinamenti di giustizia,* and not even the later relaxations had allowed him access to the more important appointments. If he had wished, however, he could have joined a guild and taken an active part in political life through one of the true nerve-centers of "popular" power. He must have received several such invitations. The chronicler Dino Compagni, for example, sent him a double sonnet (*sonetto rinterzato*), *Se mia laude scusasse te sovente,* in which, in effect, he complains that Cavalcanti is not placing his great virtues at the service of the community by "working" (*ovrere*), in other words joining a guild: you don't need to be of noble blood and have a great following, Dino tells him, because you are already noble as you are and, with the qualities you have, you could have been a great merchant. If God—he continues—were to lead every person to their right purpose, then, in balancing the differences, he would give courtliness (*cortesia*), which is plentiful in you, to the artisans and would make you a worker, a member of a guild, so that you don't stop earning money, rather like me, who, though I have to work for my living, am also generous (*cortese*) in giving. But haughty Cavalcanti wouldn't hear of such a thing. Not that he remained aloof, nor that he, a magnate, supported his own side— indeed, he was politically allied to the Cerchi, who were regarded as more open to the demands of the *popolo*—though his view of the political conflict was decidedly oriented toward the magnates. He was prone to quarreling (even violently), to provocation, and to the fine individual gesture of boldness mixed with arrogance. In his loathing of the rival faction, his personal hatred of Corso Donati counted perhaps more than purely political motives. In short, an individualist like him could not have been an integral part of any organization.

Guido, precisely because of his elitist nobility of spirit, cultivated almost in solitude, might have agreed with all the accusations Dante made against the Florentine knightly class, but he would have found it hard to accept that his friend and associate could place his learning and skill as a poet at the service of the *popolo*, whom he probably regarded as vulgar, an unworthy ally for an intellectual. And so he must have felt a certain rancor. In one famous sonnet (*I' vegno 'l giorno a te 'nfinite volte*—I visit you countless times each day) he criticizes Dante for "thinking too basely" and mixing with "boring people," a man who had once kept his distance from the throng. We don't know when or for what reason the sonnet was written, which is why there have been so many conflicting interpretations. One of these, and perhaps the best founded, suggests that Guido is criticizing Dante, who several years earlier had shared his aristocratic view of culture, for subscribing to the new "democratic" idea of politics.[13]

It should be said, however, that, of the two paths that opened before him at the end of the *Vita Nova,* if he had taken that of the eschatological vision rather than producing moral verse, this would have done nothing to prevent his rift with Guido. It was written in the heavens that this pair, so instrumental in the newborn vernacular literature, would

split. Cavalcanti, rational and skeptical, would not have approved of a
theological-philosophical poem, all the more so if written in Latin. But
already in the *Vita Nova* the protests of an identical vision and claims of
fellow feeling do nothing to hide the existence of differences. There was
already a deep gulf that separated Guido's pessimistic, irrational, and
pathological concept of love from that of Dante's praise, centered on the
assurance that love is an instrument of moral elevation. The instructive
canzone *Donna me prega* is certainly evidence of this: it has been pointed
out that "it is difficult to imagine more contrary propositions than the
treatise on love which is Dante's *Vita Nova* and Cavalcanti's canzone of
love." Indeed, it is possible that *Donna me prega* was composed specifically to refute the notion of love that Dante expresses in his *nove rime*
and that it therefore represents the most obvious point of discord between the two friends.[14] On the other hand, even though the *Vita Nova*
is almost dedicated to him, Dante's claim that Guido had been his John
the Baptist, made moreover with the specious interpretation of an in-
nocuous occasional sonnet, can be read (and could have been read by
the party concerned) as homage in appearance only. A homage which,
in effect, is basically saying that the young pupil had overtaken his older
master and, no less importantly, that he had done so by taking a direction he certainly wouldn't have liked, is a very strange homage.[15]

On the brink of financial ruin

The income from two farms and a couple of small houses wouldn't have
given him a particularly good standard of living. Yet Dante didn't seem
especially careful with money (which, anyway, he would have always
had in modest quantities, since it was likely that the fields would have
provided him with food more than anything else). He didn't shy away
from the costs of taking a horse with him to war, nor those of at least
one stay in Bologna. He may never have bought books, objects that were
prohibitively expensive, but to write he needed paper, which was also
fairly expensive. He would also have had to buy decent clothing to mix
with the smart society of Cavalcanti and his kind, and to attend assemblies and public councils. And there was also the increasing responsibility of a growing family.

During the second half of the 1290s, the Alighieri brothers (who jointly held their inherited assets) had to face a financial crisis of worrying proportions. It is clear that Dante hadn't gained much from his political activity, which then as now could offer many good opportunities. There again, political advantages—then as now—went above all to those who already enjoyed substantial wealth. The situation deteriorated in 1297. On April 11, Dante and Francesco received a loan of 227½ gold florins; in 1300 they were again insolvent, and a case was brought before a civil judge in the district of Porta del Duomo. Meanwhile, toward the end of 1297, on December 23, the brothers negotiated another loan, with Jacopo di Litto dei Corbizzi, for the substantial sum of 480 gold florins.[16] In less than a year they were therefore forced to borrow 707½ gold florins. In the second half of the previous year Dante had entered the Consiglio dei Cento. To take part in this assembly it was necessary to pay a tax of at least 100 *libbre* or lire, which was equivalent to a taxable income of 1,200 lire. At that time 1,200 lire had an effective value of 600 gold florins. Dante's wealth, even assuming it wasn't as low as the required minimum, must not have been much more than that. This sum, in fact, is consistent with the value of properties in Pagnolle calculated on the depreciated value of florins in the 1330s.[17] It is almost certain, therefore, that the 707½ florins of debt (though perhaps there was more) amounted to the whole of the Alighieri brothers' wealth.

Behind these figures can be seen the magnitude of a crisis that was in danger of ruining the whole family. Dante and Francesco were saved by the help of Durante degli Abati, their maternal grandfather, and Manetto dei Donati, the father of Gemma. In other words, the two well-to-do branches into which the Alighieri had married now joined forces to help out their children and grandchildren. It was they who guaranteed such a substantial loan, together with two other people: Noddo degli Arnoldi and Alamanno degli Adimari, the latter a magnate and fierce rival of the Cerchi. And then there were other relations by marriage, given that the lender Iacopo Corbizzi was acting for himself as well as on behalf of Pannocchia Riccomanni, who was the brother of Lapo Riccomanni, husband of Tana, Dante's sister. Besides, the Corbizzi were also neighbors of the Alighieri family: Litto, deceased father of the lender Iacopo, had bequeathed lands adjacent to those owned by Dante and Francesco at Pagnolle.[18] There is a clear impression that a family net-work had come into operation and that this network, involving the Ghibelline Abati, Donati, and Adimari families, was linked to a social and political circle that was not only extraneous but even hostile to the political realm in which Dante's sympathies lay. And perhaps we have grounds for believing that when Forese Donati, in one of his of-fensive sonnets, sarcastically hoped that God would preserve Tana and Francesco (*Rime* 25d, 10; "se Dio ti salvi la Tana e 'l Francesco"), he was referring to a situation, already apparent to Florentines for some time, in which Dante was dependent on his brother and sister.

The business of the 480-florin loan would last for decades: in 1315, in the will of Maria, widow of Manetto Donati and mother of Gemma, we learn not only that the surety given by her husband was still effective, but that he had guaranteed another loan for 46 florins, and another 90 had been guaranteed by a certain Perso Ubaldini. Only in 1332 would Francesco repay Iacopo Corbizzi half of the amount he had received thirty-five years earlier.

But the string of loans did not end there: on October 23, 1299, it was Francesco who received 53 florins—whether for himself or also for his brother is not clear. Meanwhile, Francesco had become independent and had begun to carry out the family's traditional trade of small-time mer-chant and moneylender, and so it was he who lent Dante 125 florins on March 14, 1300 (though a few days later, on March 30, he himself took out a loan for 20 florins) and another 90 florins on June 11. Dante would be appointed as prior four days later, on June 15. Of the two brothers, it was the more famous one who suffered the greater financial difficulty. The closeness of relations with Durante degli Abati is confirmed by the fact that in March 1301 it was Dante and Francesco who made guaran-tees to Cerbino di Tencino of San Pier Maggiore for a loan granted to him for an unspecified amount, and in July of the same year, Francesco received a loan of 13 gold florins from the same Cerbino di Tencino.[19]

A power struggle

Even before Campaldino (in 1289), there was no longer an organized Ghibelline party in Florence. The only remaining united party was the so-called Guelf party, with its own offices, self-governing structures, and headquarters. Despite the formal distinctions, in reality the party had become fully identified with the commune. After Campaldino, there had been an upheaval in Florentine political life, which until then had revolved around the tense and unequal relationship between the banking oligarchy and the great property investors, who together monopolized the power within the party, and the trading classes, represented by the guild corporations. This upheaval was caused by the claims of the so-called *popolo grasso* (merchants and industrialists) in alliance with the *popolo minuto* (artisans and small businesses). Party dialectic therefore gave way to class conflict. The oligarchy came out of it defeated, so that its members were banned from government posts after the *Ordinamenti di giustizia* of 1293. This didn't mean members of the oligarchy were excluded from the actual operation of power. The magnates, in fact, continued to be the party's ruling group, and the party, whose members had great weight in the guilds, in particular the larger ones, had considerable influence in the choice of political appointments. But the subsequent regulations against the magnates, from 1293 onward, had the effect of splitting the party's ruling group. The dividing line between the two factions was marked by questions about how to respond to this discriminatory treatment and what relationship to have with the *popolo*. The more uncompromising wing was headed by the Donati, while the more moderate—though it would be better to say more unclear and uncertain—approach was that of the Cerchi. They might have been seen as no more than differing attitudes, except that, as so often happened in Florence's history at that time, the disagreement degenerated into out-and-out civil war. Tensions became aggravated by numerous factors to the point where a settlement could not be reached. First among these was the long-standing rivalry that divided the two main families, who both happened to live in the same *sestiere* of San Pier Maggiore; then there was the fact that the two factions, each of which contained leading members of Florence's main banking companies, represented separate and distinct financial interests; lastly, there was interference from outside. Florence was one of Europe's financial capitals, and it was therefore inevitable that domestic political events would be affected by outside ambitions and interests. In the same way that the war between the Guelfs and Ghibellines had been exacerbated by the interference of the Angevin rulers of Naples, likewise it would be the continual intervention of Pope Boniface VIII that determined the victory of one of the two factions of the Guelf party.

The Cerchi headed Florence's largest banking company, but could boast no illustrious ancestry: they were the exact prototype of that "gente nuova" whom Dante would accuse of having caused Florence's degeneration with their "quick gains" (*Inf.* XVI 73; "sùbiti guadagni"). Arriving in the city from the Val di Sieve, the "parish of Acone" (*Para.* XVI 65; "piovier d'Acone") at the beginning of the century, their economic and social rise had been so meteoric that in 1280 they could purchase the houses of the Guidi family, close to where Dante lived. Every day, over the door that had once belonged to such a noble family, he was obliged to see a coat of arms steeped in "cowardice" (*fellonia*), that of the new owners. He is not the only one, however, to accuse the Cerchi of cowardice: Dino Compagni, too, who in the tumultuous years of internecine conflict was tied to their fate, would write in his *Cronica* that they avoided taking the title of lords of the city, but "more for cowardice than civic love, since they feared their rivals." The accusation was directed toward the head of the family, Vieri, who at Campaldino had demonstrated great physical courage but now, during the complex events over the last years of the century, which could have enabled him to take control of the city, was acting in a dithering, cautious, and above all contradictory manner, trusting in his enormous financial power.

The story of their neighbors, the Donati, is quite the opposite, as is the story of Corso, their head. With no great economic resources, the Donati were members of the city's ancient aristocracy, and behaved in the arrogant and scornful manner of aristocrats. Corso was the true model of a knight, bold and courageous, but also violent and well aware of his class superiority. Accustomed to holding the office of *podestà* in many Italian cities, and therefore to being in command, reluctant to respect the laws, which he regarded as beneath him, and enterprising in spirit (the victory at Campaldino was largely thanks to his initiative), he was a proud opponent of the *Ordinamenti di giustizia* and of all the regulations against the magnates. Like Vieri he remained aloof from the *popolo*, but unlike Vieri he did nothing to conceal his aversion toward them. He found himself as leader of the hard-line faction almost by nature, more through character than out of deliberate political choice.[20]

The first and decisive rift in the Guelf faction happened in July 1295 when, taking advantage of popular discontent caused by Corso's excesses, the magnates tried to abolish the legislation that penalized them. They succeeded only in part, so that their attempt could be described as a failure. On that occasion, Vieri dei Cerchi kept his distance, but this was enough for public opinion to label him as a friend of the "people." Personal and family rivalry between the two thus began to take on a distinct political complexion, resulting in the birth of two separate organized formations.

At first, after the expulsion of Giano della Bella, the prudence shown by Vieri increased his power in the Guelf party and in the city. But soon the magnates loyal to Corso gained the upper hand, partly because many bankers in that party (in particular the Spini and Mozzi families, who held the monopoly over papal finance) enjoyed the support of the pope, as did Corso himself. In fact, the alliance between the Donati faction and Boniface VIII, which would come out into the open in the early years of the next century, had been firmly established from the first days of the new papacy—indeed, it dated back to the financial agreements reached by Cardinal Benedetto Caetani, as he then was, even before his ascent to the throne of Saint Peter. From the end of 1296 to spring 1299, Florence was gripped by an atmosphere of tension that saw successive armed clashes and killings on both sides. In December 1296, for example, the funeral vigil for a woman of the Frescobaldi house degenerated into a brawl and then a riot, ending in an attack on the Donati houses. In December 1298, several young men of the Cerchi party died in prison, where they had been sent following violence in the streets: the circumstances were not clear but popular opinion put the blame on the Donati. Corso, by then, had effective control of the city.[21]

In particular, it was Corso's men who held the office of *podestà*—during the second half of 1298 it was Cante dei Gabrielli (who would play a crucial role in Dante's conviction and in the bloody repression of "White" rebels), and during the first half of 1299 it was Monfiorito da Coderta of Treviso. Both men were notorious for their biased application of the law. The former, Cante dei Gabrielli, passed a death sentence in November 1298 on Neri Diodati, son of Gherardino, a well-known member of the Cerchi party who lived in Dante's *sestiere,* on accusations later shown to be baseless. Neri managed to escape, and it was Dante himself who, three years later, pleaded his innocence. The latter, Monfiorito da Coderta, was particularly hated for his greed and unscrupulous behavior. In March 1299 he convicted Giovanna degli Ubertini di Gaville, the mother-in-law of Corso, whom he had accused of theft and of appropriating documents. It is not suggested there had been any abuse of power (Giovanna seems, in fact, to have acted under the influence of the Cerchi), but the sentence nevertheless caused a public outrage. Monfiorito was put in prison. The episode led to Corso's sudden disgrace when, on being called before the court, he openly admitted corrupting the *podestà*.[22] He was convicted but refused to pay the fine, so that in March of that year he was banished from the city (though Boniface VIII promptly appointed him first *podestà* of Orvieto and then rector of Massa Trabaria). Such a strong reaction to a case of corrupt justice, at a time when abuse of power, bribery, and partial justice were commonplace, can only be explained by the hatred that Corso had succeeded in arousing among the "popular" classes, as well as among the magnates of the rival party.

It is worth describing an event that took place during these very months, once again involving Monfiorito, since it also includes the lawyer Baldo d'Aguglione, whom Dante would describe in the *Commedia* as having infected Florence with his "stink." During the investigation against him, Monfiorito confessed to a certain Pietro Manzuolo, who was interrogating him, that during a criminal trial he had arranged for evidence to be entered into the records of judge Nicola Acciaioli that both he and the judge knew to be false. The confession of the former *podestà* was embarrassing since Acciaioli was Manzuolo's son-in-law. The fact was kept quiet, however, so that a few months later, on August 15, 1299, Acciaioli was elected prior. But during his period as prior, he attempted to eliminate the compromising documents from the trial records and entrusted Baldo d'Aguglione to carry this out. The latter, himself several times prior, was one of the authors of Giano della Bella's *Ordinamenti di giustizia*, but had then played a key role in relaxing the effect of their more controversial provisions and in bringing about Giano's downfall, allying himself with the magnates. Baldo managed to obtain the trial record from Acciaioli, removed the compromising parts, and returned it to the chancery archive. The interference was discovered and both were convicted.[23] But the conviction didn't prevent Acciaioli from holding important offices as soon as the Donati were back in power, distinguishing himself in the judicial persecution of the Cerchi, nor did it prevent Baldo, also an ally of the Donati, from pursuing a brilliant political career (the following year he was already involved in the process of reviewing the case between Corso Donati and Giovanna degli Ubertini). Dante would recall this episode in the *Commedia* when he says that the steps up to San Miniato al Monte were built at a time when in Florence "the record book and the measuring stick were safe" (*Purg.* XII 105; "era sicuro il quaderno e la doga"): in other words, when you could still trust public record books and measures (a reference to a scandal involving the salt monopoly).[24]

Priorship, "cause and origin" of all ills

Once Corso was out of the way, the Cerchi faction remained the holders of power. But the fight wasn't over: indeed, in 1300 it worsened.

For Dante, this was a fateful year—if we look at the consequences it had upon his life, we might even say fatal. He had just reached thirty-five when, on June 15, he began his term of office as prior. Co-opted into the Florentine ruling elite, he had the prospect of a promising future. And yet in exile he would somberly declare: "the cause and origin of all my ills and all my hardships came from my unfortunate appointment as prior."[25]

The year 1300 was a turning point for the Cerchi. After an initial period of active political involvement during 1295–1296, Corso's bullying had kept them well in the background. Now, with Corso out of the way, they could once again take the initiative. It is interesting to note that Dante's political activity—which began between 1295 and 1297 and resumed, after a period of absence, in May 1300—coincides with that of the Cerchi party's first rise to power and their predominance in the city after the crisis with the Donati. The silence of almost three years from his last public involvement in 1297 could, of course, be largely due to the loss of documentary records, but one is still left with the impression that the correlation between his emergence in a public role and the periods when the Cerchi had greatest political influence is not entirely coincidental. This means that Dante, in reality, was not an intellectual *super partes* like Brunetto Latini, motivated purely by civic feeling, but was one of the Cerchi's men.

The Cerchi followed two distinct political paths. In external affairs, they followed the line adopted by the city in previous years, of financial and armed support in the "private" wars stirred up by Boniface VIII in central Italy. In the same way that the city in 1297–1298 had supported his relentless war (elevated to the status of a "crusade") against the Colonna family, which ended with the complete and ruthless destruction of Palestrina (it is during these hostile events that we find Guido da Montefeltro's fraudulent advice: "promise much, keep little"—*Inf.* XXVII 110; "lunga promessa con l'attender corto"), likewise the Cerchi would support the war of pillage against the Aldobrandeschi, the great feudal lords and Palatine counts of the Maremma. Such amenability arose from the need to protect the considerable interest connected to the papacy that the Florentine banks on both sides had to protect. But an essential role was also played by the fear already circulating in the early years of Boniface's papacy (which turned out to be well-founded) that he was seeking an alliance with the king of France, Philip IV (Philip the Fair), in order to capture Florence with the armed intervention of his brother Charles of Valois. In domestic matters, however, the Cerchi were firm in defending Florentine institutions against papal interference, and they didn't seem overly concerned about the undisguised support the pope was giving to their enemies. The contradiction between these two stances would be one of the main reasons for their downfall.

Around mid-March 1300, a delegation was sent to Rome on a secret mission to find out whether any Florentines in the papal curia were plotting against the Cerchi. It included Lapo Saltarelli and Lippo di Rinuccio Becca. It seems that the envoys carried out their task well and, on returning to Florence, they made accusations of treachery against four people linked to the Spini family bank, one of the companies most closely involved in the pope's financial affairs. The trial (promoted in particular by the lawyer Saltarelli) led to convictions with fines, and three of the four were sentenced to have their tongues cut out. The sentences were passed on April 18 without paying any heed to the serious threats being made by the pope who, with some justification, considered the trial to be directed against him. The pope threatened the priors and, in particular, accused Saltarelli of heresy. Saltarelli had been appointed prior for the two-month period from April 15 to June 14 (the period immediately preceding Dante's appointment). As a further sign of independence from the pope, the other prior, elected alongside Saltarelli, was Gherardino Diodati, the politician whom Cante dei Gabrielli had sought to attack a couple of years earlier by sentencing his son Neri to death. The sentence could not be carried out because the accused lived in Rome, but nevertheless it was a blatant challenge to the pope and to the Donati faction. Vieri, meanwhile, was summoned by Boniface VIII to Rome. To the pope, who had received him with much ceremony and had asked him to sign a peace treaty with Corso, Vieri denied that there was any war between himself and Donati: on that occasion—comments the chronicler Villani—Vieri was "imprudent, and too harsh and quick-tempered," so that the pope "was most indignant against him and against his party."[26]

Tensions in Florence ran extremely high. Toward the evening of May 1, during the dancing to celebrate May Day, in the square in front of the Vallombrosian convent church of Santa Trinita, a group of young men of the Donati house and their friends attacked a group of Cerchi, wounding an older member of the family by the name of Ricoverino.[27] About a week later, the Donati faction met at the same convent in front of which the fight had broken out. The abbot of Santa Trinita was Ruggero dei Buondelmonti, one of the most fanatical supporters of the Donati. Their plan was an armed plot to bring an end to Cerchi rule. It envisaged the use of armed forces from outside, led by Guido di Battifolle, one of the Casentine branches of the great family of Guidi counts, who would enter the city and provide support for the internal insurgents. Among the main conspirators was Simone dei Bardi, who we already know as the husband of Bice Portinari. But the plot was discovered: many of the conspirators were immediately put on trial and convicted. Simone dei Bardi and Guido di Battifolle were fined; Corso Donati, who was with the pope in Rome and considered to be the true instigator, was sentenced to death. It was impossible to proceed against him, but his houses in San Pier Maggiore were razed to the ground and his lands confiscated.

The response from Boniface VIII was immediate: on May 23 he appointed Matteo d'Acquasparta, minister-general of the Franciscan order, as legate for Tuscany and Romagna and sent him straight to Florence on a peace mission. But when he arrived in Florence in early June, everyone knew what his true purpose was. The legate revealed his position immediately, proposing that the forthcoming appointment of new priors (on June 13) should be decided not through election, which would have assured an ample majority for the Cerchi, but by drawing lots, which would have had an unpredictable result. It was an extremely difficult moment for the Cerchi, who nevertheless found the courage to object, above all thanks to Lapo Saltarelli, both prior and the Cerchi's real political guide during those months. To thwart the papal threat it was necessary to hold complete control over the College of Priors, ensuring that those elected were loyal and resolute. Dante's name was one of those that came out of the vote. It is doubtful, however, that those chosen were of proven loyalty, since two of them would defect to the rival party. As for Dante, his appointment at that critical moment shows that the Cerchi regarded him as one of their most trusty followers. About a month earlier, on May 7, he had been sent as ambassador to San Gimignano with the task of persuading the city to take part in a conference of the *Taglia* (the alliance) of Tuscan Guelfs concerning the wars started by Boniface VIII.[28] It was an administrative appointment on behalf of the city government. The role of prior was also administrative, but rarely had the circumstances surrounding the appointment been so strongly political as on this occasion.[29] Had there been instance of "barratry," as it was called in the language of the time? Were deals made in exchange for favors in the process? It is quite clear that Saltarelli and his men had played some part in Dante's election. But the conviction against Dante, which accused him of barratry during the elections of priors or of *gonfalonieri,* is blatant hypocrisy. The election of city councilors at that time was never going to be a free, democratic game. A great Dante scholar has spoken the final word on this matter: "It is certain that all was prearranged to ensure the winners were those who were needed."[30]

The new priors immediately found out the importance of decisiveness. On the very day they took office, a notary from the Camera del Comune, the office in the Palazzo del Podestà that managed public finances and therefore had the task of collecting fines, handed them the written sentence of April against the defendants linked to the Spini family that had so infuriated the pope.[31] It had to be enforced, at least so far as the financial part. Whatever they did, the situation was very tricky. And there was still violence in the streets. Only a week after the beginning of their mandate, on June 23, the eve of the solemn feast of Saint John, the consuls of the city guilds were attacked, first verbally and then physically, by a group of magnates as they paraded toward the baptistery in the traditional procession in which the corporations carried offerings to the church of the saint. The magnates shouted out: "we are the ones who brought victory at Campaldino; and you have stripped us of the offices and honors of our city."[32] There was some truth in it. It was they, the backbone of the Florentine army, who were the main authors of the victory over the people of Arezzo and the Ghibellines, those same magnates who just a few years earlier had been ousted from public office. This spectacular protest had almost certainly been organized by the Donati, but it is also possible that this stand against the "popular" government was also supported by magnates from the other party. The priors, in the face of such an unprecedented gesture, having called a special assembly of "wise men" (among whom was Dino Compagni), decided to strike at both factions. They ordered eight members of the Donati faction and "their consorts," family and closest followers, to be interned at Castel della Pieve (today's Città della Pieve) in Umbria, and seven members of the Cerchi faction and "their consorts" to be interned at Sarzana, on the outskirts of the Lunigiana region. If this measure was intended to relieve tension, it cannot be said to have achieved its aim. The Donati resisted: with the help of the cardinal legate, they asked Lucca to intervene on their behalf, and only the decisive response of the priors, who warned Lucca against taking action (and strengthened the borders for good measure), finally persuaded them to give in. A few months later, due to a serious misjudgment by the next College of Priors, that order would result in even greater tension.

Among those interned from the Cerchi party was Guido Cavalcanti. The story of the friendship between Dante and Guido ended in tragedy. At Sarzana, a marshland area, Guido would develop malaria, and he most probably died there—if not there, he died shortly after his return to Florence. It is probable, therefore, that the two never saw each other again. Events turned out in such a way that the metaphor of the pupil who kills his master became reality.

The first effect of the serious events at the feast of Saint John was a softening in the attitude of the city rulers toward Matteo da Acquasparta.

For some time he had been claiming full powers, and so, toward the end of June, some of his requests were finally granted, though with many restrictions. But a strange event took place in July. One day "some [unnamed] person of not much wit" shot a crossbow in the direction of a window of the bishop's palace where the legate was staying. The arrow lodged itself in the shutter. The frightened cardinal hurried off across the Arno to take up residence in the palace of the Mozzi family, who were banking associates of the Spini. The gesture by the anonymous attacker had all the air of a provocation, though it forced the priors to make amends with a gift of 2,000 florins to the cardinal. But the firm line toward the pope and the legate remained unchanged. Boniface VIII urged Acquasparta to be tougher and more zealous, and the only response of the priors (and this was one of the last decisions during Dante's period as prior) was to send ambassadors to Bologna to negotiate a diplomatic and military alliance that seemed almost like a sneer, seeing that Acquasparta was legate for Romagna as well as Tuscany. The alliance would be formally signed on August 25, ten days after Dante's term of office had come to an end. One biographer wrote that "on leaving the palace," Dante must have had "the impression of having won, indeed triumphed."[33] If this were so, just a few days would have been enough to undeceive him. Very soon, in fact, the political situation would further deteriorate, but we have not a single document to shed any light on what Dante did over the next few months. After a long silence, he reappears on the political scene in April 1301.

The last medieval pope

Readers of the *Commedia* will have a very poor opinion of Boniface VIII. Dante is savage with his enemies, and since he considers Boniface to be his worst enemy, his attack on him is unremitting.

Cardinal Benedetto Caetani was elected pope in Naples on December 24, 1294, taking the name Boniface VIII, and was crowned in Rome a month later, on January 23. His predecessor had been Celestine V, the hermit Pietro da Morrone, a saintly man who had been supported by the Franciscan "spirituals" and by the Church's reformist movement. But he was unskilled in ecclesiastical and international affairs and had been heavily manipulated by the king of Naples, Charles II of Anjou. He had stepped down after only a few months as pontiff (July 5–December 13, 1294). Cardinal Caetani, who was consulted as an expert on canon law, had judged his resignation to be admissible and valid: a view that would weigh heavily on him throughout his papacy. His many enemies, particularly the Franciscan "spirituals," the Colonna family, and the king of France, would claim that he had convinced Celestine to resign so that he himself could succeed him, and that his election must therefore be considered invalid. The question of legitimacy would pursue him to the grave (and beyond). It is true that Boniface, after being elected pope, had Celestine arrested and kept in confinement (it was Charles Martel, whom Dante had met a few months earlier in Florence, that had taken him prisoner in February 1295), but he was persuaded to do so not just out of fear that Celestine might change his mind but also in case the presence of two popes might create confusion among the faithful.

Boniface VIII was a controversial figure. His deep conviction that the church and the papacy had the task of giving universal guidance to humanity lived side-by-side with more worldly ambitions for territorial expansion, both for the papacy and for his own family. His relentless conflict with the Colonna family and war against the Aldobrandeschi were motivated above all by personal interests. Perhaps his interference in Florentine domestic affairs was part of a design to bring Tuscany under the control of the Church.[34] His papacy was characterized, more than anything else, by a theocratic notion, zealously proclaimed and implemented, according to which the pope was above kings and kingdoms and therefore had to have preeminence and control over the whole earth and over every soul. From this point of view Boniface can be regarded as the last great medieval pope, following the line of popes who had fought against the German emperors to claim the supremacy of the spiritual over the temporal realm. But the temporal power to be subjugated was no longer that of the emperor but of the new monarchies.

Conflict first broke out with the king of France. Philip the Fair, with whom Boniface had an ambiguous relationship, ended up reacting harshly to the pope's theocractic aspirations, thus launching a violent and relentless attack, attempting to prove the illegitimacy of the pope's election and destroy his name with allegations of heresy, sodomy, and even of satanic practices (the attack would continue even after his death, when Philip the Fair and Clement V began an interminable posthumous trial against him that finally ended in 1311 without arriving at a decision). The conflict reached its climax with an attack on the papal palace at Anagni (on September 7, 1303) and the temporary capture of the pope by the French envoy, Guillaume de Nogaret, and Sciarra Colonna, who thus avenged the persecution of his family. The story that the pope was slapped by Colonna is probably a legend. But Boniface never recovered from the insult and died barely a month later (on October 11). While his predecessors had won their dispute with the Hohenstaufen emperors, Boniface VIII lost his with the French monarchy. It was a defeat that had far-reaching consequences for the history of the Church and for Europe. After the brief reign of Niccolò di Boccasio from Treviso (Benedict XI, October 1303–April 1304), the election of Bertrand de Got (Clement V) marked the beginning of a long series of French popes heavily influenced by the king of France, to such an extent that the papal residence would eventually be moved to Avignon, where it would remain until 1377.

Dante, as I mentioned, considered Boniface VIII to be his worst enemy. So greatly did he hate him that he was compelled to forecast Hell for him when (in the fiction of the *Commedia*) he was still alive: it is Pope Nicholas III (the Orsini pope with whom Cardinal Caetani had had close links), thrust head-first in one of the holes into which the simoniacs had been put, who mistakes the voice of the pilgrim Dante for that of the one who ought to have taken his place: "is that you already standing there, / is that you already standing there, Boniface?" [*Inf.* XIX 52–53; "sè tu già costì ritto, / sè tu già costì ritto, Bonifazio?"] Dante does not forgive the pope for having behaved underhandedly, hypocritically ("the prince of the new Pharisees"—*Inf.* XXVII 85; "lo principe d'i novi Farisei"), in favor of the Donati party which, Ciacco foretells, will win the day thanks to the support of "one who now keeps close to the shore" (*Inf.* VI 69; "di tal che testé piaggia"), of one who now, in 1300, pretends to be impartial. At times he seems to interpret events in Florence as a personal conflict between himself and the pope, so that he goes as far as stating, through the mouth of Cacciaguida, that his banishment from the city was already being planned in 1300, and would soon be carried out: "This is willed and this is already sought, / and soon it will be done by he who is planning it [Boniface] / in the place where each day Christ is sold" (*Para.* XVII 49–51; "Questo si vuole e questo già si cerca, / e tosto verrà fatto a chi ciò pensa [Bonifacio] / là dove Cristo tutto dì si merca"). Boniface, who has no qualms about declaring a crusade in the heart of the Church ("in the Lateran" [*Inf.* XXVII 86; "presso a Laterano"]), had transformed the tomb of Peter into a "cesspool / of blood and stench" (*Para.* XXVII 25–26; "cloaca / del sangue e de la puzza"). What Dante gets Saint Peter to pronounce is perhaps the most violent invective ever launched against a pope—one unworthy of Peter's throne: "he who on earth usurps my place, / my place, my place which is vacant / in the sight of the Son of God" (*Para.* XXVII 22–24; "Quelli ch'usurpa in terra il luogo mio, / il luogo mio, il luogo mio che vaca / ne la presenza del Figliuol di Dio"). Though he seems to give credence to the accusations of having duped Celestine with his legal counsel: "you did not fear fraudulently to / take the fair lady [the Church] and then strip her apart" (*Inf.* XIX 56–57; "non temesti tòrre a 'nganno / la bella donna, e poi di farne strazio"), Dante never questions Boniface's lawful right to be pope. The insult at Anagni is a reenactment of the Passion of Christ in the person of his vicar: "I see in Alagna the fleur-de-lis, / and in his vicar Christ taken captive. / I see him mocked again; / I see the vinegar and gall renewed, / and him being killed between living thieves" (*Purg.* XX 86–90; "veggio in Alagna intrar lo fiordaliso, / e nel vicario suo Cristo esser catto. / Veggiolo un'altra volta esser deriso; / veggio rinovellar l'aceto e 'l fiele, / e tra vivi ladroni esser anciso"). Personal rancor, political hatred and moral disdain are not enough for a Christian of such solid faith as Dante to deviate from the most rigorous orthodoxy. In this he is not alone: Iacopone da Todi—the most famous thirteenth-century writer of lauds and, after Dante, the poet most frequently read over the next two centuries—whose support for the Colonna family led to his imprisonment during the capture of Palestrina (in summer 1299) where he was held in terrible conditions until the death of Boniface, attacks him in his verses with rare virulence ("a new Lucifer on the papal throne"), yet without ever questioning his legitimacy as a successor of Saint Peter.[35] And Pietro di Giovanni Olivi, one of the great champions of the "spiritual" movement, also took a position on several occasions in favor of the validity of Celestine's resignation, in opposition to his Franciscan brothers.

1300, the Jubilee year

The proclamation of the Church's first Jubilee was the act for which Boniface VIII is most remembered.

With the approach of the centenary year—a year of much symbolic importance—pilgrims began to gather in ever greater numbers around the tomb of the first pope in the belief that their visit in that year would allow them to earn a Jubilee (an indulgence) that was particularly special. It is unclear what was the origin or basis of this belief (though it was certainly encouraged by the clergy at Saint Peter's); but the influx of penitents grew more and more each day, particularly as Christmas approached. Boniface VIII, who had studied law, ordered the archives to be searched for any document that might give support to the popular belief. Finding nothing, he decided all the same to take advantage of this religious upsurge and so, on February 22, 1300, he issued a bull in which he decreed that every hundred years the Church would grant a plenary indulgence for all the sins of those who, over a period of thirty days (if resident in Rome), or fifteen (if living outside), made daily visits in pilgrimage to the basilicas of Saint Peter and Saint Paul, and repented and confessed their sins. The bull, acknowledging that the Jubilee year had already been launched by believers, decreed that the indulgence could be earned from the previous Christmas (December 25, 1299) and up to Christmas Eve of that year. As with many of his decisions, alongside the strictly religious motives were also considerations of a political nature: the Jubilee, in fact, was a way of reaffirming Rome's central role and of solemnly reasserting the fullness of the pope's powers. The Vicar of Christ stood over and above nations and human institutions and, at the same time, exercised full spiritual jurisdiction over the soul, with the power even to affect its destiny after the human body had died.

A Jubilee was nothing new; many had already been granted in the past. What was new was the extent of the indulgence. Until then, the remission of temporal punishments—namely those punishments that were to be expiated either through works in this life or through the sufferings of Purgatory once the absolution obtained through the sacrament of confession had cancelled out eternal punishment—had only been granted for limited periods of time, which were brief (the largest indulgence granted before that year had cancelled out little more than three years of punishment). The indulgence for the centenary year, however, remitted all punishment. Rulers and men of government recognized above all the political aspect of the pope's decision and therefore kept away, but the mass of believers responded in an extraordinary and unexpected way. In a profoundly religious society, the announcement not only that all sins would be pardoned but that all punishment for them would be cancelled had an enormous effect. Thousands of people traveled to Rome from every part of Europe. The number of penitents who gathered there that year became etched on the collective memory: such an enormous crowd had never ever been seen. Eye witnesses and chroniclers told how the numbers of men and women (the vast presence of women was also something new) who thronged the streets of Rome were so great that, in spite of measures to ease the flow (such as opening a special gateway in the walls), many ended up being trampled under-foot. Though most had walked, there was insufficient forage to feed the large numbers of horses brought to the city. The chronicles also give figures: over the course of the year, the population of Rome steadily in-creased to two hundred thousand, not counting "those who were coming and going on foot"; each day thirty thousand pilgrims would arrive and the same number would leave; on Christmas Eve of 1300 there were said to have been more than two million men and women.[36] These figures are extravagant and farfetched, but they give a clear idea of the astonishment caused at the sight of these human masses, at a time when the numbers we are now accustomed to were completely unimaginable.

Dante was also among those thousands of pilgrims. The description of the bridge at Castel Sant'Angelo with barriers to control the great flow of pilgrims crossing it toward Saint Peter's has the flavor of an eyewit-ness account:

> like the Romans for the great throng
> in the year of the Jubilee, on the bridge
> ensure the people pass more easily,
>   who on one side all have their faces
> to the castle, and walk to St Peter's;
> and on the other move toward the mount.
>
>   come i Roman per l'essercito molto,
> l'anno del giubileo, su per lo ponte
> hanno a passar la gente modo colto,

che da l'un lato tutti hanno la fronte
verso 'l castello e vanno a Santo Pietro,
da l'altra sponda vanno verso 'l monte.

—*Inf.* XVIII 28–33

His journey to Rome, more than a mere possibility, seems a certainty. But we don't know what time of the year he went. According to the (few) records we have, nothing would have prevented Dante from taking a month off (fifteen days travel and fifteen to visit the basilicas) during the periods from March to April or September to Christmas to carry out that penitential journey. On March 14 he was in Florence, where he received a loan from his brother Francesco: it's an interesting idea that this money might have been for the pilgrimage, and perhaps he might even have reached Rome on the very day, March 25, when his journey into the next world begins in the *Commedia*.[37]

"In the middle of the journey of our life"

The journey, in a dream, as told in the poem, begins on March 25—traditionally the day of both Christ's incarnation and his death, and the day on which the Florentines began their new year—and it ends a week later, on March 31. Many reasons could have prompted Dante to set his extraordinary journey during the height of the Jubilee year. But of crucial importance must have been his awareness that 1300 was also the thirty-fifth year of his life, which he described as the "middle of the journey." The coincidence could, in fact, have a very particular significance for someone who had felt for some time he was endowed with particular qualities and was destined to leave his mark. And that thirty-fifth year in which he, the first member of his family, had been elected prior marked a turning-point in his life, the beginning of a new phase.

Dante could obviously have made these reflections at some distance of time after 1300. And in fact, while early biographers and commentators suggested that the *Commedia* was begun that year or close after, and in any event before his exile, modern scholars are almost unanimous in considering that it was composed much later: for some in 1304, for the

majority between 1306 and 1307.[38] The early commentators take the
author's claims literally, and their testimony is therefore not of great
value; nevertheless the suggestion that the idea for setting it during the
Jubilee—and therefore that a poem was born or at least was beginning
to form as an idea in Dante's mind shortly after the journey to Rome—
would correspond very well with his tendency to write in the heat of
the moment, immediately after events: after his pilgrimage, but before
his banishment into exile, since that momentous year would later appear under quite a different light.

Let us be clear: the *Commedia* that we read is the one that Dante began
writing almost certainly from 1306–1307 until just before his death. There
is no trace whatsoever of an earlier text. Despite this, the notion that he
had sketched out at least an outline of the poem or a series of preparatory drawings or cartoons, as painters might say, in a period shortly after
his journey to Rome seems reasonable in the light of what we know
about his personality and his ideological and political development. All
the more so when this can also be supported by textual considerations,
namely the recognizable differences between the early cantos and the
remainder of the poem. This could have been a sort of preparatory work,
forcibly interrupted by political events which Dante would then have
made use of when he settled down, several years later, to start the great
work without further interruption. The idea of an early stage would considerably mitigate the sensation of a mature idea transmitted almost
instantly by a *Commedia* that suddenly emerged on Dante's intellectual
and creative horizon. Against this it could be said that Dante would perhaps have had other concerns during years of such disorder as those of
1300–1301, but this would ignore, on the one hand, the fact that Dante
invariably worked on the *Commedia* in situations of similar upheaval and,
on the other, that during those two years political activity wasn't always
so intense, either for Dante or for the Florentines.[39]

Daily life, the administration of the city and business in general were
not disrupted to the extent we might imagine when we look at political
events. For example, on April 28, 1301, Dante was appointed as "over-
seer" of works requested by a group of citizens to straighten a tortuous
road between Borgo della Piagentina and the Affrico torrent.[40] Dante's
task was to supervise their performance on behalf of the priors: he
was appointed because he himself was one of the interested parties,

owning property in the parish of Sant'Ambrogio near Piagentina. The date is interesting: April 1301. We are close to the height of the decisive political crisis, and yet life in Florence, and for Dante himself, seems to be carrying on as usual. If he could find time for works of this kind, why couldn't he have found time for poetry?

I repeat: the *Commedia* that we read, including its first cantos, was written around 1306–1307; what Dante could have written previously must have been almost entirely reworked. Almost entirely, because in the first cantos of the final *Commedia* one glimpses between the lines something of its earlier form and, indeed, a few surviving textual fragments. These fragments suggest that the idea of the poem and the early stages of its writing can be no later than *Convivio* and *De vulgari eloquentia,* which were composed between 1304 and 1306. They can be no later because his vision of the political and institutional structure of Christianity that is still apparent in the poem's prologue jars with the one elaborated by Dante in his two treatises.

The political scheme of *Convivio,* which is the same as that of *De vulgari,* can be summarized as follows: "the Italian nobility, leaving aside its disunity, despite the differences between its individual members, must become what it potentially already is, and what in effect it used to be—namely, the class that, under the aegis of the Empire, guarantees the existence of a *civilitas* that is human, cohesive and peaceable, against the centrifugal and disruptive forces of new powers that are above all economic and as a result political."[41] This presupposes that Dante had developed, or was developing, an idea of the centrality of the imperial establishment. And yet, in 1306–1307, having laid aside *Convivio* for the *Commedia,* he would forget what he had just declared (and what he would declare even more forcefully a little later): to write a poem that begins (Canto II) with declarations of more plainly Guelf sentiment. The Roman Empire would not be created, as we would expect from the author of *Convivio,* as a supreme guarantor of peace and human happiness on earth, but as a function of the Church and the papacy:

> [Aeneas] was elected in the Empyrean heaven
> to be father of mother Rome and her empire:
>   both Rome and empire were in truth

established to be the holy place
where the successor of great Peter sits.

    And for this journey that you now describe
he learned those things that would bring
victory for him and for the papal mantle.

e' fu de l'alma Roma e di suo impero
ne l'empireo ciel per padre eletto:
    la quale e 'l quale, a voler dir lo vero,
fu stabilita per lo loco santo
u' siede il successor del maggior Piero.
    Per quest'andata onde li dai tu vanto,
intese cose che furon cagione
di sua vittoria e del papale ammanto

—*Inf.* II 20–27

Rome and the Empire established by Divine Providence "to be the holy place / where the successor of great Peter sits": it has been said that this is "a formula that couldn't be more Guelf."[42] Such an affirmation, if it had been written in or around 1307, would have been a sudden and unjustified retreat from what Dante had thought only a year or two before (and would continue to think a year or two later). There would be no contradiction, on the other hand, if those lines had been written earlier still and had been left in the final version of the *Commedia* as a remnant of a view he no longer held.

Boccaccio's "little notebook"

The suggestion that the *Commedia*—or rather, a verse poem that would later become the *Commedia*—was started before *Convivio* and *De vulgari eloquentia* doesn't in itself mean that it was started in Florence before his exile. This possibility is made more plausible, however, from an account by Boccaccio.

    Twice, in a space of a several years, first in his biography of Dante and then in *Esposizioni sopra la Comedia,* he refers to an episode that happened "five or more years" after Dante's banishment: this indication of time, though vague—showing that his sources didn't agree or were uncertain—points to around 1306–1307. The second fuller and more detailed version describes how Gemma Donati, fearing that their house would be sacked after her husband's conviction, took away "several coffers with certain things of more value and with Dante's writings" and had them hidden in a safe place. After "five years or more" Gemma tried to obtain the income she was owed on confiscated property that was part of her dowry, but to pursue the case she had to produce certain documents that were kept in those coffers. So she appointed a friend or relative, in the company of a lawyer, to carry out the search. The coffers contained, among other things "several sonnets and canzoni" in vernacular and a "little notebook" containing the first seven cantos of *Inferno*.[43] The little notebook was shown to Dino Frescobaldi, a *stil novo* poet ("a most famous reciter in rhyme") and scion of a prominent family of "Black" bankers. Dino, having admired what he had read, first made copies and distributed them to friends, then decided to let Dante have it back so that he could continue the composition that had been interrupted. Discovering that Dante was staying in the Lunigiana with Marchese Moroello Malaspina, he sent it to the marchese, who, also filled with admiration, urged Dante to resume writing the poem.

Scholars, with few exceptions, are skeptical about the reliability of this story. It certainly shouldn't be taken literally, but it would be too hasty to dismiss it as a "legend." In the first place, it should be considered carefully because Boccaccio is, as always, scrupulous about quoting his sources. Two different people (both claiming credit for the rediscovery) told him the story at different times, "but point for point, with hardly anything altered": he heard it the first time from the lawyer Dino Perini, the second time from Dante's nephew, Andrea Poggi. He limited himself to reporting, without expressing a view ("I don't know which I ought to prefer"); indeed, he expresses some doubt about the truth of what he had heard, and this is the best proof that it is not an invention, but that news had been handed down in Florence about the recovery of the early cantos of the poem. Secondly, the historical references seem plausible: five years after his banishment, Dante was indeed staying in the Lunigiana with Moroello; Dino Frescobaldi, as a member of the oligarchy in power, would certainly have had an opportunity to contact Malaspina, who at that time was the *capitano* of the Black Guelf army in Florence.[44]

More doubtful, however, is the news that the first seven cantos of *Inferno* had been found and that Dante then resumed writing from the eighth. The cloak of mystery around how and when the poem was composed does not allow any certainty. No one can establish for sure whether—if this is the case—work resumed from precisely the point at which it had been interrupted, or at what point it had been interrupted, or whether the written parts were only a draft or already complete, or whether and to what extent they had been revised and redone.[45] What cannot be ignored, however, is that the outside evidence fits the information that can be gleaned from the text.

It is enough, too, to examine the critical bibliography to notice how widely it is acknowledged that the first cantos of *Inferno,* more or less up to the city of Dis, have a series of characteristics in terms of form, structure, and content that distinguish them from what comes after. The differences are so considerable that one intelligent reader would write that "there are two entrances to Hell, almost two different beginnings to the poem. First we enter through the unhinged gate, then through the gates of the city of Dis."[46] The differences relate more or less to all aspects of the text: from the way it is told, structured at first on a medieval vision, then abandoned in favor of a more complex poetic development, to the portrayal, characterized by an infernal geography that is still unclear and, above all, by the author's uncertainty in finding narrative solutions for the transition from one canto to the next; from the behavior of Dante the character, who wavers between excessive piety and excessively vindictive fury, to the unclearly defined character of Virgil and the demons themselves; from the moral order of punishments and sins, which Dante must then in part correct, to a use of the terza rima which is a long way from the extraordinary versatility he will later demonstrate in his use of this meter, and so forth.[47] All of this could be put down to a Dante who was still settling in to his task, a Dante who had not yet found his own style, who had not yet acquired full command over the methods of representation and the overall project itself. And yet it is true that the obvious leap in quality and structural layout, at least from the Farinata canto onward, seems to suggest the existence of a gap in time, and that the reworking of the first cantos, however thorough it might have been, did not correct the uncertainties in that early stage of writing.

A Florentine poem

The final version of the early draft retained, above all, the point of view of the author, of a Florentine who was writing for his fellow citizens.

The whole *Inferno* is Florentine, but the cantos up to Canto X, involving Farinata, are more strongly so: in this part of the poem, the characters are indeed (almost) entirely from Florence. The fact they are Florentine is, so to speak, highlighted by the fact that they are the only recently damned souls. In effect, the opening part of *Inferno* is not exactly depopulated, but it ends up giving this impression because it is inhabited above all by souls that come from the biblical and classical world, and from fiction: as though Dante felt a reticence toward his contemporaries.

The neutral souls are recognizable—"After I had recognized several of them" (*Inf.* III 58; "Poscia ch'io v'ebbi alcun riconosciuto")—but are not worthy of being identified, with the partial exception of "he / who in cowardice made the great refusal" (*Inf.* III 59–60; "di colui / che fece per viltade il gran rifiuto"), in other words, Celestine V.[48] They are even less worthy of being named; the avaricious and the prodigal of the fourth circle are not even recognizable: "the ignoble life that befouled them makes them dark now to all recognition" (*Inf.* VII 53–54; "la sconoscente vita che i fé sozzi, / ad ogne conoscenza or li fa bruni"), so that in one canto where there would have been plenty of material ("these were clerics, who have no covering / of hair on their heads, and popes and cardinals, / in whom avarice excelled" [*Inf.* VII 46–48; "Questi fuor cherci, che non han coperchio / piloso al capo, e papi e cardinali, / in cui usa avarizia il suo soperchio"]), not a single name appears. Most reticent of all is his political discussion. References to his great rivals are so cryptic ("one who now keeps close to the shore" [*Inf.* VI 69; "che testé piaggia"]) that no certain identification can be made (just like "he / who in cowardice made the great refusal"); the possible saviors are hidden behind the allegory of the Greyhound. In the early cantos, it would seem that Dante was being most cautious in describing the all-Florentine political conflict of that moment.

The canto describing Ciacco confirms the feeling of a Dante who is very circumspect in talking about contemporary Florence. It is the first time that the "divided city" appears on the scene, the first time that Florence's political events are told explicitly, the first time that readers can see "avarice," the "beast" which "envy" (*Inf.* I 110–111; "fin che l'avrà rimessa ne lo 'nferno, / là onde 'nvidia prima dipartilla") had released from Hell and let circulate around the world, at work upon the city's social fabric. And yet this anticipation is satisfied only in part by the words of a Florentine who, though referred to by name, nevertheless remains substantially anonymous. But Dante's earliest intentions were perhaps to give Ciacco—a figure who is given very few political characteristics—a discourse not centered on factional conflict but directed toward a purpose that was more civic (in the broadest sense): a moral judgment on the decline of the aristocracy (the magnates) in Florence.

Who was Ciacco? various suggestions have been made: the most convincing is that he was a "courtier," in other words a "client" of some great prosperous family.[49] He is there, then, thanks to his sin of gluttony, to embody the way of life of the rich Florentines, or those who have become rich and hold sumptuous court—in other words, the world of *luxus* and extravagance. The sin of greed exposes a more serious social sin. The way of life symbolized by sumptuous courts is a reference to that of the nobility, referring therefore to *cortesia* in the sense of munificence, generosity, liberality, but betraying its true spirit: if to "give" and "bestow" are central to the courtly ideal, then *cortesia* requires moderation to prevent it from becoming transformed into unreasonable and culpable prodigality. Dante would protest that "new people and quick gains / have generated pride and excess" (*Inf.* XVI 73–74; "la gente nuova e i sùbiti guadagni / orgoglio e dismisura han generata"). And "pride," it should be remembered, is the description that would be given to the behavior of Filippo Argenti.

Dante's request for news about the fate of various leading figures of the magnate class who had lived in Florence around the middle of the century (Farinata, Tegghiaio Aldobrandi, Iacopo Rusticucci, Arrigo, Mosca dei Lamberti) is seen in a clearer light if we consider it as part of a general analysis of the decline of the aristocratic class. The characters are not described as political figures (Dante is, nevertheless, heavily critical of the conduct of some), but as citizens "who were so worthy" and "so set on doing good." They were illustrious citizens through personal merit, and also through family name: they were all from great families of the magnate aristocracy, knights and lords. They therefore also represented the past of those same families who now flaunted their wealth and kept clients like Ciacco: they are a clear point of reference for measuring how much the city's nobility had deteriorated.[50]

Filippo Argenti was also a member of a great magnate clan, the Adimari, one of Florence's leading Guelf families. Dante would show a dislike for the Adimari that develops into withering contempt but here, in Canto VIII, he doesn't seem to want to attack them through the figure of one of their own family. Indeed, Tegghiaio Aldobrandi belonged to the same family: he is recalled in Canto VI among those "so set on doing good" and who in Canto XVI would be found in the company of people whose "works . . . and honored names," says Dante, "I [always] repeated and heard with affection" (*Inf.* XVI 59–60: "e sempre mai / l'ovra di voi e li onorati nomi / con affezion ritrassi e ascoltai").[51] While Tegghiaio degli Adimari was, as Villani writes, "a wise knight and brave in arms and of great authority," his descendant Argenti, also a knight, was, according to Dante, "in the world a proud person" (*Inf.* VIII 46; "fu al mondo persona orgogliosa") quick-tempered (*Inf.* VIII 62; "spirito bizzarro"), and violent. Boccaccio adds that Filippo was so rich that "he sometimes had the horse he rode on shod with silver [*argento*] and from this came his nickname": his pride was therefore also displayed in an empty ostentation of wealth.[52] The comparison between two people of the same clan, and both knighted, was therefore inevitable. Argenti's pride is here to show us to what extent the customs of the Florentine ruling class—indeed the highest of that class—had declined from the times when their actions and social relationships had once been inspired by valor and courtesy until that present time, when Florence was dominated and ruined by "pride, envy, and avarice" (*Inf.* VI 74; "superbia, invidia e avarizia").

Florence's centrality would seem to be undermined by the fact that the first modern (or rather, contemporary) sinners to appear in the poem are from Romagna. We know that the killing of Francesca da Polenta and Paolo Malatesta by Gianciotto had passed unobserved by the society of that period. No local chronicle records it; no document bears any trace of it; the ancient commentators know no more about it than what Dante recounts. For contemporaries, therefore, it was not a particularly remarkable episode: in any event, the cases of husbands, especially those of rank, wiping away tainted honor with blood were hardly rare. Yet if there was a place, other than where it had happened, in which news of such a crime could have caused a certain stir, it was Florence itself. Here the protagonists in this story of love and death were well known: we know that Francesca's lover had been the city's *capitano* between 1282 and 1283 and that between July and November 1290 (only a few years after the murder of 1285) Francesca's father had held the office of *podestà*.

The countless interpretations of Canto V dwell, rightly, on the themes of love and the literature of love, but they underestimate its other important aspects, such as adultery, incest (the lovers are brother and sister-in-law) and murder. The sin of lust is individual, but has adverse effects on society. The satisfaction of sexual impulses (the subjugation of reason to "fancy") can lead to adultery, incest, murder. It is not therefore a simple sin of immoderation in relation to desire, but a sin that undermines social order, family harmony, and the rules of coexistence. In *De amore* Andrea Cappellano had written that many social ills and even crimes arose from lust: "It often leads to murder and adultery . . . incestuous relationships are also caused by it: in fact no one is so well versed in the word of God that, if aroused by the sting of love through the urge of the spirit of evil, they can keep a hold on the lustful desire toward women who are of the same or kindred blood or consecrated to God."[53] Incest between brother and sister-in-law was one of the crimes induced by licentious sexual behavior.

The fact that two members of the nobility had indulged in such behavior, provoking the violent reaction of the wronged husband, was an indication of the way in which the life of the feudal nobility had degenerated, much like that of the city nobility.

The viewpoint from which, in the early cantos of *Inferno,* Dante studies the decline of traditional values among aristocrats, both urban and feudal, is still the same as that from which Dante had earlier composed the canzone on *gentilezza* (*Le dolci rime d'amor ch'i' solia*—*The sweet rhymes of love I must forsake*) and *leggiadria* (*Poscia ch'Amor del tutto m'ha lasciato*—*Since love has wholly abandoned me*). Gluttony (Ciacco), lust (Francesca), anger, pride, and ostentation of wealth (Argenti): the scenes in Hell exemplify the vices typical of nobles who think they are behaving as *leggiadri* and yet are ignorant of the basics of true charm. In his canzoni, Dante sought to give instruction on nobility to those in power in Florence, whether noblemen or newly rich; in the cantos of *Inferno,* the prevailing voice is one of criticism, censure, but the ideological framework is the same. Here the picture was extended to the ancient nobility, whom the knights of Florence looked upon as a model. The story of Francesca and Paolo marks the decline of their own particular class; the figure of Filippo Argenti marks that of the ancient and honorable families of city magnates; the courtier Ciacco stigmatizes the way of life of the Florentine parvenus, of the new rich families that have no past. They are people who imitate the life of noble people in a debased fashion, who seek self-ennoblement through the social use of wealth, but confuse liberality with ostentation. Between the *canzoni morali* and the early cantos of *Inferno* there is an ideological continuity; these cantos are written from the point of view of a Florentine addressing his fellow citizens.

In the *Vita Nova,* Dante managed to bring together into one single project the various lines along which his cultural interests had been moving until then. But immediately after the publication of that book, the path had divided: what seemed to have been a great vocation for Latin poetry and for theological and visionary themes was almost immediately overtaken by more worldly concerns of a civic nature. Someone like Dante, with a systematic mind almost obsessed by unity and coherence, must have found it difficult to deal with such a split situation. The Jubilee, with its message of individual and universal renewal, offered powerful encouragement to conceive a work that would bring together the two contrasting inspirations. That work, which would become the *Commedia,* and of which—I repeat—we can glimpse only a faint outline, had to combine the story of Beatrice (and find its crowning glory in a text more worthy than the *Vita Nova*) with the moral and civic commitment that had already been expressed in the *canzoni morali.* The vision of the next world conferred a prophetic aura on the autobiographical figure that was its protagonist. The restless and confused political situation in Florence, the social tensions that pervaded it, the evil effects of economic development that cancelled out the city's traditional values—these were the ground on which the character could exercise his critical instructive role. Dante embarked on a journey among the dead to save the living, to save the people of Florence who were living through a dramatic, though not yet desperate, domestic crisis. The course of events would be such that a poem conceived for Florence, and to honor Florence, would be transformed into the most bitterly and violently anti-Florentine book ever written.

4

Condemned to
the Stake

1301–1302

. . . that he be burnt with fire until he dies

. . . *igne comburatur sic quod moriatur*

—Conviction of March 10, 1302

Whites and Blacks: Rehearsals for civil war

In mid-August 1300, at the end of his term of office as prior, Dante may have felt satisfied. During the two months that he served, the interference of the cardinal legate had been curbed, negotiations had begun for an alliance with Bologna (they would be concluded ten days later), and the Cerchi faction seemed to be firmly in power. But the Cerchi were feeling a little too safe, and their overconfidence led them to commit a grave error: between August and September they persuaded the new priors, all lackluster figures, to allow their political comrades back from internment at Sarzana, while leaving the representatives of the rival party at Castel della Pieve.[1] A decision so brazenly biased could only create tension, and it would indeed be one of the reasons that led to a new outbreak of violence within just a few months. Everyone knew that Dante and Guido Cavalcanti (one of those interned at Sarzana) were close friends, and word spread that Dante, just out of office as prior, was one of those behind the order. The new college of priors was certainly open to influence and clearly didn't make the decision alone, but it is by no means sure that Dante was one of its prime movers. That episode would, however, be thrown back at him during his period of political disgrace so that, in the earlier mentioned lost letter of which Leonardo Bruni summarized numerous passages, he would feel bound to recall "that, when those from Serezzana were called back [he] was out of the office of prior and mustn't be held responsible for it." And the fact he was accused precisely because of his friendship with Cavalcanti is made clear from the additional words: "he says moreover that their return was due to the infirmity and death of Guido Cavalcanti, who fell sick at Serezzana for the bad air and died soon after," words that make it seem as if the tendentious order could have been inspired by compassion for the sick friend, though they end up almost confirming Dante's intervention on Cavalcanti's behalf.[2]

The lifting of the banishment solely for political allies was one of the immediate causes that led the legate Matteo d'Acquasparta, on September 23, to excommunicate the governors of Florence, to issue an interdict on the city (namely, the prohibition of all public religious manifestations, including the administration of the sacraments), and to move to Bologna. Many attempts were made to mollify both the legate and, above all, the pope. Among other things it was decided to send a diplomatic mission to Rome which included representatives from Bologna, Lucca, and Siena. Boniface VIII received the ambassadors in private at the Lateran palace on November 11, showed himself to be conciliatory, and granted a temporary suspension of the interdict. The pope's amenability can be explained, on the one hand, by the fact that a second "private" war was about to be waged against the Aldobrandeschi for which he needed the military support of Florence. On the other hand, he had at last reached an agreement with the king of France that allowed his brother Charles of Valois to lead a military expedition, ostensibly to help the Angevins of Naples, who were at war with the Aragonese of Sicily, but in reality to take control of Tuscany or, at least, Florence. And indeed the following months were relatively calm (Charles's preparations took longer than expected), allowing the Cerchi to imagine they had resolved the whole business in their favor.

The truce came to an end in May 1301, and once again it was an error of judgment by the Cerchi that rekindled the conflict. Pistoia, a Guelf city, had been rent apart in the 1290s by a clash between the leading factions of two branches of the Cancellieri family, the white Cancellieri and the black Cancellieri. Before the events in Pistoia, the words "white" and "black" had no political nuance: they were generally used to distinguish two branches of the same family or two sections of the same banking or trading company. In short, they were neutral terms, like A and B. In the 1280s, for example, the Cerchi banking company, which was the largest in Florence, had been divided into white Cerchi and black Cerchi so as to better manage its vast range of interests. Curiously, Vieri, who was head of the black branch of the company, would find himself at the head of the white Guelfs. In Pistoia, as a result of the internecine conflicts, the adjectives "white" and "black" had ended up indicating the two branches of the Guelf party headed by the Cancellieri. In 1296, to deal with the domestic disorder, the people of Pistoia had decided to hand over control of the city, the power of government, to Florence for a period of five years. The magistrates appointed by Florence managed to maintain the balance between the whites and the blacks by sending off the leaders of the two parties to be interned. Many of them had moved to Florence itself, and here the whites of Pistoia had formed links with followers of the Cerchi, while the blacks had moved closer to the Donati. In this way the names of the political parties of Pistoia had also begun to be used to identify the two opposing factions in Florence. With the expulsion of the blacks from Pistoia, supported by the Cerchi and strongly opposed by the Donati, the practice of calling the former "Whites" and the latter "Blacks" would be established for good. Eventually, as soon as the Guelfs led by the Cerchi had been banished from Florence, they would formally use that name to distinguish themselves from those inside the city, and from that moment the records themselves would describe them as Whites.

In May 1301, the period of control over Pistoia came to an end. During the previous year, the Cerchi faction—from now on we will call them "Whites"—had already begun openly favoring the Whites of Pistoia. As the deadline approached, the problem of control of that city became increasingly urgent, above all since the lands of Pistoia, which included the Apennine passes to Emilia, were of strategic importance in ensuring that the alliance agreed just a few months earlier between the Whites of Florence and Bologna could, if necessary, be made militarily effective. The Whites of Florence then, without the support of the Donati (the

Blacks), took a series of measures against the Blacks of Pistoia which culminated in May 1301 with the expulsion first of the magnates of the Black party and then with a merciless persecution of their followers in the city and the surrounding countryside. The operation, carried out with particular cruelty, lasted for months: around thirty Blacks were sentenced and put to death; an enormous number of houses and properties were razed to the ground, and there were countless acts of pillage and vengeance.[3] The Donati, with some justification, interpreted the violence as directed against them, and would not forgive the Cerchi for it. In short, Pistoia became the rehearsal ground for civil war in Florence. Dante was well aware of this: in the *Commedia* he would write: "Pistoia first thins itself of Blacks; / then Florence renews its people and laws" (*Inf.* XXIV 143–144; "Pistoia in pria d'i Neri si dimagra; / poi Fiorenza rinova gente e modi").

We don't know what position Dante took in the debate that had divided the ruling White group over the policy to be followed in Pistoia. The trial on January 27, 1302, would also convict him, along with Palmiero degli Altoviti, Lippo di Rinuccio Becca, and Orlanduccio di Orlando, of having "worked to divide the city of Pistoia into parts breaking its previous union, having elected the elders of said city all of a single party, ordered and made to carry out the expulsion from said city of faithful Blacks devoted to the Roman Church, and separated said city from the union with the city of Florence and from subjection to the Roman Church and to Messer Charles, peacemaker in Tuscany."[4] The tough line against the Blacks of Pistoia had begun earlier during the priorship of Saltarelli (from April 15 to June 14, 1300) and had continued during later priorships—including those of Dante (from June to August 1300) and Orlanduccio di Orlando (from December 1300 to February 1301)—but it has to be said that the only one of those convicted who had direct political responsibility in that affair was Palmiero degli Altoviti, who was a prior during the months when the decision to banish the Blacks was taken and carried out. We may presume, however, that Dante bore some responsibility, however indirect, if only because during those months he was very close to Saltarelli, with whom he shared the hard line against the Blacks and Boniface VIII. And then, he must have considered the alliance with Bologna, which had led to the coup in Pistoia, as being almost his own creation, as one of the high points of his period as prior. Having said this, it must be pointed out that all the judgments by the *podestà* Cante dei Gabrielli between January and February 1302 convicted those accused in practically identical terms, of having plotted against the Blacks of Pistoia. They are carbon-copy sentences handed down with a spirit of vengeance.

After Dante's period as prior, there is no record of any further political activity by him until April 1301, when on the fourteenth of that month he speaks, in the role of "elder" (*savio*), at a meeting of the Consiglio delle Capitudini. For the second time we find him giving advice on problems of a procedural nature: on the agenda, in fact, is the method to be adopted for electing the priors who would be chosen the following day.[5] The question was a delicate one: the period of control over Pistoia was coming to an end and the priors to be elected would be required in fact, though not by law, to advise the Florentine *capitano* of that city, Andrea Filippi dei Gherardini, about what measures to take against the Blacks. Two men to be elected to the college (Palmiero degli Altoviti and Guido Bruno di Forese Falconieri) would later be condemned to death along with Dante: it is likely that in this situation the elections had been influenced more than usually, thus giving Cante dei Gabrielli the pretext for accusing Dante and the two others of fraud.

Against Boniface VIII

After the events in Pistoia, there was strong disagreement among the Whites about what approach to adopt in relation to the pope and the Blacks. By early June it seemed almost certain that Charles of Valois would arrive in Italy and that the true aim of Boniface VIII was to overthrow the government of the Whites; the Blacks, heartened by the prospect of the French expedition, became more aggressive. While Vieri dei Cerchi, relying on his enormous financial resources, seemed to be pursuing a line of compromise, a growing minority was demanding a much tougher policy. Dante was among them.

A question of apparent secondary importance—whether or not to give some modest military support to the pope in his war against the Aldobrandeschi—opened up the split among the Whites.

It is worth describing what led to this, since it neatly demonstrates how private and public interests became tangled and, therefore, how a (successful) attempt at bullying over a simple question of property ended up interfering with the pope's foreign policy until it involved cities like Florence and the whole Guelf alliance in Tuscany.

At the centre of this highly complex affair was a storybook character, Margherita Aldobrandeschi, Countess of Sovana, feudal dame of a vast territory that stretched from Monte Argentario across to Monte Amiata, to Lake Bolsena and almost as far as Civitavecchia, an area that both the cities of Siena (to the north) and Orvieto (to the east) had in their sights.[6] In 1270, Margherita had married Guy de Montfort, who would go down in history for his revenge killing, the following year, of Prince Henry of Cornwall, nephew of Henry III, king of England, in Viterbo Cathedral, in the presence of Philip III of France and Charles of Anjou.[7] Cardinal Caetani, appointed by Nicholas IV in 1291 to administer the property of Margherita, who had been widowed that year, had tried to marry her to one of his nephews but had been beaten to it by the Orsini family, so that the rich heiress had contracted a second marriage to Orsello Orsini in 1293. But he died suddenly a couple of years later, so that Caetani, who had meanwhile been elected pope, was free to celebrate Margherita's third marriage (even though she was over forty) to his great-nephew Roffredo III Caetani, in 1296. Barely two years passed before there was another dramatic turn of events. Boniface VIII ordered that if it were shown that Margherita was already bound to others by sacramental obligation, then her marriage with his great-nephew would be annulled. The rumor promptly spread that, after the death of Orsini, Margherita had secretly married one of her lovers, Nello dei Pannocchieschi, lord of feudal estates in the Maremma. The marriage was said to have been kept secret because Nello was already married to Pia dei Tolomei whom, according to a legend retold by Dante, he then killed ("remember me, I am Pia; Siena made me, Maremma undid me: / he knows it well the one who married me / placing first his ring upon my finger" [*Purg.* V 133–136; "ricorditi di me, che son la Pia; / Siena mi fé, disfecemi Maremma: / salsi colui che 'nnanellata pria / disposando m'avea con la sua gemma"]). At this point the wedding with Roffredo was annulled (in 1298), and he was free to marry (in October 1299) Giovanna of Aquila, a rich heiress from Fondi. But to ensure the Caetani family didn't lose the substantial Aldobrandeschi revenues, the pope accused Margherita of bigamy and stripped her of her noble titles (in October 1300). The Aldobrandeschi family naturally retaliated and war broke out, in which Orvieto also joined in, and which dragged on until May 1, 1302: Margherita (who had meanwhile married her cousin Guido di Santa Fiora) was imprisoned and then forced to (re)marry Nello dei Pannocchieschi. This marriage proved in a certain sense that the divorce decreed several years earlier had been legitimate.

In June 1301 we are in the midst of war. The cardinal legate Matteo d'Acquasparta sends a letter from Bologna asking for the knights sent by the city of Florence in early May to reinforce the papal troops for a period of two months to remain in service there beyond the expiry of that term. The request was discussed on June 19 during a session of the Consiglio dei Cento that had been expanded to include the Consiglio delle Capitudini. Dante spoke against the advice of the priors to accept the request. In the second session, the same day, the proposal was discussed by the Consiglio dei Cento alone: Dante once again spoke against, but those in favor eventually won by forty-nine votes to thirty-two. Finally, once again on June 19, the other councilors were assembled and the proposal was then ratified by a wide majority. The scale of the minority shows, nevertheless, that the Whites were divided. As for Dante, he took positions far removed from those of Vieri dei Cerchi, who was ready to compromise. His position of open and repeated opposition to Boniface VIII probably also weighed on the sentence he would eventually receive: with these interventions, in fact, Dante had identified himself with the more extreme section of the Whites.

On September 13, 20, and 28 he would speak again in the Consiglio dei Cento, in both extended and limited session, on questions that didn't directly touch upon the general political situation, except for one matter, discussed on September 28, that had clear political implications. In this session, the various items on the agenda included the granting of an amnesty to Neri di Gherardino Diodati, condemned to death in September 1298 with a sentence that many believed the then *podestà*, Cante dei Gabrielli, had passed in order to do political harm to Neri's father. Dante and the judge Albizzo Corbinelli supported the proposal of the priors to grant the amnesty, approved by seventy-three votes to seven.[8] That September Dante could never have imagined that only four or five months later, the same Cante dei Gabrielli would sentence him, along with Gherardino Diodati himself, to be burned at the stake.

A "policing" operation

In June 1301 Charles of Valois began his march to Italy.[9] He was traveling with his pregnant wife (who would give birth in Siena in October) and a meager band of troops, no more than 500 knights. In July he was in Turin and then Milan, governed by the Visconti; by the end of the month he had traveled through Modena (welcomed by the Este, enemies of Bologna) and arrived in Bologna. Bologna, bound by treaty to the Whites of Florence and suspicious of his meeting with the Este a few days earlier, showed no particular warmth. Charles crossed the Apennines by the passes controlled by Pistoia (keeping well away from the city itself, which was in the hands of the Whites), crossed Florentine territory and then, in August, stopped at Siena, Orvieto, and Viterbo. On September 2 he reached Anagni, Boniface's home town and summer residence. Here the pope appointed him captain general of the Papal States, peacemaker of Tuscany, and rector of Romagna. Valois now had full title to carry out his mission—a formidable one, as it no doubt seemed—of overthrowing the White government of Florence. By September 19 he was already on his way north. His first stop, not surprisingly, was Castel della Pieve (October 4), where members of the Black party had been interned since their banishment during Dante's period as prior, and where Corso Donati was living. Here his forces joined with those of the exiled Donati faction. On October 16 they halted at Siena.

In the face of approaching danger, the political line followed by the Florentine Whites was confused and hesitant. Furthermore, since none of the Guelf cities of Tuscany had given their support, the only ally they could count on was Bologna. Their hopes lay in the negotiations they tried to establish with Valois and with the pope. As a sign of reconciliation, they brought forward the election of the new priors (to October 7 instead of October 15); moreover, they elected a college that was not openly loyal to the Cerchi. One of the new priors was Dino Compagni who, in commenting on the messages sent out by the new priors to their fellow citizens, would write: "We showed our intention to negotiate for peace, when we should have been sharpening our swords."[10]

Perhaps a few days before these elections, a diplomatic mission had left Florence for Rome. The records are unclear and incomplete. It was, in fact, a joint mission from Florence and Bologna. We know that Bologna had approved it on October 11, and that their ambassadors had left the city on the fifteenth. Dante was one of the group from Florence. They were received by Boniface in Rome, at the Lateran (and not at Anagni, as many claim), perhaps shortly after October 20.[11] The pope, in substance, asked the Florentine legates for the obedience of their city governors, and immediately sent two of them, Guido Ubaldini da Signa, nicknamed Il Corazza, and Maso di Ruggerino Minerbetti, back to Florence to convey this demand. Boniface was probably trying to reach a favorable solution without having to involve Valois—in other words, without having to become indebted to the French crown. But it was now rather late for a diplomatic solution.

Valois was close to the walls of Florence, where he asked to enter as peacemaker. Confusion reigned in the city: many Whites began to side with the opposition, and the priors were not sure what to do. They didn't feel able to decide alone and consulted many parties, including the guilds. In the end it was decided to agree to the request, and Valois entered the city on November 1, welcomed with full honors. Opening the gates would prove to be the gravest error committed by Vieri and by the heads of the White party. The armed troops available to the French would have been wholly inadequate for an attack on a large, well-supplied city like Florence. White Pistoia would later reject a similar demand, and the Blacks would become embroiled in a war lasting five years to break its resistance.

The White Florentines may have realized they had made a mistake as soon as they saw the procession of infamous characters in Valois's retinue. We already know of Baldo d'Aguglione and Cante dei Gabrielli: with them were Musciatto Franzesi, a madcap financier, usurer, and merchant in France who was the financial coordinator of Charles's expedition and known to his comrades as the "evil knight" (Musciatto had given one of his sisters in marriage to Simone dei Bardi, widower of Beatrice); Maghinardo Pagani da Susinana, a Ghibelline from Romagna ready to move from one side to the other ("who changes sides from summer to winter" [*Inf.* XXVII 51; "che muta parte da la state al verno"]); Malatestino Malatesta, brother of Gianciotto and Paolo (whose dark story Dante had written perhaps only a few months earlier).[12]

As a first move, Valois used his few troops to occupy the bridges and gates of the Oltrarno. The Cerchi, in a desperate last move, wrote to the pope, asking him urgently to send the general of the Friars Minor, Cardinal Gentile da Montefiore, to Florence to negotiate a surrender. The Blacks, having been tipped off, were determined to waste no time. They persuaded Valois to demand full powers. In response, the priors called a grand assembly for November 5 to consider what to do. At this point the Blacks decided it was time to act. They wanted no outside intervention that might deprive them of complete victory. And so on the night of November 4 and 5 they carried out a genuine coup. Corso Donati, who was waiting with his troops just outside Florence, entered the city through the gates guarded by the French. The operation, according to Dante, had been carried out with Valois's agreement: he, who had come from France with no army, "unarmed," carrying only the "lance" of "Judas" (in other words, of betrayal), speared Florence for no gain, except for guilt and shame ("Thus no land, but sin and shame / shall he earn" [*Purg.* XX 76–77; "Quindi non terra, ma peccato e onta / guadagnerà"]). For six days the Blacks roused a series of attacks of unprecedented violence, after which, once the convictions against them had been annulled (recall that Corso had been sentenced to death), they began to prepare a judicial persecution that would last for months. Many followers of the Cerchi meanwhile changed sides, including Noffo di Guido Bonafedi and Neri di Jacopo del Giudice, who had served with Dante as priors. Most notable of all was the betrayal of Lapo Saltarelli (who would not manage, however, to escape the death sentence), a betrayal that Dante must have found particularly painful, so that he would use his comrade in arms as an example that typified the moral decline of Florence. He would write in the *Commedia* that during the time when Cacciaguida was alive, a "Lapo Saltarello" would have aroused the same "wonder" that now, in the corrupt Florence of 1300, a "Cincinnatus" stirs.[13]

The Blacks didn't touch the city's *Ordinamenti di giustizia,* but they occupied all public offices. The *podestà* became the executive arm of the cleansing operation that was carried out. Charles of Valois first gave this appointment to Cante dei Gabrielli, one of Corso's faithful followers. Cante served in this role from November 9, 1301 to June 30, 1302, and by January 18, 1302, he was already able, after an investigation based almost always on public gossip ("fama publica referente"), to hand out the first convictions. His successor, Gherardino da Gambara di Brescia, would be even more zealous.[14] In 1302, a total of 559 death sentences were passed, but only a small number were carried out since those convicted had already fled the city. Added to the sentences of death were those of exile and internment imposed on some 600 people, not to mention all those who went into voluntary exile. It went without saying that every conviction carried with it a penalty of destruction and confiscation of property.

The exodus was equal only to that of the Guelfs after the defeat at Montaperti. One historian has written that, "as had already happened with the Ghibellines, the exile imposed on the Whites involved not just the expulsion of a limited group or individual people. Instead a whole mass of the ruling class and of the most influential families of the greatest European financial power was sent away."[15] The White diaspora was therefore not without consequences for the city's economic and cultural life, both immediately and over the coming decades. Most of those forced to leave Florence were affluent. Before their departure they tried to sell their properties; those who were members of banking and mercantile companies tried to sell their share of the capital; everyone drew their money from the banks, so long as they were in time. It wasn't therefore just an exodus of people but also of capital: it is said that Vieri dei Cerchi alone took the enormous sum of 600,000 gold florins with him to Arezzo.[16] Perhaps it wasn't as much as 600,000, but the figure gives an idea of what impression the outflow of White capital must have left on the people of Florence. The exodus of capital was of such proportions that between 1302 and 1303 many finance companies went bankrupt or found themselves in serious difficulties. It also had a powerful effect on cultural life. With Bono Giamboni, Brunetto Latini, and Guido Cavalcanti now dead, the only personalities left were almost all in exile (as Dante would soon be, or Francesco da Barberino a few years later) or ostracized, like Dino Compagni. Many White exiles, like Ser Petracco, father of Francesco Petrarch, in exile from October 1302, like Convenevole da Prato, who would be Petrarch's first teacher, and like Sennuccio del Bene (in exile perhaps at the time of the invasion of Henry VII), would later find themselves at the papal court in Avignon under the protection of Cardinal Niccolò da Prato (one of the key political and cultural figures of the early decades of the 1300s) and would take part there in the birth of that revolutionary cultural movement known as "humanism."[17] Florence, however, remained extraneous. Deprived of its best intellectuals, it formed no part of the new cultural networks developing between Avignon, Rome, and Venice. Many decades were to pass before knowledge of the classical authors, mastery of a Latin language purified by their example, and a more general critical approach toward authority could take root in a city that remained locked in a provincial perspective.[18]

Sentenced to death

We know Dante was a member of the diplomatic mission sent to Boniface VIII, but we don't know how long he remained in Rome or what were his next movements. He was almost certainly still in Rome at the time of the coup in early November; Leonardo Bruni recounts that Dante, having left Rome, had arrived in Siena when he came to hear the situation in Florence was beyond repair, and that he decided to join his party comrades who had meanwhile left the city. Together with them, Bruni relates, he met up with representatives of old Ghibelline refugees at Gargonza. Bruni condenses events that occurred over three or four months into just a few lines, and this reduces the reliability of his account.[19] In particular, it seems difficult to imagine that Dante, in a situation so delicate and so full of risk for his family, would not have gone back to the city. It is not entirely true, in fact, that in November he could see "no remedy": the Blacks had certainly taken control of the city, but the game wasn't completely over. The Whites were larger in number, they controlled Pistoia, and their leaders were still in Florence. But above all, even though the Donati seemed to be acting in full agreement with Valois, it was by no means certain they saw eye to eye with Boniface VIII. In early December the pope once again sent his legate Matteo d'Acquasparta to Florence with the task of aiding reconciliation between the parties. For about a month the cardinal tried to convince the victorious Blacks to share some of the public positions with the Whites and worked to bring peace between the rival families. He even managed to interest the Cerchi and Donati families, and perhaps he would have achieved his aim if a bloody episode—the killing of Simone, one of Corso's children, while he was in the act of killing his hated uncle Niccolò dei Cerchi—hadn't dashed all hope of reconciliation. During the same month, the legate had also tried in vain to sort things out in Pistoia by enabling the banished Blacks to return.[20] In short, up to the end of 1301 or the beginning of the following year, while the situation in Florence was not exactly in the balance, there was still hope of avoiding disaster. It is almost certain that many Whites, feeling under threat, left the city in November and December, but it is hard to imagine a flow of refugees large enough for Dante to join them. And we can be sure that this was not a period in which Whites going into voluntary exile would have contemplated negotiations with the Ghibellines.

But the situation changed with the new year when the Blacks set the judicial machinery in motion. The first convictions were on January 18, 1302, and like those that followed, defendants were convicted in their absence. The exodus of those most at risk must therefore have begun some time just before. Dante, as a former prior, was among those at risk, and it is likely that he too may have left the city between the end of 1301 and early 1302.

The judicial crusade orchestrated by Cante dei Gabrielli struck the White leaders who had held public office (and therefore didn't affect the real heads of the party, like Vieri dei Cerchi, who as a magnate had been excluded from key judicial appointments). On January 18, two separate trials convicted, first of all, three ex-priors for barratry, illegal gain, and extortion, and then Andrea Filippi dei Gherardini, who had been the Florentine *capitano* of Pistoia and the one who had been most responsible for the persecution of Blacks in that city (hence his nickname Cacciaguelfi, or Guelf-hunter). Barratry and actions against the Blacks of Pistoia would be the leitmotiv for all the convictions until mid-March. Trials on January 27 convicted first an ex-prior, Gherardino Diodati, for barratry and then, on the same day, Palmiero degli Altoviti, Dante Alighieri, Lippo di Rinuccio Becca, and Orlanduccio di Orlando, all of whom were ex-priors (Lippo had taken part in the mission that had uncovered the Spini agents at the papal court in Rome). The accusations against these four were: barratry, illegal gain, and extortion; the approval of allocations of money against the sovereign pope and against Charles of Valois to obstruct his arrival; and the attempt to divide Pistoia and to expel the Blacks.[21]

The defendants were convicted in absentia, following the rules of Florentine criminal procedure, which deemed failing to appear to be a confession of guilt. The sentence provided for a fine of 5,000 small florins, to be paid to the municipal authority within three days: in the event of the fine remaining unpaid within the prescribed period, there would be proceedings for confiscation, depredation, and destruction of the defendant's property, internment outside Tuscany for two years, the inscription of their name and offense in the public register, and exclusion from public offices and benefits for life. The judgments handed out by Cante dei Gabrielli throughout the month of February (like that against Lapo Saltarelli the previous month) were all based on the same line of accusation and ordered more or less the same penalties: a fine of 2,000 to 5,000 small florins and around two years internment (6,000 florins and three years for Saltarelli).[22]

The political purpose of the trials was clear: to purge the White ruling class. No one was sentenced to death, and the fines were relatively small. The fine of 5,000 small florins was equivalent to around 170 gold florins, a very large sum for Dante's meager finances, but certainly affordable for almost everyone else convicted. In any event, the disproportion between the size of the fine and the value of those properties to be razed to the ground in the event of non-payment is evident: and yet no one came to pay the fine to save their properties. Everyone knew that compliance with the judgment, in that climate of scant legality, would have given them no guarantee. It was apparent, in any event, that the Blacks had no interest in physically eliminating their adversaries. Their purpose seemed to be one of depriving the White ruling group of its leadership and forcing them to emigrate and keep well away from the city.

All of a sudden, in March 1302, the attitude of the investigators became much tougher. On June 10, Cante issued a sentence against fifteen defendants, including Dante. All of them had already been sentenced to fines and internment, but now they were to die at the stake, all because they hadn't turned up to prove their innocence. The accusation against each of them was the same: barratry and illegal gain. It was a short, poorly-reasoned judgment, with an air of vengeance about it. All convictions over the following days would also be sentences of death. The Blacks had moved from purge to vendetta. Something must have happened between February 10 (the date of the last fines and internment) and March 10 to drive them to such harshness.

It is more than likely that the meeting at Gargonza, between White and Ghibelline refugees, had happened precisely then. Gargonza is a castle situated on a hill in the Val di Chiana, close to Arezzo: it belonged to the Ubertini and Pazzi families, who were Ghibellines and fiercely hostile to the Florentine Guelfs. During that time, the Ubertini and Pazzi were conducting a guerrilla campaign in the upper Arno Valley that had enabled them to recapture several castles taken by the Florentines a decade earlier. We have no evidence as to what those erstwhile enemies said and what agreements they had reached. They had probably established the basis for an alliance against Florence that would be concluded in early June in the Mugello. Nor do we have any proof that Dante was there: the only evidence in that respect is his sentence of death, perhaps in retaliation for his involvement in that meeting.

Even in the absence of information, it can be sensed that the Gargonza meeting marked a radical turning point in Guelf and Ghibelline policy, a turning point which to contemporary eyes must have seemed unprecedented. The Cerchi had reached agreements in the past with the Ghibellines (at Pistoia, for example, against the Blacks), but they were momentary and made for ulterior motives. At Gargonza, for the first time, a Florentine Guelf party allied itself with Florence's sworn enemies and, moreover, for the purpose of taking up arms against its own city. In the eyes of the Florentines this was tantamount to treason. The agreement, though still to be finalized, took effect immediately, with the guerrilla action by the Ghibelline forces redirected from April onward against the Florentine castles and garrisons in the upper Arno Valley. It was inevitable that the people of Florence, who felt a deep-rooted hatred of the Ghibellines since the massacre at Montaperti, would identify more closely with the Black faction, seen now as bastion of their city's Guelf identity. The response of the Blacks, strengthened by popular support, was immediate judicial reprisal, followed then by harsh repression. The countless death sentences that ensued from April onward, becoming more frequent over the summer months, were the judicial reaction to the guerrilla warfare being fought on the outskirts of the Florentine territory.[23]

Part Two

EXILE

5

At War with Florence

1302–1304

vile and worthless company

la compagnia malvagia e scempia

—*Para.* XVII 62

Arezzo and the anti-Florentine geopolitical block

MANY FLORENTINE exiles sought shelter in White Pistoia, many more in Ghibelline Arezzo. Arezzo was the key center for an extensive regional area that included the upper Arno Valley and the large mountain zone that stretched north as far as Romagna. Our picture of the area that includes the Casentino, the Upper Mugello, the lands of Montefeltro, the mountain ridges of the Apennines, and the foothills of Romagna is shaped by today's administrative boundaries (Tuscany, Emilia-Romagna, and the Marches) and by the communication links built in modern times between northeast and central Italy. We tend to divide up an area that was once regarded as one and give marginal significance to a region that in Dante's time still had a remarkable political and strategic influence. In this area, devoid of major urban centers, a feudal-based political system still survived, weak but far from dead, that depended on various great noble families. Despite much disparity, anti-Guelf feeling prevailed, which stood solidly against papal and Angevin claims in the Montefeltro and Romagna areas and Florentine expansionism in Tuscany.

The most powerful faction in the region was that of the Guidi, the
Palatine counts. By the beginning of the 1300s they were no longer the
great united family whose estates, in the twelfth century, had stretched
over great expanses of Romagna and Tuscany, but, though they had
shrunk to the area between the Casentino and the Apennine foothills
of Faenza and Forlì, they still controlled a substantial territory. Their
decline had started in the early 1200s when, with other feudal dynasties, they had split into various branches, each of which kept the title of
count: of Bagno, of Battifolle, of Modigliana-Porciano, of Romena, of
Dovadola. Their economic interests and political allegiances were
also divided: while the Guidi of Modigliana-Porciano were staunch Ghibellines, those of Dovadola and Battifolle were Guelfs; other branches,
such as the Guidi of Romena, moved from one side to the other according
to circumstance and convenience.[1]

The estates of the great Ghibelline Ubaldini family stretched between
the Mugello and the Apennines of Bologna. Those of the Pila branch
(whose most illustrious member had been Cardinal Ottaviano, named
together with Frederick II in Canto X of *Inferno*) had their territorial base
in the Mugello area. Less prominent were the families of Montefeltro,
who supplemented their limited land revenues with earnings from their
skills in arms. We have referred several times to the great condottiere
Guido da Montefeltro and his son Buonconte; the outstanding figure
around 1300 was Uguccione della Faggiola, the feudal lord of Massa
Trabaria whose main residence was at Corneto.[2]

The situation in the upper Arno Valley was different. Living here, in
fact, were families less powerful than those of the Tuscan-Romagna
mountains. These included the Ubertini and the Pazzi (not the Pazzi of
Florence who were linked to the Black faction), who were both under
the control of the Guidi. Florence had progressively stripped these families of many rights and much of their estates, and so they were carrying
out a sort of guerrilla campaign which the Florentines regarded as
banditry.

It was therefore in the nature of things that the Whites of Florence,
the great feudal lords of the Tuscan-Romagna mountains, the rebels of
the Arno Valley, and the old Ghibelline exiles should meet at Arezzo.
What probably drove the Cerchi to seek an immediate agreement with
forces who, for one reason or another, were hostile to Florence was their

confidence that they could rapidly reverse the situation by uniting their financial power with the military experience of the Ghibelline exiles and the mountain lords. And this was to be their worst of many errors. From exiles who were trying legitimately to return home, they became rebels, enemies not only of the Black faction but of the whole city.

The successful capture of several castles in the upper Arno Valley in spring 1302 seemed to prove them right. But they soon had to understand that nothing would be resolved by sporadic actions so far away from the city. They also had to understand that the Ubertini and Pazzi were motivated above all by self-interest. They were allies of little significance from a military point of view, and not to be trusted. Proof of this would come in July 1302, when Carlino dei Pazzi, in return for the promise of money, the restitution of confiscated estates, and the release of a son captured shortly before, handed to Gherardino da Gambara, *podestà* of Florence, the fortress of Castel del Piano (or Pian tra Vigne), which the Florentines had been besieging in vain for three weeks.[3] Imprisonments and executions would follow. In *Inferno,* Camicione dei Pazzi, thrust into the ice of Caina as betrayer of his relatives, would tell Dante to "await" the arrival of his kinsman Carlino, whose guilt would make his own seem lighter, even though it is most serious. In short, the Whites needed to associate with anti-Florentine forces who were more reliable and more incisive. And, above all, to bring the war closer to Florence.

The Coalition of the White Guelfs

The Whites had meanwhile organized themselves by establishing a Coalition of the White Party of Florence (Universitas partis Alborum de Florentia), probably in Arezzo, where their leading figures, including Vieri dei Cerchi, had converged.[4] This was an association that regulated internal affairs and managed relations with Ghibelline exiles, the feudal lords, and allied cities. The founding of a *universitas,* modeled in the same way as the party had been organized in Florence, was more or less the norm for the Guelfs as well as for the Ghibelline exiles. The novel aspect was that this coalition pitted one Guelf party against another. It was symptomatic that, while the Whites would extol their Guelfism, the Blacks would accuse them of Ghibellinism, to the point of calling them Ghibellines. Another development was the formal semantic transformation of the word "white" from a neutral description (as when it was used to distinguish the Cerchi family's "white" banking company from their "black" one) to a strong political identifier. The Coalition was governed by a secret council of four members, by a great council of twelve, and by a *capitano* who led its army. The Ghibelline Alessandro dei Guidi di Romena was appointed as the first *capitano*. This appointment, made during the time when the Coalition was based in Arezzo, would have been influenced by the fact that the bishop of the city was Ildebrandino, Alessandro's younger brother, who was also a Ghibelline.

Once established, the Whites regarded the feudal families of the Apennines as their true allies. On June 8, 1302, eighteen leading members of the White and Ghibelline party met at San Godenzo, a village in the Mugello almost on the Apennine summits, close to the present-day Muraglione pass. The house where they met belonged to the Guidi of Modigliana-Porciano and was known as Palazzo dello Specchio because of its windows, a rarity at that time. Representing the Whites were Dante and other familiar names such as Vieri dei Cerchi and Andrea dei Gherardini; the Ghibelline exiles included Lapo di Azzolino degli Uberti, nephew of Farinata, who may have been present at the meeting at Gargonza. They were men, therefore, who had once fought violently against each other and who were now signing a document in front of a notary in which they undertook to compensate Ugolino degli Ubaldini for any damage that his properties in the Mugello might sustain in the forthcoming war against the Blacks of Florence.[5] Thus began the first Mugello campaign, fought between June and September 1302. It would involve many battles but, all in all, would end inconclusively, so that the Blacks would come out stronger.

The Blacks were also beginning to achieve significant success on another battlefront—against Pistoia. Here, another character appears on the scene—Marchese Moroello Malaspina di Giovagallo of Lunigiana, who would play a major part in Dante's life. A skilled professional condottiere, like many great feudal lords, he went to serve the cities of Lucca and Florence in 1302, assuming the position of *capitano generale* in the war against White Pistoia. In early September, after a long siege, he forced the castle of Serravalle to surrender: Dante, who from 1306 would be his guest and enjoy his protection, would refer in the *Commedia* to that victory against his political allies in an almost triumphant tone, comparing Moroello to a thunderbolt that forms in the Magra valley and suddenly strikes the lands of Pistoia "so that every White will be stricken by it" (*Inf.* XXIV 145–150; "sì ch'ogne Bianco ne sarà feruto").[6] To worsen the situation of the Whites was the attitude of Uguccione. After having long fought among the Ghibelline ranks in Romagna against the papal and Angevin armies, in 1302 he was appointed *podestà* of Arezzo. The Whites, who thought of him as a safe ally, were unaware that during those months while they were sheltering in his city, Uguccione had restored his links with the Church and the Guelfs and had begun negotiations with Boniface VIII that would be advantageous to himself, his son and the city of Arezzo. Having reached an agreement with the Church, Uguccione began to make life difficult for the exiles. Between the end of 1302 and early 1303, the Coalition therefore moved across the Apennines and set up its base in Forlì, which had for many years been the Ghibelline center in Romagna. It was the lord of the city himself, Scarpetta Ordelaffi, who assumed the position of *capitano*.[7]

Under his command the second Mugello campaign was soon under way, but the exiles immediately suffered their first setbacks. Particularly serious was their failure to occupy the castle of Pulicciano, not far from Borgo San Lorenzo, which would have allowed them to control the main communication route through the Mugello. Here, in mid-March 1303, the Whites and their allies were routed by the Florentines under the leadership of the *podestà*, Fulcieri da Calboli. It was a battle not just between Florentines but also between rival forces from Forlì, since the Guelf Calboli family were enemies of the Ghibelline Ordelaffi family and had been banished by them from Forlì in 1294. The hatred toward the Ordelaffi may also explain the particular cruelty with which Fulcieri treated those defeated, a cruelty, what is more, that Fulcieri would demonstrate throughout his time as *podestà,* so that the chroniclers recall him as a "ferocious and cruel man" and Dante, in *Purgatorio,* gives a pitiless portrayal of him as a "hunter" of human flesh.[8]

During that same month of March, however, the Whites began negotiations with Bologna that led in May to the creation of a broad anti-Florentine alliance between them, Bologna, the Ubaldini, White Pistoia, the Ghibelline cities of Romagna (Forlì, Faenza, Imola), and Cervia, ruled by the Guelf Polentani family.[9] At the head of their army was Salinguerra dei Salinguerri, who was from Ferrara but an enemy of the Este family. The alliance, however, though impressive on paper, did not produce significant results. It seems, moreover, that the Whites were beginning to run short of money, so that between May and June they were forced to take out loans, though not for large amounts: on June 18 there was a full meeting of their leaders, including Ordelaffi, to agree on a loan for just 450 florins. On the Pistoia front, the Whites then had to come to terms with another Pazzi betrayal: this time it was Pazzino dei Pazzi who, in May, handed over the castle of Montale, halfway between Prato and Pistoia, for money. In short, the second year of fighting failed once again to bring success. Among the few positive pieces of news for the Whites was the fact that Uguccione della Faggiola, having ended his brief liaison with the papacy, had returned to the Ghibelline faith and had joined the alliance of exiles: Arezzo reopened its gates, so that once again the Whites could use it as one of their main operational bases. In November 1303, the *capitano* of the Coalition was no longer Scarpetta Ordelaffi but Aghinolfo dei Guidi di Romena, brother of the first *capitano* Alessandro.[10]

The event that marked a real turning point in the war between Whites and Blacks occurred in fall, and had nothing to do with the parties themselves. Boniface VIII died on October 11, 1303, shortly after the insult at Anagni. On the 22nd of the same month, after a particularly swift conclave, the Dominican Niccolò di Boccasio, a close collaborator of Boniface but of little political weight, was elected pope and took the name Benedict XI. During the first months of his papacy he intervened in the complex Florentine question in an attempt to promote a reconciliation between the parties.[11] The attempt raised great hopes for the Whites, but it soon proved unrealistic and provoked an even more deadly return to war.

Solitude of the exile

Dante left Florence before the judgments of January 18, 1302 and joined the other exiles in Arezzo. Was he alone or did he go with his family? The sentences didn't affect his brother Francesco, who remained in Florence. We don't know whether Francesco lived there peacefully or suffered any retorsions: one cousin, Cione di Brunetto, was fined in 1306 for being a Ghibelline (a name also given to the White rebels);

but it seems that other members of the Alighieri family, such as Cione di Bello, even served among the ranks of the Blacks.[12]

About Gemma, Boccaccio had no doubts: "[Dante] having left there [in Florence] his wife, with the rest of the family, unable to leave by reason of their young age, sure about her, since she was related by blood to one of the leaders of the opposing party, he himself uncertain where to go, wandered here and there in Tuscany." According to Boccaccio, he therefore left his wife and young children in Florence and went alone into exile. Boccaccio would have had this information from the same people who had told him about the finding of the little notebook. In effect, the story fits. It would have been "friends and relatives," evidently in Dante's absence, who advised Gemma to hide the most valuable things in a safe place. The first version of his *Trattatello* states that the strongboxes had been taken to "holy places": this could have been the Franciscan monastery of Santa Croce, where there was Friar Bernardo Riccomanni, Tana's son, the same person to whom Dante could have sent (though this is mere conjecture) the letter "to a Florentine friend" in 1315. We have seen that Tana and her husband Lapo, through his brother Pannocchia, had given financial help to Dante; it would therefore be no surprise if in those difficult times they had offered their help in persuading their son to hide Dante's belongings in the monastery for safekeeping.[13]

It would seem sufficiently clear that Dante's plan was to leave his wife and children in Florence: Corso Donati had been the true master of the city since the early days of November 1301, and Gemma, after all, was still a Donati. It is reasonable to suppose that a family network of protection would have extended to her. It is possible that Gemma's father, Manetto Donati, had sought reassurances. Besides, it would have been very difficult indeed for Dante's close family to leave Florence to follow an exile who had no financial resources and, above all, no patron with whom they, or even he, could live.

But the developing political situation would bring an end to this state of affairs. Soon there would be Gargonza, the guerrilla campaign would erupt in the upper Arno Valley, and the attitude of the Blacks would radically change. The Blacks would no longer be prosecuting rivals in order to distance them from the political struggle, but pursuing enemies who had betrayed their homeland. This is what brought the systematic death sentences and a repression that would also involve the relatives of those convicted.

On June 9, 1302 the Commune appointed an official with the task of managing the assets of those convicted of barratry, or for political offences, and to expel their children aged over fourteen and their wives: these provisions would be further toughened the following January. The fact that one of the instigators of this resolution was the same Nicola Acciaioli who several years before, with the help of Baldo d'Aguglione, had tampered with compromising court records is an indication of the integrity of Corso's fellow rulers. Gemma was forced to leave Florence in June. It is unlikely, for the reasons indicated, that she joined Dante, who at that time was moving between Arezzo, the Mugello, and the Casentino. The Donati or Riccomanni family had probably found a place for her and the children outside Florence and had taken on the responsibility of their financial support.[14] We have no clear information about the relationship between Dante and his family after that date. According to Boccaccio, he never saw his wife again. But the assertion is his, and still has to be proved. Some evidence to the contrary tends to suggest that, a few years later, the family moved temporarily back together again.

Into the fray

Dante went straight into action. He almost certainly took part in the meeting at Gargonza, and was definitely involved in forming the Coalition of the Whites. He, like his companions, must have been convinced that an immediate show of force was capable of reversing the situation. Or perhaps his desire for vengeance was such that he failed to properly gauge the effect of an agreement made in the heat of the moment with Ghibelline exiles and rebel families from the Valdarno. Who knows what he felt when he found himself at the same table as Lapo degli Uberti, against whom he had fought barely ten years before on the Campaldino plain: either he thought the alliance with his Ghibelline enemies would be expedient and short-lived, as it had been in the past, or his feeling of having suffered an injustice was so deep-rooted that he felt no sense of betrayal against his own city.

In the Coalition of the Whites he occupied a governing role as member of the Council of Twelve.[15] It appears certain that he was its secretary or registrar, in other words that he wrote the official letters, minutes, and dispatches. There couldn't have been many, among the bankers and merchants in the White ruling group, who were capable of carrying out this technical and political task. Lapo Saltarelli could have done it, but this fine lawyer, though not entirely ostracized after his attempt to move to the other side, seems no longer to have been included among the governing group. Dante had political experience and, above all, he was able to dictate letters in Latin of unparalleled elegance with ease. It is likely that the job of registrar or secretary was remunerated and that this was his source of income for nearly two years.

Certainly, if he had ever questioned the strangeness of finding himself working in collaboration with Lapo degli Uberti, Dante must have been aware that his present situation ran counter to the hopes he had fostered over the past fifteen years of becoming an intellectual whose expertise lay in rhetoric, poetry, and philosophy. Dante had set his sights on succeeding Brunetto as the city's critical conscience, of being a "wise man" who placed his knowledge at the service of the community, but was now reduced to playing a partisan role, making himself in effect partly responsible for the division of the city. He was using even his letter-writing skills against the city, making himself partly responsible also for the revanchist ardor of the Ghibellines, Florence's traditional and bitterest enemies.

As registrar, Dante was closely involved in the decision-making process and, probably, also in the areas of military operation. In June, in fact, we find him at San Godenzo acting as guarantor (on behalf of the Party, of course, and not personally) for the Ubaldini. He would have had close contact, in particular, with the Guidi family of Romena, which provided, as indicated above, two *capitani* of the Coalition. We also know he had dealings with Oberto and Guido, sons of Aghinolfo.

Yet his days in the Casentino would not have been filled with politics alone. At Romena or in the family's other castles (such as Montegranelli, where Oberto lived) he would have been haunted by those ghosts that had occupied his imagination since his youth in Florence and which, most probably, had taken form in the poem he had started and then had to abandon. Oberto was, in fact, married to Margherita, daughter of Paolo Malatesta, lover of Francesca da Polenta, and Alessandro's second marriage was to Caterina Fantolini, daughter in the first marriage of

Zambrasina Zambrasi who, on becoming a widow, had married Gianciotto the year after he had killed his wife.[16]

Over the coming years, Dante would have various opinions about the family clans—the Guidi branches of Romena and Modigliana-Porciano—that he had known during his early period in the Casentino. He would be particularly hard on the Romena brothers. But he would always feel a sentimental attachment to the landscape of the Casentino and the Tuscan-Romagna Apennines (places he would visit more and more often). Their waters were fixed in his mind: from Fonte Branda, which gushes below the very walls of Romena Castle and whose water the thirsty Master Adam would willingly forego if he could only see the still-living Alessandro and Aghinolfo punished along with him, to the "little streams that from the green hills / of the Casentino flow down into the Arno, / making their channels cold and soft" (*Inf.* XXX 64–66; "ruscelletti che d'i verdi colli / del Casentin discendon giuso in Arno, / faccendo i lor canali freddi e molli"), and as far as the waterfall at Acquacheta (in the valley of Montone, the lands of the Guidi family of Dovadola) which "roars there above San Benedetto / de l'Alpe to drop in one descent / where it ought to have fallen in a thousand" (*Inf.* XVI 100–102; "rimbomba là sovra San Benedetto / de l'Alpe per cadere ad una scesa / ove dovea per mille esser recetto").[17] The roar of Acquacheta was perhaps, for Dante, one of the most familiar sounds along the road that winds down to Forlì, a road he must have traveled many times in both directions between the spring of 1302 and spring of 1303.

He and the whole Coalition left Arezzo and moved to Forlì at the end of 1302 or in early 1303. As secretary he would have attended the court of the new *capitano* Ordelaffi and would have had dealings with his chancery, at the head of which was one Pellegrino Calvi about whom we can add no more.[18]

Mission to Verona

Dante was not present at the great gathering of June 18, 1303, at which 131 Whites and almost every member of their Council took part. He had probably already left on a diplomatic mission to Verona.[19] Biondo Flavio, the fifteenth-century historian from Forlì, refers to a diplomatic assignment to Verona.[20]

The Ghibelline Della Scala family had become lords of Verona (though they had no automatic hereditary title) with Alberto in 1277. To avoid the problem of no hereditary title, Alberto gave joint power to his eldest son Bartolomeo, who became sole lord from September 1301 until his death (on March 7, 1304). He was succeeded by his brother Alboino, who lived until 1311 but ruled jointly from 1308 with his younger brother Cangrande. Dante therefore arrived at the court of Bartolomeo. When he wrote in *Paradiso* that he found refuge in "the courtesy of the great Lombard / who on the ladder carries the holy bird" (*Para.* XVII 71–72; "nella cortesia del gran Lombardo / che 'n su la scala porta il santo uc-cello"), namely the imperial eagle, he would be identifying Bartolomeo himself who, having married Costanza, great grand-daughter of Em-peror Frederick II, was the only member of his family to have a coat of arms with an eagle on the fourth rung of a ladder.[21] Yet the other infor-mation in that canto certainly doesn't correspond with what actually happened on that first trip to Verona. Cacciaguida (prophesying) would say that the generous hospitality of that great man would be, for Dante, "the first . . . refuge and the first shelter" (*Para.* XVII 70; "lo primo tuo rifugio e 'l primo ostello"), yet in the middle of 1303, Dante was seeking neither refuge nor hospitality (he would return to Verona as a guest and an exile in 1316). In that year he was firmly established in the White gov-ernment in exile, and it was as its representative that he was sent to Verona for the purpose of persuading Bartolomeo to become a member of the anti-Florentine alliance that had recently been formed between the Whites, Bologna, and the cities of Romagna. Bartolomeo, so far as we know, was not persuaded. Dante, who could have dealt swiftly with the task in hand, nevertheless stayed in Verona for some ten months.

Cacciaguida would also express great praise for the liberality of Bar-tolomeo, whose generosity toward Dante is shown in a sort of contest in which his gifts would always succeed in arriving in advance of the requests of his protégé. And this too has all the air of another distortion by Dante, whose admiration for the Della Scala dates from his second stay in Verona. A series of indications suggests, in fact, that the first visit was really somewhat different.

In *Convivio*, to refute the suggestion that "noble" means "being named and known by many," Dante states that, if this were true, then it would also be true that Bartolomeo of Parma, nicknamed Asdente, an illiterate cobbler who was famous because he foretold the future, would be more noble than his fellow citizens and that "Albuino della Scala would be more noble than Guido da Castello di Reggio" (*Conv.* IV XVI 6; "Albuino della Scala sarebbe più nobile che Guido da Castello di Reggio"). To claim that the lord of the powerful city of Verona, well known to everyone by reason of his position, could not compete in terms of nobility with a figure from Reggio Emilia who, though perhaps obscure, was among the last to be able to testify to the values of the "ancient age" was a rather restrictive judgment. It is probable that this is "to be linked to negative experiences from his first visit to Verona."[22]

The treatment that Dante gives to Alberto della Scala, father of Bartolomeo, Alboino, and Cangrande, is insulting and contemptuous. A so-called "abbot at San Zeno at Verona / under the imperial reign of good Barbarossa" (*Purg.* XVIII 118–119; "abate in San Zeno a Verona / sotto lo 'mperio del buon Barbarossa"), foretelling his imminent death (in September 1301) and condemnation to Hell, accuses him of having appointed an illegitimate son (Giuseppe) as abbot of San Zeno, contrary to canon law, who moreover was "diseased in his whole body, / and worse in mind, and ill-born" (*Purg.* XVIII 124–125; "mal del corpo intero, / e de la mente peggio, e che mal nacque"), in other words, a bastard, crippled and morally if not mentally diseased. And all for greed, so that he could control this abbey's substantial estates. Would he have insulted the father of his own patrons so harshly unless they had given him good reason? Could the hospitality in Verona on that first occasion have been much less courteous than Dante would want it to be thought twelve or so years later? But if this is so, why did Dante stay so long at that court instead of returning to Forlì or Arezzo?[23]

The irresistible charm of a library

The poet Cecco Angiolieri of Siena replied in rhyme, literally and metaphorically, to a lost sonnet in which Dante harshly attacked him. Dante's attack and Cecco's answer (*Dante Alleghier, s'i' so' buon begolardo* [*Dante Alighieri, if I am a charlatan*]) date from the time of his stay in Verona: "if I am Roman, and you Lombard" ("s'io so' fatto romano, e tu Lombardo"), writes Cecco, and we know that the people of Verona were regarded as Lombards. Replying one by one to the accusations against him, Cecco tells Dante: if I'm a braggart, then you're no different to me, indeed it's true that our behavior is identical: I, as you say, dine at the table of others, but you are a regular at that table; I try to get myself the best morsels, but you aim for the fat, the best part; I try to gain the maximum profit from it, and you even more. Let us therefore stop reproaching each other for what we do: if we are reduced to such a state, it's through misfortune or our dimwittedness. From Angiolieri's argument it would seem that both are in the service or employment of someone (Cecco perhaps in Rome, Dante in Verona) so that Dante cannot start giving himself airs of grandeur and teaching others about life: he too is managing as best he can as a client-parasite. But a third rhymester intervenes in the dispute, Guelfo Taviani of Pistoia (known for having corresponded in rhyme with his fellow citizen Cino). Addressing Cecco (*Cecco Angelier, tu mi pari un musardo* [*Cecco Angiolieri, you seem to me a fool*]), he defends Dante: Cecco cannot start criticizing a great philosopher while forgetting that philosophers scorn wealth and use their minds not for material gain but solely to improve their knowledge. This is a naive position, and yet, just for once, the simplicity of a sincere admirer seems to have hit the mark much more than Angiolieri's smart cynicism. It is likely in fact that it was his very love of "knowledge" that kept Dante in that "Lombard" city in which he received few satisfactions.[24]

From the day he left Florence, Dante had had to interrupt his studies. This must have been a sad sacrifice for someone who, for over ten years, had devoted almost all his time to philosophy and literature. No libraries in the castles of the Tuscan-Romagna Apennines or in the cities of Romagna could have matched his needs, and he certainly couldn't have afforded his own books.

In Verona Dante found one of the most extraordinary libraries existing at that time in Europe, the Biblioteca Capitolare, consisting of works dating back to the fifth and sixth centuries amassed by the cathedral chapter. By the mid-1200s, its collection of books, including a wealth of classical texts, had given great momentum to the rediscovery of ancient authors, and would continue to do so during the time of Petrarch. There, Dante would have found books unknown in Florence or even in Bologna, and we can imagine him becoming absorbed in reading them. In *De vulgari eloquentia,* written not long after his first stay in Verona, and which some scholars even date to that visit, he lists a number of Latin writers—Livy, Pliny (whether the Elder or the Younger isn't clear), Frontinus, and Orosius—all of whom, except for Orosius, were hardly known at that time, who in his words "have produced the highest prose," and he alludes to "many others" that a "solicitous friend" invited him to read. Books by these authors were to be found precisely here, at the Biblioteca Capitolare in Verona, and the friend who took the trouble to guide his reading might even have been someone connected to that library, someone he had come to know there, who carried on advising him (by letter?) even after he had moved away from Verona.[25]

One of the typical features of Dante's personality, which qualifies him as an "intellectual" in the modern sense of the word, is his endless reflection on what he is doing, both as an author and as a man. The main motivations for his writing come from what he himself has seen, experienced, and said; and so he relies on the *hic et nunc,* on what is happening around him, on public and private accounts of events. Another characteristic is that of arranging the details of an experience into a theoretical or conceptual framework that explains them, and thus of rising to higher levels of generalization. Bearing in mind these aspects of his way of conceiving literature and intellectual practice, it is difficult to imagine that his studies in Verona were ends in themselves, dictated simply by a love of knowledge. It is more likely that he had developed or was developing a project, and that his studies were in fact directed toward accomplishing it—a project that started off from a reflection on what he had seen and experienced since he had become an exile at war against his own city. Dante would have reflected on the strange involvement of the parties in that war, financed and politically managed by bankers, and fought on the field by local feudal lords and soldiers of noble birth; he would have reflected on the fact that while the bankers obtained no appreciable advantage, the feudal lords and noblemen could settle old scores with Florence, carry out long-awaited vendettas, and earn vast amounts of money, passing with ease from one side to the other. And this would have led him to think about the incurable blindness of a "middle" class that thought everything could be sorted out through the power of wealth, and the lack of vision of a noble and feudal class that had no special political project of its own and had in fact placed itself at the service of its enemy cities. In short, he would have begun to meditate on the role of the nobility, on how to save it from decline and bring it back to being the fulcrum of a society ordered and governed by values that were not just those of money. From this came the seed of *Convivio*, and it is by no means improbable that he had begun to write it during those very months spent in Verona. From his point of view as an intellectual, it was a way of continuing the battle, indeed with more ambitious objectives. This doesn't rule out the possibility that, from a practical point of view, it was also a way of withdrawing. In other words, weariness and dissatisfaction may have had something to do with his decision to prolong his stay in that city.

Traveling around the Venetian cities

In the first book of *De vulgari eloquentia* (a work we can ascribe to the second half of 1304), Dante demonstrates a remarkable familiarity with the dialects of the Veneto region, so that he can give precise and accurate phonetic details about the dialects of Padua, Treviso, and Venice.[26] Only a few years later, in *Convivio* and *Inferno*, he would also show a great knowledge of places: he would describe Treviso, naming the rivers Sile and Cagnano (now Botteniga) that converge there; he would describe the dikes the people of Padua built along the Brenta before the thaw that swells the rivers with Alpine water, the landslide that occurred south of Trento (and not far from Verona) on the left bank of the Adige, and the feverish labor of the workers at the Arsenale in Venice. Linguistic skill and familiarity with places presupposes a direct experience, which Dante may have gained during his stay in Verona.[27]

But we cannot imagine Dante traveling as he pleased around the cities of Venice, spurred along by interest or curiosity, for at least two good reasons. First, Dante had been banished and was under sentence of death, and this meant he no longer enjoyed the protection of Florence. He could be killed legitimately, and therefore with impunity, by anyone. A banished person living under constant threat of death had to carefully consider every movement and, so far as possible, travel under the protection of friends. In the midst of the current war, could a White fugitive like Dante have appeared in Treviso at the court of Gherardo and Rizzardo da Camino, who were well known for their close links both with the Blacks but in particular with the Este family of Ferrara, among the bitterest enemies of the Whites? And yet we can suppose that he did, and indeed that he was received with a "courtesy" greater than that shown by the Della Scala family, as his praises for the Camino brothers a few years later testify. Second, we cannot imagine Dante as a tourist for obvious but very practical economic reasons. As he had not returned from his mission to Verona, it is probable that the Coalition of the Whites had stopped paying him, bringing an end to his only source of support. With what resources would he have traveled between Verona and Venice?

These considerations give credence to the idea that, in exchange for hospitality and maybe some gratuity, Dante might have carried out some occasional services for the Della Scala family. If, among these services, there had been some diplomatic assignment, this would then explain how, equipped with a safe-conduct, he could have moved freely around the region.

At that very time, in the summer of 1303, a dispute had begun between Padua and Venice over control of the salt trade from Chioggia, over which Venice held a monopoly.[28] On that occasion, Treviso and Verona offered to act as mediators. The matter dragged on with much changing of positions (Treviso sided with Venice, and Verona with Padua) until 1306. The idea that Dante, well informed about the background that influenced the movements of the Della Scala and Camino families in the affair, was sent by Verona to visit Treviso, Padua, and Venice in connection with the negotiations that were going on between those cities would therefore not be out of the question. The lords of Treviso ended up siding with Venice, persuaded above all by their grudge against the Paduans, a grudge caused by the fact that certain bankers and money-lenders in Padua kept a hold over those lords for money they had loaned them twenty years earlier. First among these moneylenders was Reginaldo degli Scrovegni, whose son Enrico is known to history not for being a banker but for having built a family chapel that he commissioned Giotto to decorate.[29]

"Color of ash is how the Whites have become"

From the early months of his papacy, Benedict XI sent clear signs of wanting to change his predecessor's policy in regard to Romagna, Montefeltro, and Tuscany. His councilor was a learned fellow Dominican, Niccolò da Prato, whom he had elevated to cardinal shortly after being elected to the papal throne. The new cardinal would play a most important role, from the papacy of Clement V onward, in making Avignon the most dynamic and innovative cultural center in Europe.[30] For the moment he had a reputation for being a Ghibelline sympathizer and friend of the Whites. Such friendship could be ascribed to the pope himself, who ousted the traditional Black bankers (in particular the Spini and Bardi) from managing the papal finances and replaced them with the White Cerchi. Benedict decided to intervene directly in the complex Florentine question and appointed Niccolò da Prato on January 31, 1304 as apostolic legate in Tuscany, Romagna, and in the March of Treviso, with the specific task of restoring peace in Florence. The legate, however, would only make his solemn entry into Florence a month later, on March 2. What delayed his arrival was the outbreak of violent internal clashes in the Black faction.

A constant feature of Florentine history during the period of the commune is that the political winners, having once eliminated their adversaries, split into opposing factions, and the new rivalry led, as before, to armed fighting. The Blacks were no exception. The two parties into which they divided were headed by Corso Donati and Rosso Della Tosa.[31] In February of that year, supporters of the Donati and Tosa factions fought in armed combat through the streets of the city. Murder, looting, and arson followed, and the fighting calmed down only thanks to the intervention of troops from Lucca, who occupied the city, though only briefly.

On March 2, 1304, the cardinal legate was welcomed with great pomp by a population tired of living in the midst of violence; on March 17 he was granted full control of the city. Having achieved his purpose of restoring peace between the factions, the cardinal began to carry out his ambitious but ill-considered plan to reconcile the Blacks with the White and Ghibelline exiles. It was a plan that envisaged a formal peace conference, to be held in Florence, at which representatives of all parties concerned would have to take part, each to be invited by letter or, better still, by personal summons.[32]

In practical terms, the negotiations between the cardinal legate and the parties for the arrangement of the peace meeting must have been fairly arduous. This can be gleaned from the letter dictated by Dante in which the *capitano* (who at that time must have been Aghinolfo di Romena), the Council, and the Coalition of the Whites, in obedience to the requests made to them by the cardinal himself by letter and in person by his envoy, "a man of holy piety, friar L. councilor of urbanity and peace," declare that they would "refrain from every act of war" and "submit to the decision" of the cardinal "with spontaneous and sincere willingness," as "the aforesaid friar L." would be able to confirm.[33] This nuncio who enjoyed the full trust of the cardinal must almost certainly have been the Dominican friar Lapo da Prato, appointed advocate general in 1303, and a close, lifelong collaborator of Niccolò da Prato, as well as the executor of his will.[34] The writer of the letter felt it necessary to apologize for the "unforgivable delay" and for "lacking due swiftness" in responding, and invites the illustrious recipient to consider, as an excuse, "what and how many opinions and points of view, given the sincerity of our alliance, are necessary for our Brotherhood to proceed properly; and after having given due consideration to the questions we face."[35] And so, all of a sudden, a narrow crack appears, through which we can catch a glimpse of how the Coalition of the Whites operated, and we can at least imagine how slow and laborious the decision-making process must have been, with its meetings, opinions, and discussions.

Twelve representatives of the Ghibellines and Whites converged, at last, on Florence to negotiate with twelve members of the Blacks. The White delegates included (as secretary?) the notary Petracco di Parenzo, who was soon to become father of Petrarch. A climate of optimism spread across the city. Almost a century of hatred seemed magically to disappear. Lapo di Azzolino degli Uberti, banished as long before as 1283 and now returning as a member of the Ghibelline delegation, was respectfully received as he passed through the city streets. A population worn out by continual conflicts wanted to cancel out the memory of violence in February that had stained the city with blood.

The urge for peace among the lower classes had also stirred the magnates of the Black party. Now faced by a growing movement in favor of negotiation, Corso Donati and Rosso Della Tosa quickly settled their differences and put themselves at the head of the opposing faction. They realized that any agreement would involve some concession of power to their defeated enemies, and they had no intention whatsoever of giving way. So they began to hinder the cardinal's work more and more persistently, first, to gain time, by persuading him to go to Prato to carry out his peacekeeping there as well, and then by creating an atmosphere of growing fear and tension around the exiled delegates and the families in the city who were supporting them. The situation deteriorated to the point where Niccolò da Prato decided to safeguard the delegates by accommodating them in Palazzo Mozzi, where he himself was staying. But this was not enough to deal with the disorder that the Blacks had begun to stir up, and on June 8 Niccolò had to advise the Whites and Ghibellines to leave Florence. At this point the violence grew in intensity and was directed against traditionally White families such as the Cavalcanti and the Cerchi. On June 10 the cardinal himself fled the city, against which he imposed an interdict.

That same day, even before the cardinal had left the city, the Blacks began setting fire to the houses of the Whites. Fire destroyed the homes of the Caponsacchi, Abati, and Sacchetti families and then spread through the many properties of the Cavalcanti. Within a short time the city center was ablaze and, fanned by the wind, it gutted an extensive area between the new marketplace and the Arno. Over 1,400 houses, palaces, towers, workshops, and warehouses were burned down that day. Naturally, there were many deaths and many acts of looting. The manufacturing center of Florence was destroyed since "in those buildings there was almost the whole mercantile trade." "In short," in the words of Villani, "the whole marrow and yolk and places dear in the city of Florence burned down."[36] For the Cavalcanti family, whose income came from renting workshops and houses, it was a very heavy blow.

In the face of such a disaster, we might expect it to have brought some kind of civic solidarity. But the word "solidarity" was unknown in Florence during that period. After the fire, Guido Orlandi, a Black politician belonging to the Rustichelli family of magnates from the Porta San Piero district and a writer of old-fashioned verse, often in dispute with Guido Cavalcanti, began a sonnet that oozes political hatred with the words: "Color of ash is how the Whites have become."[37]

The Blacks had won the battle against the cardinal legate, but they had also discovered that their power in the city could be questioned and had seen the danger of a coalition that enjoyed the open support of the pope. So they tightened their traditional links with the Angevin rulers of Naples and, having reorganized the Guelf league of Tuscan cities, they elected Robert, Duke of Calabria and heir to Charles II of France, as its head.

The Whites had lost the battle, but not the war. The pope, outraged by what had happened, summoned to Perugia representatives of the Commune and of the families that had taken part in the conflicts, and they obeyed. But Benedict XI died unexpectedly on July 7.

The situation for the Whites had become critical. After internal debate in which there must have been conflicting views, they made a hurried decision to set up a military alliance. Having gained the support of Pistoia, Bologna, Arezzo, and Pisa, they decided, rightly, that the best solution would be to move quickly and attack Florence before Robert arrived from Naples with his troops. At that moment the city lacked military defenses. And so on July 19 they camped at La Lastra, three kilometers from the walls of Florence, on the Bologna road. Their forces were overwhelming, but they made two disastrous errors: they failed to wait for all the allied forces to arrive before attacking on several fronts, in closed ranks, nor did they even exploit the element of surprise. On July 20, in full daylight, the exiles attacked from the north while the troops from Bologna, having just arrived, decided to wait for the troops from Pisa and Pistoia. The exiles entered the city and fought in the center of Florence, in the square in front of the Baptistery. But the attackers were eventually forced to withdraw. Their retreat led the troops from Bologna and Pistoia to believe the battle was lost, and they decided to turn back. So an easy victory was transformed into defeat. The Whites and Ghibellines would continue fighting for many years, but after the defeat at La Lastra their prospects of success diminished almost to the point of vanishing.

On the day of that battle, Francesco Petrarca (Petrarch) was born in Arezzo.

"Sad poverty"

In mid-February 1304 Dante was still in Verona. On February 15 he watched the famous race that took place on the first Sunday of Lent, the winner of which was awarded a length of green cloth; he would recall it when describing how quickly Brunetto Latini ran off naked over the burning sand: "Then he turned back, and seemed one of those / who runs at Verona for the green cloth / through the countryside; and he seemed to be / the one among them that wins, not he who loses" (*Inf.* XV 121–124; "Poi si rivolse, e parve di coloro / che corrono a Verona il drappo verde / per la campagna; e parve di costoro / quelli che vince, non colui che perde"). Bartolomeo della Scala died on March 7 and power passed to Alboino, who was little loved by Dante. But what persuaded him to leave Verona and return to his companions in the Coalition must have been the news that Cardinal Niccolò da Prato had been appointed peacemaker and had entered Florence on March 2. In the face of an event that brought real hope of an end to his exile, Dante could hardly keep away. He moved, perhaps in early March, from Verona to Arezzo, where Aghinolfo, the *capitano* who succeeded Ordelaffi, had safely set up his operational base. The difficulties with Uguccione were more or less over, now that he had sided with the White and Ghibelline alliance, and the Whites could also count on the support of the bishop, his brother Ildebrandino (the true politician among the Guidi of Romena).[38] Dante's long absence (though he had presumably continued to keep in written contact) had not damaged his relations with the ruling group, so much so that it was he who composed (in early April?) the important letter with which the Coalition informed the legate that it accepted all his conditions. It is unclear whether he always remained part of the Council, but he was certainly still the intellectual on whom the alliance relied.

It seems unlikely, however, that he continued to enjoy any regular financial income. Indeed, it would appear that Dante was beset by economic difficulties on his return to Arezzo. This can be deduced from a letter of condolence sent (perhaps in April, though there is no evidence as to the date) to Oberto and Guido di Aghinolfo di Romena on the death of their uncle Alessandro, to whom they were heirs. We can imagine that Dante was in Arezzo and that Alessandro's funeral would have taken place in one of the Guidi castles in the Casentino.

The letter opens with high-flown and lavish praise of the deceased, whom Dante recognized as his lord ("dominus") and whose memory he would preserve as long as he lived. It was a heavy loss, but "the highest nobility of Tuscany, made resplendent by such a man," his friends and

subjects, and he [Dante] himself who, "driven from his home and guilt-
lessly exiled," had found hope in him, can yet console themselves with
the thought that "he who in Tuscany was Palatine count of the Roman
[Imperial] court, now stands in glory, residing in the eternal palace, in
the celestial Jerusalem with the princes of the blessed."[39] But the tone of
the letter then changes: Dante apologizes to his interlocutors for not
being able to take part in the funeral service for their kinsman. His absence is due neither to "negligence" nor "ingratitude" but to the poverty to which his condition of exile has reduced him, and which prevents
him from owning "arms and horses" with which to travel or even from
being presentable at a funeral procession. He is certainly trying to release himself from the slavery into which "merciless" misfortune has
cast him, but his efforts until now have come to nothing.[40] In expressing
once again his loyalty to his patrons, Dante asks for some practical help
to relieve his state of poverty. It is the letter of a "client"; if we were at a
lord's court, rather than in surroundings that were still feudal, we might
describe it as the letter of a "courtier."[41]

The Guidi gave him no help, and Dante would not forgive this lack
of kindness. He would take his revenge in *Inferno*, where he retells an
old story going back to 1281. In that year the Guidi brothers, with the
help of a "relative," a certain Adam de Anglia (Master Adam), had minted
counterfeit gold florins in their castle at Romena, of twenty-one instead
of twenty-four carats. For this extremely serious offense they were convicted in their absence but then, thanks to their conversion to Guelfism,
were soon not only pardoned by amnesty but also awarded public
offices. Dante, however, did not forgive them. He would put Master Adam
the forger in hell for the sole purpose of accusing his masters: it was they,
he says, who at Romena "induced me to mint the florins / that had three
carats of dross" (*Inf.* XXX 89–90; "indussero a batter li fiorini / ch'avean
tre carati di mondiglia") for which he was burned at the stake, and now
his only consolation would be to see there with him "the evil soul /
of Guido or of Alessandro or of their brother" (*Inf.* XXX 76–77; "l'anima
trista / di Guido o d'alessandro o di lor frate"), in other words Guido,
Alessandro, and Aghinolfo. In truth, continues Master Adam, one soul
is already there, that of the oldest brother Guido (who may have died at
Campaldino), but though he (Adam) cannot move because the pain of

dropsy prevents him from walking, that doesn't stop his satisfaction at the thought of going off in search of him to enjoy his suffering. Master Adam's hatred is the same as Dante's himself, who has no hesitation in predicting hell for that very same Alessandro who, just a few years earlier, he had put in the celestial court.[42] And it should be remembered that at the time he was writing *Inferno*—indeed, at the time of its "publication" in the second half of 1314—Aghinolfo was still alive; he would die an old man in 1338. When he placed his one-time patrons in Hell, Dante would have been stirred by political motives: not those of a Florentine devoted to his coinage but, as we shall see, those of a banished Florentine who in trying to return to his home city casts off and condemns his comrades in arms. At the same time he would be moved by more personal motives, those of a client and kinsman betrayed, who wreaks his revenge for the lack of generosity with which he was treated.

Apparent in the letter to Alessandro's heirs is also the reason for his poverty caused by his state as an exile. This theme is to be found, in more or less veiled terms, in much of his subsequent output, but it is particularly desperate and insistent in the years 1303 and 1304. In the early pages of *Convivio* he admits to all his hardships and, what is more, all his shame, since in those times a "punishment of exile and poverty" led to such a state: "a wanderer, almost a beggar, I went about, showing unwillingly the wound of fortune, for which the person wounded is often unjustly held responsible. In truth I have been a ship with no sail and with no rudder, carried to various ports and inlets and shores by the dry wind that blows sad poverty" (*Conv.* I III 4–5; "peregrine, quasi mendicando, sono andato, mostrando contra mia voglia la piaga della fortuna, che suole ingiustamente al piagato molte volte essere imputata. // Veramente io sono stato legno sanza vela e sanza governo, portato a diversi porti e foci e liti dal vento secco che vapora la dolorosa povertade"). In the spring of 1304, Dante's financial situation had become so unbearable that his brother Francesco was forced to leave Florence and go to Arezzo to his aid. There, on May 13, at the house of a notary, in the presence of two witnesses—an apothecary from Arezzo with a German name and a second from Arezzo, by the name of Baldinetto di Scorzone—Francesco contracted a loan with Foglione di Giobbo, apothecary, of twelve gold florins, guaranteed by a surety bond signed by

Capontozzo dei Lamberti of Florence.[43] Was the presence of so many apothecaries coincidental? Perhaps it is more likely that Dante's enrollment with that guild a decade earlier had created around him a network of relationships which he had partly maintained after his exile. In short, those apothecaries, whether lenders or guarantors, were there for him, not for Francesco. Francesco is simply a nominee, since someone in Dante's situation could certainly not have had access to any kind of credit. Twelve gold florins was not a large amount, but neither was it exactly negligible. Dante may have had some debts to pay, but what was left over would have given him enough resources for some time.

It has been suggested that he wanted the money his brother obtained to get away from the other exiles—in other words, that Dante had decided to get out of active politics. It is true that in Verona he had rediscovered the pleasure of study, that he had planned out the great philosophical treatise that would become *Convivio* and which, most probably, he had even started to write. It is therefore understandable that he should want to return as soon as possible to an intellectual life in a city where there were books, and people who could read and understand them. Nevertheless, bearing in mind the time needed for Francesco to get to Arezzo and the time required by the procedures for the loan, that decision would have been taken in April or early May at the latest, in other words during the height of the peace negotiations being carried out in Florence. Dante must have been following these negotiations through the dispatches sent by the delegates. He had moved from the Veneto precisely to be close to events, and perhaps to influence them with his counsel and advice. Would he have decided to distance himself at such a moment when all was still possible and his great desire to return home was still attainable? That seems hard to believe.

Dante certainly did take the decision to break from the party leadership and distance himself from the theater of war, but that must have been later, at least after Niccolò da Prato's flight from Florence on June 10, or even after the pope's death on July 7. We know nothing about his relations with his companions during the stage leading up to his departure. It is possible that, in the discussion within the alliance following the failure of Niccolò da Prato's mediation, he had opposed the decision to move quickly and attack Florence before the arrival of the Angevin reinforcements. It is possible, in other words, that even after the death of Benedict XI he had wanted to support the peacekeeping initiatives of the legate and, more generally, of the Church. From the early commentaries there seems to be a vague suggestion of disagreements between him and the others. Whatever happened, it is almost certain that on the day of the defeat at La Lastra he was already a long way away.[44]

6

Return to Study
and Writing

1304–1306

it will be good for you
to have made a party unto yourself

a te fia bello
averti fatta parte per te stesso

—*Para.* XVII 68–69

Dante's tutor

ONCE DANTE has parted company with his companions in exile, the already scarce documentation thins to the point of almost disappearing. From now on, we can fill in the details of his life only through circumstantial reconstruction. Even the first stop on his wanderings, after leaving his companions in the middle of 1304, can be worked out only by conjecture. But everything leads us to think it was Bologna.[1]

Dante had stayed there during the 1280s and had perhaps gone back during the 1290s: it was therefore a place he knew and where he was known, both as poet and politician.[2] The descendants of Bellino di Lapo had lived there for several decades, moving between the city and San Giovanni in Persiceto, and perhaps also the children of Cione di Bello, brother of the murdered Geri. Dante could therefore have relied on this branch of the Alighieri clan if necessary.[3] Bologna was also a good place for finding an income, a problem faced each time he moved.[4] The city was full of university students who had to acquire a good command of Latin, and to whom he could have given private grammar lessons.[5] But the intellectual atmosphere in Bologna was valuable for other reasons: busy with his project for the philosophical treatise, only in Bologna could he have found the people with whom to discuss and develop his ideas, as well as the modern philosophy texts he couldn't have found even at the library in Verona, specializing as it did in the classics. Lastly—though this was essential for an exile convicted as a rebel—in Bologna he found a regime friendly to the Whites, to the extent that Bologna had fought beside them and the Ghibellines in the campaign that had ended in the disastrous defeat at La Lastra.

We might object, as some have done, that if Dante had entered Bologna in early summer of 1304, having just split from his own political party, he would have been regarded by the Whites, including those of Bologna, as a traitor, and would have been treated as such. In *Paradiso,* through the mouth of Cacciaguida, he not only expresses contempt for his ex-comrades in arms—"wicked and foolish company" (*Para.* XVII 62; "la compagnia malvagia e scempia")—but speaks specifically of an angry, irrational, and heartless reaction toward him: "that all ungrateful, all mad and pitiless / they will turn on you" (*Para.* XVII 64–65; "che tutta ingrata, tutta matta ed empia / si farà contr' a te"). These, however, are comments made quite some time after the event (around 1316), and so the relationship the author Dante seems to establish in that canto between the hostility of his comrades and the events leading up to the defeat at La Lastra has to be interpreted in the light of an attitude (Dante's self-fashioning as prophet) that tempers his relationship with that far-off historic moment. Closer however (dating perhaps from 1307) is the reconstruction in the canto in *Inferno,* where Brunetto Latini would say to Dante that both factions, both Black and White, wanted to devour him but that he would escape from their hunger—"one party and the other will be hungry / for you; but keep the grass far from the goat" (*Inf.* XV 71–72; "l'una parte e l'altra avranno fame / di te; ma lungi fia dal becco l'erba"), though without specifying when this would happen. Now it is true that his ex-comrades rose against him, and Dante did in effect become a traitor, but not in 1304, after La Lastra. The angry and pitiless attitude he describes presupposes a public gesture, in word or deed, of breaking ties which seriously harmed the honor of the Whites and, above all, which tainted its author with an air of betrayal. At this moment, Dante's departure from his companions was not accompanied or followed by anything of the kind: he had already been off for many months the previous year, and this had had no adverse effect on his relationship with the Coalition of the Whites.

Instruction for the Italian nobility: *Convivio*

Dante had had many important experiences over the previous four or five years.[6] He had discovered to his cost how the structure of the commune system tended to lead to division and how internal rivalry spilled out into continual warring between one city and another, and between cities and the remnants of ancient feudal dominions. He had seen how a society whose primary objective was economic gain knew no other rules than those of competition, and how a capitalism whose aim was to amass wealth was not interested in the values of culture and public ethics. There were no restraints that could at least curb the constant succession of civil conflicts and warring between cities, the alternation of regimes that wavered between despotism and oligarchy, the smashing of alliances and continual acts of betrayal—in short, everything that seemed to him to mark disorder and chaos. But, worse than that, the very institutions that should have had a controlling function were fueling these conflicts. Now that the central power of the empire had diminished, Europe was split into monarchies that followed the same policies of rivalry and bullying as those of the Italian cities and feudal lords, but on a much wider scale. The Church, instead of playing a role that fostered peace and security, was itself the cause of instability, as events in Florence had shown: its intrusions, often without even the slightest lawful justification, stirred up discord and divided Christendom.

But Dante had also discovered a different political and social reality during his years in exile. Among the descendants of the great feudal domains of the Tuscan and Romagna Apennines he had come to know a world which, unlike that of Florence, did not appear to place economic advantage at the top of its list of values, which guaranteed a hierarchical order in a society where there was no place for parties and factions, which regulated or claimed to regulate public affairs according to a code of honor based on "worth" and merit, on "courtesy" and loyalty of conduct and, above all, which assured the continuity of institutions and styles of government. In short, a different world to the one he had seen until then. Or rather, potentially different. Dante, in fact, clearly understood how the market logic of the cities had profoundly corrupted the behavior of the nobility, that what survived was no more than a relic of the past, that their politics were either subordinate to those of the economic and financial centers or strongly influenced by them, or else anchored to a vision of the world that was destined to disappear. And yet he believed that this class was still capable of returning to the center of political and social life, and would therefore be able to reestablish an ordered and peaceful society. To do so, it had to become aware of what its values were: to rebuild a culture of its own that had been largely lost and, above all, to rediscover a cohesion that had been shattered by the pressure of the city communes.

The philosophical treatise on which he worked in Bologna, *Convivio* (*The Banquet*), is addressed to a readership that is scattered across the map but which is socially well-defined: "princes, barons, knights, and many other noble folk, not just men but women, who are many in this language, who know only the vernacular and are not learned" (*Conv.* I IX 5; "principi, baroni, cavalieri, e molt'altra nobile gente, non solamente maschi ma femmine, che sono molti e molte in questa lingua, volgari, e non litterati"); he seeks to stimulate their awareness by offering them a cultural base. This will be the "food" served to all those who, to satisfy their hunger for knowledge, would sit at this "table" and take part in the "banquet."

It was Dante himself, in the years before his exile, who had sought to teach the powerful men of Florence what true nobility was, and what behavior was proper for a nobleman. In those years, as a man of the commune, he identified nobility with gentility of spirit, in other words with sensibility and refinement that could be acquired through culture. Dante was therefore describing himself, but standing before a completely different audience and with very different purposes. His position now was anti-municipal. The pivot of the argument in *Convivio*, in fact, is that

Italian nobles—nobles by birth, of course—must become the class which under the protection of the Empire guarantees "the existence of a *civilitas* that is human, cohesive and peaceful."[7]

The horizon had therefore broadened out to encompass the political and institutional framework of the whole of Christendom. To ensure that disruptive pressures are controlled and that peace reigns among the people of God, one needs to have a universal institution that regulates the relationships between monarchies and individual states on the basis of a common good and which, at the same time, controls the over-arching power of the Church, which is the cause of conflict and corruption, returning it to the spiritual realm and keeping temporal jurisdiction for itself alone. This institution can only be the empire, all the more since it is the source of the legitimate power of the great feudal dynasties who constitute the mainstays of this utopian design. For a man brought up in an Italian city commune, the sudden ideological change of tack couldn't be more clear-cut. With this, Dante becomes a Ghibelline: his utopia, in effect, envisages overcoming party divisions, beginning with the ruinous division between the "party of the empire" and the "party of the Church."

The empire, however, was inactive, distant, and for many years had shown no interest in Italy. In the absence of those unifying poles of the imperial *aula* (the court) and its *curia* (the administration), the scattered Italian nobility had to find other forms of aggregation, to establish a virtual court on a shared cultural foundation. The key points in the plan were two: a redefinition of the concept of nobility and of the implications arising from it in terms of conduct (it has been suggested that Dante wanted to "explain what was true nobility to an audience of nobles"), and the identification of the vernacular language as the instrument with which to unify the scattered members of the Italian nobility.

The ethics of giving

The original plan for *Convivio*—to be written in prose and verse, like the *Vita Nova*—consisted of fourteen books preceded by an introduction: each book was to open with a canzone followed by a commentary in vernacular prose. But work stopped at the end of the fourth book. Dante had already written most, though not all, of the canzoni in 1303–1304.

One of those that he wrote now, specifically for the treatise he was working on (which he would probably have commented on in the final book) dealt with a topic closely linked to that of nobility.

The canzone *Doglia mi reca ne lo core ardire* (*Pain stirs boldness in my heart*) is a bitter and resentful attack on meanness, the worst of uncourtly vices, which kills generosity, one of the foundations of noble behavior.[8] It is an attack, not against the "powerful men" of the city, those to whom his canzoni of ten years earlier had been addressed, in which Dante had set himself up as a teacher of "courtesy" to those city aristocrats who needed to learn the rules and values of true noble behavior, but against the heirs of the ancient feudal nobility who ought to be the natural depositaries in those values and, yet, have forgotten or misconstrued them. It is symptomatic that, whereas in the canzone on charm (*leggadria*), *Poscia ch'Amor del tutto m'ha lasciato* (*Since love has wholly abandoned me*), he had stigmatized the improper use of wealth by "knights" and Florentine parvenus, exhibitionists, and prodigals, all devoted to luxury and extravagance, Dante now, in addressing those who were noble by tradition, concentrated on the opposite vice, that of avarice and on the lack of generosity, on the "immoderate" tendency to accumulate. The main prerogative of courteous conduct is the gift, the just and proper largition of money, spontaneously offered: these days, however, nobles resolve to give only on being asked, showing in their countenance how much that gesture is a burden to them, and thus they transform the gift into something that resembles a sale—and moreover at a high price, as he who receives that charity well knows: "those with delay and those with vain look, / those with sad expression / turn giving into sale and he who buys / alone knows how it costs him dear" (*Rime* 46, 119–122; "chi con tardare e chi con vana vista, / chi con sembianza trista / volge 'l donare in vender tanto caro / quanto sa sol chi tal compera paga"). This is not the behavior of a nobleman but of a merchant or a businessman. Dante sees clearly that the feudal nobility on which his project of social regeneration depends is deeply tainted by the logic of the market economy. He sees it because he has experienced it personally. In the lines quoted, one feels the "unmistakable flavor of a painful autobiographical experience."[9]

The canzone must have been written in the second half of 1304, after Dante had suffered disappointment at the courts of the Della Scala and the Guidi of Romena. And there is an explicit reference to the Guidi in the closing lines: "Dear song, there is a lady near here / who is from our land; / beautiful, wise and courteous / is how they all call her, and no one notices / when they use her name / calling Bianca, Giovanna, Contessa. / Go you to her, demure and honest" (*Rime* 46, 148–154; "Canzone, presso di qui è una donna / ch'è del nostro paese; / bella, saggia e cortese / la chiaman tutti, e neun se n'accorge / quando suo nome porge / Bianca, Giovanna, Contessa chiamando. / A costei te ne va chiusa e onesta"). The Tuscan lady ("from our land"), to whom the canzone is sent, lives in a place close to where Dante is writing ("near here"); her name is Bianca Giovanna Contessa, a name which, translated, means "beautiful, wise, courteous."[10] Countess Bianca Giovanna was, in fact, a Guidi of the Ghibelline branch from Bagno. She was daughter of Count Guido Novello (son-in-law of Manfredi) and sister of Federico Novello, who would be recalled in Canto VI of *Purgatorio* among those killed violently. Her second marriage had been to Saracino, one of the Ghibelline family of Bonacolsi of Mantua.[11] Both Saracino and his father Tagino had fled from Mantua after a family feud and taken refuge in Ferrara at the court of Azzo VIII d'Este, therefore close to Bologna.

The dedication to Countess Bianca Giovanna is part of the general line of the canzone, which, while dealing with moral, social, and philosophical issues, takes the form of a lesson to women, who are invited to assess carefully the courtly worth of their suitors and grant their love only to those who actually show they possess it. But Dante's choice of a woman in the Guidi family to carry out this role of certifying the true inner nobility of men who claim themselves to be noble seems significant: the question of nobility now lies entirely within feudal bounds and can only be clearly answered within such bounds.

The question of nobility was something very close to Dante's heart, something with which he felt intimately involved: it should be remembered that nobility, for him, was the basis of virtue, and not vice versa, as we might perhaps think. *Convivio* represents a transitional stage between the positions he held during his years in Florence and those he would take in *Paradiso*. At first sight, although his interlocutors had changed, Dante doesn't seem to have altered his ideas about nobility. Of the instructive canzoni written in Florence only *Le dolci rime* is included and commented in the part of *Convivio* that he actually wrote. The ideas put forward in the commentary don't differ very much from those put forward in the canzone. Yet there is a notable change in the context in which the arguments on nobility are expressed. While he, the urban Guelf, treated Emperor Frederick II with condescension in the canzone ("A certain emperor described nobility . . ."), in *Convivio* the comment itself is preceded by a long preamble in which Dante, though he distances himself from the emperor, speaks of the historical need for the empire and discusses its providential origin. That imperial ideology, which would lead him to profoundly rethink his ideas on nobility, here takes on a complete form for the first time. But one revision, of no small account, has in fact already been made. Dante goes on to say that nobility is a personal gift which is not transmittable "by stock," in other words not dependent on birth and lineage, but he now thinks that God and nature concentrate the gift of nobility "for the most part" in those born of good lineage and that the quality of a lineage is obtained by the number of individuals of nobility that the family has generated. In this way he opens the way to a new evaluation of hereditary nobility.

Promotion of the vernacular

Over the previous five years, at least since his pilgrimage to Rome for the Jubilee, Dante had made another discovery—that the Italian language was much more fragmented than he had believed when he knew only the Tuscan and Bologna dialects.[12] There is a sense almost of amazement in the words with which he asks why "the speech of the right side of Italy [differs] from that of the left (for example the people of Padua speak one way and those of Pisa another); and why also those who live close together still differ in their speech, such as the people of Milan and Verona, or of Rome and Florence, and even those who belong to the same people, such as those of Naples and Gaeta, Ravenna and Faenza, and lastly, what is most astonishing, those living in the same city, like the Bolognese of Borgo San Felice and the Bolognese of Strada Maggiore" (*VE* I IX 4; "et quare quelibet istarum variationum in se ipsa variatur, puta dextre Ytalie locutio ab ea que est sinistre (nam aliter Paduani et aliter Pisani locuntur); et quare vicinius habitantes adhuc discrepant in loquendo, ut Mediolanenses et Veronenses, Romani et Florentini, nec non convenientes in eodem genere gentis, ut Neapoletani et Caetani, Ravennates et Faventini, et, quod mirabilius est, sub eadem civilitate morantes, ut Bononienses Burgi sancti Felicis et Bononienses Strate Maioris"). The man who had lived almost entirely within the walls of a single city finds unexpected horizons opening before him; other cities and other cultural and linguistic traditions attract his attention, arouse his interest: the municipal man regards himself as a citizen of the world ("nos autem, cui mundus est patria").[13]

Dante realizes that the Italian ruling classes have no common language. In the past it had been Latin, but now he has to admit—and as author of elaborate diplomatic letters written on behalf of the Coalition of the Whites, he was well aware of it—that "princes, barons, knights, and many other noble people" are people who "speak the vernacular, are not learned"; they know no Latin. From being a language of communication for the upper classes, Latin had become a specialist language, the prerogative of university academics and the higher professional ranks. For these cultural elites, whom Dante identifies as "lawyers, doctors, and almost all clerics" (*Conv.* III XI 10; "legisti, li medici e quasi tutti li religiosi"), the purpose of knowing Latin is not the pursuit of individual "happiness" and the common good, but that of advantage and gain: "they do not acquire the [Latin] language for its own sake, but for that of gaining money or status" (*Conv.* I IX 3; "non acquistano la lettera per lo suo uso, ma in quanto per quella guadagnano denari o dignitate"). In short, the direction that high culture was taking through the university system was of no use for rebuilding a common fabric for the scattered Italian nobility.

To unify a nobility that was politically, geographically, and linguistically divided it was necessary, in the face of so many forms of vernacular language, to have a new instrument with a role similar to that played by Latin in the past: a language was required that contained the characteristics of selectivity, uniformity, dignity, and stability. This language didn't yet exist, but in Dante's brilliant utopian vision it would be a reformed vernacular, purified of local particularities and features, rendered "illustrious," stable and uniform like Latin, which was an artificial language and therefore described as "grammar." This vernacular could become the instrument for political and cultural communication among those noble classes who, thanks to its distinguishing influence, could once again be the backbone of society. In short, Dante's vision was that the nobility could be regenerated by giving new form to the language of merchants, of bankers, of the city middle classes, in other words by appropriating the weapons of its traditional enemies. His utopian dream envisaged a reformed vernacular that could even eventually supersede Latin: "This will be a new light, a new sun, which will rise where the old one set, and it will give light to those who are in darkness and obscurity, for the old sun that doesn't shine on them" (*Conv.* I XIII 12; "Questo sarà luce nuova, sole nuovo, lo quale surgerà là dove l'usato tramonterà, e darà lume a coloro che sono in tenebre e in oscuritade, per lo usato sole che a loro non luce").

De vulgari eloquentia

While Dante was discovering how extremely fragmented the natural languages were, he also conceived the idea that their diversification and instability was due to their change over time. To understand how brilliant this idea was, it has to be remembered that he used concepts and ways of investigation that were entirely unconventional. The idea that spoken languages had a history—an idea that was exclusively his—would be enough in itself to make him a great linguist. But this discovery raised a problem for him. If natural languages are not only different within one and the same city, but each of them changes over time to such an extent that "if the ancient citizens of Pavia were to rise from the grave today, they would speak in a language that was separate and distinct from that of modern Pavians" (*VE* I IX 7; "quod si vetustissimi Papienses nunc resurgerent, sermone vario vel diverso cum modernis Papiensibus loquerentur"), how can a shared language be constructed that is like Latin in its stability and uniformity and yet, as an artificial language, doesn't vary over time and space? This is the crux of the problem around which *De vulgari eloquentia* revolves.

Dante's treatise on language is announced in *Convivio*: "This will be more fully discussed elsewhere in a book that I intend to write, God willing, on Eloquence in the Vernacular" (*Conv.* I V 10; "Di questo si parlerà altrove più compiutamente in uno libello ch'io intendo di fare, Dio concedente, di Volgare Eloquenza"). This treatise continues Dante's basic political motivation but is addressed to an audience of specialists, so that the two treatises appear as two parts of one political and cultural design. The search for a vernacular that is "illustre, cardinale, aulicum et curiale" (*VE* I XVII 1)—in other words, for a vernacular that illuminates other Italian vernaculars with its excellence, that regulates them as Latin does and is capable of carrying out that unifying role that would be required of it if, in Italy, there were an imperial court as well as nobles who attended it—ought to have continued over four or probably five books, to create a treatise in which it is easy to recognize the systematic and exhaustive *forma mentis* that governed the idea of that other immense treatise which was to become *Convivio*.[14] The plan appears confidently outlined. All of the linguistic material would be set out within a twofold scheme: the first distributes the vernacular words on the basis of a decreasing scale of values from the most universal to the most particular, so that, from the broad consideration of those words of higher value, which extends over several books, the discussion passes down to inferior vernacular words. The second rhetorical scheme follows the traditional tripartite division of styles. The treatise, however, was left incomplete. But even as it is, we have to admire Dante's theoretical intuitions and the absolute novelty of what today we would call field research.

It might seem odd that the first textbook dedicated to a vernacular language is written in Latin. To our own way of thinking, this might appear to indicate defeat; and yet in the cultural context in which that treatise was written, even the use of Latin was a sign of something new. Dante was right when he extolled the originality of his book: indeed, a systematic treatise that brought together the subjects of *locutio* (the natural language of communication) and *eloquentia* (its regulated expressive use), and did so by galvanizing a theoretical and philosophical structure with a strong political motivation, with detailed analysis of meter and rhetoric and with direct observations on usage, had never been seen before. But he went too far when he claimed in the opening lines that no one before him had ever attempted in any way to cultivate the doctrine of eloquence in the vernacular.[15] There had been a certain tradition which couldn't be entirely dismissed, except that it related to texts written in the vernacular addressed to readers who already used the vernacular for practical or literary purposes. Dante, on the other hand, was addressing a readership who had yet to be convinced about the use of the vernacular.

University professors

The need to talk to people face to face or, at least, to a close readership, is one of the main characteristics of Dante's writing. Each of his works, in the first instance, defines a particular environment: in the *Vita Nova* it is that of his contemporaries in Florence who shared his way of life and his idea about literature; in the *Commedia* it is the families of his patrons and the political parties he encountered from time to time along his path as an exile. And the two treatises are no exception, as we shall see. It should be added that he sometimes seems to be seeking the support, if not the collaboration, of a specific interlocutor: in the *Vita Nova* it was Cavalcanti; in *De vulgari* it is Cino da Pistoia.

Cino is often mentioned in it as a writer of vernacular verse, indeed he is even acclaimed as the champion of love poetry, whereas Dante acclaims himself as the poet of rectitude. But he wasn't known just as a lyric poet.[16] In the years when Dante was writing *De vulgari,* he was best known as a lawyer. A lawyer who trained in Bologna. He had studied there at the university during the second half of the 1280s, obtaining a first-class degree (*licentiatus in iure*) in the early 1290s; he probably taught there as a freelance lecturer, as we would call him today, around the turn of the century and finally received his doctorate at the end of 1317 (later, he would teach as *magister* at many Italian universities: Siena, Perugia, Naples, and perhaps also Florence). In short, around 1304–1306 he was not an unfamiliar figure in Bologna university circles.[17] And for Dante, as he wrote *Convivio* and *De vulgari,* this aspect was at least as relevant as his friend's poetical excellence, since university professors were precisely the readership he wanted to interest in his project of promoting the vernacular, even though the task of winning them over to the vernacular was almost impossible. That project would never have got off the ground if Dante had immediately run up against the narrow-minded opposition of the university circles. For them only Latin, over which they held a sort of exclusive secular right, could be regarded as a language of culture. This, then, is how Dante attempted to convince them, by presenting his linguistic proposal in Latin guise. It would not have assured its success, but he hoped at least that it would have prevented the book from being rejected out of hand, as would happen with the *Commedia,* which was rejected from the outset for having being written in the vernacular.[18]

Dante the verse writer had his own readership in Bologna, as the transcriptions of his compositions made by the lawyers in the records office testify. His name as a politician also circulated among the ruling classes, but he had no credentials among university professors as a man of natural science and philosophy. Only one person recognized by the institution could have introduced him, acted as his guarantor, and encouraged the interest of those he wanted to approach. Of all Dante's friends, this person could only have been Cino. We don't know whether Cino had spent time in Bologna during the period from 1303 to 1306 when he had been exiled as a Black from Pistoia; it seems he preferred the cities of Prato and Florence. But at least one significant piece of evidence suggests that he was able to give Dante some assistance in Bologna.[19] During his years in exile, Cino sent Dante a sonnet (*Dante, quando per caso s'abandona*—*Dante, when by chance one abandons*), not easily interpretable, in which he basically seems to be asking his friend "whether it is right to abandon an old love in favor of a new love"[20]; Dante replies in verse (*Io sono stato con Amore insieme*—*I have kept company with love*) that love, as he knows through experience, cannot be resisted. But the point of interest is not the sonnet in reply, but the letter in Latin that he sends to his friend as an introduction: "to a Pistoian exile, the Florentine exiled without reason" (*Ep.* III: "exulanti Pistoriensi Florentinus exul inmeritus"). The Latin text, in itself, raises the poetic exchange to a higher level, emphasizing its philosophical significance. In the letter, Dante says exactly that by asking him "if the soul can be transformed from one passion to the other" (*Ep.* III 1: "utrum de passione in passionem possit anima transformari"). Cino had raised a philosophical question whose solution he was better able to answer than Dante, but then adds that he also understands that with this request, which obliges him to take a public position in "a very doubtful case," Cino was seeking to "give more fame" to his name, and shows extreme gratitude for this intention on the part of his friend.[21]

In short, by Dante's own declaration, Cino is working to create and spread Dante's reputation as a philosopher poet.

7

The Penitent

1306–1310

if wrong dies because man repents

se colpa muore perché l'uom si penta

—*Rime* 44, 90

Escape from Bologna

FATE PREVENTED DANTE from discovering whether his bold political and cultural project would find an audience among the *magistri* of Bologna. In the early months of 1306, after almost two strangely tranquil years—so tranquil that one could even wonder whether his family might have joined him in Bologna—his life was once again torn apart by public events. His dreams of being recognized by the higher academic circles were shattered by the reality of his state of banishment. *Convivio* and *De vulgari* remained unfinished and were never made public.

Bologna had been governed from the beginning of the century by a moderate Guelf faction—joined by the party headed by the Ghibelline Lambertazzi family—which openly supported the Whites of Florence, despite their banishment, though their main reason for doing so was to limit the ambitions of the Este of Ferrara. But there was strong internal opposition, led by the Geremei family, in the form of a hard-line Guelfism (anti-Ghibelline and anti-White) and consequently linked to the Este and the Blacks of Florence. One of its leading members was Venedico dei

Caccianemici, whom Dante, in *Inferno,* brands a pimp for having persuaded his sister Ghisolabella to succumb to the wishes of Marchese Obizzo II d'Este, father of Azzo VIII: "I was the one who induced Ghisolabella / to do the marchese's will, / as the shameful story goes" (*Inf.* XVIII 55–57; "i' fui colui che la Ghisolabella / condussi a far la voglia del marchese, / come che suoni la sconcia novella").[1] The understanding between the parties collapsed in early 1306. Tensions worsened in early February and exploded into violent disorder at the beginning of March. The Lambertazzi were expelled from Bologna on March 2 and replaced by a Guelf government hostile to the Whites and the Ghibellines. By March 10, the Black cities of Bologna, Florence, Lucca, Prato, and Siena had resolved "to exterminate forever the Ghibellines and the Whites" ("ad exterminium atque mortem perpetuam Ghibilinorum et alborum").[2]

The situation for Dante and the Whites soon worsened when White Pistoia, worn down by a long siege with intermittent acts of brutality, surrendered on April 10 to the Florentine troops under the command of Moroello Malaspina. For the Whites, the loss of Bologna and Pistoia was a disastrous blow; Dante was faced once again with the prospect of having to look for a place to live, wandering among those few cities or courts that were not yet hostile. But where could he go? To some Ghibelline despot in Romagna? To Ghibelline Verona? Alboino ruled there, and Dante had already experienced his lack of "courtesy." To Ghibelline Arezzo? His relations with the Guidi of Romena—de facto lords of the city through its bishop Ildebrandino—had been broken off a couple of years earlier. To staunchly Ghibelline Pisa, where many White exiles had already taken refuge? But it was a city that Dante didn't know: who would have sheltered him there? Who would have given him a living?

It was a very difficult situation without any obvious answer. But an urgent solution had to be found. It is true that on October 6 the Bologna city commune was still issuing public notices banning any Tuscan of the White party from crossing, stopping, or living in the city or surrounding area, a clear sign that many had not complied with previous injunctions—and besides, it couldn't have been easy for someone in the precarious situation of an exile to find another place to go at short notice—but it must be remembered that Dante, though he wasn't a leading politician, was nevertheless a White of some prominence, and it would have been fairly dangerous for him to remain in Bologna after the political unrest. It is likely, therefore, that he left the city quite soon, no later than May 1306.

The pope's envoy

Despite the loss of Bologna and Pistoia, the hopes of the Whites had not altogether faded. There were no more White cities on which to depend, but there was still a vast alignment of Ghibelline forces, from Romagna to the Casentino, the Mugello, the upper Arno valley, Arezzo, and Pisa. But what gave most hope of all in 1306 was the position of the new pope, Clement V. After a long and agonizing conclave in Perugia, Bertrand de Got of Gascony was elected in June 1305 as successor to Benedict XI and consecrated at Lyon in November, taking the name Clement V. He was the first of that long series of French popes (interrupted only by Urban VI in 1378) who at first informally, and then officially, established the papal residence in Avignon (Clement VI would remain in France and never set foot in Italy). Dante would be scathing about the man he described as "a lawless shepherd" (*Inf.* XIX 83; "pastor sanza legge"), though that was only later. He must have felt far from displeased during the first years of his papacy. Pope Clement, indeed, continued the policy begun by his predecessor on the advice of Cardinal Niccolò da Prato of restoring peace in Florence. For about five years, from 1304, there was therefore a strange reversal between the parties: the Blacks, who had leaped to power thanks to the support of a pope (Boniface VIII), were now forced to defend themselves, even with force, against the support given by two more popes (Benedict and Clement) to the White exiles and even to the Ghibellines.

The papal intervention became more determined in February 1306, when Clement appointed Cardinal Napoleone degli Orsini di Marino as legate in Romagna and Tuscany, with wide-ranging powers. A nephew of Niccolò III and cousin of Cardinal Latino, who had drawn up the first peace between Guelfs and Ghibellines in 1280, Napoleone Orsini was the most powerful cardinal at the papal court. He remained there for a remarkably long time, from 1288 to 1342. As leader of the faction against Boniface, he did nothing to hide his sympathies for the Whites nor even, to judge from his alliances, for the Ghibellines. His aim was the same as that of Niccolò da Prato: to bring the exiles back to Florence. But instead of using diplomatic means, he moved with a constant display of force. Reaching Bologna shortly after the expulsion of Lambertazzi, he showed immediate hostility toward Florence. The Florentines, in return, to forestall any armed attack by him, besieged the Castle of Montaccianico, in the Mugello, which had been held by the Ubaldini and by White forces. After three months of siege, they stormed it and razed it to the ground: the Mugello was too close to Florence and would have been an ideal base for any expedition by the legate. In Bologna, meanwhile, Orsini tried to restore peace to the city, but his action was interpreted by the people of Bologna as an attempt to overthrow its government in favor of the banished Lambertazzi. Popular discontent grew to the point that an uprising on May 23 forced him to flee the city (where the *podestà* by this time was Bernardino da Polenta, brother of Francesca da Rimini) and seek shelter in Imola.[3]

It is reasonable to imagine that Dante was still in Bologna during Orsini's stay and that he followed events with much interest and with his full support, as he had also done with Niccolò da Prato. It would be no surprise if he had sought his protection. He must therefore have regarded his escape as evidence that all potential roads back to Florence were closed. In any event, he couldn't have remained in Bologna after the uprising against Orsini.

A request for pardon

Dante began to nurture the idea of finding a personal solution—of being granted a pardon. Such an idea must have grown out of desperation, but it could only be achieved if he knew people in Florence who would share and support it and who, through their authority and prestige, could negotiate with someone in power who could grant his return from exile. A banished man couldn't apply directly to the city governors.

In Florence, Dante had several people and families he could count on: the wealthy Riccomanni family, though Lapo, husband of Tana, would die toward the end of 1315; on Gemma's Donati relations, including her father Manetto, who appears still to have been alive in 1306, her brother Foresino, and his son Niccolò, who remained close to Gemma and her children; on the admiration of various intellectuals (for example, the Black banker and poet Dino Frescobaldi).[4] In particular, he could depend on his friendship with Cino da Pistoia, who for political reasons was most probably living in Florence at that time. Cino must have been in contact with Marchese Moroello Malaspina who, since March 1306, had been the *capitano* in charge of levying the Guelf tribute, and was therefore an influential person. We don't know how strong their relationship was, but we do know that a few months after the events we are speaking of, Cino sent a sonnet (*Cercando di trovar miniera in oro—As I was searching out a mine of gold*) to Moroello at Lunigiana that is not easy to interpret. It would seem to refer to his new love for a female member of the Malaspina family. Dante, in keeping with a widespread practice, replied on Moroello's behalf with another sonnet (*Degno fa voi trovare ogni tesoro—Worthy you are to find any treasure*). It would be going too far to suggest that this three-way exchange denotes a particular familiarity among the authors, but it is not too much to interpret it as indicating a literary association that extended into real life.[5] The relationship between Cino and Moroello began on a political footing: the marchese was the man appointed by the Blacks of Florence and Pistoia to "liberate" the city, and Cino, if not actually a Black leader, was certainly close to key members of that party (to such an extent that having reentered Pistoia, he was appointed as judge for civil cases, though only for a few months).[6] In short, it seems plausible that Cino, more than anyone else, worked hard to persuade the marchese to espouse Dante's cause. Moroello could play a crucial role: indeed, he was in a position to speak directly to Corso Donati.

In my view, Dante and his supporters would first have played the family card. Gemma was a Donati, a third cousin of Corso, and her readmission to the city would have done no harm to the family prestige: indeed, if anything, it would have increased it. By allowing considerations of kinship to prevail, Corso would have shown himself to be the true man of strength in Florence.

Boccaccio's account of the recovery of the "little notebook" would seem to suggest the operation was successful.[7] Gemma's return was necessary before she could search around for the documents hidden away at the time of her husband's escape. We know that "five years or more" after Dante went into exile, Gemma was advised to exert her rights over confiscated assets that were part of her dowry: "that she, at least for the reasons of her dowry, should ask for the return of Dante's assets." The text isn't clear: Boccaccio didn't want to suggest that Gemma was asking to reassert ownership over that part of the confiscated assets on which her dowry was assured (something that was impossible under Florentine law), but rather the use of the income from that portion of assets. In order to bring a case, Gemma obviously had to be in Florence and must therefore have returned to the city. The Black regime doesn't appear to have changed its attitude toward rebels and their families around 1306, as Boccaccio suggests ("the city having a more accommodating government than it had when Dante was convicted"), therefore, if we give credit to the account, we must assume that the Donati in power had managed to obtain clemency for their kinswoman.[8]

Such an act of conciliation would have much raised Dante's own hopes for the future. But it is also clear that private (or almost private) negotiations would not have been enough for someone banished to be readmitted into the community. Family prestige and affection were of little help for Dante. A public act was needed—a gesture of repentance and obedience, a request for pardon submitted with full official blessing.

And that's exactly what Dante did.

"My people, what have I done to you?"

Leonardo Bruni wrote that Dante "reduced himself to great humility, seeking by good works and good conduct to regain the favor to be able to return to Florence by free revocation of those who ruled the city," and added that for that purpose he wrote several times, not only "to particular citizens and government, but to the people," and among the letters he cites one "very long" that began with the words "Popule mee, quid feci tibi?" This lost letter has all the appearance of being that official request for pardon that Dante was obliged to make.

Bruni knew about it because in the early decades of the 1400s it was kept in the chancery of the Signoria in Florence: this means that the letter had originally been sent to the priors. During the same period as Bruni—and quite independently—it was also known to Biondo Flavio, who may have read it in what had been the chancery of the Ordelaffi at Forlì. It is unthinkable that Dante would have sent his former *capitano*

Scarpetta Ordelaffi a copy of a letter in which he condemned his alliance with him and the other Ghibellines of Romagna and Florence. It is more likely that the Blacks themselves took the initiative of circulating among their enemies a text that placed the former member of the council of the Coalition of the Whites in the position of a traitor. And confirmation that the letter caused a stir comes also from the fact it was also known to the chronicler Villani.[9] In short, this was the act that sparked the anger of the Whites and Ghibellines against Dante—and, from their point of view, with good reason.

Though the letter is lost, we can form an idea of its tone and, to some extent, its reasoning from references (with several apparent quotes) made by Bruni. Starting off with a quotation from the book of the prophet Micah ("Populus meus, quid feci tibi?"), it must have been a sort of memoir in which Dante went back over the stages of his life as a citizen and as a politician proud of his membership in the Guelf faction.[10] He recalled his honorable involvement in the battle of Campaldino and how he had been an important part of Guelf history in Florence, he defended his actions as prior from the accusations that had been leveled against him, repeated his extraneousness to the decision to allow the return of the Cerchi followers, including Cavalcanti, from internment at Sarzana, and emphasized how exile had reduced him to destitution whereas his house in Florence had been equipped with "abundant and valuable furnishings." So far we cannot detect the "humble" manner to which Bruni refers: indeed, one has the impression that Dante is justifying his conduct as a law-abiding citizen and a public figure devoted to the common good, conceding nothing, almost in self-justification.

His humility must have been apparent in the next part of the letter, to which Bruni makes no mention, where Dante asked for the banishment against him to be revoked and his wrongs pardoned. "Wrong" ("colpa") is a significant word, used by Dante himself a little later in a text relating to this same matter.[11] But for what wrong is he seeking pardon? Not for having committed offenses or injustices during his period as prior, not for having belonged to a rival faction (perfectly normal and not blameworthy in itself), nor even for having sought to return to Florence by force ("but expelled citizens wanting to return to their home cannot be condemned to death," wrote Dino Compagni);[12] the wrong was having allied himself with the Ghibellines, Florence's traditional enemies, and therefore having betrayed not only the Guelf faction, but the whole city—to be Florentine and to be Guelf were one and the same thing from at least the time of Campaldino.[13] The Guelfs could fight, banish, and kill each other, but their mutual hatred couldn't match the hatred that separated them from the Ghibellines. "Now we have found men, who are of the Guelf and Ghibelline party, who would willingly, if they could, immediately kill all the men of the other side: they would kill all of them immediately, if they could": these are words spoken from the pulpit, in the first decade of the 1300s, by the Dominican Giordano da Pisa.[14]

If Dante was asking to be pardoned for this wrong, it is understandable that the Ghibellines and the Whites he had disavowed should show great hostility toward someone who, to remove the blemish of having betrayed Florence, had no hesitation in betraying them.

Dante's request for a pardon was only the beginning of a story that would continue for another two years.

At the foot of the "mountains of Luni"

One of the very few records to have survived shows that in early October 1306 Dante was with the Malaspina family in the Lunigiana.[15] This doesn't prove that Moroello Malaspina had been involved in the (perhaps successful) attempt to allow Gemma to return to Florence, but it does prove that a relationship had been effectively established between Dante and the marchese in 1306, perhaps through Cino's mediation.[16]

Having fled from Bologna, Dante therefore moved to the Lunigiana. We could even suggest a date: June, after the May revolt against Orsini, a month in which Moroello—who until April had been busy with the siege of Pistoia and was not yet involved in the attack on the castle at Montaccianico in the Mugello—could have found himself on his estates in the Lunigiana. Here, according to the account given by Dante's son Pietro (though this is the third version of his commentary to the *Commedia,* and open to the suspicion of having been reworked), Dante stayed there "for no short time."[17] It was the first time he had visited this part of Italy, which he would later get to know well.

When we discuss places in Dante—except, of course, Florence—we immediately think of cities like Verona, Arezzo, or Ravenna; rarely do we recall that Dante spent many years in the Apennine mountains of Tuscany, Emilia, and Romagna. It is important to stress the significance of the Apennines in Dante's life not merely as a matter of interest or even just historical accuracy: the picture of his life would be incomplete without remembering that it was here that the mercantile and business world of the city "bourgeoisie" came into contact with the feudal jurisdictions of these mountain districts. If the distinguishing feature of Florence was profit, that of the Apennines was honor. The relationship and conflict between these two worlds had a deep effect on Dante.

The mountain landscape of the Lunigiana area is similar to that of the Casentino. It is a wide valley (between Tuscany and Liguria) through which the river Magra runs, flowing down from the Apennine heights to the then-marshy plain of Sarzana. Its position, like that of the Casentino, was strategically important since the one who held it was assured control of the communication routes between Tuscany and Emilia and between Tuscany and Liguria. The Lunigiana was ruled by one great family, the Malaspina; its lands extended over both sides of the Apennine ridge in the same way as those of the Guidi. In 1221 (around the same time as the Guidi had become divided) the Malaspina formed themselves into two main branches: those of the "Spino Secco" (withered thorn) and the "Spino Fiorito" (thorn in flower). Dante's hosts were members of the first branch which, in turn, had subdivided in 1266 into four further branches: Mulazzo, Villafranca, Giovagallo, and Val di Trebbia. Moroello di Manfredi, who was Dante's main (though not his only) patron, belonged to the Giovagallo branch. Like the Guidi family, the Malaspina were also politically divided: while Moroello was a Guelf close to the Black party, Franceschino di Mulazzo was a staunch Ghibelline.

Dante visited the Lunigiana many times, and for long periods, but the landscape of the Magra valley doesn't seem to have affected him as much as that of the river Arno in the Casentino. His memories, if anything, were linked to the more southerly area: to the peaks of the Apuan Alps (the "mountains of Luni") and, above all, to the white marble quarries and the view of the sea, and of the sky that opens wide over the mountains that tower above Carrara.[18] What counted in the Lunigiana was the human landscape. Dante established a happy relationship with the Malaspina family which—unusually for him—he never repudiated.

That ancient noble family still observed true virtue and courtly behavior. They embodied values and conduct that Dante judged to be worthy of the best feudal traditions, not least because he benefited from them. His meeting in Purgatory with the soul of Corrado II Malaspina, who died in 1294 and was the cousin of his patrons Moroello and Franceschino, would provide him with the opportunity for a high-flown eulogy on the honor of the dynasty, famed throughout Europe, and justly so, since that family, in a world that had lost the path of virtue, "alone walks upright and scorns the way of evil" (*Purg.* VIII 132; "sola va dritta e 'l mal cammin dispregia"). The Malaspina's greatest claim to glory was for having maintained the "value of the purse and of the sword" (*Purg.* VIII 129; "pregio de la borsa e de la spade"), in other words, of still cultivating the two main qualities that distinguish true noble behavior: the use of arms (not just for Moroello, who used them professionally so to speak, but also for his cousin Franceschino, who had been involved in warfare almost the whole of his life, and other members of the Malaspina family whom we will have occasion to meet, such as Spinetta dello Spino Fiorito) and the practice of open-handedness.[19] With the expression "value of the purse" Dante wanted to distinguish between generosity motivated by the recognition of merit in the person benefited, and that form of giving that crosses the line into payment for services and even into charity, already condemned in the canzone *Doglia mi reca*. Dante's service to the Malaspina family, and particularly to Moroello, took the form of literary services, in a relationship that was not without a sort of complicity: it involved both the marchese's involvement in the poetical correspondence between Dante and Cino, and also, as suggested in a letter sent by Dante to Moroello from the Casentino, that at his "court" it was proper for him "to attend to literary services" to attract the "admiration" of his host (*Ep.* IV 2; in qua [Moroello's court], velud sepe sub admiratione vidistis, fas fuit sequi libertatis officia). It is doubtful whether a gathering of people in those castles on the mountain border with Liguria was really such as to merit the title of "court" ("curia"), not least because the various members of the Malaspina family did not generally live in one or more castles owned individually or as a family, but in properties held in part-ownership with other branches of the family. It has to be acknowledged, however, that Dante's idealized description of it can only come from his feeling of being recognized at last as an intellectual and as a poet—indeed, it was here that he returned to writing the *Commedia*.

The literary services did not exempt him from more concrete practical tasks. We know of at least one delicate and onerous assignment given to him by the Malaspina cousins. The fact that it was given to someone who had just arrived in the Lunigiana and was therefore not particularly familiar with local issues is the best demonstration that there couldn't have been many educated and experienced people in that "court" or in those "courts."

A complicated dispute between the Spino Secco branch of the Malaspina family and Antonio di Nuvolone da Camilla of Genoa (who was the Bishop Count of Luni, a cousin of Alagia Fieschi, wife of Moroello, and protected by the powerful Fieschi counts of Lavagna) had been going on for years in a state of endemic war and family feud (fueled above all by the Malaspina family). On October 6, 1306, the parties managed to arrive at a peace settlement.[20] Dante carried out the final negotiations and signed the document on behalf of the Malaspina family, acting on the basis of a letter of attorney. The event occurred and was concluded at two separate times and places, but on the same day. On the morning of the sixth, in the main piazza in Sarzana (Piazza della Calcandola), the notary of Sarzana, Giovanni di Parente di Stupio (the Malaspina family did not have their own chancery) drafted a letter of attorney in front of witnesses in which Marchese Franceschino di Mulazzo, who was also acting on behalf of Marchese Moroello di Giovagallo and Marchese Corradino di Villafranca, appointed as his "lawful procurator executor and special envoy Dante Alighieri of Florence." This took place at seven, before mass. Then Dante and the notary went to Castelnuovo where, at the Bishop's palace, Dante and the bishop exchanged the kiss of peace and, at nine, they signed the legal document. Since it contained precautionary clauses such as "Signor Franceschino shall persuade—if he can—the said Signor Moroello to ratify" and "on condition that the aforesaid Signor Franceschino and Signori Corradino and Moroello—if they wish to accept all matters set out above and to be written below—do the same," it is clear that the signing could be carried out so speedily because the negotiations had already taken place and the agreements already reached. In short, Dante took part in the final stage because he had the necessary experience to keep an eye on what the notary was doing. Indeed, there seems to be some ground for the suggestion that the introductory part of the peace agreement (technically called the *arenga*) was actually drafted by him, and that he passed it to the notary for a fair copy to be made.

This assignment may have taken Dante to Sarzana for the first time in his life, and it is almost certain he would have found himself thinking about Guido Cavalcanti, who had died or become fatally ill there just six years before. Dante would even perhaps have pondered the extent of his own responsibility in his friend's death.

"Pardon is fine victory in war"

Dante had sent his request for pardon, but the months passed—"many moons" (*Rime* 44, 89; "più lune")—and either no response arrived from the Blacks in Florence, or the answer was negative.

Dante perhaps had no other choice in his desperation than to turn to Corso Donati, but he was not the right person at that moment to achieve the repatriation of an exile accused of Ghibellinism. Corso's rift with Della Tosa (which had already degenerated into armed conflict in early 1304) had further deepened. He felt he had been pushed to one side, and, as usual, he reacted with great determination. He hadn't abandoned his long-held hope to become lord of the city, and for this purpose had built (and continued to build over those months) a vast network of internal and external alliances that stretched from the Guelfs of Prato and Lucca to the Blacks of Pistoia, not excluding the Ghibellines of Arezzo, the Guidi, and even the White exiles. In short, the suspicions of the Florentines against him were not ill-founded. His third marriage to a daughter of the Ghibelline leader Uguccione della Faggiola (it will be recalled that Corso had been appointed by Boniface VIII as rector of Massa Trabaria) had increased distrust among the Della Tosa faction, fueled by rumors that he was plotting with the Ghibellines. In short, it was extremely difficult for Corso in 1306 to give Dante any firm help. At most, he could have cooperated with the Malaspina and other feudal families connected to him (or them) to provide him with a network of protection outside Florence.

But Dante wanted to return to Florence.

The canzone *Tre donne intorno al cor mi son venute* (*Three women around my heart are come*), known as the "exile canzone," is one of Dante's most impenetrable poems, and not because the text is obscure but because the autobiographical references are obscure. The structure of the canzone is unusual. The first four stanzas are taken up with a dialogue that takes place in the heart (and it is therefore a dramatized thought) between two abstract entities: Love (to be construed not in the erotic sense, but as *caritas,* general love which includes human love) and Rectitude, or Justice. Rectitude is accompanied by a daughter and a granddaughter: these are the "three women" of the opening line, emblems of the tripartition of Justice into divine, natural, and human law. The allegorical beings complain that Justice and the other virtues born from the same lineage as Love and Rectitude—such as Generosity and Temperance, which were once loved—are now hated and despised by a world that has banished them, forcing them as exiles to wander about begging. In the fifth and the last stanza the discourse suddenly abandons the level of allegory and refers to Dante's own situation. In listening to the lament of such excellent exiles—writes the poet—I consider it an honor to be condemned to such exile; if God or Destiny wish the world to transform white flowers into black, in other words to turn values upside down and make the guilty innocent (but the allusion to the two Guelf parties seems obvious), then to fall from the side of justice is, despite everything, honorable: "And for I who hear / among such noble outcasts / divine words of comfort and sorrow, / the exile given me brings me honor: / For if judgment or force of destiny / ordain that the world turns / white flowers dark, / then to fall with the good is worthy praise indeed" (*Rime* 44, 73–80; "Ed io ch'ascolto nel parlar divino / consolarsi e dolersi / così alti dispersi / l'essilio che m'è dato onor mi tegno: / che se giudicio o forza di destino / vuol pur che 'l mondo versi / li bianchi fiori in persi, / cader co' buoni è pur di lode degno").[21] They are proud words, similar to those spoken by Brunetto Latini in *Inferno* when he tells Dante of his forthcoming exile: "your destiny holds so much honor for you, / that the one side and the other will hunger / for you" (*Inf.* XV 70–72; "la tua fortuna tanto onor ti serba, / che l'una parte e l'altra avranno fame / di te"). It is no surprise that these are similar, given that the lines of *Inferno* must have been written around the same time as those of the canzone.

Dante is therefore confirming the rightness of his actions, inspired by Rectitude and Love, and the injustice of the sentence against him, a sign of how values were being subverted in the world. No concessions are being made by the person who nevertheless expects to be pardoned. Except that—the narrator continues—this honored exile, which I consider a minor thing, is turning into a torment for me, since I am far away from the fine object that my eyes desire to see and whose absence consumes me:

> And were it not that the fair object of my eyes
> had been removed by distance from my sight,
> which has set me on fire,
> all that weighs upon me I would count as light;
> but this fire has already
> so consumed my flesh and bone,
> that Death against my breast has placed his key.

> E se non che degli occhi miei 'l bel segno
> per lontananza m'è tolto dal viso,
> che m'have in foco miso,
> lieve mi conteria ciò che m'è grave;
> ma questo foco m'have
> sì consumato già l'ossa e la polpa,
> che Morte al petto m'ha posto la chiave.

—*Rime* 44, 81–87

There is no doubt that Dante is talking here about a woman, a woman he loves and from whom he is separated since she is in the city where he is prevented from going. Dante has been away from Florence for many years, and in his love poems written in exile there is no trace of a love in Florence that continues to stir his passion; so who can this woman be?[22]

The next lines continue as follows:

> And so, if I did wrong,
> many moons have turned the sun since it was spent,
> if guilt dies because the man repents.

Onde, s'io ebbi colpa,
più lune ha volte il sol poi che fu spenta,
se colpa muore perché l'uom si penta.

—*Rime* 44, 88–90

If it is true that repentance wipes out wrong, then any wrong I have
done has been canceled out for many months ("many moons"), and I
should therefore be allowed to return to Florence to that woman. The
many months are to be counted from the moment when he made his
public repentance, in other words, when he sent the letter to the priors,
and so this canzone must date from at least the last months of 1306, during
his stay in the Lunigiana. The last lines are like a sort of appeal, a plea
to someone who might have been supporting Dante's case. It ends
rather strangely. Here the poet invites the canzone to keep its inner
meaning hidden except to a "virtuous friend." But it has been observed
that the canzone is "not particularly difficult nor does it seem to have
hidden meanings" and therefore whatever it is that can be revealed only
to "virtuous" friends is probably none other than the appeal, motivated
by reasons of love, that ends it.[23] These reasons could only be clear to
the true recipients, those who knew the biographical background to
which Dante alludes. The recipients could only be Corso and his friends.

Now, it would seem highly unlikely that Dante would ask them to
help him return to Florence to bring an end to the amorous sufferings
caused by an unknown fellow citizen. But there would be good reason
for the request if the woman to whom Dante wanted to return was
Gemma, who had been allowed back into the city that very year. Dante
would once again, after a distance of time, be playing the family card.
It might be objected that this is the only lyrical composition of the early
centuries in which a poet not only speaks about his own wife, but speaks
of her with words that poetry reserves for amorous passion. It is true
that declarations of love for a wife appear to be wholly exceptional in
early literature, and so they remain, even taking into account the ulterior purposes they might have served. But it mustn't be forgotten that
Dante was exceptional. How otherwise can we describe a writer who
seems determined to break rules and customs in everything he writes?
So much passion toward his wife would have seemed scandalous to

anyone who could correctly decipher the text at that time, but wouldn't
it have seemed equally scandalous that he had given the identity of one
of his sisters to the *Donna pietosa* who figures in the opening lines of the
"nightmare canzone" in the *Vita Nova*?

The canzone circulated in this form, with a single ending, but Dante
later added a second. It is not possible to establish when this happened,
but there is certainly a link between the decision to add this second
ending and the effects produced by the canzone on the first recipients.
The second ending is entirely political:

> Dear song, go hawking with white feathered birds,
> dear song, go hunting with black hounds,
> who banished me,
> but still can grant me peace.
> Yet they don't, who don't know who I am:
> the room for pardon a wise man never locks,
> since to pardon is fine victory in war.

> Canzone, uccella con le bianche penne,
> canzone, caccia con li neri veltri,
> che fuggir mi convenne,
> ma far mi poterian di pace dono.
> Però nol fan, ché non san quel ch'io sono:
> camera di perdon savio uom non serra,
> ché perdonare è bel vincer di guerra.

—*Rime* 44, 101–107

One gets the impression that Dante is answering some negative message he has received from the first recipients (besides, if he was in the
Lunigiana, the communication link with his supporters in Florence, via
Moroello, would have been continually open). He acknowledges that he
cannot be reunited with his family since the tough line of the Blacks
hasn't softened, but yet, while repeating his Guelf allegiance over and
above all party differences, he cannot resist making a further almost pa-
thetic attempt to move the hearts of his adversaries: here, as Bruni
writes, Dante really is "reduced to humility." He, who goes "hawking"
("uccella") with the Whites, would like to go "hunting" ("caccia") also

with the Blacks, but they don't want him; they won't grant him the gift of peace. They do not know, in fact, how changed he is. This plea to consider the sincerity of his feelings, the good faith of a heartfelt repentance appears tragically painful when we remember it is addressed to a world that seems to know only the language of hatred and vengeance.

"Love terrible and imperious"

The patronage of the Malaspina family meant much more than their hospitality in the Lunigiana. Thanks to them Dante benefited from a network of relationships that opened the doors to homes owned by the Black nobility which he would otherwise have found firmly closed. The moral support of the Malaspina ensured, in effect, that the pardon denied him by the Blacks of Florence was granted by the Blacks outside.

In 1307—we don't know exactly when or why—Dante left the Lunigiana valley for the Casentino. In effect, very little is known about this visit. We can only guess which families gave him accommodation. Our source is Boccaccio, according to whom, after his stay in Verona (Boccaccio makes no mention of Bologna), Dante, "when with Count Salvatico in Casentino, when with Marchese Morruello Malespina in Lunigiana, when with the della Faggiuola family in the mountains near Orbino . . . was much honored."[24] This information fits perfectly with the new political position assumed by Dante upon his request for pardon. It is clear, in fact, that after having publicly distanced himself from the Whites and Ghibellines, he must have kept clear of those who had been his first patrons in the region, namely the Ghibelline Guidi of Modigliana, Porciano, and Romena, and instead looked toward the families living mainly on the Romagna side of the Apennines and in the Montefeltro area, such as the Guidi of Dovadola (which included Guido Salvatico) and the Faggiolani. These families were loyal to the Black Guelfs and, not surprisingly, were linked politically and by family ties to the Malaspina and to Corso Donati.

Dante never mentions Uguccione della Faggiola in his writings, but in Canto XII of *Inferno,* along with "Rinier Pazzo," he refers to a "Rinier da Corneto," saying that both "made much war on the roads" (*Inf.* XII 137–138; "a Rinier da Corneto, a Rinier Pazzo, / che fecero a le strade tanta guerra"). While the first Rinieri had been an important Ghibelline

head of the Pazzi family of Valdarno, the other is not an obscure
"outlaw" ("bandito") from the Maremma but the father of Uguccione,
who died in 1292. Corneto, in the Montefeltro region, was the main castle
of the Faggiolani, their headquarters.[25] And it shouldn't be imagined that
the reference was dishonorable: Dante isn't talking about highway rob-
bers, but about great feudal lords (not surprisingly Ghibelline), fighting
against the territorial expansion of the city communes, and therefore
"rebels" in the political sense of the word.

The Guidi of Dovadola were a Guelf branch closely linked to the
Blacks of Florence (Ruggero II, son of Guido Salvatico, Dante's host, had
been *podestà* there in 1304). It is easy to imagine that Dante would not
have been welcome there if he hadn't enjoyed the protection of Moroello, to whom they were linked by shared political allegiance as well as
by family ties.[26] Dante doesn't name Guido Salvatico either but, in the
same way that he had recalled Uguccione's father, he gives a most honorable mention to Salvatico's uncle Guido Guerra, who died in 1272, one
of the champions of Florentine Guelfism, a sort of anti-Farinata. And
he puts him in the same circle as Brunetto, in a canto composed at
more or less the same time as his stay with the Dovadola family.[27]

Uguccione della Faggiola and Guidi di Dovadola don't really take us
to the Casentino, but toward the other side of the Apennine ridge, toward
Romagna and the Marches, "in the mountains near Orbino." And yet
the only text by Dante that we know with certainty to have been composed during this stay in the Tuscan-Romagna Apennines, the canzone
Amor, da che convien pur ch'io mi doglia (*Love, since I must suffer*), which
Dante himself called "la montanina" ("mountain song"; *Rime* 50, 76) refers us to the Tuscan side, in the Casentino valley of the Arno: "Thus
you have bound me, love, among the Alps, / in the river valley / along
which you've always held me firm" (*Rime* 50, 61–63; "Così m'ha' concio,
Amore, in mezzo l'alpi, / nella valle del fiume / lungo 'l qual sempre
sopra me sè forte").[28] We cannot establish with any certainty where and
with whom Dante was staying when he wrote these lines, but the lands
of Guido Salvatico, though mostly in the valley of Montone on the Adriatic side of the Apennines, also included the castle of Pratovecchio in
the Casentino. The castle stood on the left bank of the Arno, overlooked
by the nearby towers of Romena. The canzone was sent to Moroello accompanied by a letter in Latin in which Dante writes that, upon his

arrival from the Lunigiana, he fell in love as soon as he set foot "in the current of the Arno" (*Ep.* IV 2; "cum primum pedes iuxta Sarni fluenta . . . defigerem"). At this point, it might be considered a simple coincidence that the writer of an anonymous commentary on *Purgatorio* in the thirteen or fourteen hundreds states that Dante loved "a woman from Prato Vecchio" for whom he had written this very canzone.[29]

The letter to Moroello gives various biographical details. The canzone, to which we have already referred in relation to the psychophysical crises of an epileptic or apoplectic kind described in several of Dante's love poems, describes the condition into which the poet fell, struck by a sudden and unexpected flash of love in that same Arno valley where, many years earlier, he had fallen in love with Beatrice. The letter describes the circumstances of the new love: "To me, therefore, having left the gates of the court, then much missed, in which, as you often saw with pleasure, I was allowed to carry out literary tasks, barely had I surely and incautiously placed my feet in the current of the Arno, than all of a sudden, alas, a woman, like lightning from above, appeared, I don't know how, meeting all my desires in manner and beauty. O how amazed I was at that apparition! But the amazement ceased for terror of the thunder that followed. Since thunder immediately follows flashes of lightning by day, thus, when I saw the flame of this beauty, Love terrible and imperious took hold of me, and whatever . . . had been opposed to him within me he killed or banished or imprisoned."[30] "Surely and incautiously" it proceeded, like Francesca and Paolo reading Galeotto's book "without any suspicion" (*Inf.* V 129; "sanza alcun sospetto"). It is pointless investigating who this *femme fatale* could have been: someone had told Boccaccio—though leaving him doubtful—that it was a "mountain woman" with a "fine face" but "goitered." Goitered or not, from Pratovecchio or not, she would have been a noblewoman or *domina* from that area. But it is important to note how the nostalgia expressed in the letter for the Malaspina "court" he has only just left behind also suggests the great difference between the cultural state of the Lunigiana and that of the Casentino. This also happens in the canzone, where the writer complains that in the mountains where he now finds himself there is no one who understands about love, nor a female audience able to understand and console: "But oh! I see no women here, nor men of worth / to whom I can lament my grief" (*Rime* 50, 67–68; "Lasso!, non donne qui, non genti accorte / veggio a cui mi lamenti del mio male"). In short, yet again the Casentino appears to Dante to be lacking in courtly places and customs.

By sudden contrast the conclusion moves the discourse to the poet's situation of exile:

> Oh mountain song, you can go:
> Perhaps you'll see Florence, my home,
> that has locked me out,
> loveless and devoid of compassion.

> O montanina mia canzon, tu vai:
> forse vedrai Fiorenza, la mia terra,
> che fuor di sé mi serra,
> vota d'amore e nuda di pietate.

—*Rime* 50, 76–79

The canzone, therefore, on its journey from the Casentino to the Lunigiana, would probably have passed through Florence (we can imagine a package carried by a courier along the Consuma road that wound up in front of Pratovecchio). Although the poem contains no dedication, it would seem, like the letter, to be addressed to Moroello himself. We know with certainty that the marchese was in Val di Magra in May 1307, "busy with his financial interests in the Lunigiana," so it is plausible to suggest the canzone and letter had been written in late spring or early summer of that year.[31]

The canzone would perhaps see the city that denies the poet's return as being devoid of love and compassion. To this pitiless Florence, the canzone (if it ever entered) could say that she had nothing more to fear from its author since, imprisoned as he was by an amorous chain, even if the cruelty of his home city were to disappear, that would never make him return: "If you go inside, say: 'the one / who made me can no longer fight you: / there, from whence I come, he is so enchained, / that even if your cruelty were to bend, / he is not free to return'" (*Rime* 50, 80–84; "se vi vai dentro, va dicendo: 'Omai / non vi può fare il mio fattor più guerra: / là ond'io vegno una catena il serra / tal, che se piega vostra crudeltate, / non ha di ritornar qui libertate'"). If it ever did enter Florence, in other words, if it ever succeeded in being read by those people to whom Dante had sent his pleas, the canzone would now pass on nothing more than a message of surrender. Here again, there was also a play on feelings: his love for a woman drew him powerfully toward Florence, his love for another kept him away from Florence. In a similar ending there is an implicit courtly homage to the recipient: if love should indeed prevent him from returning to the city which stands at the summit of his desires, it is excusable that he should remain far away from his patron or that he might appear "negligent": "so that certain things related through others," he writes in the letter to Moroello, "things that are very often apt to breed false opinions, must not let any thought of negligence be made against he who is in fact a prisoner" (*Ep.* IV 1; "ne alia relata pro aliis, que falsarum oppinionum seminaria frequentius esse solent, negligentem predicent carceratum"). And yet it must also be recognized that in the canzone Dante is speaking of a real, burning love. The crisis that hits him when he approaches this woman, a fulguration that takes him out of his senses, is exactly the same as what he says he felt in the youthful canzone *E' m'incresce di me* on the day when Beatrice was born. It cannot be a casual coincidence: we have to admit that this Dante, well into his forties, in Pratovecchio, has fallen in love with the same intensity with which he had fallen in love as a young man (and perhaps we might also think of a relapse into that illness of an epileptic kind where the youthful canzone seemed to suggest sudden fainting followed by a slow return to consciousness). From the amorous screen, however, another also appears, a sort of disillusioned resignation: Dante is aware that it is impossible to overcome the resistance of the Blacks. Perhaps it is not a surrender, since he would always cultivate the hope of being able to return to his home city, but it is certainly an acknowledgment that his condition at that time is irreversible. It is also therefore probable that the canzone dates from late 1307, when the political weakness of Corso Donati was already apparent.[32]

Under the umbrella of the Malaspina

In the same way that in Canto VIII of *Purgatorio* Corrado II Malaspina predicts to Dante that within seven years from their meeting (in March 1300) he personally would find out how well established was his family's fame, so too would Bonagiunta Orbicciani, the verse writer from Lucca, in Canto XXIV, after whispering the name of a woman, Gentucca, reveal to Dante that the woman by that name, still a child in 1300 ("doesn't yet wear a headcloth") would make him find his city pleasing (*Purg.* XXIV 43–45; "'Femmina è nata, e non porta ancor benda,' / cominciò el, 'che ti farà piacere / la mia città'"). Dante therefore stayed at Lucca.[33]

Apart from that, he was well informed about men and events in Lucca. The canto about the barraters immersed in the pitch of Malebolge (*Inferno* XXI) is an entirely negative description of people from Lucca. Most of the people in the canto about the flatterers immersed in excrement (*Inferno* XVIII) are also from Lucca. Both of these cantos seethe with contempt for the city, in both the part represented by White knights such as Alessio degli Interminelli as well as that of the Black *popolari* such as Bonturo Dati. But more than his contemptuous attitude, which was clearly politically motivated, it is interesting that Dante shows he had first-hand information. He could have known Interminelli in Florence at the end of the 1290s, but his knowledge of Bonturo Dati, against whom there is a sarcastic quip about Lucca—where "every man is a barrater there, apart from Bonturo" (*Inf.* XXI 41; "ogn'uom v'è barattier, fuor che Bonturo")—was picked up in that city where Bonturo, who had links with the Blacks of Florence and was still alive when Dante was writing (he would die in 1325), would be city governor until 1314.[34] And only in Lucca could he have gathered such precise and detailed information about the death of Martino Bottaio that enabled him to construct one of the most extraordinary narrative devices of the poem.

In the bolgia of the barraters, Virgil invites Dante to look at something that was happening; Dante then turns and sees a "black devil" carrying on his shoulders a "sinner" who had just reached Hell. He is a leading magistrate from the city of Lucca, whose name is not given. But experts on Lucchese affairs, when told by Dante himself that the events he had witnessed in the bolgia took place on Holy Saturday, five hours before midday, can identify him as Martino Bottaio (who, wrote Francesco da Buti, was "a great citizen of Lucca in his time and, along with Bonturo Dati and other men of lowly birth, then ruled Lucca"). He in fact died on March 26, 1300. Dante, the character, watches this man's soul arriving in Hell in "real time," as we would say today.[35]

Only someone with a deep understanding of Lucchese society could work out that the names of the demons, starting with that group of Malebranche, corresponded with those of local families or nicknames circulating in the city.[36] And yet, if there was one city in which a banished White ought not to have set foot, it was Lucca, the most loyal and active ally of the Blacks of Florence. If Dante stayed there—and it would seem to have been for quite some time—it was because someone in a position of power and authority was protecting him. His guarantor could only have been Moroello, whose word must have counted for much in a city whose troops he had commanded in the war against Pistoia in 1302 and where more recently, in 1306, he had held the office of *capitano del popolo*. And it is even likely that Moroello himself had found Dante a job, perhaps with the mysterious Gentucca of whom Bonagiunta speaks. All of this must have happened in 1308, after his stay in the Casentino.

Who was Gentucca? Research has provided no answer. The canto in *Purgatorio,* with its mysterious and vaguely erotic atmosphere, is in danger of being misinterpreted. It is inappropriate to ask whether Dante is offering thanks for a hospitality received or hinting at a private, intimate affair in a canto which, moreover, speaks of love poetry. Gentucca's secret is to be found almost certainly in the relationships that linked her family with the Malaspina, and cannot be resolved unless new documents come to light.[37]

Equally mysterious is the mention of a certain Giovanni, son of Dante Alighieri of Florence, as a witness in a legal document drawn up in Lucca on October 21, 1308. Certainly, the date fits with that of Dante's stay, and we could therefore even think that this Giovanni is his eldest son, forced to leave Florence because he had reached the fateful age of fourteen, who had then joined his father. That there is no news about him before this date is problematic; but the fact that there is no news about him afterward arouses considerable suspicion. Since his name does not appear among those excluded from the amnesty of 1311, we must necessarily assume that he either died young before that date or was the son of someone else by the same name. Nevertheless, it seems too much of a coincidence that in those same years there could have been two Dante Alighieri of Florence traveling around Tuscany, each with a son named Giovanni: the possibility that this is the eldest son of our Dante seems therefore to be the most convenient hypothesis. The fact that Giovanni was living in Lucca with his father doesn't in itself mean that all the family were back together in that city. If Gemma had actually managed to get back into Florence, it is hard to believe she would have moved away again just a couple of years later.

Hopes fade

From Lucca, Dante watched the gradual weakening of Corso's political influence and his final ruin. Donati had left Florence in the first half of 1308 to take up the position of *podestà* at Treviso, ruled by his friend Rizzardo da Camino. It was a prestigious position, but if Corso had felt the need to distance himself from the city it was a sign that he no longer felt so powerful. And indeed shortly after his return the situation worsened. Corso fell victim to a plot hatched by two of his bitterest enemies, Pazzino dei Pazzi and Betto Brunelleschi. They had him arrested with the accusation that he owed them money. Corso was soon released, but it led to a quarrel that degenerated into violence between his supporters and those of the Della Tosa. Corso sought military help from his outside supporters, and in particular from Uguccione della Faggiola, who was in Arezzo. His enemies then moved one step ahead, and on October 6, having obtained a judgment charging him with treason for his links with the Ghibellines, they attacked the towers where he was barricaded. By a trick they managed to persuade Uguccione, who was close to Florence, to turn back; seeing he had lost, Corso tried to escape but was pursued, caught, and imprisoned just outside the city walls. As he was being led back to the city, he fell from his horse, which dragged him along until the strike of a lance put an end to him.[38] Dante describes his agony, from the mouth of his brother Forese, in Shakespearian tones:

> "Look," he said; "the guiltiest of them all,
> I see dragged at the tail of a beast
> toward the pit that never pardons sin.
> The beast with every stride moves faster,
> ever increasing, until she kicks it free
> and leaves the corpse vilely disfigured."

> 'Or va,' diss' el; 'che quei che più n'ha colpa,
> vegg' ïo a coda d'una bestia tratto

inver' la valle ove mai non si scolpa.
La bestia ad ogne passo va più ratto,
crescendo sempre, fin ch'ella il percuote,
e lascia il corpo vilmente disfatto.'

—*Purg.* XXIV 82–87

In Dante's version, Corso, caught in a stirrup, is dragged by the runaway horse in a race toward Hell. We are in the same canto of *Purgatorio* in which Bonagiunta speaks of Gentucca: only at this point of the poem does Dante abandon his reticence. He clearly indicates Corso as "the guiltiest of them all" for the fact that the place where he was born "is day by day stripped more of virtue / and seems disposed to sad ruin" (*Purg.* XXIV 79–82; "di giorno in giorno più di ben si spolpa, / e a trista ruina par disposto"). Dante must have been long convinced that Corso was most to blame for the civil war in Florence, but he couldn't make written accusations against the one from whom he expected concrete help to return to the city.

With Donati's death, all hope of obtaining a personal amnesty had finally gone. A few months later any hope of White exiles being readmitted to Florence came to an end as a result of the action of the papal legate. Napoleone Orsini, expelled from Bologna, had moved to Imola but was forced to leave there too, and had established himself in the Casentino (at Romena, with Aghinolfo who had been *capitano* of the Whites), and at Arezzo. A vast array of forces had gathered round him ranging from the White exiles to the Ghibelline families of the Mugello (the Ubaldini) and the Ghibellines of Arezzo; it was said that even Corso Donati had been in contact with him. Orsini had in effect set up a military expedition that threatened Florence itself. There were many skirmishes between the Florentines and the allies of the legate. But it was a badly managed expedition that not only suffered setbacks in the field but failed to take advantage of the opportunity, when it arose, of a decisive attack on Florence. At the beginning of 1309, having created much mayhem between the Mugello and the upper Arno Valley, the cardinal was removed from his post.

Dante had chosen to look for a personal solution, and had therefore not been involved directly in the legate's military and diplomatic moves. He couldn't appear in Romena, where Orsini had established

his headquarters, nor even less could he turn to the Ghibelline lords he
had publicly condemned. But it was in the castles of the Faggiolani that
he came to know about the contact between Corso and the cardinal.
The legate's failure was therefore a severe blow for him as well. He must
have had the distinct feeling that one phase of his life had come to an end.

Soon his stay at Lucca would also be coming to a sudden close.

Paris or Avignon?

On March 31, 1309, an edict of the commune of Lucca required Florentine refugees to leave the city and the surrounding area. Not even Moroello's authority could exempt Dante from the order. Destiny was
continually against him: each time he found somewhere appropriate
and conducive to study (Lucca was not short of libraries), he was forced
to flee for political reasons that had nothing to do with his own wishes.[39]
The banishment from Lucca was, however, less traumatic than his expulsion from Bologna three years earlier: close at hand were the castles
of the Malaspina family, and their "courtly" benevolence was no less
lacking. But Dante's plans had changed. With no prospect of being able
to return to Florence, it seems he was no longer interested in spending
his life with feudal families in the Apennines, whether in the Lunigiana
or in the Casentino. The rewarding time he had spent in Bologna must
have made him all the more aware of the shortage of intellectual stimulus in those tiny provincial courts, despite making every effort to ide-
alize them. He felt the need to widen his horizons, for richer and more
stimulating surroundings and opportunities.

Almost all of the early biographers agree that Dante went to study in
Paris. But the claim is supported by no evidence, apart from a reference
in the *Commedia* to "Straw Street" (*Para.* X 137; "nel Vico de li Strami"),
or rue du Fouarre, where the Faculty of Arts had been based. In reality
it is very doubtful that Dante attended university lectures in Paris; a
recent scholar has quite rightly asked: "a man of over forty among young-
sters (aged between fourteen and twenty) at the Faculty of Arts? A married man among the seminarians and clerics at the Faculty of Theology?"
But if it were not for the university, what other reason would have taken
Dante to Paris? Might the idea of Dante being attracted by the philosophers and theologians of Paris be just a legend created by his admirers

to build up the picture of an extraordinary wisdom? At that time, a touch of Paris was essential for any philosopher worthy of the name.[40]

This probable legend could have been given an aura of truth by Dante undertaking a real journey to France. There is no document to help us, but in *Purgatorio* there are traces of a journey from the Lunigiana which meanders through Liguria to Provence. The rough mountainous route leaves Lerici, on the eastern border of Liguria (still ruled until very shortly beforehand by the Malaspina family), and arrives at Turbìa (La Turbie), in the western corner of France, close to Nice. Describing the steepness of the Mountain of Purgatory, Dante writes: "Between Lerice and Turbìa the wildest, / roughest crag is a stairway / compared to that, easy and open" (*Purg.* III 49–51; "tra Lerice e Turbìa la più diserta, / la più rotta ruina è una scala, / verso di quella, agevole e aperta"). Between these two points the road crosses the Lavagna torrent, which flows down to the sea between Sestri and Chiavari: "Between Sïestri and Chiavari there descends / a lovely stream" (*Purg.* XIX 100–101; "Intra Sïestri e Chiavari s'adima / una fiumana bella"), and then runs across high ground, passing west of Savona, above the town of Noli, which has to be reached down a steep slope: "Climb up to Sanleo and down to Noli . . . by foot"; *Purg.* IV 25–27; "Vassi in Sanleo e discendesi in Noli . . . con esso i piè").[41] The route is exactly that of the ancient Roman road that led to Provence. In short, there seem to be traces in the cantos of *Purgatorio* of a long and tiring journey by land. It is unanimously agreed that the only period in which Dante could have gone to France was between 1309 and 1310, immediately after he had left Lucca. The fact that the abovementioned geographical pointers are scattered among verses of the poem composed during the very same two-year period strengthens the conjecture.

But the evidence comes to an end at the border with Provence. Vague suggestions of a knowledge of the region of Provence can be found in *Paradiso*.[42] Yet the most substantial and relevant evidence, which would seem to presuppose an actual visit, is to be found in *Inferno* and consists of the brief description of the necropolis of the Alyscamps at Arles, which Dante compares to the expanse of open tombs in the circle of the heretics: "As at Arles, where the Rhone stops flowing, / as at Pola, near the Quarnaro, / which encloses Italy and washes its boundaries, / tombs variegate the whole place" (*Inf.* IX 112–115; "Sì come ad Arli, ove Rodano stagna, / sì com' a Pola, presso del Carnaro, / ch'Italia chiude e suoi

termini bagna, // fanno i sepulcri tutt' il loco varo"). Apart from the
fact that it's extremely doubtful that Dante ever saw Pola in Istria, to
accept here that he is recalling a visit to the Provencal city brings us up
against chronological obstacles that are very hard to overcome: the
cantos that recount his entry to the city of Dis were in fact most probably composed before the date of his journey to France. This means
either that Dante is using information from books or that the cantos in
question underwent a subsequent, if only partial, rewriting. This
second hypothesis is possible, though most problematic. In any event,
there is no sign in the *Commedia* of any impressions or memories of
the journey that would have taken Dante from Provence to Paris. In
1309, Dante left the Malaspina court and departed for France. If there is
no evidence that he continued on as far as Paris, could his destination
have been Avignon?[43]

Avignon at that time, where, by March 1309, Clement V had finally
established himself, was on its way to becoming the new cultural capital of Europe. (Recall that Provence was governed by the Angevins of
Naples and not by the king of France.) It had begun to attract intellectuals and those looking for professional opportunities. The White exiles of Florence were much aware of the attraction of the city, where they
could count on the sympathy of two of the most powerful cardinals in
the papal entourage, Niccolò da Prato and Napoleone Orsini. Avignon
and its court would have presented the most suitable answer for someone
like Dante, who was looking for a place in which his intellectual gifts
and learning would be appreciated, and for whom Bologna was out of
the question. He would have had no political hindrances here: at worst,
he was known for his stance against Boniface VIII, but the court of
Clement was, in any event, pro-French and anti-Boniface. The problem,
if any, would have been that of obtaining an introduction.

Dante certainly had close links with the Dominican Lapo da Prato,
who had been sent by Niccolò da Prato on a mission as envoy to the Coalition of the Whites in April 1304, but there is no evidence he had ever
personally met the cardinal; he may have had contact in Bologna with
Napoleone Orsini at the beginning of his legation, though if this had happened, it would only have been a fleeting contact. In short, although
there was no shortage of acquaintances who could have acted as go-
betweens, he would seem not to have had easy access to any of the

main channels that would have assisted in introducing a White exile into Avignon society.

There again, however, Dante still had the Malaspina family. While they could have done very little to assist him during any stay in Paris, the Malaspina could have intervened in his favor if he had gone to Avignon. One of the most influential cardinals at the papal court, Luca Fieschi (nephew of Ottobono Fieschi, descendant of the counts of Lavagna, who had become Pope Hadrian V in 1276), was in fact the brother of Alagia, the wife of Moroello. Relations between the Fieschi and Malaspina clans, being the lords of neighboring territories, were not easy, but Moroello and his wife's family remained on good terms, maintaining mutual respect and support.[44] It would be no surprise, then, if Alagia and her husband had asked their powerful kinsman to give assistance to someone under their protection.

But it is pointless asking whether Dante succeeded in getting anything. His very presence at Avignon remains mere conjecture.[45] The only likelihood, though unproven, is that in spring 1309, or shortly after, he left Italy for France or Provence.

A new king of Germany

Dante was still in Lucca when there was a turn of events in Europe to which he seems to have given little importance at the time. These events were destined, however, to have an effect on his life almost as far-reaching as his banishment in 1302.

On May 1, 1308, Albert I of Habsburg, King of the Romans (a title given to uncrowned emperors) was assassinated by a nephew. Henry of Luxembourg, strongly supported by one of the seven prince-electors and his brother Baldwin, Archbishop of Trier—perhaps also with the secret support of the pope, once again on the advice of Niccolò da Prato—was elected king of Germany at Frankfurt on November 27. He would be crowned in Aachen early the following year. Henry, whose language and culture was French, was a vassal of the king of France, Philip the Fair. The important factor, however, was not the election of a new king of Germany but that it took place against the will of the French king, whose own candidate for the throne had been his brother, Charles of Valois, whom we have already seen in action in Florence as peacemaker.

Dante's reaction seems to have been rather lukewarm. Canto VI of *Purgatorio* contains the famous apostrophe: "Ah slavish Italy, home of grief, / ship with no helmsman in a great storm, / not ruler of provinces, but whore!" (*Purg.* VI 76–78; "Ahi serva Italia, di dolore ostello, /nave sanza nocchiere in gran tempesta, /non donna di provincie, ma bordello!") He compares Italy with a horse, but in the same way that the ship has no helmsman, so too the horse has no knight: "the saddle is empty" (*Purg.* VI 89; "la sella è vòta"). The knight who ought to be "sitting . . . in the seat" is "Caesar" (*Purg.* VI 90; "e lasciar seder Cesare in la sella"), the emperor. At the time he was writing these lines, Dante was therefore still convinced the imperial throne was vacant: he clearly didn't know that the newly elected Henry intended to travel down to Italy to take the imperial crown, which wasn't formally arranged until the summer of 1309.[46] But he knew that a king of Germany had been elected: in the apostrophe, he in fact addresses Albert of Habsburg (who was still alive in 1300), threatening upon his blood the "just judgment" of heaven as punishment for having abandoned Italy, for not having mounted the saddle of that wild and untamed horse that it had become. The punishment would be "such that your successor shall fear it!" (*Purg.* VI 102; "tal che 'l tuo successor temenza n'aggia"). This threat, written after the killing of the Habsburg king (preceded a year earlier by the death of his son Rudolf) was written to give substance to the prophecy, and written after Henry had been elected the new king of Germany.[47]

In short, between 1308 and the early months of 1309, the election of a German king was not enough for Dante to consider the vacancy in the empire—which had lasted from the end of the Hohenstaufen dynasty—as having finally ended. After the death of Frederick II in 1250, three kings of the Romans had been elected (Rudolf of Habsburg in 1273; Adolf of Nassau in 1291, and Albert of Habsburg in 1298), none of whom had received the imperial crown; there was nothing to indicate that the weak Count of Luxembourg would have been successful where each of his predecessors had failed. This was the reason for Dante's indifference, almost disinterest. Moreover, he was not alone in such a feeling. It is significant that when, about a year later, news began to spread that the newly elected king would actually be coming south to Italy, it caused astonishment among people—they weren't expecting an event like this, which hadn't occurred in living memory.[48]

Writing about current affairs: The *Commedia*

For Dante the man, the years of "repentance" were an interlude that was soon over and forgotten. Once all hope of obtaining a pardon from the Blacks had gone, the speed with which he returned to political and ideological positions similar to those expressed between 1304 and 1306 in *Convivio* and in *De vulgari eloquentia* suggests there was a strong ulterior factor in that supposed repentance, despite his protests of sincerity. For Dante the poet, on the other hand, the years of repentance marked an irreversible transition. His attempt to move the hearts of his enemies led him to return to the poem he had begun before his exile and then abandoned: "incomplete," in fact, precisely because, having been conceived by a Florentine Guelf untroubled by ideological or political doubts, it could now become the pedestal on which to build the self-portrait of a loyal Guelf, offered as an assurance of his faithful adherence to the values of Florence. Let us be clear—the *Commedia,* as we know it, may be the development of a past project, but in reality it was born in exile, and with very different intentions to those of the original project. The most crucial of these intentions was perhaps Dante's urge to distance himself from the slur of treachery. That he conceived such a work under the stimulus of contingent needs while pursuing practical objectives says much about his state of mind and about how close the relationship was between his creativity and his daily life. But it also tells us how painful was his situation as an exile and how fervently he desired to end it, out of which perhaps came that false repentance. Although certain general ideas of the *Commedia,* including its visionary quality, may have been conceived before his exile, without the experience of exile the poem wouldn't have been what it is.[49]

The nexus between the *Commedia* and Dante's ambition to return to his home city is true for *Inferno,* but not for the other two parts. In *Purgatorio* he already had other political concerns and ideals. This is no surprise. The poem, imbued with autobiographical detail more than any other work by Dante, faithfully records its author's changes of allegiance and, above all, his continually varying expectations. Although it gives the idea of being a rigidly structured organism and therefore devised and planned at one single moment, in reality it was developed day by day, with constant changes of direction. From this point of view, it is the work that best expresses Dante's need to talk about himself, about what he has done, has said, and has experienced; about his political allegiances, his ideals, and his changing vision of the world. The *Commedia* is therefore a poem with two fronts: it talks about human destinies from an eschatological point of view and, at the same time, is a detailed and insistent interpretation of what was actually happening around him. It is a work of fiction, but no other works of fiction in the medieval period record facts of contemporary history, politics, and intellectual and social life in such a systematic, immediate, and detailed manner—and, moreover, without being afraid to use background details heard only through rumor or what today we would call political and social gossip. In many ways it resembles the modern-day "instant book." Readers at that time could recognize events that had occurred a short time before and the outline of many figures who had recently died or were indeed still very much alive. Yet as he wrote, Dante very often changed his ideas, moved from one political faction to another or from one protector to another (who was perhaps an enemy of the previous one). The author's biographical journey, his shifts of position, his contradictions, are all recorded in the book, which takes the form of a prophetical reading of human history and, at the same time, an autobiography. But it is a most unusual autobiography since it records the actions and thoughts of the protagonist, destined to be a man with the exceptional gift of prophecy.

The *Commedia* is a book written with a view to the future, but addressed to a readership close to the author at the time of writing. This readership changed over time as Dante changed the place where he was living, his political allegiance, his ideals. Yet the way that Dante connects writing to current affairs in his depiction of extra-literary reality remains just the same. This is absorbed into the text through nods and winks, allusions, cryptic messages, innuendos: Dante, in fact, is aware that he is writing for an audience that varies over time but is always well-informed, therefore able to unravel hidden messages and understand allusions to the present moment. It should be emphasized that the references and allusions scattered throughout the poem relate to recent (sometimes very recent) facts: many could be understood with ease only at the time of the events (and a large part of the historical references have, in fact, been lost with the passage of time). Dante could not have imagined his entire life would be devoted to writing the book and that *Paradiso* would have been published only after his death, but he certainly expected that it would have taken him many years to complete. And so why did he take so much care to "keep up with the news," knowing that the text would only be read after that news was no longer so important? It is reasonable to suppose that he didn't agree to the copying of individual cantos or groups of cantos, but that during the many years of work he gave readings to a keen and limited audience. It would be easier, then, to understand why he included political messages in many passages in the book that became important for being pronounced there and then, as events happened.

The Guelf *Inferno*

During his stay in the Lunigiana, Dante may indeed have retrieved material from Florence, as Boccaccio describes, and this could have encouraged him to resume work on the poem he had been writing.[50] In his letter of 1307 from the Casentino to Moroello Malaspina, which accompanied the "montanina" canzone, he admits to the marchese that the new passionate love that has suddenly seized him had "cruelly banished, as though they were suspect, the constant meditations with which I was considering earthly and heavenly things" (*Ep.* IV 2; "ac meditationes assiduas, quibus tam celestia quam terrestria intuebar, quasi suspectas, impie relegavit").[51] "Tam celestia quam terrestria": these words are so in tune with the definition Dante would use to describe the *Commedia* many years later—"a sacred poem / to which heaven and earth have set their hand" (*Para.* XXV 1–2; "poema sacro / al quale ha posto mano e Cielo e terra")—that it is quite possible he was talking about this same work—a work that was on his mind when he was overcome by love. The resumption of *Inferno* therefore seems to have occurred in the Lunigiana itself, perhaps in the second half of 1306. Its composition, apart from small interventions, corrections, and even subsequent major rewritings, must be regarded, from internal indications, as having been completed at the end of 1308 or early 1309, in the final period of his stay in Lucca (though Dante waited several more years until he published it, probably in the second half of 1314). The writing of *Purgatorio* followed straight after and proceeded over many years: it would only be published, in fact, between the end of 1315 and the first half of 1316.[52]

We know that for almost three years, living between the Lunigiana, the Casentino, and Lucca, Dante was trying to gain favor with the
Blacks, in particular with the faction led by Corso and with his external
allies, in an attempt to cancel out his Ghibelline reputation and indeed
to be credited as a true Guelf. Finding that the whole of the *Inferno*
gives a portrait of the author perfectly in keeping with what Dante
wanted to offer his political adversaries, it becomes clear what was the
real impetus behind his urge to return to the poem he had been working
on. We don't know how he proceeded in reworking what had already
been written: something, however, seems to have been retained since
the underlying layout of that poem, or draft poem, is still apparent in
the final version of the early cantos. Since it contained a moral and political discourse aimed at his fellow citizens, that layout could now become the starting point for a poem in which an exiled Guelf reasserted
his loyalty to Florentine ideals and his feeling, though banished, of still
being a member of the community. It is, as has been stated, a "Guelf"
Inferno, but with one important qualification: it is Guelf in a political
sense. Dante had already written *Convivio* and *De vulgari,* he had already developed convictions that were pro-imperial or, at any event,
very different from those of the party of the Church. These convictions
are neither asserted nor denied in the first part of the *Commedia;* he
limits his discussion, for tactical reasons, simply to the level of political
allegiance. Nor does he repudiate his membership in the Whites either
here or elsewhere in those texts in which he confesses his wrong and
asks forgiveness. Instead, he insists that he is a fervent follower of the
Guelf tradition to which the Florentine community had belonged for
decades, over and above internal divisions.

Two model figures of Florentine history

The canto in *Inferno* where Dante, among the heretics, encounters Farinata degli Uberti, the figure symbolizing Florentine Ghibellinism, must
have been one of the earliest to be composed after he resumed work. A
tense cut-and-thrust dialogue, a real political dispute, develops between
Dante and the great Ghibelline.[53] The underlying message is absolutely
clear: Dante the author is declaring to his protectors and enemies that
he has broken away from his dangerous past connections once and for

all. (Recall that Dante had fought against Florence side by side with Lapo degli Uberti, nephew of Farinata.) Cavalcante, too, who is condemned to the same fiery tomb as Farinata, was a famous party leader, but on the Guelf side. Dante seems to adopt an impartial attitude by pairing up a Guelf and a Ghibelline, but it's an impartiality in appearance only. Cavalcante was certainly a Guelf, but a White Guelf of the same faction as Dante. That two old adversaries should share the same fate represents then the moral and political condemnation of their descendants, who joined together to fight Florence. But Dante had to distance himself from the Ghibellines more than from the Whites. This is why—and without a single word of explanation—the condemned heretics also include Cardinal Ottaviano degli Ubaldini, a champion of Tuscan Ghibellinism, and Emperor Frederick II of Swabia, the supreme authority for the Ghibellines—"in here is the second Frederick / and the Cardinal" (*Inf.* X 119–120; "qua dentro è 'l secondo Federico / e 'l Cardinal"). Why these two great Ghibellines now both find themselves in Hell is easily understandable when we consider that only a short time before, in *Convivio*, Frederick II had been treated with much personal respect and with reverence for the position he had held, and in *De vulgari* he and his son Manfred had even been the subject of enthusiastic and high-flown praise.[54]

In Canto XV, composed shortly after the Farinata canto, another of the most illustrious figures of Florentine history, Brunetto Latini, appears. While Farinata is the quintessential Ghibelline, Brunetto is the intellectual who best represents Florentine Guelfism. He too is therefore a symbol. In the *Commedia,* and in the story of Dante's political and intellectual development, this reference to Brunetto is, in reality, a reversal.

In the 1290s, during the period of his canzoni on social morals, Dante regarded Latini as representing the archetypal sage who offered his wisdom and worldly experience to the city in order to heighten its moral and intellectual standing. This was the model that Dante still had clearly in mind when, while still in Florence, he drafted the first cantos of the poem that would become the *Commedia.* The famous opening—"Midway along the journey of our life / I found myself in a dark wood, / for the straight path was lost" (*Inf.* I 1–3; "Nel mezzo del cammin di nostra vita / mi ritrovai per una selva oscura, / ché la diritta via era smarrita")—is in fact a hidden allusion to the beginning of the *Tesoretto,* where Latini

tells how, while returning from a diplomatic mission conducted on behalf of the city to Alfonso X of Castile, on being told by a student "who
was coming from Bologna" of the defeat of the Florentine Guelfs at Montaperti and their expulsion from the city, the sorrow had made him
lose his direction and, having left the main road, he had found himself,
without realizing it, in a terrifying wood. Dante's allusion—letting a
glimpse of serious political disorder be seen behind a moral and exis-
tential disorientation—goes well beyond simple literary homage: in effect, to begin the poem in the shadow of Florence's most illustrious Guelf
intellectual was not a neutral gesture. It would seem like a way of proclaiming himself his heir.[55]

Dante's allusion to Brunetto's work was written at the beginning of
the century but, only a few years later, Dante seems to have forgotten
it. There is no trace of Brunetto in *Convivio,* and in *De vulgari eloquentia*
he is even named as one of those Tuscans who, in their madness, claim
for themselves the popular title of "illustrious" while writing verses
merely for a local audience. Harsh words indeed. Now, on returning to
the poem, his attitude is once again reversed. Brunetto becomes one of
the central figures in supporting Dante's claim to be part of that political
and cultural tradition personified by his old master himself. In Hell,
Dante emphasizes Brunetto's role as his master—"my master" (*Inf.* XV
97: "lo mio maestro")—with magniloquent expressions: "you taught me
how one makes oneself eternal" (*Inf.* XV 85: "m'insegnavate come
l'uom s'etterna"). The master's praises are accompanied by a repeated
demonstration of the filial relationship he feels he has toward him: "O
my son . . . ," "O son . . . ," "the dear kind paternal image" (*Inf.* XV 31:
"O figliuol mio . . . ,"; 37: "O figliuol . . . ,"; 83: "la cara e buona imagine
paterna"). Describing himself as Brunetto's son means declaring himself as his heir—it means pointing to himself, though a banished citizen, as the true interpreter of the city's traditional Guelf values. Brunetto judges the banishment inflicted on his pupil for his "just actions" to
be an honor, and with this he labels him as an upright citizen, faithful
to the principles of the Florentine community. Whites and Blacks, continues Brunetto, "will hunger for you" (*Inf.* XV 71–72; "avranno fame di
te"); they will both want to destroy you, demonstrating—and this is
the underlying idea—that Dante doesn't belong to any faction and that
his political rectitude is that of one who, like Brunetto, has at heart the

fortunes of his home city as a whole, and not just a part of it.[56] Dante can point to himself as Latini's heir not despite his banishment, but because of his banishment.

A significant reticence

We learn from the encounter with Farinata that Dante is an exile. The Ghibelline, in fact, predicts that he too, within four years from their meeting, will learn how "heavy" is the "art" of "returning," in other words what pain and suffering an exile is forced to endure in order to return home. Farinata's words relate to the period in Dante's life when he was vainly seeking pardon. But Farinata says nothing about when, why, and by whom Dante would be banished. The strange thing is that in none of the earlier cantos had this information been given: Ciacco had predicted that the Cerchi party would fall within three years and that the oppression of the victorious Donati party would last for much time, but he made no mention of any banishment being imposed on Dante himself. After Farinata, Brunetto would also remain silent on the why and wherefore of Dante's expulsion from Florence, limiting himself to referring to "ungrateful, malicious people" who, precisely because of his "just actions," would "become [his] enemy" (*Inf.* XV 61; "ingrato popolo maligno"; 64: "si farà, per tuo ben far, nimico"). He would dwell instead on the hostile reactions of Whites and Blacks to his betrayal. In *Inferno,* Dante the author never speaks about the circumstances or causes or responsibilities for his sentence. As a result, the story puts a character on stage about whom it is foretold that he will face serious difficulties in trying to return to his homeland, though without anyone predicting that he would actually be banished. Indeed throughout the *Commedia,* and not just in *Inferno,* there is a great gap, something unspoken that is highly significant: Dante makes no historical or political comment about the crucial years from his priorship to his exile. Brunetto blames all the "people" of Florence without distinction, as though no specific "part" of that people had banished the other; Cacciaguida would conceal the individual responsibilities of men and parties behind a generic "stepmother" (*Para.* XVII 47; "noverca") Florence. The reason for so much reticence is obvious: if he had spoken about those events, Dante couldn't have avoided blaming Corso Donati and his party. But during the two years in which he was composing *Inferno* it was from Corso himself, as pointed out earlier, that he hoped to receive the vital help to return.[57] And in any event, it was hardly appropriate for an exile looking for an amnesty to rake over the actions of the Blacks at that critical moment. Only in *Purgatorio,* from the mouth of his brother Forese, would Donati be pointed out as "that one who is most . . . to blame" for the ruin of Florence; but when Dante came to write that canto, Corso would be dead.

The first version of the Ciacco canto was written before Florence had been plunged into political turmoil. We have to presume, therefore, that the lines in which the glutton replies to Dante's question about "what will become / of the citizens of the divided city" (*Inf.* VI 60–61; "a che verranno // li cittadin de la città partita") were written during the re-working of the first part of *Inferno,* after 1306. The glutton's answer was: "after much strife / they will come to bloodshed, and the rustic party [the Cerchi or Whites] / will expel the other [the Donati or Blacks] with much offense. / Then next this falls / within three suns, and the other rises" (*Inf.* VI 64–68; "Dopo lunga tencione / verranno al sangue, e la parte selvaggia / caccerà l'altra con molta offensione. // Poi appresso convien che questa caggia / infra tre soli, e che l'altra sormonti").[58] It is surprising to see the claim in these lines that the Whites would expel the Blacks with "much offense," since, as one medieval historian has pointed out, that event "never happened," and so it is "strange that, after referring to an 'expulsion,' which, collectively as it is described, never took place, Ciacco, and Dante on his behalf, presents the revenge of the losers of that time [the Blacks] as if one side of the scales had risen while the other side had fallen ["Then next this falls / . . . and the other rises"], or in a turn of the wheel of fortune, without any reference [. . .] to the expulsion of the Whites [. . .] which, in this case, really did happen."[59] Well, the reconstruction of events by Ciacco-Dante is entirely under-standable if we recognize that those lines had been written by someone, five or six years after being exiled, who was judging the events of that time with prudence, seeking to return to his home city. It is in this spirit of (forced) reconciliation that he gives substantially the same weight to facts he knew to have been very different, and he presents the coup by the Blacks as a natural reaction to the equivalent violence supposedly inflicted by the Whites.

Almost a retraction: The first cantos of *Purgatorio*

Dante began writing *Purgatorio* immediately after *Inferno,* therefore between 1308 and 1309, in Lucca.[60] The continuity of writing gives even greater prominence to the political and ideological discontinuity between the second and the first part. In *Inferno,* there is no mention of the empire and its universal role, or rather, it is mentioned in Canto II to argue that it was created by God for the papacy: "she [Rome] and it [the empire], to speak the truth, / were established as the holy place / where sits the successor of great Peter" (*Inf.* II 22–24; "la quale e 'l quale, a voler dir lo vero, / fu stabilita per lo loco santo / u' siede il successor del maggior Piero").[61] If this formulation dates from the first Florentine draft of the canto, as seems likely, then these lines can be regarded as a remnant of Dante's staunchly Guelf thinking of that time. But during the composition of *Convivio* and *De vulgari eloquentia*—in other words, before his resumption of the *Commedia*—he had significantly changed his ideas about the empire, which he began to consider as necessary in order for men to attain earthly happiness, and had expressed very positive opinions about those whom the Church regarded as its worst enemies. But there is no trace of this pro-imperial attitude in the *Inferno* written after 1306. It's not that Dante had changed his mind and slipped back to positions held before his banishment, but in a certain sense he censored himself. Let us say that, in order to obtain a personal amnesty, he sought to provide a picture of himself that was politically correct. At the same time, he felt it inappropriate to express new beliefs that he was developing on the relationship between the empire and the papacy.

From the very first cantos of *Purgatorio,* on the other hand, his proimperial viewpoint is clear. It is as though Dante, having closed a parenthesis, had returned to the line of thought begun with his treatises. In Canto XVI, a character called Marco Lombardo, about whom we know almost nothing, expounds the theory of the two "suns": at one time the Roman Empire was illuminated by two "suns." One (the emperor) showed the way "of the world" and the other (the pope) that of God, but then one sun, the pope, "extinguished" the other, assuming for himself both spiritual and temporal power, and this is what "has made the world evil" (*Purg.* XVI 104; "'l mondo ha fatto reo"). The moral and political crisis into which the world has been plunged has a date of birth—that of the war waged by the pope against Emperor Frederick II. Marco Lombardo explains that "the land where the Adige and Po run, / once flowed with valor and courtesy, / before Frederick was disturbed" (*Purg.* XVI 115–117; "in sul paese ch'Adice e Po riga, / solea valore e cortesia trovarsi, / prima che Federigo avesse briga"): in other words, in Lombardy (though this is true for the whole of Italy) courtly values remained in favor until the Church entered into dispute with the Swabian emperor. The watershed is all the more significant when we consider that this same emperor, whose defeat turns out to be so disastrous for the public good, was sent down to Hell as a heretic in the first part of the *Commedia*.

The first half of *Purgatorio* (including, perhaps, the canto of Marco Lombardo) was written in haste, by the end of summer 1310. The abrupt about-turn was not therefore a result of the expectation aroused by Henry VII's journey down to Italy, but preceded it. In reality, the events that brought Dante back to his ideological position of two or three years before were of much more limited historical significance: not the hope of a new start for humanity, but the certainty, produced by the death of Corso Donati and the defeat of Cardinal Orsini, that his personal situation would remain unchanged. Once all possibility of a personal amnesty and all prospect of the entire White party being allowed back had vanished, it was as if Dante felt free to express his real convictions. And this is why he begins the next part of the *Commedia* in almost a tone of recantation.

In the Canto X of *Inferno*, as already stated, Frederick II was placed among the fiery tombs of the heretics in the company of Farinata, Ottaviano degli Ubaldini, and Cavalcante Cavalcanti. We know why Dante had put the Guelf Cavalcanti beside those political rivals of his, in the same way that we know why he cast the disturbing shadow of heresy over the Ghibelline-Imperial party. From the 1250s onward, it had become the political practice of papal legates and the judicial practice of the Inquisition to regard heresy and Ghibellinism as the same thing.[62] Dante was therefore simply following the commonplaces of anti-imperial propaganda. He did so in order to keep his distance from the Ghibelline party. Yet, at the very beginning of *Purgatorio*, in Canto III, he meets Manfred, the natural son of Frederick II, who was even more of an enemy of the Church than his father and a true bastion of the imperial cause. There is a clear feeling of sympathy toward this person—"he was blond and handsome and of noble aspect" (*Purg.* III 107; "biondo era e bello e di gentile aspetto")—as well as a clear respect and admiration for his family—"grandson of the Empress Constance" (*Purg.* III 113; "nepote di Costanza imperadrice"), whom he would describe in *Paradiso* as "great Constance / who by the second wind of Swabia [Henry VI of Swabia] / generated the third and last power [Frederick II]" (*Para.* III 118–120; "gran Costanza / che del secondo vento di Soave / generò 'l terzo e l'ultima possanza"). Equally clear is the condemnation of Pope Clement IV and his legate Bartolomeo Pignatelli, "shepherd of Cosenza" (*Purg.* III 124; "pastor di Cosenza"), who with "light dimmed," according to the procedure laid down for the excommunicated dead, had Manfred's body exhumed, denying him a Christian burial. In short, such a description also denotes an emotional commitment to the imperial cause that Dante would not have expressed a few months earlier. Once again we see the same Dante who in 1304, in *De vulgari eloquentia,* referred to both "Emperor Frederick and his worthy son Manfred" as "illustrious heroes" who "so long as fortune allowed them, had pursued what is human, disdaining all that is vile" (*VE* I XII 4; "Siquidem illustres heroes, Fredericus Cesar et benegenitus eius Manfredus . . . donec fortuna permisit humana secuti sunt, brutalia dedignantes"). While Farinata had been the charismatic head of the Ghibellines in Florence, the leading Italian Ghibelline after Manfred's downfall was Guido da Montefeltro. He had fought for a quarter of a century against Guelf and Angevin expansionism, first as Conradin of Swabia's deputy, then as military head of the Ghibellines in Romagna and, finally, as *capitano generale* of the Pisans against the Florentines. There is therefore a precise political strategy behind the fact that, in extreme contrast to *Inferno,* juxtaposed with the episode involving Farinata is another centered on Montefeltro, which relates to it in a similarly negative manner. Guido, who only a short time before, in *Convivio,* had been described as "our most noble Latin" (*Conv.* IV XXVIII 8), meaning perhaps "the most noble of Italians", is now reduced to a fraudster who had spent his whole life working not as a lion but as a fox, and who indeed had placed his skills at the service of his enemy Boniface VIII.[63] The fact is that his famous advice ("promise much, keep little"—*Inf.* XXVII 110; "lunga promessa con l'attender corto"), given to the pope who asked him how to destroy Palestrina (the fortress of his Colonna enemies), may have been invented by Dante. This possible invention reveals how much Dante wanted to disgrace one of Florence's greatest Ghibelline enemies, deliberately attacking his reputation.

The reversal of judgment—but we might say the restitution of the honor of the Montefeltro family—occurs once again, as it had for Frederick II, through the figure of a son, Buonconte, whom Dante meets in Canto V of *Purgatorio*. Buonconte had fought at Campaldino among the Ghibelline ranks, dying there, but also finding eternal salvation, in the battle that was to prove decisive for the Guelfs of Florence. The absolution that Dante grants him is obviously also a political recognition, and reflects upon other personalities who are not named in the poem and, above all, on those still living—for example, on Lapo degli Uberti, who had also fought at Campaldino, with whom Dante had found himself collaborating during the wars of the exiles. It was from Lapo and others like him that Dante wanted to keep a distance in clashing with the dead Farinata. Unlike Manfred, who rejoices at his own "beautiful daughter" (*Purg.* III 115: "bella figlia"), Buonconte wanders about among the other souls "with head bowed" in shame because—as he himself declares— on earth "neither Giovanna nor others have any concern for me" (*Purg.* V 89–90; "Giovanna o altri non ha di me cura, / per ch'io vo tra costor con bassa fronte"). We are unable to decipher who and what this refers to; we don't even know whether the Giovanna he names was his wife or a daughter. But there is no doubt that the unspecified "others" refers to some of his family. A daughter called Manentessa had married Guido Salvatico of Dovadola with whom Dante had stayed a year or two before composing this canto. Could it therefore be that he wanted to pepper the rehabilitation of the old Ghibelline enemy with a gibe against that part of the Guidi family, hostile to the Whites, from whom he had been obliged to seek help, and from whom, once his plan to obtain a pardon had failed, he now felt psychologically and politically distant?

Gratitude and resentment

If the gibe was directed against the Guidi of Dovadola, then Dante trod carefully: the meaning was apparent only to those well informed about Montefeltro and Dovadola family affairs. He trod carefully because that branch of the Guidi were related to the Malaspina of Giovagallo, and never in the *Commedia* is Dante disrespectful to this family.[64] On the contrary, *Inferno* and *Purgatorio* are set under the sign of the Malaspina, in the same way that *Paradiso*—or rather, a part of it—will appear under the aegis of the Della Scala family.

Dante is unremitting against his personal or political enemies but is generous in acknowledging his friends and patrons. Yet since the *Commedia* was written over a number of years, the objects of Dante's condemnation and praise varied with the alteration in his patrons, enemies, or political views; at times, he even completely repudiates his earlier opinions. His treatment of the Malaspina and the Della Scala families is typical of this.

After 1316, Dante would stay for some time in Verona as the guest of Cangrande della Scala, and it would be there that he wrote the canto of *Paradiso* in which Cacciaguida predicts his banishment and his sufferings in exile. Well, Cacciaguida would speak of his "first . . . refuge" with Bartolomeo della Scala and of the great "benefits" (*Para.* XVII 88; "a' suoi benefici") he would receive from Cangrande, but he would make not a single mention of the long and important time that Dante would spend in the Lunigiana and the support he would receive from the Malaspina family. When he wrote the Cacciaguida canto, however, Dante had not only already written but also published *Inferno* and *Purgatorio,* and we know that Canto VIII of *Purgatorio* contains not only high-flown praise of the valor and virtue of that house but also the prediction that he personally would find out how well-deserved was the fame that "honors" it. Yet also in *Purgatorio,* the abbot of San Zeno in Verona had spoken words of contempt against Alberto (father of Bartolomeo, Alboino, and Cangrande), and therefore against the whole Della Scala family. There had therefore been a complete about-turn.

Dante expresses his gratitude to the marchesi of Lunigiana first of all through the praises in the canto of Corrado II and the grim, though objectively celebratory description of Moroello, who strikes like lightning upon the people of Pistoia, and through a complex series of references to the Malaspina family. The honorable mention of their friends and allies is countered by criticism and harsh condemnation of their enemies and rivals. In the same canto in which he talks with Corrado, Dante meets the soul of Nino Visconti, former lord (judge) of Gallura. Having escaped the plot by Archbishop Ruggieri, Nino had taken refuge in Florence (where Dante might have known him) and had organized the alliance against Pisa. It is no coincidence that Nino appears together with Corrado. There were in fact close links between the Visconti of Pisa and the Malaspina, following a complicated affair having to do with the Sardinian estates of the Gherardeschi, the Visconti, and the Malaspina (an affair that involved the interests not only of these families but also of the people of Pisa and the crown of Aragon). The bond between the Visconti and the Malaspina families was also sealed by a series of matrimonial contracts upon which Dante—who came to learn about his hosts' family stories and interests during his stay in the Lunigiana—constructed a significant part of the episode in *Purgatorio*. Nino talks to Dante with affection about his daughter Giovanna: "my Giovanna" (*Purg.* VIII 71; "Giovanna mia") and harshly about his wife Beatrice: "I don't believe her [Giovanna's] mother loves me any more . . . Through her it is quite easy to understand / how long the female fire of love lasts, / if sight and touch don't regularly kindle it" (*Purg.* VIII 73–78; "non credo che la sua madre più m'ami . . . Per lei assai di lieve si comprende / quanto in femmina foco d'amor dura, / se l'occhio o 'l tatto spesso non l'accende"), both of whom were still alive at the time Dante was writing (Beatrice would die in 1334 and Giovanna in 1339). It is a family snapshot full of political implications. Beatrice d'Este, the widow of Nino, had remarried Galeazzo Visconti of Milan. But in Dante's eyes—and, above all, in those of his Malaspina patrons—the real offence of that woman was not one of remarrying, but of marrying a member of a Ghibelline family who were allied to the Doria family of Genoa, their enemies. On the other hand, their daughter Giovanna (ruler of the Visconti feudal estates in Sardinia), who had been earlier betrothed to Corradino Malaspina (to whom Corrado II was uncle), after an intricate negotiation carried out during the same years in which Dante was staying in the Lunigiana, had married the lord of Treviso, Rizzardo da Camino, a leading member of a Guelf family allied to the Malaspina of Giovagallo in November 1309. As we can see, Dante was referring to events that happened only a few months before he wrote the canto.

I realize it is difficult to navigate the maze of direct and indirect family relationships, marriages negotiated and marriages celebrated, and yet to fully understand what Dante is talking about we need to project this web of genealogical connections onto his verses, bearing in mind that in the interrelationship between ancient feudal families (such as the Malaspina) and new despots (such as the Visconti of Milan) every link made or broken or denied had far-reaching political and financial repercussions. This is why women play such an important role in these historical events, as well as in the way Dante portrays them.

In *Purgatorio,* Dante puts on stage Pope Hadrian V, who refers to a niece of his, Alagia, a virtuous girl, unlike the rest of his family: "I have a niece back there called Alagia, / a good girl, so long as our house / doesn't set her a bad example" (*Purg.* XIX 142–145; "Nepote ho io di là c'ha nome Alagia, / buona da sé, pur che la nostra casa / non faccia lei per essempro malvagia"). It is not difficult to understand why only Alagia is saved from the adverse judgment against the whole of his family once it is remembered that she is the wife of Moroello Malaspina. And who are the other "bad" ones? One of them is Beatrice d'Este herself. She and her brother Azzo VIII were in fact children of one of Hadrian V's sisters, and therefore Alagia's aunt and uncle. But still worse for the Malaspina family (and therefore for Dante) must have been Eleonora, Alagia's cousin, married to Bernabò, son of the odious Branca Doria of Genoa.[65]

He, together with Alberico dei Manfredi of Romagna, is the key figure in one of the poem's most extraordinary narrative inventions: the souls of both of them are stuck in the ice of the Ptolomea, whereas their bodies are still alive but inhabited by a devil. Doria, who would outlive Dante, dying in 1325, is placed among the worst sinners of Hell as a betrayer of guests. He is said to have murdered his brother-in-law, Michele Zanche, lord of Logudoro in Sardinia (who is also placed in Hell, in the bolgia of the barraters), after having invited him to a banquet, so that he could seize his lands in Sardinia. This is therefore, once again, a story linked to the question of Sardinia. But there is no mention of this grim event in the chronicles and documentary records, so that the only sources are Dante's own account, and commentaries on the *Commedia*. Dante might therefore have come to hear about it from the Malaspina family, who were distant relatives of Zanche.[66] Would it have been the barbarity of the crime that prompted Dante to portray Branca exceptionally as "living dead"? That is not very plausible. Generally his condemnations, like his absolutions, depended either on political considerations or on personal feelings of resentment (or gratitude). It is probable, however, that there are implications unknown to us behind this dark episode, involving Malaspina family interests or alliances. We do know that Branca Doria had forcibly occupied the Malaspina castle at Lerici in 1307: once again, Dante was writing shortly afterward, just a few months after an event that had seriously harmed his patrons.

In more general terms, the difficult relationship between the Spino Secco branch of the Malaspina family and the neighboring city of Genoa forms the context for certain malicious gibes and infamous accusations, and it is precisely against this background that the address to the people of Genoa which ends the Branca Doria canto acquires its full meaning: "Ah, people of Genoa, men devoid / of all decency and full of every vice, / why can't the world be rid of you?" (*Inf.* XXXIII 151–153; "Ahi Genovesi, uomini diversi / d'ogne costume e pien d'ogne magagna, / perché non siete voi del mondo spersi?") There would be a similar discourse for Pisa, another traditional Malaspina enemy. It is no coincidence that this canto also contains the account of the tragedy of Ugolino della Gherardesca, closely linked to judge Nino Visconti, and where, by perfect parallel, the story ends with the famous invective: "Oh Pisa, disgrace of the peoples / of the fine land where *sì* is spoken [Italy], / since your neighbors are slow to punish you, / let Capraia and Gorgona move, / and dam up the Arno at its mouth, / so that it may drown every one of you!" (*Inf.* XXXIII 79–84; "Ahi Pisa, vituperio delle genti / del bel paese là dove 'l sì suona, / poi che i vicini a te punir son lenti, // muovasi la Capraia e la Gorgona, / e faccian siepe ad Arno in su la foce, / sì ch'elli annieghi in te ogne persona!")

A delicate question

We certainly can't include the Donati family among Dante's patrons. If anything they, or rather their main branch, can be listed among his bitterest political adversaries. They opposed him during his years in Florence and, with Corso, they were among the people most responsible for his banishment. Together with the Della Tosa faction, they thwarted the attempt by Cardinal Niccolò da Prato to bring about a reconciliation. Dante would therefore have had every right to regard them as enemies, to the same extent as Boniface VIII. And yet in the *Commedia* they are treated differently from Boniface.

What attitude to take toward the Donati must have been a particularly difficult problem for Dante to resolve. We cannot forget that Gemma was a Donati and that, thanks to that marriage, he, the son of a small-time businessman, had became attached to one of the city's most noble and influential clans. In short, it was an awkward question, to be treated with delicacy.

His overall approach is one of great respect, made all the more significant by the disdainful manner in which he refers to the Cerchi, though they had been the heads of his own political party and were the people he had to thank for his public appointments. In *Paradiso*—during the years when those passions that had fired him during the Florentine troubles and the civil war must have gone, or at least been much diminished—he would still condemn them for cowardice. Then, during the course of the poem, he dwells on their lowly origins and how they had only recently immigrated from the countryside, unlike the Donati, an ancient city family of unquestionable social standing.[67]

The most complex problem was obviously that of Corso. Only in *Purgatorio* does Forese predict his death and damnation. Corso's soul could only be consigned to Hell, and yet the context of the prediction is most significant. The fact that it is announced by his brother should not be construed as some sort of retaliation. On the contrary, the friendly figure of Forese, by his presence, seems to soften any sense of grievance at that rightful and inevitable condemnation. Corso's damnation to Hell is counterbalanced by his brother who is safely in Purgatory, while in *Paradiso,* the first soul that Dante meets is their sister Piccarda, not only blessed but in the company of Costanza, mother of Frederick II. It has been written that in *Purgatorio* and *Paradiso* Dante weaves an "authentic apologia for the family of Forese and Corso." Though talk of an apologia might be going too far, it is right to emphasize how in his encounters with the Donati brother and sister he displays a familiarity that seems to hint at something more than friendship.[68] His meeting with Forese is friendly and fraternal; so too is his meeting with Piccarda. The recollection of a past familiarity, even a shared companionship—"if you recall / what you used to be to me, and what I was to you" (*Purg.* XXIII 115–116; "Se tu riduci a mente / qual fosti meco, e qual io teco fui"), Dante says to his friend—softens the inevitable accusations against the head of the family. These accusations are hidden "people then, more used to evil than to good" (*Para.* III 106; "uomini poi, a mal più ch'a bene usi"), and Dante extends a veil of goodness, fraternity, and friendship over the evil of the Donati family.

Forese yields to a violent invective against "the brazen women of Florence" (*Purg.* XXIII 101; "le sfacciate donne fiorentine") and praises, by contrast, the modesty of his wife Nella: "As dear and beloved to God / is my sweet widow, whom I so loved / as she is quite unique in doing good" (*Purg.* XXIII 91–93; "Tanto è a Dio più cara e più diletta / la vedovella mia, che molto amai, / quanto in bene operare è più soletta), who was still alive in 1300 and perhaps even when Dante was writing. How should this praise of Nella be interpreted? As a way of retracting and compensating for Dante's unflattering portrayal of her in the tenzone of insulting sonnets he exchanged many years earlier with her husband? He had described her as a poor unfortunate woman, cold even in the height of summer because her husband didn't warm her up. It is possible that this praise in *Purgatorio* also has this significance, but it should be remembered that Cacciaguida also rails against the immodesty of Florentine women with fiery words, using as a supreme example the licentiousness of a certain "Cianghella": "A Cianghella would have been held then in such wonder" (*Para.* XV 127–128; "Saria tenuta allor tal meraviglia / una Cianghella"). This name means little to us—the passage of time has reduced it to a symbol—but it meant much to Dante's contemporaries, especially in Florence. Cianghella, like Forese's widow, was still alive and belonged to the powerful Della Tosa family, who were archrivals of the Donati and the staunchest upholders of the ban against the Whites.[69] In short, in reality, behind what might seem to us today as no more than a belated friendly attempt at making amends (to Nella) or hauling out an almost proverbial figure (Cianghella) are concealed Dante's political strategies and the biting judgments he reserved for his adversaries.[70]

The writing of *Purgatorio* proceeded smoothly until the end of summer 1310, after which Dante slowed down considerably and, for some time, seems even to have stopped. These delays and pauses coincided with the period of Dante's complete involvement in the adventure of Henry VII.

8

An Emperor Arrives

1310–1313

signs appear of consolation and peace

signa surgunt consolationis et pacis

—*Ep.* V I

A game for four

IT WAS THE PRACTICE for the king of Germany to take the title of King of the Romans, a title granted by the pope and necessary in order to proceed to his coronation as emperor.[1] The emperor-elect Henry of Luxembourg did not have the pope's "confirmation" (*confirmatio*), but it did not take long to arrive. After brief negotiations—during which Henry made many concessions to the pope, even modifying the traditional symbol of the two celestial bodies so that the brighter (the sun) represented the pope while the emperor was only the moon—Clement V issued an encyclical (*Exultet in gloria*) at the end of July 1309 in which he not only recognized Henry's title as King of the Romans but fixed the date of the coronation in Rome for February 2, 1312, the Day of the Feast of the Purification.[2]

There were now four players—Henry of Luxembourg, Clement V, King Philip the Fair of France, and Robert of Anjou—in the game that had deeply affected the political life of the Italian peninsula for around four years. Henry, who ruled a small state which had no financial and military resources, needed the support of the pope in order to play an effective role in Germany. This support was also essential for him to re-establish imperial rights over that portion of Italy that still looked, for-mally, to the empire, namely the northern and central regions (excluding therefore the dominions of Saint Peter, the kingdoms of Anjou in the south, and of Aragon in Sicily); such an undertaking would have given him an authority that none of his predecessors had had since Frederick II. The pope also needed Henry. He planned, in fact, to free himself from the protection of the king of France: to this end he encouraged an alli-ance between the German emperor and the king of Naples, who was a vassal of the Church and its traditional source of armed support. This would have been a complete reversal of the Church's usual policy: until then, to protect its lands in Italy and the supremacy of spiritual over tem-poral power, the papacy had sought to hold imperial power in check by using the Guelph Angevin-French bloc against it. On the other hand, the king of France, the ruler of the strongest European power, had every-thing to lose if Clement V's plan had been realized: the rebirth of an effective supranational power would have reduced the power of the young monarchies and, in particular, that of France itself, whose point of strength was its role in protecting the pope, and the alliance with the Angevins. The position of Robert of Anjou, who had recently succeeded his father Charles II (he had died on May 5, 1308) to the throne of Naples was the most awkward: he could not break with the pope but, at the same time, was in danger of losing his role as leader and protector of the Guelf faction in Italy. To further complicate his foreign policy, there was also the old question of Sicily in the hands of the kings of Aragon, a problem which these new developments—depending on how events unfolded—could have proved advantageous for him or could have ended in outright defeat. For these reasons he moved cautiously and ambiva-lently for some time, and only later did he openly oppose the emperor, even with force. In reality, there were five players, since Florence was also in the game. Florence and the Guelf (but also some Ghibelline) com-munes of Tuscany and northern Italy were in no doubt: the emperor's descent into Italy could be a serious blow to the independence they had now enjoyed for many decades; Florence therefore took an immediate stand against any question of the emperor returning and assumed the task of leading the opposition.

During the summer of 1309—while these events were taking place at the papal court and Henry had begun to plan his journey to Italy at a specially assembled diet at Spira in August—Dante may have been in Avignon, on his way to Paris, or already there. Wherever he was, those events couldn't have made much more impression on him than the news of the election of the new king of Germany had done six months earlier. It is true that there was official talk now of a coronation in Rome, but this had been planned for three years hence, and experience showed that it was one thing to make a promise and another to keep it.

Besides, the next few months seemed to confirm Dante's skepticism. Henry was occupied with affairs in Germany for almost a year, and the expedition to Italy, at least so far as the focus of international public opinion was concerned, passed into the background. In reality, the king of the Romans had no choice. To establish his authority over German territories was an absolute priority. Henry proved himself able, managed to find agreement with the Habsburgs—who had been accustomed until then to regard the imperial throne as theirs almost by hereditary right—and to obtain the kingdom of Bohemia for his son John. The journey down to Italy wouldn't be so easy: it wasn't just a matter of taking part in a coronation (an event that just in itself had the greatest symbolic and political significance, which was the reason why popes had been refusing to celebrate it for almost a century) but of reasserting imperial rights over cities, lands, and feudal jurisdictions that had long refused to recognize him or had given him only formal recognition. In order to reach Rome, having first "pacified" Italy in the name of imperial justice, it was necessary to carry out a long and patient diplomatic operation that would smooth the way so far as possible and, at the same time, to establish a full military expeditionary force.

By the early spring of 1310, Henry VII felt he was ready, and decided to speed things up. A series of official delegations visited the cities of the Po Valley and Tuscany to inform them, one by one, of the king of the Romans' decision to come down to Italy for the purpose of restoring peace. Peace was the central word in Henry's message: he presented himself as the man whom God had destined to bring an end to disputes between cities and factional wars, to bring down the despots (those regimes established by force and with no legitimation), and to restore peace, inside and outside the city walls, through impartial justice. His greatest concern was to show he stood above the parties, whether Guelf or Ghibelline. The realization that the emperor-elect really did intend to carry the imperial banner to Italy, after so much lack of interest from his predecessors and, above all, that his plan enjoyed the support of the pope, stirred reactions of amazement at first, followed by sporadic manifestations of genuine enthusiasm. Particularly happy, of course, were the Ghibellines, whether in government or exile, as well as those Guelfs who had been banished. There were also those who made the best of a difficult situation, as was to be expected. But the Guelf cities of Tuscany, of Umbria, and Bologna were far from happy: by March 1310 they had established an anti-imperial alliance (supported, though not yet openly, by the king of France and by Robert of Anjou). Florence had no intention of even putting on a brave face. The ambassadors, on their tour of Tuscany, stopped at Ghibelline Pisa, where they were given a triumphal welcome; Lucca, where they were received with formal correctness; and San Miniato, a traditional imperial stronghold. They arrived in Florence on July 2, where the atmosphere was completely different. Their reception was extremely cool, to the point where the appointed orator, Betto Brunelleschi, one of those responsible for Corso's downfall, responded with discourtesy to the requests of Henry's envoys. They left Florence for Arezzo empty handed, without even the undertaking of an appearance at a full assembly that Henry proposed to call at Lausanne (and which in fact took place that autumn without the Florentines). Things could hardly have been helped by the presence in the imperial delegation of Simone di Filippo Reali, a Pistoian White who had been banished by the Florentines three years earlier and played a conspicuous role in Henry's court, perhaps as a counselor.[3] We begin to get a glimpse of the contradictions that would befall the policy of a king who, in the inextricable tangle of hatred and division in Italy, wanted to appear *super partes* but inevitably offended one side or the other, and sometimes both at the same time. Another member of the imperial legation was Louis of Savoy (nephew of Count Amadeus V, Henry's brother-in-law), who was on his way to Rome to take up an appointment as a senator, clearly in view of the future coronation.[4]

Not even the actions of Clement V were entirely free of ambiguity and contradiction. He had appointed Robert of Anjou as rector of Romagna on August 19, 1310: it was a way of making sure that the territories of the Church would not be touched. Nevertheless, whether he intended it or not, that decision created, in military terms, a front, which, by welding together Romagna, Bologna, and Florence, had closed most of the Apennine passes to the imperial army, leaving free only the Tyrrhenian coastal corridor on the western side of the peninsula. Moreover, in late spring Robert had left Provence (where he had been during the months of Henry's election and the pope's acknowledgment) to return to Naples, and during the journey he had formed pacts with many cities in Piedmont. On September 30 he entered Florence in triumph, where he remained for almost two months, and it was here that he received the official insignia of Papal Vicar in Romagna. In this city—where he had been five years earlier as Duke of Calabria, called there to bring help against the Whites, who had been stirred by the mission of Niccolò da Prato—Robert devoted much of his time to what must have been his passion, preaching. Almost three hundred of his Latin sermons survive, and he climbed to the pulpit of Santa Maria Novella at least three times. With wicked sarcasm, Dante would describe him as a king "of sermonizing" (*Para.* VIII 147; "re . . . da sermone") and therefore unfit to wield the sword, and Dante wouldn't be the only one to mock him in this way. In Florence the new king of Naples would spend time on matters more substantial than preaching: he would start to organize future resistance against Henry, though still with great circumspection, leaving the way open for potential compromises.

Waiting for the emperor

In spring 1310, the buildup of news that the king of the Romans would soon be actually arriving in Italy must now have begun to make some impression on Dante. He had only just finished complaining in *Purgatorio* about the lack of interest shown by emperors toward Italy and about the empty imperial throne. For several years he had been examining the tragic consequences brought to Christianity by the political oppression of the Church, but now, all of a sudden, the dreams of reform seemed to be coming true. Dante couldn't help but see the hand of the divine in this. An emperor who declared he wanted to settle discord and restore peace to divided cities offered him some solid and unexpected hope, after his miserable failure to obtain a personal amnesty, that his exile might be at an end. For this reason—and also because Dante, wherever he was, seemed incapable of remaining far from events—he must have decided that his place was in Italy. We don't know from where he set off, nor what road he took, nor even precisely when in 1310 he began his journey, but we know that in July of that year he was in Forlì, governed still by Scarpetta Ordelaffi.[5]

Biondo Flavio describes in great detail the mission of Henry VII's envoys to Florence in July 1310, after which he refers to the harsh judgment that Dante, who was then (in July 1310 or shortly after) living in Forlì ("Fori Livii tunc agens"), had made upon the contemptuous response by the Florentines to the envoys, which he condemned as impudent, petulant, and blind in a letter to Cangrande della Scala in his own name and that of the exiles of the White party ("partis Albae extorrum et suo nomine data"). What is most certain about this valuable evidence is the information relating to Dante's presence in Forlì in the summer of 1310; more controversial, however, is the possibility that Dante had written to Cangrande at that time, and that he had done so also on behalf of the White exiles.[6]

Alboino della Scala and his brother Cangrande were the mainstays of Ghibellinism in northern Italy, equivalent to what Pisa and Arezzo represented in Tuscany. They would be among the first to pay homage to Henry on Italian soil (in Asti, in early December 1310), but in July, at the same time as the imperial mission to Florence, they had already given a great ceremonial welcome to the imperial envoys who were visiting the cities of the north. It would be no surprise, then, that Dante should write to Cangrande to inform him about the outcome of the meeting that had taken place in Florence in parallel with the one in Verona.[7] It would be no surprise, of course, provided it was not a personal initiative but a message sent on behalf of the Florentine exiles and their Ghibelline friends. Besides, why should Dante have gone to Forlì, the very city in which he had been most closely involved with the Coalition of the Whites, unless he was driven there by specific political interests? The imminent arrival of the emperor certainly stirred in him expectations of a personal nature, but it must have been clear to him, now that the time for personal initiatives was over, that these interests could only be achieved as part of a collective design. It was natural, then, that on his return to Italy, he would have gone to a place where he could have received the support of organized groups. These concentrated mainly in Pisa, the main center for Ghibelline exiles, and in Romagna and the Casentino. Dante had no real contacts in Pisa (from which his special relationship over recent years with the Malaspina family had also kept him at a distance), but he had plenty of contacts spread widely across Romagna and Tuscany. And it was in the very places he had left when he had abandoned politics that he began his new involvement, alongside his old comrades.[8]

With old comrades

To anyone who might argue that it wouldn't have been so easy to repair such a clean break as the one that had split Dante and the other exiles (and one, moreover, that had led to acts of open hostility) we could reply that generally speaking, then as now, about-turns, splits, and reconciliations were part of political life: the rule in politics that there's no such word as "never" was just as true in Dante's time. In this specific case, in the summer of 1310, it was clear to everyone—those who wanted it as well as those who feared it—that the arrival of Henry of Luxembourg would have upset the balance in many places. The waters of Italian politics were already calming, old divisions seemed be coming to an end. The general word circulating among the courts, cities, and political groups during those months was to break down the obstacles between Guelfs and Ghibellines and between Whites and Blacks with a view to a complete reordering of Italian society (history would soon bring a swift end to such hopes).

It is more than probable, therefore, that Dante had returned among the ranks, so to speak, and was once again offering the Whites and Ghibellines his skills as wordsmith and intellectual. We might say that he had returned to his job as secretary and public relations officer. He himself confirms this in the letter he would send to Henry in April 1311: not only does he declare in the *salutatio* that Dante Alighieri and "all Tuscans who desire peace" (*Ep.* VII; "devotissimi sui Dantes Alagherii Florentinus et exul immeritus ac universaliter omnes Tusci qui pacem desiderant, terre osculum ante pedes") prostrate themselves at his feet, but in the body of the letter he states that he is writing on behalf of himself and others: "I who write for myself and for the others" (*Ep.* VII 2;

"Nam et ego qui scribo tam pro me quam pro aliis"). The Forlì to which Dante returned after six or seven years was no longer the same as when he had left it. Scarpetta was still the strongman of the city, but the Calboli, expelled by the Ordelaffi, were pressing to return. When the appointment of Robert of Anjou as rector of Romagna became effective in September, his vicar, Niccolò Caracciolo, would insist among other things that Scarpetta should allow the return of the Calboli, led by Fulcieri.[9] In such conditions it is unlikely that Dante remained in Forlì for very long. But the new and growing spirit of unity enabled him to visit Ghibelline families on the Adriatic side of the Apennines, such as the Guidi of Modigliana-Porciano, the Guidi of Bagno, and the Faggiolani, who would never otherwise have welcomed him after his declaration of regret at having joined forces with them. And in the Casentino, the castle gates of the Guidi of Romena could again be opened to him. It should be added that the prospect of Henry's arrival couldn't (and didn't) fail to stir the interest even of those Guidi families (such as the Dovadola or the Battifolle) who had allied themselves with the Blacks of Florence: after all, they were still palatine counts, with imperial insignia, and they too were bound to respond to the call of the future emperor. Dante may therefore have left Forlì during the second half of 1310 for the feudal courts of Romagna and the Casentino.

The iron crown

Henry of Luxembourg left Geneva in early October 1310 at the head of a small army, crossing the lands ruled by his brother-in-law Amadeus V of Savoy, and over the Alps. On the thirtieth of that month he solemnly entered Turin.[10]

He had been preceded by an encyclical letter, addressed on September 1 to all clergy and laymen of whatever status, in which Clement V asked the subjects of the king of the Romans to assist him in the work of reconciliation he would be carrying out during his journey toward Rome, where he would be crowned emperor. The pope was therefore officially sanctioning Henry's journey into Italy before the expected time, though without making any pronouncement on the request to bring forward the date of the coronation.

From Turin, moving slowly, and pausing at Chieri, Asti, Casale, Vercelli, Novara, and Magenta, the imperial procession reached Milan two days before Christmas. The march through Piedmont and Lombardy had been a success. Henry had considerably enlarged the number of his troops, and also considerably enriched his meager finances with gifts and levies. Above all, he had stirred great enthusiasm: at every place he stopped, those who came to pay homage included not only the local dignitaries but also representatives from many other central or northern cities or feudal jurisdictions as well, of course, as exiles of both political colors. Moroello Malaspina, for example, went to Vercelli and then joined the procession as far as Milan and, before that, his Ghibelline cousin Franceschino had been to pay homage. Thus far in Italy Henry had shown that the political reconciliation he promised was actually feasible: in individual cities he had succeeded in smoothing serious differences between factions. He imposed his authority through a method which he had first used in Chieri and which then became his standard, of appointing an imperial vicar with full powers who presided over councils, governed finance, dispensed justice, and commanded the armed forces. He had moved adroitly, had shown he did not incline toward any of the parties concerned (whereas everyone had expected him to favor the Ghibellines) and had thus strengthened the image of a sovereign devoted to the public good, which the propaganda circulating for months through documents and diplomatic missions had already proclaimed. The procession that arrived in Milan was therefore much larger and more representative than the one that had descended the Alps from Moncenisio. In Milan, he had to intervene once again in the city's domestic affairs, compelling the de facto Guelf rulers, the Della Torre, to allow back the Ghibelline Visconti who had been expelled. (Matteo Visconti had entered the city with him and had become one of his most trusted men.)

Henry chose Milan because it was there that he wanted to be crowned king of Italy. According to an old but obsolete custom, emperors had to be crowned three times: in Aachen, with the silver crown as king of Germany; in Rome, with the gold crown as emperor; and in Milan (or Monza or Pavia) with the iron crown as king of Italy.[11] In reality, the coronation as king of Italy, which conferred no further title or rights that hadn't already been acquired upon investiture as king of Germany and of the Romans, had a significance that was more symbolic than legal or political, so much so that few emperors after Charlemagne had required it. It was purely a matter of image, which allowed Henry nonetheless to reinforce the sense of his restorative action in Italy.

The date of the ceremony was set for January 6, 1311, the Feast of the Epiphany, in the Basilica of Sant'Ambrogio. So much time had passed since the last coronation of a king of Italy (that of Henry VI of Swabia in 1186, while his father Frederick Barbarossa was still alive and reigning) that no one could remember how to celebrate the event. Nor could the legendary "iron crown" be found, so that a new one had to be made in great haste. The coronation in Milan was, more than anything else, a great celebration that sought to consolidate pro-imperial feeling. It was attended by ambassadors from throughout the so-called *Regnum Italiae,* but not from Florence or the other Guelf cities allied to it.

A political manifesto

Was Dante there? We have no evidence either to confirm or deny it. In the letter he would send to Henry in April, Dante states that he had the honor to be received by him in an audience.[12] This could have taken place in Milan during the days of the coronation, but also in one of the many places the procession had passed through after Turin. To obtain an interview with the king, Dante must have been presented by someone who had been well placed in the court. It could have been Moroello—at Vercelli (on December 16, 1310), from where he could have followed the court to Milan—or one of his influential acquaintances (such as Uguccione della Faggiola) who gathered around Henry during his stay in Milan. More than the place where the meeting took place, it is important to establish in what capacity Henry had received him. Was Dante granted the audience in a personal capacity or as spokesman for a political group?

Dante would not have arrived empty-handed. After Clement V's encyclical of September 1, 1310, and before Henry's arrival in Turin, he had written a letter, a sort of pro-imperial manifesto, addressed "to all and every king of Italy, to senators of the mother city of Rome, to dukes, marquises and counts and to the communes" (*Ep.* V; "Universis et singulis Ytalie Regibus et Senatoribus alme Urbis nec non Ducibus Marchionibus

Comitibus atque Populis"), in other words, to the entire ruling class of the peninsula. It was, in substance, a general call for reconciliation, made possible by the sun that was appearing on the horizon. The letter explicitly follows the line of the Papal encyclical of September, which is even cited in the closing lines. To emphasize the need for peace between the two supreme powers, he uses the image of the two celestial bodies—the sun (pope) and the moon (emperor)—used by Clement in the encyclical of July of the previous year, where he had recognized Henry's title as King of the Romans.[13] One fixed point in all of Dante's writings throughout Henry's adventure in Italy was that pope and emperor had to work together.

The points set out in the letter are few, but clear. "The godless" and the "wicked" will be punished by the new Caesar, who will "scatter [them] with his sword" and "he will hand over his vineyard to other cultivators"—therefore, the emperor will proceed, where necessary, to change the rulers currently in office—but the new Caesar will be compassionate and "will pardon all those who beg for mercy" (*Ep.* V 2; "prope est qui liberabit te de carcere impiorum; qui percutiens malignitates in ore gladii perdet eos, et vineam suam aliis locabit agricolis"). The "oppressed," namely all "those who," like the writer, "have suffered injustice," must humble themselves, break the circle of hatred and animosity, and "pardon as from now" (*Ep.* V 5; "Parcite, parcite iam ex nunc, o carissimi, qui mecum iniuriam passi estis"). The emperor can do justice because the enjoyment of "public goods" and the possession of "private" goods depend upon his laws (*Ep.* V 7; "qui publicis quibuscunque gaudentis, et res privatas vinculo sue legis, non aliter, possidetis"). It is clear that Dante is not speaking personally, but in the name of the exiles. He looks forward to a political program—easily discernible if seen from the point of view of the Florentine exiles—that envisages a change of attitude by both parties: he asks the victors who are in government to accept the new order, and therefore to readmit the exiles, and promises Henry—more than those in government—that the exiles will carry out no acts of revenge.[14]

If we interpret the letter as a message of total support for Henry VII's line of reconciliation, made by the Florentine exiles (apparently without distinction between Guelfs and Ghibellines), in other words, written in the name of all those who "have suffered injustice," we can reasonably suppose that the purpose of the audience had been to officially present this document (which was probably already in circulation) to the sovereign and give him verbal reassurance of the full support of those banished from Florence. This would seem to confirm that Dante had resumed contact with his old comrades in 1310 and had indeed returned to his role as spokesman and political strategist.[15] The mediators for the meeting should be sought, then, among the circle of exiles or their sympathizers well connected to the court, and it is therefore plausible that the audience took place in Milan.[16]

A victor vanquished

The Florentines weren't altogether wrong to keep away from the coronation ceremony. A large number of Ghibellines and White Guelfs from both Florence and Pistoia had gathered around the new king of Italy. That group of political exiles that appeared to have scattered after the defeat at La Lastra was back together again.[17] Old acquaintances were renewed, but essentially under the Ghibelline shield. The Florentine Blacks would have been all the more distrustful due to the fact that many leading figures in that composite universe occupied a large number of political and administrative offices, exercising a growing influence over the sovereign.[18] It is easy to understand why so many exiles had crowded around Henry's court when we consider that one of the first acts after the coronation was a decree, dated January 23, in which the sovereign declared "null and void all orders, judgments, convictions, banishments, trials against any citizen, issued by any *podestà* or other official for accusations of rebellion, war, pillage, arson, wounding or other offense committed in any city brought under his obedience." It followed that confiscated properties had to be returned to their lawful owners (and the imperial jurists would argue long over this thorny question).[19] The vast presence of Ghibellines in power and of Whites and Ghibellines in exile was in danger of compromising the image of neutral arbiter that Henry was trying to build—an image that was finally destroyed by what took place during 1311.

Henry pressed the pope to bring forward the date of his coronation in Rome, and even succeeded, but the pattern of events in Lombardy ruled out both the first date set by Clement (May 10) as well as the second (August 15). His success in obtaining an earlier date, many months earlier, was nevertheless an achievement: in the encyclical of 1309, Clement V had set the date of the ceremony at three years hence for the reason that he himself wanted to crown him but couldn't get to Rome before the end of the ecumenical council he had called in France, at Vienne (the council would be held between October 16, 1311 and May 6, 1312). Now, in agreeing to be represented by cardinals, he assured the emperor-elect that there would be no further delay to the ceremony. And in fact three cardinals (including Niccolò da Prato and Luca Fieschi) arrived in August, appointed to act on the pope's behalf. But they found Henry in the midst of a war. The situation in Lombardy prevented the king of the Romans from taking advantage of that diplomatic success. He couldn't continue down to Rome without being assured of the loyalty of that region. He had proceeded there, as he had done before reaching Milan, by requiring cities to recognize his imperial rights. But this proved more difficult than expected. Many cities, shortly after bowing to his demands, had rebelled and returned to their previous position of independence. From February, there had been a steady flow of revolts (in Milan, Lodi, Crema, and Bergamo), which Henry had nevertheless managed to contain without resorting to excessive force, thus preserving his image as a peaceable and, above all, peacemaking king. But his attitude changed when Cremona rebelled between February and March. Even though the revolt came to an end by itself, partly through the lack of support promised by the Blacks of Florence, Henry—who had been lenient until then—became intransigent. He imagined that punishment by example would prevent further revolts. He entered the city at the end of April, demolished the city walls and towers (except for the "Torrazzo"), took three hundred hostages and imposed a harsh levy. This was a great success for Guelf and Angevin propaganda: Henry, from this moment, was no longer seen as an impartial emperor but as the head of the Ghibellines. It was a success that further grew when Henry, bound by now to a policy of repression, fell into the trap he had made for himself when Brescia also rebelled. The climate of unity during his first months in Italy was rapidly falling apart, and the two traditional factions were beginning to form again, with Ghibelline-imperial forces on one side and

Guelf-Angevin forces on the other. This second bloc was still not clear, since the policy of the pope was apparently pro-imperial and Robert of Anjou continued to play a double game.

Henry, who had hoped to resolve the problem in haste, was instead held back for four months, from mid-May to early September, in a siege at Brescia that wore down his political prestige, reduced his modest military forces (also hit by an outbreak of plague) and undermined once and for all his reputation as a man of reason. One episode caused a scandal. The head of the Brescian Guelfs, Tebaldo dei Brusati, who had even been one of Henry's trusty followers, was captured by chance during the siege. Despite pleas for clemency from various figures, including the queen, Henry was inflexible: Tebaldo was stitched into an ox hide, tied to the tail of a donkey, dragged through the military camp, then beheaded and ripped apart by four bulls driven in opposite directions, and finally, as though that were not enough, his intestines were burned and shreds of his body were put on display. One historian has written that, when Henry finally managed to occupy Brescia, he was "a victor vanquished."[20] He no longer had the strength to attack Florence or to travel to Rome. Instead, he resolved to move his court and army to Genoa, not least because the western corridor down the Tyrrhenian coast was the only route he could take once he decided to move south. He left behind him a Lombardy that had not yielded, in which only two great strongholds remained loyal to him: Milan (where, after various vicissitudes, he had appointed Matteo Visconti as his imperial vicar in July) and Verona, under the control of the Della Scala family.

A diehard Ghibelline

Did Dante remain at court after the audience? If so, for how long? If not, where did he go? It is unlikely that he returned to Forlì: Robert of Anjou's deputies had a firm grip on Romagna and it has to be remembered that Dante was a banished convict under constant threat of death.[21] We can be quite sure, however, that he was in the Casentino between March and May 1311.

From there he sent two manifesto-letters, the first addressed to the "most villainous Florentines" ("scelestissimis Florentinis"), the second to Henry of Luxembourg. The first is dated "March 31, on the Tuscan boundary, at the springs of the Arno, in the first year of the most auspicious descent of Caesar Henry into Italy" (*Ep.* VI; "Scriptum pridie Kalendas Apriles in finibus Tuscie sub fontem Sarni, faustissimi cursus Henrici Cesaris ad Ytaliam anno primo"); the second is dated "April 17, in Tuscany, at the springs of the Arno, in the first year of the most auspicious journey of Emperor Henry to Italy" (*Ep.* VII; "Scriptum in Tuscia sub fonte Sarni XV Kalendas Maias, divi Henrici faustissimi cursus ad Ytaliam anno primo"). Both letters are violently anti-Florentine. This, together with geographical factors, is the main reason to rule out the suggestion often made that they were written and sent from the castle of the Guidi of Battifolle at Poppi. Poppi is not near the springs of the Arno—indeed it is many kilometers away—whereas the castle of Porciano, belonging to the Guidi of Modigliana, is directly beneath the springs of Falterona, not far from the Apennine ridge marking the boundary ("in finibus") with Romagna. Whereas Dante could not have sent letters of this kind from a castle belonging to the Battifolle family, he would have had no such worries at Ghibelline Porciano.[22]

The almost prophetic tone and apocalyptic style of the letters mustn't obscure the fact that they deal with actual concrete political problems.[23] The Dante who is writing them is not a lone prophet but someone interpreting the thinking of a whole political movement and acting accordingly.

Henry wanted Tuscany and Lombardy to reaffirm the rights of the empire in a manner that was not just formal—that was not limited to acts of deference and the payment of a few taxes, without compromising the independence won by the city communes or despots over two centuries of conflict. Quite the contrary. He was cultivating a plan, perfectly clear to the Florentines, for a true restoration. The replacement of elected magistrates with imperial vicars who were directly responsible to him was a demonstration of it. Even more intolerable, especially for Florence—the financial capital, thanks to the florin—was the plan for monetary reform on which the imperial jurists were working. In whatever way it was carried out (decrees concerning it would be issued in August 1311), the plan to mint imperial money in place of the currencies then in circulation would have had a terrible impact on the Florentine economy.[24] But the most difficult problem of all involved the rights cities claimed for themselves and the recognition of those of the empire.

The cities of central and northern Italy had expanded, appropriating—through financial negotiations or, more often, by force—castles, towers, rural villages, and feudal estates directly subject to the empire. From the legal point of view, they were unlawful and unjustifiable: the feudal lords and others deprived of such rights had suffered an injustice (all the more since those who resisted were branded as rebels or even outlaws). But this expansion and the resulting phenomena of urbanization had provided cities with a territorial base that guaranteed their security, their source of supplies and, in short, their economic growth. The king of the Romans regarded all of this as robbery and usurpation, claimed that the rights of the empire had not been lost merely for the fact that they were no longer being exercised, and demanded their restitution. A document of the imperial chancery of 1312 would list—for Florence alone—as many as 158 castles and 60 rural communities over which the empire claimed once again to exert its rights. On this point, Florence and the other cities (including those under Ghibelline rule, which indeed had also rebelled) had to take a hard line: those rights that Henry's lawyers claimed still to be in force had in their view lapsed.[25]

It was precisely this question of the inalienability or limitability of "imperial rights" (*publica iura*) that formed the central argument in Dante's letter to the Florentines. With a vehemence that to our ears sounds almost like insanity, but which should instead be construed in the context of the biblical-prophetic style found in much medieval epistolography, and the certainty of one who believes he holds the truth, Dante predicts destruction, death, banishment, and slavery for his fellow citizens, unless they give up their blind and mulish opposition and repent, however late it might be. It is not a general opposition to Henry that is to be punished so terribly, but the specific "folly of rebellion" consisting in the fact that the Florentines, "in appealing to the right of prescription," deny "the duty of due submission" (*Ep.* VI 2; "atque iure prescriptionis utentes, debite subiectionis officium denegando, in rebellionis vesaniam maluistis insurgere.") "Do they perhaps not know," asks Dante, "wretched madmen, that the rights of sovereignty will terminate only with the end of time, and are not subject to any notion of prescription?" "The rights of sovereignty," he declares, "though long forgotten, can never be extinguished nor, though weakened, be challenged" (*Ep.* V; "An ignoratis, amentes et discoli, publica iura cum sola temporis terminazione finiri, et nullius prescriptionis calculo fore obnoxia? . . . publica rerum dominia, quantalibet diuturnitate neglecta, numquam posse vanescere vel abstenuata conquiri"). Dante is not therefore venting his spleen as an impatient intellectual who has lost touch with reality, but is entering into the midst of a bitter legal and political debate. He is expressing positions that must have been not so much those of the Guelf exiles—who, after all, were still citizens brought up in the culture of independence—but those of the groups of Ghibelline nobles and feudal lords. It is amazing, however, that Dante, who only two or three years earlier was protesting his Guelfism, now, in the heat of the conflict, has no hesitation in portraying himself, as has been said, as a "diehard Ghibelline."[26]

The defense of the inalienability of imperial rights must have pleased the Guidi, palatine counts whose estates and jurisdictions had been curtailed by the expansion of Florence which, heedless of their imperial rights, was constantly and systematically usurping—indeed sucking like a "bloodsucker," as the great jurist Boncompagno da Signa had written around a century earlier—larger and larger portions of their estates.[27] It certainly pleased the Guidi of Porciano, of Bagno, and of Romena, but it could hardly have displeased even those of Battifolle. They, however, as already pointed out, would never have allowed an open letter so hostile in tone and substance to be sent from their castle to Florence. And even less would they have endorsed the one sent to Henry on April 17. The dignity of the palatine counts had almost compelled them to support the imperial side, but it must have pained them. The Battifolle, who had broken away from the more prestigious Ghibelline branch of Bagno in 1275, had always followed a Guelf and pro-Florentine position. Guido then had close links with the Donati faction (it will be remembered that the plot in 1300 involved his armed intervention) and later with the Della Tosa faction. In any event, Battifolle support for Henry's cause would be short-lived: by the winter of 1311 and 1312, Guido di Battifolle was at war in the upper Arno Valley, along with Guido Salvatico of Dovadola (another Guelf branch that had sided with the Blacks), against the imperial forces. The story would end in 1315 with Battifolle becoming Robert of Anjou's vicar in Tuscany.

The second letter to Henry, written at the time when he was moving against the rebels at Cremona, is a strong and desperate appeal for him to realize who his true enemies are and to act accordingly. The Tuscans see him holding back in the Po Valley and ask "with amazement" whether he has "forgotten" their region, as if "the imperial rights to be preserved were limited to the confines of Liguria" (*Ep.* VII 3; "Sed quid tam sera moretur segnities admiramur, quando iam dudum in valle victor Eridani non secus Tusciam derelinquis, pretermittis et negligis, quam si iura tutanda imperii circumscribi Ligurum finibus arbitreris"), in other words to northern Italy. Florence is taking advantage of his delay "and every day, fomenting the pride of villains, is building up new forces" (*Ep.* VII 4; "et cotidie malignantium cohortando superbiam vires novas accumulat") and acquiring allies. The decision, after the winter, to remain in Milan through the spring, seeking to subdue the rebel cities one by one, like cutting off each single head of the hydra, would bring Henry no decisive victory: as soon as one city is retaken, others rebel. He doesn't seem to realize that the "fox" producing the stench that is infecting Italy comes not from the Po nor the Tiber but from the Arno, and that this fox "is called Florence" (*Ep.* VII 7; "An ignoras . . . ubi vulpecula fetoris istius, venantium secura, recumbat? . . . et Florentia, forte nescis?, dira hec pernicies nuncupatur"). So crush this viper, this diseased sheep, this Myrrha who rejects her legitimate husband and couples incestuously with the pope, father of all. Dante is urging Henry, therefore, to take his own city by force.

Once again, the letter should not be regarded as the isolated gesture of someone who, to obtain an audience, feels authorized to advise, even to teach, an emperor: besides, Dante himself states that he is writing on behalf of himself and others. It forms part of a strategy elaborated at that particular time by the Tuscan exiles to put further pressure on Henry to convince him to adopt a different course in his expedition. On April 14, three days before the date of Dante's letter, the priors of Florence had written to ambassadors from Naples, and to Robert of Anjou himself, that "all the Ghibellines of Tuscany and Lombardy, as well as the king's counselors, are daily doing all they can to persuade Henry to embark on a campaign against Florence."[28] The Tuscan exiles may have been right to urge him to make a direct attack on Florence: Henry, if nothing else, wouldn't have been caught up in the siege of Brescia and he wouldn't have lost what remained of his reputation as an even-handed sovereign.

If we are surprised by Dante the Ghibelline in his letter to the Florentines, what do we make of this instigation to war against his own city? Read what he wrote about Florence, as an exile recently defeated and, moreover, while at the same time criticizing his city: we "love Florence to the point that, because we have loved it, we suffer exile unjustly . . . for our pleasure or for the peace of our senses there is no dearer place than Florence" (*VE* I VI 3; "quanquam . . . Florentiam adeo diligamus ut, quia dileximus, exilium patiamur iniuste . . . Et quamvis ad voluptatem nostram sive nostre sensualitatis quietem in terris amenior locus quam Florentia non existat"). And remember that this person, who loved his city until very recently, had humbled himself to ask for pardon in order to return. This helps us to understand what explosive mixture of intellectual vision, personal rancor, and impatience for revenge had formed within him with the unexpected arrival of the emperor—an almost legendary character, a figure from stories of the past, who had now miraculously reappeared, as though history had turned full circle and gone back to where it had left off, after the downfall of the Swabians.

During the months spent in the Casentino, Dante therefore also crossed that gateway of the castle at Poppi that had remained closed to him when he had wandered the valley as a White exile. In May we find him as the guest of Guido di Battifolle and his wife Gherardesca (daughter of the Pisan count Ugolino). As usual, there at Poppi, he earned his board and lodging by working as secretary and registrar. There are three short letters—or rather, three versions of the same letter—sent by Gherardesca to the queen of the Romans, Margaret of Brabant, Henry's wife, in reply to her message. While the first two are undated, the final draft carries the date May 18, from the castle of Poppi. Dante must have been its author. The writing of this brief letter must, it seems, have given rise to considerable debate at the Guidi family court. By comparing the rough copies we glimpse the traces of a discussion between the writer, Dante, who tries to introduce various details that are specifically political and pro-Empire, and the family who want them removed. The first draft ends (remember that it is being sent by Countess Gherardesca) with a plea that God, "who subjugated the barbarian nations and the citizens of the Roman Empire, in defense of mortals, may change the human family for the better in this delirious age, with the triumph and the glory of his Henry" (*Ep.* VIII; "ut qui romani principatus imperio barbaras nationes et cives in mortalium tutamenta subegit, delirantis evi familiam sub triumphis et gloria sui Henrici reformet in melius"). They are typically Dantean concepts, and they are concepts that are politically very much in character. In the next draft there is a reference to "celestial Providence" which "has ordained that human society should have one Prince alone" (*Ep.* IX; "que humane civilitati de Principe singulari providit"). In the version actually sent there is no (or almost no) trace of any of this. "Inform her good and serene Majesty of the Romans," writes Dante-Gherardesca, "since she asks it, that at the moment of dispatch of this letter my dearest consort and I, by the Lord's blessing, were in good health, enjoying the flourishing condition of our children, more happy than usual since the signs of the resurgent empire were already promising better times" (*Ep.* X; "Audiat, ex quo iubet, Romanorum pia et serena Maiestas, quoniam tempore missionis presentium coniunx predilectus et ego, Dei dono, vigebamus incolumes, liberorum sospitate gaudentes, tanto solito letiores quanto signa resurgentis imperii meliora iam secula promittebant"). There had to be some reference to Henry's expedition but, confined as it is to a family context and reduced to a motive for private satisfaction, it has lost its political bite. Guido of Battifolle didn't want to run any risks, knowing the letter would end up in the archives of the imperial chancery.[29]

Baldo d'Aguglione's amnesty

In the year when Henry's prospects were beginning to fail, the other actors on the scene were busy in diplomatic exchanges and some major military activity.

Clement V continued in his attempt to forge an alliance between Henry and Robert of Anjou, cementing it with a marriage between Robert's son Charles, Duke of Calabria, and Henry's daughter Beatrice. The pope's plans (though not those of the emperor) were that Beatrice would bring as a dowry the kingdom of Arles, a vast area of lands extending east of the Rhone, which included large estates such as those of the counts of Provence, Burgundy, and Savoy, which were part of the empire, but over which the emperor had exercised only nominal rights since the times of the Swabians.[30] The most powerful lords of the area were the Angevins themselves, the counts of Provence, who with such a marriage (already previously attempted with the Habsburgs) would have controlled the whole area. The project was bound to incur the hostility of Philip the Fair, who was extending the power of the French monarchy into those territories, using military means as well. And so, in May 1311, Clement would be forced to recant by declaring publicly that he would never have allowed the king of the Romans to concede any rights whatsoever over the kingdom of Arles to any prince who wasn't the Roman Church. And this was one of the clearest indications that his attitude toward Henry was changing and that the influence of the king of France was having an effect.

Robert of Anjou continued to play a double game. He didn't want to clash with the pope, sent diplomatic missions of reconciliation to Henry, and made his own proposals for marriage alliances in exchange for the appointment of his son Charles as imperial vicar for Tuscany. In short, he expressed willingness, on these conditions, to let the imperial entourage travel to Rome unhindered. But at the same time he was committing acts tantamount to blackmail: together with Florence he sent a large contingent of Catalan mercenaries in the pay of the Guelfs to occupy Versilia, thus closing the only land corridor still open to the imperial army, and sent an armed force to Rome under the command of his brother John, Count of Gravina, with the excuse of assuring Henry's safety during his stay in Rome, but in reality (as would become clear) with the intention of preventing the coronation from going ahead.

Florence was working on two fronts: externally, it extended the network of Guelf alliances (at the end of March, a few days after Dante's letter to the Florentines, a parliament of Guelf cities had been held in Florence itself); internally, it strengthened the city wall and united the people of the city as far as possible.

One of the most disturbing aspects of Florentine life was the fact that the conflict between political parties or rival families continued unabated within its walls, sometimes violently, even during the city's most difficult moments. Even in 1311, private vendettas gave rise to disturbances and riots.[31] In view of the increasing likelihood of conflict with the imperial army, the commune decided to encourage domestic reconciliation and ordered an amnesty. Enacted on September 2, it was known as the Baldo d'Aguglione Reform: he was the jurist, in his capacity as prior, who was most responsible for it. The amnesty (conditional on payment of a tax calculated on a percentage of the fine the offender had been sentenced to pay) related to both ordinary and political offenses, and therefore involved several thousand people in the city and surrounding areas.[32] In this way the commune hoped to reduce the forces that the exiles were able to recruit and to strengthen internal unity. To ensure there was no risk to domestic peace, the Ghibellines were excluded from this order. Some of the Guelfs were excluded as well. The order ended, in fact, with a long list of around two hundred families, divided by *sestieri,* who were described as rebels and expressly excluded. Appearing there was the name Dante Alighieri, along with the sons of Cione di Bello ("filii domini Cionis del Bello et Dante Allegherii"). We don't know why the nephews of Geri del Bello were excluded from the amnesty; on the other hand, if we think about his propaganda work in support of the emperor and against Florence over the previous months, it is easy to imagine why the political convict Dante had been excluded. Indeed, we would have been amazed if he hadn't.

It is surprising, however, that in a long and very exact list that includes whole family clans or large groups within one and the same family, and in which the names of individuals are almost always followed by additional words such as "et filii" (by far the most common), "et fratres," "et consortes," "et nepotes," and even with such specifications as "et consortes, excepto . . . ," Dante's name appears with no additional words. This is surprising because Dante had children, and the Florentine law was very strict about the children of a person who had been banished: when they reached the age of fourteen, males had to leave the city. We might think, then, that Iacopo and Pietro, unlike their father, had been granted an amnesty, but this goes against the fact that four years later, in 1315, they too would be affected by the death sentence passed once again on their father. It can only be supposed that they hadn't yet reached the age of fourteen in September 1311, so that the provision couldn't apply, and that they had reached that age by 1315.[33] The case of the supposed eldest son, Giovanni, is different: if he were actually the son of Dante, he would have been already affected by the banishment before 1308; and if he doesn't appear in this order, it is because in the meantime he must have died. This reconstruction would suggest that the other two sons

were born a long time after the presumed date of Dante's marriage to
Gemma, namely between 1297 and 1300–1301.

Shadow of the past

It has been suggested that Dante, who was still in the Casentino in late
spring of 1311, had left later that year because he had begun to find the
Guidi undependable. In the castle at Poppi, he had seen how unenthu-
siastic the Guelf branches of the family were about joining the imperial
ranks; nevertheless, in the summer to autumn of 1311, none of them had
made any open gesture of dissociation or (as would happen a year later)
of defiance. And there again, even if he had decided to leave the Casentino, where would he have found shelter? Henry was garrisoned in Lombardy; Romagna was controlled by Robert of Anjou; even the access
roads to the Malaspina family in the Lunigiana were being controlled
by mercenaries sent from Florence. That left only Pisa, where many exiles had concentrated. But Dante had to think twice before going there.
It was highly unlikely that the Pisans would have welcomed him with
open arms after he had described their city as a "disgrace" to Italians:
"disgrace to the peoples / of the fine land where sì is spoken" (*Inf.* XXXIII
79–80; "vituperio de le genti / del bel paese là dove 'l sì suona"). At that
time, as the hard-line Guelf he had then seemed, he rubbed salt into a
wound still open in his description of the death of Count Ugolino.[34] Can
it be imagined that Dante hadn't read that canto of *Inferno* to Guido di
Battifolle and his wife Gherardesca, daughter of Ugolino? That he hadn't
read it in the house of Moroello, who was also related to one of the
count's sons?[35] Can it be imagined, considering the many relatives the
Gherardesca family had in Pisa, that at least news of it hadn't spread
there? And then, apart from the anti-Pisan sentiment in *Inferno*, Dante
would have been compromised by his close links with the Malaspina:
how would the Pisans have treated a White Guelf who had lived peacefully for over a year in Lucca, their age-old enemy? It wasn't easy for
Dante to free himself from the shadow of the recent past. It is therefore
likely he remained in the Casentino until at least the autumn.[36]

Toward the end of October 1311, several envoys sent by Henry to the
cities of Tuscany, while he was on his way to Genoa, arrived by chance,
after various mishaps, on the borders of the Casentino. The legation

included two bishops: Pandolfo Savelli (the Savelli family in Rome would openly support Henry during the armed conflicts prior to his coronation) and Nicholas, bishop of Butrint in Albania (a Dominican friar from Luxembourg who would later write a detailed account for Clement V about Henry VII's exploits in Italy). After a perilous journey to Florence, following the open hostility shown by the people of Bologna, the imperial envoys were declared public enemies, stripped of their horses and money, and thrown into prison. On their release, they were conducted through the Mugello as far as San Godenzo, where they could at last enjoy the hospitality and protection of Count Tegrimo II of Modigliana-Porciano. Over the next few days they were welcomed by the Guidi brothers (Tancredi, Bandino, and Ruggero who, apart from Ruggero, were Ghibellines), by the Guelf Guido Salvatico, and by Guido of Battifolle. The Guidi declared their allegiance to Henry, to whom they promised help as soon as he arrived in Tuscany. In his report to the pope, Nicholas of Butrint emphasized how the Guelf branches showed themselves on that occasion to be the most fervent supporters of the imperial cause, only to disavow their promises and side in the end with Florence. The legates crossed the whole of the Casentino from north to south, arriving in Arezzo at the palace of Bishop Ildebrandino of Romena.[37] If Dante was still staying at the castles of the Guidi family in October and November, he would certainly have been present at those meetings. One daring possibility—though by no means out of the question—is that he joined the imperial expedition on its way back to the court, and accompanied them to Genoa. For someone like Dante, in need of protection (and perhaps with no means of transport), to travel in such company (the Guidi supplied horses for them and their retinue) would have been the ideal solution. If this is what happened, Dante would have reached Genoa toward the end of November or early December, very shortly after Henry had establish court there.

Among the Genoese "full of every vice"

Henry arrived in Genoa toward the end of October 1311: he would remain there until February 15, 1312, when the imperial entourage set off for Pisa. Here too, in Genoa, Henry asked for full powers (and obtained them, though not without resistance). His demand was justified by the need to put an end to the dispute that divided the Spinola and Doria families. (The strongman of the city at that time was Bernabò Doria, son of Branca, the "living dead").[38] Once again, Henry played the role of the sovereign peacemaker. But his time in Genoa was not easy, worsened by the fact that the imperial army had brought with it the plague, which had broken out beneath the walls of Brescia. (It was from that disease, contracted at Brescia, that Margeret of Brabant would die on December 14.) Later, however, there would also be tensions in imperial Pisa. Henry may perhaps have been the mild-mannered peacemaker, as the chronicles described, but he could act roughly even toward his friends. Nevertheless, in Genoa, he was able to reorganize his troops, boost his finances, and prepare for the military expedition to Rome. The empire's declaration against Florence on Christmas Eve of 1311 was more of a gesture than a real threat, but it was a clear message to everyone about what his future political and military moves would be.

During the winter between 1311 and 1312, Dante too was in Genoa. This is established by a very special witness. In a letter to Boccaccio, Petrarch writes that he met Dante only once in his life, when he was still a child. He doesn't specify where or when, but states only that Dante and his father were friends and were both in exile. Yet from what he says about his childhood in other letters, we can be sure that Ser Petracco and Dante met in Genoa that very winter, in the presence of young Francesco. Petrarch and his family were waiting to board a ship for Avignon. It was expected to be a difficult crossing because of the rough sea conditions, and they would indeed be shipwrecked not far from Marseilles. Now, that Dante and Ser Petracco were great friends was perhaps not altogether true, but they would certainly have had much to talk about: their paths had crossed several times during the years when they were members of the Coalition of the Whites. Henry's arrival had stirred the same hopes in each of them, and each had been excluded from the recent amnesty in Florence. We can imagine, nevertheless, that they wouldn't have talked only of politics. If the theory about Dante's stay in Avignon is correct, then Ser Petracco, on his way to a city unknown to him, would have been interested in forming a picture of what awaited him from someone who had been there not many months earlier.[39]

Dante would have spent time at Genoa in the company of the exiles (some of whom would have been friends and acquaintances) who gravitated around the imperial court. It is most unlikely, however, that he had established any meaningful links with members of the city's ruling families; there is reason to think that his relations with the Genoese were not entirely easy. According to certain legends, for example, he was given a beating by friends and servants of Branca Doria in revenge for the way he had insulted them in *Inferno* (or, in other versions, that Dante had taken his revenge in *Inferno* for an attack in Genoa).[40] Such legends cannot be trusted (besides, the second version is disproven by the fact that the canto was written before 1311), but neither can we entirely discount them: stories that are obviously baseless nevertheless always give some measure of the general climate. And nor can the question be settled by arguing that Doria couldn't have held such resentment because, at that time, *Inferno* hadn't yet been published. We tend to admire the integrity and courage with which Dante openly attacks powerful people who are still alive at the time of writing, making scathing judgments and hurling out-and-out insults with supreme disregard for the consequences. But we rarely ask what consequences and repercussions those judgments could have had upon his life—perhaps because there is no evidence on the matter. He himself suggests that such reactions had taken place when, in *Paradiso,* he tells Cacciaguida that he fears that the truth, declared without simulation and with words that those concerned consider "harsh," "brings to many people a most bitter taste" (*Para.* XVII 117; "a molti fia sapor di forte agrume"). The attacks upon the Doria, the Fieschi, and the people of Genoa in general—"men devoid / of all decency and full of every vice, / why can't the world be rid of you?" (*Inf.* XXXIII 151–153; "uomini diversi / d'ogne costume e pien d'ogne magagna, / perché non siete voi del mondo spersi?")—wouldn't have remained closed inside a secret book, awaiting future publication. In the *Commedia,* Dante is constantly concerned with current affairs. When he speaks of past events, he does so from the political perspective of the present or in relation to the situation unfolding at the time he is writing. It is unthinkable that he kept under lock and key the pages of something we have already compared to the "instant books" of today. He would at least have read his anti-Genoese verses to the Malaspina, and in the narrow world of the medieval aristocracy, intimately linked through kinship and marriage, sentiments of such "bitter taste" as these would have circulated wide. The Doria may not have had him beaten, but it's very doubtful the Ghibelline rulers of Genoa would have given a particularly warm welcome to a Florentine like him, a person not only banished but linked to Guelf families who were their rivals. In short, Dante must have paid a price for his constant moving about between different and even opposing political positions and for the debts he contracted with his patrons. If, between 1306 and 1308, he had felt the consequences of his previous alliance with the Ghibelline exiles, now it was his expression of whole-hearted Guelfism and loyalty to the Malaspina that worked against him. A defenseless exile like him, in Genoa but also a little later in Pisa, would have been kept out of difficulty only through the protection of the imperial court or court circles. And there again, if it weren't for the presence of the court, what other reason would have driven him to that city?

Toward the elaboration of a theory

What reason had driven Dante to Genoa if it wasn't to get away from the Guidi? It is a constant feature of his life that periods when he throws himself into the political arena are followed by others when he withdraws to study and to write. Having spent a couple of years fighting among the ranks of the exiles, he felt the need to give order to the new experiences gained over that period, to organize the feelings, the sensations, and the knowledge he had accumulated into a single conceptual framework. He had retired to Bologna and dedicated himself to the composition of *Convivio* and *De vulgari eloquentia*. He always felt a pressing intellectual need to arrange, organize, raise day-to-day experiences to higher levels of generalization. But it became more urgent in periods of transition when the social panorama around him changed and, above all, when his inner perspectives and the criteria with which he saw reality changed. The year 1311 was one of these moments.

Until 1310, Dante's attitude—as city dweller and as exile—was that of a municipal man. It is true that he had fought against Florence, but the idea of depriving it of its autonomy had never occurred to him. Even as an exile, he considered Florence the focal point in his view of history. With the arrival of the emperor, he saw the role and destiny of his city from a new perspective. From that moment he had invoked a universal temporal power, a peace assured by an institution devoted to the common good, the restoration of an imperial right that would have shattered a well-settled political and state geography; in short, through his writings and his actions, he had supported Henry's political and institutional program. But for someone like Dante this had to involve a deep reflection on the legitimacy and founding principles of that program. He had begun to think about the role of the empire from the time of *Convivio*; during 1311, at the height of the conflict, he had formed various specific ideas about it. For example, in the letter to the Florentines he had declared in no uncertain terms the providential origin of the empire, ordained by the Lord "so that mortals shall have peace, in the serenity of so great a protection, and wherever it is given civilly, respecting the laws of nature" (*Ep.* VI 1; "Eterni pia providentia Regis . . . sacrosancto Romanorum Imperio res humanas disposuit gubernandas, ut sub tanti serenitate presidii genus mortale quiesceret, et ubique, natura poscente, civiliste degeretur"); but he had not outlined a systematic historical, legal and, in certain respects, theological context into which to place and justify, in the light of certain incontrovertible truths, both Henry's actions and his own. He would draw a full picture of this in a treatise specifically dedicated to "monarchy," which he regarded as "being subject to one single principality and one prince" (*Conv.* IV IV 4; "uno solo principato e uno prencipe avere"). He had probably already begun to think about its contents in 1311, in the valleys of the Casentino. In a work of this kind, the legal aspects were particularly important. Dante therefore needed access to a law library in order to expand what may already have been a partial knowledge but was almost certainly insufficient to deal with such weighty arguments. Would he have found the works he needed in the castles of the Guidi, from the *Digest* of Roman Law to the writings of Accursius and of Odofredus Denari? Henry's chancery, with its impressive output of legal texts, was certainly well-stocked with such works. And not only that. The imperial court, for obvious reasons, was in continual contact with the chanceries of European monarchs and with the headquarters of the imperial council at Vienne, and was therefore the first to receive draft decrees and council documents. And these kinds of documents would have been most valuable for anyone contemplating a work that was theoretical but also firmly anchored in current events.

Coronation and catastrophe

Henry sailed from Genoa on February 15, 1312. He reached Porto Pisano, after a slow voyage, on March 5. The following day, the entourage left the basilica of San Piero a Grado by the port, arriving at the city's cathedral amid great joy and celebration. It couldn't have been otherwise—Pisa had always sided with the imperial cause. But the warmth of the Pisans cooled considerably in the face of Henry's economic claims and, above all, his firm and uncompromising decision to exercise full power over the city. His stay in Pisa, where a large number of Tuscan Ghibellines had gathered (including Count Tegrimo II Guidi di Modigliana-Porciano from the Casentino and also Bishop Ildebrandino di Romena from Arezzo, who would die there a year later), allowed him to reorganize his troops in preparation for the expedition to Rome. He and his army moved off on April 23, taking the road through the Maremma and reaching Rome on May 6.

Senator Louis of Savoy had been at work there for several months, with the support of the Colonna family. His task was to take control of the city before the coronation, which was to be held at Saint Peter's Basilica, but the king of Naples had sent a military contingent the previous December under the command of his brother, John of Gravina, to prevent it from taking place. The Angevin troops, actively supported by the Orsini, age-old rivals of the Colonna, had occupied a large part of the city, including the so-called Borgo, the area between the Tiber and Saint Peter's. In the absence of an agreement, Henry would have to open the way by force. Only the pope had the power to compel the Angevins to withdraw, and Clement V seemed prepared at first to take this step, but then, under pressure from the king of France, he changed his mind. Instead, toward the end of March, he warned Henry that the king of Naples was a beloved son and vassal of the Church and could not therefore be attacked. It was clear from this moment that the pope had yielded to Philip the Fair and had withdrawn his support from the king of the Romans. Henry was left with no choice but to fight. After a period of preparations, during which he succeeded in occupying the Capitoline Hill and other baronial fortresses, he attacked the Angevin forces on May 26 with the support of Colonna troops, in an attempt to open the road toward Saint Peter's which was blocked by the Orsini defenses. But "the greatest battle ever to have taken place in the streets of Rome" ended in defeat for Henry, who failed in his attempt to storm the Borgo.[41] He decided to abandon the idea of Saint Peter's—the traditional place of coronations—and make do with the basilica of Saint John Lateran. On June 29, 1312, Henry of Luxembourg became the seventh ruler to take the name Emperor of the Romans.

From the legal point of view, the ceremony, presided over by cardinal legates, gave the king of the Romans all imperial powers and sanctions: in his letter of the same day to the sovereigns of Europe announcing that his coronation had taken place, Henry VII solemnly proclaimed the sovereignty of the emperor, answerable to God alone, over all monarchs. Philip IV replied that France recognized no one above its own king.[42] From the symbolic point of view, a coronation not performed by the pope and not at Saint Peter's was something of a nonevent, considering in particular that this was the first time in almost a hundred years that a king of the Romans had received the imperial diadem (the last one had been Frederick II in 1220). Nor was the basilica of Saint John Lateran the most fitting place for such a solemn investiture. Half-destroyed by fire four years before (on May 6, 1308), it was still awaiting proper restoration: it may even have been without its roof, which had collapsed among the flames. Accounts of the banquet held after the ceremony give a fairly clear idea of the atmosphere in which the festivities took place. "The grand banquet was arranged outdoors at the Convent of Santa Sabina, on the Aventine [Hill], owned by the Savelli . . . But enemy slingsmen and archers, positioned on the highest points of the Aventine, hurled stones at the spectators who had gathered in curiosity around the guests, and disrupted the banquet with sounds of jeering . . . the open-air banquet had to be suspended and continued inside protective walls."[43]

The emperor remained in Rome and its surrounding district until late August. Many German princes defected during this period and returned to Germany with their few troops: Henry's already meager army became further depleted. He decided, nevertheless, to move against Florence. His strength allowed him to win the numerous battles in open countryside and in the district around Florence, but it was not enough to attack the city or to surround it with an effective siege. From mid-September, he camped for around forty days beneath the walls of Florence, though without closing off all access routes. That pointless siege wore down his army and struck a serious blow to his imperial image. Toward the end of October he abandoned the siege but remained in the area for several months: he captured many castles and towns but failed to make any real breakthrough in an enterprise that was proving more and more disastrous. It wasn't until early March 1313 that he returned to Pisa.

Meanwhile, however, something extraordinary had happened. From late 1311, Henry had been involved in negotiations with Frederick III of Aragon, the king of Sicily (at the same time as negotiations the pope had been encouraging Frederick to carry out with Robert of Anjou). The Angevins had sought in vain, since the time of the Sicilian Vespers, to regain possession of the island over which the kings of Aragon had ruled (in their view) illegitimately. A few days after the coronation ceremony, on July 4, 1312, the negotiations were concluded with the signing of a military alliance between the king of Aragon and the emperor. The objective was to invade the kingdom of Naples from both north and south at the same time.

The alliance signed with Frederick of Aragon gave the emperor the chance to strike a decisive blow against the one who had turned out to be his real and most powerful enemy. And so, having passed a sentence of death by decapitation against him (on April 26, 1313) as traitor of the empire, Henry officially announced the start of the military expedition on August 1. On the same day, the Sicilian fleet set sail from Messina and Frederick's army invaded Calabria. It all seemed as though Robert of Anjou would be crushed by this pincer attack and Henry VII would succeed in his design to become master of the whole peninsula. Except that the emperor fell sick on the march south, and died at Buonconvento, near Siena, on August 24.

The imperial army fell apart. The Ghibellines who had joined the emperor went back to their cities, and the exiles also left: only the Teutonic knights remained to escort the body on its journey to Pisa, setting off immediately. To prevent the body from decomposing, the entrails were removed and it was boiled in wine and herbs. At Pisa, a solemn funeral took place, and Henry's body was entombed in the cathedral, where it remains today, in a sarcophagus that the commune commissioned to be carved by Tino di Camaino. The climate of grief around the city was further aggravated by the rumor which had immediately

begun to circulate (and would continue for centuries) that Henry had
not died of sickness (perhaps from some form of malaria contracted the
previous year during his stay in the Roman countryside) but from poisoning. The finger of blame pointed to his confessor, the Dominican
friar Bernardino da Montepulciano, who was said to have administered
a poisoned host.[44] The rumor, though discounted among imperial circles, continued to spread. In many cities, the Dominicans (perhaps also
at the instigation of their rivals, the Franciscans), became the target of
this accusation, were attacked and injured, and even their churches and
monasteries were not left unscathed.

An obscure passage in *Purgatorio,* found moreover in the context of a
very obscure prophecy, the famous one of the "five hundred ten and
five," could suggest—but here the conditional tense is essential—that
even Dante thought Henry had been killed: "know that the vessel the
serpent broke, / was and is not; but let him whose fault it is, believe /
that God's vengeance fears no sop" (*Purg.* XXXIII 34–36; "Sappi che 'l vaso
che 'l serpente ruppe, / fu e non è; ma chi n'ha colpa, creda / che vendetta di Dio non teme suppe"). A sop is a piece of food dipped in a liquid,
so that, if the prophecy in *Purgatorio* was written after the death of Henry
VII, Dante might be alluding to the rumors about the poisoning of the
host: those to blame for the ruin of the Church (the "vessel" broken by
the serpent-demon, namely Satan) will not be spared from divine vengeance only because they had freed themselves with the poison of the
person who was appointed to carry it out.[45]

Monarchia

Dante was almost certainly present at the imperial funeral. He must
have followed the imperial court to Pisa in early March 1312.[46] So far as
we know, it was the first time he had set foot in this city. Almost a quarter
of a century before, as a young cavalier, after witnessing the surrender
of Caprona, he and the Florentine army had pushed forward as far as its
walls, which were ably defended by Guido da Montefeltro, but hadn't
entered the city either then or later. Now he did so, not as a Guelf enemy,
but as an ally. In Genoa, he had probably already found some position,
if not in the sovereign's immediate entourage then in one of the court
circles, and had had some contact with the notaries and lawyers of the

imperial chancery. He had no lack of acquaintances, such as Palmiero degli Altoviti, for example, who could have helped to introduce him. He may also have had some assistance from Cardinal Niccolò da Prato, described by the great Paduan intellectual Albertino Mussato (there in Genoa as an ambassador) as a key figure for Ghibellines arriving in that city, and in particular for those from Tuscany.[47] And it is also likely that he continued to use those contacts in Pisa.

Dante doesn't seem to have witnessed the many events that occurred outside Pisa, such as the coronation in Rome, the siege of Florence, or the death of Henry VII. He was certainly not with the imperial army at the siege of Florence. According to Leonardo Bruni, "he didn't want to be there" because "he felt reverence for the city."[48]

In Pisa he devoted himself to that philosophical and legal treatise on the question of "monarchy" which he had presumably left the Casentino in order to write.[49]

The treatise is divided into three books, each of which answers a question (questio). They are in the following order: whether the Monarchy (or Empire) "is necessary for the good state of the world"; "whether the Roman people have claimed the office of Monarch for themselves as of right"; and "whether the authority of the Monarch comes from God directly or from a minister or vicar of God" (Mn. I II 3; "an ad bene esse mundi necessaria sit . . . an romanus populus de iure Monarche offitium sibi asciverit . . . an auctoritas Monarche dependeat a Deo inmediate vel ab alio, Dei ministro seu vicario"). Following a rigorously syllogistic-deductive procedure, starting off therefore from the abstract and universal principles of a moral, philosophical, and theological nature, and with the support of historical considerations, Dante, having first stated that "universal peace is the greatest of blessings ordained for human beatitude" (Mn. I IV 2; "pax universalis est optimum eorum que ad nostram beatitudinem ordinantur"), makes three points. First, government by a single person, the Emperor (or Monarch), is necessary for the good order of the world since it assures (unlike kings, princes or oligarchic and elective regimes) the highest degree of justice, maximum freedom, harmony between parties, and therefore universal peace (Book I). Second, the Roman people did not use force and violence (as would kings and princes) to obtain dominion over the world, but this privilege was conferred by Divine Providence, so that, by subduing all peoples, peace was established, and that Christ himself, having chosen to be born under the Empire, sanctioned its full right to govern the human race (and consequently Christians and men of the Church who attack or vilify the Empire commit a grave sin, since it is explicitly approved by Christ) (Book II). Lastly, in Book III, regarding the problem of the relationship between the two great "luminaries" (the Roman Pontiff and the Roman Prince) who illuminate and guide the world, he demonstrates that the authority of the Prince comes directly from God and "does not depend in any way upon the Church," a view contrary to that of many doctors of the Church, according to whom "in the same way that the moon, which is the lesser luminary, has no light except for that which it receives from the sun, so neither does the temporal regime have authority, except for that which it receives from the spiritual regime" (*Mn.* III IV 3; "quemadmodum luna, que est luminare minus, non habet lucem nisi prout recipit a sole, sic nec regnum temporale auctoritatem habet nisi prout recipit a spirituali regimine"). It follows that popes "cannot annul or fetter the decrees of the Empire, or its laws" (*Mn.* III VIII 11; "non tamen propter hoc sequitur quod [successor Petri] possit solvere seu ligare decreta Imperii sive leges"), nor can they appeal to the fact that Constantine had given "Rome, seat of the Empire, with many other dignities of the Empire," as a donation to the Church, since "Constantine could not alienate the power of the Empire nor could the Church receive it" (*Mn.* III X 1–4; "Dicunt adhuc quidam quod Constantinus imperator . . . Imperii sedem, scilicet Romam, donavit Ecclesie cum multis aliis Imperii dignitatibus . . . Constantinus alienare non poterat Imperii dignitatem, nec Ecclesia recipere"). The two scopes of power were clearly distinct: man pursues "the beatitude of this life" and the "beatitude of eternal life" (*Mn.* III XVI 7; "beatitudinem scilicet huius vite . . . et beatitudinem vite ecterne"), and therefore, in order that he can achieve this twofold purpose, Providence has given him two guides, that "of the supreme Pontiff, who according to those things revealed to him leads the human race to eternal life, and that of the Emperor, who directs the human race toward temporal happiness according to the teachings of philosophy" (*Mn.* III XVI 10; "Propter quod opus fuit homini duplici directivo secundum duplicem finem: scilicet summo Pontifice, qui secundum revelata humanum genus perduceret ad vitam ecternam, et imperatore, qui secundum phylosophica documenta genus humanum ad temporalem felicitatem dirigeret").

"Truths never attempted by others"

It has been said with regard to his vernacular lyric poetry—but the observation is true for his entire output—that Dante is "the poet who succeeded more than anyone else in freeing himself from the set forms imposed upon him by tradition." Whether he was working within a genre or writing a text that fitted into no pre-established genre, he nevertheless strove to be new and original. And his works are indeed new—none of them can be completely contained within a pre-existing genre.[50] Only *Monarchia,* with such a rigidly consequential progression and such a didactic style of text that it could have started its life in the classrooms of a *Studium,* would seem to provide an exception. It moves within the confines of a single discourse, avoiding any overlap with different traditions and influences. And yet, even here, Dante couldn't avoid declaring its novelty, which would bring him glory: "I have sought . . . to reveal truths never attempted by others" (*Mn.* I I 3; "publice utilitati non modo turgescere, quinymo fructificare desidero, et intemptatas ab aliis ostendere veritates"). The claim to originality is justified. It is true that with *Monarchia* Dante enters a wider debate involving the leading jurists of the eleventh and twelfth century; but in what other political and legal work does "the Digest stand beside Livy, Virgil, Ovid, Lucan, and Boethius, beside Aristotle and his interpreters, beside Seneca and Cicero"?[51] And above all, what other work of this kind distills a subject like the one addressed in *Monarchia*—a subject imbued with such passion, vested interest, hatred—to the level of the highest and most objective formal and philosophical speculation? Apart from Dante's capacity to open up new horizons in every subject to which he turns, this book clearly exhibits Dante's most typical characteristic, which is that of interconnecting direct and personal experience of current events with the reflection that arranges it into a firm and definitive conceptual system. *Monarchia* is a prime example of this for the very reason that its rigorous logical argument, its creation of a rigid hierarchy of values based on general principles, and its cold "scientific" detachment conceal the fact that its purpose arises from a contingent situation that is chaotic, contradictory, and above all, suffused with passion. It is no surprise, then, that there is debate as to whether the underlying historical events relate to Henry VII or rather to those in which Cangrande della Scala is the key player.

In reality, many factors point to Henry's years. And it may be possible to further identify the period when the last book, if not the whole treatise, was composed. There is a consistency between his central thesis (namely, that imperial power, established by God to assure peace among men, comes directly from God without any mediation from his vicars) and the state of relations between Henry VII and Clement V after the imperial coronation. At first, the two of them seemed to be in agreement. Henry repeatedly asked for the papal *confirmatio* and the pope seemed willing to grant a recognition that would thus confirm the superiority of spiritual over temporal power. But in the period of agitation leading up to the coronation when the pope gave in to pressure from the French, as well as later, the two protagonists became entrenched in opposing positions. The new emperor claimed that his powers were fully autonomous, and the pope emphasized that they were subordinate to his. And it was during these very months that the open opposition of the kings (Philip IV of France and Robert of Anjou) became apparent, denounced in the book with the words of Psalm 2: "Why do the nations rage and the peoples plot in vain? The kings of the earth rise up, and the princes conspire against the Lord and against his Anointed one" (*Mn.* II I 1: "Quare fremuerunt gentes, et populi meditati sunt inania? Astiterunt reges terre, et principes convenerunt in unum, adversus Dominum et adversus Cristum eius").[52]

Monarchia demanded not only a large baggage of doctrinal, legal, philosophical, historical, and theological learning; Dante must also have had access to a series of documents, decrees, letters, and legislative measures produced by the emperor, the pope, the previously mentioned kings, and above all, those documents produced between the summers of 1312 and 1313. This meant access to the "Pisan constitutions," enacted by Henry on April 2, 1313 (which sanctioned the subjection of every man to the emperor, the basis for Robert's deposition and condemnation), access to the various *petitiones* to the pope in which the king of Naples not only applied for a declaration that the coronation was illegitimate, but even rejected the necessity of a universal empire (created, moreover, by force and not, as Dante argued, by right) in a new world of "national" monarchies (as we would call them today), and access to the decrees by which, after the Council of Vienne, Clement V annulled the imperial ruling against King Robert and, in particular, reasserted his duty-right to exercise paternal power over the Christian nations. In light of this mass of available documents (to which others could be added, such as Philip the Fair's answer to the imperial encyclical announcing that the coronation had been carried out), all produced in a period of months, many of Dante's arguments seem to be best dated to the spring of 1313.[53]

The documents that *Monarchia* allows us to glimpse in the background could be regarded as proof that Dante was in actual contact with the imperial chancery: after all, where else could letters, decrees and assorted documents arrive with such rapidity, even—as in the case of the pope's decrees—before being published? But the real question is: contact or collaboration? *Monarchia* had—or rather, should have had—a strong propagandistic impact, and this would be evidence in favor of the fact that there was some kind of collaboration between the chancery and Dante. It is probable not so much that Dante was writing on commission, but that he was able to consult Henry's lawyers and receive material from them.

That Dante intended to write a piece of propaganda should be excluded. His aim was much higher. But it is clear that the treatise could be put to such a use. The author seems to have been aware of this and even seems concerned that the effect of the book could be counterproductive. In his final comments, after having demonstrated the independence of the emperor's temporal power from the pope's spiritual power (in metaphorical terms, that Christianity is illuminated by two "suns" and not by a "sun" and by a "moon"), he feels it necessary to warn readers that this "truth . . . must not be construed in too narrow a sense, that the Roman Prince is in no respect subject to the Roman Pontiff, since this mortal happiness is in some way ordered to an immortal happiness," and he therefore exhorts the emperor to give the pope "that reverence that the eldest son must use toward the father" (*Mn.* III XVI 17–18; "Que quidem veritas ultime questionis non sic stricte recipienda est, ut romanus Princeps in aliquo romano Pontifici non subiaceat, cum mortalis ista felicitas quodammodo ad inmortalem felicitatem ordinetur. Illa igitur reverentia Cesar utatur ad Petrum qua primogenitus filius debet uti ad patrem"). The invitation is motivated by his deep religiosity and his unfailing sense of orthodoxy (even Boniface VIII was untouchable since he was the vicar of Christ), but it probably also reflects the concern that his radical arguments on the division of the two powers could be exploited and might worsen the already difficult relations between Henry and Clement. Such concern was perhaps also shared by the imperial side, which never pushed as far as an open breach with the pope. Having said this, it is a fact that *Monarchia* lent itself, objectively, for use as a propaganda weapon in the political struggle. It is no surprise that it would be drawn upon toward the end of the 1320s in a diatribe between the pope and Emperor Louis of Bavaria. Boccaccio says that its appropriation in those circumstances by Ghibellines brought "great fame" to a book "that until then was hardly known."[54] Why then, it might be asked, was no use made of it during the years when it naturally lent itself to being used, so that it passed almost unnoticed? Perhaps the answer is that there wasn't enough time for it to be published: Henry's sudden, unexpected death rendered it irrelevant.[55]

By hereditary right

Monarchia is perhaps Dante's only book with no obviously autobiographical passages. But since there is not a single book in which Dante resists the need to talk about himself, the autobiographical elements have to be searched out, sought in the recesses of his ideological arguments, in the same way that references to current events have to be unearthed from beneath his detached legal and philosophical reasoning.

His reflection on the definition of nobility and who is noble runs like a thread throughout Dante's works. Dante uses nobility (of mind, or by birth) as a way of probing social relationships and identifying what might be the optimal state for a well-ordered society, but there is a strong suspicion that he is motivated by personal or private interests.[56] In other words, that his is not just an intellectual need to define nobility but also a need to define his own social standing. Underlying his reflection, therefore, are the feelings of unease he seems to have experienced since he was young, and his difficulty in identifying his position in the city hierarchies and, later, in the feudal courts.

His numerous writings over the years were accompanied, like a leit-motiv, by Aristotle's saying: "nobility is virtue and ancient wealth." In his canzone *Le dolci rime* of the 1290s, Dante had firmly and rather scorn-fully challenged that saying, which he then attributed to Frederick II, "that emperor who held that nobility, / in his view, / meant ancestral wealth / with pleasing manners" (*Conv.* canz. III, 21–24; "Tale imperò che gentilezza volse, / secondo 'l suo parere, / che fosse antica possession d'avere / con reggimenti belli"). Dante, at that time, was a Guelf advocate of the commune, a determined champion of nobility of spirit, a nobility that went beyond considerations of family and wealth. In *Convivio*, com-menting on these same lines, he had distanced himself from the emper-or's assertion, but with caution and deference, and had begun to open the way for a reassessment of the hereditary aspect of nobility. Now, in *Monar-chia*, at the beginning of the book in which he discusses the right of the Roman people to claim the dignity of Empire, he once again quotes the saying, attributing it correctly to Aristotle, in these terms: "It is known that men become noble through virtue, namely their own virtue and that of their forebears. Nobility is in fact virtue and ancient wealth, according to the Philosopher in *Politica*, and according to Juvenal: 'the sole and only virtue is nobility of mind.' Sayings, these two, that give rise to two dif-ferent nobilities: man's own and that of his forebears. Nobles therefore, by reason of the cause, are entitled to the reward of preferment" (*Mn.* II III 4; "Est enim nobilitas virtus et divitie antique, iuxta Phylosophum in *Politicis*; et iuxta Iuvenalem: 'nobilitas animi sola est atque unica virtus.' Que due sententie ad duas nobilitates dantur: propriam scilicet et maiorum. Ergo nobilibus ratione cause premium prelationis conveniens est"). That this is a complete reassessment of hereditary nobility is also clear when, on the next page, Dante emphasizes the fact that Aeneas, a figure standing at the origin of the Empire, was noble by reason of his personal virtue but also due to that inherited from his ancestors and acquired from his wives.[57] Let it be clear: Dante would never simply accept that true nobility is that acquired by birth and lineage—for him, the principle of personal virtue would always prevail—and yet, since *virtus* is a prerogative subordinate to *nobilitas*, blood comes to represent a special condition for the attain-ment of full nobility, provided that individual worth exists.

Dante well knew that he had given ample proof during the course of his public life, in his political action and his intellectual activity, that he possessed those virtues that demonstrate nobility of mind. If, to this, he could have added a lineage, a recognized noble ancestry, he would have fulfilled every aspect of the requirements borne out by his words: a Dante who was not only virtuous but noble, like Aeneas, would have had every right to proclaim the need to return to that order whose origins went back to Aeneas. Dante would take that step from the theoretical revaluation of heredity to the proclamation of his own nobility by birth only a few years later, during the writing of *Paradiso*. Canto XVI would open with a prologue in which his character expresses proud satisfaction when he learns that his great-grandfather, Cacciaguida, had been a knight, and moreover of imperial investiture:

> O our petty nobility of blood,
> if you make men glory in you
> here below where affection is feeble,
>   it will not make me marvel:
> there where yearning is unbent,
> I say in heaven, I gloried in it.

> O poca nostra nobiltà di sangue,
> se glorïar di te la gente fai
> qua giù dove l'affetto nostro langue,
>   mirabil cosa non mi sarà mai:
> ché là dove appetito non si torce,
> dico nel cielo, io me ne gloriai

—*Para.* XVI 1–6

Nobility of blood may count for little, but he gloried in having it, even in Heaven! The author's comment reinforces the feeling of the character. And we note that, when speaking of the nobility of his family, Dante is more explicit than anywhere else—in fact, this is the only place, in both his vernacular and Latin writings, where he uses the expression "nobility of blood."

The young man who had started out as a poet proclaiming himself to be noble in mind, and therefore a member of a close circle of cultural aristocrats, ends his career as a man of letters with the very doubtful claim to being noble by birth. The result of this long journey shows incontrovertibly that the municipal man, the man who even as an exile had kept his eyes fixed firmly on Florence and who judged political events and the movements of society following a code that was still substantially that of the Florentine world, had changed once and for all his parameters of judgment and, above all, had identified the social environment which he felt at last was his. After more than ten years spent in contact with great (and less great) feudal families and, in particular, after Henry's imperial plan had seemed to bring new impetus and meaning to an organization of society and a world that seemed to be falling into irremediable decline, Dante felt himself to be an integral part of that vast portion of society for whom hereditary nobility was an ideological mainstay, a way of life, and a political ideal.

9

The Prophet

1314–1315

a five hundred ten and five
messenger of God

un cinquecento diece e cinque,
messo di Dio

—*Purg.* XXXIII 43–44

Awareness of a mission

THE SUDDEN DEATH OF HENRY VII must have been a terrible blow for
Dante, the worst of many blows that life had inflicted on him over the
previous ten years. The unexpected fading of a dream that seemed about
to come true would have left him in a state of shock. Then again, all of
the emperor's supporters were left bewildered and demoralized. Cino
da Pistoia, in his canzone *Per la morte de lo imperatore Henrico da Lucim-*
burgo, writes that Henry is not dead, because he "lives blessed" in heaven
and his "name" will live on, but it is his followers who are dead: "Dead
are those who still live, / since they had their whole faith lodged in
him . . . / each thus remains as if in shock" ("Ma que' son morti e' qua'
vivono ancora, / ch'avean tutta lor fé in lui fermata . . . però ciascun
come smarrito regna").[1]

Nothing, however, allows us to portray Dante in despair, abandoning
the plans and ambitions of a short time before. On the contrary, his writ-

ings of this period give the picture of a man in fighting form, even more eager about the mission he feels he has been given. His words have the fervor and harshness of a prophet.

Less than a year after Henry's death, Dante was writing an impassioned letter to the Italian cardinals who had gathered in conclave.[2] Clement V had died on April 20, 1314, and ten days later, twenty-three cardinals gathered at the bishop's palace in Carpentras to elect his successor. They were split into three groups: the Gascons (cardinals appointed by Clement, who were largest in number), the Italians, and the French. Dante's letter was addressed to the eight Italian cardinals and it specifically named two Roman cardinals, Iacopo Caetani Stefaneschi and Napoleone Orsini. Though the letter was sent after the Conclave had already started, it almost certainly reached those to whom it was addressed.[3] Describing the Conclave as a combat, Dante states that "fighting has already begun" (*Ep.* XI 11; "iam cepti certaminis".) It is no surprise that Dante talks about combat: his letter is indeed a passionate plea to the Italian cardinals to fight manfully to elect an Italian pope who would bring Peter's throne back to Rome. Rome, he writes, is widowed and abandoned—doubly abandoned since, with the death of Henry VII and the transfer of the apostolic see to Avignon, it is "now deprived of one and the other sun" (*Ep.* XI 10; "Romam urbem, nunc utroque lumine destitutam"). The entire Church is in a grave condition, almost nearing its funeral ("in matris Ecclesie quasi funere"). Greed is rampant among priests, who, instead of defending and guiding their flocks, drag them with them into the abyss. There has to be a revival of dignity, especially among those like the two Roman cardinals who, though members of opposing groups, had been most responsible for the election of the last pope at the conclave in Perugia. They must therefore fight against the Gascons, against their demand that the leaders of the Church maintain that "opprobrium" which had been one of the major causes of its decline, and that of Rome. This letter marked the beginning of a series of ferocious attacks on Clement V who, at the time of *Monarchia,* had still been treated with respect; Dante now blamed his treachery as the cause of Henry VII's defeat.

At first it seemed the Italian cardinals had won the day with the election of a prelate who was French, but was also the cardinal of Palestrina, near Rome. Once this attempt had failed, the various factions continued to quarrel without success until July 14, when a group of armed soldiers in the pay of two powerful nephews of Clement V, taking advantage of disorder in the city, broke into the conclave shouting: "Death to the Italian cardinals; we want the Pope, we want the Pope," and forcing the Italians to escape.[4] The assembly dispersed and the papal throne remained vacant for over two years, until Jacques Duèse of Cahors was elected in August 1316, taking the name John XXII.[5]

Dante's letter implies that he had reflected on recent political events, that he had identified a close link between the moral and spiritual decline of the Church institution and its political dependence on the French monarchy, and that he had also understood how the alliance between the papacy and the French monarchy (with its Angevin satellite) was the obstacle that stifled every attempt to reform society. The political question of the dependence of the papacy had to be resolved: that was why it was essential to return the papal see to Rome. Unless that question was resolved, the moral crisis in which the Church found itself could not be cured and, vice versa, unless there was a revival in the Church, and a rediscovery of its true spiritual role, there was no hope for any successful reordering of civil society. The diagnosis was correct, but was one that could also prove paralyzing from the point of view of the remedy. On the one hand, it could lead to discouragement and the abandonment of any practical action, while on the other, it could result in visions of general *renovatio* that were purely theoretical and utopian. Yet Dante doesn't hold back in the face of the enormity of the task, nor does he resort to a utopian vision, despite the already strongly prophetic flavor of the letter. It is true that there is, at this stage, an overriding visionary voluntarism and the feeling of a mission to be carried out despite all the evidence to the contrary, but it is also true that he never misses an opportunity (like the election of a new pope) to develop those contacts that might transform a personal and abstract vision into a feasible political project.

An intricate political situation

The situation in Italy over the two years after the death of Henry VII did indeed offer him several opportunities. He could, at least, give the impression that not all the hopes raised by the emperor's accession were lost.

Henry had one son, John, Count of Luxembourg, king of Bohemia and, from 1310, imperial vicar general for Germany. From Henry, he had received the title of "Eldest Son of the King of the Romans," which underlined his claim to succeed him. In his second letter to Henry, Dante also referred to John as his father's legitimate successor who would continue the fight against the enemies of the empire. John had been called to help his father and had mustered an army, but had received news of his father's death in September 1313 while he was marching toward Italy. He had turned back, not through lack of interest in the Italian question, but to play his cards better in the forthcoming election of the king of Germany.[6] His absence, however, had transformed the struggle between the imperial and Guelf-Angevin forces from a game played out on an international chessboard into a predominantly Italian question.

Another who had gone to help Henry in August 1313 was Frederick of Aragon, king of Trinacria. Having set sail with his fleet for Pisa, he too heard of the emperor's death during the journey. Arriving in Pisa, he learned that John of Bohemia and his army would not be arriving in Italy, refused the Pisan invitation to take command of the Ghibelline faction, and sailed back to Sicily on September 26. But this wasn't the end of his warring with Robert of Anjou, who was claiming his right to the possession of Sicily; indeed, in August 1314 he assumed the title of King of Sicily instead of that of King of Trinacria. Until at least the end of 1314, when he signed a truce with his rival on December 16, Frederick of Aragon would remain the key figure for the Ghibelline and pro-imperial forces of the peninsula. In September 1313 Dante was almost certainly in Pisa, and therefore, even if he hadn't encountered the Aragonese king, he would have had many opportunities to meet members of his retinue and to understand his political intentions at first hand.[7] This understanding replaced the antipathy expressed earlier, before Frederick had become Henry VII's most trusty and important ally. But after the truce signed at the end of 1314, Dante would change his opinion once again, accusing Frederick of meanness, cowardice, and bad government. It was one of Dante's well-known ambivalences of judgment dictated by the political situation of the moment.

Frederick of Aragon shifted his theater of war with the Angevins between Sicily and Calabria, and thus the main battlefield was still Tuscany. The scenario was similar to that seen at various times over the previous century, with Florence, the Angevins of Naples, and the Guelf cities on one side, and Pisa and the Ghibelline forces on the other. What now reemerged was something that was almost a standard feature of Italian history between the twelve and thirteen hundreds. Even the domestic political and military arrangements of the two factions replicated situations already seen in the past—in May 1313, Florence entrusted the Signoria of the city (the power to appoint the *podestà*) to Robert of Anjou (who would keep it for the next eight and a half years) in exactly the same way as it had granted it almost fifty years before (in 1267) to Robert's grandfather, Charles I of Anjou; Pisa, meanwhile, after the failed attempt to involve Frederick of Aragon, handed itself over to an external *capitano,* Uguccione della Faggiola, granting him the powers of *podestà, capitano di guerra,* and *capitano del popolo,* repeating what it had done a quarter century earlier with Guido da Montefeltro. And Uguccione, though now over sixty, conducted a brilliant military campaign in exactly the same way as Montefeltro had done in his time. In June 1314 he captured Lucca (thanks also to the internal support of the Ghibelline leader, Castruccio Castracani degli Antelminelli), which then formed an alliance with Pisa in which he himself was the *capitano.* Having effectively become lord of both cities, Uguccione proceeded from victory to victory until he defeated the joint forces of Florence and Robert of Anjou (whom the pope had meanwhile appointed imperial vicar for Italy) in a pitched battle fought at Montecatini on August 29, 1315. This victory marked the peak of the Ghibelline offensive and of Uguccione's power, which would then plummet. Within a few months, internal opposition would grow in both Pisa and Lucca, where strong disagreements began to develop between him and Castruccio, so that in April of the following year Uguccione would be deposed in both cities on the same day.

An ardent visionary

Between the summers of 1313 and 1315 the political and military outlook much favored the Ghibelline forces. Dante may therefore have felt encouraged not to abandon his political commitment. Even if there was no sign of any change comparable to what Henry VII would have brought to Italian affairs, the situation seemed to offer much hope. And yet it wasn't sufficient to justify the fervor and visionary impetus that pervade Dante's writing in this period.

The letter to the Italian cardinals doesn't seem much different from the manifesto-letters written three years before. The political problem that prompts it, the need to elect an Italian pope, has the same immediacy as those dealt with in the earlier letters (limitation of imperial rights, the need to wage war in Tuscany); the style is also similar, padded with biblical quotes and persistent use of heavy religious metaphor. The biblical and prophetic wording and tone are much more emphatic in this letter, but the underlying structure is the same as before.[8] Yet the figure of the author is radically different.

In the letters to Henry VII and to the Florentines, Dante spoke on behalf of others. He was the interpreter and spokesman for organized groups. But this time, addressing the cardinals, Dante is one man alone, who stresses this solitude because it is precisely this condition that legitimizes his words: "one single voice," his own, "solitary and devout, and this private voice is heard almost at the funeral of Mother Church" (*Ep.* XI 6; "una sola vox, sola pia, et hec privata, in matris Ecclesie quasi funere audiatur"). A "private" person has neither the authority of a "shepherd"—indeed "in the pastures of Jesus Christ" he is "the last of the flock" (*Ep.* XI 5; "Quippe de ovibus in pascuis Iesu Christi minima una sum"—nor power or wealth, and yet he dares to use bitter and angry words to the prelates who govern the Church. He does so because—he writes, paraphrasing Saint Paul—"by the grace of God I am what I am" and because—he adds, quoting the Psalms—"the zeal for his house eats me up" (*Ep.* XI 5; "Non ergo divitiarum, sed 'gratia Dei sum id quod sum' [I *Cor* 15:9] et 'zelus domus eius comedit me' [*Ps* 69:10]"). The solitary voice that speaks through divine impulse, and who dares to stand up against those in power by declaring that they are to blame, is the voice of the biblical prophets. And like the prophets, Dante doesn't speak in the name of social or religious or political groups, but expresses what people think and don't have the courage to say: "But, O fathers, don't consider me a phoenix on earth; everyone, in fact, mutters or whispers or thinks or dreams what I tell, and they don't declare what they've seen" (*Ep.* XI 8; "Sed, o patres, ne me phenicem extimetis in orbe terrarum; omnes enim

que garrio murmurant aut mussant aut cogitant aut somniant, et que
inventa non attestantur"). In short, the letter is not being written by a
politician behaving like a prophet, but by someone who actually feels
he has a prophetic mission. Someone whose exceptionality is not derived
from particular intellectual gifts or acquired merits but, like Saint Paul,
from being what he is by grace of God.

The letter to the cardinals is the culmination of a process that had
already started in Dante's youth. We have seen on several occasions how
he had a strong feeling of being different, how he had interpreted illnesses and personal events over the years as signs that marked out his
uniqueness, how he had felt the hand of destiny in the death of a woman
he loved, how he had claimed to have visionary powers and how, in the
end, he had conceived a poem whose structure, from the outset, included
a strong prophetic component. It is possible that all this was a sort of
reaction against his sense of social and family disadvantage, that a feeling
of inadequacy was transformed into an overwhelming need for self-
affirmation: egocentricity is an indelible characteristic of Dante's
writing. The fact that the prophetic voice becomes clearer and more resolute at the moment of deep disappointment after Henry VII's downfall corresponds well with what we sense about Dante's character, about
his way of reacting to defeat, about his urge to make the best of the situation and look toward the future. This could perhaps have been a way
of escaping from reality. The more he is alone and isolated, the more he
claims to speak in the name of everyone. In the *Commedia* he goes as far
as claiming to speak in the name of God.

Whatever the underlying causes and the psychological processes that
made it happen, the ultimate result was the construction of an autobiographical character endowed with prophetic charisma. It is impossible
to establish whether Dante truly felt himself to be a prophet; but it is
undeniable that in the *Commedia* he declares this several times: he is a
prophet not because he has the ability to read the future and predict
events, but because he can tell the living about the prophecies heard in
the afterlife. Beatrice at the end of *Purgatorio,* and Cacciaguida and Saint
Peter in *Paradiso,* specifically appoint him to carry out that task.[9] And
since the *Commedia* is the fulfillment of the appointed task, the investiture given to the character ends up falling upon the author himself.

But the fact remains that this all takes place within a *fictio,* and is
therefore a self-investiture. It has been said that "in order for Dante to

be elevated to the rank of prophet, his will as author is not enough . . .
Dante the prophet has to show to his contemporaries some objective,
irrefutable sign—one independent of his will that is not, however, hidden
from his intelligence: the concrete mark of his privilege."[10] The only true
sign of Dante's role as a prophet is the account of the smashing of the
baptismal font, told in *Inferno* in the canto of the simoniacs. If his message had not been deciphered for centuries, this was not because Dante
wanted to be cryptic but quite simply because, over the passage of time,
knowledge about the shape of the baptismal font at San Giovanni had
been lost. The description of how he had broken one of the amphorae
full of holy water in order to save a person (presumably a child) who
was drowning has a twofold objective. Since that gesture was carried
out in public and had probably caused a scandal, Dante now wanted to
re-establish the truth about what happened: "and may this be a seal to
undeceive all men" (*Inf.* XIX 21; "e questo sia suggel ch'ogn' omo sganni").
But in the meantime he had realized that his gesture of that time had
repeated that of the prophet Jeremiah, and he had convinced himself that
his own gesture had been prophetic—the sign that God, in that holy
place, had given him the task of denouncing simony in the Church. And
thus an action that might have seemed a scandal would be transformed,
in the eyes of those who knew how to read God's signs in history, into
proof of the prophetic nature of what he had done.[11]

Further on in the canto, Pope Nicholas III, stuck head down in one of
the circular holes dug into the wall of the bolgia, predicts to Dante,
who is leaning over him so as to better hear his words, that Boniface
(who died in 1303) will arrive in Hell, followed then by that pope "of
fouler action" (*Inf.* XIX 82; "di più laida opra"), elected, like Jason in the
Bible, thanks to those practices of simony that had procured him the support of the king of France.[12] This is Clement V, who, as pope, is further
condemned as "a lawless shepherd" (*Inf.* XIX 83; "pastor sanza legge")—
as someone who respects no human and divine limit. Dante uses this
expression to refer to the "treachery" Clement carried out (or would
carry out, according to the prophecy) against Henry VII: "but before the
Gascon tricks noble Henry" he would write in *Paradiso* (*Para.* XVII 82;
"ma pria che 'l Guasco l'alto Arrigo inganni"). If the canto about the
simoniacs was composed between 1308–1309, the lines that angrily denounced Clement's actions must date from a later revision. Were they
written before or after the pope's death in April 1314? In the first case,

this would have been a fairly safe prophecy (the death of the pope), but nevertheless to be interpreted as such; in the second case, it would have been Dante's usual way of foretelling events that had already happened. And this second possibility, which seems more likely, would lead us to conclude that the canto was revised during the late spring of 1314, during more or less the same months that Dante wrote his letter to the cardinals. It may be significant, then, that the lines of the *Commedia* dwell more on his simoniacal election than on the pope's volte-face in relation to the emperor—significant because the same conclave in Perugia that had elected him provides the historical background to which the letter to the cardinals refers, the wrong that the Rome cardinals now had to rectify in the new conclave just opened. If we accept the possibility that in spring 1314 Dante had been reworking the canto of a few years earlier, it would be by no means strange that during the months in which he was publicly manifesting his prophetic charisma, he had also added the autobiographical digression about the smashed font as an objective sign that he was a prophet.[13] It would provide confirmation that Dante's prophetic character was taking form and, above all, being expressed in the months after Henry's death, as a voluntaristic protest, as an act of faith despite everything.

Purgatorio and the vacancy in the empire

Dante began writing *Purgatorio* between 1308 and 1309, and proceeded rapidly: he had composed more than two-thirds of it by the time of Henry VII's arrival. Between 1311 and 1313 work seems to have slowed down considerably: Dante would have been distracted from the poem by his new political and intellectual activity (apparent from the letters and *Monarchia*).[14] But it is possible he may also have had difficulty readjusting the political and ideological framework he had sketched out prior to Henry's appearance, which had lost its relevance with the unexpected arrival of an emperor.

Much of *Purgatorio* revolves around the theme of the vacancy in the empire and the seriously negative effects it had had, and continued to have, on Christianity. Compared with the staunchly Guelf and fervently anti-Ghibelline viewpoint of *Inferno* it marks an almost complete volte-face. After observing that "the saddle [of the empire] is empty" (*Purg.* VI

89; "la sella è vòta"), that Albert of Austria had no concern for Italy and allowed the "garden of the empire to go to waste" (*Purg.* VI 105; "'l giardin de lo 'mperio sia diserto"), that Rudolf of Habsburg had also "neglected what he should have done" (*Purg.* VII 92; "negletto ciò che far dovea"), which was to come to Italy, and above all, that one of the two "suns" from which humanity is illuminated had extinguished the other, so that "the sword is joined / to the shepherd's crook" (*Purg.* XVI 109–110; "è giunta la spada / col pasturale"), Dante continues with a bitter and depressing analysis of the current situation in Italy and Europe.[15]

Most of the historical pictures painted in *Purgatorio* are devoted to lamenting the sad state in which Italy had found herself at the end of the Swabian dynasty. The famous apostrophe in Canto VI paints her wracked by war (no "part [of it] enjoys peace"—*Purg.* XVI 87; "alcuna parte in te di pace gode"), trapped in the fighting between factions ("and now in you they cannot stay without war / those alive, each torments the other / locked within one wall and one moat"—*Purg.* XVI 82–84; "e ora in te non stanno sanza guerra/ li vivi tuoi, e l'un l'altro si rode / di quei ch'un muro e una fossa serra!"), an Italy in which the great feudal dynasties are "obscured" and impoverished. Rome grieves, "a widow and alone" (*Purg.* XVI 113; "vedova e sola"), the cities are filled with "tyrants," the political rulers are newcomers with no history. Almost halfway through *Purgatorio*, Guido del Duca descends the Arno and describes the inhabitants of that "accursed and wretched ditch" (*Purg.* XIV 51; "maladetta e sventurata fossa") with a bestiary of insults: the people of the Casentino are "pigs," those of Arezzo "mongrels," the Florentines "wolves," the Pisans "foxes." Then he portrays the bleak situation in Romagna: in the past, "love and courtesy" went to cultivate the virtues of chivalry and courtly pleasures: "ladies and knights, the labors and pleasures / that love and courtesy once inspired" (*Purg.* XIV 109–110; "le donne e 'cavalier, li affanni e li agi / che ne 'nvogliava amore e cortesia"), whereas now hearts "have turned so vile" (*Purg.* XIV 111; "son fatti sì malvagi"). A little later it is Marco Lombardo who notes how in Lombardy and the March of Treviso—regions where, prior to the conflict between Frederick II and the pope, "valor and courtesy used to be found" (*Purg.* XVI 116; "solea valore e cortesia trovarsi")—no scoundrel need now fear shame. Tuscany, Romagna, Lombardy, the March of Treviso: these are

Dante's regions, the places where he pursued his political activity after his banishment.[16]

The representation of post-imperial decline also extends to Europe, or rather, to the Europe of the monarchies. And here too, the picture is one of decline. The crowned or princely heads gathered in the Valley of the Princes in Canto VII stand out neither for their virtue nor their capacity to govern: indeed, quite the opposite. Almost all correspond to the old adage according to which feckless fathers are succeeded by even more feckless sons.[17] Dante hadn't needed to wait for Henry VII's ill-fated expedition to understand that one of the worst effects (from his point of view, of course) of the imperial vacancy had been the establishment of independent monarchies. It is no surprise that the protagonist in one canto that condemns greed, the "old she-wolf" whose "hunger" is "never sated" (*Purg.* XX 10–12; "fame sanza fine cupa"), is Hugh Capet, the "son . . . of a Paris butcher" (*Purg.* XX 52; "figliuol fu'io d'un beccaio di Parigi"), from whom "were born the Philips and the Louis / by whom France in recent times is ruled" (*Purg.* XX 50–51; "di me son nati i Filippi e i Luigi / per cui novellamente è Francia retta"). Three Charles's in succession exemplify the guilt of the Capets, the Valois, and the Anjou: Charles I of Anjou, who condemned Conradin of Swabia and, according to Dante, had Saint Thomas Aquinas poisoned; Charles of Valois, who carried out the coup in Florence, earning only "sin and shame" (*Purg.* XX 76; "peccato e onta"); and Charles II of Anjou who, worse than a pirate, sold Azzo VIII d'Este not a slave, but his own daughter Beatrice. Yet none of the crimes committed by them bears comparison with those of Philip the Fair, who first insults the vicar of Christ at Anagni and then, out of simple greed, forcibly and arbitrarily abolishes the Order of Templars.[18]

The picture of decline of Italy and Europe is completed by glimpses of city life, dominated by savage violence (Fulcieri da Calboli who rages against the Whites of Florence) and envy (Sapia of Siena who prays for the defeat of her fellow citizens and rejoices in their misery), on the moral decline of the feudal houses (the Aldobrandeschi, the counts of Lavagna, though with the glaring exception of the Malaspina), and on the arrogance of the new despots (the Della Scala).[19]

Condemnations, accusations, bitter sarcasm. It would seem that the outlook for Italian and European public life could only be bleak. Such a depressing view fits well with the grim prospects that marked the period beginning with Corso Donati's death and Cardinal Orsini's final defeat, and ending with Henry VII's descent into Italy. But if some of the above-mentioned cantos must have been written several months later, when it was certain that the king of the Romans would be arriving or, indeed, when Henry was already in Italy, we have to infer that Dante, in the face of a sudden and radical change in the political situation, was still unable to adjust his sights, to give a positive shift to the pessimistic story he was working on.

There is a strong feeling that Dante slowed down his pace of composition after the canto in which he meets Forese—in other words, two-thirds of the way through *Purgatorio*—or that he even stopped for a while. It is certain, however, that the last third of the book follows a road that leads him away from the politics and the historic events of that moment. In the foreground, now, is his account of the purifying ascent of Dante's character, while space is also given to a discussion of the author's past activity as a vernacular poet.[20] Bonagiunta, Guinizelli, and Arnaut Daniel move in a tonal aura and in a conceptual universe that has little to do with the grim representation of political decline produced by the absence of empire.[21] Almost no part of *Purgatorio* is animated by prophetic inspiration.

Beatrice's prophecy

Almost no part, that is, because the prophetic vision explodes—unexpectedly, one might say—when Dante the character arrives at the top of the mountain and enters earthly paradise. The great symbolical and allegorical actions that take place in Eden are bound together, showing, by way of prophecy, the path to individual salvation for the character and the path of destiny for mankind. It is while the allegorical scenes are taking place that Beatrice twice gives Dante the task of recording and reporting to those on Earth what he has seen and heard; and it is in relation to the allegorical visions that Beatrice makes an obscure (like all prophecies) but solemn prediction about the forthcoming deliverance of Christianity.[22]

In Eden, Dante the character comes across a strange symbolic procession that moves toward him along the edge of the Lethe: seven luminous candelabra precede twenty-four old men dressed in white and crowned with lilies (the twenty-four books of the Old Testament), followed by four strange animals (the Gospels) who escort a triumphal two-wheel chariot (the Church) pulled by a griffin with the body of a lion and the head and wings of an eagle (Jesus Christ); three women (the theological virtues) dance to one side of the chariot, and four (the cardinal virtues) to the other; lastly, following behind the chariot are seven more figures dressed in white (Acts of the Apostles, Letters of Saint Paul, Peter, John, James and Judas, Revelations). Having confessed his wrongs to Beatrice, Dante joins the procession which, having turned around, returns the way it came. The griffin ties the chariot to a completely bare tree which immediately blossoms. Then, while many of the figures rise up into the sky, an eagle (the Roman Empire) plunges down against the chariot, striking it with force: soon after it is a fox (heresy) that hurls itself against it. The eagle drops down a second time, but does not damage the chariot, indeed it leaves some of its feathers on it (the gift of Constantine). A dragon appears from the ground, breaks the base of the chariot and takes part of it away; the chariot becomes covered with the eagle feathers and is transformed into a seven-headed monster (the seven deadly sins). Finally, seated on the chariot, a lecherous half-dressed "whore" exchanges lascivious kisses with a "giant":

> Secure, like a high mountain fortress,
> I saw a shameless whore sitting there
> with eyes glancing readily in all directions;
> and as if to ensure she wasn't taken from him,
> I saw right there beside her a giant;
> and they kissed together several times.

> Sicura, quasi rocca in alto monte,
> seder sovresso una puttana sciolta
> m'apparve con le ciglia intorno pronte;
> e come perché non li fosse tolta,
> vidi di costa a lei dritto un gigante;
> e basciavansi insieme alcuna volta.

—*Purg.* XXXII 148–153

The scene with the chariot retells the long saga of the Church in allegorical form. During the age of the martyrs, the Church resisted pagan persecution as well as crimes of heresy, but from the gift of Constantine onward, from the time when material wealth compromised its purity, it slipped down into a gradual and relentless process of degeneration, culminating in illicit acts of love and actual slavery in which the papal court (the whore) has subjected her wishes to the base desires of the giant. It culminates, therefore, in present times, since there is no doubt that the giant represents Philip the Fair or, at least, the French monarchy. The giant, realizing that the whore was looking at Dante with hungry eyes, loses his temper, whips her from head to toe, and finally hauls the chariot into a forest:

> But since she turned her covetous
> and roaming eye to me, that savage lover
> whipped her from head to toe;
>   then, filled with suspicion and raw anger,
> he loosened the monster [the chariot], and dragged it to the wood,
> so that its trees alone became a shield
>   for the whore and the strange beast.

> Ma perché l'occhio cupido e vagante
> a me rivolse, quel feroce drudo
> la flagellò dal capo infin le piante;
>   poi, di sospetto pieno e d'ira crudo,
> disciolse il mostro, e trassel per la selva,
> tanto che sol di lei mi fece scudo
>   a la puttana e a la nova belva.

—*Purg.* XXXII 154–160

The forest into which the giant drags the chariot of the Church would seem to be a clear allusion to the papal court being moved from Rome to Avignon, where the papacy was held almost a prisoner.

Beatrice comments upon the allegorical actions of the chariot of the Church (which she calls "vessel") broken by the dragon (which she calls "serpent") and upon the whore enslaved to the giant's desires with a mysterious prophecy, made even more opaque by the introduction of a technical conundrum:

> Know that the vessel the serpent broke,
> was and is not; but let him whose fault it is, believe
> that God's vengeance fears no sop.
> The eagle who left his feathers on the chariot
> that then became a monster and then prey
> will not forever be without an heir;
> I plainly see, and therefore tell you this,
> stars, already close, show a time,
> safe from every hindrance and every barrier,
> in which a five hundred ten and five,
> messenger of God, will kill the thief
> with that giant who consorts with her.

> Sappi che 'l vaso che 'l serpente ruppe,
> fu e non è; ma chi n'ha colpa, creda
> che vendetta di Dio non teme suppe.
> Non sarà tutto tempo sanza reda
> l'aguglia che lasciò le penne al carro,
> per che divenne mostro e poscia preda;
> ch'io veggio certamente, e però il narro,
> a darne tempo già stelle propinque,
> secure d'ogn' intoppo e d'ogne sbarro,
> nel quale un cinquecento diece e cinque,
> messo di Dio, anciderà la fuia
> con quel gigante che con lei delinque.

—*Purg.* XXXIII 34–45

Beatrice is prophesying that the empire (the eagle) will soon have an heir, a new emperor who will kill the prostitute and the giant. The prophecy is obscure but not vague (like that of the greyhound in the first canto of *Inferno*): concealed beneath the number puzzle is the name of a historic character.[23]

Purgatorio is set entirely between the initial lament over the absence of the empire after the death of Frederick II and the final anticipation of an "heir." From the narrative point of view—don't forget the action takes place in 1300—the story line is completely consistent: the death of Albert of Habsburg puts the spotlight on the problem of the imperial vacancy, which the mysterious person concealed behind the "five hundred ten and five" will soon remedy.[24] But in terms of the historical periods to which it refers, we have to ask whether Dante is talking about the same vacancy or about two different periods—about that long vacancy which began with the end of the Swabians and that very recent vacancy caused by the death of Henry VII. A persuasive answer could only come from solving the puzzle, but up until now, despite many impressive attempts, no one has been able to provide an entirely convincing explanation.

Most scholars think that the "messenger of God" is Henry VII, whose identity could be indicated by the Roman numerals DXV (fifty, ten, five), an anagram of DVX, "leader, commander." Here the emperor, who had appeared on the historical scene when *Purgatorio* was well on the way to being finished and, up until these lines, had never been named, is said to be receiving the solemn homage of his faithful follower. Such homage obviously implies that Henry was still alive and that *Inferno* and *Purgatorio* had been published in their entirety (even if not yet widely circulated) prior to August 1313. By publishing them Dante would be seeking "also to show his personal loyalty to the emperor." Indeed, the historical events following the coronation in June 1312 would seem consistent with Dante's allegorical account: that tumultuous and ill-destined coronation showed beyond any possible doubt that Clement V, and therefore the papal court, had altered their attitude to Henry, and that Church policy was once again subservient to the wishes of the French king.[25] Beatrice's prophecy is said to take account of this situation and to urge the new emperor to free the Church from the state of servitude into which it had been cast.

We might ask, however, whether Henry VII and, more generally, the imperial court, would have welcomed such homage. According to the prophecy, the emperor, whose arrival had been awaited for half a century (in 1300) so that he could restore peace to strife-torn Europe and open the road to earthly happiness, is said to be called by destiny to perform one single action: to kill the "thief" and the "giant who consorts with her." Two such blows, delivered both together to a corrupt papal court and the king of France, would certainly be sensational, and enough to revolutionize the whole political structure. It is also certain that Dante thought it necessary to release the Church from its bondage to France in order to reestablish imperial authority. But perhaps such blows would, on the one hand, be rather too revolutionary if considered in 1312–1313. Yet on the other hand, paradoxically, such actions would be rather limited in terms of the universal mission of the empire. In the climate of acute tension between Henry on one side and Philip the Fair, Robert of Anjou, and Clement V on the other, Beatrice's prophecy, for the very fact that it limits the salvific mission of the "messenger of God" to this one action, could even seem like the prophecy of vengeance. It would be too crushing, therefore, in its contingency and too unmindful of the task of restoring peace between men and between peoples, which ought to have constituted the heart of Henry's mission. We might therefore ask whether the emperor would really have welcomed such homage that painted him as an enemy of the Church and indeed as a "killer," albeit metaphorical, of its leaders. *Monarchia* seems much more in tune with the political line between 1312 and 1313, where the prince's positions are, unsurprisingly, softened with a final plea for reciprocal respect between the two supreme authorities.

But Beatrice's prophecy could have been written after the death of Henry VII and therefore predict the arrival of another person. It is important to emphasize that the whole allegorical structure of the cantos of Eden and the same prophetic interpretation that Beatrice gives of them are centered on the Church, not on the empire. This is because, as the letter to the cardinals shows, it is as a consequence of Henry's downfall that Dante directs his political and religious reflection upon the condition of the Church, upon the moral crisis that threatens it, its political dependency and the need to remedy it.[26] The cantos of Earthly Paradise would fit very well into this period, both for what they say as well as what they tend to suggest about the author's state of mind. The bitter, angry prophecy in the last canto of *Purgatorio* fits perfectly with the way Dante reacted to the catastrophe: not only did he refuse to give up, but he clung to the tiniest positive signs that might have fueled the hope stirred by Henry VII. That this hope is nourished by a voluntaristic and visionary tension that leads to prophetic zeal is the most characteristic feature of this phase of Dante's life. Even if it were dated after Henry's death, the predicted mission of the "messenger of God" would continue to appear overwhelmed by the events of history, but in this case the sense of revenge that comes from Beatrice's words would be attributed more to the anger and scorn of the writer than to the vengeful prophet.

Once moved forward in time, there is an interesting possibility that hidden behind the "messenger of God"—an expression that echoes the "missus a Deo" as John's Gospel names John the Baptist—is Henry's son, John of Bohemia. This impression is reinforced by taking the name Johannes as the technical key to the puzzle and using a cipher book that was widely used by the ecclesiastical hierarchy for sending messages. It is then possible to translate the string of numbers "five hundred ten and five" into the initials f i e, which could stand for f(ilius) i(mperatoris) e(nrici).[27] This identification would take us to the period when Dante believed it still possible that John of Bohemia would succeed his father and continue his mission, in other words, to the months between late summer of 1313 and late summer of 1314. In early fall of 1314, John's chances of becoming emperor quickly faded as those of Frederick of Habsburg and Louis of Wittelsbach (known as the Bavarian) strengthened—both were elected king of Germany in opposition to each other on almost the same day: the Bavarian on October 19 at Aachen; the Habsburg on October 20 at Bonn. In this way, the end of *Purgatorio* would date to a time close to that of the composition of the letter to the cardinals.

We would have incontrovertible proof if it were possible to link Beatrice's prophecy to the events about which the letter speaks. Some evidence in that sense—though only circumstantial—can be glimpsed in Dante's lines. The "shameless whore" is modeled on the "meretrix magna" with which the kings of the earth flirt in the Book of Revelation: while "in Revelation it is the figure of imperial Rome, in Dante . . . it is the figure of the corrupt Roman papal court," therefore the figure of a collective entity and not of a pope (incorporated into the concept of papal court).[28] The absence of direct references to the pope would seem to point to the period when the throne was vacant after the death of Clement V. And the allegorical scene of the "giant" who whips his lover and then hides her in the forest because he is angered by the fact that she gave Dante's character a look filled with desire could be a reference to the conclave. The meaning of that glance is far from clear. For those who suggest that the "messenger of God" is Henry VII, Dante's character could represent here a collective self, those many people who had been deceived and had believed in the good faith of Clement V; this is possible, but Dante's character would, in that case, deviate from the autobiographical role of the character, which in the *Commedia* is always Dante himself. That character could, in fact, certainly be the representative of a human collectivity, even the whole of humanity, but without ever ignoring his actual biographical experiences. Dante the writer places Dante the character into a particular narrative context when certain things he says, writes, or does have an actual relationship to the historical situation to which that context refers. Well, what would Dante have done and said and written for the papal curia to look upon him with favor, indeed with desire? Is there any concrete event in his biography that could relate to the seductive gaze of the curia-prostitute? Perhaps there is something, given that we needn't worry about overestimating Dante's egocentric nature. It will be remembered that the conclave at Carpentras had been interrupted in July 1314 by an armed irruption against the Italian cardinals who were attempting to elect a pope acceptable to them. It fits well with Dante's psychology for him to believe that the attempt by the Italian cardinals had been influenced by his letter (thus the "covetous and roaming eye" of a papal court that would have been spurred by the words of that lone prophet to break off the relationship with the giant) and therefore that the brutal reaction of the giant (an allegorical transposition of the armed irruption of the French powers and the scattering of the college of cardinals) had been determined by him.[29]

One hesitation about accepting the idea that the prophecy came after the death of Henry VII could arise from the observation that, if that were so, a canticle entirely dominated by the problem of the eclipse of imperial power would never record the only real attempt that Dante knew to restore it.[30] Henry VII would become a sort of vast gap in a narration that would totally ignore him, leaping from what had happened before him to what had happened immediately after. And yet the structure of *Inferno* isn't much different. This canticle hinges around the civil war in Florence and Dante's subsequent exile: yet we know that Dante gives no detailed description of those crucial years between 1300 and 1302 and never talks directly about his banishment or the responsibility of those who expelled him.[31] In *Inferno,* at the center of the discussion, there is something unsaid, a gap; here too the historical and biographical nucleus that determines the meaning of the canticle and the story itself are hidden beneath the surface of the text.

The tribulations of a bishop

Where was Dante during those months when John of Bohemia was pursuing his dream to become emperor, when Frederick III of Aragon was at war with Robert of Anjou, and when Uguccione was at war with Florence? He was most probably in Pisa until the time of Henry VII's funeral in September 1313. Did he stay there after, and for how long? There is a total lack of documentation; all we can do is guess.

Many think that in 1314 he was already in Verona, at the court of Cangrande della Scala;[32] some, though few, think he had gone to Ravenna that year: but the letter on which they rely, supposedly by Dante, is clearly false.[33] It is not unlikely that he had prolonged his stay in Pisa. By September, Uguccione had in effect become its lord, and he and Dante had known each other since 1307, when Dante had been his guest at Massa Trabaria, an acquaintance they could have developed during the years of Henry VII. He could have provided Dante, therefore, with the protection assured until then by the imperial court, and with it, perhaps, some material help. Once Dante's link with Henry's entourage had gone, we don't know what kind of support he might have relied upon. He needed help, however, seeing that his sons had been forced to leave Florence by at least 1314, and it is therefore reasonable to assume they had joined him.[34] He would have received some support from his family, as in the past—from his brother and sister (more from well-to-do Tana than from Francesco), as well as from Gemma's brothers and nephews (from Niccolò Donati, son of Foresino, for example, whom we know was attentive toward the needs of those Alighieri in exile).[35]

The Lunigiana is not very far from Pisa, and it can't be ruled out that Dante may have benefited once more from the hospitality of the Malaspina family. Indeed, a very slender pointer to what really happened during 1314 might be found between the lines of the letter to the Italian cardinals.

The Church produces sons (the prelates) to be ashamed of, and this is because they marry neither charity nor justice, but the "daughters of the bloodsucker" (*Ep.* XI 7; "filie sanguisuge"), in other words, lust and greed, born from the devil. And the degeneracy of the sons born from these unions is demonstrated by all prelates, all "apart from the Bishop of Luni" (*Ep.* XI 7; "que quales pariant tibi fetus, preter Lunensem pontificem omnes alii contestantur")—which is the same ironic stylistic form as "every man there is a barrater, apart from Bonturo" (*Inf.* XXI 41; "ogn' uom v'è barattier, fuor che Bonturo"). What is striking, above all, is the inconsistency of tone between this sarcastic parenthesis and the high, eloquent, prophetic manner of the letter. It is striking because it is the only leap in tone throughout the whole letter. But the Bishop of Luni is also the only named example of degeneracy among the high clergy, and this stands out in a letter in which just two other names appear, though these are the recipients (Iacopo Caetani Stefaneschi and Napoleone Orsini).[36] In a discussion that deals with issues crucial to the destiny of the Church, what is the relevance of the bishop of a place like Luni, important no doubt in Liguria, but hardly significant for the future of Christianity? It is worth pausing to consider this figure of the bishop-count, and also to resolve a recurring misunderstanding that it is a reference to a member of the Malaspina family of Lunigiana.

In 1307, after the death of Bishop Antonio Nuvolone da Camilla—with whom Dante had concluded the peace agreement on behalf of the Malaspina—the canons of Sarzana could not agree on the choice of a successor: some of them had voted for the friar minor Guglielmo Malaspina di Villafranca, cousin of Moroello and of Franceschino di Mulazzo (the same person who had been a witness at the peace agreement between his relatives and the late bishop); the others, supported by the people of Lucca, had voted for Gherardino Malaspina, who belonged to a Guelf faction in Lucca. The first had Ghibelline sympathies, whereas the second supported the Blacks. The dispute between them dragged on until 1312, when Clement V finally appointed Gherardino. With the arrival of Henry VII, the position of the Guelf bishop-count became difficult. He refused to provide soldiers for the emperor, and Henry declared him a rebel at Poggibonsi in February 1313 and had him banished. The bishop fled to Lucca, and many profited from his lands once he was out of the way, in particular Marchese Spinetta Malaspina di Fosdinovo, one of Henry's followers, who took military control of a large part of them. In the letter, however, Dante seems to be referring to a later situation that had arisen during the actual time of writing. Shortly after

mid-June 1314 Uguccione captured Lucca and became its lord. The city's
Guelfs and their followers moved en masse to Fucecchio. Among them
was Gherardino. Uguccione appointed Castruccio Castracani as viscount
for the jurisdiction of Luni, whom the deposed bishop, from Fucecchio,
decided to invest with the office of "vicar and administrator of the bishop's castle and its lands" on July 4. It seems that he had done so for payment, "perhaps to save some part of his revenues."[37]

Were the sad tribulations of the bishop-count of Luni significant
enough to merit a mention as the only example of avarice in a letter of
such weight?

The offensive reference might perhaps have amused Napoleone Orsini, since he had been involved in the dispute between Gherardino and
friar Guglielmo several years earlier (when he supported the latter), but
in a dramatic situation such as that of the conclave it would have given
him only fleeting satisfaction. In reality, bearing in mind that the letter
was intended for publication, those for whom the sarcasm against bishop
Gherardino was really aimed would seem to have been Uguccione and,
even more, the Malaspina family, who had emerged on the losing side
in the quarrel over the bishopric. If Dante had been far away from the
scene of these local events, would he have had any interest in quoting
them and, above all, would he have known about facts that were happening at exactly the time he was writing? The most convenient answer
is that he was staying in the Lunigiana with Franceschino or Moroello.

It is possible, and perhaps probable, that at least until the end of spring
or summer 1314 Dante was still in western Tuscany, between Pisa and
the Lunigiana. After that, we don't have enough evidence even to hazard
a guess. Unless, that is, we accept what the good friar Ilaro writes in his
letter to Uguccione. The events he describes would have taken place between the end of 1314 and early 1315, so if Dante gave the friar a copy of
Inferno with the task of delivering it to Uguccione, it means he put at
least the final touches to the canticle outside Pisa. And this would add
weight to the suggestion he was staying in the Lunigiana. Ilaro writes,
however, that Dante was passing the hermitage of Bocca di Magra on
his way "ad partes ultramontanas": to interpret this expression, however,
as meaning "beyond the Apennines" goes against the fact that, according
to the almost formulaic manner in which it was used in late medieval
texts, this can only indicate the lands beyond the Alps. But that Dante

was on his way to France on that date is almost impossible. It would be quite another thing if he was heading in the direction of France, in other words, about to take the road leading to France. In this case, Ilaro could either have misunderstood the destination or given a general indication of direction. Moroello Malaspina died on April 8, 1315. His body was interred in Genoa at the church of San Francesco in Castelletto, the pantheon of the great Genoese families, especially the Guelfs (though Henry VII's wife had also been interred there in 1311), and in particular of the Fieschi. It can be inferred that relations between the Moroello and the Fieschi families, which had always been close, had been further strengthened over the last period of Moroello's life, since he died in Genoa in one of their houses. From the monastery of Santa Croce al Corvo there was a stretch of road that meandered over the hills of the eastern coastline of Liguria to Sestri (and then on to Genoa).[38] There is no evidence to support—nor any strong reasons against—the suggestion that Dante had made a journey to Genoa to visit his patron.

The second sentence of death

Where Dante lived and traveled in 1315 is a complete blank. This is a shame, since various orders and judicial proceedings that year were to prove crucial to his life and that of his family.

In May 1315, in one of the most critical moments in the war against Pisa and Lucca, Florence issued a measure revoking orders of banishment, partly in an effort to reduce their enemies' forces. The Florentines resorted to this type of amnesty fairly often, either in the form of a general order of revocation or, more frequently, in relation to individual categories (for example, prisoners). We don't have the text of the resolution of May 1315, but we know of a similar order made on June 2, 1316, which established that convicts, in order to extinguish the offense, had to pay twelve denari for every lira of the full sum fixed by the sentence (in other words, 5 percent of the amount payable). The money was then "offered" (oblati) to the patron saint in the Baptistery during a ceremony to be held on the Feast of Saint John (June 24). On this occasion the banished person who was to be pardoned had to appear dressed in sackcloth, holding a candle and a cowl that he had to continue to wear for a certain period and which, however humiliating (as Dante saw it), served

nevertheless to make it clear to everyone that the person wearing it had
his civil rights restored to him and was therefore no longer exposed to
acts of vengeance and violence. The amnesty of 1316 also contained
various exclusion clauses: it specified that it was not applicable to those
convicted of rebellion or barratry and to those convicted by Cante dei
Gabrielli in 1302. We don't know whether the order of 1315 contained the
same provisions, but we do know that many friends hurried to write to
Dante to inform him about the "order just made in Florence on the absolution of those banished" (*Ep.* XII 2; "per litteras vestras meique nepotis nec non aliorum quamplurium amicorum, significatum est michi
per ordinamentum nuper factum Florentie super absolutione banni-
torum") and inviting him to apply.[39] Therefore, either his friends had
failed to notice when they wrote to him that the amnesty excluded those
convicted by Cante or, more probably, that exclusion was not attached
to the first order. It is worth emphasizing that after almost fifteen years
of exile, Dante still had friends and admirers in Florence, people who
were still concerned about him and knew where he lived. This makes it
plain that his hopes, ten years earlier, of obtaining a personal pardon
were not entirely unfounded.

Dante proudly refused the city's offer, setting out the reasons in a
letter sent to a person called "pater" and probably therefore a priest who,
in the absence of evidence sufficient to reveal his identity, is usually
referred to as his Florentine friend.[40] But of more interest than the recipient are Dante's arguments. He finds it intolerable that he would have to
pay to obtain an amnesty and shameful that he would be "offered" in the
Baptistery of San Giovanni: "Is this perhaps the much awaited revocation
for which Dante Alighieri is called back to his home after having suffered exile for almost fifteen years? Is this the reward for an innocence
obvious to anyone? This for the continual sweat and toil of study? Far
from him, a man familiar with philosophy, a baseness of spirit so foolish
as to oblige him, almost bound, to be put on show like some Ciolo or
other such scoundrel. Far from him, a man who preaches justice, the
idea of paying, after having suffered injustices, villains who have wronged
him as though they were benefactors. This is not the path back home,
dear father; but if first you and then others find another path, one that
does not limit the fame and honor of Dante, then I will tread it, not
with slow feet; and if one doesn't enter Florence by such a path, I will

never enter Florence."[41] Dante dwells upon his studies, on his familiarity with philosophy, on the fame he enjoys. But what work, in late spring of 1315, could have made him a famous philosopher? Not his youthful prose and verse, nor his *canzoni morali* which, however philosophical they might have been, were still not comparable with true works of wisdom; *Convivio* and *De vulgari* had been left unfinished; *Monarchia* doesn't seem to have had much immediate success. A few months earlier, however, he had published *Inferno* (and perhaps also *Purgatorio*), and the effect must have been great. The letter to his Florentine friend is certainly evidence of Dante's moral determination. At the same time, he claimed the path for a dignified return home might be not only through the recognition of his innocence but also through that of his intellectual merit. Dante was forming the idea that the *Commedia* would open wide those gates that politics hadn't succeeded in even unlocking.

At the end of August 1315, the Florentines and the Angevins suffered a terrible defeat at Montecatini. At this critical moment, in order to strengthen the home front and weaken the enemy forces, the Florentines once again—as they had done in 1311 under threat from Henry VII—promptly resorted to an amnesty (which therefore followed shortly after the revocation of the banishments of May). In early September the priors put the machinery of justice into action, and during the course of the month they issued a first order, which has not survived. They established that the death sentences passed by Cante dei Gabrielli were to be commuted to internment, provided that those convicted made an appearance and paid a surety to guarantee they would respect the internment ordered against them. It was a measure of very cautious clemency: it was careful not to allow rebels and Ghibellines within the walls and tended instead to distance them from the Uguccione faction. The choice of the place of compulsory residence, which could be in Tuscany but also outside, was obviously left to the discretion of the judge, Ranieri di Zaccaria of Orvieto, appointed by Robert of Anjou (who had been "lord" of Florence for two years). A list was therefore drawn up of those rebels condemned to death who were eligible to have their sentences commuted, and they were told to appear before the judge. Dante was included in the list but did not appear, and so, for his failure to comply with the order, he and his sons were convicted by Ranieri on October 15 and sentenced to death by decapitation ("caput a spatulis amputetur"). On November 6, as a result of this, Ranieri passed a sentence of banishment on Dante and his sons, giving license to anyone to "offend" them in property and in person, freely and with impunity.[42] This time, it must have been a question of convenience rather than pride that persuaded Dante not to comply with the offer to commute the sentence. He wouldn't, in any event, have been allowed back into the city. He would have been sent somewhere not his choice, which might have been entirely inappropriate for his studies and for the ambitions of a poet who was beginning to taste success.

10

Courtier

1316–1321

how hard is the way
down and up someone else's stairs

come è duro calle
lo scendere e 'l salir per l'altrui scale

—*Para.* XVII 59–60

On the other side of the Apennines

MOROELLO MALASPINA died in 1315, and Uguccione's political fortunes began to wane after his victory at Montecatini. Dante's refusal to make use of the clemency laws widened the rift between him and Florence; the judgments in the fall of that year exposed him and his sons to new dangers. The ties that bound him to Tuscany gradually frayed and broke. In May, ending the letter to his Florentine friend, he declared that even if he didn't return to Florence, he would have no shortage of bread.[1] The problem of bread, however, was not quite so easy to solve. Equally important was the question of safety—his own and his family's. The only region that could give him any guarantee at that time, at least regarding this last point, was Lombardy. There were still two great Ghibelline strongholds there: Milan, ruled by Matteo Visconti who, thanks to his appointment as imperial vicar, had managed to take control of the city, and Verona, ruled by Cangrande della Scala who, likewise, thanks to Henry's appointment, had transformed his family's de facto power into a hereditary despotism. Dante seems to have had no contact with Visconti, but Verona was different—he had stayed there between 1303 and 1304. If he decided to leave Tuscany, this would have been his natural destination.

Dante knew Verona, but may not have known its ruler. Cangrande della Scala had been a boy of thirteen or fourteen during Dante's stay as Bartolomeo's guest. He had not attended Henry VII's coronation in Milan, and though he had followed Henry to Genoa in November 1311, he had left straight away, due to the fatal illness of his brother Alboino. He and Dante would, at most, have crossed paths, but any personal contact would have been unlikely. Their contact seems to have been only by letter and, moreover, through official letters written by Dante on behalf of others.[2] And perhaps not even Dante's growing fame as a poet and philosopher would have been enough to encourage the patronage of a lord who is praised by contemporary sources for his talents as a military leader and his "courtliness"; in other words, a disinterest in money, but no artistic and cultural sensibilities. In short, to enter the court, Dante would have needed the help of someone who mattered.

Who might have assumed the task of recommending him? And when did Dante cross the Apennines in the direction of Verona? We are groping in the dark. As a pure guess, we might imagine that it was Uguccione who had helped him out, and perhaps even that Dante had gone with him to Verona. In April 1316, Uguccione della Faggiuola, expelled from Pisa by a kind of conspiracy hatched by his former protégé Castruccio Castracani, and armed with a safe-conduct signed by Castruccio himself, had taken shelter in the Lunigiana with Spinetta Malaspina (who had fought beside him at Montecatini). But a little later, pursued by Castruccio's troops, he was forced to escape: crossing the Apennines for Modena and Mantova, he took shelter in Verona, where he entered the service of Cangrande. It is not so unlikely that Dante had joined the retinue (at Pisa or in the Lunigiana) of the person who, on Moroello's death, remained his most important patron, all the more since Uguccione knew Cangrande well enough that he could speak in Dante's favor.[3]

Necessary praise

The role played by Cangrande in Dante's life and in his poetical and intellectual life has been, and (to some extent) continues to be, emphasized and perhaps overstated. Some suggest that *Paradiso* was dedicated to him, indeed that the whole canticle was written for him; he is said to be the person hidden behind the "five hundred ten and five" and even the greyhound in *Inferno*; and Dante is said to have written *Monarchia* to defend him from the attacks of Pope John XXII. In short, a whole Della Scala legend has been built up over the centuries.[4] It most probably gathered its first momentum shortly after Dante's death, from those very groups who gravitated around the lord of Verona and who sought to associate him with the intellectual authority of someone known to all for his pro-imperial and Ghibelline positions, as well as to bask in the glory of a poet who had now become famous.[5]

The Cangrande legend rests on two pillars: one, entirely solid, is the high-flown praise of him pronounced by Cacciaguida, and the other, much weaker, is a letter where Dante is said to have dedicated *Paradiso* to him.[6]

Reams have been written about the authenticity of the letter, without any agreed solution. The text is divided into two parts. In the first, the writer addresses Cangrande: "Magnificent and victorious lord . . . vicar general of the most holy Prince Emperor in the city of Verona and the city of Vicenza" (*Ep.* XIII; "Magnifico atque victorioso domino domino Cani Grandi de la Scala sacratissimi Cesarei Principatus in urbe Verona et civitate Vicentie Vicario generali"), expressing his devout friendship, his most fervent wish that it might be reciprocated, and his commitment to do all he can to preserve it. To this end he offers to dedicate *Paradiso* to him as a gift. The second part, which is very long, almost a mini-treatise, contains a rhetorical exposition on the whole poem, followed by an analysis of the first canto of *Paradiso*. It therefore deals with many arguments: these include the "subject" of the work, which can be interpreted literally or on a secondary level ("allegorical or moral or anagogic"), and the title ("comedy"), with regard to its literary genre. The arguments in this second part look very much as though they are a compilation, almost like a collection of commonplaces: and it is this comparison between their lack of originality and the extraordinary insights contained in *Convivio* and *De vulgari eloquentia* that raises strong doubts about whether Dante was the author of a large part of the letter. Not all of it, however, since there is nothing about the beginning to suggest that it's a fake. A reasonable compromise argument could therefore be that the letter as a whole is "a montage of one authentic part (though most probably re-written) . . . and one part grafted on to confirm not just the dedication of the poem to Cangrande . . . but also the less 'extreme' interpretations of the whole work." The allegorical interpretation, in effect, softened the prophetic and doctrinal aspects, which the Church authorities regarded as dangerous (in 1335 the provincial chapter of the Dominicans in Florence forbade monks to read Dante's vernacular works).[7]

The early paragraphs, behind the screen of lively and elaborate rhe-torical construction, give glimpses of Dante's attempt to ingratiate himself with a lord he has only recently known, whom he looks to for protection and for material help. The letter could therefore date from the early months of his stay in Verona. The high-flown words of praise, however, suggest the writer feels a certain embarrassment. It seems as though Dante is seeking to justify his past coolness to the lord he is addressing. He declares, in fact, that he now recognizes that the great praises he had heard of him in the past were well founded—praises that once, before he knew him, seemed excessive: "Once I thought that this praise, which exceeds every enterprise of people today, was much greater than the truth. And therefore so that an excessive uncertainty would not keep me long in suspense . . . I came to Verona, to verify with my own eyes what I had heard; and here I saw your greatness, and at the same time I saw and experienced the favors bestowed; and whereas first I sus-pected a disproportionate gossip, so later I had to acknowledge that the works were beyond proportion."[8] From the admission of his past doubts, Dante certainly finds a way of constructing a most effective eulogy, but would he have recorded his old uncertainties if he hadn't been almost forced to do so—in other words, if not to do so would have undermined the sincerity of the praise? Well, Dante had good reason to be embarrassed.[9]

At the time of the letter, *Purgatorio* was still "fresh off the press"—as we would say today—and in that canticle, as we know, Dante expressed a less-than-flattering view of Alberto della Scala, father of Cangrande, who was guilty of having appointed his illegitimate son Giuseppe as abbot of San Zeno. The judgment was offensive in itself, but to Can-grande it must have seemed doubly so, since, when Giuseppe died in 1313, he behaved in just the same way as his father in appointing another abbot of illegitimate birth, the son of his dead half-brother, for that most prosperous abbey. In such circumstances, Cangrande could hardly have been well disposed to a mendicant, even if he was a poet, who offered to immortalize him in his verse. In short, here too in Verona, as had happened elsewhere, Dante had to face up to the reactions aroused by his poem.[10] This time the question was particularly difficult, since the person to whom he was looking for help was one of the sons of someone he had insulted.

He managed to obtain help from Cangrande, but it's by no means clear that he won his affection. Each time Dante comes into contact with the Della Scala family there seems to be a feeling of unease; even the echoes of the praise he lavished on Cangrande are muted by a sort of veil: it may be no coincidence that the most wretched description of his life as an exile is to be found in the canto that celebrates the "courtesy of the great Lombard" (Bartolomeo della Scala) as well as the "incredible" exploits of Cangrande:

> You'll learn that there is salt
> in others' bread, and how hard is the way
> down and up other people's stairs.
>
> Tu proverai sì come sa di sale
> lo pane altrui, e come è duro calle
> lo scendere e 'l salir per l'altrui scale.
>
> —*Para.* XVII 58–60

There may be no particular importance to the fact that many of the anecdotes around Dante's life are set in the Della Scala court and describe events in which Dante finds himself in a situation of disadvantage. They are all part of a well-established repertory. But the testimony of Francesco Petrarch has quite a different value. The tale he includes in *Res memorande* about a "caustic" reply that Dante is said to have made to Cangrande is also traditional; but Petrarch's comments in introducing it are uniquely his, and far from obvious: "Dante Alighieri, that very fellow citizen of mine, who lived not long ago . . . an exile from his homeland, residing with Cangrande of Verona, then a common place of refuge for those in distress and exile, had at first been received with honor, then little by little had begun to lose favor and day by day to be less pleasing to the lord."[11] Petrarch, writing sometime between early 1343 and the spring of 1345, shows himself well informed about the situation in Verona. Many veterans of Henry's imperial expedition had gathered around Cangrande, including soldiers like Uguccione and Spinetta Malaspina, and Henry's old chamberlain, Simone di Filippo Reali, a White Guelf from Pistoia). But at that time Petrarch had not yet been to Verona, and he would therefore have obtained his information in Avignon—where many clergy and intellectuals kept in contact and corresponded with Verona through the usual channel of Cardinal Niccolò da Prato (to whom Petrarch had been a client before entering into service with the Colonna family)—as well as in Bologna, where he may have attended the lectures of Giovanni del Virgilio, an admirer of Dante. In short, his evidence is not to be underestimated.

Besides, the picture of a lone Dante is confirmed by other indications. Unlike what happened with Scarpetta Ordelaffi, with the Guidi family of Battifolle, and with the court of Henry VII, there is no evidence that Dante had even indirect relations with the chancery in Verona, nor that he held any appointments as procurator or ambassador of the kind he had carried out for the Malaspina family and perhaps even for Bartolomeo della Scala during his first stay in Verona, and would later carry out for Guido Novello da Polenta. This sense of his isolation is further heightened by the lack of any information about his relations with the city's cultural circles. There is no trace of any involvement, even indirect, in that pre-humanist movement that was taking root in the cities of the Veneto where he was staying at the time: Mussato and Dante ignored each other, even though they would have been in close proximity on several occasions, or may actually have met.[12]

Under the sign of Mars

Dante certainly worked very hard to make himself worthy of his new lord's friendship. He erected a sort of monument in one of the most important cantos of *Paradiso* (and of the entire *Commedia*), where his great-grandfather Cacciaguida foretells the course of his life as an exile. Not surprisingly, it begins there in Verona. "Your first refuge and first sanctuary" (*Para.* XVII 70; "Lo primo tuo refugio e 'l primo ostello"), he tells him, will be with Bartolomeo della Scala; and beside him, he continues, you will see a boy who is now (in 1300) only nine years old, so deeply marked by the influence of Mars that his wartime exploits will be worth recording. But in addition to his military valor, whose first signs will already be seen "before the Gascon [Clement V] deceives noble Henry" (*Para.* XVII 82; "pria che 'l Guasco l'alto Arrigo inganni"), in other words, before 1312, Cangrande will become known for his "magnificence." At this point, the words Dante puts into Cacciaguida's mouth are unmistakably those of a courtier: "Look you to him and to his benefactions; / through him many men are transformed, / rich men and beggars changing their condition" (*Para.* XVII 88–90; "A lui t'aspetta e a' suoi benefici; / per lui fia trasmutata molta gente, / cambiando condizion ricchi e mendici"). Never had Dante used the poem to convey such explicit requests to a lord whose guest he was. His celebration "of the value of the purse and of the sword" (*Purg.* VIII 129; "del pregio de la borsa e de la spada") in praising the Malaspina was of quite another cut, though the substance was the same. Still not satisfied, Dante the writer recounts how Cacciaguida told him "things" about this boy that were so "incredible" that they could not be revealed: if even those future eyewitnesses would not be able to believe their eyes, then we can only imagine the reaction of those who knew about them in the form of a prediction!

So far as the Malaspina are concerned, Dante shows an astonishing lack of gratitude toward them. For almost a decade they had given him hospitality and support, had admired his intellectual talent and his writings, had introduced him into the circle of great feudal families in which they moved, had helped in his desperate attempt to obtain a pardon from Florence. *Inferno* and *Purgatorio* are largely inspired by the Malaspina, so that the information given by Ilaro that Dante had intended to dedicate the second canticle to Moroello, if accurate, would come as no surprise. Well, in Verona, Dante wipes away all trace of the Malaspina family. His journey as an exile, as predicted by Cacciaguida, contemplates only the Della Scala court, there at the beginning and— so Dante perhaps still believed—at the end of a long period of his life in which there is no shadow of any other family or any other protector.

Having left the sky of Mars, where he had met Cacciaguida, Dante rises to that of Jupiter, from which the influences of justice descend. And here, having described the vision of the blessed souls that move in such a way as, firstly, to form the thirty-five letters of the verse of scripture, "Diligite iustitiam qui iudicatis terram" ("Love justice you who judge the earth"), and then the figure of an eagle, the author turns to the blessed souls, asking them to pray for mortals "led astray by bad example" (*Para.* XVIII 126; "sviati dietro al malo essemplo"), by the bad example of popes who are so corrupt that they use their power of excommunication as though it were a weapon.[13] At this point the narrator launches a searing attack on a pope who writes only "to cancel out," who issues excommunications only to make money from their annulment, and whose faith lies not in Peter and Paul, the founders of the Church, but in John the Baptist, whose image appears on the florin:

> But you who write only to cancel out,
> remember that Peter and Paul, who died
> for the vineyard you destroy, are still alive.
>> Well may you say: "My desire is so fixed
> on him who wished to live alone
> and who by leaps [because Salome had danced] was led to
>   martyrdom,
>> that I know not the fisherman nor Paul."

> Ma tu che sol per cancellare scrivi,
> pensa che Pietro e Paulo, che moriro
> per la vigna che guasti, ancor son vivi.
>> Ben puoi tu dire: "i' ho fermo 'l disiro
> sì a colui che volle viver solo
> e che per salti fu tratto al martiro,
>> ch'io non conosco il pescator né Polo."

—*Para.* XVIII 130–136

The pope so strenuously loyal to the Baptist florin is John XXII. What remains is to understand why Dante turns upon him so violently and, all in all, without his attack having any cogent connection to the rest of the canto. The reason is to be found in the relationship between the pope and Cangrande.

In 1316, a Guelf offensive, inspired and supported by the pope himself, had been launched against the alliance of the three Ghibelline lords of Milan, Mantua, and Verona. The conflict had further worsened in early 1317, after Cangrande had paid homage to Frederick of Habsburg, from whom, in March, he had obtained reconfirmation of the title of imperial vicar granted to him by Henry VII. Cangrande had then refused the pope's repeated requests to renounce the vicariate for the period during which the imperial throne remained vacant, so that he was excommunicated on April 6, 1318. Dante's attack on John XXII therefore refers to this particular excommunication: it is a declaration of support for his patron, and has all the appearance of being written close to the time of the event, in other words, in spring 1318.[14]

But the flurry of praise in the central cantos of *Paradiso* comes to a sudden end. After the attack on John XXII there are no further references, direct or indirect, either to Cangrande or to other historical events. Indeed, the whole of the last part of the canticle avoids commenting on current affairs and focuses exclusively on the great themes of Church and Empire.

Cunizza's predictions

Dante promised in his letter to Cangrande to dedicate *Paradiso* to him. Ilaro, on the other hand, wrote that Dante had intended to dedicate it to Frederick III of Aragon; even assuming this to be true, it would be understandable, however, that Dante had changed his mind once the king of Sicily had come to an agreement with Robert of Anjou and abandoned the imperial cause. But the fact remains that *Paradiso* would not be dedicated to Cangrande or anybody else. In 1316, Dante had no idea that he would finish the poem in another city and, what is more, at the very end of his life. Neither did the other two canticles have dedicatees: the dedications that Ilaro referred to were therefore just intentions never carried out.

Even the widely held idea that the whole of *Paradiso* was written in Verona goes against what are clearly the facts. When he arrived there, around the middle of 1316, Dante had already written a large portion of it.

In Canto VI, Justinian—in order to show Dante the guilt borne by those who "move against" the imperial emblem (the eagle), whether misusing it or fighting against it—traces the history of that glorious institution from Ascanius, son of Aeneas, who founded Alba Longa, to Char-lemagne, who founded the Holy Roman Empire in continuation of the Roman Empire. It is a story of courage and virtue that enables him to deplore the conduct of one who "against the public emblem [the eagle] opposes the yellow lilies [of the kings of France]" and one who "appropri-ates that part" (*Para.* VI 100–101; "al pubblico segno i gigli gialli / oppone, e l'altro appropria quello a parte"), in other words, uses it as a party symbol. The accusation is against the Guelfs and Ghibellines together. And Justinian rails angrily against both of them:

> Let the Ghibellines do their work
> under another sign, for he ill follows that [imperial sign]
> where justice and he are split;
>> and let not this new Charles [Charles II of Anjou] strike it [the sign] down
> with his Guelfs, but let him fear the claws
> that flayed a much mightier lion.

> Faccian li Ghibellin, faccian lor arte
> sott'altro segno, ché mal segue quello
> sempre chi la giustizia e lui diparte;
>> e non l'abbatta esto Carlo novello
> coi Guelfi suoi, ma tema de li artigli
> ch'a più alto leon trasser lo vello.

—*Para.* VI 103–108

Such scathing anti-Ghibelline words could not have been written in Verona, the capital of Italian Ghibellinism. Dante couldn't have accused the head of the Ghibelline faction of using the imperial shield to carry out actions that were partisan and, moreover, unjust, at the same time as he was seeking its protection. This canto is earlier than 1316, dating from a period when Dante was already convinced that the two factions had become no more than instruments that pursued specific interests and that the great question of the two universal powers had to be placed on another footing.[15] It was the period after the deaths of Henry VII and Clement V, when the keenness of political analysis becomes associ-ated, in the absence of true figures of importance, with a strong prophetic and visionary charge: even the tone ("but let him fear the claws") refers to the prophecies in the cantos of Eden ("let him whose fault it is, believe / that God's vengeance fears no sop").

Canto IX would already seem to be influenced by and indeed be favorable to the Della Scala court. Here, the sister of Ezzelino da Romano, Cunizza (of whom Dante had heard during his childhood in Florence), prophesies grave misfortune to the population of the March of Treviso.[16] The Paduans, guilty of not having recognized Cangrande's power as imperial vicar, would be badly defeated by him in the marshes near Vicenza (in December 1314); the lord of Treviso, Rizzardo da Camino, son of Gherardo, would be killed in a plot (in 1312), perhaps "for having taken sides with Henry VII whose vicar he had become, thereby abandoning his own, his family's and his city's traditional Guelph allegiances"; the Guelf Alessandro Novello of Treviso, bishop of Feltre, would betray the Ghibelline exiles of Ferrara who had taken refuge with him and would deliver them up to the Black Florentine Guelf, Pinuccio Della Tosa, Robert of Anjou's vicar in that city (in 1314), who would have them slaughtered. If we think of Cunizza's predictions as written in Verona, they certainly fit into a consistent political picture: they would be lines favorable to Cangrande, who had to stand up against a Guelf alignment that stretched "from Feltre to Padua and Treviso after its rule by the Caminesi, supported by Ferrara, in the hands of the Este family and, for a period, of the Angevins."[17] And yet the beginning of the canto tends to suggest it was composed before 1316 and, therefore, that Cunizza's prophecy, though appearing as an objective political statement in favor of the Della Scala, had not been written from the viewpoint of a "courtier."

Much of the canto immediately before is taken up with a speech by Charles Martel of Anjou, whom Dante had known in Florence in 1294. The young king first states that many disasters caused by his family, such as the popular uprising in Sicily, would not have happened without his premature death, then warns his brother Robert, king of Naples, of the risks to which his avarice is exposing the realm and, lastly, in order to explain how a miser like Robert could be born from a royal lineage known for its generosity, he embarks on a disquisition about the various inclinations that the heavens bring down on particular individuals. The conclusion of the discourse marks the end of the canto. The next canto, in which Dante meets Cunizza, opens without introduction or any transitional passage, with the narrator addressing the wife of Charles Martel, Clemence of Habsburg (whom Dante also knew in Florence): "After your Charles, fair Clemence, / had enlightened me, he told me of the betrayals / his progeny would have to suffer; / but said: 'Say nothing and let the years pass'; / so that all I can say is that / deserved grief will follow your sufferings" (*Para.* IX 1–6; "Da poi che Carlo tuo, bella Clemenza, / m'ebbe chiarito, mi narrò li 'nganni / che ricever dovea la sua semenza; / ma disse: 'Taci e lascia muover li anni'; / sì ch'io non posso dir se non che pianto / giusto verrà di retro ai vostri danni"). Charles, having cleared up the doubt about how a generous man can produce a mean son, therefore tells Dante that Charles's descendants would be betrayed, but predicts that it will be followed by just revenge. But he also tells him not to reveal what this consists of, so that Dante, in obedience, cannot say more except that it will be painful. There is not the slightest indication of this prediction in the preceding words of Charles Martel. In narrative fictional terms, he would have continued talking without Dante the author writing down what he said. This fact is unusual in the *Commedia,* so much so that the link between the two cantos seems rather unconvincing. There is the feeling that Dante wanted to communicate some news at the beginning of Canto IX which he hadn't been aware of when he was writing Canto VIII and which he couldn't introduce into that canto through a partial reworking because it was completely filled, to the very last line, with the long discussion about inclinations and free will. The news would obviously not be about the "betrayals" suffered by Charles Martel's descendants—going back to 1296, when his son Charles Robert was deprived of the right to the throne of Naples in favor of Robert—but would concern the just revenge for the injustices suffered. This would be seen in the defeat inflicted by Uguccione della Faggiola upon the Guelfs of Florence, Lucca, and their Angevin allies at the battle of Montecatini on August 12, 1315.[18] For Charles Martel, it was a defeat that brought the death of his brother (Peter, Count of Eboli) and Charles of Acaia, son of Philip of Taranto, commander of the Angevin troops and brother of King Robert, and was a serious blow to the prestige of the Anjou king, which might have seemed like revenge. But Dante wasn't particularly concerned about domestic quarrels between members of the Anjou family; for him the great victory by the Ghibelline forces—the first since the death of Henry

VII—had enormous political value. It is understandable, then, that he wanted to record it, even beneath the veil of an allusive prediction, and that he wanted to record it straight away, a very short time after the event. The meeting he had just recounted with Charles Martel gave him the chance to do so. And this confirms once again that, in certain respects, the *Commedia* really is an "instant book."

If this is how things went, then we can infer that in September 1315, before he moved to Verona, Dante was still working on the canto of Cunizza. The allusion to the battle was also a way of paying homage to the author of the victory, his protector Uguccione. This, then, is a further indication that until the end of that summer Dante was still living in Tuscany.[19]

After the attack on John XXII (in spring of 1318), *Paradiso* contains no more references to current political events. Cangrande disappears from the poem. And yet the events of the years immediately afterward would have provided considerable material for someone like Dante, who was always interested in what was happening around him and, above all, always ready to praise his lord. How do we interpret this? As the effect of a sudden change in the form of the poem or as a sign that relations with Cangrande had cooled or even ended?

Fame as a sorcerer

We learn from the records of an investigation by cardinals that Matteo Visconti, lord of Milan, and his eldest son Galeazzo wanted to kill John XXII by sorcery, and for this purpose Galeazzo had expressed the intention in May 1320 to summon *magister* Dante Alighieri of Florence to Piacenza. We can only laugh at the fact that someone could think of killing their enemies through necromancy and sorcery, but the pope and the court around him were evidently not of the same opinion: magic was considered to be an effective and dangerous diabolical art. It cannot be believed that Dante (who doesn't in fact seem to have gone to Piacenza) was involved in black magic. Nevertheless, this affair, which happened between Avignon, Milan, and Verona, is verified by official investigations, so that Dante's fame as a necromancer is also in a certain sense documented.[20]

Such notoriety shouldn't be surprising. For one thing, he had a reputation as an expert in astrology, and we know that this discipline could easily spill over into magical and necromantic practices. And then, above all, he was famous after the publication of *Inferno* for having descended live into the realms of the afterlife and for having encountered devils there, the souls of the damned, and having spoken to them. It must have been a rumor widely spread and also disturbing. It seems, according to Boccaccio, that the women who used to pass him in the street would say to each other: Look, "he who goes into Hell, and returns whenever he likes, and brings back news of those who are down there"; to which one of them might answer: It's quite true, "don't you see how his beard is frizzled and his complexion browned by the heat and smoke down there?" It is more than probable that gossip of this kind circulated among ordinary folk, and that Dante made no attempt to deny it: "hearing these words behind him, and knowing that they came from the women's simple belief, being amused by it, and almost pleased that they were of such an opinion, smiling somewhat, he continued on."[21] After all, he had always tried to create the self-image of a man who was exceptional and different from the others. But any kind of involvement with demons automatically placed him among those who practiced black magic, or could do so if they wished. Not only ordinary women believed this, but also popes, rulers, judges, and doctors, and so anyone who had taken the account of his journey to hell as true would have called him a necromancer.[22] This is why the early commentators on the poem (including the person who composed the second part of the letter to Cangrande) are almost unanimous in interpreting his journey into the underworld allegorically: as already stated, it was a way of "preventing a literal interpretation of the *Commedia*," that is, of dissuading anyone from "imagining an actual journey of the poet into the afterlife," with the implications that we have just seen.[23]

The last refuge

Galeazzo Visconti's intention (since it seems to have been no more than an intention) to involve Dante in the witchcraft he was planning is too vague for us to make any inferences about timescale—for example, that

Dante was still in Verona in early 1320 (at most, we can infer that Gale-azzo thought he was there at that time).[24] In reality, it seems that Dante had been living in Ravenna for more than a year—since at least 1319, if not the latter part of 1318. He would therefore have lived in Ravenna, where he died, for around three years, and this would confirm what Boccaccio—an expert on what was going on in Ravenna—stated twice, namely that Polenta let him stay with him "for several years" and that Dante "lived [there] several years."[25] In truth, the date when Dante moved there is the subject of much debate: most Dante scholars give it as either 1318 or the early months of 1320. There are arguments in favor of both possibilities but, as usual, nothing is certain.[26]

Dante went to Ravenna perhaps in the company of his family, and certainly with his son Pietro.[27] In early January 1321, Pietro was in fact recorded as being the beneficiary, as rector, of the incomes from two churches in Ravenna: Santa Maria in Zenzanigola and San Simone al Muro. We know that he and others were excommunicated by the vicar of the Archbishop of Ravenna on January 4 for not having paid church taxes on those incomes to the legate Bertrando del Poggetto.[28] We don't know exactly how long Pietro had enjoyed those benefices: it is certain only that he was receiving them already during the summer of 1320. Young Alighieri would obviously have benefited from them not through his own merits, but in consideration of those of his father. This generous gesture would have been arranged by the Polenta family and various relatives. Even assuming, as seems likely, that the grant of such bene-fits had been decided before Dante's arrival in Ravenna, a certain period of time would have been needed to complete the necessary bureaucratic formalities. It would, in fact, have been a double procedure, since the rights for the churches were granted by two different people, though related, namely the cousins Caterina and Idana Malvicini di Bagnaca-vallo. In short, these considerations also support the view that 1319 is the most probable date for Dante's move.

Added to this, at the end of 1319 (or in early 1320, at the latest), the rhetorician Giovanni del Virgilio sent a poem to Dante from Bologna in Latin hexameters in which he recalled the promise he had made on the occasion of their meeting in Ravenna to send some of his writings: "if, however, in the city encircled by the Po [Ravenna] you gave me hope that you might deign to visit me with friendly words . . . may it please you to reply to me" (*Ec.* I 47–51; "Si tamen Eridani michi spem mediamne dedisti / quod visare notis me dignareris amicis . . . rispondere velis"). The meeting could only have taken place in 1319.

The fall of Lucifer

Everything would fit together nicely if it weren't for the so-called *Questio de aqua et terra*. This is a scientific text that discusses and resolves, in its own way, following a logical-syllogistic procedure, the cosmological problem about why, in the inhabited hemisphere, many lands emerge from the surface of the sea. Theory would have it that around the center of the earth, which is also the center of the universe, there is a concentric arrangement of spheres of elements, from the heaviest to the lightest (earth, water, air, fire), so that water, being external to the earth, ought to cover the whole of its surface. Experience, however, shows that it is not like this. The solution proposed is that emersion depends upon the attraction exercised by the heavens, and in particular from that of the fixed stars.

The text, though mixed up with other genres, has the appearance primarily of an academic *questio*: a teacher would set the topic in advance, which would then undergo discussion, during which he would answer the objections of those taking part. In a later session, he would reorganize the arguments put forward during the disputation, disprove them and put forward his own reasoning, which would thus rise to the status of "determined" truth; finally he would put his reasoning in writing. The story of how this text came into existence relates to this kind of scientific and educational procedure: in Mantua, Dante found himself involved in a debate (not at a university) on the question of lands above sea level. The discussion remained unresolved, without any conclusion being presented by a teacher, so he took it upon himself to "determine it" and on January 20, 1320, in the small church of Sant' Elena beside the cathedral, he publicly presented his argument (which he then put in writing).

From the moment it first became known in 1508, in an edition published in Venice by the Augustinian theologian Giovanni Benedetto Moncetti, there has been a strong suspicion, almost a certainty, of the text being a fake.[29] Indeed, there is no shortage of reasons for thinking this. It has come down to us in that edition alone, taken moreover from an unknown manuscript. Before that time, nobody—with one single exception—seems to have known or even heard of it. Then, in comparison to the normal *questio,* this one by Dante bears remarkable anomalies,[30] starting from the fact that the solution to the problem was given in a city different from that in which the disputation was held (and therefore in front of an audience who, with few presumable exceptions, couldn't have taken part in it) and ending with the way that Dante, with annoying insistence, confirms that he is the author, to the point of emphasizing that the text was written in his own hand.[31] Finally—one of the reasons that raises the most doubt—the solution proposed not only fails to take into account what Dante had written in the final lines of *Inferno* with regard to the great devastation wrought by the fall of Lucifer, but seems even to contradict it.[32] It is true that he often changed his mind, even on questions of science and doctrine, but these were always changes and reversals of opinion either within works never published or between the *Commedia* and the unpublished *Convivio* and *De vulgari,* and therefore never made public. This would be the only case of a public recantation or change of position, which, moreover, would relate to one of the most conspicuous points in a work only recently published.

And yet, doubts and uncertainties ought to be resolved by what is unanimously regarded as the best evidence of the authenticity of the *Questio,* which is the fact that Pietro Alighieri, commenting on the lines on the fall of Lucifer, refers to an actual disputation held by his father "an terra esset altior aqua vel contra" and refers to certain arguments that resemble passages of the *Questio.*[33] Pietro, in Verona, was most probably there himself at the lecture given by his father, and this is why his evidence counters all objections. If this is how it was, we ought either to accept that Dante had made a special journey to Verona at the beginning of 1320—which frankly seems too much to suggest—or that on that date he hadn't yet moved.

I have used the conditional tense because, in reality, Pietro's evidence doesn't have the authority attributed to it; indeed, it could be the proof that on that January of 1320 Dante had not spoken at the church in Verona. Of the three distinct versions of his commentary of the *Commedia,* in fact, it seems that only the first, datable between 1339 and 1341, is attributable to him, whereas the other two have been heavily re-written, if not entirely reworked by others. The reference to the *Questio* is to be found only in the third, written around 1360, and this removes Pietro's qualification as eyewitness. And not only that: the fact that he says nothing in the commentary that is certainly his own can be inter-preted as very strong evidence, if not proof, that it was not written by Dante. Why does Pietro remain silent? If the Alighieri family were still in Verona in early 1320, Pietro would have been present at the event; if it had already moved to Ravenna, Pietro would certainly have known about his father's journey and the reason why he had made it.

A cultured despot

Dante left a grand court—the political capital of Italian Ghibellines—to move to a small city (Ravenna then had less than 7,000 inhabitants), governed moreover by a well-known Guelf family.[34] This time, politics played no part in his decision. Dante had never been Ghibelline in the sense of belonging to the party; during these years he had been pro-empire and against the *pars Ecclesiae*—against the Guelf-Angevin alli-ance. But political involvement no longer seemed to interest him: in the last cantos of the *Commedia* there is no trace of the wars and diplomatic conflicts between the pope, the Della Scala, and the Visconti, or of the quarrel between the German pretenders to the imperial throne. His con-cern was now centered on the great question—cultural more than political—of Church reform as the necessary prerequisite for the resto-ration of imperial order. Whether his host and patron was Guelf or Ghibelline couldn't have worried him very much from the ideological point of view. But he must have been far more interested when a Guelf patron like Guido Novello da Polenta was prepared to give him ample assurances about his own and his children's safety.[35] At the height of clashes between the pope and the Ghibelline lords, a man as politically compromised as Dante couldn't move to a region like Romagna, under the hold of the Angevins, without prior guarantees. Having obtained them, his decision would have been influenced by such considerations as the possibility of better conditions for himself and his family, the op-portunity of devoting himself without too much distraction to his work on *Paradiso,* on which he was now absorbed, and the advantages of obtaining access to books essential to that work. Ravenna probably offered all of these.

Dante didn't have any personal acquaintance with Guido Novello da Polenta, but he must have had plenty of opportunity to meet other members of the family. He had stayed for long periods in Romagna and in the Casentino: the noble families in those regions were bound together by common interests and often by family relationships that crossed the bounds of shifting political allegiances.[36] And he probably made trips to Ravenna or nearby cities.

Guido Novello, who was a nephew of Francesca, had become head of the family and of the city of Ravenna too late for Dante to have had earlier dealings with him. Only in June 1316 had he been appointed *podestà,* an office thanks to which he exercised his control over the city. It was most probably he who had taken an interest in Dante, now famous through the publication of the first two canticles, rather than the other way around. Guido Novello was different from the usual type of despot who emerged in northern Italy during that period: he was a poet and loved literature. Unlike Moroello Malaspina and many others, who liked vernacular poetry but had to resort to Dante's pen to respond in rhyme to the sonnets sent him by Cino da Pistoia, Novello wrote verse that was his own and also of a certain quality. His poetry still has to be fully explored: he certainly wrote six ballate which reveal a familiarity with the *stilnovo* poetry of Guido Cavalcanti, Cino da Pistoia, and Dante himself.[37] The atmosphere among his circle was therefore quite different to that of Cangrande della Scala.

Dante became familiar with very different kinds of social and cultural surroundings during his life. Being schooled in the city life of Bono Giamboni, of Brunetto Latini, of love poets like Guido Cavalcanti, growing up in a society dominated by trade, in which intellectuals sought to offer instruments that would make it more cultured, he had then moved into the declining world of the feudal courts, where courtly values had by that time become remnants of the past and where low levels of education hampered the creation of new prospects. In the university city of Bologna he had experienced the hostility of academics in his attempts to revive the new vernacular culture in which he strongly believed; in the palaces of northern Italian despots, caught up in a daily battle for survival, he had seen their lack of interest in questions of philosophy and literature. And he himself, on the other hand, through his stubborn interest in the vernacular, had shown no interest in the seeds of the pre-humanistic revival which had begun to sprout in those same Venetian cities where he was staying. He failed—or refused—to understand that a new culture was being spread through Latin. Now, in the last years of his life, he found himself in a situation that resembled (remotely, of course) that in which Petrarch would find himself several decades later while he was staying at the courts of the Visconti in Milan and the Carraresi in Padua. Guido Novello was not a "lord" in the full sense of the word (unlike the Visconti and the Della Scala who, as imperial vicars, had obtained a sort of legitimate dynastic power), so that there was not a formal court with clearly defined rules and responsibilities. His was a sort of feudal "family" who, unlike those who lived in castles, exercised its own jurisdiction (without any true legitimate right) over a city and its surrounding territory. Feudal-style bonds of loyalty merged ambiguously with relationships of paid employment. Yet it was a family in which cultural and artistic merits seem to have received higher recognition than they would have done in other institutions of this kind. From this point of view, it would anticipate to some extent what would later happen in the larger courts, when the presence of intellectuals and men of letters was regarded as a value in itself (and therefore also a reason for economic investment). We can suppose that the relationship between Dante and Guido Novello da Polenta was a sort of halfway between the traditional "service" of a loyal follower or client and the "freelance provision" of intellectual services. It may then be significant that in *Paradiso*—for which many cantos still had to be written at the time of his arrival in Ravenna—Dante never mentions Guido Novello or his family. It is indicative of the fact that his relationship with this lord was of a kind that could ignore the shameless courtly praises lavished on Cangrande, or the elegant expressions of gratitude given to the Malaspina family. We can trust Boccaccio when he writes that Guido Novello da Polenta, "schooled in the liberal arts, honored highly men of worth."[38]

The importance of having a poet as guest

Boccaccio adds that it was the lord of Ravenna who invited Dante, "having for a long time known his worth by reputation."[39] The notion that it was he who made the first move is somewhat puzzling: his would be an almost pre-Renaissance gesture of patronage, too advanced for the despotic minds of the early Trecento, however enlightened they might have been. Perhaps things had gone differently.

The decision to grant Dante, through his son Pietro, the enjoyment of benefices of the churches of Santa Maria in Zenzanigola and San Simone al Muro didn't depend only on the Polentani and their closest relatives. The holders of the rights were, as already stated, the cousins Caterina and Idana Malvicini di Bagnacavallo, who had inherited them in the absence of male heirs in the Bagnacavallo family. In *Purgatorio,* deploring the state of Romagna, "where hearts are made so evil" (*Purg.* XIV III; "dove i cuor son fatti sì malvagi"), Guido del Duca had declared: "Bagnacavallo does well to beget no sons" (*Purg.* XIV 115; "Ben fa Bagnacaval, che non rifiglia"). If it weren't for the fact that those lines date from many years before, "it would have been said that Dante had extremely good reason to be thankful for the extinction of the males in the Malvicini *domus.*"[40] Caterina had married Guido Novello around 1309–1310; Idana was the second wife of Aghinolfo di Romena, the old *capitano* of the White exiles and the Ghibellines. The two cousins couldn't have acted without the agreement of their husbands; it would, moreover, have been the agreement between Polenta and Guidi that determined their act of generosity. To grant a rectorate required the approval of the diocesan office in Ravenna: it just so happened that the right-hand man of Bishop Rinaldo da Concorezzo—who lived forty kilometers away at Argenta and very rarely set foot in the city—and the person who really controlled the Church in Ravenna was the archdeacon, Rinaldo da Polenta, Guido's brother. So the diocesan office certainly wouldn't have created obstacles. That act of munificence for an old client or faithful follower of the Romena family who had become a renowned poet and philosopher seems to have been performed to reconcile the feudal sense of honor of the Guidi counts as well as to fulfill Guido da Polenta's hopes for cultural prestige. We must therefore suppose that Dante had reestablished contact—we don't know how—with his old patrons and that they had worked (contributing also in material terms) for a grant of hospitality from the lord of Ravenna with added financial support. For both, it was an investment in which the reasons of "courtesy" merged with the expectation of furtherance for the family name.[41]

This meant, of course, that Aghinolfo, with whom Dante would have had dealings during the years of Henry VII, must have ignored the insults that his protégé had made in the poem. The lines where Master Adam had accused him of counterfeiting the florin and labeled him, along with his brother Guido and Alessandro, as a "wretched soul" (*Inf.* XXX 76; "anima trista") must have been known to him since at least 1314 or 1315. Only a few years had passed, but many things had changed in Aghinolfo's life. The old Ghibelline soldier who had battled alongside the emperor during the fighting in Rome and at the siege of Florence and had then joined the army of Uguccione della Faggiola (one of whose sons had married one of his daughters), had eventually yielded to a political situation which had brought Ghibelline fortunes in Tuscany to an end. First he had been forced to sell his castles and estates in the upper Arno Valley, and then, taken prisoner, he had agreed to join forces with Florence in 1318, in exchange for cancellation of the banishments against him. And he would remain loyal to Florence until his death, as an old man, in 1338. During the years leading up to Dante's arrival in Ravenna, he was no longer actively involved in politics or in military combat, but a simple feudal lord whose powers were much reduced, who lived on his estates in the Casentino under continual threat from neighboring relatives. Dante Alighieri had become a resource for him too.

A moment of calm

In none of Dante's other places of exile did he enjoy the calm and serenity that he found in Ravenna. Here he resolved the financial problem that had always afflicted him. The rectorate of the two churches was granted to his eldest son Pietro—though he never embarked upon a career in the Church—partly because it would have been impossible to grant ecclesiastical benefices to his father, who had famously placed himself against the Church. It is clear, however, that the revenues went to support the whole family. We can also suppose that the arrangement for Dante's daughter Antonia at the convent of Santo Stefano had been a gesture of patronage by Guido Novello or someone else in Ravenna.[42]

It is certain, however, that Dante lived in Ravenna surrounded by his children. Since the group also included Antonia (who, as a girl, was not subject to the banishment that affected the sons), the whole family, including Gemma, were probably now reunited (though it cannot be ruled out that the family had come back together during the last period of his stay in Tuscany or, immediately afterward, in Verona). The reassembly of the family may have been helped by the fact that Dante now had the use of a house.[43]

Apart from family affection, Dante was surrounded by the warmth of a substantial group of friends and admirers. All of them were men of letters who looked upon him as a teacher. Boccaccio wrote that in Ravenna Dante "had many pupils in poetry and especially in the vernacular," and that "he showed many the way of composing in rhyme." This has prompted the question of whether he gave public lessons in rhetoric, especially in the vernacular. Some have suggested the possibility of a private school paid for by the pupils themselves rather than an institution paid for by the city, though some have even suggested he was a lecturer in vernacular rhetoric at the *Studio*. But we have no proof of any of this. It is a fact, however, that many young men congregated around him, almost all doctors and notaries: some are named, in pastoral disguise, in the eclogues he exchanged with Giovanni del Virgilio.[44]

We have already come across the Florentine notary Dino Perini, Boccaccio's informant (on the rediscovery of the "little notebook" containing the first seven cantos of *Inferno*), who, "according to what he said, had been as familiar as was possible and a friend of Dante."[45] Perini was not boasting, to judge from the role of confidant and assistant that Dante gives him in the eclogues, under the pseudonym of Meliboeus, from which, however, it emerges that he wasn't particularly expert either in Latin poetry or, more generally, in literature. Not much different is the intellectual standing of another notary, Pietro Giardini of Ravenna, who was also one of Boccaccio's informants. He would certainly have been "one of the closest friends and servants that Dante had in Ravenna," though there is no evidence he had any particular interest in poetry or, even less, in writing it.[46] Of quite a different caliber were two figures who we know to have been in contact with Dante. One of them, Menghino Mezzani of Ravenna, was also a notary—the humanist Coluccio Salutati, in a letter written at the end of the 1300s to a clerk in the Polenta household, states that he had been a "familiaris et socius Dantis nostri" and that he had even written about the *Commedia*. And indeed

Mezzani, who enjoyed composing verse in Latin and, especially, in vernacular, and had known both Boccaccio and Petrarch, left various poetical writings on Dantean subjects (two summaries of *Inferno* and *Purgatorio* in terza rima), while it is unclear whether he also wrote a commentary on the poem. The other figure, who appears in the eclogues under the name Alphesiboeus, is the Bologna doctor and philosopher Fiduccio dei Milotti. He was a distinguished contemporary of Dante who had business links with Ravenna (as well as other cities in Romagna, such as Forlì and Imola), but he was also the father-in-law of Giovanni da Polenta, the brother of Guido Novello. The eclogues show that Dante regarded him as an intimate friend and someone whose advice was to be taken seriously. He seems not to have pursued literature, but his scientific and philosophical interests (he probably moved in university circles) are apparent from the lavish library (split up between the cities where he generally spent his time) which he left in his will. There is no documentary evidence of any relationship between Dante and another Ravenna doctor, Guido Vacchetta, who wrote poetry and was on friendly terms with Pietro Giardini and his family. But since we know he exchanged a few Latin poems with Giovanni del Virgilio, it is more than likely that he had some dealings with Dante.

This picture shows that Dante was surrounded more or less permanently by a group of people with strong intellectual, and in many cases literary, interests. Some of them would also keep contact with each other after Dante's death and in his memory. The fourteenth-century poet Antonio Beccari, known as Maestro Antonio da Ferrara, who kept a long verse correspondence with Menghino Mezzani, invokes the muse Calliope, in one sonnet to him, that she might help a noble "fellowship" of vernacular poets to follow flawlessly and effortlessly in the footsteps of "father Dante."[47] We can't imagine that Beccari was alluding to an academy, or anything of that kind, but his verses nevertheless suggest that at least some of the group that had gathered around Dante in the last years of his life continued to honor his memory, writing a vernacular poetry that was inspired by him.

In Ravenna, therefore, Dante had around him a small but significant circle of friends and admirers. And yet, in no other period of his life as that in Ravenna does he give the impression of being a man alone and largely misunderstood.

An invitation and a challenge

The grammarian and Latin poet Giovanni di Antonio, known as Giovanni del Virgilio, went to visit Dante in Ravenna in 1319. The author of grammar treatises, of an *Ars dictaminis* and a commentary on Ovid's *Metamorphoses,* as well as correspondence in Latin verse, Giovanni lectured at the *Studio* in Bologna. He wasn't a *magister,* therefore, but an ordinary teacher (and badly paid as well, it would seem), yet he had connections with the leading figures of the emerging humanist movement, mostly from Padua, and had extraordinary rhetorical and literary ability. He must have enjoyed a certain prestige in Bologna, and not only there, since he corresponded in verse with Albertino Mussato. He was an avid admirer of Dante. This admiration was probably shared with others in Bologna; in any event, he came from those academic circles that Dante had always looked upon with interest—an interest that hadn't been reciprocated. We don't know why he went to Ravenna (though we know he moved between Bologna and the Romagna and would spend two years, between 1324 and 1325, teaching in Cesena). Perhaps he was looking for work.[48]

Indirectly, we can glean something of what Giovanni and Dante probably had to say to each other. They would have talked about vernacular literature and its relationship with Latin literature. Dante would have tried to persuade Giovanni about the dignity of the vernacular and its appropriateness in writing literature. To overcome Giovanni's doubts, he must even have let him read (or have read to him) *De vulgari eloquentia* which, so far as we know, he still kept well hidden. Yet Giovanni del Virgilio doesn't seem to have changed his opinion on the unworthiness of that language.

Dante promised to send him some verses. But since he delayed in keeping his promise, Giovanni, once back in Bologna, sent him his own verse, toward the end of 1319, an epistle in the style of Horace in which he urged him to stop addressing ordinary people and throwing pearls before wild boar ("nec margaritas profliga prodigus apris"; *Ec.* I 21), to abandon vernacular language ("carmine . . . laico"; *Ec.* I 15) taken from the marketplace ("sermone forensi"; *Ec.* I 18) and finally to compose cantos in Latin that were worthy of an intelligent public.[49] In particular, he suggested he should write an epic poem on a modern theme: with such a work, Dante could obtain the poet's crown (Albertino Mussato

had been crowned in Padua only a few years before, in December 1315).
If Dante agreed to move to Bologna, he himself would introduce him
into academic circles.

Giovanni del Virgilio, as I said, was an admirer of Dante, and this
makes his comments even more significant. He gives voice to what the
magistri at the *Studio* thought of Dante's poem, rejected by them above
all because it was written in vernacular: "learning scorns vulgar idioms"
("clerus vulgaria tempnit"; *Ec.* I 15).[50]

Though motivated by the best intentions, such an invitation—
addressed to a poet who had always wagered his success on the vernacular and who, until then, had never written or at least published any
Latin verse—was, in objective terms, a provocation. Dante accepted the
implicit challenge and replied to the Horatian verse with an eclogue in
the style of Virgil. His reasoning seems to have been more or less as follows: if the challenge involved demonstrating that he was also a great
poet in Latin, then, since his vernacular poem had already successfully
measured up to the epic poet Virgil, he could win by reviving another
Virgilian genre, that of pastoral poetry, which no one for centuries had
dared to attempt. He was also subtly rebuking his interlocutor, who,
though calling himself Virgilianus, had written an epistle in the style
of Horace—by answering with an eclogue, he could demonstrate who,
in truth, was worthy of that name.

In his reply, Dante calls himself Tityrus (the shepherd in Virgil's first
eclogue) and his interlocutor Mopsus (the name of another Virgilian
shepherd), and makes no mention at all of the criticisms made against
him for using the vernacular. He uses not a single word to refute the
accusation of having used "words of comedy," words to be avoided
"because they wear heavily on the lips of women, and because the
Castalian sisters [the Muses] are ashamed to accept them" (*Ec.* II 52–54;
"Comica nonne vides ipsum reprehendere verba, / tum quia femineo
resonant ut trita labello, / tum quia Castalias pudet acceptare sorores?")
And yet, what better occasion could he have had to defend and give the
reasons for such a scandalous choice? Would he have allowed such a direct attack by an academic, however obsequious, to pass without comment at the time of *Convivio* or *De vulgari*?

The fact is that Dante makes no reference to the *Commedia*, not even
to defend it.[51] While his other works almost always generated reflections
on poetry, literary history, language—in other words, were accompanied

and justified by a work of historical and theoretic nature—the *Commedia* does not give rise to a critical thought that places it in context. And yet he never stops talking about his past poetical writing, his friends and his rivals; several times he talks about himself as writer—about the difficulty of the subject, the inadequacy of his "words" and the true impossibility of fully communicating his vision. And he often lets technical terms fall from his pen with regard to the art of writing in general, and particular situations in which he finds himself in his current writing. But this doesn't form into a systematic reflection on what is so original about the text he is composing. Dante knows that for a "sacred poem, / to which Heaven and earth have set their hand" (*Para.* XXV 1–2; "poema sacro / al quale ha posto mano e Cielo e terra"), any reference to poetical or rhetorical style is aleatoric, that no genre can wholly contain it. Its poetic identity is so novel that perhaps no one can truly understand it.

But well aware of the value of what he is doing, he is also convinced that the power of his poetry is enough in itself to assure its success. He makes no reply to the criticisms of Giovanni del Virgilio, proudly declaring instead that the much maligned *Commedia* is what will bring him the poet's laurel: once *Paradiso* is complete and published—with all due respect to Mopsus—his head will be crowned with ivy and laurel.[52]

Tityrus-Dante refuses his interlocutor's invitation to write a Latin epic, but courtesy requires him to reciprocate the friendly gesture. So he decides to send him a gift of ten jars of milk from his favorite ewe ("ovis gratissima"). The early commentators, who adhered strictly to the pastoral code fixed by academic practice, saw in these lines an allusion to ten eclogues that Dante had decided to write, equal in number to Virgil's Eclogues.[53] The context, however, suggests that Dante is referring to ten cantos of *Paradiso* that had not yet been published. Besides, Tityrus says something about that "ovis gratissima" which fits extraordinarily well with the physiognomy of the *Commedia:* "separate from every flock, not accustomed to any fence, never compelled by force, she is accustomed to come freely in order to ask to be milked" (*Ec.* II 61–62; "Nulli iuncta gregi nullis assuetaque caulis, / sponte venire solet, nunquam vi, poscere mulctram"). It belongs to no flock, no tradition, and its freedom is limited by no fence, no barrier.

In early 1320, *Paradiso* was therefore still unpublished. This is also what Boccaccio understood: according to him, Dante "was unable to make

sufficient haste to publish the whole of it [the *Commedia*] before his death."
Unpublished, but not perhaps unknown to friends in Ravenna, and to
Guido Novello himself.[54] Whether they really understood the revolutionary impact of the poem is doubtful. They were doctors and lawyers,
less discerning than a rhetorician like Giovanni del Virgilio, whose
criticisms, however, were not the result of cultural conservatism. On
the contrary, they grew out of that cultural neo-humanism that would
very soon find success. What seemed scandalously popular and, so to
speak, pre-artistic to the old culture of lawyers and doctor-philosophers
at the universities was seen as old-fashioned and anachronistic to expo-
nents of nascent Latin classicism.

Farewell to history

In Ravenna, Dante had no Guido Cavalcanti or Cino da Pistoia with
whom to talk and compare work. He had friends, perhaps even disciples, but no cultural context that he could regard as his own. And he
didn't even have political figures that might offer him the hope of
changing his life and the structure of society. All he had left was a stubborn faith in his own mission, the conviction that he, alone, would
triumph in the end, that his poem would reverse the apparently un-
changeable state of affairs. In *Paradiso*, starting from the first cantos
written in Ravenna, all of this is clearly legible.

Cantos XXI and XXII are the only ones in which personalities appear
(Saint Peter Damian and Saint Romuald) who had been born in Ravenna
and had made her famous. Peter Damian, having recalled the Camal-
dolese hermitage of Fonte Avellana, mentions his stay, under the name
of Peter the Sinner, in the monastery of Santa Maria in Porto, on the
coast near the city ("In that place [Fonte Avellana] I was Peter Damian,
/ and Peter the Sinner was I in the house / of our Lady on the Adriatic
coast" (*Para.* XXI 121–123; "In quel loco fu' io Pietro Damiano, / e Pietro
Peccator fu' ne la casa / di nostra Donna in sul lito adriano"). Dante
was probably drawing on a local legend that identified Peter Damian
with a Peter the Sinner who was said to have founded the church of Santa
Maria al Porto; whatever the truth, the impression remains that he
wanted to pay homage to the city where he had recently arrived.[55] In
locating the hermitage on the slopes of Monte Catria, an Apennine

mountain visible in the distance from Ravenna, Peter Damian found a way of pleasing his interlocutor by recalling his home city: "between the two coasts of Italy rise crags, / not far from your home city . . . and form a hump called Catria, / beneath which lies a hermitage" (*Para.* XXI 106–110; "Tra' due liti d'Italia surgon sassi, / e non molto distanti a la tua patria . . . e fanno un gibbo che si chiama Catria, / di sotto al quale è consacrato un ermo"). That incongruous and pointless reference to Florence reveals how strong Dante's nostalgia is.

The cantos of Peter Damian and Romuald (or rather Saint Benedict, who mentions Romuald) mark a sort of dividing line: current events do not pass beyond it or, at least, not apparently so. After hearing Saint Benedict's stern condemnation of corruption in the order he had founded, Dante rises up to the heaven of fixed stars and, on Beatrice's invitation, he turns to look back down the path he had taken. Looking down from heaven to heaven he sees below "the threshing floor that makes us so fierce" (*Para.* XXII 151; "l'aiuola che ci fa tanto feroci"). This is his last glimpse of the Earth, a sort of final farewell.[56] And indeed, from this moment, theological questions and mystical aspects of the vision clearly prevail over references to current historical events. Renouncing current events, however, doesn't mean renouncing history: on the contrary, the prophetic component intensifies. But, at the same time, it becomes more specific: Church and Empire, the two "suns," become the sole targets of his reproaches and the sole objects of his prophecies. It is significant that the last historical figure in the poem is Emperor Henry VII, whose throne Dante sees, waiting to receive him, in the Empyrean. The celestial glory of "noble Henry" makes the knowledge of his failure on earth all the more bitter: "he'll come to set Italy straight / before she's ready" (*Para.* XXX 137–138; "a drizzare Italia / verrà in prima ch'ella sia disposta"). It would be—it had been, from the writer's point of view—the "cupidity" of the Italians and the maneuverings of a pope, Clement V, "who openly and secretly / will not tread one path with him" (*Para.* XXX 143–144; "che palese e coverto / non anderà con lui per un cammino"), that caused the ruin of a project which could have saved not only Italy but the whole of Christendom. And God would punish Pope Clement, making him die shortly after Henry and damning him among the simoniacs: stuck there in the hole—with clear reference to the story told in *Inferno*—"he will push that one of Alagna [Boniface VIII] deeper down" (*Para.* XXX 148; "farà quel d'Alagna intrar più giuso"). The final part of the *Commedia* resounds with what for Dante had been the disastrous effect of that failure. Henry's death, in effect, marked the collapse of the pillar that supported Dante's political vision (and the personal hopes that went with it). His prophecies are more assured and peremptory in tone, but their substance becomes increasingly vague and indeterminate. He has no doubt that divine justice will happen—and will happen soon—but he is no longer able to indicate what earthly instrument it will choose: he no longer talks of a greyhound and even less of a real historic figure such as the "messenger of God." Peter Damian, a cardinal, having denounced the luxury of the modern clergy, announces an imminent divine "vengeance," so imminent that Dante would see it before he dies: "the vengeance / that you will see before you die" (*Para.* XXII 14–15; "la vendetta / che tu vedrai innanzi che tu muoi"), but without specifying its ways and instruments. This is similar to what Cacciaguida had done when, in foretelling the sure divine "vengeance" against those Florentines who would slander Dante: ("but the vengeance / shall be witness to the truth it bears," *Para.* XVII 53–54; "ma la vendetta / fia testimonio al ver che la dispensa"), he had refrained from placing it in any context of time and space. Beatrice expresses certainty that soon the "human family," which is corrupt because "on earth there is no one who governs," will radically change its way of life, and that "the real fruit will come after the flower" (*Para.* XXVII 148; "vero frutto verrà dopo 'l fiore"); but this will happen without human intermediation, through the indeterminate influences and benefits of the stars. It is the same as the prophetic style of Saint Peter, who limits himself to forecasting that "soon" "high Providence . . . will bring help" (*Para.* XXVII 60–63; "l'alta Provedenza . . . soccorrà tosto"). In short, it was human politics that had failed. The disappearance of any practicable solution is therefore translated into a voluntaristic affirmation of faith.

The great disappointment also gave rise to scorn and resentment against those responsible for that defeat. In the Empyrean, Dante gives vent to this with the harshest and bitterest words he had ever used. It is the first pope who exclaims that Boniface VIII "usurps [his] place on earth" and has "turned [Peter's] burial place into a sewer / of blood and stench" (*Para.* XXVII 22, 25–26; "usurpa in terra il luogo mio; fatt' ha del cimitero mio cloaca / del sangue e de la puzza"). Boniface is Dante's personal enemy, and is therefore present everywhere in the poem, but since the sore spot at this point in time is Henry's defeat, this is why Peter has no hesitation in foretelling the arrival of "those from Cahors and Gascony" who "are prepared to drink" the blood of martyrs (*Para.* XXVII 58–59; "Del sangue nostro Caorsini e Guaschi / s'apparecchian di bere!"). John XXII, the pope at the time of writing, came from Cahors, while Clement V was from Gascony.

The political debacle had had a serious effect on his personal prospects. His banishment now began to seem like an irreversible situation or, at any event, a situation that no one but Dante himself could change. Even personal redemption therefore has a utopian tinge to it.

The reason for his banishment, which is not mentioned at all in *Purgatorio*, becomes central in the meeting with his ancestor Cacciaguida in *Paradiso*. Here the conversation becomes expansive, with a wealth of arguments that earlier anticipations didn't have. Talking about the future, Cacciaguida retraces the long road that Dante had taken from Florence in 1302 to Verona after the death of Henry VII. But he doesn't stop at foretelling the events; he also reveals their significance. And the ultimate reason for having suffered injustice is contained in the prophetic mission which he gives to Dante, renewing the task given him by Beatrice in the final cantos of *Purgatorio* and anticipating what Saint Peter would say ten cantos later: "let all you have seen be clear; / and let them scratch where it hurts" (*Para.* XVII 128–129: "tutta tua visïon fa manifesta; / e lascia pur grattar dov'è la rogna"). Cacciaguida's charge is similar to that of Beatrice, but its tone is different: more than a confirmation, it seems to be investing him with a new task, more difficult and onerous than before. The prophetic mission in the last cantos of *Purgatorio* was still associated with the idea, embodied in the coming of the "messenger of God," of a possible and imminent political change: in it was an inherent hope of actually being able to influence "the world that lives badly" (*Purg.* XXXII 103; "del mondo che mal vive"). The words of Cacciaguida present Dante's prophetic vision not as a sign of palingenesis and renewal, but as an arduous moral duty, as an ethical need to bear witness to the truth. Dante would be a lone and helpless prophet. He could not rely on divine messengers to endorse his words: he would have to strike like wind against "the highest peaks" (*Para.* XVII 134; "le più alte cime"), but at his own risk, trusting in the fact that, despite everything, his "importunate voice" will prove to be "vital nutriment" (*Para.* XVII 130–132: "la voce tua sarà molesta / nel primo gusto, vital nodrimento / lascerà poi"). It is not surprising, therefore, that Cacciaguida suggests only personal reward: "and this is no small reason for honor" (*Para.* XVII 135; "e ciò non fa d'onor poco argomento").

And yet Cacciaguida also points to a possibility of redemption, allowing for even a hope of victory. Added to the personal feeling of honor will be public fame and glory among coming generations: the *Commedia* will project Dante into a future in which the persecutions inflicted by his fellow citizens will have little significance in comparison.

Nostalgia for the "fair fold"

Toward the end of *Paradiso,* Dante would express the hope—almost a certainty—that a public coronation in Florence would recognize his merit as "bard" of the vernacular language. The poem would moderate the "cruel" hearts of the Florentines who have kept him outside the "fair fold" where he was born:

> If it ever happens that the sacred poem
> to which Heaven and earth have set their hand,
> making me thin for many years,
>   wins over the cruelty that locks me out
> of the fair fold where I slept as a lamb,
> foe to the wolves that make war against it;
>   with other voice then, with other fleece
> I will return as poet, and over the font
> of my baptism I will take the cap.

> "Se mai continga che 'l poema sacro
> al quale ha posto mano e Cielo e terra,
> sì che m'ha fatto per molti anni macro,
>   vinca la crudeltà che fuor mi serra
> del bello ovile ov' io dormi' agnello,
> nimico ai lupi che li danno guerra;

con altra voce omai, con altro vello
ritornerò poeta, e in sul fonte
del mio battesmo prenderò 'l cappello"

—*Para.* xxv 1–9

There is a return to that theme of the "offer" which, in the letter to his Florentine friend, he regarded as shameful and ignominious. In his church of San Giovanni he would be crowned "poet," but with a very particular crown: in the Baptistery in which, by breaking the font, he had demonstrated his prophetic power, he would proudly wear, as the highest proof of his innocence, that "cap" that pardoned exiles were compelled to wear in humility.[57] Dante seems to be adopting the words of Cacciaguida; indeed, more than that, it is as though he knew his ancestor's hopes and premonitions were true. But one thing is essential: Dante's return to Florence, if it ever occurs, will happen only through his merits; only the poem will restore him to his "fold"—not the action of a pope, an emperor, or a powerful lord.

The symbolic center of the "fold" is the Baptistery. That church has a central place in Dante's vision of Florence. His hope is that San Giovanni will be the place of regeneration—his own, the city's, and that of the Church itself. The *Commedia* is the prophetic work that could overturn the depraved course of history and return Florence (and with it the Church, for whose moral decline Florence is largely responsible) to the good ways of a time when the Baptistery and the statue of Mars "on the Arno bridge" (*Inf.* XIII 146; "sul passo d'Arno") marked the boundary of a community: "the fold of San Giovanni" (*Para.* XVI 25; "l'ovil di San Giovanni") that was close-knit and not yet torn apart by greed. Dante recalls the Baptistery, therefore, not just for nostalgic reasons. Or rather, those reasons were metabolized and transformed into political and ideological substance.[58] And yet, the fact that toward the end of his life he could imagine no other place to celebrate his victory than the "font" of his "baptism" goes to show just how deep the roots of his attachment were.

But his insistence on San Giovanni also shows something else—how someone exiled for many years can remain bound to myths and symbols that, in the meantime, have lost their value for those still living in the city. It is true that San Giovanni was the city's church par excellence from the twelfth century, from the time when that church, though managed by the diocese, was administered by the Opera di San Giovanni, in other words by the city administration. But during the years straddling the eleventh and twelfth centuries, Santa Reparata had, after a long process, gained supremacy over its sister church. This process had culminated in the transformation of the old building into the new church of Santa Maria del Fiore (1296). Within a few years, this would be the new cathedral, representing the city from a religious as well as a political and civic point of view.[59]

Dante mentions neither Santa Reparata nor Santa Maria del Fiore. Toward the end of his life, at a time when the symbolic and functional changes of the baptistery and cathedral complex were by now consolidated, he continued to think of his deliverance in the place that was still for him the city's main church. Maybe he didn't know about those changes; maybe he didn't want to accept them. There is something very touching about this loyalty of an exile to myths and images that now lived only within him.

A reluctant refusal

Giovanni del Virgilio, having received Dante's reply in the form of an eclogue, took the hint and responded accordingly. In the spring and summer of 1320 he, in turn, replied with a pastoral composition. After recognizing that the milk Dante sent to him as a gift "had not been milked for a long time" (*Ec.* III 19–21: "lac . . . quale nec a longo meminerunt tempore mulsum/custodes gregium"), meaning, that kind of pastoral verse had not been tried out for centuries, Giovanni-Mopsus expresses the hope that Tityrus-Dante will once again be able to see the "pastures of the Arno" he had been denied: "shame upon the ungrateful city!" (*Ec.* III 37–38; "pascua Sarni . . . ingrate dedecus urbi"). While waiting for his hope to come true, he invites him to join him in the happy caverns in which he lives. Young and old shepherds, devotees of the cult of the Muses, will rush to make his acquaintance, to admire his "new poems" and to study "his old ones" (*Ec.* III 67–69: "huc venient, qui te pervisere gliscent, / Parrhasii iuvenesque senes, et carmina leti / qui nova mirari cupiantque antiqua doceri"). Dante would find an audience of devoted followers who already know his writings and are anxious to find out from him directly about his new works. But Giovanni knew that Dante was reluctant to go to Bologna, since he regarded the city as dangerous for him, and so he goes on to declare that he would find no perils or threats there: "Come here and do not be frightened, Tityrus, of our cliffs . . . Here there are no perils, there is no violence, as you believe" (*Ec.* III 72–76; "Huc ades, et nostros timeas neque, Tityre, saltus . . . Non hic insidie, non hic iniuria, quantas / esse putas"). Dante-Tityrus is exaggerating the dangers, which are much less than he thinks.

There was, in fact, a reference in Dante's reply to his fear of finding himself between cliffs and fields that do not know gods, but it was only a passing reference, and also very vague. It is probable that the two, thanks to the mediation of friends, had carried out some sort of negotiation, and that the very question of safety had been a central issue.[60] It should be remembered that Bologna was a staunch ally of Black Florence, and had been the headquarters since July 1319 of Cardinal Del Poggetto, who was pursuing a tough offensive against the Ghibellines on behalf of John XXII. With his eclogue, Giovanni del Virgilio would have been making a final attempt to persuade his interlocutor. Of particular relevance among the reasons used by Dante to justify his refusal—as well as his fear about personal safety—must have been the opposition of Guido Novello, who would obviously have been displeased that his guest was leaving him after so short a time. Giovanni must have known this, since he confidently declares in the eclogue that Iolas (the pseudonym for Guido Novello) would not allow Tityrus to go away: "Mopsus, why are you raving?" he says to himself. "Since Iolas will surely not allow it" (*Ec.* III 80; "Mopse, quid es demens? Quia non permittet Iollas").[61] Dante must have found the idea of returning to Bologna most attractive. He had addressed—or at least would have liked to address—his revolutionary proposals to the *magistri* at the *Studio;* he had always hoped that his poem might gain the approval of the leading academics at the university, but had so far received only criticism and disapproval from such quarters. And now a member of the *Studio* had given him an invitation, assuring him he would find disciples and admirers in Bologna. Whether or not to accept the invitation must have been the subject of much reflection and also of discussion with his friends in Ravenna. And these reflections and discussions must have lasted quite some time. An academic commentary tells us that Dante didn't write his eclogue in reply to Giovanni until a year later (therefore around summer of 1321) and didn't even manage to send it before his death.[62]

Dante refused the invitation, but it must have been a difficult and painful decision. Tityrus discusses with Alphesiboeus (Fiduccio dei Milotti)—therefore, not surprisingly, with someone from Bologna—whether it is appropriate to move there. Alphesiboeus heartily encourages him not to do so: he is worried for him. He reminds him of the fondness of those in Ravenna toward him, the pain his departure would cause to his friends: "with you absent the mountains will grieve [for you], our cliffs for you, the rivers for you, and the nymphs who with me fear the worst . . . we, the shepherds will be sorry to have known you. O fortunate old man, do not take your everlasting name away from springs and pastures known!" (*Ec.* IV 57–62; "Te iuga, te saltus nostri, te flumina flebunt / absentem et Nymphe mecum peiora timentes . . . nos quoque pastores te cognovisse pigebit. / Fortunate senex, fontes et pabula nota / desertare tuo vivaci nomine nolis"). And so the appeals of the one whom Tityrus regards as his dearest friend would not be enough to hold him back: he is persuaded by the fear instilled in him by a certain Polyphemus, "accustomed to staining his savage jaws with human blood" (*Ec.* IV 77; "assuetum rictus humano sanguine tingui").

Who is this wild Polyphemus that lives in Bologna?

After the riot on July 17, 1321, which had banished Romeo dei Pepoli (an extremely wealthy banker who for ten years had been ruling the city from behind the scenes), the office of *capitano del popolo* of Bologna was given to an old acquaintance of ours, and of Dante, Fulcieri da Calboli.[63] Polyphemus, with his jaws smeared in human blood, bears too close a resemblance to that savage who killed the Whites "like an ancient beast" and then left the scene of the "bloody" (*Purg.* XIV 62, 64) slaughter, for us not to think the two might be the same person. The presence of such a ruthless persecutor of Whites and the intensification of Guelph feeling among the people of Bologna was certainly enough to dissuade Dante from venturing into that city. Such advice may have come from Guido Novello himself, who appears at the end of the eclogue, under his usual name of Iolas, listening secretly to the dialogue between Tityrus and Alphesiboeus.

Dante, once again, could not free himself from the past. The long shadow of the civil war still hung over him and shattered his dream of taking a place among the learned men of Bologna.

Dante didn't go to Bologna, but his eclogues did, including the last. Giovanni del Virgilio read them at the *Studio,* commented on them and circulated them: in 1327, he would remind Albertino Mussato—by no coincidence in an eclogue, too—that Dante had been the first to revive that forgotten poetical genre.[64] An exegetic tradition developed around Giovanni del Virgilio, and would strengthen over the course of the century, thanks to the information he more than anyone else possessed. Soon, however, Dante's eclogues moved beyond academic and university circles: already by the 1340s they had reached Boccaccio and then Petrarch, inspiring them to compose their pastoral writings in Latin. From Petrarch and Boccaccio the new genre spread fast (also in the vernacular), becoming one of the most important in Renaissance literature. Thus Dante's destiny became shaped by a chapter at odds with the image of a writer resistant to cultural changes, through the cultural ferment that the rediscovery of antiquity had stirred around him. In the last years of his life, with two poetic writings of great value, yet still of marginal relevance, Dante crossed paths with the emerging humanist awareness, established an unsought contact with new poets and, in this way, became attached to a literary period that for him was essentially alien.

The last embassy

In August 1321, Guido Novello sent Dante as an ambassador to Venice. His departure from Ravenna may have prevented him from putting the final touches to the last eclogue. The embassy had become necessary to avoid a war with Venice, an ally of Forlì and Rimini, that would have been fatal for Ravenna. Guido relied on Dante's experience and oratorical skills, as other lords had done in the past. War, indeed, was averted: Ravenna and Venice would reach an agreement in October. But Dante was not its author. He took ill during his return over land, perhaps with malaria contracted in the marshy Po delta. He lay ill for some time and then died, on September 13, after sunset.[65]

Guido Novello gave him a solemn funeral in the church of San Francesco, where the Polenta family were interred. At the end of the ceremony he went to the house where Dante had lived, and there he gave an "ornate and long sermon" in which he announced his intention to erect an impressive tomb for him. It seems he organized a form of competition to find the epitaph to be carved on it, and that it was the start of a sort of contest among the most famous poets of Romagna, fueled—comments Boccaccio—by the desire of each to display their own brilliance, to show their esteem for Dante, and to ingratiate themselves with Guido Novello. At least two written epitaphs were presented straight away: one by Giovanni del Virgilio and another attributable to Menghino Mezzani; a third perhaps dates from several years later, attributable to the grammarian Rinaldo Cavalchini da Villafranca from Verona. There was also another, written much later, of which we know only the first four lines, composed by the Vicenza historian Ferreto dei Ferreti.[66]

But Dante was no more fortunate in death than in life. Guido Novello moved to Bologna in spring 1322 for a six-month appointment as *capitano del popolo*. He temporarily handed over the city government to his brother, who was already archdeacon and had been elected archbishop three days after Dante's death. He was assassinated in September by his cousin, Ostasio, who seized power and ordered Guido Novello never to set foot again in Ravenna. The planned tomb was never built and the epitaphs remained on paper.

Paradiso refound

It seems certain that Dante had left the last eclogue for Giovanni del Virgilio hidden away, and that it was one of his sons, perhaps Iacopo, who had it sent to its destination. The question of *Paradiso* remains open. It is certain that Dante had finished it before he died; what is not so clear is whether it had been circulated. He certainly hadn't published it before the first half of 1320, not least because the canticle must still have been unfinished. If we have to rely on Boccaccio, then after Dante's death, "sons and disciples" searched for a long time among his papers for the last cantos—thirteen to be exact—only to find them thanks to a dream of Iacopo, in which his father is said to have revealed to him that they were hidden in a "small opening" ("finestretta") in the wall of his bedroom, covered by a mat, and "in such manner the work, composed over many years, was seen complete." The miraculous discovery is said to have taken place "after the eighth month" from Dante's death.[67] It is a fact, and not legend, however, that after eight months Iacopo Alighieri sent Guido Novello in Bologna, on the day on which he took up office as *capitano del popolo* (on April 1, 1322), a composition in terza rima (*Divisione*) which was "a little guide" to the *Commedia,* together with a dedicatory sonnet from which it is apparent that Guido Novello already had "a complete knowledge of the whole poem," including *Paradiso.*[68]

Dante had therefore completed it in the final year of his life. He had not circulated it outside Ravenna, but had given readings of it to his patron and to friends.[69] Iacopo's prompt promotional action would set off a process that in very few years would transform the *Commedia* into the most famous and most widely read vernacular book of its time.

Appendix

GENEALOGICAL TABLES

ALIGHIERI

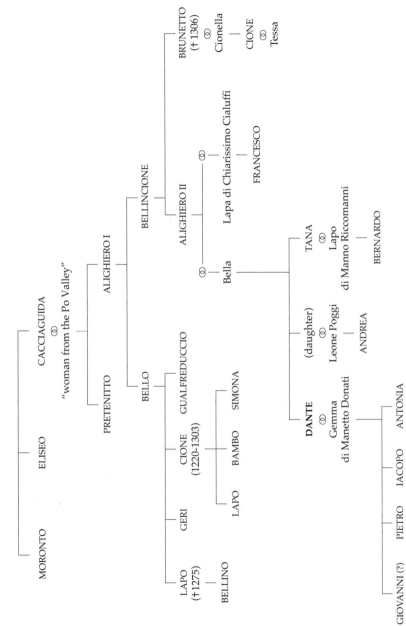

DONATI

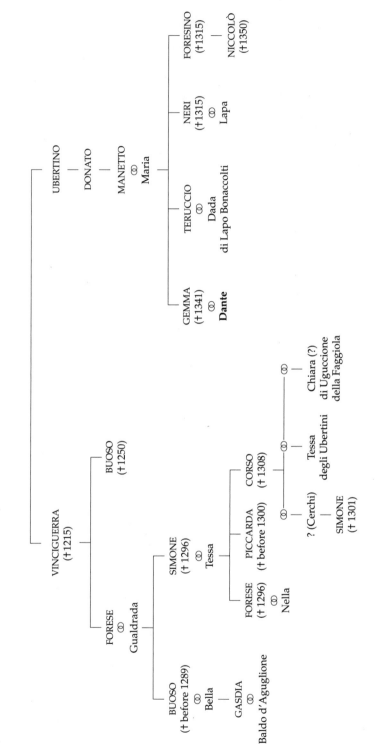

GUIDI
(GENERAL OUTLINE)

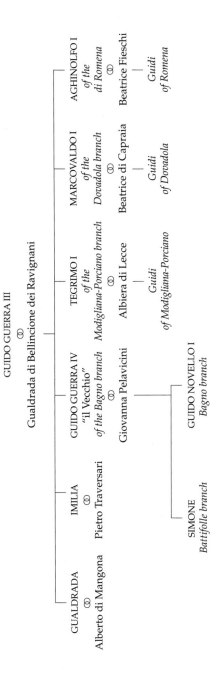

GUIDO GUERRA III
∞
Gualdrada di Bellincione dei Ravignani

GUALDRADA
∞
Alberto di Mangona

IMILIA
∞
Pietro Traversari

GUIDO GUERRA IV
"il Vecchio"
of the Bagno branch
∞
Giovanna Pelavicini

TEGRIMO I
*of the
Modigliana-Porciano branch*
∞
Albiera di Lecce

MARCOVALDO I
*of the
Dovadola branch*
∞
Beatrice di Capraia

AGHINOLFO I
*of the
di Romena*
∞
Beatrice Fieschi

SIMONE
Battifolle branch

GUIDO NOVELLO I
Bagno branch

*Guidi
of Modigliana-Porciano*

*Guidi
of Dovadola*

*Guidi
of Romena*

GUIDI OF BAGNO AND BATTIFOLLE

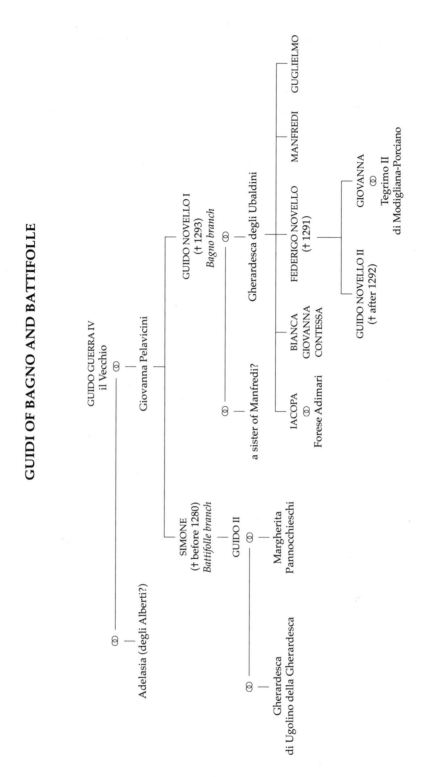

GUIDI OF MODIGLIANA-PORCIANO

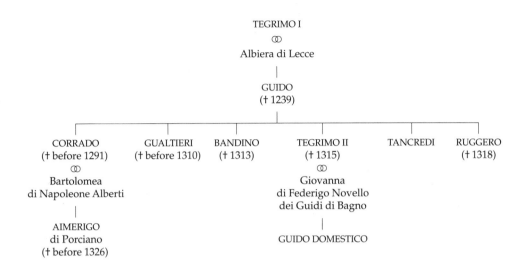

TEGRIMO I
⚭
Albiera di Lecce
|
GUIDO
(† 1239)

CORRADO († before 1291)	GUALTIERI († before 1310)	BANDINO († 1313)	TEGRIMO II († 1315)	TANCREDI	RUGGERO († 1318)

CORRADO
(† before 1291)
⚭
Bartolomea
di Napoleone Alberti
|
AIMERIGO
di Porciano
(† before 1326)

TEGRIMO II
(† 1315)
⚭
Giovanna
di Federigo Novello
dei Guidi di Bagno
|
GUIDO DOMESTICO

GUIDI OF DOVADOLA

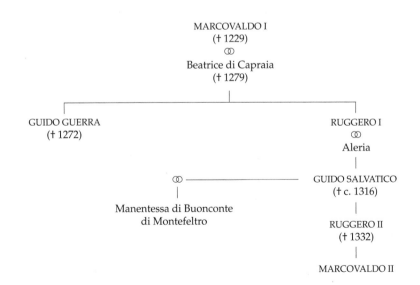

MARCOVALDO I
(† 1229)
⚭
Beatrice di Capraia
(† 1279)

GUIDO GUERRA
(† 1272)

RUGGERO I
⚭
Aleria
|

⚭ ——————————— GUIDO SALVATICO
| († c. 1316)
Manentessa di Buonconte |
di Montefeltro   RUGGERO II
                             († 1332)
                                  |
                          MARCOVALDO II

GUIDI OF ROMENA

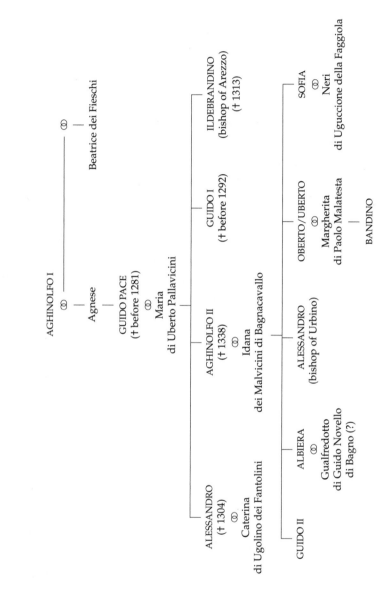

MALASPINA
(GENERAL OUTLINE)

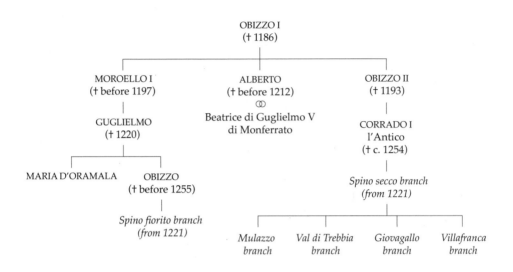

OBIZZO I
(† 1186)

MOROELLO I
(† before 1197)

ALBERTO
(† before 1212)
∞
Beatrice di Guglielmo V
di Monferrato

OBIZZO II
(† 1193)

GUGLIELMO
(† 1220)

CORRADO I
l'Antico
(† c. 1254)

MARIA D'ORAMALA

OBIZZO
(† before 1255)

*Spino secco branch
(from 1221)*

*Spino fiorito branch
(from 1221)*

*Mulazzo
branch*

*Val di Trebbia
branch*

*Giovagallo
branch*

*Villafranca
branch*

MALASPINA DELLO SPINO FIORITO

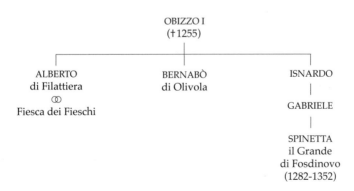

OBIZZO I
(†1255)

ALBERTO
di Filattiera
∞
Fiesca dei Fieschi

BERNABÒ
di Olivola

ISNARDO

GABRIELE

SPINETTA
il Grande
di Fosdinovo
(1282-1352)

MALASPINA DELLO SPINO SECCO

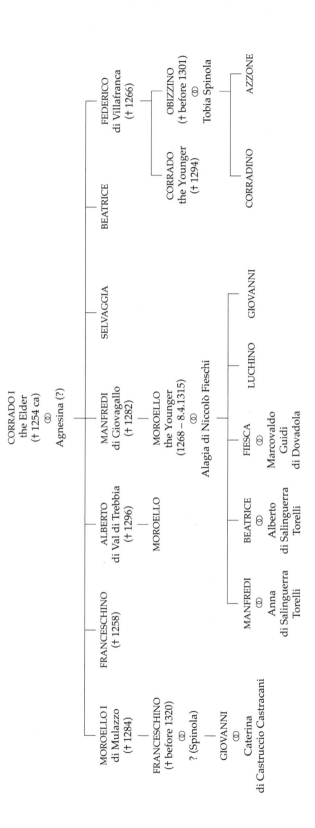

Abbreviations in Notes

Works by Dante and Reference Editions

Works Dante Alighieri, *Opere,* edition directed by Marco Santagata (Milan: Mondadori) : I, *Rime, Vita Nova, De vulgari eloquentia,* edited by Claudio Giunta, Guglielmo Gorni, Mirko Tavoni, 2011; II, *Convivio,* edited by Gianfranco Fioravanti and Claudio Giunta, *Monarchia,* edited by Diego Quaglioni, *Epistole,* edited by Claudia Villa, *Egloge,* edited by Gabriella Albanese, 2014.

Minor works Dante Alighieri, *Opere minori* (Milan-Naples: Ricciardi): I 1, edited by Domenico De Robertis and Gianfranco Contini, 1984; I 2, edited by Cesare Vasoli and Domenico De Robertis, 1988; II, edited by Pier Vincenzo Mengaldo, Bruno Nardi, Arsenio Frugoni, Giorgio Brugnoli, Enzo Cecchini, Francesco Mazzoni, 1979.

Commedia Dante Alighieri, *La Commedia secondo l'antica vulgata,* edited by Giorgio Petrocchi. Edizione nazionale edited by the Società Dantesca Italiana (Florence: Le Lettere, 1994) 4 vols. (1st edition Milan, 1966–67): *Inf.* = Inferno, *Purg.* = Purgatorio, *Para.* = Paradiso.

Conv. Dante Alighieri, *Convivio,* edited by Franca Brambilla Ageno, Edizione nazionale edited by the Società Dantesca Italiana (Florence: Le Lettere, 2003), 2 vols.

Ec. Dante Alighieri, *Egloge,* edited by Enzo Cecchini, in *Opere minori,* II, pp. 645–689.

Ep. Dante Alighieri, *Epistole,* edited by Arsenio Frugoni and Giorgio Brugnoli, in *Opere minori,* II, pp. 505–643.

Mn.   Dante Alighieri, *Monarchia,* edited by Prue Shaw, Edizione nazio-
                 nale edited by the Società Dantesca Italiana (Florence: Le Lettere,
                 2009).

Questio   Dante Alighieri, *Questio de aqua et terra,* edited by Francesco Maz-
                 zoni, in *Opere minori,* II, pp. 693–880.

Rime   Dante Alighieri, *Rime,* edited by Claudio Giunta, in *Opere,* I,
                 pp. 7–744.

VE   Dante Alighieri, *De vulgari eloquentia,* edited by Mirko Tavoni, in
                 Opere, I, pp. 1065–1547.

VN   Dante Alighieri, *Vita Nova,* edited by Guglielmo Gorni, in *Opere,* I,
                 pp. 745–1063.

For *Monarchia, Epistole, Egloge,* and *Questio de aqua et terra* I have made free use of
unpublished translations by Diego Quaglioni, Claudia Villa, Gabriella Albanese,
and Stefano Caroti.

Journals and Reference Works

CCD   *Censimento dei commenti danteschi. 1. I commenti di tradizione mano-
                scritta (fino al 1480),* edited by Enrico Malato and Andrea Mazzucchi
                (Rome: Salerno Editrice, 2011), 2 vols.

DBI   *Dizionario biografico degli italiani* (Rome: Istituto della Enciclopedia
                Italiana, 1960 et seq.).

ED   *Enciclopedia dantesca* (Rome: Istituto della Enciclopedia Italiana,
                1970–78), 6 vols.

EP   *Enciclopedia dei papi* (Rome: Istituto della Enciclopedia Italiana,
                2000), 3 vols.

GSLI   *Giornale storico della letteratura italiana*

IMU   *Italia medioevale e umanistica*

NRLI   *Nuova Rivista di Letteratura Italiana*

RLI   *Rivista di Letteratura Italiana*

RSD   *Rivista di studi danteschi*

SD   *Studi danteschi*

Other Sources

BARBI[1]   Michele Barbi, *Problemi di critica dantesca. Prima serie (1893–1918)* (Florence: Sansoni, 1934; anastatic reprint 1975).

BARBI[2]   Michele Barbi, *Problemi di critica dantesca. Seconda serie (1920–1937)* (Florence: Sansoni, 1941; anastatic reprint 1975).

BELLOMO   Saverio Bellomo, *Dizionario dei commentatori danteschi. L'esegesi della* Commedia *da Iacopo Alighieri a Nidobeato* (Florence: Olschki, 2004).

BOCCACCIO[1]   Giovanni Boccaccio, "Trattatello in laude di Dante" (first version), edited by Pier Giorgio Ricci, in *Tutte le opere di Giovanni Boccaccio,* edited by Vittore Branca (Milan: Mondadori, III, 1974), pp. 423–496.

BOCCACCIO[2]   Giovanni Boccaccio, "Trattatello in laude di Dante" (second version), edited by Pier Giorgio Ricci, in *Tutte le opere di Giovanni Boccaccio,* edited by Vittore Branca (Milan: Mondadori, III, 1974), pp. 497–538.

BOCCACCIO[3]   Giovanni Boccaccio, "Esposizioni sopra la Comedia di Dante," edited by Giorgio Padoan, in *Tutte le opere di Giovanni Boccaccio,* vol. 6, edited by Vittore Branca (Milan: Mondadori, 1965).

BRUNI   Leonardo Bruni, *Vite di Dante e del Petrarca,* in *Opere letterarie e politiche di Leonardo Bruni,* edited by Paolo Viti (Turin: UTET, 1996), pp. 537–560.

CARPI   Umberto Carpi, *La nobiltà di Dante* (Florence: Edizioni Polistampa, 2004), 2 vols.

CASADEI   Alberto Casadei, "Questioni di cronologia dantesca: da *Paradiso* XVIII a *Purgatorio* XXXIII," *L'Alighieri* 38 (2011): 123–141.

COMPAGNI   Dino Compagni, *Cronica,* edited by Gino Luzzatto (Turin: Einaudi, 1968).

DAVIDSOHN   Robert Davidsohn, *Storia di Firenze* (Florence: Sansoni, 1956–68) (First edition, Berlin, 1896–1927), 8 vols.

DAVIS   Charles T. Davis, *Dante's Italy and Other Essays* (Philadelphia: University of Pennsylvania Press, 1984).

FIORAVANTI   Dante Alighieri, *Convivio,* edited by Gianfranco Fioravanti, in *Opere,* II (Milan: Mondadori, 2014).

GIUNTA   Dante Alighieri, *Rime,* edited by Claudio Giunta, in *Opere,* I (Milan: Mondadori, 2014), pp. 7–744.

GORNI   Guglielmo Gorni, *Dante. Storia di un visionario* (Rome-Bari: Laterza, 2008).

INDIZIO[1]   Giuseppe Indizio, "Le tappe venete dell'esilio di Dante," *Miscellanea Marciana* 19 (2004): 35–64.

INDIZIO[2]   Giuseppe Indizio, "Dante secondo i suoi antichi (e moderni) biografi: saggio per un nuovo canone dantesco," SD 70 (2005): 237–294.

INDIZIO[3]   Giuseppe Indizio, "Pietro Alighieri autore del *Comentum* e fonte minore per la vita di Dante," SD 73 (2008): 187–250.

PADOAN   Giorgio Padoan, *Il lungo cammino del "poema sacro." Studi danteschi* (Florence: Olschki, 1993).

PASQUINI   Emilio Pasquini, *Dante e le figure del vero. La fabbrica della* Commedia (Milan: Bruno Mondadori, 2001).

PETROCCHI   Giorgio Petrocchi, *Vita di Dante* (Rome-Bari: Laterza, 1983).

PIATTOLI   Renato Piattoli, *Codice Diplomatico Dantesco* (Florence: L. Gonnelli, 1940; rev. ed. 1950).

RAVEGGI et al. Sergio Raveggi, Massimo Tarassi, Daniela Medici, and Patrizia Parenti, *Ghibellini, Guelfi e Popolo grasso. I detentori del potere politico a Firenze nella seconda metà del Dugento* (Florence: La Nuova Italia, 1978).

SANTAGATA   Marco Santagata, *L'io e il mondo. Un'interpretazione di Dante* (Bologna: il Mulino, 2011).

TAVONI   Dante Alighieri, *De vulgari eloquentia,* edited by Mirko Tavoni, in *Opere,* I (Milan: Mondadori, 2014), pp. 1065–1547.

VILLANI   Giovanni Villani, *Nuova cronica,* critical edition by Giuseppe Porta (Parma: Fondazione Pietro Bembo/Guanda editore, [1990–91] 2007), 3 vols.

ZINGARELLI   Nicola Zingarelli, *Dante* (Milan: Vallardi, 1904).

When no reference edition is indicated, the early commentaries are quoted from the text database of the Dartmouth Dante Project (http://dante.dartmouth .edu/).

Notes

1. Childhood

1. In 1265 the constellation of Gemini shone between May 14 and June 13. That Dante was born in May is supported by the account given to Boccaccio by Pietro Giardini, a Ravenna notary who was close to Dante during his final years (see the entry on him in ED: "Giardini, Pietro" by Andrea Ciotti): On his deathbed, in September 1321, Dante is said to have revealed his exact age, counting in years and months from May (BOCCACCIO³, I 1 5). All newborn children in Florence were baptized in San Giovanni in a large joint ceremony that took place twice a year, the first on Holy Saturday, the second on the Sunday of Pentecost. Dante was probably baptized the following year, when Holy Saturday fell on March 26.

2. Evidence that his baptism name was Durante (perhaps after his maternal grandfather) comes from his son Iacopo who, in a legal document, drawn up twenty years after his father's death (on January 9, 1343), gives both names for greater precision: "Durante, olim vocatus Dante" (Durante, commonly called Dante); PIATTOLI, no. 183.

3. For the significance of the name Beatrice, I refer to Guglielmo Gorni, *Lettera, nome, numero. L'ordine delle cose in Dante* (Bologna: il Mulino, 1990), pp. 19–44. Among the various interpretations of the name Dante are those of BOCCACCIO³, *Accessus* 37: "each person, who with a free spirit offers those things which he himself has received by grace of God, is worthy of being called 'Dante'" ("ciascuna persona, la quale con liberale animo dona di quelle cose, le quali egli ha di grazia ricevute da Dio, puote essere meritamente appellato 'Dante'") and the anonymous fourteenth-century sonnet (wrongly attributed to Pietro Faitinelli): "O gentle spirit, o true *dante* / to us mortals the fruit of life, / giving to you the great infinite goodness, / as a fitting and worthy means" ("O spirito gentile, o vero dante / a noi mortali il frutto della vita, / dandolo a te l'alta bontà infinita, / come congruo e degno medïante," lines 1–4; *Rime di ser Pietro de' Faytinelli detto*

Mugnone, edited by Leone Del Prete [Bologna, Gaetano Romagnoli, 1874], p. 111). The question of the double name Dante/Durante wouldn't itself be relevant if it were not implicated in one of the most thorny philological problems concerning Dante: the authorship of the so-called *Fiore.* The fact that the narrator-protagonist of *Fiore* twice calls himself Durante is considered to be one of the most significant pieces of evidence in favor of Dante as its author.

4. For the kind of influence exercised by Gemini, see the entry in ED, "Gemelli" by Emmanuel Poulle. One testimony close to Dante is the author of the so-called *Ottimo commento* (who could be the Florentine notary Andrea Lancia, but the question remains open), who in relation to *Para.* XXII 112–116 notes: "The author wishes to show how the secondary causes, namely the influences of Heaven, grant him the dispositions to be suited to literary science . . . Gemini is house of Mercury, which is signifier, according to the astrologers, of writing, of science and of knowledge . . . and especially when the Sun finds itself there" ("Vuole mostrare l'autore come le seconde cause, cioè le influenze del Cielo, li conferiscono sue disposizioni ad essere adatto a scienza litterale . . . Gemini è casa di Mercurio, che è significatore, secondo li astrolaghi, di scrittura e di scienza e di cognoscibilitade . . . e maggiormente quando il Sole vi si truova") (on the versions of the commentary, date and identification of the author, see BELLOMO, pp. 304–313, 354–374, and CCD, entry "Andrea Lancia" by Luca Azzetta and Ottimo Commento by Massimiliano Corradi).

5. The portrait of Dante is in VILLANI, X CXXXVI ("si dilettò in quella Commedia di garrire e sclamare a guisa di poeta, forse in parte più che non si convenia; ma forse il suo esilio gliele fece. Fece ancora la Monarchia, ove trattò de l'oficio degli 'mperadori. Questo Dante per lo suo savere fue alquanto presuntuoso e schifo e isdegnoso, e quasi a guisa di filosofo mal grazioso non bene sapea conversare co' laici"); that Giovanni was a friend of Dante is confirmed, with perhaps some exaggeration, by his nephew Filippo Villani in the preface to his Latin commentary on the *Commedia* written toward the end of the 1300s and left unfinished after the first canto (Filippo Villani, *Expositio seu comentum super "Comedia" Dantis Allegherii,* edited by Saverio Bellomo [Florence: Le Lettere, 1989], Prefatio, 225). The portrait of Dante's manner and character in BOCCACCIO[1], at paras. 117–170; a physical portrait at paras. 111–113 ("Il suo volto fu lungo, e il naso aquilino, e gli occhi anzi grossi che piccioli, le mascelle grandi, e dal labro di sotto era quel di sopra avanzato; e il colore era bruno, e i capelli e la barba spessi, neri e crespi, e sempre nella faccia malinconico e pensoso"); on Andrea Poggi (for which see the entries in ED, "Poggi, Andrea" and "Poggi, Leone" by Renato Piattoli) and on his resemblance with Dante see BOCCACCIO[3], VIII I 3–4; further, according to BRUNI (p. 548) Dante "spoke seldom and slowly" ("parlatore rado et tardo") (a careful study of the biographies of Dante by Villani, Boccaccio, and Bruni are found in INDIZIO[2]). Dante confesses himself guilty of the sin of pride in *Purg.* XIII 136–138.

6. For the discovery of the figure in the Palazzo dell'Arte dei Giudici e dei Notai, its relationship with that of the Palazzo del Podestà and for the more general tradition of portraying Dante, see the essential works of Maria Monica Donato: "Famosi Cives. Testi, frammenti e cicli perduti a Firenze fra Tre e Quattrocento," *Ricerche di storia dell'arte* 30 (1986): 27–42; Donato, "Per la fortuna monumentale di Giovanni Boccaccio fra i grandi fiorentini: notizie e problemi," *Studi sul Boccaccio* 17 (1988): 287–342; "Dante nell'arte civica toscana. Parole, temi, ritratti," in Maria Monica Donato, Lucia Battaglia Ricci, Michelangelo Picone, and Giuseppa Z. Za-nichelli, *Dante e le arti visive* (Milan: Unicopli, 2006), pp. 9–42. The graffito of SS. Annunziata (no longer discernible today) was accompanied by the inscription "Nobilis est ille . . . nobilitat," a Latin motto also to be found (as "Nobilis est ille, quem sua virtus nobilitavit") in the *Carmina Burana* (I VII): see the *Registro di Entrata e Uscita di Santa Maria di Cafaggio* (REU) 1286–1290, transcription, comment notes, and glossary edited by Eugenio M. Casalini (Florence Convento della SS. Annunziata, 1998) figs. 13 and 14. A portrait by Taddeo Gaddi was to be seen in the church of Santa Croce until 1556 (BRUNI, p. 548).

7. In 1865—the year of the sixth centenary of Dante's birth—in the space behind a walled-up gateway not far from the poet's tomb in the church of San Francesco, Ravenna, a wooden box was discovered by chance containing bones (including skull) which two inscriptions of 1766 described as belonging to Dante Alighieri. An initial scientific examination of the bones was carried out in the same year; this was followed by a second examination, more accurate and reliable from the methodological point of view, carried out in 1921, on the sixth centenary of Dante's death, by the anthropologists Giuseppe Sergi and Fabio Frassetto. From the re-port, published in Fabio Frassetto, *Dantis Ossa. La forma corporea di Dante* (Bologna: Tipografia L. Parma, 1933), it appears that Dante was of medium height (1.64–1.65 m), with long limbs, sloping shoulders, and an arthritic stiffness that made him walk with a stoop. The overall picture is of a man prematurely aged. The head showed a brain of large capacity, broad forehead, long face, large eyes, aqui-line nose, prominent cheekbones: in short, many of the features established by the earliest iconography. Recently, on the basis of Frassetto's reconstruction of the skull, the paleontologist Francesco Mallegni has carried out a digital reconstruc-tion of what Dante's face probably looked like. For further information, see: Giorgio Gruppioni, "Dantis Ossa. Una ricognizione delle ricognizioni dei resti di Dante" and Francesco Mallegni, "La ricostruzione fisiognomica del volto di Dante tramite tecniche manuali," both in *Dante e la fabbrica della* Commedia, edited by Alfredo Cottignoli, Donatino Domini, and Giorgio Gruppioni (Ravenna: Longo Editore, 2008), respectively at pages 255–267 and 277–281.

8. The shared ownership that Dante had with Francesco saved the house from destruction. The question of property that was owned jointly between convicted persons and others was the subject of much legal debate at the time. So far as the

destruction of buildings owned or enjoyed by a sibling of the convicted person, see *Tractatus maleficiorum* by Alberto Gandino, a famous lawyer who, among other appointments, was also a judge in Bologna in 1289 and between 1294 and 1295 (see the entry on him in DBI by Diego Quaglioni): in his collection of questions, under the heading "De bonis malefactorum," he deals with the question of whether a house or a tower owned jointly between a convicted person and sibling can be wholly or just partially destroyed, and concludes, relying among other things on the authority of Odofredo Denari, that the joint owner cannot be harmed (Hermann Kantorowicz, *Albertus Gandinus und das Strafrecht der Scholastik,* vol. 2: *Die Theorie. Kritische Ausgabe des Tractatus de maleficiis nebst textkritischer Einleitung,* (Berlin: Walter De Gruyter & Co., [1926] 1981), pp. 356–357).

9. Leonardo Alighieri, who was born in 1395 and died in 1441 (see the entry in ED on Leonardo by Serego Alighieri), was the son of Dante, the youngest son of Pietro, the poet's eldest son (BRUNI, p. 552; at p. 547 the statement that the Alighieri house was "very respectable"). So far as the references to the "room" into which Dante often withdrew, see: *VN* 1, 13; 5, 9; 7, 9. On the lack of privacy in medieval houses see Arsenio Frugoni in the introduction to Arsenio and Chiara Frugoni, *Storia di un giorno in una città medieval* (Rome-Bari: Laterza, [1997] 2011), 9. He writes: "the medieval house has this characteristic: absence of differentiated space and of different functions (even in the bedroom, on the upper floor of the house, there was no privacy, except perhaps for the upper classes); bear in mind also that privacy did not exist in a city where people lived "almost continually under the eyes of everyone" (Ernesto Sestan, "Dante e Firenze," a 1965 essay in Sestan, *Italia medievale* [Naples: ESU, 1968], 270–291; quotation at p. 278).

10. On the families living in the *sestiere* of San Pier Maggiore, see the investigations of RAVEGGI et al., p. 143, information on the property owned by the Cerchi. The relationship between the Cerchi and Donati, in the light of the property investments of the former, is described by Jean-Claude Maire Vigueur, *Cavaliers et citoyens. Guerre, conflits et societé dans l'Italie communal, XIIe–XIIIe siècles* (Paris: Ecoles des Hautes Etudes en Sciences Sociale [EHESS], 2003), pp. 324–315. For Baldo d'Aguglione I refer to the entry in DBI by Roberto Abbondanza; to that in ED by Arnaldo d'Addario, and to RAVEGGI et al., p. 251 and passim.

11. The dynamics of urban expansion in Florence during the second half of the 1200s is the subject of an important study by Franek Sznura, *L'espansione urbana di Firenze nel Dugento,* presentation by Elio Conti (Florence: La Nuova Italia, 1975), which is a useful addition to the volumes of DAVIDSOHN and the entry on Florence ("L'aspetto urbano di Firenze dai tempi di Cacciaguida a quelli di Dante") in ED by Ugo Procacci.

12. On the military role of the city's towers, see Maire Vigueur, *Cavaliers et citoyens,* pp. 287–290.

13. Population figures are obviously very approximate and the figures vary considerably according to the sources. I rely substantially on DAVIDSOHN, III, pp. 229–230.

14. The Florentines had begun minting silver florins around 1237, whereas the only currency circulating in the city before then was from outside, especially from Pisa. For the florin and its history, I refer to Arrigo Castellani, *Nuovi testi fiorentini del Dugento* (Florence: Sansoni, 1952) pp. 869–876. The comments on the florin by Remigio dei Girolami (for whom see the entry in DBI by Sonia Gentili) are reported by DAVIS, p. 112, who also notes that only in Dante does one find, "in addition to denunciations of faction and civic corruption, what might be called an extended negative theory of thirteenth and early fourteenth century Florentine history."

15. With regard to the purchase by the Cerchi of the property from the Guidi family, Massimo Tarassi writes: "the purchase deed, drawn up between the family that personifies more than anyone else those 'nouveau riche' who had made their money with 'quick gains,' and an ancient feudal family, is a tangible sign of the change in the city's political and social picture and represents, in a certain sense, the transition of powers between the old and the new political world" (Massimo Tarassi, "Il regime guelfo," in RAVEGGI et al., pp. 73–164; quote from p. 143).

16. The idea of transformation of cultural phenomena over time, which is central in *De vulgari eloquentia,* is exemplified in the *Commedia* by various pairs of artists and poets, one of whom has outdone the other: see *Purg.* XI 82–84, 94–99 and *Purg.* XXIV 55–57.

17. It is calculated that after Montaperti 103 palaces, 580 houses, 85 towers, 9 shops, 1 warehouse, 10 textile factories, 22 mills, and 7 castles were destroyed in the city and surrounding countryside, without counting those palaces, towers, warehouses and factories only partially demolished: the figures on the destruction of Guelf and Ghibelline properties are from DAVIDSOHN, II, pp. 453, 707–708; see also DAVIDSOHN, II for the description of Florence strewn with rubble (at p. 708). For the destruction carried out by the Ghibellines between September 1260 and November 1266, see Isidoro Del Lungo, *Una vendetta in Firenze il giorno di San Giovanni del 1295* (1887), and Del Lungo, *Dal secolo e dal poema di Dante* (Bologna: Zanichelli, 1898), pp. 63–145, in particular pp. 66–74.

18. In *Inf.* XXIII 103–108 Dante writes that the pleasure-seeking friars Catalano dei Malavolti and Loderingo degli Andalò, specially appointed to cover the role of *podestà* in 1266, behaved in such a way "that it still appears around the Gardingo" ("ch'ancor si pare intorno dal Gardingo")—in other words, that in 1300, around what is now Piazza della Signoria, you could still see the ruins of the Uberti houses they had ordered to be destroyed.

19. A detailed reconstruction of historical events in Florence against the background of those in Italy is found in the monumental history of Florence by DAVIDSOHN; a succinct outline of events in Florence is found in the entries in ED, "Firenze" ("Storia") by Ernesto Sestan and "Guelfi e ghibellini" by Guido Pampaloni.

20. In the communes of central and northern Italy the *podestà*, elected by the Consiglio generale for a period of six months or a year, exercised executive and judicial power. In order to guarantee his independence, he was elected from among people who did not belong to the city "podestà forestiero"): he received substantial remuneration for himself and his assistants, who were also outsiders. Members of the more prestigious city oligarchies and feudal families regarded it as a great honor to be appointed *podestà*, but it also brought considerable financial gain. The *capitano del popolo*, elected by the Consiglio del popolo, also came from outside: he shared judicial responsibility with the *podestà* and commanded the city's military forces.

21. For the amount of compensation to the Alighieri, less than 500 lire, see RAVEGGI et al., p. 162; the document of 1269, which, among the properties of the Guelfs in exile damaged by the Ghibellines, lists the house of Geri di Bello or del Bello (for whom see the entry in ED, "Alighieri, Geri" by Renato Piattoli), is published in PIATTOLI, no. 35. With regard to the Guelfism of the Alighieri, Ernesto Sestan ("Dante e Firenze," p. 275) writes that "Dante was not born into a family marked by hard-line Guelfism, by Guelfism resulting from the early experience of exile."

22. The information that Cacciaguida gives about himself is concentrated in *Para.* XV 134–148: "and in your ancient Baptistery / I became both a Christian and Cacciaguida. / Moronto and Eliseo were my brothers; / my wife came from the Po valley, / and thus I took your surname. / Then I served the emperor Conrad, / and he made me a knight in his army, / so pleased he was by my deeds. / Following him I fought the evil / of that law whose people usurp, / through the sin of the shepherds, your justice. / There was I by that base folk / delivered from the deceiving world, / the love for which corrupts many souls; / and I came from martyrdom unto this peace" ("e ne l'antico vostro Batisteo / insieme fui cristiano e Cacciaguida. / Moronto fu mio frate ed Eliseo; / mia donna venne a me di val di Pado, / e quindi il sopranome tuo si feo. / Poi seguitai lo 'mperador Currado; / ed el mi cinse de la sua milizia, / tanto per bene ovrar li venni in grado. / Dietro li andai incontro a la nequizia / di quella legge il cui popolo usurpa, / per colpa d'i pastor, vostra giustizia. / Quivi fu' io da quella gente turpa / disviluppato dal mondo fallace, / lo cui amor molt' anime deturpa; / e venni dal martiro a questa pace"). He refers to his son Alighiero I in lines 91–94: "He from whom you take / your family name and who for a hundred years and more / has been circling the first terrace of this mountain, / was my son and your great-grandfather" ("Quel da cui si dice / tua cognazione e che cent'anni e piùe / girato ha 'l monte in la prima cornice, / mio figlio fu e tuo bisavol fue"). The view that Dante was furthering a strategy, here and elsewhere in his work, of ennobling his family is put forward very convincingly by CARPI, particularly in ch 1 (pp. 13–252); other scholars, however, tend to give credit to the words put into the mouth of Cacciaguida: see

ZINGARELLI, p. 19, and Ernesto Sestan, "Dante e i conti Guidi", a 1965 essay in Sestan, *Italia medievale* [Naples: ESU, 1968], pp. 334–355, particularly pp. 336–337, who think that Cacciaguida's crusade was the one with Corrado III. I would add that Giuseppe Indizio, another scholar well versed in the life of Dante and the Alighieri family history (see "Note di storia degli Alighieri: le origini [1100–1300]," SD 74 [2009], pp. 227–273, in particular p. 242; INDIZIO[3], pp. 240–242), thinks it possible that Cacciaguida left for the crusade "with Conrad of Hohenstaufen" and that he was killed "in the defeat between 1147 and 1148 inflicted on the armies of the German king and Louis VII of France."

23. There is information (not always reliable) on Dante's family in ED, through the "Alighieri" entry by Arnaldo d'Addario and, above all, thanks to many entries on his ancestors, descendants, relatives (actual or claimed) through marriage. The most reliable are those compiled by Renato Piattoli: his entries also include "Abati, Durante degli" and "Poggi, Leone" (husband of an unidentified sister of Dante) and "Riccomanni, Lapo" (husband of Tana). An important contribution—which also corrects errors and inaccuracies in ED—is that of Indizio, "Note di storia degli Alighieri"; from here, at p. 244, I take the quote relating to Alighiero I ("he had houses in San Martino del Vescovo . . ."). This work by Indizio and also INDIZIO[3], pp. 239–240, demonstrates the groundlessness of the information, reported in ED and in most traditional accounts, that Alighiero I married a daughter of Bellincione Berti dei Ravignani, a leading member of an ancient and illustrious landed family, another daughter of which, by the name of Gualdrada, had married none other than Guido Guerra III of the Guidi counts, in other words a member of the highest aristocracy. See also, again from Giuseppe Indizio, the persuasive note on Dante's older sister, "Tana Alighieri sorella di Dante," SD 65 (2000), pp. 169–176. Piattoli thinks he has identified the mysterious sister of Dante who married Leone Poggi as a certain Ravenna, daughter of Alighiero II's first marriage, who is thought to have been born around 1240 and would therefore have been much older than Dante: it is suggested she married Poggi between 1255 and 1260 and died around 1300; but this Ravenna is almost certainly the first wife of Poggi. The unidentified sister could be Dante's "young and gracious lady . . . very closely related by birth" ("donna giovane e gentile . . . di propinquissima sanguinità congiunta") who looks after him during a "painful" illness.

24. The evidence indicating that Alighiero II died in the period of 1275–1280 (but closer to the beginning than the end) is examined by Indizio, "Note di storia degli Alighieri," pp. 270–272.

25. I have taken the information on Dante's wealth from Michele Barbi, "La condizione economica di Dante e della sua famiglia" (1892 and 1917), then in BARBI[1], pp. 157–188.

26. The consideration of dialogue and communication in medieval verse is at the center of the book by Claudio Giunta, *Versi a un destinatario. Saggio sulla poesia*

italiana del Medioevo (Bologna: il Mulino, 2002). The most persuasive interpretation of the tenzone with Forese (which some have dated to 1294) is at GIUNTA, pp. 286–317.

27. Dante's references to childhood are at: *Purg.* XI 105; *Purg.* XXX 43–45; *Purg.* XXXI 64–66; *Para.* XV 121–123; *VN* 5, 9.

28. According to Dante, one of the two reasons that allow a writer to talk about himself is "when, by speaking about oneself, great benefit is brought to others by way of instruction" ("quando, per ragionare di sé, grandissima utilitade ne segue altrui per via di dottrina") (*Conv.* I II 14 OK).

29. For the state of education in Florence and for Dante's studies, read: DA-VIDSOHN, VII, pp. 211–243 (with a certain caution); Paul Renucci, *Dante disciple et juge du monde gréco-latin* (Paris: Les Belles Lettres, 1954), pp. 22–27; DAVIS, pp. 137–165; Rosa Casapullo, *Il Medioevo (Storia della lingua italiana)*, edited by Francesco Bruni (Bologna: il Mulino, 1999), pp. 85–109; FIORAVANTI.

30. Petrarch wrote to Zanobi da Strada (*Fam.* XII 3, 15–16): "Hi puerorum manus instabiles, oculos vagos et confusum murmur observent, quos labor ille delectat et pulvis et strepitus et sub ferula gementium clamor precibus mixtus ac lacrimis . . . quos . . . iuvat preesse minoribus, semper habere quos terreant, quos crucient, quos affligant, quibus imperent, qui eos oderint dum metuant." (Zanobi followed Petrarch's advice: in 1349 he left teaching to become secretary to the king of Naples, then vicar to the bishop of Montecassino and, finally, papal secretary.)

31. Several examples of teachers' poor pay: two grammar teachers, one called Bartolo and the other Bandino da Tignano, who taught in the Servite convent of Santa Maria di Cafaggio in the late 1280s received a salary of one and a half soldi a month (*Registro di Entrata e Uscita di Santa Maria di Cafaggio [REU] 1286–1290*, pp. 35 and 62); the private teacher named Benno who, between 1290 and 1295, taught Perotto, the orphaned child of Paghino Ammannati, to write, received a payment of nine soldi for three months (remember that one gold florin was worth a little more than thirty-eight soldi)—the figures appear in an expense book kept by Compagno Ricevuti, guardian to the brothers Perotto and Fina Ammannati (Castellani, *Nuovi testi fiorentini del Dugento*, p. 566).

32. The young friars of Cafaggio, after their second cycle of schooling, were often sent, at the expense of the convent, to continue their theological studies at the University of Paris: see *Ricordanze di Santa Maria di Cafaggio (1295–1332)*, edited by Eugenio M. Casalini, in Eugenio M. Casalini OSM, Iginia Dina, Paola Ircani Menichini, *Testi dei "Servi della Donna di Cafaggio"* (Florence: Convento della SS Annunziata, 1955), pp. 56–57.

33. A more detailed examination of these matters can be found in Marco Santagata, *Folgorazioni e svenimenti. La malattia in Dante tra patologia e metafora*, in *Scientia, Fides, Theologia. Studi di filosofia medievale in onore di Gianfranco Fioravanti*, edited by Stefano Perfetti (Pisa: Edizioni ETS, 2011), pp. 387–399.

34. In *Conv.* III IX 15 Dante states that he suffered eye strain the same year as the "birth" of his canzone *Amor che nella mente mi ragiona.*

35. In the prologue in Heaven to the journey into the afterlife, Dante recounts that the Madonna, pained at seeing him lost in the forest of sin, called upon Saint Lucy, who then turned to Beatrice (*Inf.* II 97–102). In addition, it will be Saint Lucy who transports Dante asleep from the valley of the princes to the gate of Purgatory (*Purg.* IX 55–57), and the last glorious soul named by Saint Bernard before reciting the prayer to the Virgin (*Para.* XXXII 136–138) will be hers. And yet the symbolic significance of the figure of Saint Lucy is not established thanks to any characteristic or distinctive features, as can be seen from the variety of interpretations that have been given to it. Other saints could aspire to her role. If the choice has fallen on her, in the absence of pressing theological and symbolical reasons, we may think that this depends upon the particular devotion that Dante professes toward her. As confirmation we could quote what the Bologna notary Graziolo Bambaglioli wrote in 1324 in his commentary on *Inferno:* "Beata Lucia, in qua ipse Dantes in tempore vite sue habuit maximam devotionem," bearing in mind, however, that the notary's source could be Dante's own lines: "Your faithful one now needs / you" ("Or ha bisogno il tuo fedele / di te") *Inf.* II 98–99 (Graziolo Bambaglioli, *Commento all'* Inferno *di Dante,* edited by Luca Carlo Rossi [Pisa: Scuola Normale Superiore, 1998], p. 36).

36. On the reasons why Dante wanted his readers to identify the "Donna pietosa e di novella etate" of the canzone with that of "propinquissima sanguinità congiunta" in the introductory prose, so that we are faced with a canzone in "tragic" style which opens with the mention of a member of the author's close family—something totally unheard of in ancient verse tradition—read Marco Santagata, *Amate e amanti. Figure della lirica amorosa fra Dante e Petrarca* (Bologna: il Mulino, 2000), pp. 113–139. For the impossibility of the sister in the *Vita Nova* being Tana, see Indizio, "Tana Alighieri sorella di Dante," p. 176; as for the unidentified sister, since her son Andrea was an adult in 1304, it is likely that the marriage with Leone Poggi had been celebrated before 1283.

37. The two psychophysical crises are described in *E' m'incresce di me sì duramente* (*Rime* 19, 57–69): "the day she came into the world, / as we find / in the ever-fading book of the mind, /my young person felt / a new passion, / so that I was filled with terror; / that all my virtues were halted / so suddenly that I fell to the ground / for a light that struck my heart; / and if the book doesn't err, / the great spirit shook so strongly / that it well seemed that death / had arrived for him in this world . . ." ("Lo giorno che costei nel mondo venne, / secondo che si truova / nel libro della mente che vien meno, / la mia persona pargola sostenne / una passïon nova, / tal ch'io rimasi di paura pieno; / ch'a tutte mie virtù fu posto un freno / subitamente sì ch'io caddi in terra / per una luce che nel cuor percosse; / e se 'l libro non erra, / lo spirito maggior tremò sì forte / che parve ben che morte / per

lui in questo mondo giunta fosse . . .") and in *Amor, da che convien pur ch'io mi doglia* (*Rime* 50, 43–60): "then I turn to see who / can help me; and am struck / by eyes that slay me most wrongly. / That I become so wounded, my love, / you alone know, and not me, / for you remain to see me lifeless; / and though the soul then returns to the heart, / ignorance and oblivion / has been with it, while it is gone. / As I come back to life, and gaze at the wound / that undid me when I was struck, / I can find no comfort / so that the whole of me shakes with fear. / And then my face drained of color / shows what was that thunder that had struck me down; / which though moved by a sweet smile, / remains dark long afterward, / for the spirit is not reassured." ("Allor mi volgo per vedere a cui / mi raccomandi; e 'ntanto sono scorto / da li occhi che m'ancidono a gran torto. / Qual io divegno sì feruto, Amore, / sailo tu, e non io, / che rimani a veder me sanza vita; / e se l'anima torna poscia al core, / ignoranza ed oblio / stato è con lei, mentre ch'ella è partita. / Com'io risurgo, e miro la ferita / che mi disfece quand'io fui percosso, / confortar non mi posso / sì ch'io non triemi tutto di paura. / E mostra poi la faccia scolorita / qual fu quel trono che mi giunse a dosso; / che se con dolce riso è stato mosso, / lunga fiata poi rimane oscura, / perché lo spirto non si rassicura.")

38. For the interferences between medical and poetical views of love, I refer to Mary Frances Wack, *Lovesickness in the Middle Ages. The* Viaticum *and Its Commentaries* (Philadelphia: University of Pennsylvania Press, 1990); for Dante and Cavalcanti, see Natascia Tonelli, "'De Guidone de Cavalcantibus physic' (con una noterella su Giacomo da Lentini)," in *Per Domenico De Robertis. Studi offerti dagli allievi fiorentini,* edited by Isabella Becherucci, Simone Giusti, and Natascia Tonelli (Florence: Le Lettere, 2000), pp. 459–508; Tonelli, "Fisiologia dell'amore doloroso in Cavalcanti e in Dante: fonti mediche ed enciclopediche, in Guido Cavalcanti laico e le origini della poesia europea nel 7° centenario della morte." *Poesia, filosofia, scienza e ricezione,* proceedings of the international conference, Barcelona, October 16–20, 2001, edited by Rossend Arqués (Alessandria: Edizioni dell'Orso, 2004), pp. 63–117.

39. A tenuous hint from the French doctor and Dante scholar Maxime Durand-Fardel offered Cesare Lombroso the opportunity to intervene with a brief note in which he stated that it could be inferred from the *Commedia* (without however quoting the passage about Vanni Fucci) that the poet suffered from attacks of epilepsy (*La nevrosi in Dante e Michelangelo,* "Gazzetta Letteraria," November 25, 1893). The idea was picked up, repeated and further argued (with references to the *Commedia*—including Vanni Fucci—and also to the *Rime,* including *E' m'incresce di me*) by one of his students, Bernardo Chiara ("Dante e la psichiatria. Lettera a Cesare Lombroso," *Gazzetta Letteraria,* April 14, 1894). It was obvious that this would immediately raise cries of scandal: "Dante mad?" asked Giuseppe De Leonardis ("Dante matto?!" and "Dante isterico," *Giornale dantesco* 2 [4: 1894]: 211–213;

2 [5: 1895]: 156–158). The question, it has to be said, wasn't so impertinent, since Dante as epileptic was useful to Lombroso and his school to support the theory about the pathology of genius, a theory that had epilepsy as one of its mainstays. GIUNTA (pp. 233–237) is one of the few Dante scholars who formulated the hypothesis of epilepsy independently of Lombroso.

40. In the vast bibliography on the history of epileptic illness, the most fundamental are Owsei Temkin, *The Falling Sickness. A History of Epilepsy from the Greeks to the Beginnings of Modern Neurology* (Baltimore: The Johns Hopkins University Press, 2nd ed. rev., 1994), pp. 85–183, and Lynn Thorndike, *A History of Magic and Experimental Science during the First Thirteen Centuries of our Era* (New York: Columbia University Press, vol. 2, 1923). For the theory of Hildegard of Bingen, see Temkin, *The Falling Sickness,* pp. 97–98, who suggests that Dante had the same condition (here, the quote about the devil's "breath").

41. The word "oppilazione" is documented only in *La santà del corpo* by Zucchero Bencivenni to indicate, five times, the obstruction of the spleen and of the liver (Rossella Baldini, "Zucchero Bencivenni, 'La santà del corpo,' volgarizzamento del 'Régime du corps' di Aldobrandino da Siena [a. 1310] nella copia coeva di Lapo di Neri Corsini [Laur. Pl. LXXIII 47]," *Studi di lessicografia italiana* 15 [1998]: 21–300).

42. Barbara Reynolds, in *Dante: The Poet, the Political Thinker, the Man* (London: I. B. Tauris, 2006), wonders whether Dante's "experiences of heightened awareness" may have been further stimulated by the taking of some "psychedelic substance" (pp. 339, 376).

43. The dynamics of the breaking of the baptismal font and the prophetic significance of that gesture are considered and explained by Mirko Tavoni, "Effrazione battesimale tra i simoniaci (If XIX 13–21)," RLI 10 (1992): 457–512, then, with the title "Sul fonte battesimale di Dante / On Dante's Baptismal Font," in *Il Battistero di San Giovanni a Firenze / The Baptistery of San Giovanni Florence* (Mirabilia Italiae, 2), edited by Antonio Paolucci (Modena: Franco Cosimo Panini, 1994) vol. 2, *Testi,* pp. 205–228. The biblical account of Jeremiah's gesture in Jeremiah 19,1–13. On the dynamics of the event, see also the observations of Giuseppe Indizio, "La profezia di Niccolò e i tempi della stesura del canto XIX dell'*Inferno,*" SD 67 (2002): 73–97, in particular pp. 85–88.

44. On the relationship between epilepsy and prophecy see once again Temkin, *The Falling Sickness,* pp. 148–161.

45. The first meeting with Beatrice is told in *VN* 1, 2–3; the second in *VN* 1, 12.

46. For the date of the *Vita Nova* and the complex issues over its writing, I refer to SANTAGATA, pp. 113–141; in this same book (at pp. 141–191) wide consideration is also given to the relationship between reality and fiction, which is the key aspect of the story.

47. The account of the May Day festival is found in BOCCACCIO[1], 30–34, and, more briefly, in BOCCACCIO[2], 27–28; it was DAVIDSOHN (VII, p. 560) who pointed out that "the May Day festival was celebrated in solemn form only after 1290."

48. In *VN* 19, 6, Dante states that the number nine "was she [Beatrice] herself," ("fue ella medesima"), in other words "that she was nine": for the symbolism of this number I refer to SANTAGATA, pp. 206–209; for the symbolism of the number six in Petrarch, to Marco Santagata, *I frammenti dell'anima. Storia e racconto nel Canzoniere di Petrarca* (Bologna: il Mulino, [1992] 2011, pp. 125–127. As an example of the modern (and incorrect) approach to medieval symbolism, see what Harold Bloom has to say in *Genius: A Mosaic of One Hundred Exemplary Creative Minds* (London: Fourth Estate, 2002), p. 93: "They first meet as nine-year-olds, though that 'nine' is a warning against any literalization of this story."

49. Francesco Barberino's novelette and considerations on the age of puberty among young women can be found in *Reggimento e costumi di donna,* critical edition by Giuseppe E. Sansone, 2nd rev. ed. (Rome: Zauli Editore, 1995), pp. 9, 16–17.

50. Dante's particular autobiographical approach, which cancels the dividing line between fiction and reality, is widely covered in SANTAGATA, in particular at pp. 9–13.

51. The date of Beatrice's death is given in *VN* 19, 4.

52. Among the early commentaries on the *Commedia,* one of the first and few to have talked about Beatrice is that, already referred to, by Graziolo Bambaglioli, dating from the early 1320s; unfortunately it has a gap, perhaps intentional, in relation to the name of her father ("anima olim generose domine Beatrice, filie condam domini . . .") and is silent about her husband (Bambaglioli, *Commento all'*Inferno *di Dante,* pp. lxii, 35). Knowledge about the historical existence of Beatrice appears, however, in other commentaries, in which, here and there, there is information about her family of origin and her husband's family (see INDIZIO[3], pp. 236–238). Nevertheless, for more detailed information we have to wait for the mid-1300s. The two best-informed exegetics are Pietro Alighieri and Giovanni Boccaccio: the first was Dante's son, the second was connected, though distantly, to the Bardi and Portinari families. In the second version of his commentary on the *Commedia,* Pietro states that a certain "domina nomine Beatrix . . . nata de domo quorundam civium Florentinorum qui dicuntur Portinari" was loved by Dante, who in praise of her "multa fecit cantilenas [canzoni]." There are various doubts about the authorship of this version, which is datable to around 1345–1350 (INDIZIO[3], pp. 215–216), so the starting point for any investigation is the evidence of Boccaccio. In the passage of the *Trattatello* that describes the first meeting between Dante and Beatrice, he writes that "among the crowd of children" ("intra la turba de' giovinetti") gathered at the house of Folco Portinari to celebrate May Day was "a young daughter of the aforesaid Folco, whose name was Bice, though he [Dante] always

called her by her original name, Beatrice" ("una figliola del sopraddetto Folco, il cui nome era Bice, come che egli sempre del suo primitivo, cioè Beatrice la nominasse"; BOCCACCIO[1], 32). The first version of the work dates from the years 1351–1355; two decades later, in October 1373, Boccaccio began his public reading of Dante, which forms the basis of his *Esposizioni*. Here, commenting on *Inf* II 57, he notes: "It was therefore this lady, according to the report of a reliable person, who knew her and was closely related to her, daughter of a worthy man called Folco Portinari, old citizen of Florence . . . and was wife of a de' Bardi knight, called messer Simone" ("Fu adunque questa donna, secondo la relazione di fededegna persona, la quale la conobbe e fu per consanguinità strettissima a lei, figliuola di un valente uomo chiamato Folco Portinari, antico cittadino di Firenze . . . e fu moglie d'un cavaliere de' Bardi, chiamato messer Simone"; BOCCACCIO[3] II I 83–84). Boccaccio's testimony is reliable because it reports information that he could have obtained from the Bardi family, with whom his father, Boccaccino di Chelino, was professionally linked, as well as from the Portinari family, since Boccaccino had married a woman related, on her mother's side, to this same family (see Michele Barbi, "Sulla 'fededegna persona' che rivelò a Boccaccio la Beatrice dantesca" [1920], then in BARBI[2], pp. 415–420). Both pieces of information given by Boccaccio (that Beatrice was the daughter of Folco Portinari and the wife of Simone dei Bardi) were confirmed by the discovery of Folco's will, drawn up on January 15, 1288. Among other provisions, Folco leaves fifty lire in florins to her daughter Bice, married to messer Simone dei Bardi: "Item, dominae Bici etiam filiae suae et uxori domini Simonis de Bardis legavit de bonis suis libras L ad florenos" (see ED, entry "Bardi, Simone" by Arnaldo d'Addario).

53. Dante alludes to Folco's generosity (confirmed also by the founding of the hospital) in *VN* 13, 2; as to her brother Manetto, in *VN* 21, 1 Dante says: "he is a friend to me immediately after the first [Guido Cavalcanti]" ("è amico a me immediatamente dopo lo primo"). For Folco and Manetto, see in ED the entries (though not without inaccuracies) "Portinari, Folco" and "Portinari, Manetto" by Arnaldo d'Addario; for Folco also RAVEGGI et al., p. 191.

54. Among the many people with the name 'Simone dei Bardi' and living in Florence at that time, only Simone di Geri could claim the title of *messere* or *dominus*, the prerogative of knights and judges, and therefore Isidoro Del Lungo, in "Beatrice nella vita e nella poesia del secolo XIII," in *La donna fiorentina del buon tempo antico* (Florence: Bemporad, 1906), pp. 105–156, has inferred that this is the "knight" whom Boccaccio describes as Beatrice's husband. Compagni's "canzone del pregio" appears in *Poeti minori del Trecento,* edited by Natalino Sapegno (Milan-Naples: Ricciardi, 1964), pp. 281–288.

55. That Beatrice and Simone were already married in 1280 would seem to be confirmed by news published in a Florence newspaper (Domenico Savini,

"Beatrice l'ultimo segreto," *Corriere fiorentino,* March 4, 2008) of the discovery of a legal document which states that "Mone de' Bardi in 1280 gives land to Cecchino his brother and Madonna Bice, wife of said Mone, consents." News of this document has circulated on the Internet, but since the author of the article doesn't indicate the source, it cannot be checked. It may perhaps be the result of a misunderstanding or a misinterpretation. Indeed, Roberta Cella informs me that in the State Archive in Florence she has found a legal document drawn up by the notary Giunta di Spigliato, dated June 17, 1280, which records the sale of land with adjoining building in the *popolo* (parish) of Ripoli by Bartolo of the late Iacopo di Ricco Bardi to "Simone qui Mone dicitur et Ceccho qui dicitur Cecchino fratribus filis domini Geri Ricchi Bardi": in this document as well, the wife of the seller, Tessa, consents (Archivio di Stato di Firenze [ASFL], *Archivio generale dei contratti,* 1280 giugno 17). The coincidence of the year and the similarity of the transaction cast substantial doubt on the first legal document.

56. The account of the pilgrims crossing the city on their way to Rome is in *VN* 29; for the route they followed see SANTAGATA, pp. 204–206; for the hospitals situated along that road, DAVIDSOHN, VII, p. 96; for the church of Santa Lucia, Giuseppe Richa, *Notizie istoriche delle chiese fiorentine divise ne' suoi quartieri* (Florence: Viviani, 1762) vol. 10, part 2 (anastatic reprint, Roma: Multigrafica Editrice, 1989), p. 291; information that the houses of the Bardi were close to the church of Santa Lucia is in VILLANI, V VIII.

57. The anecdote about Guido Cavalcanti attacking Corso Donati is told in COMPAGNI I, XX.

58. There is information about Gemma and her father Manetto in ED, under the headings "Donati, Gemma" and "Donati, Manetto," written by Renato Piattoli.

59. To emphasize Ubertino Donati's high nobility in *Para.* XVI 115–120, referring to the Adimari family, Dante writes: "That arrogant breed who rage like a dragon / behind those who flee, and to those that show their teeth / or purse, become quiet as a lamb, / was already rising up, but were lowly folk: / so that Ubertin Donato was not pleased / that then his father-in-law [Bellincione Berti] made him a relative of theirs" ("L'oltracotata schiatta che s'indraca / dietro a chi fugge, e a chi mostra 'l dente / o ver la borsa, com' agnel si placa, / già venia sù, ma di picciola gente: / sì che non piacque ad Ubertin Donato / che poï il suocero il fé lor parente").

60. The documents relating to Gemma's dowry are published in PIATTOLI, nos. 43, 146.

61. I am indebted to Roberta Cella for the considerations that lead us to think that the negotiation for the marriage settlement between Dante and Gemma was carried out not by his father Alighiero, but by a guardian whose ideas and social standing were similar to those of his grandfather Durante degli Abati.

2. A Strange Florentine

1. It is calculated that around three thousand Ghibellines were interned or banished in 1267: see Isidoro Del Lungo, *Una vendetta in Firenze il giorno di San Giovanni del 1295* (1887), p. 79.

2. The trial proceedings of Salomone da Lucca between 1282 and 1285, including that of Farinata, are recounted, with various inaccuracies, by DAVIDSOHN, III, pp. 376–382; better documented is the contribution by Giuseppe Indizio, "Supplemento a *Fiore*, CXXIV e CXXV: l'Inquisizione tra fede e azione politica," RSD I: 2009: 99–113.

3. For the legal bases for the exhumation of convicted people who are dead and the confiscation of property inherited from convicted people, see the entries "Defunti," by Andrea Errera, and "Confisca dei beni," by Vincenzo Lavenia, in *Dizionario storico dell'Inquisizione,* directed by Adriano Prosperi, with the collaboration of Vincenzo Lavenia and John Tedeschi (Pisa: Edizioni della Normale, 2010), 3 vols.

4. For institutional changes and the social dynamics of Florence after the Peace of Cardinal Latino, essential reading is Gaetano Salvemini, *Magnati e popolani in Firenze dal 1280 al 1295. Seguito da "La dignità cavalleresca nel Comune di Firenze,"* introductory essay by Ernesto Sestan (Turin: Einaudi, 1960). The first edition of *Magnati e popolani* was published in 1899. See also DAVIDSOHN, III, and essays in RAVEGGI et al. An overview of the system of guilds is in Viktor I. Rutenburg, *Arti e corporazioni,* in *Storia d'Italia,* vol. 5, *I documenti* I (Turin: Einaudi, 1973), pp. 613–642.

5. For the Malatesta brothers see DBI, entry on "Malatesta (de Malatestis), Paolo" and "Malatesta (de Malatestis), Giovanni" by Anna Falcioni, and for Giano della Bella under the entry by Giuliano Pinto.

6. On the cavalry, or rather, on the *militia* during the commune period until the early thirteenth century, read the essential research in Jean-Claude Maire Vigueur, *Cavaliers et citoyens. Guerre, conflits et societé dans l'Italie communal, XIIe–XIIIe siècles* (Paris: Ecoles des Hautes Etudes en Sciences Sociale (EHESS), 2003); on the status of knights in Florence in the age of Dante, see Salvemini, *La dignità cavalleresca nel Comune di Firenze,* pp. 339–482, and the concise but comprehensive observations of GIUNTA, pp. 331–334. I have taken the statistical information about knights from DAVIDSOHN, III, pp. 337, 576. The description of their lifestyle is in VILLANI, VIII LXXXIX.

7. The Alighieri were not among the group of magnates in part because they had no knight in the family: Cione, brother of Geri di Bello, and therefore cousin of Dante's father, would be knighted, but only later, at the turn of the century (see the entry in ED, "Alighieri, Cione" by Renato Piattoli).

8. The Tuscan wars between Guelfs and Ghibellines and the events in Pisa are told in DAVIDSOHN, III; for biographies of Guido and Buonconte da Montefeltro,

see the respective entries in ED: also the entry on Guido, written by Aldo Rossi, and that on Buonconte, by Giorgio Petrocchi.

9. The inscription commemorating the battle of Campaldino is referred to in BRUNI, pp. 540–541.

10. For count Ugolino Della Gherardesca, see the entry in DBI by Maria Luisa Ceccarelli Lemut and Nello Toscanelli, *I conti di Donoratico signori di Pisa* (Pisa: Nistri-Lischi, 1937), pp. 85–200; for Nino Visconti, see Michele Tamponi, *Nino Visconti di Gallura. Il dantesco Giudice Nin gentil tra Pisa e Sardegna, guelfi e ghibellini, faide cittadine e lotte isolane,* presentation by Diego Quaglioni (Rome: Viella, 2010).

11. The legal document in which Dante passed on the credit inherited from his father is in PIATTOLI, no. 47: the story of the loan is reconstructed by ZINGARELLI, p. 80, who also establishes that Tedaldo Orlandi Rustichelli was brother of Guido Orlandi, a politician and writer of verse, in poetical contact with Guido Cavalcanti, and that as notary he would also write out the will of Folco Portinari.

12. For the date of marriage of Tana, I refer to Giuseppe Indizio, "Tana Alighieri sorella di Dante," SD 65 (2000), and for the amount of the dowry to the entries in ED, "Alighieri, Tana" and "Riccomanni, Lapo" by Renato Piattoli.

13. The question of the supposed son Giovanni is discussed by Michele Barbi, "Un altro figlio di Dante?" (1922), then in BARBI², pp. 347–370, and by Renato Piattoli, in the entry in ED, "Giovanni di Dante di Alighiero da Firenze"; the notary's document recording the presence in Lucca of this Giovanni in 1308 is published in PIATTOLI, appendix II 1. Some also suggest there existed a fifth son called Gabriello, referred to in few documents in the mid-1300s (ED, entry "Gabriello di Dante di Alighiero" by Renato Piattoli).

14. Barbi, in "Un altro figlio di Dante?" (1922), in BARBI², pp. 355–358, suggests that Gemma followed her husband into exile and returned to Florence only after his death; DAVIDSOHN, IV, pp. 280–281, suggests that she, too, was banished in June 1302 and returned to Florence later.

15. For portraits of Iacopo and Pietro Alighieri, see BELLOMO, pp. 62–91, and those of CCD; for the latter, it is essential also to refer to INDIZIO³; for Antonia, see entry in ED, "Alighieri, Antonia (suor Beatrice)." Petrarch sent Pietro a short letter in Latin verse (*Epyst.* III 7), for which see the entry in ED, "Petrarca, Francesco," by Michele Feo.

16. Charles Martel would be the protagonist in Canto VIII of *Paradiso,* where he would also refer (lines 34–36) to Dante's canzone *Voi che 'ntendendo il terzo ciel movete,* which makes it plausible that this canzone, collected and commented on in *Conv.* II, was one of the pieces of verse that Dante recited to him in Florence; Dante would address Clemence of Austria at the beginning of Canto IX (lines 1–6): see SANTAGATA, pp. 116, 375–376.

17. In *Inf.* XXVII 55–57 Dante shows that he didn't know Guido da Montefeltro: "Now please tell us who you are; / be no harder than others have been, / so that

your name can hold its own on earth" ("Or chi se', ti priego che ne conte; / non esser duro più ch'altri sia stato, / se 'l nome tuo nel mondo tegna fronte").

18. The murder of Geri and the long story that led, first, to the killing of a Sacchetti and, finally, to the signing of the peace settlement of 1342 are reconstructed by Marco Santagata, "Geri del Bello, un'offesa vendicata," NRLI 13 (2011): 199–209.

19. For Geri and his brother Cione, see the entries in ED, "Alighieri, Cione" and "Alighieri, Geri" by Renato Piattoli; the record of the trial proceedings in Prato is published in PIATTOLI, no. 45. The date of Geri's death is found in the note, dated April 15, 1287, "It a la sepultura di Gieri del Bello, s. xiijj" in *Registro di Entrata e Uscita di Santa M ria di Cafaggio (REU) 1286–1290,* transcription, comment, notes, and glossary edited by ̄ugenio M. Casalini (Florence: Convento della SS. Annunziata, 1998), p. 133.

20. With regard to the particular tendency of the Florentines to take vengeance, BOCCACCIO[3] (VII II 118) writes: "Of which curse [to take vengeance] the Tuscans are cruelly tainted, and among them in particular the Florentines, who for any rebuke made to us we know not how to pardon" ("Della qual maladizione fieramente son maculati i toscani, e tra loro in singularità i Fiorentini, li quali per alcuno ammaestramento datoci non ci sappiamo recare a perdonare"); and Iacomo della Lana of Bologna states "that the Florentines are so jealous, that all the family regard themselves as offended, and so they condemn the whole family of the offender: and so every relative of the offended party is ready to take vengeance on the offender or his relatives" ("che Fiorentini hanno tale uxo, che tutto il parentado si reputa l'offesa, e così la si imputano da tutti li parenti dello offenditore: e però ciascun parente della parte offesa s'apronta di fare vendetta in lo offenditore o in li suoi parenti") (Iacomo della Lana, *Commento alla* Commedia, edited by Mirko Volpi, with the collaboration of Arianna Terzi (Rome: Salerno Editrice, 2010) vol. I, p. 436).

21. For Forese's accusation against Dante of cowardice, see *Rime* 25f, 1–8, and the comment in GIUNTA, pp. 313–317.

22. The theory about Brodario's motive is put forward by Michele Barbi, "Per una più precisa interpretazione della *Divina Commedia*" (1905), then in BARBI[1], pp. 197–303; the quote appears at pp. 275–276. For the Sacchetti, see ED, entry by Arnaldo d'Addario, and RAVEGGI et al., pp. 118–119.

23. On Dante's wishes to raise his family to nobility, see CARPI, p. 135 (where, at pp. 283–285, he includes a selected bibliography on the question of vengeance): "the vengeance to be carried out against the noble Sacchetti family for the murder of Geri . . . was an indirect sign, though immediately perceptible to the Florentine sensibility of that time, of nobility and awareness of nobility, of being part of the system of ruling class families allowed [required?] to exercise vengeance. Hence the show of *pietas* toward Geri; hence the endorsement of the nobility of the Sacchetti."

24. For Bambo and Lapo di Cione, see the entries in ED written by Renato Piattoli. The story of the Velluti revenge is told by Del Lungo, *Una vendetta in Firenze*; the proverb ("vendetta di cento anni tiene lattaiuoli") is quoted in *Ottimo commento* (first version) in the commentary on *Inf.* XXIX 31–34.

25. The peace settlement with the Sacchetti is published in PIATTOLI, no. 182.

26. That Dante took part on several occasions in the war against Arezzo is considered more than likely by CARPI, pp. 366, 564; for Lano, identified as a certain Arcolano di Squarcia Maconi, a wealthy man from Siena, see the entry in ED, "Lano," by Renato Piattoli. The only slim evidence of the fact that Dante could have been present at Poggio Santa Cecilia comes from the prose introduction to the sonnet *Cavalcando l'altrier per un cammino* (*Riding the other day along a path*) (VN 4). It has been pointed out that various words used in the prose sound like the language used by documents and chronicles of the time to describe war, and it has been inferred that his riding in the "company of many" ("compagnia di molti") in which he was obliged to take part ("something happened that required me to leave"—"avvenne cosa per la quale me convenne partire") was in reality a military expedition from the city. The cavaliers would have followed the line of the river Arno, the "river fine and swift and crystal clear" ("fiume bello e corrente e chiarissimo"), either down toward Pisa or, more probably, by climbing back toward Arezzo, therefore in the direction of the castle to be attacked (see Isidoro Del Lungo, *La donna fiorentina del buon tempo antico* (Florence: Bemporad, 1906, pp. 121–128, and PETROCCHI, pp. 21–22).

27. The account of Buonconte who, wounded in the throat, dragged himself as far as the point where the Archiano torrent flows into the Arno, who dies "in the name of Mary" ("nel nome di Maria"), and whose body is carried by the swollen waters rushing down after a storm over Mount Pratomagno, is in *Purg.* V 94–129. On Iacopo del Cassero (who had previously taken part in the expedition against Arezzo of 1288), see the entry in DBI by Lorenzo Paolini, and especially the observations by CARPI, pp. 365–366, 413.

28. The letter quoted in BRUNI (pp. 540–542) ("ove ebbe temenza molta et nella fine grandissima allegrezza per li varii casi di quella battaglia") is probably that which began "Popule mee, quid feci tibi?" to which I will return several times later. The letter was also known to Biondo Flavio who, on the very basis of it, describes the Battle of Campaldino: see Rosetta Migliorini Fissi, "Dante e il Casentino," in *Dante e le città dell'esilio*, proceedings of the international research conference, Ravenna, September 11–13, 1987, technical director Guido Di Pino (Ravenna: Longo Editore, 1989), pp. 114–146, in particular p. 118, and INDIZIO[2], pp. 276–277. I have taken the information on cavaliers, on the role of Vieri dei Cerchi, and on compensation payments to soldiers from DAVIDSOHN, III, pp. 458–463; here also, at p. 483, information on the punishment of the Pisan defenders of Caprona accused of betrayal and cowardice.

29. A detailed description of the outfit worn by a mounted soldier is provided by Migliorini Fissi, "Dante e il Casentino," pp. 119–120. For an idea of costs, bear in mind that in 1291 a shod horse (with grey coat and therefore much prized) was valued at around the substantial sum of seventy-five gold florins, and at the time of the wars against Arezzo and Pisa the "cavallate" (i.e., the military obligations) imposed by the commune on an increasing number of citizens included maintaining a horse worth between thirty-five and seventy florins or the payment of an equivalent tax to avoid going to war. I have taken this information on the value of a destrier from Arrigo Castellani, *Nuovi testi fiorentini del Dugento* (Florence: Sansoni, 1952),p. 637; for the value of the "cavallate" see the *Registro di Entrata e Uscita di Santa Maria di Cafaggio (REU) 1286–1290*, pp. 63–64, 82.

30. The quotation about the power and wealth of the Cavalcanti ("le più possenti case di genti, e di possessioni, e d'avere di Firenze") is by VILLANI, IX LXXI. For the Sigibuldi family, see Guido Zaccagnini, *Cino da Pistoia. Studio biografico* (Pistoia: Pagnini, 1918), at pp. 30–31 the references to Cino's bank deposits.

31. On how Dante would have seen his social condition, see the observations of Tommaso Gallarati Scotti, *Vita di Dante* (Milan: Treves, 1929) pp. 4–6; DAVIS, who at p. 27 refers to the insecurity of his social position; and above all, Ernesto Sestan, "Dante e Firenze," a 1965 essay in Sestan, *Italia medievale* [Naples: ESU, 1968], 270–291, p. 279: "Dante at a very young age must soon have had the feeling, disagreeable to his pride, that his family, far from being able to compete with the great Guelf clans, wasn't even included among that hybrid group of rich nobles and merchants that dominated Florentine politics . . . it can be reckoned that Dante had already in his youth mitigated and compensated the pride offended by the mediocrity of his social position by exalting the nobility of his origins."

32. On Lapo Gianni, see the entry in ED by Mario Marti. COMPAGNI, III VIII refers to the "houses and palaces and workshops, which for the high rents, for the cramped space, kept [the Cavalcanti] rich" ("case e palagi e botteghe, le quali per le gran pigioni, per lo stretto luogo, tenean ricchi").

33. So far as Dante living beyond his means, there is an evocative, though imaginary, reconstruction by Piero Bargellini, " 'Il figliuol d'Alaghieri': Dante, uomo privato, in *Il processo di Dante. Celebrato il 16 aprile 1966 nella Basilica di S. Francesco in Arezzo*, edited by Morris L. Ghezzi (Milan-Udine: Mimesis Edizioni, 2011), pp. 40–43.

34. Dante's meeting with Beatrice when she was eighteen is described in *VN* I, 12.

35. Cappellano writes: "Dico tamen et firmiter assero, quod masculus ante decimum octavum annum verus esse non potest amans" (Andrea Cappellano, *De amore*, edited by Graziano Ruffini [Milan: Guanda, 1980], p. 14). The quote by Francesco da Barberino is in *Reggimento e costumi di donna*, critical edition by Giuseppe E. Sansone, 2nd rev. ed. (Rome: Zauli Editore, 1995), Ip. 20 ("giovane che

venuta è già nel tempo del maritaggio ... e s'egli avien che colla madre sua per alcun luogo passi, non si inframmetta d'alcun salutare"). See also what Barberino writes about the married woman (pp. 47–48): "Leaving then her house. / Now I ask, must she greet / when passing on the street, or what manner [must she] keep? / On this I have found many varied customs / and varied opinions, / but it can be said / it depends on the custom of her homeland / and of the place where she is sent, / and that is tempered with the other ... and others say that if she is a girl / from twelve or thereabout / she is not obliged to any greeting." ("Movesi poi da casa sua. / Mo ti domando se de' salutare / per via passando, o che modo tenere. / Di ciò ho trovato molte varie usanze / e di varie openioni, / però dir si porria / dimandi della sua terra l'usanza / e del paese dov'ell'è menata, / e quella servi com' può temp[e]rata ... e altri dicon che s'ell'è fanciulla / da dodici anni o intorno di quelli / non è tenuta d'alcun salutare,")

36. The circular and anonymous request to interpret a dream has all the air of an academic exercise, an intellectual game in which the symbols and conundrums require either no real experience or only a vague experience. *A ciascun'alma presa e gentil core* seems, as do others, to be an intentionally obscure riddle. "It is all too obvious," writes Michele Barbi in *Rime della* Vita nuova *e della giovinezza,* edited by Michele Barbi and Francesco Maggini (Florence: Le Monnier, 1956), p. 9, "that the poet here, instead of expressing feelings experienced or imagined in a real life situation or a painful personal premonition, is composing something difficult to submit for the interpretation of those faithful to love ... an invention to test out the subtlety of the verse writers of his time." An invention so subtle and specious as to irritate Dante da Maiano, who in his reply accuses Dante of "raving" and, rather impolitely, advises (*Di ciò che stato sei* 7–9): "that you wash your balls thoroughly, / so that the fever fades and passes / which will make your stories better" ("che lavi la tua coglia largamente, / a ciò che stinga e passi lo vapore, / lo qual ti fa favoleggiar loquendo"). His poems are published in Dante da Maiano, *Rime,* edited by Rosanna Bettarini (Florence: Le Monnier, 1969). The sonnets in reply to Dante, including *Vedeste, al mio parer, onne valore* by Cavalcanti, are to be found, with commentary, in Dante Alighieri, *Rime,* with commentary edited by Domenico De Robertis (Florence: SISMEL-Edizioni del Galluzzo, 2005). So far as the use of anonymity, note that, even in a tenzone with Dante da Maiano, Dante shows he doesn't know the identity of the sender: in *Rime* 2b, 1: "Whoever you are, friend ..." ("Qual che voi siate, amico ..."); in *Rime* 2d, 1: "not knowing, friend, your name" ("non conoscendo, amico, vostro nomo"); and likewise Cavalcanti in a sonnet replying to Guido Orlandi (*Di vil matera mi conven parlare* 13) writes: "whoever you are ..." ("qual che voi siate ..."). On this phenomenon, see GIUNTA, p. 98, to which I also refer for the reason behind sonnets containing a dream to be interpreted.

37. The possible tenzone with Chiaro Davanzati is to be found in *Rime dubbie* XIIIa–XIIId; for Chiaro, see the DBI entry by Pasquale Stoppelli. For Guido Orlandi, who was also in correspondence with Cavalcanti, see: Valentina Pollidori, "Le rime di Guido Orlandi" [critical edition], *Studi di filologia italiana* 53 (1994): 55–202, and Guido Cavalcanti, *Rime. Con le rime di Iacopo Cavalcanti,* edited by Domenico De Robertis (Turin: Einaudi, 1986), pp. 187–205; for Ser Cione, see the entry "Cione di Baglione" in DBI by Mario Pagano; for Terino, *Poeti del Duecento,* edited by Gianfranco Contini (Milan-Naples: Ricciardi, 1960), vol. I, pp. 393–395.

38. For Puccio Bellondi, see GIUNTA, pp. 728–733. Dante's *rime* sent to correspondents not identifiable with any certainty are *Rime* 4; 16; 39; those exchanged with Bellondi or Dante da Maiano are *Rime dubbie* XIVa–b.

39. Dante refers to the sirventes in *VN* 2, 11.

40. In the prose that introduces the sonnet *Io mi senti' svegliar dentro allo core* (*VN* 15), Love tells Dante that the name of Cavalcanti's beloved, Giovanna, "comes from that Giovanni [John] who preceded the true light saying: 'I am the voice crying out in the wilderness: prepare ye the way of the Lord'" ("è da quello Giovanni lo quale precedette la verace luce dicendo: 'ego vox clamantis in deserto: parate viam Domini'") Now, since the sonnet recounts how Vanna (Giovanna) preceded Beatrice, there follows a double symmetry: Vanna is to Beatrice what John the Baptist is to Christ and, at the same time, if Giovanna was the one who preceded Beatrice, the poetry of Guido preceded that of Dante. For the dating of *Donne ch'avete intelletto d'amore* see SANTAGATA, pp. 131–135; for Pietro Alegranze and his transcription on the legal register, see *Rime due e trecentesche tratte dall'Archivio di Stato di Bologna,* critical edition by Sandro Orlando, with archive consultancy by Giorgio Marcon, Bologna, Commissione per i testi di lingua, 2005, and Armando Antonelli, *Rime estravaganti di Dante provenienti dall'Archivio di Stato di Bologna (con un approfondimento di ricerca sul sonetto della Garisenda vergato da Enrichetto delle Querce),* in *Le rime di Dante,* Gargnano del Garda (25–27 September 2008), edited by Claudia Berra and Paolo Borsa (Milan: Cisalpino, 2010), pp. 83–115.

The second half of the 1280s is the most appropriate period for the composition of *Il Fiore* and *Detto d'Amore,* if they are by Dante. *Il Fiore* is a sequence of 232 sonnets which compose a free summary of the French poem *Roman de la Rose,* the subject of which is itself condensed into the 240 seven-syllable couplets of the related *Detto d'Amore.* (The *Romance of the Rose,* begun by Guillaume de Lorris between 1225 and 1230 and continued by Jean de Meun between the 1260s and 1270s, was the most famous book in the whole of European vernacular literature at the time of Dante.) Since they were discovered in 1878, found in a single manuscript, the two texts have given rise to much debate on their authorship. The most fervent and influential supporter of the argument that they were written by Dante was Gianfranco Contini, who produced the critical edition of

Il Fiore and *Detto d'Amore* with the words "attributable to Dante Alighieri," where "attributable" means "to be attributed," for which see at least *Un nodo della cultura medievale: la serie* Roman de la Rose, Fiore, Divina Commedia (1973), then in Contini, *Un'idea di Dante. Saggi danteschi* (Turin: Einaudi, 1976), pp. 245–283. The question is still debated; the two most recent contributions move in opposite directions: Dante Alighieri, *Fiore, Detto d'Amore,* edited by Paola Allegretti, Edizione nazionale by the Società Dantesca Italiana (Florence: Le Lettere, 2011) is substantially in favor of Dante as author, while Pasquale Stoppelli, *Dante e la paternità del* Fiore (Rome: Salerno editrice, 2011) (to which I also refer for the bibliography on the subject), rejects his authorship.

41. With regard to the backwardness of classical studies in Florence at the end of the 1200s, Giuseppe Billanovich ("Tra Dante e Petrarca," IMU, 8 [1965]: 1–43) writes: "Dante shows himself to be an expert in prosody and Latin meter: which he must therefore have learned as an adolescent at a decent school" (p. 17), but he observes "that Florence at that time, where no serious grammar book or a monumental classical manuscript could be found—and which indeed was politically, culturally and artistically a younger creature than neighboring Lucca, Pisa and Arezzo—knew no philology equal to that of the Venetians." The statement by Renato Piattoli ("Codice Diplomatico Dantesco. Aggiunte," *Archivio storico italiano* 127, nos. 1–3 [1969]: 3–108) that Dante learned Latin "in the schools of a large monastery" (p. 82) has still to be proved.

42. For the link between rhetoric and legal studies (and vernacular translations of rhetoric texts), see Cesare Segre, *Lingua, stile e società. Studi sulla storia della prosa italiana,* new expanded edition (Milan: Feltrinelli, 1974), pp. 49–55; Segre edited the critical edition of the treatise by Bono Giamboni, *Il libro de' vizî e delle virtudi* and *Il trattato di virtù e di vizi,* edited by Cesare Segre (Turin: Einaudi, 1968); for his biography, see the entry in DBI by Simona Foà. *De consolatione Philosophiae* by Severinus Boethius was one of the most widely used texts in medieval education: it was used as a schoolbook for learning Latin and as a preparatory text for studying the major classics (see Robert Black and Gabriella Pomaro, La consolazione della filosofia *nel Medioevo e nel Rinascimento italiano. Libri di scuola e glosse nei manoscritti fiorentini* (Florence: SISMEL-Edizioni del Galluzzo, 2000). That it was not widely known in Florence at the time of Dante, as he himself suggests when he writes: "that book of Boethius not known by many" ("quello non conosciuto da molti libro di Boezio") (*Conv.* II XII 2), therefore arouses a certain doubt. Dante most probably wanted to suggest that readers underestimated the philosophical aspect of Boethius' book, due to the way in which it was used for ulterior purposes. And yet it would seem that the English Dominican Nicholas Trevet—active in Pisa and Florence around the years straddling the twelve and thirteen hundreds, later a theology teacher at Oxford and London, and author of many commentaries on *Consolatio*—had great difficulty in obtaining this text at the convent of Santa Maria

Novella (see Giuseppe Billanovich, *La tradizione del testo di Livio e le origini dell'umanesimo*, vol. 1: *Tradizione e fortuna di Livio tra Medioevo e umanesimo*, Part 1 (Padua: Editrice Antenore, 1981), pp. 34–41).

43. There is a more detailed and reliable biographical profile of Brunetto under the entry in DBI by Giorgio Inglese, to which should be added at least DAVIS, pp. 166–200, and Pietro G. Beltrami, introduction to Brunetto Latini, *Tresor*, edited by Pietro G. Beltrami, Paolo Squillacioti, Plinio Torri, and Sergio Vatteroni (Turin: Einaudi, 2007).

44. The phrase is taken from VILLANI, IX X ("sén tenuti / un poco mondanetti"), in which the expression "mondano uomo" is also found (taken from *Tesoretto*, v. 2561).

45. The homoerotic nature of the canzoni of Brunetto (*S' eo sono distretto inamoratamente*) and of Dietaiuti (*Amore, quando mi membra*)—for whom see the entry in DBI by Liana Cellerino—has been claimed by D'Arco Silvio Avalle, *Ai luoghi di delizia pieni. Saggio sulla lirica italiana del XIII secolo* (Milan-Naples: Ricciardi, 1977), pp. 87–106; for a different interpretation of Brunetto's canzone, see Luciano Rossi, *Brunetto, Bondie, Dante e il tema dell'esilio*, in *Feconde venner le carte. Studi in onore di Ottavio Besomi*, edited by Tatiana Crivelli (Bellinzona: Edizioni Casagrande, 1977), pp. 13–34, and Sergio Lubello, "Brunetto Latini, "S'eo son distretto inamoratamente" (V 181): tra lettori antichi e moderni," in *A scuola con ser Brunetto. Indagini sulla ricezione di Brunetto Latini dal Medioevo al Rinascimento*, proceedings of the international study conference, University of Basel, June 8–10, 2006 (Florence: Edizioni del Galluzzo, 2008), pp. 515–534. Both the Brunetto and Bondie Dietaiuti texts are published with comments by Sergio Lubello in *I poeti della Scuola siciliana*, vol. 3: *Poeti siculo-toscani*, critical edition with commentary directed by Rosario Coluccia (Milan: Mondadori, 2008), pp. 306–326.

46. Given that the practice of compiling documents and letters would become a genuine employment for Dante in exile, Giorgio Padoan ("Tra Dante e Mussato. I. Tonalità dantesche nell' *Historia Augusta* di Albertino Mussato," *Quaderni veneti* 24 [1966]: 27–45) confesses that it would be no surprise "if one day it is found that Alighieri had some kind of qualification as a notary," and adds as a footnote the testimony of the great scholar and philologist Augusto Campana, who "held a similar opinion" and had one day confided in him "that he had found documentary evidence of it (but wanted first to examine it, fearing it was by someone else of the same name)" (p. 38).

Thanks to Brunetto, Dante may also have improved his knowledge of French, a language much used in a city which had special relations with the Angevins of Naples and the kings of France, and for which France was an important market. Brunetto, who had lived in that country and, above all, had written his most important work in that language, could have transmitted to him a competence that went far beyond the commercial French of traders. Dante also learned Provencal in his youth, though we don't know to what level. At this time it was still an essential language for anyone who wanted to be seriously involved in writing lyric poetry, and it would therefore have been normal for him to search out and read anthologies of poets who wrote in Langue d'oc. Among the friends of Brunetto—who, don't forget, also wrote vernacular verse—Dante da Maiano wrote in Provencal and Bondie Dietaiuti translated, or rather reworked, Occitan lyric compositions: Latini could therefore also have been an important means for learning about Provencal poetry and language.

Some suggest that Brunetto may have introduced Dante to a very particular work, *The Book of Muhammad's Ladder,* a text of Arabic origin which is said to have influenced his conception of the *Commedia,* or he may at least have told him about the Arab legends about which the book gives one of many versions. It is a legendary account that brings together the tradition of a miraculous night journey by Muhammad from Mecca to Jerusalem and the Prophet's equally miraculous ascent into Heaven. *The Book of Muhammad's Ladder,* which contains one version of the journey into the afterworld, comes from a lost Arabic original which, thanks to the king of Castile, Alfonso X the Wise, was translated by a certain Bonaventura of Siena into Castilian (also lost), from which French and Latin versions were made. The text is available in English translation as *The Prophet of Islam in Old French: The Romance of Muhammad (1258) and The Book of Muhammad's Ladder (1264),* translated and with introduction by Reginald Hyatte (Leiden; New York; Köln: Brill, 1997). It is possible that Dante was familiar with one of these translations and was influenced by it; it is most unlikely, however, that this had happened through Brunetto. It is suggested that Brunetto could have been the vehicle because the city had sent him as ambassador to Alfonso X in 1259 or 1260 (it was during his return from that mission that he received news of the rout at Montaperti), and he could have learned about the legends of the journeys of Muhammad from that highly cultured sovereign, who was responsible for a vast program of translation of Arabic and Hebrew texts into Castilian. But apart from the fact that we don't know whether he met the king, and therefore what relations he had with him, he couldn't have spoken to Dante about this book in particular since the Castilian version appeared after his stay in Spain. He could, however, have told him stories that he had heard, though even this seems unlikely. In 1305, when he wrote *De vulgari eloquentia,* Dante was still unaware of the existence of the Castilian language: for him the "Yspani," in other words, all those inhabitants of the Spanish peninsula, used Langue d'oc, namely that Provencal in fact spoken in Catalonia (*VE* I VIII 5). If Brunetto hadn't even told him of the existence of Castilian, would he really have talked about those Arabic legends? On *The Book of Muhammad's Ladder,* on the relationship between the *Commedia* and the Arabic legends of Muhammad's journey, and on the supposed role of Brunetto Latini, see Miguel Asín Palacios, *Dante e l'Islam,* vol. 1: *L'escatologia islamica nella* Divina Commedia; vol.

2: *Storia e critica di una polemica* (Parma: Pratiche Editrice, 1994); Enrico Cerulli, *Il "Libro della Scala" e la questione delle fonti arabo-spagnole della* Divina Commedia (Vatican City: 1949); Cesare Segre, *Fuori del mondo. I modelli nella follia e nelle immagini dell'aldilà* (Turin: Einaudi, 1990); Maria Corti, *Percorsi dell'invenzione. Il linguaggio poetico e Dante* (Turin: Einaudi, 1993), pp. 126, 160. Dante's ignorance of the existence of Castilian is stressed in TAVONI, pp. 1206–1209.

47. On the reasons that led the notaries of Bologna, who worked on the register of public records ("il Memoriale") to transcribe poetic texts into it, on their criteria of choice and purpose, see the observations in *Rime due e trecentesche tratte dall'Archivio di Stato di Bologna,* pp. xxiv-lx. For the problem of the linguistic guise of Dante's sonnet on the Garisenda and for an analysis of the various interpretations proposed, I refer to GIUNTA, pp. 155–159; for Enrichetto delle Querce, see Antonelli, *Rime estravaganti di Dante provenienti dall'Archivio di Stato di Bologna.*

48. For the inns where Florentines stayed in the area around the Garisenda Tower, see Giovanni Livi, *Dante, suoi primi cultori, sua gente in Bologna* (Bologna: Cappelli, 1918), pp. 158–165.

49. For his stay in Bologna, see BOCCACCIO¹, 25, and BOCCACCIO², 20.

50. The poetry of Monte Andrea can be found in Monte Andrea da Firenze, *Le rime,* critical edition by Francesco Filippo Minetti (Florence: Accademia della Crusca, 1979).

51. With the same verse (*Quomodo sedet sola civitas plena populo! Facta est quasi vidua domina gentium*) Dante would begin his letter to the Italian cardinals (*Ep* XI) in which he grieves for Rome's widowhood.

52. The possible identity of the person or persons to whom the Latin epistle was addressed is discussed more fully in SANTAGATA, pp. 203–204; information on Cino dei Bardi in *I Priori di Firenze (1282–1343),* edited by Sergio Raveggi (www.storia.unisi.it) and in RAVEGGI et al., pp. 107–108.

53. For the welcoming delegation for Charles Martel, see *Dino Compagni e la sua Cronica,* edited by Isidoro Del Lungo (Florence: Le Monnier, 1879), vol. 2, pp. 503–504.

54. The quotes are from BRUNI, p. 548 ("dilettossi di musica e di suoni . . . et di sua mano egregiamente disegnava"); at p. 540, referring to Dante's description of the battles of Campaldino in a lost letter already mentioned, Bruni states that Dante "draws the form of the battle" (it could have been a sketch attached to the letter).

55. On the practice of "clothing" (*rivestire*) lyrical texts with music, see GIUNTA, pp. 123–128. With regard to Dante's relationship with music, it should be emphasized, as pointed out at several points in *De vulgari eloquentia,* that music is an element within the poetical text, incorporated into its rhythmical and rhetorical structure, and therefore the figure of the poet combines grammatical, rhetorical, and musical skills, whereas the figure of the person appointed to compose the

actual notes of accompaniment is merely an external, secondary executor; for the intrinsic relationship between meter and music as described in *De vulgari,* some fundamental observations are made in TAVONI (in particular pp. 1490–1493). The encounter with Casella is told in *Purg.* II 76–133.

56. Dante also knew painters of renown: he seems to have been on familiar terms with the illuminator Oderisi da Gubbio (was he another of those he met in Bologna?), whose art was later superseded by a certain Franco Bolognese, about whom we know little; the same fate befell Cimabue, whose fame was outclassed by Giotto. In Florence, Dante could have seen Cimabue's *Maestà* at Santa Trinita and his *Crucifixion* at Santa Croce; he could also have seen his *Crucifixion* at San Domenico in Arezzo. He may have had some personal acquaintance with Giotto, who was the same age, and whose *Crucifixion* he would certainly have seen at Santa Maria Novella. This could have taken place in Rome in the Jubilee year, or in Padua between the end of 1303 and early 1304, during the period when Giotto was frescoing the Scrovegni Chapel. But this is mere conjecture. We cannot rely on an anecdote told by Benvenuto da Imola: when asked jokingly by Dante why he painted figures so beautiful yet produced such ugly children, Giotto is supposed to have answered: "Because I paint by day and procreate by night." The same anecdote, as Benvenuto moreover recognized, had indeed already been told, in relation to the painter Mallius, by the fifth century Roman writer Macrobius in a sort of encyclopedia entitled *Saturnali,* and Petrarch had also repeated it twice in his *Epistolae familiares.* For Oderisi (who died in 1299) I refer to the entry in ED by Isa Barsali Belli, and to Stefano Bottari, "Per la cultura di Oderisi da Gubbio e di Franco Bolognese," in *Dante e Bologna nei tempi di Dante,* edited by the Faculty of Literature and Philosophy of Bologna (Bologna: Commissione per i testi di lingua, 1967), pp. 53–59. The anecdote about Giotto's ugly children is to be found in Benvenuto's commentary on *Purg.* XI 94–96; Petrarch refers to Macrobius (2, 2, 10) in *Epistolae familiares* V 17 6–7; XIX 7 1. (Benvenuto seems to have been inspired by the first letter, where, in the passage referring to the anecdote about Mallius, the name Giotto appears among those painters known by Petrarch who were distinguished but not handsome.) For the biography of Giotto, I refer to the entry in DBI by Miklós Boskovits; for the possibility that he and Dante met in Padua, to INDIZIO[1], p. 41, and INDIZIO[2], pp. 256–257 (much more cautious).

57. The account of Dante drawing angels is told in *VN* 23, 1–3.

58. The phrases by Cennino are taken from *Libro dell'arte, o trattato della pittura di Cennino Cennini da Colle di Valdelsa,* republished with many corrections and the addition of further chapters taken from Florentine manuscripts, edited by Gaetano and Carlo Milanesi (Florence: Le Monnier, 1859), chs. IV, V, VI, VIII.

59. The suggestion that the place where Dante is drawing is an open workshop comes from Vincent Moleta, " 'Oggi fa l'anno che nel ciel salisti': una rilettura della *Vita nuova* XXVII–XXXIV," in GSLI 161 (1984): 78–104.

60. The account of the episode in Siena is in BOCCACCIO[1], 121–122; on the relationship between apothecaries and books, see ZINGARELLI, p. 161.

61. Several passages in Dante reveal a sure technical knowledge of colors and their preparation. Particularly enlightening in this respect is the detailed analysis of *Purg.* VII 73–75: "Gold and fine silver, cochineal and white lead, / Indian wood bright and clear, / fresh emerald at the moment it is split" ("Oro e argento fine, cocco e biacca, / indaco, legno lucido e sereno, / fresco smeraldo in l'ora che si fiacca") made by Ignazio Baldelli, "Dante e Giotto: il canto XXIII del *Paradiso*" in *Bibliologia e critica dantesca. Saggi dedicati a Enzo Esposito,* edited by Vincenzo De Gregorio (Ravenna: Longo, 1997) vol. 2: *Saggi danteschi,* pp. 203–224. Another significant passage is *VE* I XVI 5: "and the simplest color, which is white, makes its perfume felt in the yellow more than in the green" ("et simplicissimus color, qui albus est, magis in citrino quam in viride redolet"), "where the color analysis in the mixing of the paints seems almost that of an expert" (see ED, entry "Arti" by Fortunato Bellonzi).

62. In lines 64–66 of *Purg.* XII: "What master of brush and stylus / portrayed the shadows and features which there / cause subtle minds to marvel?" ("Qual di pennel fu maestro e di stile, / che ritraesse l'ombre e' tratti ch'ivi / mirar farieno un ingegno sottile?") Dante distinguishes between the painter (master of the brush) and the drawer (master of the stylus), and "rightly attributes the effect of the shadows to the brush and the 'features' to the stylus" (Valerio Mariani, "Dante e Giotto," in *Dante e Giotto,* proceedings of the study conference promoted by the Casa di Dante in Rome and by the Società Dante Alighieri, Rome, November 9–10, 1967 [Quaderni del Veltro, 7], 1968, pp. 5–18; quote at p. 17). With regard to shadows, commenting on *Para.* XXIV 24–27: "And so my pen leaps ahead and I do not write it: / for our image of such folds, / and our speech, is too brightly colored" ("Però salta la penna e non lo scrivo: / ché l'imagine nostra a cotai pieghe, / nonché 'l parlare, è troppo color vivo"), Iacomo della Lana observes: "note that the painter, when he wants to paint folds, is better off using a color less bright than that of the dress, therefore darker, and then the folds appear" ("Commento alla *Commedia,*" in Iacomo della Lana, *Commento alla "Commedia",* edited by Mirko Volpi, with the collaboration of Arianna Terzi (Rome: Salerno Editrice, 2010), vol. 4, p. 2371). There are also some very interesting remarks on Dante's skills in drawing and colors in ZINGARELLI, pp. 71–74.

63. Bear in mind, however, that the idea that Dante may have become a member of the Guild of Doctors and Apothecaries (Arte dei medici e degli speziali) for his possible associations with painters is firmly rejected by Michele Barbi, "Dante e l'Arte dei medici e speziali" (1924 and 1934), and then in BARBI[2], pp. 379–384.

64. There are some very interesting comments on the importance of philosophical studies at Bologna University toward the end of the 1200s in the introduction to FIORAVANTI.

65. Boccaccio's views on Cavalcanti are expressed in *Decameron* X 9, and in BOC-CACCIO³, X 62; so far as his fame as a scholar, Cavalcanti was a man "devoted to study" ("intento allo studio") according to Dino Compagni (COMPAGNI I XX); "philosopher, virtuous man in many things" ("filosafo, virtudioso uomo in più cose"), according to Giovanni Villani (VILLANI, IX XLII); "one of the best logicians in the world and an excellent natural philosopher" ("un de' miglior loici che avesse il mondo e ottimo filosofo natural") and also "excellent logician and good philosopher" ("ottimo loico e buon filosofo") according to BOCCACCIO³; "most able man and philosopher" ("valentissimo uomo e filosofo") according to Franco Sacchetti (*Il Trecentonovelle* LXVIII).

66. On Cavalcanti's possible role in encouraging Dante toward philosophy, see DAVIS, p. 10. The phrase about Cavalcante's unbelief tainting his son is from Contini, *Un'idea di Dante*, p. 143; in this respect see also Domenico De Robertis, *Dal primo all'ultimo Dante* (Florence: Le Lettere, 2001), p. 155. The followers of Averroes reject the immortality of the individual soul, and so it will be no coincidence that in *Purg.* XXV 64–65, at the very point where Statius refutes the doctrine of Averroes which "separated / the possible intellect from the soul" ("fè disgiunto / da l'anima il possibile intelletto"), there is a reappearance of the phrase from Cavalcanti's canzone *Donna me prega, per ch'eo voglio dire* 22–23: "that takes—in possible intellect, / as in subject,—place and dwelling" ("che prende—nel possibile intelletto, / come in subietto,—loco e dimoranza"), the "last but fairly evocative, polemical reference to Guido in the poem" (Contini, *Un'idea di Dante*, p. 155). *Donna me prega* is edited and commented by De Robertis in Cavalcanti, *Rime*.

67. The differences of position between Guido and Iacopo da Pistoia are examined by Sonia Gentili, *L'uomo aristotelico alle origini della letteratura italiana*, preface by Peter Dronke (Rome: Carocci, 2005), pp. 187–190. Guido's medical and philosophical ideas, and gloss by Dino del Garbo, are discussed in Natascia Tonelli, "'De Guidone de Cavalcantibus physic' (con una noterella su Giacomo da Lentini)," in *Per Domenico De Robertis. Studi offerti dagli allievi fiorentini*, edited by Isabella Becherucci, Simone Giusti, and Natascia Tonelli (Florence: Le Lettere, 2000), pp. 459–508, and in Enrico Fenzi, *La canzone d'amore di Guido Cavalcanti e i suoi antichi commenti* (Genoa: Il melangolo, 1999) (which also includes *Scriptum super cantilena Guidonis de Cavalcantibus* by Dino del Garbo, with Italian translation).

68. The account of his infidelity with the *Donna pietosa* occupies paras. 24–28 of the *Vita Nova*; his repentance is told in para. 28. The reason why he had not revealed the allegorical nature of that woman is set out in *Conv.* II XII 8; the date on which "that gentle lady whom I mentioned at the end of the *Vita Nova*, first appeared . . . to my eyes and took any place in my mind" ("quella gentile donna cui feci menzione nella fine della Vita nova parve primamente . . . alli occhi miei e prese luogo alcuno nella mia mente") is given in *Conv.* II II 1; it is followed (at II II 3)

by the statement: "But since love is not born and does not grow and become perfect straight away, but needs some time and nourishment of thought, especially where there are conflicting thoughts that get in the way, it required, before this new love was perfect, much strife between the thought that fed it and that which opposed it, which the fortress of my mind still kept for that glorious Beatrice ("Ma però che non subitamente nasce amore e fassi grande e viene perfetto, ma vuole tempo alcuno e nutrimento di pensieri, massimamente là dove sono pensieri contrari che lo 'mpediscano, convenne, prima che questo nuovo amore fosse perfetto, molta battaglia intra lo pensiero del suo nutrimento e quello che li era contrario, lo quale per quella gloriosa Beatrice tenea ancora la rocca della mia mente").

69. The second account in *Convivio* occupies the whole of para XII of book II. For the problem about how to reconcile the two timescales with which *Convivio* sets the start of his philosophical studies, I refer to SANTAGATA, pp. 114–118.

70. On the organization of the monastic *Studia* in Florence, see DAVIS, pp. 137–165, and FIORAVANTI. I also refer to DAVIS (pp. 260–288) for Remigio dei Girolami, for whom see also the entry in DBI by Sonia Gentili. The phrase quoted is from CARPI, p. 56: ("l'autentico campione religioso della cultura comunale, come Brunetto nella generazione precedente ne era stato il campione laico").

71. For Pietro di Giovanni Olivi and Ubertino da Casale, see the entries in ED by Raoul Manselli, and also Sergio Cristaldi, *Dante di fronte al gioachimismo. I. Dalla "Vita Nova" alla "Monarchia"* (Caltanissetta-Rome: Salvatore Sciascia Editore, 2002). In *Para.* XII 124–126, Bonaventura, having deplored the corruption in the Franciscan order, goes on to state that some friars are still faithful to the rule, but not Matteo nor Ubertino da Casale: "but not from Casal nor from Acquasparta, / who read the scripture in such a way / that for one it is too loose and for the other too narrow" ("ma non fia da Casal né d'Acquasparta / là onde vegnon tali a la scrittura, / ch'uno la fugge e altro la coarta").

72. Dante must have had direct experience of theological disputations if the simile of the bachelor is a reference to one of these: "As the bachelor arms himself and doesn't speak / until the master gives the question, / to argue it, not determine it, / thus did I arm myself with every reason / while she [Beatrice] spoke, to be prepared / for such a questioner and such a profession" ("Sì come il baccialier s'arma e non parla / fin che 'l maestro la question propone, / per approvarla, non per terminarla, / così m'armava io d'ogne ragione / mentre ch'ella dicea, per esser presto / a tal querente e a tal professione") (*Para.* XXIV 46–51). The bachelor was in fact the student in a faculty of theology who had to take the final exam for a medium-low level course (lower than the current doctorate). The master gave the question and the bachelor, having silently gathered together, within him, the dialectic "arms," produced the evidence, to "demonstrate" it; on a later date the master resumed the argument and completed it, "determined" it. Toward the end of his

life, Dante would be attributed the role of master in "determining" a *questio* of a scientific nature, but Dante's authorship of the so-called *Questio de aqua et terra* seems very unlikely.

73. The legal document showing that Dante was present in Florence on September 6, 1291, is in PIATTOLI, no. 51. Other possible evidence that Dante was in Florence between May 1291 and May 1292 comes from the exchange of sonnets between him, *Per quella via che la Bellezza corre* (*Rime* 51), and Aldobrandino dei Mezzabati of Padua (*Lisetta voi de la vergogna sciorre*), who was *capitano del popolo* in Florence during that period: the matter, however, is very complex and almost irresolvable (the terms of the problem are discussed by GIUNTA, pp. 625–630). For Bellino di Lapo Alighieri, see the entry in ED by Renato Piattoli. Gargan regards it as certain that Dante attended the *Studio* at Bologna between 1292 and 1294—Luciano Gargan, *Per la biblioteca di Dante,* GSLI, 186 (2009): 161–193, in particular 166–173—but see the review by Giuseppe Indizio, SD 75 [2010]: 370–373).

74. Public disputations—referred to as "de quolibet," i.e., on arguments proposed by anyone, including laymen, as they wished—were carried out with particular solemnity. One of these took place in 1295 at the *Studio* of Santa Maria Novella. A young layman, whose name is not given, submitted to the reader Petrus de Trabibus (Piero delle Travi/della Trave?), about whom we know very little, except that he was in touch with Olivi, a question that was not far removed from the cultural climate of a Dominican theological *Studio.* He asked to debate the subject "Whether secular sciences or intellectual goodness are beneficial to the sanctity of the soul" ("Utrum scilicet scientia humanarum litterarum vel bonitas intellectus conferat ad sanctitatem anime"). The subject was unusual, in the first place because these words (we have to imagine a written request sent to the reader, accepted by him, and then publicly debated) are in line—especially the reference to "goodness" (nobility) of the intellect—with certain statements of the new Paris philosophers and their Bologna students about the task of philosophy in carrying human intellectual capacities to perfection. In short, they denote a faith in human rationality that ought not to have been shared by a strictly theological vision. And secondly, it is unusual in referring to the secular sciences (scientia humanarum litterarum), which could also include rhetoric and poetry. It would almost seem as though the anonymous person who had formulated the *questio* was both poet and philosopher. No one can say that this anonymous person was Dante; but the array of interests underlying such a *questio* was certainly typical of Dante in the 1290s. It is a question that he—especially if he had been able to read or listen to certain philosophers in Bologna, such as Iacopo da Pistoia—could very well have submitted to the reader in theology at Santa Maria Novella (for all of this, see Sylvain Piron, "Le poète et le théologien: un rencontre dans le 'Studium' de Santa Croce," *Picenum Seraphicum. Rivista di studi storici e francescani* 19 [2000]: 87–134).

75. On the history of the writing and the date of the *Vita Nova,* I refer to SANTA-GATA, pp. 113–141.

76. Suggested "precedents" of the *Vita Nova* include late ancient and middle Latin prose verse, the autobiographical writings of Augustine, the Gospels, the hagiographies of saints (especially female saints), Occitan *vidas* and *razos,* the university practice of *divisio textus,* and the elegiac style mediated by Boethius. Each of these aspects certainly brought something to Dante's writing, but it is equally certain that he didn't wholly subscribe to any of these. A rapid but comprehensive survey of the various answers to the question about what genre the *Vita Nova* belongs to is provided by Stefano Carrai, *Dante elegiaco. Una chiave di lettura per la "Vita nova"* (Florence: Olschki, 2006), pp. 11–15.

77. The historic importance of equal dignity that Dante gives to vernacular verse writers and Latin poets was examined by Mirko Tavoni, "Il nome di poeta in Dante," in *Studi offerti a Luigi Blasucci dai colleghi e dagli allievi pisani,* edited by Lucio Lugnani, Marco Santagata, and Alfredo Stussi (Lucca: Maria Pacini Fazzi Editore, 1996), pp. 545–577.

78. In the *Vita Nova,* Aristotle (the "Philosopher") is referred to in 16, 2 and 30, 6; the greatest concentration of philosophical terms and concepts are found in paras 11, 6 and 12, 1 (distinction between "power" and "action").

79. The evidence suggesting a final hurried writing is considered by Valeria Bertolucci Pizzorusso, "La *Vita Nova* nella cronologia dantesca. Nuove considerazioni," *Studi Mediolatini e Volgari* 56 (2010): 5–25, and by SANTAGATA, pp. 119–124.

80. The discussion on the relationship between the *Vita Nova* and the *Commedia* would be different if it were established that the last paragraph had been written in a later period, in other words, that it was shown that both were being written at the same time: a first *Vita Nova* would have ended with the episode of the *Donna pietosa,* and the later chapters (or at least the last) would have been added, according to reconstructions, either after 1308 or after 1312. In short, the picture would alter if the end of the *Vita Nova* had been added after work had started on the *Commedia.* But none of these theories have so far found any philological support, given that there is no surviving trace of the supposed original manuscript draft. The old theories of Luigi Pietrobono and Bruno Nardi in favor of the overlap have been re-proposed in recent years by Maria Corti, *La felicità mentale. Nuove prospettive per Cavalcanti e Dante* (Turin: Einaudi, 1983), pp. 146–155.

3. Municipal Man

1. Ilaro's letter has been passed down through the manuscript in the Laurentian Library (Fondo Plutei 29, 8, c. 67r); I quote it from the publication by Saverio Bellomo, "Il sorriso di Ilaro e la prima redazione in latino della *Commedia,*" *Studi*

sul Boccaccio 32 (2004): 201–235; at pp. 206–209 (reproduced in SANTAGATA, pp. 391–393). The date of the events described in the letter, if not of the letter itself, can be gleaned from the information in it: Frederick III of Aragon assumed the title of "rex Cicilie," referred to here, instead of "rex Trinacrie," on August 9, 1314; Marchese Moroello Malaspina died on April 8, 1315; the events described can therefore be placed within a fairly narrow space of time. The idea, authoritatively supported by Giuseppe Billanovich ("La leggenda dantesca del Boccaccio. Dalla lettera di Ilaro al Trattatello in laude di Dante," in Billanovich, *Prime ricerche dantesche* (Rome, Edizioni di Storia e Letteratura, 1947), then in SD 28 [1949]: 45–144), that it was a rhetorical exercise by Boccaccio, and therefore a written invention devoid of any documentary value, has now been rejected thanks above all to the work of Giorgio Padoan (by whom, see the entry "Ilaro" in ED and PADOAN, pp. 5–23). Some scholars think it may be a letter actually sent by the Benedictine friar (those in favor of its authenticity, apart from Padoan, are PASQUINI, pp. 135–137, and CARPI, pp. 444–446). But we are still a long way from satisfactorily resolving the question. There are two opposing theories: one, against the authenticity of the letter and inclined to regard it as a practical exercise either by Giovanni del Virgilio or someone in his circle, supported by Saverio Bellomo ("Il sorriso di Ilaro,"), and another oriented, though with great caution, toward recognizing the good faith of Boccaccio as well as the historical plausibility of the text passed down by him, supported by Giuseppe Indizio ("L'epistola di Ilaro: un contributo sistemico," SD 71 [2006]: 191–263). Now, it is one thing to ascertain whether at least some of the historical and biographical details provided in the letter, and it alone, are reliable, and quite another thing to establish whether that letter, in the form in which it was transcribed by Boccaccio, can be traced back, wholly or partly, to the hand of the mysterious friar Ilaro. So far as the first point, there is no shortage of arguments in favor of its reliability. That a hermit of the Pulsanese order at Santa Croce al Corvo could have sent such a precious gift to the lord of Pisa, accompanied perhaps by a request for some favor or benefit, is not surprising, since the small hermitage had depended for many years on the Abbey of San Michele degli Scalzi in Pisa. Information on the monastery can be found in Eliana M. Vecchi, "Ad pacem et veram et perpetuam concordiam devenerunt." Il cartulario del notaio Giovanni di Parente di Stupio e l'*Instrumentum pacis* del 1306," *Giornale storico della Lunigiana e del territorio lucense* 59 (2008): 69–175, in particular pp. 146–148, which refers to the tradition of hospitality there, favored by its position on an important communication route. It should be added that Uguccione (who, moreover, was a soldier with a certain degree of learning: see Carla Maria Monti, "Uguccione della Faggiola, la battaglia di Montecatini e la *Commedia* di Dante," RSD 10 (2010): 127–159) must have been amenable to requests from a monastic order in which one of his brothers, Federico, was an abbot. In short, in the difficult situation in which the convent found itself—such that it would be abandoned during the second half of the 1300s—it is very likely that Ilaro sent the gift along with a request (the *petitio* no longer existing) for material support. The promised dedications of *Inferno* to Uguccione della Faggiola, of *Purgatorio* to Moroello Malaspina, and of *Paradiso* to Frederick of Aragon, dedications that have often been assumed as evidence of its falsity or, at least, of the historical improbability of the account (in particular in relation to Frederick, bearing in mind the hostility that Dante would show him in *Para.* XIX 130–135 and XX 61–63), could, however, weigh in favor of the opposite view. After the death of Henry VII (in August 1313), Uguccione and Frederick appeared indeed to be his heirs, and to be those who would continue his work; Malaspina, though Guelf, was a supporter of the empire and, above all, Dante's greatest patron. The writer of the letter is therefore well-informed about Dante's political positions in these months, and such information could not come from his writings which, if anything, would give other contradictory information. The profile of the author of the epistle doesn't fit with the typical picture of medieval forgers, but could a man of letters in a playful mood construct a picture such as this in the absence of special sources of information? Bellomo suggests that this is not "a malicious forgery" but "an exercise, and moreover light-hearted, without the slightest intent to deceive anyone." But this doesn't mean that the text transcribed by Boccaccio corresponds with that of the letter composed by Ilaro (or whoever else it might have been), and therefore that all of the information passed down by it has to be accepted. In the first place, there is a striking series of significant contradictions in the letter, pointed out by Alberto Casadei, "Considerazioni sull'epistola di Ilaro," in *Dante: Rivista Internazionale di Studi su Dante Alighieri,* vol. 8 (Pisa: Fabrizio Serro, 2011), pp. 11–22. Secondly, we don't know what and how many passages there were before it arrived in Boccaccio's hands: with no idea about its history, we cannot rule out the possibility that the text was tampered with or modified later. Finally, even accepting that the letter in its transcribed form corresponds substantially with what Ilaro had written, we have to ask to what extent a friar in a provincial hermitage (and also very ill-informed, seeing that he himself admitted he had received news of Dante from others—"quod accepi ab aliis") could have misrepresented the conversations heard and what else he might have forgotten or distorted when, sometime after the meeting, he summarized its content. Insofar as Dante's supposed claim that he had first written the *Commedia* in Latin and the justification that he had made the subsequent transition into the vernacular ("Sed cum presentis evi conditionem rependerem, vidi cantus illustrium poetarum quasi pro nicilo esse abiectos; et hoc ideo generosi homines, quibus talia meliori tempore scribebantur, liberales artes—pro dolor!—dimisere plebeis"), an objection can be made that, if it is true that the use of the vernacular "as choice for the public who are 'noble' (and inexpert in Latin)" is "the central argument used by Dante himself in crucial pages of *Convivio* and *De vulgari*" (CARPI, p. 444), the potential rhetorician or forger would have needed to have had access to those books. And in any event the argument could be reversed: bearing in mind the extremely limited availability of two unpublished treatises at the time of Boccaccio's transcription in the early 1340s, it could be used as evidence of authenticity.

2. Boccaccio quotes the hexameters both in *Trattatello,* where he summarizes the letter (BOCCACCIO[1], 192–194; BOCCACCIO[2], 132), as well as in *Esposizioni* (BOCCACCIO[3], *Accessus* 75–76). Their similarity to several lines of the eclogue responding to the poem of Giovanni del Virgilio ("Tunc ego: 'cum mundi circumflua corpora cantu / astricoleque meo, velut infera regna, patebunt,'" *Eg* II 48–49) can itself be a double-sided argument: it could be interpreted as a phenomenon of internal memory, but also as the result of an imitation by someone familiar with that poetic exchange. The balance, however, would tip strongly toward the suggestion of a forgery if, like Bellomo, we consider that those presumed introductory lines resemble the beginning of the poem by Giovanni del Virgilio: "Pyeridum vox alma, novis qui cantibus orbem / mulces letifluum, vitali tollere ramo / dum cupis, evolvens triplicis confinia sortis / indita pro meritis animarum— sontibus Orcum, / astripetis lethen, epyphebia regna beatis" (*Eg* I 1–5). The hexameters, in fact, have all the air of having been inserted to strengthen the idea that the *Commedia* had had a Latin genesis. In conclusion, one might agree with Casadei ("Considerazioni sull'epistola di Ilaro," p. 22) when he speaks "of manipulation and not of complete forgery."

3. Filippo Villani (*Expositio seu comentum super "Comedia" Dantis Allegherii,* edited by Saverio Bellomo [Florence: Le Lettere, 1989], Prefatio, 221–225) wrote: "I remember having heard it said by Giovanni Villani, the historian, my uncle and one-time friend and companion of Dante, that the poet had once declared how, when he compared his lines of Latin with those of Virgil, Statius, Horace, Ovid and Lucan, he seemed to be placing a coarse rag beside a purple cloth. Given however that he was aware of possessing the highest excellence in vernacular poetry, he applied all of his mind to this" ("Audivi, patruo meo Iohanne Villani hystorico referente, qui Danti fuit amicus et sotius, poetam aliquando dixisse quod, collatis versibus suis cum metris Maronis, Statii, Oratii, Ovidii et Lucani, visum ei fore iuxta purpuram cilicium collocasse. Cumque se potentissimum in rithmis vulgaribus intellexisset, ipsis suum accomodavit ingenium").

4. It has been said that in lines 66–71 of *Così nel mio parlar vogli'esser aspro* Dante "imagines being able at last to satisfy his desires . . . in terms so crude and brutal that perhaps have no parallels in the lyrical romance tradition" (GIUNTA, p. 509). The so-called "rime petrose" (stony poems), a cycle to which the canzone *Così nel mio parlar* belongs, date from the winter of 1296 due to the astrological periphrasis that opens the canzone *Io son venuto al punto della rota* (*Rime* 40, 1–9); the same astral conjunction described in the periphrasis was repeated at the end of 1304, but the earlier date is regarded as the more probable (see GIUNTA, p. 465).

5. For an analysis of Beatrice's rebukes and Dante's regret and, above all, the connection between her rebukes and the forgotten promise made at the end of the *Vita Nova*, see SANTAGATA, pp. 234–241. Guglielmo Gorni, in *Dante nella selva. Il primo canto della Commedia* (Parma: Pratiche Editrice, 1995), pp. 95–97, feels that Dante's "betrayal" of Beatrice was his failure to keep a promise, but identifies the book promised and too long delayed as the *Commedia*.

6. In *VN* 16, 6 Dante claims that vernacular verse can only be about love, unlike what others, such as Guittone, think; in *VN* 19, 10 he declares that he agrees with Cavalcanti about having to write only in vernacular.

7. The phrase quoted is by Gaetano Salvemini, *Magnati e popolani in Firenze dal 1280 al 1295. Seguito da "La dignità cavalleresca nel Comune di Firenze,"* introductory essay by Ernesto Sestan (Turin: Einaudi, 1960), p. 259.

8. The documents regarding Dante's enrollment in the guild, interventions in the Consiglio delle capitudini and in the Consiglio dei cento are found in PIATTOLI, nos. 53, 56, 79. For the organization of the Florentine collective bodies and for the stages in Dante's political career, see Michele Barbi, "L'ordinamento della repubblica fiorentina e la vita politica di Dante" (1899), then in BARBI[1], pp. 141–155. Dante's membership of the restricted or special council of the *capitano del popolo* is regarded as certain by Barbi, but also by PETROCCHI, pp. 64–65; a concise but clear reconstruction of the recorded interventions by Dante in the city councils is given by Ernesto Sestan, "Comportamento e attività di Dante in Firenze come uomo politico di parte," in *Il processo di Dante. Celebrato il 16 aprile 1966 nella Basilica di S. Francesco in Arezzo,* edited by Morris L. Ghezzi (Milan-Udine: Mimesis Edizioni, 2011), pp. 33–39.

9. The *gonfaloniere di giustizia* had been created by Giano della Bella's *Ordinamenti di giustizia,* along with the *podestà* and the College of Priors, as a move against the magnates.

10. On the founding value for the *Stilnovo* of the concept of "gentilezza" I refer to Marco Santagata, *I due cominciamenti della lirica italiana* (Pisa: Edizioni ETS, 2006), pp. 35–69. The poetry of Guinizelli can be read, with a commentary, in Guido Guinizzelli, *Rime,* edited by Luciano Rossi (Turin: Einaudi, 2002).

11. *Le dolci rime* would be collected and commented on in the fourth book of *Convivio;* lines 20–24 can be paraphrased as follows: "there was an emperor who claimed that nobility consisted of ancient family fortune accompanied by a refined tone of life." It is possible that Dante planned also to include *Poscia ch'Amor (Rime* 27) in *Convivio;* on this canzone and on its implications with the Florentine social context, see Claudio Giunta, *La poesia italiana nell'età di Dante. La linea Bonagiunta-Guinizzelli* (Bologna: il Mulino, 1998), pp. 279–284; GIUNTA, pp. 330–358; Enrico Fenzi, "'Sollazzo' e 'leggiadria.' Un'interpretazione della canzone dantesca *Poscia ch'Amor,"* SD 63 (1991, but printed in 1997): 191–280. With regard to those of false charm ("i falsi leggiadri"), read lines 20–57: "Sono che per gittar via loro avere /

credon potere / capere là dove li boni stanno . . . Qual non dirà fallenza / divorar cibo ed a lussuria intendere, / ornarsi come vendere / si dovesse al mercato d'i non saggi? . . . E altri son che, per esser ridenti, / d'intendimenti / correnti voglion esser giudicati / da quei che so' ingannati / veggendo rider cosa / che lo 'ntelletto cieco non la vede. / E' parlan con vocaboli eccellenti, / vanno spiacenti, / contenti che dal vulgo sian mirati; / non sono innamorati / mai di donna amorosa; / ne' parlamenti lor tengono scede [battute irridenti]; / non moveriano il piede / per donneare a guisa di leggiadro, / ma, come al furto il ladro, / così vanno a pigliar villan diletto / —e non però che 'n donne è sì dispento / leggiadro portamento— / che paiono animal sanza intelletto." The description quoted of the "leggiadro" is from Giunta, *La poesia italiana nell'età di Dante,* p. 352.

12. For the attitude of Brunetto and Lapo Saltarelli in the argument over the *grandi,* see CARPI, pp. 101–105. In the 1290s, shortly before his collaboration with Saltarelli, Dante must have felt well-disposed toward Giano della Bella; but his attitude would change, so that in *Paradiso* (XVI 127–132) he would display open malice toward a character who, though wearing the heraldic insignia of the "great baron" Hugh of Brandenburg, Marquis of Tuscany (tenth century), had betrayed his party by "gathering with the people" ("col popolo di rauni"). It was Dante's ideological position that had changed: by 1310 he had full sympathy for the feudal nobility and the knightly class (see also CARPI, pp. 100–101; GORNI, pp. 35–36).

13. On the political positions of Guido Cavalcanti, read Michele Barbi, "Guido Cavalcanti e Dante di fronte al governo popolare" (1920) (though not all of it can be agreed with), then BARBI[2], pp. 371–378. I must point out, however, that the hitherto accepted biography of Guido would be radically upset by the archive research of Francesco Velardi ("I 'due Guidi' Cavalcanti e la data di morte del necrologio di Santa Reparata", SD 72 [2007]: 239–263), research that is said to show that "the person who married the daughter of Farinata degli Uberti . . . was not Dante's friend but a 'second' Guido Cavalcanti, to whom the date of death relates (though it is August 29, 1310) recorded at 41r. of the Registro Obituario di S. Reparata" (p. 239). The sonnet by Dino Compagni to Cavalcanti is published and commented on in Guido Cavalcanti, *Rime. Con le rime di Iacopo Cavalcanti,* edited by Domenico De Robertis (Turin: Einaudi, 1986), pp. 211–214; De Robertis, in the introductory section (pp. 158–159), reviews the various suggested interpretations of *I' vegno 'l giorno a te 'nfinite volte.*

14. The quote on the radical difference between the conception of love in the *Vita Nova* and that in *Donna me prega* is from Domenico De Robertis, *Dal primo all'ultimo Dante* (Florence: Le lettere, 2001), p. 31. On the question as to whether Guido's canzone is a polemical response to the *Vita Nova,* there is now a substantial bibliography; see at least: Giuliano Tanturli, "Guido Cavalcanti contro Dante," in *Le tradizioni del testo. Studi di letteratura italiana offerti a Domenico De*

Robertis, edited by Franco Gavazzeni and Guglielmo Gorni (Milan-Naples: Ricciardi, 1993), pp. 3–13; Enrico Malato, *Dante e Guido Cavalcanti. Il dissidio per la "Vita Nuova" e il "disdegno" di Guido* (Rome: Salerno Editrice, 1997); Nicolò Pasero, "Dante in Cavalcanti," *Medioevo romanzo* 22 (1998): 388–414; Enrico Fenzi, *La canzone d'amore di Guido Cavalcanti e i suoi antichi commenti* (Genoa: Il melangolo, 1999).

15. The role of forerunner, but surpassed, is given to Guido in *VN* 15, forcing the interpretation of the occasional sonnet *Io mi senti' svegliar dentro allo core.*

16. The documents showing the debts are published by PIATTOLI, nos. 57, 58.

17. I take the information on the level of taxation necessary to be admitted to the Consiglio dei cento from DAVIDSOHN, III, p. 581; the calculation of how much 1,200 *libbre* or lire was worth in gold florins was done for me by Roberta Cella. Information on Dante's properties and their value are provided by Michele Barbi, *La condizione economica di Dante e della sua famiglia* (1892 and 1917), then in BARBI[1].

18. On the lands owned by Litto Corbizzi, see ZINGARELLI, p. 31; for Alamanno degli Adimari see DAVIDSOHN, IV, pp. 145, 149.

19. The will of Gemma's mother is in PIATTOLI, no. 113; the receipt issued by Iacopo Corbizzi in 1332 is in PIATTOLI, no. 155; the debt contracted by Francesco in 1299 is in PIATTOLI, no. 71; for other loans, see the documents in PIATTOLI, nos. 72, 74, 78, 85.

20. For the Cerchi family and for Vieri, see the entries in ED by Franco Cardini; for the Donati family and for Corso, those by Renato Piattoli and Ernesto Sestan. With regard to the property acquisitions of the Cerchi, in *Para.* XVI 94–99 Dante would write: "Over the gate [of San Piero] now laden/ with new cowardice [of the Cerchi] of such weight / that soon the ship will come to grief, // lived the Ravignani, from whom is descended / count Guido and whoever / of the noble Bellincione took his name" ("Sovra la porta ch'al presente è carca/ di nova fellonia di tanto peso / che tosto fia iattura de la barca, // erano i Ravignani, ond'è disceso / il conte Guido e qualunque del nome / de l'alto Bellincione ha poscia preso")—it should be remembered that Dante claimed that Alighiero I, his father's grandfather, had married a daughter of Bellincione. The accusation of cowardice against the Cerchi ("più per viltà che per piatà, perché temevano i loro avversari") is in COMPAGNI, I XXVII.

21. The account of events in Florence from 1295 to the coup of 1301 are in DAVIDSOHN, IV; the more accurate reconstruction of the interference by Bonifacio VIII in the political conflict in Florence is by Giuseppe Indizio, " 'Con la forza di tal che testé piaggia': storia delle relazioni tra Bonifacio VIII, Firenze e Dante," *Italianistica. Rivista di letteratura italiana* 39, no. 3 (2010): 69–96.

22. With regard to the judicial proceedings that involved Corso and Giovanna degli Ubertini di Gaville, an event that "stands out as a founding element in the

division of Florence during the late Duecento," see Giuliano Milani, "Appunti per una riconsiderazione del bando di Dante," *Bollettino di italianistica. Rivista di critica, storia letteraria, filologia e linguistic*, n.s. 8, no. 2 (2011): 42–70, in particular p. 56.

23. For the Acciaioli-Aguglione affair I refer to DAVIDSOHN, IV, pp. 102–105; for Cante dei Gabrielli, see the entry in ED, "Gabrielli da Gubbio, Cante de'" by Giuseppe Inzitari.

24. The salt scandal must have happened at around the same time as Baldo and Acciaioli were tampering with the trial records: friar Durante of the Chiaramontesi or Chermontesi magnate family, who held the office of superintendent for the sale of salt, made a large fortune by changing the measure of the wooden bushel used for distribution; Dante refers to the shame that it brought on the family in *Para.* XVI 105: "and those who blush for the bushel" ("e quei ch'arrossan per lo staio"); in this respect, see DAVIDSOHN, IV, pp. 105–106, and the entry in ED, "Chiaramontesi" by Arnaldo d'Addario.

25. Dante's declaration ("tutti e mali et tutti gl'inconvenienti miei dalli infausti comitii del mio priorato ebbono cagione et principio") is recorded by BRUNI, p. 542, who translates from the lost letter already mentioned.

26. Vieri dei Cerchi's reply to the pope ("fu poco savio, e troppo duro e bizzarro, che della richesta del papa nulla volse fare, dicendo che non avea guerra con niuno; onde si tornò in Firenze, e 'l papa rimase molto isdegnato contro a·llui e contro a sua parte") in VILLANI, IX XXXIX 75–89.

27. On the date of the assembly at Santa Trinita the sources do not agree: although Dino Compagni, an eyewitness to the events of those years, places it in 1301 (COMPAGNI, I XXIII), and despite the view of eminent Dante scholars like Isidoro del Lungo (*Dino Compagni e la sua Cronica* vol. 2, (Florence: Successori Le Monnier, 1879–1887), p. 111) and Michele Barbi, "Guido Cavalcanti e Dante di fronte al governo popolare" (1920), then in BARBI², pp. 376–377, I prefer to rely on the account of VILLANI (IX XXXIX), who seems to me to reconstruct events more consistently. The date of 1301 has recently been repeated by Milani, "Appunti per una riconsiderazione del bando di Dante," pp. 54–55.

28. The record of the session of the Consiglio generale in San Gimignano is in PIATTOLI, no. 73.

29. Bear in mind that the city statutes did not lay down the way in which the priors were to be elected, and therefore "the selection of the highest governing body was renegotiated every two months by a council formed by heads of the main city guilds and by elders chosen by the outgoing priors, who were present at the sitting" (Milani, "Appunti per una riconsiderazione del bando di Dante," p. 60).

30. The great Dante scholar referred to is Michele Barbi, *Vita di Dante* (Florence: Le Lettere, 1996), p. 15 (first edition 1933).

31. The legal document of delivery of the sentence in April is published in PIATTOLI, no. 75.

32. The words of protest of the magnates ("noi siamo quelli che demo la sconfitta in campaldino; e voi ci avete rimossi degli ucîci e onori della nostra città") are reported by COMPAGNI, I XXI; he too (I XXI) reports the attack on Matteo d'Acquasparta.

33. The biographer who speaks of Dante's sense of victory is PETROCCHI, p. 82.

34. On Boniface, see the entry in EP compiled by Eugenio Dupré Theseider, and Agostino Paravicini Bagliani, *Bonifacio VIII* (Turin: Einaudi, 2003), which makes little reference however to the role of the pope in Florentine affairs; extremely useful for Boniface and Florence is Indizio, " 'Con la forza di tal che testé piaggia.' "

35. The attitude of Iacopone is examined by Paravicini Bagliani, *Bonifacio VIII,* pp. 200–203. The line quoted ("Lucifero novello a sedere en papato") is taken from the laud, of disputed authorship, *O papa Bonifazio, molt'ài iocato al mondo* (Iacopone da Todi, *Laudi, Trattato e Detti,* edited by Franca Ageno (Florence: Le Monnier, 1953).

36. Life in Rome during the Jubilee is described by Arsenio Frugoni, *Pellegrini a Roma nel 1300. Cronache del primo Giubileo,* presentation by Chiara Frugoni, edited and with an introduction by Felice Accrocca (Casale Monferrato: Piemme, 1999). Frugoni also sets out the information on numbers present and the observations of chroniclers, namely Giovanni Villani, Guglielmo Ventura from Asti, and Cardinal Iacopo Caetani Stefaneschi, whose *De centesimo seu Jubileo anno liber* appears in Italian translation in the appendix. The quote about two hundred thousand pilgrims continually present in Rome is by VILLANI, IX XXXVI; the figure of two million pilgrims is provided by Guglielmo Ventura, that of thirty thousand entering and leaving each day from the anonymous *Annales Colmarienses* (all quoted by Frugoni at pp. 55–56). The more recent contribution is by Robert M. Durling, "Dante, le jubilé de l'an 1300 et la question des indulgences", *Revue des Études italiennes* 56 (2010): 5–17.

37. The hypothesis, prudently advanced by PETROCCHI, pp. 87–88, and cautiously repeated by Enrico Malato in *Dante* (Rome: Salerno Editrice, 1999) p. 46, that Dante went to Rome in November 1300 as the member of a Florentine diplomatic delegation is disputed by INDIZIO², pp. 283–285. The document regarding the loan made to Dante by his brother on March 14, 1300, is published by PIATTOLI, no. 71.

38. I refer here and in the next paragraph to the hypothesis on the Florentine genesis of the poem, which I have more fully discussed in SANTAGATA, pp. 293–316.

39. The chronology of the fictional journey is the subject of debate among Dante scholars (a short but thorough survey of the possible timescales of the poem's genesis is contained in the entry in ED, *"Commedia"* [para. 2] by Antonio Enzo Quaglio), while early commentaries were in agreement in placing it around the middle of March 1300: see the observations of INDIZIO³, pp. 226–236, and of Saverio Bellomo, " 'La natura delle cose aromatiche' e il sapore della *Commedia*: quel che ci

dicono gli antichi commenti a Dante," *Critica del testo* 14, no. 1 (2011): 531–553, in particular pp. 536–541.

40. The business of the road works is studied by Michele Barbi, "L'ufficio di Dante per i lavori di via S. Procolo" (1921), then in BARBI², pp. 385–413.

41. The sentence on the political scheme of *Convivio* quoted at p. 120 is taken from the introduction to FIORAVANTI; it is Fioravanti once again who points out that Dante would describe Rome as "santa cittade" also in *Conv.* IV V 20, but with a substantial difference compared to the "loco santo" of the *Commedia*: Rome would receive that name in *Convivio*, "not for having been the place of the martyrdom of Peter (and Paul) and for now being the seat of his successor, but rather for being the birthplace and seat of the highest political authority, directly ordained by God."

42. The definition of "Guelf formula" is to be found in Umberto Carpi, "Un *Inferno* guelfo," NRLI 13 (2010): 95–134, in particular p. 113, an essay fundamental for interpreting the whole canticle. PASQUINI, p. 163, also points out that in Canto II Dante "still sees the Roman Empire in effect in the papacy," but previously Parodi had written: "in the whole of *Inferno* there is no mention of the empire, except for one single time, almost in passing, in the well-known words of the second canto which, while they glorify it as preordained by God, they seem however to refuse to recognize that it has any purpose . . . Dante seems to conclude that the ultimate purpose of the foundation of Rome and the institution of the empire was to prepare its seat for the vicar of Christ" (Ernesto Giacomo Parodi, *La data della composizione e le teorie politiche dell'*Inferno *e del* Purgatorio [1905], then in Parodi, *Poesia e Storia nella* Divina Commedia, edited by Gianfranco Folena and Pier Vincenzo Mengaldo (Vicenza: Neri Pozza Editore, 1965), pp. 233–324; the quote ["a formula that couldn't be more Guelf"] is at pp. 253–254).

43. Boccaccio's account of the discovery of the seven cantos is in BOCCACCIO¹, 179–183 (substantially the same in BOCCACCIO², 179–182), and in BOCCACCIO³, VIII i 6–19.

44. Boccaccio is doubtful for two reasons: because of Ciacco's prophecy on the fall of the Whites in three years ("And the doubt is this: the author introduces Ciacco in Canto VI and makes him predict that on the third year, from the day he gives, the party to which Dante belonged would come to an end and would be banished from the state; which is what happened, so that, as he said, the loss of the state of the White party and the departure [of Dante] from Florence was all one; and yet, if the author left at the predicted time, how could he have written this? And not only this, but one more canto?" ["E il dubbio è questo: introduce nel VI canto l'autore ciacco e fagli predire come, avanti che il terzo anno, dal dì che egli dice, finisca, conviene che caggia dello stato suo la setta, della quale era Dante; il che così avvenne, per ciò che, come detto, il perdere lo stato la setta Bianca e il

partirsi [di Dante] di Firenze fu tutto uno; e però, se l'autore si partì all'ora pre-
mostrata, come poteva egli avere scritto questo? E non solamente questo, ma un
canto più?"]), and because of the fact that Frescobaldi had circulated copies of the
"little notebook" when there is absolutely no trace of those copies (BOCCACCIO[3],
VIII I 14–15). On Dino di Lambertuccio Frescobaldi and his production of
verse, see Dino Frescobaldi, *Canzoni e sonetti,* edited by Furio Brugnolo (Turin:
Einaudi, 1984).

45. There is extensive debate on the reliability of Boccaccio's account, however
much it was conditioned by the judgment of being "legendary," given by Billanovich, "La leggenda dantesca del Boccaccio." I propose only to indicate the most
important contributions that give credibility to Boccaccio, and therefore to the
idea that the genesis of the *Commedia* is Florentine: particularly authoritative is
the view, expressed in 1904 by Michele Barbi ("Una nuova opera sintetica su Dante,"
then in BARBI[1], pp. 29–85, in particular pp. 69–72) in a review to ZINGARELLI,
according to which Boccaccio's account has the basis of truth and it is therefore
credible that Dante began "a poem like the *Commedia,* I don't say the *Commedia* as
such as we know it, before his exile," that he had interrupted it and then resumed
it (and this would be the actual *Commedia*) in the Lunigiana. But in 1934, when he
read the review by BARBI[1], the scholar changed his view and stated "that, even if
Dante could, before being banished from Florence, devise and commence something more complex than sonnets and canzoni in praise of glorious Beatrice in
heaven, the idea for the poem as we know it" belongs "to his exile," p. 69. The
most fervent supporter of the Florentine genesis of the poem is Giovanni Ferretti,
I due tempi della composizione della Divina Commedia (Bari: Laterza, 1935); in recent
times, this view has been accepted by Cesare Garboli, *Pianura proibita* (Milan:
Adelphi, 2002), pp. 152–163; CARPI, *passim* and, above all, Carpi, "Un *Inferno* guelfo."
PADOAN, pp. 25–37, and PASQUINI, pp. 6–8, give credit to Boccaccio, except for
relating his account with the problem of the presumed poem in Latin. Separate
consideration has to be given to the position of Raffaele Pinto, "Indizi del disegno
primitivo dell'*Inferno* (della *Commedia*): *Inf.* VII–XI," *Tenzone* 12 (2011): 105–152, who
advances the "suggestion of a double structural design of *Inferno,* the first operating up to canto VI, the second (and final) operating from canto VIII," a change
of plan that took place while work was in progress, but not referable to the time
break suggested by an earlier Florentine draft (besides, Pinto fully shares Billanovich's view about the Boccaccio "legend").

46. The intelligent reader quoted is Garboli, *Pianura proibita,* p. 158.

47. The features that differentiate the cantos preceding the city of Dis from
those after are listed above all by Ferretti, *I due tempi della composizione della Divina
Commedia;* by Edward Moore, *Studies on Dante,* 2nd series (Oxford: Clarendon,
1899), pp. 170–174; and from a different viewpoint, by Luigi Blasucci, "Per una

tipologia degli esordi nei canti danteschi," *La parola del testo,* 4 (2000): 17–46, and Pinto," Indizi del disegno primitivo dell'*Inferno*".

48. The anonymity of Celestine V contrasts strongly with the assertive words with which the character is introduced: "I saw and knew the shade of him / who by cowardice made the great refusal" ("vidi e conobbi l'ombra di colui / che fece per viltade il gran rifiuto"; *Inf.* III 59–60): "I saw and knew" in its Latin form ("vidi et cognovi") was the technical legal formula used by a lawyer or a judge to confirm he had seen something with his own eyes, in particular for confirming the presence and identity of the defendants, or their absence. The use of this formula, far from going to prove that Dante had actually met the pope in life, seems, on the contrary, to be a way of giving greater credibility to his recognition. It is not at all necessary, therefore, to suggest that Dante had personally met Celestine, perhaps in Naples in October 1294 as a member of the Florentine delegation (on this question, see PETROCCHI, pp. 61–62). It should be pointed out, however, that Dante couldn't have seen Mount Cacume (or Caccume), recalled in *Purg.* IV 26, from Anagni during the embassy to Boniface VIII in 1301, because at the time when the embassy took place the pope wasn't residing in his home city but at Rome in the Lateran. The other unanswered problem is why at the moment of publication of *Inferno,* after 1313, Dante hadn't intervened on the canto, given that Clement V had that year proclaimed Celestine a saint: it is indeed impossible that he could have placed a saint canonized by the Church in Hell: on this question, see Giorgio Petrocchi, *Itinerari danteschi,* introduced and edited by Carlo Ossola (Milan: Franco Angeli, 1994) [first edition Bari: Laterza, 1969], pp. 41–59.

49. The identification of Ciacco as a courtier is done by *Ottimo commento,* of which see the third and final version: "This Ciacco was of the city of Florence, a courtier, and behaved to gentlemen with much charm, and the author saw him in life and he was most corrupted by the vice of gluttony, which is the true vice of such kind of people" ("Questo Ciacco fue della cittade di Firenze, huomo di corte, et usoe con li gentili huomeni leggiadramente, e l'auctore il vide in vita et fue molto corrocto al vitio della gola, il quale è proprio vitio di così facta gente"). The latest edition is: *Ottimo commento. Chiose sopra la Comedia di Dante Alleghieri fiorentino tracte da diversi ghiosatori. Inferno,* critical edition by Claudia Di Fonzo (Ravenna: Longo Editore, 2008) p. 97), and with a rather different emphasis, from Boccaccio, apart from in *Decameron* IX 8, in *Esposizioni:*

"This man was not exactly a courtier; but, since he had little to spend and he had, as he himself says, taken totally to the vice of gluttony, he was a man of wit and always spent his time with wealthy gentlemen, especially with those who ate and drank lavishly and finely" ("Fu costui uomo non del tutto di corte; ma, per ciò che poco avea da spendere erasi, come egli stesso dice, dato del tutto al vizio della gola, era morditore e le sue usanze erano sempre co' gentili uomini e ricchi, e massimamente con quelli che splendidamente e delicatamente mangiavano e beveano") (BOCCACCIO³, VI I 25). On the figure of Ciacco and on his role in the *Commedia*, there are some very interesting and pertinent observations by André Pézard in the entry under that heading in ED.

50. Dante asks Ciacco: "Farinata and Tegghiaio, who were so worthy, / Iacopo Rusticucci, Arrigo and Mosca / and the others so set on doing good, / tell me where they are" ("Farinata e 'l Tegghiaio, che fuor sì degni, / Iacopo Rusticucci, Arrigo e 'l Mosca / e li altri ch'a ben far puoser li 'ngegni, / dimmi ove sono"), and Ciacco replies: "They are among the blacker souls; / different sins weigh them down to the bottom: / if you carry on down, you'll see them there" ("Ei son tra l'anime più nere; / diverse colpe giù li grava al fondo: / se tanto scendi, là i potrai vedere"; *Inf.* VI 79–82, 85–87).

51. His scorn for the Adimari ("arrogant breed") is fully expressed in *Para.* XVI 115–118, where Dante accuses them of being haughty to the weak and servile to the strong, and reminds them of their humble origins.

52. The phrase on Tegghiaio degli Adimari ("cavaliere savio e prode in arme e di grande autoritate") is in VILLANI, VII LXXVII; the portrait of Argenti ("alcuna volta fece il cavallo, il quale usava di cavalcare, ferrare d'ariento e da questo trasse il sopranome") is in BOCCACCIO³, VIII I 68.

53. For the story of Paolo and Francesca and for Canto V, I refer to Antonio Enzo Quaglio, *Al di là di Francesca e Laura* (Padua: Liviana, 1973); Ignazio Baldelli, *Dante e Francesca* (Florence: Olschki, 1999); CARPI, pp. 700–701; SANTAGATA, pp. 312–316. The many interpretations of the canto are reviewed by Lorenzo Renzi, *Le conseguenze di un bacio. L'episodio di Francesca nella "Commedia" di Dante* (Bologna: il Mulino, 2007). The quote from Andrea Cappellano ("Nam constat homicidium et adulterium inde saepius provenire . . . Sed et constat, incestus inde maxime provenire; non enim reperitur aliquis adeo divinis eloquiis eruditus, si maligno spiritu concitante amoris aculeis incitetur, qui contra mulieres cognatas sibi et affines ac Deo dedicatas feminas sciat unquam frena continere luxuriate") is taken from *De amore,* edited by Graziano Ruffini (Milan: Guanda, 1980), p. 298.

4. Condemned to the Stake

1. For the reconstruction of events in this chapter, the main sources of reference are DAVIDSOHN, IV and Giuseppe Indizio, " 'Con la forza di tal che testé piaggia': storia delle relazioni tra Bonifacio VIII, Firenze e Dante," *Italianistica. Rivista di letteratura italiana* 39, no. 3 (2010): 69–96.

2. The summary of the lost letter ("A questo risponde Dante che, quando quelli da Serezzana furono rivocati, esso era fuori dell'oficio del Priorato et che a lui non si debba imputare. Più dice, che la ritornata loro fu per la infirmità et morte di Guido Cavalcanti, il quale ammalò a Serezzana per l'aere cattiva et poco appresso morì") is in BRUNI, pp. 544–545.

3. For the distinction between Whites and Blacks see the "Cerchi" entry in ED by Franco Cardini. The events in Pistoia are recounted by DAVIDSOHN, IV, pp. 202–206.

4. The conviction against Dante is published in PIATTOLI, no. 90 (there is a partial Italian translation in *Il processo di Dante. Celebrato il 16 aprile 1966 nella Basilica di S. Francesco in Arezzo,* edited by Morris L. Ghezzi (Milan-Udine: Mimesis Edizioni, 2011), pp. 23–26).

5. The document regarding Dante's interventions in the Consiglio delle Capitudini of April 14 is in PIATTOLI, nos. 81, 82.

6. For the complex affair involving Margherita Aldobrandeschi, see Agostino Paravicini Bagliani, *Bonifacio VIII* (Turin: Einaudi, 2003), pp. 37, 48, 140, 194–195, and CARPI, *passim.*

7. The heart of Henry of Cornwall had been taken to London, where he was still held in honor when Dante wrote: "That one cleft in the bosom of God / his heart that still drips blood upon the Thames" ("Colui fesse in grembo a Dio / lo cor che 'n su Tamisi ancor si cola"; *Inf.* XII 119–120): for the murder in Viterbo see CARPI, pp. 336–341.

8. The documents on Dante's interventions in the various councils in PIATTOLI, nos. 83, 84, 86, 87, 88.

9. For the story of events in Florence during the months between June 1301 and summer of 1302, I rely essentially on DAVIDSOHN, IV and Indizio, "'Con la forza di tal che testé piaggia.'"

10. The quote ("Demo loro intendimento di trattare pace, quando convenìa arrotare i ferri") is taken from COMPAGNI, II V.

11. It is recorded that in 1301 Boniface VIII stayed at the Lateran from October 11 to December 27: see Agostino Paravicini Bagliani, "La mobilità della curia romana nel secolo XIII. Riflessi locali," in Società e istituzioni dell'Italia comunale: l'esempio di Perugia (secoli XII–XIV)," Congresso Storico Internazionale (Perugia 6–9 November 1985), Perugia, Deputazione di storia patria per l'Umbria, 1988, vol. 1, pp. 155–278.

12. For Musciatto Franzesi, see CARPI, pp. 146–147; the description of "evil" ("malvagio") in COMPAGNI, II IV; Musciatto, "a very prosperous and great merchant in France" is the one who, on having to follow Charles of Valois to Tuscany, appointed the notary Cepparello da Prato, nicknamed Ciappelletto, to collect the loans owing to him by "several Burgundians" (Boccaccio, *Decameron* I 1). For Maghinardo see the heading in ED, "Pagani, Maghinardo" by Arnaldo d'Addario.

13. About Saltarelli, Dante would write: "A Cianghella would have been held then in such wonder, / or a Lapo Santarello, / as Cincinnatus or Cornelia would now be" ("Saria tenuta allor tal meraviglia / una Cianghella, un Lapo Saltarello, / qual or saria Cincinnato e Corniglia"; *Para.* XV 127–129).

14. On Gherardino da Gambara, see the DBI entry, "Gambara, Gherardo" by Gabriele Archetti.

15. The quote is from CARPI, p. 488.

16. The information on the financial crisis caused by the exodus of the Whites is described by DAVIDSOHN, IV, pp. 297–304. With regard to Vieri's 600,000 florins, by way of comparison, it is worth recalling that on May 3, 1297, close to the tomb of Cecilia Metella on the Appian Way, in what Jean-Claude Maire Viguer has described as "one of the greatest armed robberies of all time," Stefano Colonna of Palestrina raided a convoy that was carrying around 200,000 florins belonging to Boniface VIII: it was the event that sparked off the war which ended with the destruction of Palestrina. That vast fortune consisted of the savings amassed by a greedy and unscrupulous man like Boniface over thirteen years as cardinal. Remember also that "in 1313 the revenues of the city of Pisa totaled the astonishing figure of 240,000 florins and that at the end of the thirteenth century a budget of 20,000 florins was enough to cover the ordinary expenses of a city like Perugia": see Jean-Claude Maire Viguer, *L'autre Rome: une histoire des Romains à l'époque des communes. XIIe–XIVe siècle* (Tallandier: Paris, 2010), pp. 241–243.

17. An analysis of the negative effects that the exile of the Whites caused to the Florentine cultural fabric may be found in Giuseppe Billanovich, "Tra Dante e Petrarca," IMU, 8 [1965]: 1–43.

18. The main personalities in the events that took place between 1300 and 1302 in Florence—events that seem momentous if read from Dante's viewpoint, but which in reality had no major effect on the international political panorama of the time—had no great future success. Charles of Valois, having carried out his "policing" operation between March and April 1302, left Florence and went to fight in Sicily on behalf of the pope and Charles II of Anjou, against Frederick III of Aragon. It was unsuccessful, so that the king of Naples had to resign himself, after years and years of war, to accepting a peace (at Caltabellotta on August 29, 1302) that deprived him of Sicily forever. In *VE* (II VI 4) Dante—who calls Valois the "second Totila" because, like the first Totila, king of the Goths, he too had destroyed Florence—would write: "Having snatched the greater part of the flowers from your breast, o Florence, the second Totila advanced in vain toward Trinacria" ("Eiecta maxima parte florum de sino tuo, Florentia, nequicquam Trinacriam Totila secundus adivit"), repeating what must then have been commonly said among his contemporaries; Villani would recall how he was mocked with words such as "Messer Charles came to Tuscany as peacemaker, and left the city at war; then went to Sicily to make war, and brought a shameful peace" ("Messer Carlo venne in Toscana per paciaro, e lasciòe il paese in guerra; e andòe in Cicilia per fare guerra, e reconne vergognosa pace"; VILLANI, IX I 1). The Cerchi, who for a few years were lords of the city, lost all their power in exile; the victorious Donati soon

found themselves quarreling with the new faction into which the Blacks had become divided, lead by the Della Tosa or Tosinghi, and they too, on the death of Corso (in 1308), would leave the scene; the Della Tosa would never manage to impose a lasting hegemony. Florentine political life in the twelve and thirteen hundreds was one of continual flux, of an endless succession of winners and losers: the city's *Ordinamenti di giustizia,* so long as they lasted, constantly prevented any family dynasty from achieving a stable leadership. BOCCACCIO[3] (VII I 63) would write: "In our times the Cerchi, the Donati, the Tosinghi and others were in such a position in our city that they governed small and large affairs as they wished and according to their pleasure, whereas today they are hardly remembered; and it is this power passed down in families, who were once unknown: and so it must be expected that it will pass from those who govern now on to others." ("Furon de' nostri dì i Cerchi, i Donati, i Tosinghi e altri in tanto stato nella nostra città, che essi come volevano guidavano le piccole cose e le grandi secondo il piacer loro, ove oggi appena è ricordo di loro; ed è questa grandigia trapassata in famiglie, delle quali allora non era alcun ricordo: e così da quegli, che ora son presidenti, si dee credere che trapasserà in altri.")

19. The reconstruction of Dante's movements made by BRUNI, p. 546, is almost entirely accepted by INDIZIO[2], pp. 283–285.

20. For the attempt by Cardinal d'Acquasparta at reconciliation, see DAVIDSOHN, IV, pp. 267–274.

21. The sentence of January 27, with regard to the charges, reads: "ad aures nostra set curie nostre notitia, fama publica referente, pervenit, quod predicti, dum ipsi vel aliquis eorum existentes in offitio prioratus vel non existentes vel ipso offitio prioratus deposito, temporibus in inquisizione contentis, commiserunt per se vel alium baractarias, lucra illicita, iniquas extorsiones in pecunia vel in rebus. Et quod ipsi vel aliquis ipsorum receperunt pecuniam vel res aliquas vel scriptam libri vel tacitam promissionem de aliqua pecunia vel re pro aliqua electione aliquorum novorum priorum et vexilliferi seu vexilliferorum facienda, licet sub alio nomine vel voce. Et quod ipsi vel aliquis eorum recepissent aliquid indebite, illicite vel iniuste pro aliquibus offitialibus erigendi vel ponendis in civitate vel comitatu Florentie vel districtu vel alibi, pro aliquibus stantia mentis, reformationibus vel ordinamentis faciendis vel non faciendis, vel pro aliquibus apodixis missis ad aliquem rectorem vel offitialem comunis Florentie vel concessis alicui. Et quod propterea dedissent, promisissent vel solvissent seu dari vel solvi fecissent in pecunia vel in rebus vel scriptam libri alicuius mercatoris fecissent, offitio durante vel eo deposito. Et super eo quod recepissent a camera comunis Florentie vel de domo et palatio priorum et vexilliferi ultra vel aliter quam comunis Florentie stantiamenta dictent. Et quod commiserint vel commicti fecerint fraudem vel baractariam in pecunia vel rebus comunis Florentie, vel quod darentur sive expenderentur contra summun pontificem et d. Karolum pro resistentia sui ad-

centus vel contra statum pacificum civitatis Florentie et partis guelforum. Quodque ipsi vel ipsorum aliquis habuissent vel recepissent aliquid in pecunia vel rebus ab aliqua spetiali persona, collegio vel universitate occasione vel ratione aliquarum minarum consussionis terrarum, quas vel quos intulissent vel de inferendo per priores, comune et populum minati essent. Super eoque quod commisissent vel commicti fecissent vel fieri fecissent fraudem, falsitatem, dolum vel malitiam, baractariam vel inlicitam extorsionem; et tractassent ipsi vel ipsorum aliquis quod civitas Pistorii divideretur et scinderetur infra se et ab unione quam habebant insimul; et tractassent quod anziani et vexilliferi dicte civitatis Pistorii essent ex una parte tantum; fecissentque tractari, fieri seu ordinari expulsionem de dicta civitate eorum qui dicuntur Nigri, fidelium devotorum sancte Romane ecclesie; dividi quoque fecissent dictam civitatem ab unione et volutate civitatis Florentie et subiectione sancte Romane ecclesie vel d. Karoli in Tuscia paciari" (PIATTOLI, no. 90). All the sentences of conviction in 1302 are collected in a parchment register known as *Il libro del chiodo,* into which are also transcribed the convictions against the Ghibellines of 1268 and other documents such as the Baldo d'Aguglione reform of September 2, 1311. The latest edition is: *Il libro del chiodo,* facsimile reproduction with critical edition by Francesca Klein, in collaboration with Simone Sartini, introduction by Riccardo Fubini (Florence: Edizioni Polistampa, 2004); the sentence of March 10 is also found in PIATTOLI, no. 91, while all other sentences of conviction of 1302 can be found in Maurizio Campanelli, "Le sentenze contro i Bianchi fiorentini del 1302," *Bullettino dell'istituto storico italiano per il Medio evo,* 108 (2006): 187–377. On the criteria by which the sentences against the Ghibellines and those relating to the conflicts between Whites and Blacks were collected together in the fourteenth century (of which *Il libro del chiodo* is the third in order of time) and the underlying political reasons, essential reading is Giuliano Milani, "Appunti per una riconsiderazione del bando di Dante," *Bollettino di italianistica. Rivista di critica, storia letteraria, filologia e linguistic,* n.s. 8, no. 2 (2011): 42–70; see pp. 43–49.

22. There is one detail in the sentences handed out that seems of little relevance to us today, but which to a Florentine of that period must have seemed not just strange, but an insult. Cante's sentences of January, February, and March are dated "dalla Natività" and not "dall'Incarnazione": the first style of dating began the year on Christmas Day, whereas the second began it on March 25, the Feast of the Annunciation, and therefore of Christ's Incarnation. The second style, from the Incarnation, was the one used in Florence in the Middle Ages, and it was so typical of the city (where it remained in use from the tenth century until 1749) that it was known as the "Florentine style." That of the Nativity, on the other hand, was used in the Papal States, but only under the papacy of Boniface VIII. Cante dei Gabrielli came from Gubbio, and his notaries and registrars were Umbrian: it was therefore natural for them to count from the Nativity, but to do so in Florence when it had such a strong political connotation seems like blatant provocation. It would

be as if judges in Florence today were to hand out judgments dated according to a calendar that put March 24, 2012 into the year 2011.

23. On the date of the meeting at Gargonza and the effects it must have had in aggravating the Black repression, the question has been clarified by Guido Pampaloni, "I primi anni dell'esilio di Dante," in *Conferenze aretine 1965* (Arezzo: Zilli, 1966), pp. 133–145; Pampaloni, "I primi tempi dell'esilio. Da Gargonza a S. Godenzo. L'Universitas Partis Alborum e il 'governo' bianco in Arezzo," in *Il processo di Dante*, pp. 45–47. The "shocking" effect of the alliance between the Whites and the Ghibellines is the subject of a careful study by CARPI, pp. 483–488. For fundamental observations on the substantial difference between convictions for barratry handed out in March 1302 and the convictions later on, relating to "criminal conduct more explicitly directed against the city and its government," see Milani, "Appunti per una riconsiderazione del bando di Dante," pp. 56–64.

5. At War with Florence

1. On the great Guidi family, see Ernesto Sestan, "I conti Guidi e il Casentino," an essay from 1956 in Ernesto Sestan, *Italia medievale* (Naples: ESU, 1968), pp. 356–378.

2. Information about the Ubaldini in the ED entry by Renato Piattoli. For Uguccione della Faggiuola (or Faggiola) I refer to Carla Maria Monti, "Uguccione della Faggiola, la battaglia di Montecatini e la *Commedia* di Dante," RSD 10 (2010): 127–159 and the DBI entry by Christine E. Meek.

3. The betrayal of Carlino dei Pazzi is told by DAVIDSOHN, IV, pp. 318–319; the damned soul of Camicione speaks to Dante in *Inf.* XXXII 66–69.

4. For a reconstruction of the history of the Whites immediately after their exile, see: DAVIDSOHN, IV; Guido Pampaloni, "I primi anni dell'esilio di Dante," in *Conferenze aretine 1965* (Arezzo: Zilli, 1966), pp. 133–145; Giuseppe Indizio, "Sul mittente dell'epistola I di Dante (e la cronologia della I e della II)," RSD 2 (2002): 134–145, and also: Giorgio Petrocchi, "La vicenda biografica di Dante nel Veneto," in Giorgio Petrocchi, *Itinerari danteschi,* introduced and edited by Carlo Ossola (Milan: Franco Angeli, 1994; first edition Bari: Laterza, 1969), pp. 88–103, and Francesco Bruni, *La città divisa. Le parti e il bene comune da Dante a Guicciardini* (Bologna: il Mulino, 2003), to which I refer for Ildebrandino Bishop of Arezzo and for the practice among exiles of establishing *universitates* (pp. 54–56). For Vieri dei Cerchi's move to Arezzo, see Cino Rinuccini, *Ricordi (1282–1460)* (Florence: Piatti, 1840), p. vii: "On the 4th day of April 1302 Messer Vieri de' Cerchi was expelled from Florence and all his family, and all the assets of the said Messer Vieri were seized and held by the city, and he went to Arezzo and issued an announcement that anyone who owed him money should send it there and he would be duly paid; and so each one was paid, and it is said he paid out more than 80,000 florins, and it is said his

wealth was more than 600,000 florins." ("A dì 4 d'Aprile 1302 fu cacciato di Firenze Messer Vieri de' Cerchi e tutti i suoi consorti, e confiscato tutti i beni di detto Messer Vieri e messi in comune, il quale se n'andò a Arezzo e vi mandò un bando, che qualunche avessi avere da lui, mandassi là e sarebbe pagato cortesemente; e così fece pagare ognuno, e dicesi che pagò più di 80.000 fiorini, e dicesi che fu ricco di più di 600.000 fiorini.")

5. The contract signed at San Godenzo is published by PIATTOLI, no. 92.

6. The military career of Moroello Malaspina can be summarized as follows: "he was *capitano* of Florence in 1288 against the Ghibellines of Arezzo, *capitano generale di guerra* of the Guelfs of Bologna against the Este in 1297 and later *podestà*. Then *capitano generale* for Matteo Visconti in the league against the marchesi of Monferrato and their allies in 1299, *capitano generale* of the Black Guelf party of Lucca and Florence against Pistoia between 1302 and 1306, *capitano del popolo* of Pistoia" (Eliana M. Vecchi, *Alagia Fieschi marchesa Malaspina. Una "domina" di Lunigiana nell'età di Dante* [Lucca: Maria Pacini Fazzi Editore, 2003], p. 40); there is a full entry on Moroello in the DBI by Enrica Salvatori. Vanni Fucci would predict to Dante: "Mars shall draw steam from Val di Magra / which is wrapped in thick clouds, / and with swift and raging violence / will battle over Campo Piceno; / whence suddenly he will rend the mist / so that every White will be stricken by it" ("Tragge Marte vapor di Val di Magra / ch'è di torbidi nuvoli involuto; / e con tempesta impetüosa e agra / sovra Campo Picen fia combattuto; / ond' ei repente spezzerà la nebbia, / sì ch'ogne Bianco ne sarà feruto"; *Inf.* XXIV 145–150).

7. For Scarpetta Ordelaffi, see the "Ordelaffi" entry in ED by Augusto Vasina.

8. The chronicler who refers to the cruelty of Fulcieri da Calboli is VILLANI, IV LIX. In *Purg.* XIV 58–63, Guido del Duca says to Rinieri da Calboli: "I see your nephew who's become / a hunter of those wolves [the Whites] along the banks / of the fierce river [Arno], and he frightens them all. / He sells their flesh while it's still alive; / then he kills them like aging cattle; / he deprives many of life and himself of merit." ("Io veggio tuo nepote che diventa / cacciator di quei lupi in su la riva / del fiero fiume, e tutti li sgomenta. / Vende la carne loro essendo viva; / poscia li ancide come antica belva; / molti di vita e sé di pregio priva.")

9. With regard to the Polentani, alongside Scarpetta is "Bernardino da Polenta, *podestà* and lord of Cervia, brother of Francesca, and also husband in due course of a certain Maddalena Malatesta, sister of Gianciotto and Paolo" (CARPI, pp. 623–624).

10. On Aghinolfo di Romena, see the entry in DBI, "Guidi, Aghinolfo," by Marco Bicchierai.

11. For the biography of Benedict XI, I refer to the entry in EP by Ingeborg Walter.

12. For the Cione di Bello and Cione di Brunetto, see the entries in ED by Renato Piattoli.

13. The quote regarding Gemma ("Lasciatavi la sua donna, insieme con l'altra famiglia, male per picciolà età alla fuga disposta, di lei sicuro, perciò che di con-sanguineità la sapeva ad alcuno de' prencipi della parte avversa congiunta, di se medesimo or qua or là incerto, andava vagando per Toscana") is by BOCCACCIO[1], 72; the reference to "holy places" ("luoghi sacri") is in BOCCACCIO[1], 180. The pres-ence of Bernardo Riccomanni at Santa Croce is recorded only up to the end of 1299, and this has raised the possibility that "he, having at the end of the century become a priest and joined the higher orders, had been sent to another convent, to another place" (Renato Piattoli, "Codice Diplomatico Dantesco. Aggiunte," *Archivio storico italiano* 127, nos. 1–2 [1969], pp. 3–108—the quotation is at p. 83; see also the entry in ED, "Riccomanni, Bernardo" by Piattoli). The suggestion is there-fore not entirely unsubstantiated; during the period after 1310, friar Bernardo seems to have resided at Santa Croce. According to Giorgio Padoan, *Introduzione a Dante* (Florence: Sansoni, 1975), p. 47, the words "holy places" mean "among rela-tives and friends in the Church."

14. For the laws concerning the relatives of those convicted and the movements of Gemma, see DAVIDSOHN, IV, pp. 280–281 (to whom I refer also for the role of Acciaioli, p. 307), and above all Michele Barbi, "Un altro figlio di Dante?" in BARBI[2], pp. 347–370.

15. Confirmation that Dante was part of the Council of Twelve is found in BRUNI, p. 546.

16. For the matrimonial links between the Guidi and Malatesta families, see Ignazio Baldelli, *Dante e Francesca* (Florence: Olschki, 1999), pp. 26–27.

17. The Guidi of Romena had property at San Benedetto, according to BOC-CACCIO[3], XVI 74–75, and planned to build a large castle: there might be a reference to this unfulfilled project in the line "where it ought to have fallen in a thousand" ("ove dovea per mille esser recetto"). For Fonte Branda, see Giorgio Varanini, "Dante e la fonte Branda di Romena," in Varanini, *L'acceso strale. Saggi e ricerche sulla* Commedia (Naples: Federico & Ardia, 1984), pp. 228–252.

18. The collaboration between Dante and Pellegrino Calvi has perhaps been more valuable for us than it was for Dante himself: the letters collected by Calvi in his chancery and some of his written chronicles, all lost, were known to the fifteenth-century Forlì humanist Biondo Flavio, who was a great friend of Leo-nardo Bruni. Biondo kept a record of some of those documents, thanks to which we can reconstruct certain details of Dante's life, such as his mission as ambas-sador to Verona: see the important entries in ED "Biondo Flavio" and "Calvi, Pel-legrino" by Augusto Campana, but also ZINGARELLI, p. 188.

19. Of fundamental importance in reconstructing Dante's stays in Verona are Petrocchi, "La vicenda biografica di Dante nel Veneto," INDIZIO[1], and CARPI.

20. Biondo Flavio, in *Historiarum ab inclinatione Romani imperii decades quattuor* (Basileae: Froben, 1531), decade II, book IX, p. 338, after having stated that the facts

"testified by the words of Dante Alighieri, poet of Florence, are certainly more believable than what we see described by Villani and Tolomeo da Lucca," writes that "Cangrande della Scala, who at that time had only recently become lord of Verona, on the request of all those aforesaid who were working at Forlì for the intermediary of an embassy by Dante, granted military help of horse and infantry" ("multa sunt secuta, quae Dantis Aldegherii, poetae Florentini, verbis dictata certioris notitiae sunt quam a Villano Ptolemaeoque Lucensi referri videamus . . . et Canis Grandis Scaliger, Veronae tunc primum dominio potitus, a praedictis omnibus Fori Livii agentibus per Dantis legationem oratus, auxilia equitum peditumque concessit"). Biondo Flavio is obviously confusing Bartolomeo della Scala with the more famous Cangrande, nor does there seem to be any basis for the information that the Della Scala family sent the military help requested, but there is no reason to doubt the validity of the information about Dante's embassy. It is notable that Biondo places so much trust in Dante's letters—known to him through the transcription made by Calvi—that he claims Dante to be more reliable than the chroniclers Giovanni Villani and Tolomeo da Lucca (i.e., Bartolomeo Fiadoni).

21. There is still much debate among Dante scholars about whether Dante's first host in Verona was Bartolomeo or his brother Alboino, even though the reference to the coat of arms ought to remove all doubt in this respect; see the entry "Della Scala, Bartolomeo" in ED, and INDIZIO[3], p. 224; Alboino is preferred as candidate by CARPI, pp. 71–74, 125 (see pp. 72–73 for the criticisms expressed by Dante in relation to the Della Scala). The eagle would also appear on the coat of arms of Cangrande, Bartolomeo's brother, who married a daughter (Giovanna) of Conrad of Antioch, grandson of Frederick II and cousin of Federico della Scala, husband of Imperatrice (see CARPI, p. 82), though this was somewhat later. Finally, it is no surprise that Dante refers to someone from Verona as a "Lombard": Verona, at that time, was regarded as Lombard territory and therefore distinct from the March of Treviso, present-day Veneto; see the observations by Gianfranco Folena, "La presenza di Dante nel Veneto,"*Atti e memorie dell'accademia patavina di scienze, lettere ed arti* 78 (1965–1966): 483–509 (at pp. 487–488), and TAVONI, pp. 1248–1249, 1303–1304.

22. Asdente will be placed among the soothsayers in *Inf.* XX (lines 118–120); Guido da Castello will return, together with Gherardo da Camino and Corrado da Palazzo, in *Purg.* XVI 121–126. For the period in Dante's life when he was a Guelf supporter and critical of the Della Scala, see CARPI, pp. 517–520; the quote about negative experiences is by FIORAVANTI, commentary on *Conv.* IV XVI 6.

23. With regard to the extension of his stay in Verona, Michele Barbi ("Una nuova opera sintetica su Dante," then in BARBI[1], pp. 29–85) does not disapprove of the idea "that Dante either, from being an ambassador, almost immediately became a guest once the reason for the embassy had gone, or that he returned to Verona shortly after the defeat at Pulicciano, and then rejoined the other exiles

before March 1304," also because, according to him, "it is likely that Dante began his wanderings while he was still with his companions: he came and went according to need" (pp. 44–45).

24. The sonnet from Angiolieri to Dante is commented on by De Robertis in Dante Alighieri, *Rime*, with commentary edited by Domenico De Robertis (Florence: SISMEL-Edizioni del Galluzzo, 2005), pp. 477–478; published here, at pp. 481–482, is also the sonnet *Cecco Angiolier, tu mi pari un musardo* by Guelfo Taviani; on this exchange, see also Claudio Giunta, *Versi a un destinatario. Saggio sulla poesia italiana del Medioevo* (Bologna: il Mulino, 2002), pp. 276–277.

25. In *VE* II VI 7, in referring to the syntactical phenomenon that he calls "constructio suprema," Dante writes that it is found among those traditional poets (Virgil, Ovid of *Metamorphosis,* Statius, and Lucan), but also among great prose writers such as Livy, Pliny, Frontinus, Orosius, "and many others that a solicitous friend invites us to visit" ("et multos alios quos amica sollicitudo nos visitare invitat"). For Dante's relationship with the Biblioteca Capitolare in Verona, see Luciano Gargan, *Per la biblioteca di Dante*, GSLI, 186 (2009): 161–193, in particular p. 175–177—Gargan believes the composition of *De vulgari* was begun in Verona during this period—and especially TAVONI, pp. 1451–1455. Particularly interesting is the suggestion by Tavoni that the friend who introduced Dante to the secrets of the Biblioteca Capitolare was the notary Giovanni de Matociis, known as Giovanni Mansionario because from at least 1311 he was *mansionarius,* i.e., sacristan, of the cathedral (though his activity in Verona is earlier recorded in 1303): read the entry on him in the DBI, "Matociis, Giovanni De' (Giovanni Mansionario)" by Marino Zabbia. For Giuseppe Billanovich, however, "no evidence, nor any echo of his works proves to us that the poet of the *Commedia* crossed the threshold of the cathedral library and studied there any of the many authors, sacred or profane, known and unknown"; see *La tradizione del testo di Livio e le origini dell'umanesimo*, vol. 1: *Tradizione e fortuna di Livio tra Medioevo e umanesimo,* Part 1 (Padua: Editrice Antenore, 1981), p. 55.

26. Proof that the first book of *De vulgari eloquentia* dates to 1304 comes from the fact that it refers (at I XII 5) to Giovanni I di Monferrato, who died in January 1305, as being still alive (see the entry in DBI, "Giovanni I, marchese di Monferrato" by Aldo A. Settia).

27. For Dante's familiarity with the linguistic features of the Veneto area, read *VE* I XIV 5–6; with regard to geographical localities, for Treviso, see *Conv.* IV XIV 12 and *Para.* IX 49; for the banks of the river see Brenta, *Inf.* XV 7–9; for the "landslide" ("ruina") south of Trento, see *Inf.* XII 4–9; for the Arsenale in Venice, see *Inf.* XXI 7–15. Indizio suggests that Dante's knowledge of the geography and languages of the Veneto date from his first stay at Verona (INDIZIO[1], pp. 41–52); others suggest he stayed with the Caminesi at Treviso at some time between the second half of 1304 and the early months of 1306: this view is held, with some doubt, by

Petrocchi, "La vicenda biografica di Dante nel Veneto,"pp. 96–97, and more decisively by CARPI, who emphasizes several times that Dante would have received hospitality from the Guelfs Gherardo and Rizzardo da Camino.

28. The events relating to the salt question are described by INDIZIO[1], pp. 43–44.

29. It is no coincidence that Dante, around 1307, during a period of his life when, for political reasons, he showed particular favor to the Caminesi, puts Reginaldo among the usurers in the ditches of Hell and gets him to predict the forthcoming arrival of his brother-in-law, Vitaliano Del Dente, who was the other banker implicated in the loans to the lords of Treviso (*Inf.* XVII 64–69). In condemning Reginaldo and Vitaliano, Dante's position in favor of the Caminesi is implicit, but his stab at the Della Scala family is entirely explicit: Vitaliano, the usurer, was the father of the woman whom Bartolomeo della Scala had married on the death of his wife Costanza and shortly before his own death—therefore at the time when Dante was in Verona. On the Scrovegni and the Del Dente, who were members of the great Lemizzi family, particularly interesting is CARPI, pp. 72, 247, 408.

30. On the figure of Niccolò da Prato and his promotion of the new humanist culture, see the important research of Giuseppe Billanovich, in particular "Tra Dante e Petrarca," IMU, 8 (1965): 1–43, and *La tradizione del testo di Livio,* pp. 41–56.

31. On the conflict that saw the split between Corso Donati and Bishop Lottieri Della Tosa on one side and Rosso and Rossellino Della Tosa on the other, see CARPI, pp. 630–631.

32. The events in Florence during the months of Niccolò da Prato's mission are retold in detail by DAVIDSOHN, IV, pp. 369–390; here, at p. 384, the description of the popular reception of Lapo degli Uberti. The mediation of Niccolò da Prato was also supported by Remigio dei Girolami who, between May and June, wrote a *De bono pacis* in which he proposed an amnesty for those in exile and, in exchange, a pardon for Blacks who had expropriated property belonging to Whites (see Bruni, *La città divisa,* pp. 58–59).

33. *Ep.* I 3: "Sane, cum per sancte religionis virum fratrem L. civilitatis persuasorem et pacis, premoniti atque requisiti sumus instanter pro vobis, quemadmodum et ipse vestre littere continebant, ut ab omni guerrarum insultu cessaremus et usu, et nos ipsos in paternas manus vestras exhiberemus in totum, nos filii devotissimi vobis et pacis amatores et iusti, exuti iam gradiis, arbitrio vestro spontanea et sincera voluntate subimus, ceu relatu prefati vestri nuntii fratris L. narrabitur, et per publica instrumenta solempniter celebrata liquebit." For the problem as to whether the signatory of the letter to the cardinal is Alessandro or (as I think) his brother Aghinolfo, see Francesco Mazzoni, "Le epistole di Dante," in *Conferenze aretine 1965* (Arezzo: Zilli, 1966), pp. 47–100, in particular p. 56.

34. Emilio Panella has argued persuasively that hidden behind the "L." is the Dominican friar Lapo da Prato: see "Nuova cronologia remigiana," *Archivum*

fratrum praedicatorum 60 (1990): 221–222, and *Cronologia remigiana* (http://www
.etheca.net/emiliopanella/remigio2/re1304.htm).

35. *Ep.* I 1: "Et si negligentie sontes aut ignavie censeremur ob iniuriam tardi-
tatis, citra iudicium discretio sancta vestra preponderet; et quantis qualibusque
consiliis et responsis, observata sinceritate consortii, nostra Fraternitas decenter
procedendo indigeat, et examinatis que tangimus, ubi forte contra debitam celeri-
tatem defecisse despicimur, ut affluentia vestre Benignitatis indulgeat deprecamur."

36. The quotation ("E fu sì empito e furioso [che] arse tutto il midollo e tuorlo
e cari luoghi della città di Firenze . . . Il danno . . . fu infinito, perocché in que'
luoghi era quasi tutta la mercatantia") is from VILLANI VIII LXXI.

37. The sonnet by Guido Orlandi can be paraphrased as follows: "The Whites
are turned to ash, and timid and despicable like crabs that come out at night for
fear the lion [the Marzocco, the heraldic lion of Florence] will catch them. Until
their crime, of having turned from Guelfs into Ghibellines, is cancelled out, from
this moment on let them be called rebels, enemies of the commune, like the
Uberti" ("che non perdano mai la forfattura / —ché furon guelfi, ed or son ghibellini, / da ora innanti sian detti ribelli, / nemici del comun come gli Uberti," lines
8–11). "And so let the name of the Whites be destroyed through an irrevocable
judgment, unless they resign themselves to being 'offered' to Saint John" (Valentina Pollidori, "Le rime di Guido Orlandi," [critical edition], *Studi di filologia
italiana* 53 (1994): 55–202, sonnet XVIII; I refer to this work for the interpretation
of the text and for information on the life of its author).

38. "Ildebrandino, Bishop of Arezzo, was for over twenty years from 1290 the
leading figure for the Guidi and their generation, the only person to attempt a new
and independent policy in what was now post-imperial Italy, neither of resignation to Florence nor of obstinately holding on to residual Ghibellinism" (CARPI,
p. 575).

39. *Ep.* II 1–2: "Doleat ergo, doleat progenies maxima Tuscanorum, que tanto
viro fulgebat, et doleant omnes amici eius et subditi . . . inter quos ultimos me
miserum dolere oportet, qui a patria pulsus et exul inmeritus infortunia mea
rependens continuo, cara spe memet consolabar in illo . . . et qui Romane aule
palatinus erat in Tuscia, nunc regie sempiterne aulicus preelectus in superna
ierusalem cum beatorum principibus gloriatur."

40. *Ep.* II 3: "Ego autem, preter hec, me vestrum vestre discretioni excuso de
absentia lacrimosis exequiis; quia nec negligentia neve ingratitudo me tenuit, sed
inopina paupertas quam fecit exilium. Hec etenim, velud effera persecutrix, equis
armisque vacantem iam sue captivitatis me detrusit in antrum, et nitentem cunctis
exsurgere viribus, hucusque prevalens, impia retinere molitur."

41. In the absence of documentary evidence, the question of the date of Alessandro di Romena's death is almost impossible to answer: Indizio, "Sul mittente
dell'epistola I di Dante," suggests that Alessandro was dead in the early months

of 1303 (and, therefore, that the letter indicated in current publications as the second is in fact the first); I prefer to keep to the traditional dating due to the fact that, while Dante's financial situation in spring of 1304 justified the implied request for help contained in the letter, we can say that, at the beginning of 1303, since Dante was firmly settled into the university organization, he had no need to make that kind of request. The wording "equis armisque vacantem" used in the letter of condolence, rather than an actual lack of means of transport, could refer to the lack, for economic reasons, of respectable horse livery of the kind necessary for a gentlemen to take part in a funeral procession: see in this respect Gian Paolo Marchi, "'Equis armisque vacantem.' Postille interpretative a un passo dell'epistola di Dante a Oberto e Guido da Romena," *Testo* 32 (2011): 239–252.

42. For the counterfeiting of the florin by the Guidi di Romena and Dante's attitude toward them, I refer to Ernesto Sestan, "Dante e i conti Guidi," a 1965 essay in Sestan, *Italia medievale* (Naples: ESU, 1968), pp. 344–345, and to CARPI, pp. 535, 647; the story is reconstructed by DAVIDSOHN, III, pp. 251–253. For reasons that might have induced the Guidi to counterfeit the florin, linked essentially to the need to maintain—even in their spending—the role of a great aristocratic family, and the scarcity of resources that was increasingly troubling them, see Rosetta Migliorini Fissi, "Dante e il Casentino," in *Dante e le città dell'esilio,* proceedings of the international research conference, Ravenna, September 11–13, 1987, technical director Guido Di Pino (Ravenna: Longo Editore, 1989), pp. 139–140.

43. The legal document for the loan contracted in Arezzo by Francesco is published in PIATTOLI, no. 94.

44. *Ottimo commento,* with regard to *Para.* XVII 61–68, makes a rather unclear reference to disagreements between Dante and the White party "already at war" ("già guerreggiante"), and gives this as the reason why "he left them" ("elli si partìe da loro").

6. Return to Study and Writing

1. Dante's early biographers offer little help in reconstructing his story after the battle of La Lastra. BOCCACCIO[2], 54–55 (more ordered and correct than BOCCACCIO[1], 74), summarizes Dante's movements between 1302 and 1315–1316 as follows: "having left that city, to which he would never go back, hoping shortly to be able to return, he wandered for several years in Tuscany and Lombardy, reduced to almost extreme poverty, carrying with him deepest bitterness. He first took shelter in Verona . . . then having returned to Tuscany was for some time with Count Salvatico in Casentino. Then he was with Marchese Moruello Malespina in Lunigiana. And also for some time with the lords della Faggiuola in the mountains near Urbino. Then he went to Bologna, and from Bologna to Padua, and from Padua returned to Verona." ("uscito di quella città, nella qual mai tornar non dovea,

sperando in brieve dovere essere la ritornata, più anni per Toscana e per Lombardia, quasi da estrema povertà costretto, gravissimi sdegni portando nel petto, s'andò avvolgendo. Egli primieramente rifuggì a Verona . . . quindi in Toscana tornatosene, per alcun tempo fu col conte Salvatico in Casentino. Di quindi fu col marchese Moruello Malespina in Lunigiana. E ancora per alcuno spazio fu co' signori della Faggiuola ne' monti vicini ad Orbino. Quindi n'andò a Bologna, e da Bologna a Padova, e da Padova ancor si tornò a Verona.") BRUNI gives information on the two years of the Coalition, about which Boccaccio is silent, but knows little about the following years, and indeed names only Verona among the places where he stayed before the arrival of Henry VII.

2. Dante's reputation in Bologna for his involvement in politics must have depended largely on the fact that the basis of the treaty of alliance that would assure the Whites of support from Bologna even after their expulsion was established during his period of office as prior.

3. For the Alighieri who had settled in Bologna, see the entries by Renato Piattoli, "Alighieri, Bellino" and "Alighieri, Cione" in ED.

4. It could have been the very practice of private teacher (*praeceptor*) that gave rise to the mistake that Dante's son Pietro made in thinking that he may have held a form of "lectureship" at the *Studio*. In the canzone (*Quelle sette arti liberali—Those seven liberal arts*), written in the 1330s, after the condemnation of Dante's writings by Bertrando del Poggetto (1329) and by the Dominican Chapter in Florence (1335), Pietro Alighieri gets each of the liberal arts to lament how "their master" had been shamefully treated: astrology, in particular, complains about not being able to "foresee" the "end" (the death) "of [her] master [Dante] who read at Bologna" ("del mie maestro che lesse a Bologna"; lines 90–92). The canzone is published by Domenico De Robertis, "Un codice di rime dantesche ora ricostruito," SD 36 (1959): 137–205; pp. 196–205. De Robertis observes (at p. 204) that in the canzone "there re-emerges, through testimony much more solid than that of Ubaldo Bastiani . . . the old suggestion, raised by Zingarelli . . . and long abandoned, about Dante's teaching" (but compare ZINGARELLI, p. 209; on Pietro's canzone, see also INDIZIO[3], pp. 224–226). Pietro's words are indeed one of the most solid pieces of evidence showing that Dante stayed in Bologna (in an unspecified period which seems however to be 1304–1305), but the technical word "read" ("leggere") is misleading: it certainly cannot refer to teaching in a public institution. Either Pietro was not in Bologna with his father at that time, and was therefore making a later reconstruction based on secondhand information, or he was in Bologna but, being still a child, may have misinterpreted the fact that Dante was working privately as a tutor.

5. Ubaldo di Bastiano of Gubbio, a lawyer who trained at the *Studio* in Bologna, wrote a Latin dialogue around 1326–1327 in prose and verse form between him-

self and Death, entitled *Teleutelogio,* in which he states that he had Dante as a tutor during his adolescence. But from the dates available, which suggest that Ubaldo would have been around twenty-five to thirty when he wrote the dialogue in which the statement is made, that expression would seem not to indicate a teaching received personally in Bologna but a discipleship carried out in writing. It should also be pointed out that in *Teleutelogio* Ubaldo, who had Angevin links and was part of the Guelf bureaucracy in Florence, argues at a very early date about certain views in *Monarchia.* See Attilio Bartoli Langeli, "Ubaldo di Bastiano (o Sebastiano) da Gubbio," in ED; Leonella Coglievina, "La leggenda sui passi dell'esule," in *Dante e le città dell'esilio,* convegno internazionale, Ravenna, 11–13 September 1987, dir. Guido Di Pino (Ravenna: Longo, 1989), pp. 46–74, in particular pp. 60–64; Emiliano Bertin, "Primi appunti su Ubaldo di Bastiano da Gubbio lettore e censore della *Monarchia,*" *L'Alighieri* 48 (2007): 103–119.

6. It is persuasively argued that *De vulgari eloquentia* was written in Bologna between 1304 and 1305 by TAVONI, pp. 1091–1092, 1113–1116: he suggests—against the prevailing opinion that the first three books are earlier than 1306 (and written mostly in Bologna, as is also suggested by FIORAVANTI) and the fourth dates to 1308—that *Convivio* was written before the flight from Bologna and request for a personal pardon. On this last point, see also Mirko Tavoni, "Guido da Montefeltro dal *Convivio* all' *Inferno,*" NRLI 13 (2010): 167–198, in particular pp. 197–198. Many scholars had already suggested a stay in Bologna of around two years, during which Dante had composed the two treatises: see at least ZINGARELLI, pp. 211–212; Paul Renucci, *Dante disciple et juge du monde gréco-latin* (Paris: Les Belles Lettres, 1954), pp. 63–66; Francesco Mazzoni, *Prefazione a La Divina Commedia con il commento Scartazzini-Vandelli* (Florence: Le Lettere, 1978), p. xvi; INDIZIO[1], pp. 48–52; INDIZIO[3], pp. 225–226; for *De vulgari,* John A. Scott, *Understanding Dante* (Notre Dame, IN: University of Notre Dame Press, 2004), pp. 35–36. GORNI also writes that "everything indeed conspires toward imagining Dante in Bologna" (p. 84) during the period 1304–1306. Umberto Carpi has made a different reconstruction, based on a "political" view of Dante's movements between 1304 and 1306, for which, apart from CARPI, *passim,* see: Umberto Carpi, "Un *Inferno* guelfo," NRLI 13 (2010): 95–134 and Carpi, "*Tre donne intorno al cor mi son venute,*" in *Dante Alighieri: Le quindici canzoni: lette da diversi,* vol. 2, 8–15, ser. Quaderni per leggere (Lecce: Pensa, 2011). Carpi thinks that Dante, after the defeat at La Lastra, spent a short time in Bologna but then moved to stay with Alboino della Scala in Verona and then to Gherardo da Camino in Treviso; finally, in 1306, he arrived to stay with Moroello Malaspina in the Lunigiana and, the year after, returned once again to the Casentino. The whole reconstruction revolves around the basic factor of Dante's repentance and his search for an agreement with the Blacks of Florence for his return to the city.

7. The quote is taken from the introduction in FIORAVANTI.

8. Of relevance for the canzone *Doglia mi reca* are the studies collected in Grupo Tenzone, *Doglia mi reca ne lo core ardire*, ed. Umberto Carpi (Madrid: Departamento de Filología Italiana UCM-Asociación Complutense de Dantología, 2008); in particular, the papers of Umberto Carpi, "La destinataria del congedo e un'ipotesi di contestualizzazione," pp. 13–29, and Enrico Fenzi, "Tra etica del dono e accumulazione. Note di lettura alla canzone dantesca *Doglia mi reca*," pp. 147–211. The canzone is quoted in *VE* II II 8, and therefore before the beginning of 1305: as to the date, compare also Fenzi, "Tra etica del dono e accumulazione," pp. 147–149, who, agreeing with CARPI, pp. 75–80, considers it to have been composed in Treviso (and not in Bologna as I suggest).

9. The phrase on "autobiographical experience" is quoted from Migliorini Fissi, "Dante e il Casentino," in *Dante e le città dell'esilio*, p. 126; with regard to the same lines CARPI at p. 78 notes: "it seems to photograph Dante's experience with Alboino and the court in Verona, quite the opposite of the experience of courtly liberality that he found . . . in Treviso of the Caminesi."

10. On the person to whom the canzone was addressed, see also Carpi, "La destinataria del congedo," and Fenzi, "Tra etica del dono e accumulazione." On the other hand, Francesco Bausi, "Lettura di *Doglia mi reca*," in *Le quindici canzoni lette da diversi*, takes the view that it was addressed to Giovanna di Federico Novello, a niece of Bianca Giovanna, Contessa di Guido Novello, married by dispensation to her kinsman Tegrimo II dei Guidi di Modigliana-Porciano. Bausi also regards the canzone as dating to the mid-1290s and that only the conclusion was written in the early years of exile (late 1302 or early 1303): it is suggested it consists of a request for protection from the Guidi. Carpi (in *"Tre donne intorno al cor mi son venute"*) objects, however, that the canzone "oozes exile from every line" and points out the decisive detail that the recipient proposed by Bausi was called Giovanna and not Bianca Giovanna.

11. For the Bonacolsi of Mantua, see the entries by Ingeborg Walter, "Bonacolsi Guido, detto Bottesella" and "Bonacolsi, Tagino (Tayno)" in DBI. The choice of Bianca Giovanna as interlocutrix also perhaps implies a criticism of the Della Scala, close allies of Guido Bonacolsi at war with the Este, to whom Tagino and his son were closely linked.

12. The introduction in FIORAVANTI and TAVONI, pp. 1067–1116, are important for the observations made in this and the next section.

13. Dante's love for his home city did not prevent him from seeing its limitations which, by reaction, he tends even to emphasize: "We, however, to whom the world is our home like the sea to fish, although we drank from the Arno before we cut our teeth, and although we love Florence to the point that, because we loved her, we unjustly suffer exile, we . . . have reached the conviction, and firmly believe, that there are many regions and cities more noble and more pleasant

than Tuscany and Florence, where we were born and are a citizen, and that many nations and peoples use a language more beautiful and more useful than that of the Italians" ("Nos autem, cui mundus est patria velut piscibus equor, quanquam Sarnum biberimus ante dentes et Florentiam adeo diligamus ut, quia dileximus, exilium patiamur iniuste . . . multas esse perpendimus firmiterque censemus et magis nobiles et magis delitiosas et regiones et urbes quam Tusciam et Florentiam, unde sumus oriundus et civis, et plerasque nationes et gentes delectabiliori atque utiliori sermone uti quam Latinos"; *VE* I VI 3).

14. That the treatise was intended to have five books is suggested by TAVONI, p. 1363.

15. See Dante's claim to novelty in the opening lines of the treatise (*VE* I I 1): "So far as we are aware, no one before us has in any way cultivated the doctrine of eloquence in the vernacular" ("Cum neminem ante nos de vulgaris eloquentie doctrina quicquam inveniamus tractasse").

16. Apart from love (*venus*), salvation (*salus*) and *virtus* are the great arguments ("magnalia") which must necessarily be sung in tragic style. Each of the three sectors (love poetry, war poetry and moral poetry) had its champions: in Provencal, Arnaut Daniel for the first, Bertran de Born for the second and Giraut de Borneil for the third; in high Italian vernacular, Cino da Pistoia for love and Dante himself for rectitude (*VE* II II). In Italy, there was still no champion of war poetry or epic poetry.

17. In the absence of a modern biography of Cino da Pistoia, we must still refer to Guido Zaccagnini, *Cino da Pistoia. Studio biografico* (Pistoia: Pagnini, 1918).

18. For Dante's strategies in relation to university circles, see Pier Vincenzo Mengaldo, *Linguistica e retorica di Dante* (Pisa: Nistri-Lischi, 1978), pp. 64–65, and especially TAVONI, pp. 1364–1366, 1443–1444.

19. Cino's role as mediator between Dante and the university environments is examined by INDIZIO[1], pp. 50–51 (who rightly emphasizes Dante's gratitude toward his friend expressed in *Ep.* III), and by TAVONI in the comment; GORNI, p. 184, describes a "Cino da Pistoia eager to 'launch' his Florentine friend in the philosophical and academic sphere."

20. The phrase quoted is by GIUNTA, p. 584.

21. *Ep.* III 1; "quod quamvis ex ore tuo iustius prodire debuerat, nichilominus me illius auctorem facere voluisti, ut in declaratione rei nimium dubitate titulum mei nominis ampliares. Hoc etenim, cum cognitum, quam acceptum quamque gratum extiterit, absque importuna diminutione verba non caperent."

7. The Penitent

1. For the erratic relations between the Bologna factions of the Lambertazzi and the Geremei, see CARPI, pp. 480–481; I refer to him also for the figure of

Venedico and the role of the Caccianemici family (pp. 411, 495–498). Note that Venedico was still alive in 1300: indeed, we know he made his will in 1303. Had Dante made a mistake, or did he intentionally place him among the dead?

2. For events in Bologna and Pistoia in spring 1306, see DAVIDSOHN, IV, pp. 435–440. The banishment of the Whites and the Ghibellines is dealt with by Emilio Orioli, *Documenti bolognesi sulla fazione dei Bianchi* (Bologna: Tip. Garagnani e Figli, 1896. The extract is from "Atti e memorie della R. Deputazione di Storia Patria per le provincie di Romagna," III series, XIV, 1896, pp. 1–15, at pp. 6–7, and Giovanni Livi, *Dante, suoi primi cultori, sua gente in Bologna* (Bologna: Cappelli, 1918), p. 156.

3. The story about Orsini's legation is told by DAVIDSOHN, IV, pp. 446–475; for a historical assessment of Orsini's conduct and an analysis of the relations between him and Guelf and Ghibelline exiles, see CARPI, pp. 437–438, 579, 631–632. A brief portrait of Cardinal Orsini is drawn by Jean-Claude Maire Vigueur, *L'autre Rome: une histoire des Romains à l'époque des communes. XIIe–XIVe siècle* (Tallandier: Paris, 2010), pp. 276–278.

4. For Foresino and Niccolò Donati see Michele Barbi, "Per un passo dell'epistola all'amico fiorentino e per la parentela di Dante" (1920), then in BARBI[2], pp. 305–328, in particular pp. 309, 328, and Giorgio Padoan, *Introduzione a Dante* (Florence: Sansoni, 1975), p. 103.

5. For the exchange of sonnets between Cino and Dante (Moroello), see GIUNTA, pp. 594–600; I refer to Claudio Giunta, *Codici. Saggi sulla poesia del Medioevo* (Bologna: il Mulino, 2005), p. 178, for the practice of replying in writing "on behalf of."

6. For the political positions of Cino and his appointment as judge in Pistoia in 1307, see Guido Zaccagnini, *Cino da Pistoia. Studio biografico* (Pistoia: Pagnini, 1918), pp. 145–148.

7. The account by Boccaccio ("Ma poi, passati bene cinque anni o più, essendo la città venuta a più convenevole reggimento che quello non era quando Dante fu condennato [. . .] fu consigliata la donna che ella, almeno con le ragioni della dote sua, dovesse de' beni di Dante radomandare") is told in BOCCACCIO[1], 179–183, and BOCCACCIO[3], VIII I 6–19. The problem of returning did not affect Dante's sons, since in 1306 none of them had reached fourteen: we shall see that the act of 1311 by which Dante was excluded from Baldo d'Aguglione's amnesty does not name his sons, which means that at that date they were not yet subject to the banishment.

8. DAVIDSOHN, IV, pp. 280–281, thinks that "Gemma, certainly due to her belonging to the Donati family, could return to Florence." See, however, the arguments to the contrary by Michele Barbi, "Un altro figlio di Dante?" (1922), then in BARBI[2], pp. 357–358. The question of the rights of wives over assets seized or confiscated from those convicted was the subject of much legal debate at the time, like that of joint owners. Alberto Gandino deals with it under the heading *De bonis malefactorum del Tractatus maleficiorum*: it appears that the judicial practice was di-

vided between respecting the shared right, which required respect for the wife's dowry, and reliance on the statutes, which imposed confiscation or even destruction of the property. From the *questio* discussed in para. 3 (Hermann Kantorowicz, *Albertus Gandinus und das Strafrecht der Scholastik,* vol. 2, *Die Theorie. Kritische Ausgabe des Tractatus de maleficiis nebst textkritischer Einleitung* [Berlin: Walter De Gruyter, 1926/1981], pp. 349–350), it appeared that the wife, by virtue of the privileged position given to her by the law, especially with regard to rights over the dowry, could nevertheless recover the revenue from the portion of the assets that guaranteed her dowry, and this was exactly Gemma's situation. She failed, however, in her intent, and only after Dante's death "could she make annual requests on the deceased's assets . . . the revenue from the dowry she had brought in marrying him" (Renato Piattoli, "Donati, Gemma,"entry in ED). On the contrary, according to Padoan, *Introduzione a Dante,* p. 103, "Gemma must perhaps even have succeeded in obtaining something in return for the goods seized on the strength of her dowry, if in 1329 she was still receiving an annual allocation of 26 bushels of corn as payment from the office dealing with the assets of the rebels."

9. The quotation at the beginning of this section ("ridussesi tutto a umiltà, cercando con buone opere et con buoni portamenti racquistare la gratia di potere tornare in Firenze per spontanea revocazione di chi reggeva la terra. Et sopra questa parte s'affaticò assai, et scrisse più volte, non solamente a particulari cittadini et del reggimento, ma al popolo") and passages in the lost letter are from BRUNI, p. 546. Bruni, and those who reject the idea of the long stay in Bologna in favor of stays in Verona and Treviso, suggest that the requests for pardon, including *Popule mee,* were sent from Verona. But apart from the matters already considered which make a stay in Verona unlikely during these years, so far as the letter itself, it would be very strange indeed for Dante to have sent a text in which, as we shall see, he renounces his past alliance with the Ghibellines and asks for pardon in what the Florentines construed as an actual betrayal of Verona itself, which was one of the capitals of Italian Ghibellinism. Bruni distinguishes between letters sent to individuals, to holders of public offices, and to the people: INDIZIO[2], p. 271, considers that *Popule mee* had been sent to the people, and not to the "government" ("reggimento"), like the letter referred to by VILLANI, X CXXXVI; but Bruni's view seems conditioned by Dante's opening ("Popule"), and it seems unlikely that Dante had sent out a sort of open letter "collectively to the ruling class." It seems clear to me that both Bruni and Villani (as well as Biondo Flavio) are referring to the same letter.

10. The verse in Micah 6:3, read during the Good Friday liturgy with the words "Popule mee, quid . . .", instead of "Populus meus . . .", is also quoted in Dante's trilingual canzone *Aï faus ris, pour quoi traï aves,* lines 2–3: ". . . et quid tibi feci, / che fatta m'hai sì dispietata fraude?" To open a letter with a passage from scripture is, however, a feature of Dante's letter-writing: for example, the letter to the

Italian cardinals (*Ep.* XI) begins by quoting the first verse of Lamentations ("Quo-modo sedet sola civitas . . ."), a verse which also begins the lost letter to the "princes of the earth" on the death of Beatrice.

11. Dante uses the word "wrong" ("colpa") in the canzone *Tre donne intorno al cor mi son venute,* line 88.

12. The sentence quoted from COMPAGNI (II XXX) is a comment on the torture and beheading inflicted by Fulcieri da Calboli on Donato Alberti.

13. On Dante's wrong, see the definitive words of Umberto Carpi, *"Tre donne intorno al cor mi son venute,"* in *Dante Alighieri: Le quindici canzoni: lette da diversi,* vol. 2, *8–15,* ser. Quaderni per leggere (Lecce: Pensa, 2011).

14. The passage from the sermon of Giordano da Pisa ("Or noi avemo trovati uomini, che sono di parte Guelfi e Ghibellini, che vorrebbe volentieri, se potesse, 'n un tratto uccidere tutti gli uomini dell'altra parte: tutti gli ucciderebbe a un tratto, se potesse") is reported by Francesco Bruni, *La città divisa. Le parti e il bene comune da Dante a Guicciardini* (Bologna: Il Mulino, 2003), p. 39 (at pp. 36–37, there is a short biographical profile of the Dominican friar).

15. Dante's stay with Guido di Castello, "the simple Lombard," at his house in Reggio, could have taken place during his journey from Bologna to the Lunigiana (a journey which, after the fall of Pistoia, could not have happened after a tour of Tuscany). Benvenuto da Imola refers to it while commenting on lines 124–126 of *Purg.* XVI in which the nobleman from Reggio is remembered along with Cor-rado da Palazzo and Gherardo da Camino: "cuius liberalitatem poeta noster ex-pertus est semel, receptus et honoratus ab eo in domo sua."

16. The information on Moroello's movements during spring and summer of 1306 comes from Eliana M. Vecchi, *"Ad pacem et veram et perpetuam concordiam de-venerunt. Il cartulario del notaio Giovanni di Parente di Stupio e l'Instrumentum pacis del 1306,"* *Giornale storico della Lunigiana e del territorio lucense* 59 (2008): 69–175, p. 110. Useful information on relations between Dante and the Malaspina is found in various parts of CARPI, in particular pp. 519–528. An interesting idea has been put forward by Giuseppe Ciavorella in "Corrado Malaspina e sua *gente on-rata.* Ospitalità e profezia (*Purgatorio* VIII, 109–139)," *L'Alighieri* 51 (2010): 65–85) that Moroello consulted Cino "(while the two were at Pistoia, or nearby, during the siege) for his opinion about how to resolve the age-old disputes between the Mala-spina family and the Bishop of Luni" and that "Cino had proposed a neutral inter-mediation between the two parties . . . and had named Dante as the person who could deal with the complex question." It is suggested that the Malaspina accepted the proposal and Cino wrote to Dante, who in turn accepted the appointment (p. 75).

17. Pietro Alighieri's supposed testimony ("per non modicum tempus") is quoted by INDIZIO[3], p. 223 (to which I also refer for doubts on Pietro's actual authorship of the second and third version of the commentary on the *Commedia*).

18. In *Inf.* XXXII 28–30 he writes that the ice of Cocytus is so thick "that if Tamberlicchi [Mount Tambura] / had fallen down on it, or Pietrapana [Mount Pania della Croce], / it wouldn't even have made its edge creak" ("che se Tambernicchi / vi fosse sù caduto, o Pietrapana, / non avria pur da l'orlo fatto cricchi"). Aruns the soothsayer "in the mountains of Luni, where he works the land / the Carrarese who lives below, / had a cave of white marble / for his home; where his view of the stars / and of the sea was not cut off" ("monti di Luni, dove ronca / lo Carrarese che di sotto alberga, / ebbe tra ' bianchi marmi la spelonca / per sua dimora; onde a guardar le stelle / e 'l mar non li era la veduta tronca"; *Inf.* XX 47–51).

19. His praise of the Malaspina occupies four whole tercets of *Purg.* VIII (lines 121–132). For the military exploits of Franceschino di Mulazzo see the entry in DBI, "Malaspina, Franceschino," by Franca Ragone.

20. The power of attorney and peace settlement of October 6, 1306 are published in PIATTOLI, nos. 98, 99. The most important contribution regarding the negotiations and the documents signed is that of Vecchi, *"Ad pacem et veram et perpetuam concordiam devenerunt,"* to which I also refer for information on Antonio da Camilla (pp. 132–136); for Dante's possible authorship of the *arenga* of the peace settlement, see Emiliano Bertin, "La pace di Castelnuovo Magra (6 ottobre 1306). Otto argomenti per la paternità dantesca," IMU 46 (2005): 1–34, but also Giorgio Padoan "Tra Dante e Mussato. I. Tonalità dantesche nell' *Historia Augusta* di Albertino Mussato," *Quaderni veneti* 24 (1966): 27–45. Among the witnesses to the deed are the friar minor Guglielmo Malaspina, who we find in dispute with Gherardino Malaspina over the appointment of the Bishop of Luni after the death of Antonio da Camilla.

21. On the canzone *Tre donne* there have been some particularly interesting recent studies which relate it to the admission of wrong and request for pardon: finest of these is the essay by Carpi, *"Tre donne intorno al cor mi son venute,"* but important also are those collected in Grupo Tenzone, *"Tre donne intorno al cor mi son venute"* (Madrid: Departamento de Filología Italiana UCM-Asociación Complutense de Dantología, 2007), in particular: Umberto Carpi, "Il secondo congedo di *Tre donne*," pp. 15–26; Natascia Tonelli, *"Tre donne*, il *Convivio* e la serie delle canzoni," pp. 51–71, and Enrico Fenzi, *"Tre donne*," 73–107 la colpa, il pentimento, il perdono," pp. 91–124; and the article by Stefano Carrai, "Il doppio congedo di *Tre donne intorno al cor mi son venute,"* in Claudia Berra and Paolo Borsa, eds., *Le rime di Dante,* Conference on Italian Literature held at Gargnano del Garda, 25–27 September 2008 (Milan: Cisalpino, 2010), pp. 197–211. The dating proposed in these works, around late 1304 to early 1305, in Verona, which makes it later than the traditionally established date of 1303 to 1304, is different from my own (late 1305: the fact that the canzone is not cited in *De vulgari eloquentia* could be a further pointer in support of the suggestion that it is later than 1305) because it is based on the belief that Dante's repentance is shortly after the battle of La Lastra.

22. On the political interpretation according to which the "fair object" ("bel segno") in line 81 is said to refer to Florence, it has been rightly observed by Carpi, *"Tre donne intorno al cor mi son venute,"* that if it is paraphrased as "and if it were not for the fact that by distance it is taken from my sight . . . that fine Florence from which I have been set on fire . . . I would consider it light to bear that which, instead, lays heavily on me," we would end up with the "following, most curious hypothetical absurdity: 'if it weren't that the sight of Florence has been taken from me, not to see Florence would be easy to bear.'" That the expression "bel segno" denotes an object of female love is also corroborated by the lines (1–9) of a sonnet by Giovanni Quirini (which one of the three witnesses attributes to Dante): "if the fine aspect of this lady / whom I desire had not been taken from me, / for which in sorrow here I weep and sigh / so distant from her charming face, / that which lays heavily on me . . . / would be light to bear" ("Se il bel aspetto non mi fosse tolto / di questa donna ch'io veder desiro, / per cui dolente qui piango e sospiro / cossì lontan dal suo ligiadro volto, / ciò che mi grava . . . / mi seria leve"; cited by GIUNTA, p. 537), to which could be added those later lines of Nicolò de' Rossi: "Since I see my merits have been ignored, / and pity for me is destroyed and dead, / and humility brings me shame, / and faith in love is broken and gone, / and that hope of return has disappeared, / and the fair object no longer comforts me, / and the shadow of peace even grieves me, / little do I now care about my life" ("Da che mego veço merçé tradita, / e sopra me pietate stuta e morta, / et humeltà che ver' me sdegno porta, / e la fede d'amor rotta e falita, / e che la spene di tornare èe ita, / e 'l bel segno che plu no mi conforta, / e l'ombra de paçe starmi pur torta, / poco curo che sia ormai de mia vita"), lines 1–8; published in Furio Brugnolo, *Il canzoniere di Nicolò de' Rossi,* vol. 1: Introduction, text and glossary (Padua: Editrice Antenore, 1974), p. 217.

23. The quote on the absence of hidden meanings in the canzone is taken from GIUNTA, p. 538; GIUNTA (at p. 537) also names Gemma in relation to the woman alluded to with the expression "fine object," but he speaks of "Gemma left in the city" and not Gemma returned to the city.

24. The quotation ("quando col conte Salvatico in Casentino, quando col marchese Morruello Malespina in Lunigiana, quando con quegli della Faggiuola ne' monti vicini ad Orbino . . . onorato si stette") is taken from BOCCACCIO[1], 74.

25. Dante's relations with the Faggiolani and the Guidi di Dovadola are explored very convincingly by CARPI, pp. 360–383; it is also he who identifies Rinieri or Ranieri da Corneto as the father of Uguccione (see pp. 375–383). Corneto in the Montefeltro region is not to be confused with Corneto (Tarquinia) referred to by Dante in describing the boundaries of the Maremma: "the cultivated lands between Cecina and Corneto" ("tra Cecina e Corneto i luoghi cólti"; *Inf.* XIII 9).

26. Guido Salvatico, though Guelf, was related to the Ghibelline counts of Montefeltro by marrying Manentessa, daughter of Buonconte who died at Cam-

paldino, and therefore granddaughter of the condottiere Guido: but these were local alliances that disregarded political loyalties. A grandson of Guido Salvatico, Marcovaldo II, had married Fiesca, daughter of Moroello and Alagia Fieschi.

27. In relation to Guido Guerra, Dante would write: "he was the grandson of the good Gualdrada [the daughter of Bellincion Berti whom Dante saw as the embodiment of the good old-fashioned virtues]; Guido Guerra was his name, and in his life / he achieved much with wisdom and with the sword" ("nepote fu de la buona Gualdrada; / Guido Guerra ebbe nome, e in sua vita / fece col senno assai e con la spade"; *Inf.* XVI 37–39).

28. Of the substantial bibliography on the "montanina" I note only a few of the more recent contributions: the essays collected in Grupo Tenzone, *Amor, da che convien pur ch'io mi doglia,* ed. Emilio Pasquini (Madrid: Departamento de Filología Italiana UCM-Asociación Complutense de Dantología, 2009), in particular that of Umberto Carpi, "Un congedo da Firenze?" pp. 21–30, and the survey of the various interpretations of the canzone made by Enrico Fenzi, "La *montanina* e i suoi lettori," pp. 31–84); Dante Alighieri, *La canzone* montanina, ed. Paola Allegretti, with a preface by Guglielmo Gorni (Verbania: Tararà Edizioni, 2001); Anna Fontes Baratto, "Le Diptyque *montanino* de Dante," *Arzanà. Cahiers de littérature médiévale italienne* 12 (2007), pp. 65–97; Natascia Tonelli, "Amor, da che convien pur ch'io mi doglia. La canzone montanina di Dante Alighieri (Rime, 15): nodi problematici di un commento," *Per leggere* 10, no. 19 (2010): 7–36.

29. For Guido Salvatico's ownership of Pratovecchio, see Alfred Bassermann, *Orme di Dante in Italia. Vagabondaggi e ricognizioni,* ed. Francesco Benozzo (Sala Bolognese: Arnaldo Forni Editore, 2006; anastatic reprint of the Zanichelli edition of 1902; 1st edition Heidelberg 1897), pp. 92–93, 189. The statement by the so-called anonymous Florentine (in relation to *Purg.* XXIV 43–45) is reported by Rosetta Migliorini Fissi, "Dante e il Casentino," in *Dante e le città dell'esilio,* convegno internazionale, Ravenna, 11–13 September 1987, dir. Guido Di Pino (Ravenna: Longo, 1989) pp. 127–128; as to the identity of the anonymous person, that if he had been Antonio di San Martino a Vado then he would have been from the Casentino, see the entries in BELLOMO, pp. 97–101, and by Francesca Geymonat in CCD. Enrico Malato, *Dante* (Rome: Salerno Editrice, 1999), p. 56, suggests that the "montanina" was written "perhaps in Lunigiana."

30. *Ep.* IV 2; "Igitur michi a limine suspirate postea curie separato, in qua, velud sepe sub admiratione vidistis, fas fuit sequi libertatis officia, cum primum pedes iuxta Sarni fluenta securus et incautus defigerem, subito heu! mulier, ceu fulgur descendens, apparuit, nescio quomodo, meis auspitiis undique moribus et forma conformis. O quam in eius apparitione obstupui! Sed stupor subsequentis tonitrui terrore cessavit. Nam sicut diurnis coruscationibus illico soccedunt tonitrua, sic inspecta flamma pulcritudinis huius, Amor terribilis et imperiosus me tenuit. Atque hic ferox . . . quicquid eius contrarium fuerat intra me, vel occidit vel expulit vel ligavit."

31. A lively analysis of the destructive passion that affected Dante in the Casentino and its autobiographical truth is in Emilio Pasquini, *Vita di Dante. I giorni e le opere* (Milan: Rizzoli, 2006), pp. 53–59; CARPI, at pp. 761–762, also declares that he is convinced of the autobiographical nature of this love. Information about the "goitered" Casentino woman is found in BOCCACCIO[2], 35. The record of the presence of Moroello in the Lunigiana in May 1307 is provided by Vecchi, *"Ad pacem et veram et perpetuam concordiam devenerunt,"* p. 110.

32. For the conclusion of the "montanina," see Tonelli, "Amor, da che convien pur ch'io mi doglia," pp. 15–16; so far as the date, according to Carpi, "Un congedo da Firenze?" p. 28, "we are in all likelihood in the middle of 1307, I would say toward 1308 when there is already a prospect of defeat for the 'black' negotiator Corso inside Florence and of the 'Ghibelline' peacekeeping cardinal Napoleon Orsini outside."

33. For an overview of Dante's relationship with Lucca, see Giorgio Varanini, "Dante e Lucca," in *Dante e le città dell'esilio,* pp. 91–114.

34. Dante himself says he knew Alessio Interminelli when he was still alive (*Inf.* XVIII 120–122). For Dante's critical attitude toward the people of Lucca and for the figure of Alessio Interminelli, see CARPI, pp. 162–163, 503–505.

35. The indication of time in relation to the events taking place in the bolgia of the barraters is found in *Inf.* XXI 112–114: "yesterday, five hours later than now, / one thousand two hundred and sixty-six / years had passed since the path was broken" ("ier, più oltre cinqu' ore che quest' otta, / mille dugento con sessanta sei / anni compié che qui la via fu rotta"). The quote from Buti is taken from *Commento di Francesco da Buti sopra la* Divina Commedia *di Dante Allighieri,* ed. Crescentino Giannini, 3 vols. (Pisa: Nistri, 1858; anastatic reprint Pisa: Nistri-Lischi, 1989), vol. I, p. 548. On Buti, who was writing in the final years of the Trecento, see BELLOMO, pp. 346–359, and the entry in CCD by Fabrizio Franceschini. The extraordinary coincidence between the date of Martino Bottaio's death and his arrival in Hell is pointed out for the first time by Guido da Pisa in his comment on *Inf.* XXI 38: "Ad quorum omnium notitia est sciendun, quod anno domini MCCC, die scilicet XXVI martii, in civitate lucana mortuus est quidam popularis maximus antianus qui vocabatur Martinus Bottarius, quia vegetes faciebat": on Martino and in this episode, see Francesco Paolo Luiso, "L'Anziano di Santa Zita," in *Miscellanea lucchese di studi storici e letterari in memoria di Salvatore Bongi* (Lucca: Scuola Tipografica Artigianelli, 1931), pp. 61–75.

36. Malebranche is the name of a family in Lucca; the nicknames Cagnasso, Graffiacane and Scarmiglione appear in many records in the city archives (compare Luiso, "L'Anziano di Santa Zita," pp. 73–74; Varanini, "Dante e Lucca," p. 99; CARPI, p. 163).

37. As for the identity of Gentucca, the most accepted theory is that she was the daughter of a Ciucchino di Guglielmo Morla and then wife of Buonaccorso di Lazzaro di Fondara, known as Coscio or Cosciorino (Morla and Fondara were both

Lucca families): see Giorgio Varanini, "Dante e la fonte Branda di Romena," in *L'acceso strale. Saggi e ricerche sulla* Commedia (Naples: Federico e Ardia, 1984), pp. 130–135.

38. The death of Corso is retold in detail by DAVIDSOHN, IV, pp. 485–494.

39. The cultural life in Lucca and, in particular, its books in the Dominican convent of San Romano (seat of an important *Studium in naturis* which, in other words, studied Aristotle's treatises on physics) is described in the introduction of FIORAVANTI.

40. It is Fioravanti who expresses doubt about Dante's attendance at the university in Paris. The claims of early biographers about Dante's stay in Paris are examined by INDIZIO², pp. 281–282. Particularly important is the evidence of BOCCACCIO², 56–57: "But, several years having already passed from his leaving Florence, nor apparently having any way of being able to return, finding himself in his view betrayed, he decided to abandon Italy entirely; and, having passed the Alps, went as best he could to Paris, so that, being able to study there, he revised philosophy which other cares had caused him to put aside. He therefore heard there philosophy and some theology, not without great hardship for lack of the comforts of life. From this he was drawn away by a hope that he might return home through the power of Henry of Luxembourg, emperor. So that, having left his studies and returned to Italy . . ." ("Ma, essendo già dopo la sua partita di Firenze più anni passati, né apparendo alcuna via da potere in quella tornare, ingannato trovandosi del suo avviso, si dispose del tutto d'abandonare Italia; e, passati gli Alpi, come poté n'andò a Parigi, acciò che, quivi a suo potere studiando, alla filosofia il tempo, che nell'altre sollecitudini vane tolto l'avea, restituisse. Udì dunque quivi e filosofia e teologia alcun tempo, non senza gran disagio delle cose opportune alla vita. Da questo il tolse una speranza presa di potere in casa sua ritornare con la forza d'Arrigo di Luzimborgo, imperatore. Per che, lasciati gli studii e in Italia tornatosi . . .") Among modern scholars, the view that Dante spent time at the university in Paris is supported with great determination by CARPI, pp. 651–656, and is regarded as certain by Luciano Gargan, "Per la biblioteca di Dante," *Giornale storico della letteratura italiana* 186 (2009), p. 169.

41. A short distance from Lerici there flows the river Magra, "which for a short path / divides the Genoese from the Tuscan" ("che per cammin corto / parte lo Genovese dal Toscano"; *Para.* IX 89–90), that is, for a short stretch it marks the boundary between Tuscany and Liguria: but this is obvious for someone who, like Dante, is familiar with the Lunigiana, and doesn't relate to a clear and definite travel experience (for the interpretation of the "cammin corto" of the Magra, see Bassermann, *Orme di Dante in Italia*, pp. 348–349; there is also a careful description of the descent to Noli).

42. Apart from the reference to the exploits of the imperial eagle in the hands of Caesar witnessed by "every valley that fills the Rhone" ("ogne valle onde Rodano è pieno"; *Para.* VI 60), the clearer reference to Provence is made by Charles

Martel: "That left bank that is washed / by the Rhone then is mixed with Sorgue" ("Quella sinistra riva che si lava / di Rodano poi ch'è misto con Sorga"; *Para*. VIII 58–59).

43. CARPI (pp. 651–655), who declares that he doesn't much believe in indirect information and points out "that in those times there were no photographic archives nor the painting trips of our grandparents and great-grandparents, that travel accounts were themselves scanty and certainly didn't dwell on descriptions of landscapes," suggests that the evidence scattered throughout the *Commedia* is the result of personal experience, including the sight of the necropolis at Arles. He goes even further, suggesting that the references to Flanders, and especially Bruges—"As the Flemish between Wissant and Bruges, / fearing the tide that rises against them, / build the barrier to hold back the sea" ("Quali Fiamminghi tra Guizzante e Bruggia, / temendo 'l fiotto che 'nver' lor s'avventa, / fanno lo schermo perché 'l mar si fuggia"; *Inf*. XV 4–6); "But if Douay, Lille, Ghent and Bruges" ("Ma se Doagio, Lilla, Guanto e Bruggia"; *Purg*. XX 46)—might be evidence of "a visit from the nearby French capital, attracted also by the presence, especially in Bruges, of a colony of Florentine merchants and bankers with whom he had a certain familiarity, those Frescobaldi for example," who, through Dino, had arranged for the return to him of the "little notebook" when it was refound. Acceptance of these conjectures would mean, in any event, postulating a partial rewriting of the relevant cantos of *Inferno*. It is more difficult to accept the idea that the city of Dis, situated at the center of a marsh, might suggest the geographical position of Aigues Mortes, "a recently founded city," "built by King Louis IX of France" at the center of an immense canal: it is difficult to accept because the reference to a direct experience in this case would not only implicate a partial rewriting, but would shift the invention of the whole geography to a period after 1309.

44. On Cardinal Luca Fieschi, see the entry in DBI by Thérèse Boespflug; for relations between the Fieschi and the Malaspina di Giovagallo, see Eliana M. Vecchi, *Alagia Fieschi marchesa Malspina* (Pacini Fazzi, 2003); Vecchi, "Legami consortili fra i Malaspina e Genova nell'età di Dante," *Memorie dell'accademia lunigianese di scienze 'G. capellini'* 75 (2005): 229–252; and Vecchi, "Per la biografia del vescovo Bernabò Malaspina del Terziere (d. 1338)," *Studi Lunigianesi* 22–29 (1992–1999): 109–141, in particular pp. 121–125.

45. There is no record of any stay by Dante in Avignon; only two commentators later make a vague reference to him making a journey and staying in the city of the popes: Francesco da Buti, commenting on *Purg*. XXXII 142–160, writes that the author predicts "that soon Rome must be free from this greed [of the clergy] either that God will change their hearts, or the [papal] court will leave here" ("che tosto Roma debbe essere libera da questa avarizia o che iddio mutrà tosto li cuori loro, o che la corte si partirà quinde"), and he adds "and this I believe was the au-

thor's intention: inasmuch as he passed Avignon" ("e questo credo fusse la 'ntenzione de l'autore: imperò che passò a Vignone"); the anonymous Florentine mentioned earlier, in relation to *Inf.* III 52–57, states that "a certain commentator" claims that "the author, finding himself at Avignon, and seeing so many scoundrels as those who follow the court of the pope, [. . .] resorted to the words of the text" ("dice alcuno chiosatore che, trovandosi l'autore a Vignone, et veggendo tanti gaglioffi quanti sono quelli che seguitano la corte del Papa, egli usò di dire le parole del testo"). Neither of the two statements has any documentary value, but both are perhaps evidence of some weak oral tradition around that event.

Many Florentines whom Dante might have known before his exile were staying in Avignon during that period: for example, the Dominican and historian Bartolomeo Fiadoni, known as Tolomeo da Lucca, who had been prior of Santa Maria Novella from July 1300 to July 1302 (years when Dante certainly attended the *Studio* there), lived in Avignon from that same year of 1309: see the entry in DBI, "Fiadoni, Bartolomeo (Tolomeo, Ptolomeo da Lucca)" by Ludwig Schmugge. Also: in the early months of 1309 Francesco da Barberino, a contemporary of Dante, had traveled to Avignon, as an expert in law, to accompany a diplomatic mission from the Venetian Republic and had stopped there until at least March–April of 1313. Now, the first quotation from the *Commedia,* more precisely from *Inferno,* is to be found in a Latin note by Barberino to his *Documenti d'Amore*: this, written according to some in the second half of 1314 (but according to Alberto Casadei to be dated around June–July 1313 [oral communication]), states that in a work of his called *Commedia,* which among many things deals with matters of Hell, Dante praises Virgilio as his master ("Hunc [Virgilium] Dante Arigherij in quodam suo opere quod dicitur Comedia et de infernalibus inter cetera multa tractat, commendat protinus ut magistrum"). The note may prove that on that date *Inferno* had been published and that Barberino had seen it; see Giuseppe Indizio, "Gli argomenti esterni per la pubblicazione dell'*Inferno* e del *Purgatorio,*" SD 18 (2003): 17–47. The same note may, however, have a different explanation if, in 1309, Dante had himself been in Avignon and, due to the acquaintance they must have had (Barberino had practiced the profession of notary in Florence between 1297 and 1303) and bearing in mind also that those from the same region tended to stay together, he might have spoken about that first canticle that was now complete and might even perhaps have read some part of it to him.

46. On the dating of Canto VI of *Purgatorio* and on Dante's skeptical attitude toward the election of Henry VII, see CASADEI, pp. 125–128.

47. The reproach to Albert of Habsburg and his father Rudolf is in *Purg.* VI 97–105; with regard to the line: "so that your successor may fear it" ("tal che 'l tuo successor temenza n'aggia"), Umberto Carpi, in "Il canto VI del *Purgatorio,*" *Per leggere* 10 (2006): 5–30, agrees with those who feel it is "not at all necessary to regard [Henry VII] as having already acceded, at the moment of writing" (p. 25).

There is also a reference to Henry in Canto VII, where Rudolf of Habsburg is accused of having "neglected" Italy: "Emperor Rudolf . . . could have / healed the wounds of dead Italy, / it will be long, then, before others restore her" ("Rodolfo imperator . . . che potea / sanar le piaghe c'hanno Italia morta, / sì che tardi per altri si ricrea"; *Purg.* VII 94–96); for many, including Carpi, "Il canto VI del *Purgatorio*," pp. 24–26, the line: "sì che tardi per altri si ricrea" is to be read "as an acknowledgement of the failed effort to restore [Italy] by Henry VII." Interpreted in this way, it would be "an intervention after the event, carried out as part of that revision of *Purgatorio* which Dante is suggested to have carried out after Henry's end"; however for CASADEI, p. 127, that line can also be traced back to the "climate of skeptical expectation" which arose on the first news of the election. Finally, it should be noted that in *Convivio* Dante had commented on the absence of the empire in these terms: "Frederick of Swabia, last emperor of the Romans—last I say in relation to the present, even though Rudolf and Adolf [of Nassau] and Albert were then elected, after his death and his descendants" ("Federigo di Soave, ultimo imperatore delli Romani—ultimo dico per rispetto al tempo presente, non ostante che Ridolfo e Andolfo e Alberto poi eletti siano, apresso la sua morte e delli suoi discendenti"; IV III 6).

48. On the surprise with which the Lombards and the Italians in general received the news of the forthcoming arrival of Henry VII, see Gabriele Zanella, "L'imperatore tiranno. La parabola di Enrico VII nella storiografia coeva," in *Il viaggio di Enrico VII in Italia,* ed. Mauro Tosti-Croce, ([Città di Castello]: Edimont, 1993), pp. 43–56, in particular pp. 43–44.

49. I have developed the themes referred to in this paragraph in SANTAGATA, pp. 9–13, 343–347, 357–364.

50. "Un *Inferno* guelfo" is the title of the essential essay by Umberto Carpi (NRLI 13 (2010): 95–134), quoted here on several occasions, which in developing and reconsidering many observations contained in the book on Dante's nobility (CARPI), provides an essential interpretation of the canticle, written during the period when Dante was seeking to obtain a personal amnesty. My pages owe much to his.

51. The passage in the letter to Moroello is much debated: for some the "meditationes assiduas" are the treatises, and *Convivio* in particular (which many consider still being written in 1308), for others they are those of the *Commedia*. The first view is shared, for example, by Enrico Fenzi, "Ancora sulla Epistola a Moroello e sulla *montanina* di Dante," *Tenzone* 4 (2003): 43–84; Dante Alighieri, *Rime,* ed. and commentary by Domenico De Robertis (Florence: SISMEL-Edizioni del Galluzzo, 2005), p. 199; Giuliano Tanturli, "Come si forma il libro delle canzoni?" in Berra and Bersa, *Le rime di Dante,* pp. 117–134, in particular p. 131; those who support the second view include Giovanni Ferretti, *I due tempi della composizione della Divina Commedia* (Bari: Laterza, 1935), pp. 64–66; PADOAN, pp. 35–36; PASQUINI, pp. 9–10.

52. So far as the dating of the first two canticles, of particular interest is the suc-cinct outline by Michele Barbi, "Una nuova opera sintetica su Dante," then in BARBI[1], pp. 69–77, and repeated, expanded and also modified by Ernesto Giacomo Parodi, *La data della composizione e le teorie politiche dell'* Inferno *e del* Purgatorio (Perugia: Unione Tipografica Cooperativa, 1905), pp. 233–313. On the dates of publication of *Inferno* and *Purgatorio* there is an important study by Giuseppe In-dizio, "Gli argomenti esterni per la pubblicazione dell'*Inferno* e del *Purgatorio*." The question cannot, however, be regarded as closed: for example, CASADEI, p. 140, considers that both canticles "could have been completed and circulated by Dante even to demonstrate his personal loyalty to the emperor, therefore prior to his death" in August 1313.

53. For the political interpretation of Cantos X and XV of *Inferno,* I refer to Carpi, "Un *Inferno* guelfo," pp. 117–120; a study of the encounter with Farinata in Marco Santagata, *La letteratura nei secoli della tradizione. Dalla* Chanson de Roland *a Fos-colo* (Rome-Bari: Laterza, 2007), pp. 63–73; and SANTAGATA, pp. 330–333, 351–355.

54. In *VE* I XII 4 Dante had described Frederick II and Manfredi as "illustrious heroes . . ." who had pursued "all that is human, disdaining that which is base" ("illustres heroes . . . humana secuti sunt, brutalia dedignantes").

55. As to the *Tesoretto,* in Gianfranco Contini, ed., *Poeti del Duecento,* 2 vols. (Milan-Naples: Ricciardi, 1960), vol. 2, pp. 175–277, see lines 156–162: "he told me straight away / that Guelfs of Florence / by ill-providence / and by force of war / were banished, / and there was great loss / of prisoners and of dead" ("mi disse immantinente / che guelfi di Firenza / per mala provedenza / e per forza di guerra / eran fuor de la terra, / e 'l dannaggio era forte / di pregioni e di morte") and lines 186–190: "and I, so aggrieved, / thinking with my head bowed, / lost the main road, / and took the side path / into a strange wood" ("e io, in tal corrotto, / pen-sando a capo chino, / perdei il gran cammino, / e tenni a la traversa / d'una selva diversa"). Note also that Dante's text, shortly after the beginning, describes Flor-ence as a "city divided" ("città partita"; *Inf.* VI 61), in exactly the same way as Bru-netto speaks of a civil war as offensive to the natural desire of every man that his own city is not "divided" ("in divisa"), "since a land torn apart cannot survive" ("ché già non può scampare / terra rotta di parte"; lines 166–179). With regard to the reason for his exile in the *Tesoretto,* Giuliano Milani, "Brunetto Latini e l'esclusione politica," *Arzanà* (2012): 37–51 observes (at p. 47) how Brunetto expresses "a general consideration on the need, for a city, to be administered in harmony, without the interests of one party, whichever it is, triumphing to the exclusion of others." Giorgio Inglese refers to a "macroscopic antecedent to the opening of the *Commedia*" (entry "Latini, Brunetto" in DBI); also Beltrami (in the Introduction to Brunetto Latini, *Tresor,* ed. Pietro G. Beltrami, Paolo Squillacioti, Plinio Torri, and Sergio Vatteroni (Turin: Einaudi, 2007), p. xxv) observes how, at the begin-ning of the *Tesoretto,* there is an "immediate comparison with the beginning of

the *Commedia*," except for pointing out that the "*Tesoretto* doesn't, however, offer much more than a simple idea" for Dante's poem.

56. The foolish Tuscans who, "in their madness, lay claim to the title of owning illustrious vernacular" are "Guittone d'Arezzo, who never aimed at court vernacular, Buonagiunta da Lucca, Gallo of Pisa, Mino Mocato of Siena, Brunetto of Florence, whose verses, if there were space to study them closely, would turn out to be suited not to a court but merely to a civic council" ("qui propter amentiam suam infroniti titulum sibi vulgaris illustris arrogare videntur . . . puta Guittonem Aretinum, qui nunquam se ad curiale vulgare direxit, Bonagiuntam Lucensem, Gallum Pisanum, Minum Mocatum Senensem, Brunectum Florentinum, quorum dicta, si rimari vacaverit, non curialia sed municipalia tantum invenientur"; *VE* I XIII 1). Some scholars seek to mitigate Dante's criticism by referring not to the *Tesoretto* and the *Favolello,* but to Brunetto's verse production; TAVONI however (pp. 1282–1283), taking account of the absolute marginality of Brunetto's verse and of characters who were far from "mediocre" in the language in their few surviving examples, suggests that he is referring to the didactic poems. These are rich in civic terms and expressions, the same which, in order to describe them and without any polemical intent, Dante "will place in the mouth of Brunetto, the character in *Inferno,* cramming his conversation with popular, proverbial and idiomatic expressions."

57. The discussion on Dante's reticence about political events in Florence and his banishment is developed further in SANTAGATA, pp. 330–333. Ernesto Sestan "Dante e Firenze," in *Italia medieval* (Napoli: Edizioni scientifiche italiane, 1966), pp. 273–274, also observes that Dante in the *Commedia* passes silently over many events "that marked the political life" of the city in the years when he was living there: these include "the figure and action of people like Giano della Bella and Corso Donati; and even the ferocious conflict between Whites and Blacks." Sestan's observations were followed then by Girolamo Arnaldi, "Pace e giustizia in Firenze e in Bologna al tempo di Dante," in Facoltà di lettere e filosofia, Università di Bologna, *Dante e Bologna nei tempi di Dante* (Bologna: Commissione per i testi di lingua, 1967), pp. 163–177, in particular p. 165.

58. See the lines of Farinata's prediction: " 'If they have not mastered that art,' he said, / 'this torments me more than this bed. / But not fifty times will / the face of she who reigns be relit, / before you'll know how much that art weighs . . .' " (" 'S'elli han quell'arte,' disse, 'male appresa, / ciò mi tormenta più che questo letto. / Ma non cinquanta volte fia raccesa / la faccia de la donna che qui regge, / che tu saprai quanto que quell'arte pesa . . .' "; *Inf.* X 77–81): on the meaning of the prophecy, see Carpi, "Un *Inferno* guelfo," p. 117.

59. The medieval historian referred to is Girolamo Arnaldi, "Il canto di Ciacco (Lettura di *Inf.* VI)," *L'Alighieri* 38 (1977): 7–20; the quote is at pp. 14–15.

60. For the dating of the cantos of *Purgatorio* up to and including XVI, I refer substantially to CASADEI.

61. "In the whole of *Inferno* there is no mention of the empire, except for one single time, almost in passing, in the well-known words of the second canto which, while they glorify it as preordained by God, they seem however to refuse to recognize that it has any purpose . . . Dante seems to conclude that the ultimate purpose of the foundation of Rome and the institution of the Empire was to prepare its seat for the vicar of Christ" (Parodi, "La data della composizione e le teorie politiche dell'*Inferno* e del *Purgatorio* di Dante," pp. 253–254).

62. On the equation of Ghibellinism with heresy, see the observations of Gian Maria Varanini, under the entry "Ezzelino III da Romano," in *Dizionario storico dell'Inquisizione*, 3 vols., ed. Adriano Prosperi, with Vincenzo Lavenia and John Tedeschi (Pisa: Edizioni della Normale, 2010).

63. Canto XXVII of *Inferno* and the political position from which the figure of Guido da Montefeltro is observed are the subjects of a new study by Tavoni (Mirko Tavoni, "Guido da Montefeltro dal *Convivio* all'*Inferno*," NRLI 13 (2010): 167–198, whose basic lines I follow); it is he who suggests that the expression "lo nobilissimo nostro latino" means "il più nobile degli italiani" (p. 169).

64. So far as the kinship between the Guidi of Dovadola and the Malaspina family of Giovagallo, it should be remembered that Marcovaldo, grandson of Guido Salvatico, had married Fiesca, daughter of Moroello and Alagia.

65. The complex web of family relationships between the Malaspina, Visconti, and Fieschi, further complicated by the history of their estates in Sardinia and by the designs of the Doria of Genoa and the Este of Ferrara, can be reconstructed through the index of names and family trees in CARPI: in particular, for Alagia, Beatrice d'Este, Eleonora Fieschi, and the Doria family, see pp. 413–416, while for the intricate story of the married life of Giovanna daughter of Nino Visconti, see p. 415 (at pp. 452–453 a brief portrait of her). On the figure of Hadrian V, see the contributions of Giuseppe Indizio, "Adriano V in Dante e nel secolare commento. Leggenda e storia nel canto XIX del *Purgatorio*," *Giornale storico della Lunigiana e del territorio lucense*, n.s. (2008): 267–280, and Daniele Calcagno, "In merito alla conversione di Ottobuono Fieschi Adriano V," *Giornale storico della lunigiana e del territorio Lucense*, n.s. 59 (2008): 281–296. So far as Alagia and relations between the Malaspina and Fieschi families, I refer to Eliana M. Vecchi, *Alagia Fieschi marchesa Malaspina. Una "domina" di Lunigiana nell'età di Dante* (Lucca: Maria Pacini Fazzi, 2003).

66. Alberico introduces himself and Branca Doria in Canto XXXIII of *Inferno*, lines 118–147. Information on the hedonist friar Alberico dei Manfredi of Faenza, author of a family massacre perpetrated at the end of a banquet, appears in the entry in ED, "Alberigo, Frate" by Vincenzo Presta and in CARPI. On Michele Zanche

(for whom see also *Inf.* XXII 88), see the entry in ED by Giorgio Petrocchi. So far as the difficult relationship between the Doria and Malaspina families, it should be recalled that Branca Doria had planned to give Giovanna, daughter of Nino Visconti, in marriage to a nephew who was son of the Bernabò who was married to Eleonora Fieschi, Alagia's cousin. For the question of Lerici occupied by Branca Doria, I refer to CARPI, pp. 639–640. The sources on which the Malespina could rely for information on the mysterious affair of the death of Michele Zanche would have included the Spinola, another important Ghibelline family in Genoa with close links to the Doria—one of the Spinola was Orietta, wife of Corrado II, and one of the daughters of Michele Zanche was married to a Spinola. Dante says that Branca had committed the crime with the help of "one of his kinsmen" ("un suo prossimano"; *Inf.* XXXIII 146), and it is worth noting that he is identifiable as Giacomino Spinola.

67. In *Para.* XVI 94–98 Dante complains that over the door of the Guidi counts' house in Florence there is now (in 1300) the emblem of the Cerchi, who had bought it in 1280. As for their recent move to the city, Ciacco describes them as "the rustic party" ("la parte selvaggia"; *Inf.* VI 65), whereas Cacciaguida states that if there hadn't been that deplorable phenomenon, "the Cerchi would [still] be in the parish of Acone" ("sarieno i Cerchi nel piovier d'Acone"; *Para.* XVI 65), in the Val di Sieve. Conversely, back in the ancient Florence of Cacciaguida "the stock from which the Calfucci [to which the Donati belonged] were born / was already great" ("Lo ceppo di che nacquero i Calfucci / era già grande"; *Para.* XVI 106–107).

68. It is CARPI (p. 176) who speaks of an "apologia" for the Donati family (but see also pp. 136–138).

69. For Cianghella, cousin of Rosso Della Tosa and wife of Lito degli Alidosi, a Guelf family from Imola connected to the Della Tosa, see CARPI, pp. 175–177, and SANTAGATA, pp. 346–347.

70. Dante is temperamental and almost never able to free himself from contempt for those who have done him wrong or insulted him. And this is true even for the respected Donati family. In *Inferno* there are two people with the name Buoso Donati: the older is among those who impersonate other people; the younger is among thieves. But the first is a victim, the second a criminal. It is said that Simone Donati (father of Corso, Forese, and Piccarda) had persuaded Gianni Schicchi dei Cavalcanti to take the place of the dying Buoso di Vinciguerra Donati: Gianni, disguised so well that not even the notary was aware of the substitution, dictated a will in favor of Simone. In *Inf.* XXX 42–45 it is the alchemist Griffolino d'Arezzo (for whom see CARPI, pp. 674–675) who says to Dante: "the other there [Gianni Schicchi] who is leaving, contrives, / to gain the queen of the herd, / to disguise himself as Buoso Donati, / making and giving due form to the will" ("l'altro che là sen va, sostenne, / per guadagnar la donna de la torma, / falsificare in sé Buoso Donati, / testando e dando al testamento norma"). Even though the story, as told

by the commentators, has many aspects of a fictional tale, it must contain a kernel of truth in terms of the financial relations between two powerful families like the Donati and the Cavalcanti. We don't know why Dante so fiercely attacks the father of the Donati family. He certainly knew the background to what had happened, and equally certainly knew that the Florentines would have understood. It is entirely clear, however, why he had attacked the second Buoso (nephew of Buoso, victim of the impersonation, and paternal uncle of Corso, Forese, and Piccarda), accusing him of being a thief (*Inf.* XXV 140). Buoso di Forese Donati was father of Gasdia, who was married to Baldo d'Aguglione, and when this jurist is involved, Dante cannot resist. For the two Buoso Donati, I refer to CARPI, pp. 138–140.

8. An Emperor Arrives

1. In the extensive bibliography relating to Henry VII and his expedition, I have found the following studies particularly useful: DAVIDSOHN, IV, pp. 477–759; Francesco Cognasso, *Arrigo VII* (Milan: Dall'Oglio, 1973); the essays collected in Mauro Tosti-Croce, ed., *Il viaggio di Enrico VII in Italia* ([Città di Castello]: Edimont, 1993, in particular: Franco Cardini, "La Romfahrt di Enrico VII," pp. 1–11; Hannelore Zug Tucci, "Henricus coronatur corona ferrea," pp. 29–42; Gabriele Zanella, "L'imperatore tiranno. La parabola di Enrico VII nella storiografia coeva," pp. 43–56; and "Achille Tartaro, Dante e l'*alto Arrigo*," pp. 57–60.

2. For the concessions made by Henry to the pope on the matter of the superiority of spiritual power over temporal power, see ZINGARELLI, p. 251.

3. For Simone di Filippo Reali, see the biographical sketch by DAVIDSOHN, IV, pp. 524–525.

4. Of little importance in itself, though significant in the present context, is the fact that Henry's officers were sworn in by Aghinolfo di Romena, the former *capitano* of the White exiles. Unlike many other members of the Guidi clan, Aghinolfo and his brother, Bishop Ildebrandino, would remain faithful to the imperial cause. Aghinolfo would fight in the imperial army during the siege of Florence; Ildebrandino (who died in 1313) would be appointed vicar of Arezzo (see CARPI, pp. 578–579).

5. Suggestions that Dante may have joined the procession of Henry VII that moved down to Italy are clearly wrong: indeed, one of the few certain facts is that he was in Italy at least five or six months before Henry began his journey. Careful consideration must be given, however, to Boccaccio's evidence that Dante set off from Paris on "hearing" that the newly elected emperor was leaving Germany "to subjugate Italy"; the information, except for Paris, is substantially correct. Boccaccio then continues by saying that, "passing across the Alps again" and "having joined up with many enemies of Florence and their party," Dante, with embassies

and letters, sought to draw Henry from the siege of Brescia and to convince him to attack Florence (BOCCACCIO[1], 76–78). The siege to which he is referring is that of Cremona, and not Brescia, but this information also contains much truth, except that it doesn't relate to a period immediately after his return to Italy.

6. Biondo Flavio, who seems to base his account on a chronicle (*traditur*) written perhaps by Pellegrino Calvi, after having given a detailed description of the embassy to Florence, adds: "Dante Alighieri, who lived in Forlì at that time, in a letter addressed to Cangrande della Scala of Verona in his own name and that of the exiles of the White faction, which Pellegrino Calvi left written, says such things, with regard to the answer to the aforesaid directions of the emperor given to the Florentines who then held the power of the city, for which he accuses those who governed of imprudence, insolence and blindness, so that Benvenuto da Imola, whom I believe to have read the writings of Pellegrino, declares that Dante, from this moment on, began to call the Florentines with the epithet of 'blind'" ("Dantes Aldegherius, Fori Livii tunc agens, in epistola ad Canem Grandem Scaligerum veronensem, partis Albae extorrum et suo nomine data, quam Peregrinus Calvus scriptam reliquit, talia dicit de responsione supradictae expositioni a Florentinis urbem tenentibus tunc facta, per quae temeritatis et petulantiae ac caecitatis sedentes ad clavum notat, adeo ut Benvenutus Imolensis, quem Peregrini scripta legisse crediderim, Dantem asserat hinc cepisse Florentinos epitheto 'caecos' appellare"); Biondo Flavio, *Historiarum ab inclinatione Romani imperii decades quattuor* (Basileae: Froben, 1531), decade II, book IX, p. 342). Benvenuto da Imola makes no mention of this episode in his life of Dante, not even when he gives a lengthy explanation, in relation to *Inf.* XV 67, about the origin of the popular saying that described the Florentines as blind. As to whether Dante wrote to Cangrande in 1310, Michele Barbi is doubtful ("Sulla dimora di Dante a Forlì" (1892), in BARBI[1], pp. 189–195, in particular p. 194); CASADEI, p. 129, is very skeptical; according to him "it is most unlikely that, in the second half of 1310, Dante would have written on behalf of himself and of the exiles 'partis albae'"; here too, in his view, Biondo could have "misinterpreted the references," as had already happened when he had spoken about the diplomatic mission to Verona in 1304. There is no basis for the idea that the letter to Cangrande referred to by Biondo could have been written in spring 1310 (PETROCCHI, p. 150) or in the second half of 1311 (Giorgio Padoan "Tra Dante e Mussato. I. Tonalità dantesche nell' *Historia Augusta* di Albertino Mussato," *Quaderni veneti* 24 (1966): 37).

7. For the mission of Henry's legates to Verona, see Francesco Cognasso, *Arrigo VII* (Milan: Dall'Oglio, 1973) pp. 102–103.

8. On the fact that Dante, in the second half of 1310, was acting in a collective context and speaking on behalf of a group, which can only have been that of the exiles, the scant reference notes in INDIZIO[2] (p. 290) are highly indicative; see also PETROCCHI, p. 149.

9. The marriage had been celebrated only a year before (in 1309) between Sinibaldo, the brother of Scarpetta, and a sister of Fulcieri named Onestina. It will be remembered that Fulcieri had been the *podestà* who had been merciless against the Whites after his victory over them at Pulicciano (in 1303) and whom, in a canto of *Purgatorio* composed perhaps only a few months after his arrival in Forlì, Dante had branded as a ruthless "hunter" of his companions (*Purg.* XIV 58–66). I take the information on the Ordelaffi-Calboli marriage and on the return of the Calboli to the city from CASADEI, pp. 129–130.

10. It wasn't the first time that Henry had been to Italy: he had been there ten years earlier, on a private visit, so to speak. After a long stay in Turin, he had traveled to Rome with Louis I of Savoy-Vaud, who was on his way to Naples for his marriage to Isabella d'Aulnay on May 1, 1301 (Cognasso, *Arrigo VII,* pp. 96–97).

11. For the events surrounding the coronation and the "iron crown" which, as it was then imagined by those who had never seen it, was probably simple legend, see Cognasso, *Arrigo VII,* pp. 136–139, and especially, Zug Tucci, "Henricus coronatur corona ferrea."

12. In *Ep.* VII 2 to Henry (of April 1311) Dante writes: "I saw you most benevolent, as is fitting for the imperial majesty, and I heard you speak with absolute clemency, when my hands touched your feet and my lips paid off their debt" ("[ego] velut decet imperatoriam maiestatem benignissimum vidi et clementissimun te audivi, cum pedes tuos manus mee tractarunt et labia mea debitum persolverunt").

13. *Ep.* V (of fall 1310) ends with the following words: "He is the one whom Peter, vicar of God, exhorts us to honor; whom Clement, now successor of Peter, illuminates with the light of apostolic benediction; and where spiritual radiance not enough, there shines the light of the lesser luminary" ("Hic est quem Petrus, Dei vicarius, honorificare nos monet; quem Clemens, nunc Petri successor, luce Apostolice benedictionis illuminat; ut ubi radius spiritualis non sufficit, ibi splendor minoris luminaris illustret"). The political character of the letter was acknowledged very clearly by DAVIDSOHN, IV, pp. 562–563, though he infers too exact a program: "From this letter by the Poet, one can glimpse what the Whites and the Ghibellines, their allies, were seeking when he, their eager interpreter, paid homage to the king of the Romans. They wanted Florence to become a city free from the empire: as such, it would have been invested by the future emperor with the jurisdiction and the right to mint money and to enjoy all other royal privileges. In exchange, the city would have been obliged to pay a tribute and to supply armies on the sovereign's request." With regard to the "two luminaries," Emilio Pasquini writes (in *Vita di Dante. I giorni e le opere* (Milan: Rizzoli, 2006), p. 69): "At the end of the letter Dante seems to endorse . . . the theory of the *duo luminaria* (Sun and Moon, as symbol of Papacy and Empire), confirmed by Clement in the letter *Divine sapientie,* sent to Henry by the pope on July 26, 1309."

14. If we consider the degree and extent of reprisals carried out in commune cities with each change of regime, the value of Dante's invitation to the exiles to pardon and his assurance in that regard to Henry would be seen in their appropriate political context. It is revealing that in *Ep.* IV 2 to Moroello, he, in order to illustrate the dominion of Love over him, uses the metaphorical image of "a lord driven away from his land" who "after a long exile, upon returning to the lands that are only his, annihilates, banishes or fetters whatever thing that had been against him" ("hic ferox, tanquam dominus pulsus a patria post longum exilium sola in sua repatrians, quicquid eius contrarium fuerat . . . vel occidit vel expulit vel ligavit").

15. The meaning of Dante's letter fits perfectly with what emerges from the record of a crowded assembly of Guelf and Ghibelline exiles held in Pisa, at the church of San Michele in Borgo, on October 18, 1310. Those present—among whom we find some familiar names such as those of Lapo degli Uberti the elder, son of Farinata, Ricovero dei Cerchi, Andrea Gherardini (persecutor of the Blacks of Pistoia), Gherardino Diodati (prior along with Saltarelli, then condemned to death)—decide to send a delegation to Henry, who was shortly to arrive, headed by Lapo degli Uberti, who had power to accept all the conditions the emperor wished to place upon them and to submit themselves entirely to his will. The record of the meeting is published by PADOAN, pp. 229–235, for which see also Padoan, "Tra Dante e Mussato," pp. 30–31.

16. Possible mediators include Henry's chaplain Galasso, canon of Cambrai, from the family of the Alberti counts of Mangona, who was close to Cardinal Niccolò da Prato (by whom he was appointed vicar of Pistoia when the city had attempted to readmit the Whites in 1304), and Palmiero degli Altoviti, a close friend of Dante, a jurist, with much influence at court, who had also been a prior during the months in which the Cerchi faction had decided to banish the Blacks from Pistoia and who was jointly sentenced to death, along with Dante. For Galasso degli Alberti di Mangona, see DAVIDSOHN, IV, pp. 175, 380, 437, 567.

17. In Milan, Dante would have been able to meet up with many old friends and acquaintances: his friends included Cino da Pistoia, who was politically "black" but supported the imperial ideas in both his actions and his writings (Cino traveled from Milan to Rome to join the new senator Louis of Savoy, with whom he remained as legal advisor until the summer of the following year). His acquaintances included Sennuccio del Bene, the White Guelf and poet, who had left Florence, voluntarily or otherwise, on the arrival of the Blacks and had then taken part in the siege of his city among the ranks of the imperial army. Dante must have known him during the second half of the Duecento, when Sennuccio held various city appointments; it is unlikely, however, that Dante is the author of the sonnet *Sennuccio, la tua poca personuzza* (*Rime dubbie* 4): see GIUNTA, pp. 682–683.

18. For some idea on how much pressure the Ghibellines and White exiles placed on Henry, it is enough to look at the list of vicars appointed by him between 1311 and 1312: the Ghibelline lords Alboino and Cangrande della Scala were vicars of Verona (Cangrande also became vicar of Vicenza on the death of his brother in November 1311); Rizzardo da Camino, who had abandoned the Guelfs, was vicar of Treviso; Franceschino Malaspina was vicar of Parma; Uguccione della Faggiola vicar of Genoa; so far as Florentine exiles, Lapo degli Uberti was vicar of Mantua; Lamberto dei Cipriani vicar of Piacenza; Francesco di Tano degli Ubaldini vicar of Pisa. Many White Guelfs among the numerous Vergiolesi family from Pistoia, who were forced into exile in 1306, held the office of vicar: Guidaloste was vicar of Modena; Soffredi (or Goffredo) vicar of Cremona; Lando vicar of Bergamo. In addition, Filippo Vergiolesi (father of Selvaggia, immortalized by Cino) who, once in exile, had fought against the Florentines in the Apennines, held important diplomatic posts. Important positions were also given to Palmiero degli Altoviti of Florence. Information about Lamberto dei Cipriani in DAVIDSOHN, IV, pp. 571, 642, 776; see also pp. 488, 494, 571, 642, for information on Francesco degli Ubaldini, son of Tano; for the Vergiolesi, I refer to Vinicio Pacca, "Un ignoto corrispondente di Petrarca: Francesco Vergiolesi," NRLI 4 (2001): 151–206.

19. For the quoted decree revoking the banishments and for the question of confiscated property, I refer to Cognasso, *Arrigo VII*, pp. 151–153.

20. The historian referred to is DAVIDSOHN, IV, p. 593.

21. In July–August 1311, the new vicar of Romagna, Gilberto de Santilla, on succeeding Niccolò Caracciolo, intervened heavy-handedly in Forlì, imprisoning Scarpetta Ordelaffi and Fulcieri da Calboli (see CASADEI, p. 130).

22. Many suggest that epistles VI and VII were written in Poppi: for example, Francesco Mazzoni, "Le epistole di Dante," in *Conferenze aretine 1965* (Arezzo: Zilli, 1966), p. 67; the commentary by Arsenio Frugoni in *Ep.*, p. 550; PETROCCHI, pp. 149–150; Cardini, "La Romfahrt di Enrico VII," p. 1. But ZINGARELLI, p. 264, writes that the words "sub fontem Sarni" contained in both letters "lead us immediately to think of Porciano, five miles below the springs of the Arno"; the same view was also taken by Corrado Ricci, *L'ultimo rifugio di Dante,* new ed. (Ravenna: Edizioni "Dante" di A. Longo, 1965; 1st ed. 1891), pp. 14–17; less certain is DAVIDSOHN, IV, p. 591, who claims *Ep.* VI was written "at one of the castles of the Guidi Ghibellines in the Casentino." ZINGARELLI, pp. 263–264, rightly points out that Dante could not have expressed such radically anti-Florentine ideas while staying with the Guidi at Battifolle.

23. For the biblical and prophetical style of Dante's political letters, see the observations of Mazzoni ("Le epistole di Dante," pp. 77, 95) on the prevalence of biblical and liturgical language and phrasing in Latin registry documents.

24. Henry's monetary plans are dealt with in Cognasso, *Arrigo VII,* pp. 160–163.

25. The question of prescription of imperial rights is considered with great insight by DAVIDSOHN, IV, pp. 562–566 (it is from here that I take the list of castles over which claims for restitution had been drawn up by the imperial chancery), but see also: Cognasso, *Arrigo VII*, pp. 186, 189; Alberto Casadei, "Sicut in Paradiso Comedie iam dixi," SD, 76 (2011): 179–197, in particular pp. 186–187, and above all, the introduction by Diego Quaglioni to his commentary on *Monarchia* in Dante Alighieri, *Opere*, II. CARPI writes (at p. 561) that the Church and Florence, in attempting to establish their own claim over Romandiola and Tuscia, interpreted "as mere property of feudal lords (to be purchased or confiscated) all that over which there had been full *dominium* by imperial diploma" and they therefore reduced "administrative and government decisions to arbitrary acts or crimes."

26. The reference to a "diehard Ghibelline" is from DAVIDSOHN, IV, p. 566.

27. On the death of Guido Guerra III, his sons had asked Boncompagno da Signa, a jurist and personal acquaintance, for advice on whether it was appropriate to divide the countship: Boncompagno had replied with an epistle-treatise (*Epistola mandativa ad comites palatinos*) in which he advised caution, pointing out that divisions had already led to the decline of many families of marchesi and counts, especially in geographical areas in which there were "dominia" over cities. Such cities he branded, from a feudal point of view, as "bloodsuckers." On this episode, see the observations of CARPI, pp. 553–554; Boncompagno's epistle is published online by Steven M. Wight (http://scrineum.unipv.it/wight/epman.htm). For fundamental information on the stories of the various branches of the Guidi, their attitude toward Florence and, later, toward Henry, see CARPI (pp. 534–580); the ways in which the commune of Florence gradually succeeded in appropriating the properties and rights of the Guidi family, to the point of destroying it, are described by Ernesto Sestan, "I conti Guidi e il Casentino," an essay from 1956 in Sestan, *Italia medievale* (Naples: ESU, 1968), pp. 359–362.

28. Passages from the letter from the priors of Florence to Robert of Anjou are published by DAVIDSOHN, IV, p. 594.

29. With regard to the letter from Gherardesca to Margaret of Brabant, a good example of the view that Dante scholars have about Dante's flawless and proudly independent character is the objection made by Mazzoni ("Le epistole di Dante," p. 78) to the conjecture (whose basic arguments cannot however be accepted) of Fredi Chiappelli, "Osservazioni sulle tre epistole dantesche a Margherita Imperatrice," GSLI 140 (1963): 558–565, who suggests that the last letter is cooler toward the emperor; Mazzoni states "that Alighieri would never have been told what to say by his patrons to the extent of watering down his own enthusiasm and warmth of expression to an open-ended, diplomatic, judgment about what was happening."

30. On the question of the kingdom of Arles, see Cognasso, *Arrigo VII*, pp. 59–60, 70, 194–195 (for a history of the kingdom during the years immediately before-

hand, see Paul Fournier, *Le Royaume d'Arles et de Vienne et ses rélations avec l'Empire da la mort de Fréderic II à la mort de Rodolphe de Hasbourg [1250–1291]* (Paris: Victor Palmé éditeur, 1886).

31. Particularly serious was what occurred after the killing of Betto Brunelleschi who, in June of the previous year, had responded arrogantly to Henry's messengers. The Donati had considered that he and Pazzino dei Pazzi were responsible for the death of Corso in 1308. In February 1311, two young Donati avenged their illustrious kinsman by killing Betto. One of the attackers was, in turn, killed by a son of Brunelleschi. It led to riots in the city. Corso's body was exhumed and given a lavish funeral. The funeral, in turn, led to a long and bitter dispute between the Dominicans of Santa Maria Novella and the clergy of the chapterhouse of Santa Maria del Fiore over the division of a substantial gift of alms, which degenerated into violence. Over the next few days, the quarrel over the earnings from the funeral extended to include the whole of the city's lay clergy, and Dominicans were even banned from preaching in churches other than their own. The dispute would last ten years, reaching even the papal corridors of Avignon, and ended only in 1321 with the intervention of the general of the Order (see DAVIDSOHN, IV, pp. 546–548).

32. For the reform of September 2, see PIATTOLI, no. 106, though he publishes only the names of those excluded in the district of Porta San Piero (the full version is in *Il libro del chiodo*, facsimile reproduction with critical edition by Francesca Klein, in collaboration with Simone Sartini, introduction by Riccardo Fubini (Florence: Edizioni Polistampa, 2004) pp. 283–308).

The amnesty did not pacify the hearts of the Florentines. In January 1312, a few months after it became law and when Henry had already made the imperial decree against Florence, Pazzino dei Pazzi was also killed by vendetta. This time it was the Cavalcanti who avenged the execution of their kinsman nine years earlier, for which they held Pazzino responsible. And this time the killing of a powerful member of the oligarchy caused a popular uprising that culminated in the burning of the Cavalcanti houses, which had been rebuilt after the great fire of 1304. The flight of almost all the heads of the family and the destruction of their property caused the ruin of their commercial business (see DAVIDSOHN, IV, pp. 448–450).

33. The lack of references to Dante's sons in the reform is noted by DAVIDSOHN, IV, p. 620, according to whom Iacopo and Pietro, whom he presumes to be banished, "would then," as a result of not being named in that document, "have been able to return to the city which their father would never again be able to see."

34. As an indication of how the fate of Ugolino was still relevant, even though it happened more than thirty years earlier, it should be noted that Guelfo, one of the count's nephews who had been imprisoned in June 1288 when he was only a few months old, was still in prison in 1313, from which he would be released by Henry's intervention, after being held hostage moreover by the Ghibellines of Pisa; see DAVIDSOHN, III, p. 435; IV, p. 639.

35. Moroello's family relationship with Ugolino della Gherardesca was through his sister Manfredina, who in 1285 had married Banduccio, an illegitimate but acknowledged son of the count; see Eliana M. Vecchi, *Alagia Fieschi marchesa Malaspina. Una "domina" di Lunigiana nell'età di Dante* (Lucca: Maria Pacini Fazzi, 2003), p. 35.

36. Padoan, "Tra Dante e Mussato," p. 37, suggests that Dante left the Casentino after May 1311 to "join up with the other Tuscan exiles" (which, it would seem, happened at Forlì); CARPI, p. 664, thinks, however, that Dante's stay in the Casentino might have lasted for almost the whole year; it is also he (at pp. 669–670) who describes Pisa as "always untrustworthy and dangerous both in [Dante's] memory as an old Guelf linked to Nino Visconti (and in previous months to the daughter of Count Ugolino . . .), as well as in his recent experience as an intellectual in the anti-Pisan and pro-Luccan court of the Malaspina."

37. For the diplomatic mission which was repelled by the Florentines and ended up with the Guidi, I refer to: DAVIDSOHN, IV, pp. 605–613; Cognasso, *Arrigo VII,* pp. 251–252; CARPI, pp. 664–666 (from which is taken the extract from Butrint's report on the meeting with the Guidi); Giuseppe Indizio, "Un episodio della vita di Dante: l'incontro con Francesco Petrarca," in Indizio, *Problemi di biografia dantesca* (Ravenna: Longo Editore, 2013), pp. 115–125 (which contains the translation of the same passage cited by Carpi). For information on Butrint's *Relatio de itinere Henrici VII ad Clementem V,* see CARPI, p. 769; a detailed account of that ill-fated mission is given by Isidoro Del Lungo, *Da Bonifazio VIII ad Arrigo VII. Pagine di storia fiorentina per la vita di Dante* (Milan: Hoepli, 1899), pp. 435–441.

38. For Bernabò Doria, see Carla Maria Monti, "Uguccione della Faggiola, la battaglia di Montecatini e la *Commedia* di Dante," RSD 10 (2010): 139–141.

39. Information about the meeting with Dante is given by Petrarch in *Fam.* XXI 15, 7–8, of 1359. The reconstruction of the Petrarch family movements between 1310 and 1312 made by Arnaldo Foresti, *Aneddoti della vita di Francesco Petrarca* [1923], rev. and enl., ed. Antonia Tissoni Benvenuti (Padua: Editrice Antenore, 1977), pp. 1–7, is corrected persuasively by Indizio, "Un episodio della vita di Dante."

40. The stories about the beating that Dante is said to have received on Doria's instruction are published by Giovanni Papanti, *Dante secondo la tradizione e i novellatori* (Livorno: Vigo Editore, 1873), pp. 151–153.

41. The phrase quoted on the extent of the battle fought in the streets of Rome is by Jean-Claude Maire Vigueur, *L'autre Rome: une histoire des Romains à l'époque des communes. XIIe–XIVe siècle* (Tallandier: Paris, 2010), pp. 71–72.

42. For Henry VII's encyclical to the sovereigns and Philip IV's reply, see Cognasso, *Arrigo VII,* pp. 289–290, 303.

43. The banquet after the coronation is described by DAVIDSOHN, IV, pp. 656–657.

44. For the rumors that Henry VII had been poisoned and accusations against the Dominican order, I refer to DAVIDSOHN, IV, pp. 750–752, and to Cognasso, *Arrigo VII,* pp. 369–370. The information doesn't seem entirely ill-founded according to Indizio, "Un episodio della vita di Dante," who, indeed, speaks of "probable poisoning," despite the modern forensic opinion of Francesco Mari and Elisabetta Bertol, *Veleni. Intrighi e delitti nei secoli* (Florence: Le Lettere, 2001), pp. 37–47.

45. The meaning of "sop" and the suggestion that this term alludes to a poisoning are considered by Filippo Bognini, "Per *Purg.,* XXXIII, 1–51: Dante e Giovanni di Boemia," *Italianistica* 37 (2008): 11–48, in particular pp. 33–44; Bognini identifies the "vessel" as Henry VII, but the context leaves no doubt about the fact that the "chariot" is that of the Church.

46. The suggestion that Dante moved from Tuscany to Verona toward the middle of 1312, formulated by Giorgio Petrocchi, *Itinerari danteschi,* introduced and ed. by Carlo Ossola (Milan: Franco Angeli, 1994; Bari: Laterza, 1969), pp. 98–101, and PETROCCHI, p. 154) and put forward more recently by Enrico Malato, *Dante* (Rome: Salerno Editrice, 1999), pp. 62–63 ("during that two-year period of 1312–1313 Dante probably stayed in Verona as guest of Cangrande della Scala"), cannot be sustained in the light of the convincing arguments put forward, among others, by CARPI, pp. 666–671, and INDIZIO[1], pp. 52–59. It seems more likely, at least until Henry's death and shortly after, that Dante "had not wanted to move away from Henry VII's field of action and from Tuscany" (CARPI, p. 669) and that he had spent 1312–1313 in Pisa (Padoan, "Tra Dante e Mussato," p. 32). Indizio, "Un episodio della vita di Dante," limits this stay to the first half of 1312.

47. The passages in *Historia augusta* (V I) where Mussato describes Niccolò da Prato as the key figure for the Ghibellines are reported by Giuseppe Billanovich, *La tradizione del testo di Livio e le origini dell'umanesimo,* vol. I: *Tradizione e fortuna di Livio tra Medioevo e umanesimo,* Part I (Padua: Editrice Antenore, 1981), p. 46. The suggestion that Dante, perhaps due to the mediation of Niccolò da Prato, may have collaborated, so to speak, externally with the imperial chancery is put forward by Padoan, "Tra Dante e Mussato," pp. 38–45.

48. For Dante's absence from the siege of Florence, see BRUNI, p. 547; his absence is confirmed by the evidence that his name doesn't appear among the list of those who sided with the emperor between September 1312 and March 1313 ("Lista compilata dai Capitani di Parte guelfa nel marzo 1313 dei nomi di coloro che fra il settembre 1312 e il marzo 1313 si erano schierati con Arrigo VII di Lussemburgo," in *Il libro del chiodo,* pp. 319–334).

49. Dating Dante's works can be a hopeless task, and *Monarchia* is no exception, all the more because it is a book that has no explicit biographical references. One of the two main hypotheses, with regard to time, argues that it was composed around 1317–1318 for the purpose of supporting the rights of the

imperial vicar Cangrande della Scala in his dispute with Clement V's successor, Giovanni XXII; the other dates it to the period of Henry VII's descent into Italy. However, while the suggestion that it was written for his patron Cangrande is not corroborated by any direct or indirect reference to that dispute, a number of internal and external factors can be relied on to support the suggestion that it dates between Henry's coronation in Milan (in January 1311) and his death (in August 1313), starting from the evidence of BOCCACCIO[1], p. 195, who confidently states that "at the coming of Emperor Henry VII [Dante] wrote a book in Latin prose, whose title is *Monarchia*." For a survey of the various proposed dates for *Monarchia*, see the entry in ED by Pier Giorgio Ricci. New persuasive arguments for the dating of the treatise during the years of Henry VII have been put forward in Alberto Casadei, "Sicut in Paradiso *Comedie* iam dixi," SD 76 (2011): 179–197, and Diego Quaglioni in the commentary on *Monarchia* in Dante Alighieri, *Opere*, II. I refer to them for an analysis of the specific questions; I would point out only that both agree regarding the parenthesis at *Mn.* I 12 6—"Sicut in Paradiso *Comedie* iam dixi"—as not written by Dante, a parenthesis which, in referring to *Para.* V 19–22, would relate to a period after 1314. Quaglioni regards it as a corruption of the text, whose origin can be traced from a phrase by Dante ("iam dixi") that referred to what had just been said in the text (Diego Quaglioni, "Un nuovo testimone per l'edizione della *Monarchia* di Dante: il Ms. Additional 6891 della British Library, *Laboratoire italien* 11 (2011): 231–278).

50. The phrase about Dante freeing himself from the clichés of tradition is by GIUNTA, p. 44. On the constantly new character of Dante's writing, see SANTAGATA, pp. 98–104.

51. The phrase about the variety of sources for *Monarchia* is by Diego Quaglioni (introduction to the commentary in Dante Alighieri, *Opere,* II).

52. With regard to the passage in *Mn.* II 1–5 against the kings of the Earth and the princes who conspire against the Lord's Anointed One, the observations of Casadei, "Sicut in Paradiso *Comedie* iam dixi," pp. 182–187, should be borne in mind; he suggests, from comparisons above all with *Ep.* VI to the Florentines, that "it is important not to think of the opposition [to Henry] after his coronation of June 29, 1312" but instead of the opposition that developed between 1311 and 1312.

53. For the complex problems relating to the relationship that Dante's treatise seems to have with the *Constitutiones pisanae* and with Clement's decrees (whose dating is much debated), I refer to the introduction by Diego Quaglioni in Dante Alighieri, *Opere*, II, according to whom *Monarchia*, which "seems indeed to reflect the further radicalization of the conflict, probably before the death of the emperor," was "completed around" the period of the promulgation of the Pisan constitutions, "perhaps around [the time of] their drafting and publication." Also for DAVIDSOHN, IV, pp. 740–745, the treatise "owes its origin" to the discussions that animated the peninsula during the months of the final conflict between

Henry VII and the Angevin sovereign; he established the date of its composition as "summer 1313, perhaps July of that year." A different view is expressed by Casadei, "Sicut in Paradiso *Comedie* iam dixi," p. 190, who suggests that the treatise can be dated "only in a period that saw Henry and Clement in full function, not yet in active opposition to each other, as would happen shortly after the Roman coronation in June 1312." For relations with contemporary political affairs, see also Sergio Cristaldi, *Dante di fronte al gioachimismo. I. Dalla "Vita Nova" alla "Monarchia"* (Caltanissetta-Rome: Salvatore Sciascia Editore, 2002) pp. 400–410, who fixes the earlier limit for composition to July–August 1312, but allows the later limit to slip to 1314–1316.

54. When Clement's successor, John XXII, and Henry's successor, Louis of Wittelsbach (called the Bavarian), arrived at a point of bitter conflict, worse than that of their predecessors (with even the election of an antipope), the Bavarian and "his followers . . . began to use" to their advantage "many of the arguments" put forward by Dante in *Monarchia,* and this gave rise to a propaganda by the Church that sought to refute the ideas. Dante's book was caught up in the diatribe to the extent that the papal legate, Cardinal Bertrando del Poggetto, ordered its burning in Bologna in 1329. Dante was accused of heresy and his bones risked being disinterred and burned, as had happened to those of Farinata degli Uberti many years earlier. At Bologna, the epicenter of the conflict, between 1327 and 1334 the Dominican friar Guido Vernani wrote, probably before 1329, a *Reprobatio Monarchiae*: see in this respect Michele Maccarrone, "Dante e i teologi del XIV–XV secolo," *Studi Romani* 5 (1957): 20–28, and Casadei, "Sicut in Paradiso *Comedie* iam dixi," p. 193. The account of the "Ghibelline" success of *Monarchia* and the trial brought by Bertrando del Poggetto (whose activity is described in the entry in ED by Beniamino Pagnin) is found in BOCCACCIO[1], 195–197. The information that Dante, as a result of *Monarchia,* was "almost" convicted as a heretic is confirmed by the jurist Bartolo da Sassoferrato (for whom see the entry in DBI by Francesco Calasso).

55. DAVIDSOHN, IV, p. 743, writes: "events, immediately after the work was written, made the content [of *Monarchia*] for the moment practically unusable, whereas, in the time of Louis the Bavarian, it once again touched on burning questions of current importance."

56. CARPI is fundamentally important for Dante's revaluation of nobility of blood (not surprisingly the book is entitled *La nobiltà di Dante*).

57. About Aeneas, Dante writes (*Mn.* II III 7): "I wouldn't know how to fully describe the nobility of this most victorious and most dutiful father, considering not only his own virtue, but also that of his forebears and wives, whose nobility flowed into him by hereditary right" ("Qui quidem invictissimus atque piissimus pater quante nobilitatis vir fuerit, non solum sua considerata virtute sed progenitorum suorum atque uxorum, quorum utrorunque nobilitas hereditario iure in ipsum confluxit, explicare nequirem").

9. The Prophet

1. The canzone *Da poi che la Natura ha fine posto* by Cino da Pistoia can be found in Gianfranco Contini, ed., *Poeti del Duecento,* 2 vols. (Milan-Naples: Ricciardi, 1960), vol. 2, pp. 678–679.

2. On the letter to the cardinals, see Arsenio Frugoni, "Dante tra due Conclavi—La lettera ai Cardinali italiani," *Letture classensi* 2 (1969): 69–91; Ovidio Capitani, "Una questione non ancora chiusa: il paragrafo 10 (Ed. Toynbee) della lettera ai Cardinali italiani di Dante," *Annali della Scuola Normale Superiore di Pisa, Classe di Lettere e Filosofia,* s. 3, vol. 3 (1973): 471–485; Raffaello Morghen, "La lettera di Dante ai Cardinali italiani e la coscienza della sua missione religiosa," in Morghen, *Dante profeta tra la storia e l'eterno* (Milan: Jaca Book, 1983), pp. 109–138.

3. It appears that the letter reached its destination from the fact that it "must have been kept among the papal records, between Avignon and Rome: since Petrarch and Cola di Rienzo would soon refer to it" (Billanovich, *La tradizione del testo di Livio e le origini dell'umanesimo,* vol. I: *Tradizione e fortuna di Livio tra Medioevo e umanesimo,* Part I (Padua: Editrice Antenore, 1981), p. 46); see also Morghen, "La lettera di Dante ai Cardinali italiani," pp. 111–112.

4. The account of the Gascon irruption into the conclave, shouting "Moriantur Cardinales italici; volumus Papam, volumus Papam," is given by the cardinals themselves in an encyclical letter to the Cistercian abbeys: see Francesco Mazzoni, "Le epistole di Dante," in *Conferenze aretine 1965* (Arezzo: Zilli, 1966), p. 82.

5. For John XXII, see the entry in EP by Christian Trottmann.

6. On John of Luxembourg, see: Filippo Bognini, "Per *Purg.,* XXXIII, 1–51: Dante e Giovanni di Boemia," *Italianistica* 37 (2008): 11–48 (and related bibliographical references); and Francesco Cognasso, *Arrigo VII* (Milan: Dall'Oglio, 1973), pp. 373–374. In *Ep.* VII 5, Dante writes: "John, your royal firstborn and king, for whom the coming descendants await after the end of the day that now dawns [i.e., after the death of his father], is for us a second Ascanius [son of Aeneas], who, following the example of his great father, will roar furiously like a lion against the Turni [the Rutulians, referred to in Virgil's *Aeneid*] and, like a lion, will be meek toward the Latins" ("Iohannes namque, regius primogenitus tuus et rex, quem, post diei orientis occasum, mundi successiva posteritas prestolatur, nobis est alter Ascanius, qui vestigia magni genitoris observans, in Turnos ubique sicut leo deseviet et in Latinos velut agnus mitescet").

7. On the possible relations between Frederick III of Aragon and Dante, see the entry in ED by Raul Manselli. In *Para.* XIX 130–131, the blessed souls, arranged together to form the image of an eagle, place Frederick of Aragon among the bad Christian princes; "See the greed and cowardice / of he who guards the island of fire [Sicily]" ("Vedrassi l'avarizia e la viltate / di quei che guarda l'isola del foco"); in *Para.* XX 62–63, southern Italy, which sorrows under the rule of Charles II of

Anjou and Frederick of Aragon, fondly remembers good King William II of Haute-ville: "he was William, mourned by that land / that weeps for Charles and Federico [still being] alive" ("Guglielmo fu, cui quella terra plora / che piagne Carlo e Federigo vivo"). With regard to Dante's successive changes of view about Fred-erick, see CARPI, pp. 444–446, and TAVONI, pp. 1271–1272.

8. With regard to the prophetic tone of the letter to the Italian cardinals, Mor-ghen, "La lettera di Dante ai Cardinali italiani," p. 152, observes: "There is one doc-ument which, in my view, validates the opinion that, at a certain moment, Dante was aware of having almost had the great authority to speak to the great men of the earth and to all Christian people with the admonishing tone of a prophet: it is the epistle that he sent to the cardinals assembled for the conclave at Carpen-tras." The prophetic tone of the letter is also emphasized by Frugoni, "Dante tra due Conclavi," pp. 80, 84.

9. Beatrice appoints Dante to carry out the prophetic mission in *Purg.* XXXII 103–105 and XXXIII 52–54; Cacciaguida in *Para.* XVII 124–129; and Saint Peter in *Para.* XXVII 61–66.

10. The quoted sentence about the objective signs that Dante had to give of his prophetic charisma is by Guglielmo Gorni, *Lettera, nome, numero. L'ordine delle cose in Dante* (Bologna: il Mulino, 1990), p. 111; but Gorni identifies only one: in the Book of Daniel (12:11–12) we read: "From the moment that the daily sacrifice was abolished to establish the appalling abomination: one thousand two hundred and ninety days. Blessed is he who waits and reaches one thousand three hundred and thirty-five days." ("Et a tempore cum ablatum fuerit iuge sacrificium, et posita fuerit abominatio in desolationem, dies mille ducenti nonaginta. Beatus qui expectat et pervenit ad dies mille trecentos triginta quinque"). If "days" are translated into "years," we arrive at two dates, 1290 and 1335, which, in terms of Dante's life, would be very significant: the first is the year of Beatrice's death; the second, bearing in mind that thirty-five was the middle of Dante's life, would have been the year in which he (having been born in 1265) would have died "blessed" like Daniel. In short, "Dante, who felt chosen by God in 1300, imagined himself blessed in 1335" (p. 127). I am not altogether convinced about the existence of this relationship (even though Gorni's "very interesting discovery" is accepted by Enrico Malato, *Dante* [Rome: Salerno Editrice, 1999], pp. 381–384); in any event, that coincidence of numbers, which may not have escaped Dante's intelligence (though he makes no mention of the relationship between the two dates), is hardly the objective sign that he had to give.

11. For the significance of the breaking of the baptismal font in *Inf.* XIX, of es-sential importance is Mirko Tavoni, "Effrazione battesimale tra i simoniaci (*If* XIX 13–21)," RLI 10 (1992): 457–512.

12. Nicholas III says of Clement V: "He will be a new Jason, of whom we read / in Maccabees; and in the same way that [Jason] was indulged / by his king, so

will the ruler of France [indulge] him" ("Nuovo Iasón sarà, di cui si legge / ne'
Maccabei; e come a quel fu molle / suo re, così fia lui chi Francia regge"; *Inf.* XIX
85–87).

13. Only a few scholars support the suggestion that the whole of Canto XIX dates
to 1314 (for example, Gianluigi Berardi, "Dante, *Inferno* XIX," in *Letteratura e critica.
Studi in onore di Natalino Sapegno,* ed. Walter Binni et al., vol. 2 (Rome: Bulzoni,
1975), pp. 97–103). Saverio Bellomo, "Le muse dell'indignazione: il canto dei
simoniaci (*Inferno* XIX)," *L'Alighieri* 37 (2011): 111–131, who rightly dwells on the relationship between the canto and the epistle to the cardinals, wavers between the
idea (on the one hand) that not only the episode of the popes stuck in the holes
but "probably the whole canto, inasmuch as the figure of Clement V appears in
the final invective," had been written after April 1314, and (on the other hand) the
suggestion that the prophecy of Clement's death as well as "almost the whole"
canto are "the result of a last-minute revision, when the canticle was complete
and not yet published." A compromise position is held by Giuseppe Indizio, "La
profezia di Niccolò e i tempi della stesura del canto XIX dell'*Inferno*," SD 67
(2002): 73–97, who suggests that the canto was composed immediately after the
Council of Vienne (1312) and that the lines relating to Pope Clement were added
in spring 1314. A different reconstruction is put forward by CASADEI, pp. 138–141: in
his view, the revision of the canto was carried out before the death of Clement V,
between the second half of 1312 and August 1313 (shortly before the publication of
Inferno, which Casadei dates prior to August 1313, therefore before the death of
Henry VII). The foretelling of Clement's death would therefore be a "prophecy
ante eventum," made possible as a result of the "pope's very poor state of health,
which had much deteriorated as from April of 1312."

14. So far as the chronology of the cantos in *Purgatorio,* the bibliography is impressive and wide-ranging: a reliable overview, however, can be obtained by comparing the observations of Ernesto Giacomo Parodi, "La data della composizione
e le teorie politiche dell'*Inferno* e del *Purgatorio* di Dante," in *Studi Romanzi,* vol. 3,
ed. Ernesto Monaci (Rome: Presso la Società, 1905), 15–52, with those of CASADEI.

15. For a persuasive political interpretation of *Purg.* VI, I refer to Umberto Carpi,
"Il canto VI del *Purgatorio,*" *Per leggere* 10 (2006): 5–30.

16. For the apostrophe to Italy, see the lines: "and now no one who lives within
you / can remain without war, and those confined within / the same wall and
moat each torment the other. / Search, wretched one, around your sea shores, /
and look within you bosom, / for any part of you that enjoys peace . . . Come [Al-
bert of Germany] to see Montecchi and Cappelletti, / Monaldi and Filippeschi, o
callous man: / those already sorrowful, and these in fear! / Come, cruel man,
come, and see the distress / of your nobles, and treat their woes; / and you will
see how dark Santafiore is! / Come and see your Rome who grieves / widowed
and alone, and day and night calls out: 'My Caesar, why aren't you with me?' " ("e

ora in te non stanno sanza guerra / li vivi tuoi, e l'un l'altro si rode / di quei ch'un muro e una fossa serra. / Cerca, misera, intorno da le prode / le tue marine, e poi ti guarda in seno, / s'alcuna parte in te di pace gode . . . Vieni [Alberto tedesco] a veder Montecchi e Cappelletti, / Monaldi e Filippeschi, uom sanza cura: / color già tristi, e questi con sospetti! / Vien, crudel, vieni, e vedi la pressura / d'i tuoi gentili, e cura lor magagne; / e vedrai Santafior com'è oscura! / Vieni a veder la tua Roma che piagne / vedova e sola, e dì e notte chiama: 'Cesare mio, perché non m'accompagne?' "; *Purg.* VI 82–114). Guido del Duca compares the inhabitants of the Arno valley with animals in *Purg.* XIV 40–54; Marco Lombardo describes the situation in Lombardy in *Purg.* XVI 115–120.

17. In the valley of the princes (*Purg.* VII) Sordello names, in order, Rudolf of Habsburg, Ottokar of Bohemia, Philip III of France, Henry of Navarre, Peter III of Aragon and Sicily, Charles I of Anjou, Alfonso III of Aragon, Henry III of England, William VII of Montferrat. Only of Peter of Aragon is it said that "he carried the garter of every good" ("d'ogne valor portò cinta la corda," line 114). A worthless father—with the exceptions of Henry of England and Alfonso of Aragon—is followed by an ever more worthless son: Ottokar produces Wenceslaus, "who feeds on lust and idleness" ("cui lussuria e ozio pasce," line 102); Philip III and his father-in-law Henry of Navarre produce the "plague of France" ("mal di Francia," line 109), namely Philip the Fair; Charles II, son of Charles I of Anjou, is such that "Puglia and Provence already grieve" ("Puglia e Proenza già si dole," line 126); James and Frederick, sons of Peter of Aragon, have inherited kingdoms but "neither has the better heritage" ("del retaggio miglior nessun possiede," line 120); lastly, John of Montferrat, son of William, has sparked a bloody war on his father's account that "makes Monferrat and Canavese weep" ("fa pianger Monferrato e Canavese," line 136).

18. Hugh Capet or Ciappetta speaks of the three Charles's and the "new Pilate" (Philip), whom he sees, not satisfied with all he did at Alagni, "without decree / carrying greedy sails into the Temple" ("sanza decreto / portar nel tempio le cupide vele") in *Purg.* XX 67–93.

19. For Fulcieri da Calboli, see *Purg.* XIV 58–66; for Sapia, *Purg.* XIII 109–123; for the Aldobrandeschi, see Omberto's self-portrait in *Purg.* XI 58–72; for the Fieschi, counts of Lavagna, see the reference to their corruption made by Hadrian V in *Purg.* XIX 143–144; lastly, for the Della Scala, see the words of the abbot of San Zeno in *Purg.* XVIII 118–126.

20. The Forese cantos (*Purg.* XXIII–XXIV) are the only ones in *Purgatorio* in which Florence has a central role; the fact that the city moves into the background, in comparison to *Inferno,* can be explained by the situation of stalemate after the downfall of the Whites and Dante's own personal setback, so as to give no scope for discussing the trauma of the civil war and exile.

21. For Bonagiunta, Guinizelli, and Arnaut Daniel, see *Purg.* XXIV and XXVI.

22. For an extensive study of the cantos of Eden, of the meaning of Beatrice's prophecy, and a proposed timescale, see SANTAGATA, pp. 234–287. Important observations on the allegories in the Eden cantos are made by Lino Pertile, *La puttana e il gigante. Dal* Cantico dei Cantici *al Paradiso Terrestre di Dante* (Ravenna: Longo Editore, 1998).

23. In *Inf.* I 101–111, Virgil had predicted that a "greyhound" would kill "avarice," chasing it back to Hell from where it came: "He will not feed on land or pewter, / but on wisdom, love and virtue, / and his birthplace will be between felt and felt" ("Questi non ciberà terra né peltro, / ma sapïenza, amore e virtute, / e sua nazion sarà tra feltro e feltro").

24. The numerous theories on the significance of "five hundred ten and five," from the earliest commentaries up to those of the 1970s, are surveyed in the entry in ED, "Cinquecento diece e cinque," by Pietro Mazzamuto; those after publication of the encyclopedia, by Bognini, "Per *Purg.*, XXXIII, 1–51," pp. 12–18.

25. The theory that the "messenger of God" is Henry, and that Dante had written the last cantos of *Purgatorio* and then published the first two canticles during the period between the coronation of 1312 and the emperor's death in August 1313, is cogently supported by CASADEI (the phrase I quote about loyalty is from p. 140).

26. PASQUINI, pp. 165–166, who suggests that Canto XXXII of *Purgatorio* was composed "not later than 1314" and that the letter to the cardinals follows "shortly after," notes perceptively that the originality of detail in Dante's description of the decline of the Church in Avignon puts "into second place the same prophecy of the 'five hundred ten and five' (the Dux)."

27. The identification of the "five hundred ten and five" with John of Bohemia and the consequent deciphering of the enigma is by Bognini, "Per *Purg.*, XXXIII, 1–51," though it cannot be accepted that the "shameless whore" ("puttana sciolta") is Florence and her lover the giant is Robert of Anjou: Florence and the king of Naples would be inconsistent with the allegorical picture that represents the gradual degeneration of the Church over history. By Bognini see also: "Gli occhi di Ooliba. Una proposta per *Purg.*, XXXII 148–60 e XXXIII 44–45," RSD 7 (2007): 73–103; and Bognini, "Dante tra solitudine e protezione [*Pg* XXXII 148–160 e XXXIII 1–5]," in *Novella fronda. Studi Danteschi,* ed. Francesco Spera (Naples: D'Auria Editore, 2008), pp. 177–197). It was Gorni, *Lettera, nome, numero,* p. 121, who pointed out that "the syntagma 'messenger of God' bears an exact resemblance to the prologue of the Gospel of John, 'Fuit homo missus a Deo, cui nomen erat Iohannes.'" The cipher is found under the heading *Formate epistole,* in the *Elementarium* of Papias (dating from the mid-eleventh century): compare Bognini, "Per *Purg.*, XXXIII, 1–51," pp. 30–33.

28. For the "shameless whore," see Rev. 17: 1–5; the phrase quoted about Revelation is by Anna Maria Chiavacci Leonardi from Dante Alighieri, *Commedia,* vol.

2, *Purgatorio,* with commentary by Anna Chiavacci Leonardi (Milan: Mondadori, 1994), p. 954. According to CASADEI, p. 135, in the scene of the whore's enticement "Dante represents those who believed in the good faith of Clement V and therefore . . . supported the emperor's alliance with the Church: only then to be deceived by the events during the period of Henry's coronation in Rome. The attempted enticement therefore corresponds with the phase of possible alliance between Clement and Henry, followed by the pope ultimately distancing himself from the Italian scene because he is once again subjugated to Philip's will."

29. The reconstruction of the allegorical scene in reference to the events during the conclave at Carpentras is from Antonio Alessandro Bisceglia, "Due nuove proposte esegetiche per *Purgatorio* XXXII," *Studi e problemi di critica testuale* 77 (2008): 115–124. It should be pointed out that there are certain similarities between Dante's letter and that sent by the Italian cardinals to the Cistercian abbeys in which they describe their expulsion: the similarities are indicated by Mazzoni, "Le epistole di Dante," pp. 82–83. Moreover, the letter by Napoleone Orsini to Philip the Fair, written when the Italian cardinals found themselves in a minority at Carpentras, contains "historical emphases and judgments in many respects complementary to those of Dante's letter addressed to the Italian cardinals (or rather, above all, to Napoleone Orsini himself)" (CARPI, pp. 628–629).

30. All doubt about the prophecy being written after the death of Henry VII would disappear if line 36 "that God's vengeance fears no sop" ("che vendetta di Dio non teme suppe") is accepted as being an allusion to the emperor's poisoning.

31. CASADEI, p. 140, notes that if the first two canticles had not been completed and circulated before Henry's death, "we would arrive at the strange paradox of a 'real' Dante who was champion *toto corde* of Henry's cause who never writes about him (apart from the passing reference in *Para.* XVII, 82) before the manifestly posthumous exaltation at *Para.* XXX, 133 et seq."

32. With regard to Dante's movements after the death of Henry VII (apart from the untenable hypothesis of PETROCCHI, p. 154, that he was already in Verona in 1312) see, for example, CARPI, pp. 670–671: "On Henry's death it is very likely that Dante moved fairly quickly, if not immediately, toward the Verona of Cangrande, who was the most powerful despot in what had become the imperial north."

33. There is some indication of Dante's presence at Forlì in March 1314 in a short vernacular letter published in 1547 by Anton Francesco Doni in a volume printed by him of *Prose antiche di Dante, Petrarcha, et Boccaccio.* Dante is supposed to have sent it on March 30, 1314, to Guido Novello da Polenta during his return journey to Ravenna from Venice, where he had been to pay homage on behalf of the lord of Ravenna to the recently elected doge. The content of the missive is an invective by Dante against the Venetian ruling class who, according to him, not only know no Latin, but have only a vague knowledge of Italian. The letter had always been regarded as being a forgery by Doni until Rosetta Migliorini Fissi, in pre-

paring the critical edition of it ("La lettera pseudodantesca a Guido da Polenta. Edizione critica e ricerche attributive," SD 46 (1969): 103–272), showed that Doni had been only its publisher. That Dante is the author of the letter (which would originally have been written in Latin and then translated by someone unknown) has been claimed by PADOAN alone (pp. 57–91), followed, too confidently, by IN-DIZIO[1], pp. 54–57 (and, with reservations, by Malato, *Dante,* pp. 62–63). Their attempts to resolve the clear historical inconsistencies in the text conflict with the extreme unlikelihood that Dante would have taken the trouble to send a messenger to Ravenna for the sole purpose of delivering an invective that contains no real news and that an ambassador would express such deeply offensive views against a state with which Ravenna had a difficult and sensitive relationship, in a letter that was destined to be filed away in the chancery. But above all, they conflict with the fact that the forger, as Migliorini Fissi had already described and documented, has a clear profile and the purpose of the falsification was evident: he was a Florentine who was writing in either the early decades of the 1500s or, less probably, in the 1540s, inspired by Filippo Villani's account of an embassy to Venice on behalf of the Polentani in which it is said that Dante was prevented from speaking. The anti-Venetian political and civil sentiment relates to this period—a sentiment shared by the anti-republican circles of the Medici—as well as the observations on language, which can be framed within the heated debate revolving around Dante in which many Florentine intellectuals were involved in the early 1500s.

34. Emilio Pasquini, in *Vita di Dante. I giorni e le opere* (Milan: Rizzoli, 2006), p. 83, writes that after the sentence of death in 1315, Dante's sons "were perhaps already with him, staying with Uguccione," thus endorsing the idea that Dante was still in Pisa and that Uguccione was his patron; Corrado Ricci, *L'ultimo rifugio di Dante,* new ed. (Ravenna: Edizioni "Dante" di A. Longo, 1965; 1st ed. 1891), p. 61, had earlier written: "we think that during the war that ended with the Guelf defeat at Montecatini, Dante was in Tuscany."

35. For Niccolò Donati, see the entry in ED by Renato Piattoli and BARBI[2], p. 328. As from 1315, Gemma may also have been of financial help after receiving an inheritance from her mother Maria: we don't know when she died, but she made a will between February and May 1315 (the will is published in PIATTOLI no. 113).

36. The exception of the bishop of Luni, according to Frugoni, "Dante tra due Conclavi," p. 83, "is surprising" for the "sudden change of tone."

37. For new information on the events relating to the bishopric of Luni and the figures of Guglielmo and Gherardino Malaspina, see Eliana M. Vecchi, *"Ad pacem et veram et perpetuam concordiam devenerunt.* Il cartulario del notaio Giovanni di Parente di Stupio e l'*Instrumentum pacis* del 1306," *Giornale storico della Lunigiana e del territorio lucense* 59 (2008): 69–175. Friar Guglielmo Malaspina has sometimes been wrongly identified with Bernabò Malaspina del Terziere, bishop of Sarzana

in the 1320s and 1330s (see Eliana M. Vecchi, "Per la biografia del vescovo Bernabò Malaspina del Terziere (†1338)," *Studi Lunigianesi* 22–29 (1992–1999): 109–141). For the events involving Gherardino after the invasion of Lucca by Uguccione della Faggiola, see also DAVIDSOHN, IV, pp. 816–817; for the role of Castruccio, see the entry in DBI "Castracani degli Antelminelli, Castruccio" by Michele Luzzati. On Spinetta Malaspina, see the entry in DBI, "Malaspina, Spinetta (Spinetta il Grande di Fosdinovo)" by Franca Ragone.

38. Niccolò Fieschi, father of Alagia, was buried in the Franciscan church in Genoa in 1310, and Luchino, one of Alagia and Moroello's sons, would be interred there in 1340. Bear in mind that close to that church was the house of Manfredina, a sister of Moroello, who, after her first marriage to Gherardesca, had married Alaone Grimaldi of Genoa (and Alagia is shown to have spent much time at the house of her sister-in-law during her widowhood). I refer again to Vecchi, *"Ad pacem et veram et perpetuam concordiam devenerunt,"* pp. 145–148, for road connections to the monastery of Santa Croce al Corvo. For the meaning of the expression "ad partes ultramontanas," see Alberto Casadei, "Considerazioni sull'epistola di Ilaro," *Dante* 8 (2011): 15–18.

39. Events relating to the revocation of banishments ("ribandimento") of 1315–1316 and the amnesty of fall 1315 are reconstructed by Michele Barbi (with reference to ZINGARELLI) in "Una nuova opera sintetica su Dante," then in BARBI[1], pp. 29–85, in particular pp. 51–56.

40. "To identify the correspondent [of *Ep.* XII] it is important to establish how it is to be read: 'Per litteras vestri meique nepotis' ['From the letters of your and my nephew'], as the only manuscript reads, or 'Per litteras vestras meique nepotis necnon aliorum quamplurium amicorum' ['From your letters and [those] of my nephew and many other friends'], as Dante scholars think, especially Pistelli, the editor of the critical edition of the text, and Barbi? . . . nothing is certain in this respect. So it is better to distinguish between priest and nephew" (GORNI, p. 225). A different solution is put forward, however, by Renato Piattoli, "Codice Diplomatico Dantesco. Aggiunte," *Archivio storico italiano* 127, nos. 1–2 (1969): 3–108; pp. 75–108, correcting, in the light of new documents, the view of Michele Barbi ("Per un passo dell'epistola all'amico fiorentino e per la parentela di Dante" [1920], then in BARBI[2], pp. 305–328), namely interpreting the recipient as a cleric who is also a nephew of Dante. This would open up the possibility of identifying him—as Piattoli does—as being Bernardo Riccomanni, son of Lapo and Tana, who we have considered as having possibly helped in hiding Dante's property on the eve of his banishment, when he was a young friar at Santa Croce or another neighboring monastery.

41. *Ep.* XII 3–4; "Estne ista revocatio gratiosa qua Dantes Alagherii revocatur ad patriam, per trilustrium fere perpessus exilium? Hocne meruit innocentia manifesta quibuslibet? hoc sudor et labor continuatus in studio? Absit a viro

phylosophie domestico temeraria tantum cordis humilitas, ut more cuiusdam Cioli et aliorum infamium quasi vinctus ipse se patiatur offerri! Absit a viro predicante iustitiam ut perpessus iniurias, iniuriam inferentibus, velut benemerentibus, pecuniam suam solvat! Non est hec via redeundi ad patriam, pater mi; sed si alia per vos ante aut deinde per alios invenitur, que fame Dantisque honori non deroget, illam non lentis passibus acceptabo; quod si per nullam talem Florentia introitur, nunquam Florentiam introibo." Like the others, the person Dante names as Ciolo (who tends to be identified as Ciolo degli Abati) was certainly a common criminal: see the entry in ED, "Ciolo."

42. The sentences of October and November 1315 are in PIATTOLI, nos. 114, 115.

10. Courtier

1. The last words of the epistle to the Florentine friend are: "Quippe nec panis deficiet" (Ep. XII 4).

2. That Dante didn't know Cangrande personally is apparent also from the beginning of Ep. XIII, where he says that he had come to Verona to find out the truth about its lord's reputation.

3. The year 1316 is also indicated as the date of his move to Verona by INDIZIO[1] (at the end of a biographical profile that differs from the one I propose) and by others: for example, by GORNI, p. 184.

4. Information on Cangrande della Scala is adequately dealt with in the extensive and detailed entry in DBI by Gian Maria Varanini, to be read with that on Alboino, also by Varanini.

5. It is most interesting that Boccaccio does not subscribe to the creation of the Verona story: he also expresses doubts about the dedication of Paradiso to Cangrande (BOCCACCIO[1], pp. 193–194).

6. On Paradiso, which he promises to dedicate to Cangrande, Dante writes (Ep. XIII 3): "And I have found nothing more fitting to your greatness than the sublime canticle of the Commedia that is entitled Paradiso: which, offered with this letter, as with an epigram of dedication, I attribute, offer and also entrust to you" ("Neque ipsi preheminentie vestre congruum comperi magis quam Comedie sublimem canticam que decoratur titulo Paradisi; et illam sub presenti epistola, tanquam sub epigrammate proprio dedicatam, vobis ascribo, vobis offero, vobis denique recommend").

7. With regard to the exegetic part of the letter, and in particular the doubts surrounding the description of the work as "commedia" and the explanation of the title of the poem, see: Mirko Tavoni, "Il titolo della Commedia di Dante," NRLI I (1998): 9–34, in particular pp. 21–23; and Andrea Mazzucchi, "Tertia est satira, idest reprehensibilis, ut Oracius et Persius: Cino da Pistoia, Pietro Alighieri e Gano di Lapo da Colle," in Però convien ch'io canti per disdegno. La satira in versi tra Italia e

Spagna dal Medioevo al Seicento, ed. Antonio Gargano, with an introduction by Giancarlo Alfano (Naples: Liguori Editore, 2011), pp. 1–30. For a different viewpoint, see Claudia Villa, *La protervia di Beatrice. Studi per la biblioteca di Dante* (Florence: SISMEL-Edizioni del Galluzzo, 2009), pp. 163–181. The quotation is taken from Alberto Casadei, "Il titolo della *Commedia* e l'Epistola a Cangrande," *Allegoria* 60 (2009): 167–181, 178, which suggests most convincingly that part of the letter was written by Dante in 1316 (which must have contained "the promise of a dedication of *Paradiso* to Cangrande"), and the second exegetic part was added to it in the 1340s "perhaps as one of the numerous legends created to (re)construct the pattern of the poet's final works"; by Casadei, see also "Allegorie dantesche," in *Atlante della letteratura italiana,* ed. Sergio Luzzatto and Gabriele Pedullà, vol. 1, ed. Amedeo De Vincentiis (Turin: Einaudi, 2010), pp. 199–205.

8. *Ep.* XIII 1; "Huius quidem preconium, facta modernorum exsuperans, tanquam veri existentia latius arbitrabar aliquando superfluum. Verum ne diuturna me nimis incertitudo suspenderet . . . Veronam petii fidis oculis discursurus audita, ibique magnalia vestra vidi, vidi beneficia simul et tetigi; et quemadmodum prius dictorum ex parte suspicabar excessum, sic posterius ipsa facta excessiva cognomi."

9. The reference to his poverty at the end of the letter (*Ep.* XIII 32): "I am pressed indeed by concern over family matters, so that I am obliged to neglect this and other matters useful to the public interest" ("urget enim me rei familiaris angustia, ut hec et alia utilia reipublice derelinquere oporteat"), whether genuine or otherwise, simply expresses the situation underlying his praises at the beginning.

10. For the stories about the abbots of San Zeno and how Cangrande may have reacted to Dante's description in *Purgatorio,* see CARPI, pp. 667–668.

11. Petrarch's anecdote was already to be found, for example, in *Novellino* XLIV, but in reference to Marco Lombardo, the main figure in Canto XVI of *Purgatorio.* Giuseppe Billanovich, ("Tra Dante e Petrarca," IMU 8 (1965): 1–43, pp. 27–28) is convinced that Petrarch, with the phrases that appear in *Rerum memorandarum libri* II 83 ("Dantes Allegherius, et ipse concivis nuper meus . . . exul patria cum apud Canem Magnum veronensem, comune tunc afflictorum solamen ac profugium, versatur, primo quidem in honore habitus deinde pedetentim retrocedere ceperat minusque in dies domino placere"), is giving actual testimony to "the thankless coexistence that Dante had to endure with Cangrande and his courtiers."

12. It would be interesting to establish whether Dante, during his second stay in Verona, had renewed acquaintance with Giovanni Mansionario, mentioned earlier, with whom he may have had contact in 1303–1304. On Dante's isolation in Verona, see the observations of Girolamo Arnaldi in the entry "Verona" in ED.

13. The souls in the sphere of Jupiter form the first verse of *Liber Sapientiae* (the Book of Wisdom).

14. On the apostrophe to John XXII, see CASADEI, pp. 123–125, who observes that "the incursion into the present," consisting of the informal "you" (*tu*) accompanied by the present indicative "write" (*scrivi*), "due to its exceptional nature in the context of the poem, can only be regarded objectively as an effective immediate provocation, and only makes sense if it is imagined as being written at the time of the episode it describes, and therefore as direct support for Cangrande's cause, probably in the first half of 1318." At p. 125, Casadei writes that "Dante in practice cuts out the story after 1318." On this question, see also SANTAGATA, pp. 334–335.

15. For Dante's change of attitude toward the Guelfs and the Ghibellines, see the observations in CARPI, pp. 649–650.

16. Cunizza's prophecy is in *Para.* IX 46–60. In her final years, after a tumultuous love life characterized by an extravagant affair with the troubadour Sordello, Cunizza retired to Florence, where she died between the 1270s and 1280s. In Florence, she stayed at the house of Cavalcante dei Cavalcanti on at least one occasion. Dante didn't visit the Cavalcanti house at that time, and certainly had no opportunity of meeting Cunizza, but it's not unreasonable to suppose that Guido or his father had told him about her during the following decade: see Valter Leonardo Puccetti, *Fuga in Paradiso. Storia intertestuale di Cunizza da Romano* (Ravenna: Longo Editore, 2010).

17. The passages quoted regarding Rizzardo da Camino and the Guelf faction who fought Ghibelline Verona are by CARPI, pp. 514–515. INDIZIO[1], p. 52, also takes the view that "Canto IX of *Paradiso* presupposes [Dante's] presence in Verona and his adherence to the city's cause."

18. The battle of Montecatini is described by Uguccione in a letter sent on September 2, 1315, to the Genoese Ghibellines Gherardo Spinola and Bernabò Doria: see Carla Maria Monti, "Uguccione della Faggiola, la battaglia di Montecatini e la *Commedia* di Dante," RSD 10 (2010): 127–159 (here, at pp. 146–147, is the critical edition of the letter).

19. As for the address to Clement and the reference to the battle of Montecatini, I refer to SANTAGATA, pp. 375–377 (pointing out, however, that I took the view at that time that the canto had been written in Verona).

20. Detailed accounts of the events surrounding the attempts by the Visconti to put a curse on John XXII are in DAVIDSOHN, IV, pp. 898–900, and, especially, in Girolamo Biscaro, "Dante Alighieri e i sortilegi di Matteo e Galeazzo Visconti contro papa Giovanni XXII," *Archivio Storico Lombardo* 47 (1920): 446–481.

21. The comments made by certain women in Verona as they passed Dante, and his amused reaction, are described in BOCCACCIO[1], 113.

22. Among those best informed about the business of the curse on the pope was Cardinal del Poggetto: he had been a member of the secret investigating commission appointed by the pope, up until the time of his departure from Avignon to begin his legation in Lombardy, and had also certainly been kept informed about

developments after that date. Might it also have been due to the allegations made against Dante during that investigation that the cardinal would seek to have Dante convicted of heresy after his death?

23. The phrase about the allegorical interpretation of the poem is by Saverio Bellomo, "La *Commedia* attraverso gli occhi dei primi lettori," in *Leggere Dante*, ed. Lucia Battaglia Ricci (Ravenna: Longo Editore, 2003), pp. 73–84, quotation on p. 77.

24. On the possible chronological implications of the story of the attempted curse in terms of Dante's life, see INDIZIO[1], pp. 59–60.

25. The statements about the length of his stay in Ravenna are in BOCCACCIO[1], pp. 81, 84.

26. For the date of his move to Ravenna, I will mention only the most important references: Corrado Ricci, *L'ultimo rifugio di Dante*, new ed. (Ravenna: Edizioni "Dante" di A. Longo, 1965; 1st ed. 1891), opts for 1317; those favoring 1318, or early 1319 at the latest, include Giorgio Petrocchi, "La vicenda biografica di Dante nel Veneto," in Petrocchi, *Itinerari danteschi*, ed. and introduction by Carlo Ossola (Milan: Franco Angeli, 1994; Bari: Laterza, 1969), pp. 101–103; Alberto Casadei, "Sulla prima diffusione della *Commedia*," *Italianistica* 39 (2010): 57–66, in particular p. 63; CASADEI, p. 125; 1319 or the first half of 1320 is preferred by Girolamo Biscaro, "Dante a Ravenna," *Bullettino dell'istituto storico italiano* 41 (1921): 1–117; INDIZIO[1], pp. 57–64, also favors the early months of 1320. The information, provided by the anonymous chronicle *Annales Caesenates*, about a plague epidemic in Romagna during the period 1318–1319, which could have dissuaded Dante from moving during that time (see Ricci, *L'ultimo rifugio di Dante*, pp. 60–61), has to be placed in perspective: there was probably an epidemic, though it was limited to the city of Cesena. See Renzo Caravita, *Rinaldo da Concorezzo arcivescovo di Ravenna (1303–1321) al tempo di Dante* (Florence: Olschki, 1964), pp. 180–185; and Petrocchi, "La vicenda biografica di Dante nel Veneto," p. 102.

27. The most accurate reconstruction of Dante's years in Ravenna is that of Caravita; *Rinaldo da Concorezzo*, pp. 167–203.

28. The sentence of conviction against Pietro is published in PIATTOLI, no. 126; events relating to the benefit are reconstructed in detail by Ricci, *L'ultimo rifugio di Dante*, pp. 46–55, and, especially, by Biscaro, "Dante a Ravenna," pp. 40–51, but see also Caravita, *Rinaldo da Concorezzo*, pp. 173–177, and INDIZIO[3], pp. 188–189.

29. The authenticity of the *Questio* has been supported with great vigor, in particular, by Francesco Mazzoni (see the pages that sum up his earlier contributions in the introduction to the *Questio* published in Dante Alighieri, *Opere minori*, vol. 2) and by PADOAN, pp. 163–180 (who also wrote the entry in ED on Moncetti). Equally vigorous is the disagreement expressed by Bruno Nardi, "La caduta di Lucifero e l'autenticità della *Questio de aqua et terra*" (1959), more recently published in Nardi, *Lecturae e altri studi*, ed. Rudy Abardo, with introductory essays by Francesco Mazzoni and Aldo Vallone (Florence: Le Lettere, 1990), pp. 227–265.

30. The eccentric aspects of the *Questio* are examined by Stefano Caroti in the introduction to his commentary in Dante Alighieri, *Opere,* vol. 3 (forthcoming).

31. With regard to the autography, in *Questio* I 3 we read: "And so that the envy of many . . . does not alter what has been well said behind my back, it also seems appropriate to set down on this paper, written in my hand, what was determined by me, and to describe with the pen the terms of the whole disputation" ("Et ne livor multorum . . . post tergum bene dicta transmutent, placuit insuper in hac cedula meis digitis exarata quod determinatum fuit a me relinquere, et formam totius disputationis calamo designare").

32. Lucifer, the prince of the rebel angels, fell into the southern hemisphere, where the land then emerged, and this land, due to the fear he caused, withdrew and re-emerged in the opposite hemisphere and, so as to avoid contact with the demon, it also retracted at its center to form Mount Purgatory (*Inf.* XXXIV 121–126).

33. The passage by Pietro Alighieri can be read in Pietro Alighieri, *Comentum super poema Comedie Dantis. A Critical Edition of the Third and Final Draft of Pietro's Alighieri's Commentary on Dante's* The Divine Comedy, ed. Massimiliano Chiamenti (Tempe: Arizona Center for Medieval and Renaissance Studies, 2002), pp. 277–278. On the problem of authorship of the third version of the commentary, an essential reference is INDIZIO[3]: It should be noted, however, that Indizio believes that the testimony can be relied on, even though not directly referable to Pietro, proposing, on the basis of the Venetian origin of the only written evidence that contains it, that "the information may nevertheless come from Pietro or from another witness to the *Questio* in Verona. The information, which is authentic, was therefore introduced into the text as an element of undoubted value" (p. 218); but see also the doubts about the reliability of the testimony expressed by Enrico Malato, "Per una nuova edizione commentata delle opere di Dante," RSD 4 (2004), pp. 88–89. Casadei ("Sulla prima diffusione della *Commedia,*" p. 64) is also doubtful about whether Dante returned from Ravenna to Verona to give the lecture on this question.

34. Figures on the population of Ravenna are in Caravita, *Rinaldo da Concorezzo,* pp. 199–200.

35. Biscaro ("Dante a Ravenna," p. 55) writes: "in accepting the invitation or proposing it, Dante was convinced that Guido would never have given in to the injunctions of the papacy to hand him over to the inquisitor's henchmen."

36. With regard to Dante's relations with the noble families of Romagna, it should be noted that Benvenuto da Imola, in relation to the encounter with Pier da Medicina (*Inf.* XXVIII 70–75), states that Dante was guest at the court ("curia") of the lords ("cattani") of Medicina, "a large and prosperous villa between Bologna and Imola" ("villa grossa et pinguis inter Bononiam et Imolam").

37. It is almost certain that Dante had an opportunity to meet Bernardino da Polenta, son of Guido il Vecchio and brother of Francesca, who was a military man and for a certain period of time lord of Cervia and of Cesena. Though Guelf by conviction and by family tradition, like all the smaller landowners of Romagna he had moved back and forth between one party and the other, according to convenience. And so, having fought against the Ghibellines of Romagna led by Guido da Montefeltro and sided with the Florentines in the war against the Ghibellines of Arezzo in the latter half of the 1280s, he joined Ordelaffi and Aghinolfo di Romena in the Whites' campaign against the Blacks in the Mugello; and Dante very probably came to know him during those months. He may also have met him again in Bologna, where Bernardino, having joined the Blacks, was *podestà* and had pacified the disorder in May 1306 during which Napoleone Orsini was forced to flee. Later he had fought, in alliance with the Guidi of Dovadola and Battifolle, against Henry VII, and became *podestà* of Florence in the first half of 1313 (where he died in April of that year): much information about him is given in CARPI, throughout. The comparison between the rustle of leaves in the "divine forest" of Eden and that which "gathers from branch to branch / through the pinewood on the shore of Classe, / when Aeolus unleashes the scirocco" ("di ramo in ramo si raccoglie / per la pineta in su 'l lito di Chiassi, / quand' Ëolo scilocco fuor discioglie"; *Purg.* XXVIII 19–21) seems to suggest that by early 1314 Dante had already been to the pine forest of Classe, near Ravenna. I wonder whether Dante might have been part of the delegation from the Coalition of exiles that had negotiated the alliance against Florence with Bernardino in May 1303. The six ballads attributed to Guido Novello, as well as nine anonymous ballads, appear in Domenico De Robertis, "Il Canzoniere escorialense e la tradizione *veneziana* delle rime dello Stil novo," GSLI, suppl. 27 (1954): 210–223, and are republished by Eugenio Chiarini in the appendix to Ricci, *L'ultimo rifugio di Dante,* pp. 514–521; four of the six ballads of certain authorship are republished, with commentary, in *Rimatori del Trecento,* ed. Giuseppe Corsi (Turin: UTET, 1969), pp. 33–39.

38. The quotation about Guido Novello ("ne' liberali studii ammaestrato, sommamente i valorosi uomini onorava") is taken from BOCCACCIO[1], p. 80.

39. This quotation about Guido Novello, "avendo egli lungo tempo avante per fama conosciuto il suo valore," is also taken from BOCCACCIO[1], p. 80.

40. The ironic comment on the benefits that Dante had obtained from the extinction of the male line of the counts of Bagnacavallo is from CARPI, pp. 579–580.

41. On the question of the grant to Pietro of the rights over the two churches by the Malvicini cousins, see the observations by CARPI, pp. 579–580 and by Biscaro, "Dante a Ravenna," p. 52: "A long-standing relationship between Dante and the relatives of Guido's wife and Polentano's professed interest in the arts, cultivated with a certain success, would have been the reason for the invitation made

to Dante, according to Boccaccio's account, to accept his hospitality, even though Dante himself might have indirectly sought such an invitation by referring to his economic difficulties." Francesco Filippini, *Dante scolaro e maestro (Bologna, Parigi, Ravenna)* (Geneva: Olschki, 1929), pp. 164–165, also writes that "the long-standing family relationship with the Guidi of Romena is enough in itself to explain why Dante went to Ravenna, all the more when associated with the ecclesiastical benefit that Caterina and Idane granted to Pietro."

42. Biscaro, "Dante a Ravenna," at p. 53, writes: "the grant of the rectorship constituted the fulfillment of a condition imposed by the poet for his coming to stay with Polenta, as a guarantee that he would have enough means to live"; and also: "the benefit had been granted [to Pietro] so that his father could take advantage of the revenues" (p. 65). Biscaro confidently expresses the interesting idea, but which has yet to be proved, that "the provision of the rectorship for the son went together with the placement of the daughter Beatrice in the cloister of S. Stefano dell'Oliva, which must have happened around the same period, by intercession of Guido Novello; a placement without charge, and therefore without the conferment of the appropriate dowry that was usually required for placing young girls in monasteries." It is certain that a Suor Beatrice, daughter of Dante, was in that monastery in 1350 (when she may have been visited by Boccaccio). In 1371, Donato degli Albanzani (a friend of both Boccaccio and Petrarch) delivered three ducats to the monastery on behalf of a donor who wished to remain anonymous, who was heir to Suor Beatrice of the late Dante Alighieri: see the entry "Alighieri, Antonia (suor Beatrice)" in ED, and Ricci, *L'ultimo rifugio di Dante*, pp. 236–238.

43. On the possible presence of Gemma in Ravenna, see Giorgio Petrocchi, "Biografia" in ED, *Appendice*, p. 50. Biscaro (in "Dante a Ravenna," pp. 139–141) talks about Dante's house in Ravenna. The only evidence in this respect is from Boccaccio who refers to "the house in which Dante had lived" before he died (BOCCACCIO[1], 88; BOCCACCIO[2], 63).

44. The references to Dante as teacher of vernacular rhetoric are in BOCCACCIO[1], p. 84, and in BOCCACCIO[2], p. 62. On Dante's supposed teaching, see Ricci, *L'ultimo rifugio di Dante*, pp. 64–74 (who thinks he may actually have taught at the *Studio*); and Silvio Bernicoli, "Maestri e scuole letterarie in Ravenna nel secolo XIV," *Felix Ravenna* 32 (1927), pp. 61–63, in particular pp. 61–62. That Dante had a public teaching post is suggested also by Filippini, *Dante scolaro e maestro*, pp. 51, 173–174; Michele Barbi, *Vita di Dante* (1933; Firenze: Le Lettere, 1996), p. 31, does not exclude the possibility of a public teaching post. Augusto Campana, "Guido Vacchetta e Giovanni del Virgilio (e Dante)," *Rivista di cultura classica e medioevale* 7 (1965): 252–265, emphasizes the fact that Dante was surrounded solely by doctors and notaries, and there was a total absence of jurists.

45. The quotation regarding Perini is taken from BOCCACCIO³, VIII I 13. Dante's first eclogue tells how Meliboeus (Dino Perini) is anxious to know the content of the writing that Mopsus (Giovanni del Virgilio) has sent to Tityrus (Dante); Tityrus shows it to him, having gently mocked him for his inexperience in literature: "You don't know the meadow on which Menalus throws its shadow, hiding the setting sun with its high peak" ("Pascua sunt ignota tibi que Menalus alto / vertice declivi celator solis inumbrat"; *Ec.* II 11–12); in Dante's second eclogue, young Meliboeus is described as he arrives running and gasping, "hot and with his throat breathing tightly" ("calidus et gutture tardus anhelo"; *Ec.* IV 28), to take the text of Mopsus's reply to Tityrus and Alphesiboeus (Fiduccio dei Milotti), who are engaged in learned philosophical discussion.

46. On Giardini, see BOCCACCIO³, I I 5.

47. For Menghino Mezzani, I refer to the entry in ED by Augusto Campana, to BELLOMO, pp. 330–338, and to Andrea Mazzucchi, CCD, pp. 340–353; for Fiduccio dei Milotti, to the entry in ED by Aurelia Accame Bobbio, and to Giovanni Livi, *Dante, suoi primi cultori, sua gente in Bologna* (Bologna: Cappelli, 1918), pp. 176, 268 (as confirmation of the importance of Fiduccio, it should be noted that one of his uncles, Sinibaldo, was bishop of Imola); lastly, for Guido Vacchetta, I refer to Campana, "Guido Vacchetta e Giovanni del Virgilio (e Dante)." It seems that Dante had no dealings with the leading figure in Ravenna at that time, the archbishop, Rinaldo da Concorezzo (see Caravita, *Rinaldo da Concorezzo,* pp. 193–203). The quoted sonnet by Antonio Beccari, *Non è mester el caval de Medusa,* ("a zò che questo nobil sodalizio, / in volgar poesì, senza fatica, / seguisca 'l padre Dante, senza vizio") can be read with a commentary in *Le Rime di Maestro Antonio da Ferrara (Antonio Beccari),* introduction, text and notes by Laura Bellucci (Bologna: Pàtron, 1972).

48. For the biography of Giovanni del Virgilio I refer to Giuseppe Indizio, On the exchange of eclogues, their authenticity is now accepted, though Aldo Rossi (for which see "Dossier di un'attribuzione. Dieci anni dopo," *Paragone* 19 (1968): 61–125) had attributed the work to Boccaccio; there is an extensive biography and I record here only the most important: Carlo Battisti, "Le egloghe dantesche," SD 33 (1955): 61–111; Guido Martellotti, "Dalla tenzone al carme bucolico. Giovanni del Virgilio, Dante, Boccaccio," IMU 7 (1964): 325–336, then in the posthumous volume *Dante e Boccaccio e altri scrittori dall'Umanesimo al Romanticismo,* ed. Vittore Branca and Silvia Rizzo (Florence: Olschki, 1983); Giuseppe Velli, "Sul linguaggio letterario di Giovanni del Virgilio," IMU 24 (1981): 136–158; Luciano Gargan, "Dante e Giovanni del Virgilio: le *Egloghe,*" GSLI 127 (2010): 342–369. For the intellectual figure of Giovanni del Virgilio and his other works, see: Paul O. Kristeller, "Un'*ars dictaminis* di Giovanni del Virgilio," IMU 4 (1961): 181–200; Gian Carlo Alessio, "I trattati grammaticali di Giovanni del Virgilio," IMU 24 (1981): 159–212; Matteo

Ferretti, "Boccaccio, Paolo da Perugia e i commentari ovidiani di Giovanni del Virgilio," *Studi sul Boccaccio* 35 (2007): 85–110.

49. For the date when Giovanni's first poem was sent, useful information (in addition to the essays already cited) can be found in INDIZIO[1], pp. 61–63, and Casadei, "Sulla prima diffusione della *Commedia*," p. 63.

50. In the opening lines of the poem that he sent to Dante after their meeting (*Ec.* I 1–16): "Sacred voice of the Pierides, you who with new songs soothe the world of the dead . . . revealing the realms of the triple fate assigned according to the merits of the souls—Orcus to the guilty, Lethe to those who aspire to the stars, the realm beyond the sun to the blessed—ah, that you might continue always to spread such sublime themes among common folk, and we learned men . . . can we read nothing of your poetry as bard? . . . the learned reader despises vulgar idioms, even if they were not unstable and diversified, as in reality they are, in a thousand varieties" ("Pyeridum vox alma, novis qui cantibus orbem / mulces leti-fluum . . . evolvens triplicis confinia sortis / indita pro meritis animarum—sontibus Orcum, / astripetis Lethen, epyphebia regna beatis, / tanta quid heu semper iactabis seria vulgo? . . . clerus vulgaria tempnit, / et si non varient, cum sint ydiomata mille"). Giovanni del Virgilio shows that he understands the central, and absolutely new, idea in Dante's treatise, namely that the natural languages are fragmented in space and unstable in time (*VE* I X 7): "if we wish to count the primary and secondary and subsidiary variations of the vernacular in Italy, even only in this tiny corner of the world we would arrive at the thousandth diversification of the language, indeed we would arrive even much beyond it" ("si primas et secundarias et subsecundarias vulgaris Ytalie variationes calculare velimus, et in hoc minimo mundi angulo non solum ad millenam loquele variationem venire contigerit, sed etiam ad magis ultra"). Giovanni's adherence to Dante's text goes even as far as the hyperbole of "millenam . . . variationem." See commentary on the *Egloge* by Gabriella Albanese in Dante Alighieri, *Opere,* vol. 2. Claudia Villa (*La "Lectura Terentii,"* vol. 1, *Da Ildemaro a Francesco Petrarca* (Padua: Antenore, 1984), pp. 178–183) points out that lines 8–13 of the poem sent to Dante ("the secrets of the heaven, which Plato toiled to distil from the arcane spheres"—"et secreta poli vix experata Platoni") contain a succinct "quotation" from *Conv.* III V 4–8.

51. Around 1327, the Carmelite friar Guido da Pisa in *Declaratio* (a vernacular composition in terza rima, accompanied by Latin explanations, which takes the form of an introduction to his commentary on the *Commedia*) relates that learned men express their disdain for the literary form and language as well as for the content of the poem: "hearing this name, *Commedia,* and seeing it written in vernacular, they disregard and disdain the fruit concealed within it" ("Audientes hoc nomen *Comedie* et videntes ipsam vulgari sermone compositam, fructum qui latet in ipsa negligunt et abhorrent"); Guido da Pisa, *Declaratio super Comediam Dantis,*

critical edition by Francesco Mazzoni (Florence: Società Dantesca Italiana, 1970), p. 34.

52. Dante's certainty that he would receive the poet's laurel with the publication of *Paradiso* is clearly expressed in *Ec.* II 48–51: "When the volumes of the world that revolve in concentric circles and the souls inhabiting the stars are disclosed in my song, like the realms of Hell already, then it will be my joy to wear on my head the crown of ivy and laurel: Mopsus agrees!" ("Tunc ego: 'Cum mundi circumflua corpora cantu / astricoleque meo, velut infera regna, patebunt, / devincire caput hedera lauroque iuvabit: / concedat Mopsus'").

53. Casadei, "Sulla prima diffusione della *Commedia*," p. 65, suggests that the "ten jars" promised are to be interpreted as ten eclogues.

54. The information that the *Commedia* was still unpublished at the time of Dante's death ("né tanto si poté avacciare, che prima nol sopragiugnesse la morte che egli tutta publicare la potesse") is given by BOCCACCIO[1], p. 183; Boccaccio writes that "it was [Dante's] custom, when he had done six or eight or more or less cantos, before anyone else saw them, wherever he was, to send them to Messer Cane della Scala" ("egli era suo costume, quale ora sei o otto o più o meno canti fatti n'avea, quegli, prima che alcuno altro gli vedesse, donde che egli fosse, mandare a messer Cane della Scala"), but this last statement seems rather unlikely.

55. For the intricate question of Peter Damian/Peter the Sinner, I refer to the entry "Pier Damiano" by Arsenio Frugoni in ED.

56. Dante also turns to look at the "threshing-ground" in Canto XXVII (line 86), once again on Beatrice's invitation, but this second glimpse fixes the coordinates of the journey and doesn't therefore have the significance of a farewell, as it does in Canto XXII.

57. For the "cap" in *Para.* XXV 9, see Villa, *La protervia di Beatrice*, pp. 198–200.

58. The subordination of the church-baptistery to the cathedral was sanctioned by the liturgical reform of Bishop Antonio degli Orsi (1310), which brought an end to the centuries-old customary relationship between the two churches.

59. For relations between Santa Reparata and Santa Maria del Fiore, I refer to Anna Benvenuti, "Stratigrafie della memoria: scritture agiografiche e mutamenti architettonici nella vicenda del *Complesso cattedrale* fiorentino," in *Il bel San Giovanni e Santa Maria del Fiore. Il centro religioso a Firenze dal tardo antico al Rinascimento,* ed. Domenico Cardini (Florence: Le Lettere, 1996), pp. 95–128; Benvenuti, "Arnolfo e Reparata. Percorsi semantici nella dedicazione della cattedrale fiorentina," in *Arnolfo's Moment: Acts of an international conference, Villa I Tatti, May 26–27, 2005,* ed. David Friedman, Julian Gardner, Margaret Haines (Florence: Olschki, 2009), pp. 233–252; and to Marica S. Tacconi, *Cathedral and Civic Ritual in Late Medieval and Renaissance Florence. The Service Books of Santa Maria del Fiore* (Cambridge: Cambridge University Press, 2005).

60. Livi, *Dante, suoi primi cultori, sua gente in Bologna,* p. 175, suggests that Fiduccio dei Milotti played the role of intermediary between Giovanni del Virgilio and Dante.

61. A conspicuous number of explanatory notes collected by Boccaccio in *Zibaldone Laurenziano* enables us to identify the characters concealed behind the pastoral names. For the reception of the eclogues by scholars in the 1300s, see: Giuseppe Billanovich, "Giovanni del Virgilio, Pietro da Moglio, Francesco da Fiano," IMU 6 (1963): 203–234 and 7 (1964): 279–324; Giuseppina Brunetti, "Le *Egloghe* di Dante in un'ignota biblioteca del Trecento," *L'Ellisse. Studi storici di letteratura italiana* 1 (2006): 9–36; Giuliano Tanturli, "La corrispondenza poetica di Giovanni del Virgilio e Dante fra storia della tradizione e critica del testo," *Studi medievali* 52 (2011): 809–845. For the development of humanism: Giuseppe Velli, "Tityrus redivivus: the Rebirth of Vergilian Pastoral from Dante to Sannazaro (and Tasso)," in *Forma e parola. Studi in memoria di Fredi Chiappelli,* ed. Dennis J. Dutschke et al. (Rome: Bulzoni, 1992), pp. 68–78; Gabriella Albanese, "Tradizione e ricezione del Dante bucolico nell'Umanesimo. Nuove acquisizioni sui manoscritti della Corrispondenza poetica con Giovanni del Virgilio," NRLI 13 (2010): 238–327.

62. The note relating to the eclogue sent by Giovanni del Virgilio to Albertino Mussato, contained in Boccaccio's *Zibaldone,* reads: "Nam postquam magister Johannes misit Danti eglogam illam *Forte sub irriguos* etc. stetit Dantes per annum ante quam faceret *Velleribus colchis* et mortuus est ante quam eam micteret."

63. For the insurrection against Pepoli, see DAVIDSOHN, IV, pp. 894–895; for the date of the appointment of Fulcieri, see Casadei, "Sulla prima diffusione della *Commedia,*" p. 63. Lino Pertile ("Le *Egloghe,* Polifemo e il *Paradiso,*" SD 75 (2006): 285–302) emphasizes the incompleteness of the last eclogue.

64. The eclogue from Giovanni del Virgilio to Mussati can now be read in *La corrispondenza bucolica tra Giovanni Boccaccio e Checco di Meletto Rossi. L'egloga di Giovanni del Virgilio ad Albertino Mussato,* critical edition with commentary and introduction by Simona Lorenzini, Quaderni di Rinascimento, 49 (Florence: Olschki, 2011), pp. 175–210.

65. Evidence on his date of death varies between September 13 (the day that appears in the epitaphs composed by Giovanni del Virgilio and Menghino Mezzani) and September 14 (documented, among others, by BOCCACCIO[1], p. 86, and BOCCACCIO[2], p. 62): to reconcile the two dates, it is thought that his death occurred after sunset of the thirteenth. BOCCACCIO[1], pp. 87–91, also describes the funeral and the epitaphs composed shortly after (including that of Giovanni del Virgilio, which he quotes).

66. For events relating to the burial and epitaphs, see Saverio Bellomo, "Prime vicende del sepolcro di Dante," *Letture classensi* 28 (1999): 55–71; the complex question of the funeral epitaphs, including attribution, is considered by Giuseppe In-

dizio, "Saggio per un dizionario dantesco delle fonti minori. Gli epitafi danteschi: 1321–1483," SD 75 (2010): 269–323.

67. The account of the dream and the way in which the last cantos were found is in BOCCACCIO[1], pp. 183–185.

68. *Divisione* and the sonnet *Acciò che le bellezze, Signor mio* by Iacopo are published in Iacopo Alighieri, *Chiose all'*Inferno, ed. Saverio Bellomo (Padua: Antenore, 1990); *Divisione* also by Camilla Giunti, "*L'antica vulgate* del capitolo di Jacopo Alighieri. Con una edizione (provvisoria) del testo," in *Nuove prospettive sulla tradizione della* Commedia. *Una guida filologico-linguistica al poema dantesco,* ed. Paolo Trovato (Florence: Cesati, 2007), pp. 583–610.

69. For the reconstruction of the final stages of work and publication of *Paradiso,* I refer to Casadei, "Sulla prima diffusione della *Commedia,*" pp. 57–62.

Acknowledgments

Many friends and colleagues have helped me with their advice, suggestions, and criticisms, and have assisted in providing me with books and valuable bibliographical indications. I express my deep gratitude to all of them.

I must thank in particular my fellow Dante scholars at Pisa, with whom I have been in almost daily discussion: this has proved of great advantage for me but also, I hope, for the research on Dante in which we have been involved for several years. Each has their own ideas but are always fully prepared to discuss and, where appropriate, to accept the views of others. A thank you, therefore, to Lucia Battaglia Ricci, Gabriella Albanese, Pietro Beltrami, Umberto Carpi, Alberto Casadei, Gianfranco Fioravanti, Fabrizio Franceschini, Claudio Giunta, and Mirko Tavoni. My thanks go also to two "non-Pisans," Claudia Villa and Diego Quaglioni, with whom discussions have nevertheless been intense and rewarding.

My special gratitude to Annalisa Andreoni, Roberta Cella, Elena Salibra, Giuseppe Indizio and Vinicio Pacca, who have followed the writing of this book step by step with generosity, patience, and intelligence, and have read the various drafts. I am also obliged to Roberta and Giuseppe for the genealogical tables.

My sincerest thanks to Richard Dixon for the care he has taken over a translation which in many respects improves the Italian text.

Index

Due to the extremely large number of references to Florence, it is not included in the Index.